Money 18⁵⁰

International Production and the Multinational Enterprise

JOHN H. DUNNING

*Esmée Fairbairn Professor of International Investment
and Business Studies, University of Reading*

London
GEORGE ALLEN & UNWIN
Boston   Sydney

George Allen & Unwin (Publishers) Ltd.
40 Museum Street, London WC1A 1LU, UK

George Allen & Unwin (Publishers) Ltd.
Park Lane, Hemel Hempstead, Herts HP2 41E, UK

Allen & Unwin Inc.
9 Winchester Terrace, Winchester, Mass 01890, USA

George Allen & Unwin Australia Pty Ltd.
8 Napier Street, North Sydney, NSW 2060, Australia

First published in 1981

British Library Cataloguing in Publication Data

Dunning, John H.
    International production and the multinational
enterprise.
1. International business enterprises
I. Title
338.8′8   HD2755.5
ISBN 0-04-330319-6
ISBN 0-04-330320-X pbk

Library of Congress Cataloging in Publication Data

Dunning, John H.
    International production and the multinational
enterprise.
1. International business enterprises. I. Title.
HD2755.5.D867   338.8′8   81-8101
ISBN 0-04-330319-6   AACR2
ISBN 0-04-330320-X (pbk.)

Set in 10 on 11 point Press Roman by Alden Press, Oxford,
London and Northampton
and printed in Great Britain
by Richard Clay (The Chaucer Press) Ltd, Bungay, Suffolk

Contents

Foreword   *page* vii

PART ONE

1 The Distinctive Nature of the Multinational Enterprise   3
2 Trade, Location of Economic Activity and the Multinational
   Enterprise: A Search for an Eclectic Approach   21
3 Trade, Location of Economic Activity and the Multinational
   Enterprise: Some Empirical Tests   46
4 Explaining Changing Patterns of International Production:
   In Support of the Eclectic Theory   72
5 Explaining the International Direct Investment Position of
   Countries: Towards a Dynamic or Developmental Approach   109
6 The UK's International Direct Investment Position in the
   Mid-1970s   142

PART TWO

7 Multinational Enterprises, Market Structure, Economic Power
   and Industrial Policy   179
8 Multinational Enterprises and Domestic Capital Formation   221
9 Multinational Enterprises, Locational Strategies and
   Regional Development   249
10 Employee Compensation in US Multinationals and Indigenous
   Firms: An Exploratory Micro/Macro Analysis   272
11 Multinational Enterprises and Trade Flows of Developing
   Countries   304
12 The Consequences of International Transfer of Technology by
   Multinational Enterprises. Some Home Country Implications   321

PART THREE

13 Evaluating the Costs and Benefits of Multinational Enterprises
   to Host Countries: A 'Tool-Kit' Approach   357
14 Alternative Policy Prescriptions and the Multinational
   Enterprise   385
15 Multinational Enterprises and the Challenge of the 1980s   409

Index   426

List of Tables

1.1 The Foreign Content Ratio of 866 of the World's Largest
Industrial Enterprises, 1977   *page* 5
1.2 Indicators of Foreign Participation in Selected Industries
in Developed and Developing Countries   6
3.1 Types of International Production: Some Determining
Factors   49
3.2 US Affiliate Sales, US Exports and Total Industry Sales in
Seven Countries, 1970   51
3.3 Identifying the Main Ownership and Location Advantages   56
3.4 Determinants of Participation Ratios of US MNEs in Seven
Countries, 1970   60
3.5 Determinants of Export/Local Production Ratios of US
MNEs in Seven Countries, 1970   61
3.6 Determinants of Participation Ratios of US MNEs in Five
Advanced Countries, 1970   63
3.7 Determinants of Export/Local Production Ratios of US
MNEs in Five Advanced Countries, 1970   65
4.1 Stock of Direct Investment Abroad of Development Market
Economies, by Major Country of Origin, 1967–1978   75
4.2 The Eclectic Theory of International Production   80
4.3 Outward Direct Investment Stake of Five Industrialised
Countries by Main Manufacturing Sectors, 1975   83
4.4 Revealed Comparative Advantage Index for Outward Direct
Investment Stake (RCA(A)) of Five Industrialised
Countries, 1970 and 1975   84
4.5 Revealed Comparative Advantage Index for Exports
(RCA(X)) of Five Industrialised Countries, 1970 and 1975   85
4.6 Links between Selected Ownership-Specific Advantages and
Country-Specific Characteristics Likely to Generate and
Sustain Them   87
4.7 Export/Foreign Direct Investment Stake Ratio and
Revealed Comparative Indices (RCA(X/A)) of Five
Industrialised Countries, 1975   93
4.8 Links between Selected Location-Specific Factors and
Country-Specific Characteristics Likely to Affect Them   95
5.1 Alternative Routes of Servicing Markets   111
5.2 Some Illustrations of how OLI Characteristics may vary
according to Structural Variables   113
5.3 Direct Investment Flows 1967–78 GNP per Capita, 1971   114
5.4 Inward and Outward Direct Investment and Stages of
Economic Development   117
5.5 Direct Investment Flows per Capita and GNP per Capita
1967–75, by Economic Structure of Countries   120

5.6	Net Outward Direct Investment and Indicators of OLI-Specific Advantages and Economic Structure 1967–75; Countries grouped by GNP per Capita	126
5.7	Relationship between Investment Flows. OLI Variables and Economic Structure of Countries	130
5.8	Classification of Clusters tested by Discriminant Analysis	131
5.9	Relationship between GII, GOI and NOI and Selected O and L Variables Classified by Three Groups of Countries	132
5.10	Inward and Outward Direct Investment Flows for Selected Countries: Mid 1960s–1978	134
6.1	The UK's Direct International Stake Position 1962–79	146
6.2	The Significance of Outward and Inward Investment for the UK Economy: Selected Indicators, 1962–78	147
6.3	Distribution of UK Outward and Inward Direct Capital Stake by Broad Geographical Area, 1962–78	149
6.4	Geographical Distribution of Outward and Inward Direct Capital Stake 1971 and 1978	150
6.5	Distribution of Outward and Inward Direct Capital Stake by Economic Sector, 1965–76	152
6.6	Distribution of Outward and Inward Investment by Geographical Area and Sector of Economic Activity, 1960–78	154
6.7	Distribution within Manufacturing Industry of UK Net Assets and Investment Abroad and Foreign Net Assets and Investment in UK	156
6.8	Ratio between Net Assets Owned by UK Firms Abroad and Foreign Firms in UK (1971) and between Outward and Inward Investment (1972–8)	157
6.9	UK Foreign Investment Ratios in Manufacturing Industry, Ownership- and Location-Specific Advantages, 1961–77	160
6.10	Some Determinants of Foreign Capital and Investment Ratios classified by Industry 1971–3 and 1974–6	164
6.11	Profitability of UK and Foreign Firms in UK Manufacturing Industry and of UK Firms in Foreign Manufacturing Industry 1960–77	167
6.12	Profitability of UK Overseas Direct Investment, Foreign Investment in UK, and UK Domestic Firms, 1971–3 and 1974–6	168
6.13	Estimated Gains and Losses to UK as a Result of Outward and Inward Investment	170
7.1	Estimated Share of Production of US Affiliates and Market Structure in UK Manufacturing Industry	190
8.1	Estimated Cumulative Funds of US-Owned Affiliates Abroad, 1966–1970	222

8.2   Response of Affiliates of Multinational Enterprises, relative
to those of Indigenous Firms, to Selected Changes in Policy
on Capital Spending   232

9.1   Regional Distribution of Industrial Moves in UK, 1945–65   251

9.2   Regional Distribution of Foreign Production Units
according to Starting Year: Belgium   252

9.3   Regional Distribution of Grant-Aided Manufacturing Plants
Established in Ireland 1960–73   253

10.1 Estimated Average Hourly Compensation paid to all
Employees by Multinational and Indigenous Firms in 1966   276

10.2 Estimated Average Hourly Compensation paid to all
Employees by Multinational and Indigenous Firms in 1970   277

10.3 The Dispersion of Employee Compensation of Multinational
and Indigenous Firms in 1966 and 1970 (By Country)   278

10.4 The Dispersion of Employee Compensation of Multinational
and Indigenous Firms in 1966 and 1970 (By Industry)   280

10.5 Explanatory Power and Significance of Country, Industry
and Firm Factors shown by an Analysis of the Variance of
Wages in Six Host Countries   285

10.6 Explanatory Power and Significance of Country, Industry
and Firm Factors Shown by an Analysis of the Variance of
Wages in Seven Countries including the USA   285

10.7 Average Hourly Compensation in Manufacturing Industry
and Percentage Increase in Consumer Prices, 1966–70   293

12.1 Participation Rates of MNE Affiliates in Manufacturing
Sector of Selected Developing Countries   330

12.2 Ranking of Countries in Selected Developing Countries
according to Degree of MNE Penetration in Manufacturing
Industry and Export Performance   333

12.3 Ranking of Industries in Developed and Developing
Countries, according to Degree of MNE Penetration and
Export Performance   334

12.4 US Related-Party Imports as a Percentage of Total Imports
of Selected Manufactured Products from Selected Newly
Industrialising Countries, 1977   335

12.5 Breakdown of Foreign Direct Investments in Developing
Regions by Broad Type, 1970   337

13.1 Patterns of Foreign Direct Investment Regulation in
Selected Developing Countries   360

13.2 Best Guess Estimates of Selected Balance-of-Payments
Return of UK and US Direct Foreign Investment in
Manufacturing Industry   373

13.3 Summary of Studies Relating to Employment Effects of US
MNEs   374

Foreword

This volume contains some of my mainstream writings on the multi-national enterprise over the last eight years. It is, however, more than a collection of essays: indeed, I have tried to structure the book in such a way that the reader is provided with both a review of recent advances in the theory of multinational enterprise, and a fairly comprehensive analysis of some of the ways in which its activities impinge on, and inter-act with, the policies of governments. A final chapter of the volume speculates a little about the future prospects for international business.

Most of the chapters represent substantially revised versions of articles and chapters in books I first authored or co-authored between 1973 and 1980. The revisions include the updating of statistical material and the incorporation of new analytical insights and empirical findings. In Part One, the reader is offered an evolution of my own thinking on the theory of international production over the last four years, viz. from the time the eclectic theory was first set out in a contribution to a Nobel Symposium on the International Allocation of Economic Activity in 1976 to September 1980 when I read a paper at the Annual Conference of the International Economics Study Group at the University of Sussex Conference Centre. Inevitably, since the six chapters comprising Part One were first published separately and in different journals, there is some overlap in their contents. I have tried to eliminate this as much as possible, but I would ask the reader's forbearance for any repetition that remains.

In Part Two of the volume, I trace some of the more important con-sequences of the activities of multinational enterprises on host or home countries. Chapter 7 looks at their impact on competiton and market structure, and the following chapters discuss the ways in which these have affected domestic capital formation, the location of activity and regional development, wage levels and the international transmission of inflation, trade flows of developing countries and the international division of labour, and the economic capabilities of home countries resulting from the export of technology to developing countries. While these studies in no way exhaust the economic effects of multinational enterprises, they do give a reader a sense of the nature and form of their impact, and the reasons for the concern of home and host governments about their increas-ing participation in economic affairs.

The first two chapters of Part Three are essentially addressed to govern-ments in their dealings with multinational enterprises. They offer no direct and easy solutions; instead they suggest a kind of 'tool kit' by which governments may evaluate the contribution of foreign owned or controlled firms, and their own ability to promote unilateral policies to harmonise the activities and behaviour of such companies with their developmental and other goals. The final chapter in Part Three tries to place the postwar expansion of the multinational enterprise in an historical context, and looks at some of the possible alternatives to this institution as a vehicle of transferring intangible assets across national boundaries in the 1980s.

I am grateful to the editors of several journals and the publishers of the books, in which earlier versions of these studies first appeared, for permission to make use of this material. Three of these studies were co-authored and I much appreciate the share of George Yannopoulos, Eleanor Morgan and Martin Gilman in this volume. My intellectual debt, however, is much wider than this. I have been greatly stimulated in my ideas about the multinational enterprise in recent years by my colleagues at the University of Reading, particularly Mark Casson and Peter Buckley (now at the University of Bradford), and by comments and criticisms of colleagues and postgraduate students from a large number of universities in both the UK and abroad, at which I have presented papers. I also owe a special word of gratitude to Bob Pearce, Esmée Fairbairn Research Economist at the University of Reading, whose dedicated and invaluable assistance has made my task of writing several of the essays in this book so much easier.

The preparation of this volume has been a mammoth task. Each publication has its own particular house style for the preparation of typescripts, for example, with respect to the placing of footnotes and the citing of references, and, as students of the subject well know, there is no universal agreement even on the nomenclature of the subject under discussion. In the editorial and typing work, the brunt of the burden has fallen on Mrs Margaret Lewis, whose tireless and efficient efforts, borne with remarkable cheerfulness, have meant a great deal to me.

Much of the final writing of this book was undertaken at the Centre for International Business Studies, École des Hautes Études Commerciales, University of Montreal, where I was on leave from January to April 1980. I greatly appreciated the hospitality of the Centre, and particularly that of its Director, Professor André Poirier, during that time, and am also grateful for some financial assistance provided by the Centre towards editing and indexing this volume.

Reading   *John H. Dunning*
February 1981

PART ONE

1

The Distinctive Nature of the Multinational Enterprise

I

Why is the multinational enterprise (MNE) a subject worthy of study by economists? What new insights do its operations and effects offer on the workings of the international economy? What distinguishes this institution from other economic phenomena?

One simple answer to the first question is the importance, and increasing importance, of the MNE in the modern world economy.[1] Firms that engage in foreign direct investment — the broad definition of the MNE adopted by this book[2] — accounted for one-fifth of the world's output, excluding the centrally planned economies in the mid-1970s (UN, 1978). Their production, for some years now, has been growing at the rate of 10–12 per cent per annum — nearly twice the growth of world output and, outside the petroleum industry, half as much again as world trade.

According to *Who Owns Whom*, in 1976 there were nearly 11,000 companies which operated 82,600 foreign affiliates, a 20 per cent increase over a previous estimate of 9,481 by the Commission of the European Communities in 1973 (1976). Of this latter number of MNEs, 371 operated in twenty or more countries; these were thought to account for more than three-fifths of all sales of MNEs. In 1977, some 27 per cent of the sales of 866 of the world's largest industrial enterprises was derived from their foreign affiliates (Dunning and Pearce, 1981); of 381 enterprises with sales of more than $1 billion, 153 had a foreign content ratio (i.e. percentage of all sales, assets or employment accounted for by their foreign based activities) of more than 25 per cent, and 52 a foreign content ratio of more than one-half (UN, 1978). Some years ago, the liquid assets of all kinds of multinational institutions were estimated at twice the size of the world's gold and foreign exchange reserves (US Tariff Commission, 1973); by the end of the 1970s, the corresponding figure was probably nearer three times. In every respect, MNEs are among the most powerful economic institutions yet produced by the capitalist system.

This chapter is adapted from Chapter 1 of *Economic Analysis and the Multinational Enterprise*, J. H. Dunning (ed.) (London: Allen & Unwin, 1974).

To these data may be added others which illustrate the role that MNEs, or their affiliates, play in the particular economies in which they operate. Again the facts have been well documented.[3] To the *home* countries their importance is usually expressed, at a macro level, by the share of the gross national product accounted for by the foreign activities of domestically owned MNEs; and at a micro level, by the percentage of the sales, assets, profits or employment of a particular company or industry generated by foreign production. Table 1.1 gives some details of the proportion of sales of the world's largest industrial enterprises accounted for by their overseas operations in 1977. It can be seen that the ratios vary considerably both between home country and industry, being highest among European nations[4] and within the research intensive sectors.

Outside manufacturing industry, though indigenous (and often state owned) enterprises are increasing their participation in the petroleum and some non-fuel mineral sectors (Dunning and Pearce, 1981), eight major MNEs still accounted for 30 per cent of the oil production of market economies in 1975; in copper, the corresponding share of seven principal MNEs in 1978 was 25 per cent; while in the same year six multinationals owned or controlled 58 per cent of the world's bauxite capacity. More than one-half of all iron ore production in 1976 was accounted for by the seven largest multinationals (UNIDO, 1979). In several agribusiness activities, for example, tea, coffee, bananas, pineapples, sugar and tobacco, a few multinationals account for upwards of 60 per cent of the world output of the product in its natural or processed state. Lastly, in the services sector, most of the world's leading banks, advertising agencies, hotels, airlines, auditing firms, engineering, petrochemical and management consultants, and construction companies have major and expanding interests outside their national boundaries. Increasingly, the world is becoming one large market place with the interpenetration of national markets by international production, supplementing, and in some cases replacing, that by trade.

To many host countries, the contribution of affiliates of MNEs is a crucial one. In several economies, such affiliates account for more than one-third of the output of the manufacturing sector and/or one-half the output of their primary product industries. Examples include Australia, Belgium, Canada, Ireland, Norway and Sweden among the developed countries; Brazil, the Dominican Republic, Ethiopia, Fiji, Ghana, Honduras, Kenya, Malaysia, Mexico, Nigeria, Peru, the Philippines, Sierra Leone, Singapore, and Turkey among the less developed nations. The concentration of activity is most marked in import-substitution or export-oriented sectors supplying primary commodities, branded manufactured goods and skill-intensive services, and in which the market structure is oligopolistic. Some details published by the United Nations Centre on Transnational Corporations in 1978 are set out in Table 1.2.

Table 1.1   The Foreign Content Ratio of 866 of the World's Largest Industrial Enterprises, 1977

	Home Country of MNEs				All Countries
	USA	Europe	Japan	Other Countries	
High Research Intensity					
Aerospace	7.6	6.8	n.a.	n.a.	7.5
Office Equipment and Computers	42.2	39.3	10.0	n.a.	41.5
Petroleum	47.0	59.5	1.0	1.3	42.7
Measurement, Scientific and Photographic Equipment	35.2	21.0	8.0	n.a.	33.1
Electronics and Electrical Appliances	21.3	26.6	4.5	45.8	20.5
Chemicals and Pharmaceuticals	25.7	40.5	4.3	4.3	29.0
Total	35.8	44.0	3.6	5.2	33.5
Medium Research Intensity					
Industrial and Farm Equipment	28.1	26.9	2.8	48.5	22.9
Shipbuilding, Railroad and Transportation Equipment	5.0	1.6	7.1	31.7	8.8
Rubber	31.6	48.5	7.0	n.s.a.	34.2
Motor Vehicles and Components	21.4	20.5	17.4	n.a.	20.6
Metal Manufacturing and Products	13.7	16.8	3.3	15.2	13.5
Total	19.6	20.4	8.6	21.6	18.4
Low Research Intensity					
Building Materials	21.7	38.7	3.0	2.0	27.9
Tobacco	29.0	52.1	n.a.	n.a.	40.8
Beverages	23.6	20.5	n.s.a.	3.7	17.4
Food	18.9	55.2	2.1	5.8	28.8
Paper and Wood Products	13.6	32.8	4.0	32.4	18.1
Textiles, Apparel, Leather Goods	10.2	26.5	12.3	11.7	15.5
Publishing and Printing	6.2	15.3	4.1	n.a.	9.2
Total	17.9	44.6	4.8	13.3	25.0
Other Manufacturing	11.0	0.9	5.0	2.0	5.8
Total	27.4	35.1	6.1	11.5	26.6

n.a. not applicable.   n.s.a. not separately available.

Source: Dunning and Pearce (1981). Foreign content is defined as the percentage of sales of foreign affiliates of MNEs (excluding goods imported from the parent companies for resale) to the worldwide sales of the MNEs.

Table 1.2 Indicators of Foreign Participation in Selected Industries in Developed and Developing Countries

ISIC No.	Chemicals (351–352)	Rubber (355)	Iron and steel basic industry (371)	Non-electrical machinery (382)	Electrical machinery (383)	Motor vehicles (3843)	Year
Developed countries							
Australia	84(A)	–	72(A)	–	–	83(A)	1972/73
Austria	21(E)[a]	56(E)[a]	–	32(E)[a]	40(E)	–	1973
Belgium/Luxembourg	73(O)	70(O)	–	–	–	–	1970
Canada	33(E)	25(E)	11(E)	–	64(A)	84(A)	1973
France	33(A)	48(A)	–	37(A)	–	21(A)	1973
Germany, Federal Republic of	33(A)	–	33(R)	–	51(A)	–	1974
New Zealand	–	–	–	–	–	–	1969/70
Spain	–	–	–	–	50(O)	84(O)	1973
Sweden	–	–	14(O)	–	–	–	1973
Turkey	54(A)	59(A)	–	43(A)	–	38(A)	1974
Developing countries							
Argentina	37(O)	75(O)	–	82(O)	33(O)	84(O)	1969
Brazil	51(O)	44(O)	61(O)[b]	55(A)[b]	33(A)[b]	100(A)	1976
India	27(O)	52(O)	41(O)	25(O)	33(O)	10(O)	1973
Korea, Republic of	22(E)	–	37(O)	19(O)	–	–	1970
Mexico	67(O)	84(O)	37(O)	31(O)	63(O)	–	1973
Peru	67(S)	88(S)	–	25(S)	62(S)	–	1969
Philippines	–	73(O)	–	–	–	43(A)	1973
Singapore	46(E)	76(E)	21(E)	–	–	–	1968

[a] Employment by US majority affiliates.

[b] Based on the largest 5,113 enterprises.

O = Output, T = Turnover, R = Revenue, A = Assets, E = Employment.

Source: Table III-63 of UNCTC (1978).

II

It is, however, less the distinctive characteristics of MNEs and more their distinctive *behaviour*, and the consequences of this behaviour for national and international resource allocation, which makes them of special interest to economists and policy makers. This distinctive behaviour stems from the fact that they directly control the deployment of resources in two or more countries and the distribution of the resulting output generated between these countries.

There are three near relations to the MNE; they are:

(1)   The national enterprise which operates production units in different parts of the nation state in which it is incorporated, that is, the multi-location domestic enterprise. Like it, the multinational enterprise owns income-generating assets in more than one location and uses these, together with locally owned resources, to produce goods and/ or services. As the affiliates of multi-location domestic enterprises possess certain advantages over their local competitors, due *inter alia* to their being part of a larger economic unit and the opportunities for specialisation this confers, so do MNEs enjoy similar benefits over national enterprises. But, unlike the multi-location domestic enterprise, the MNE owns and operates its assets and controls the use of its inputs in different national states, each of which is a sovereign political unit.[5]

(2)   The national firm which produces in the country in which it is incorporated but exports part of its output, that is, the international trading firm. Like it, the MNE sells its output across national boundaries, thereby introducing an element of openness and interdependence in both the exporting and importing economies. Unlike the international trading firm, however, its activities involve a transfer of factor inputs and part of its trade is not between independent economic agents, at arm's length prices, but within the same enterprise, at transfer prices, which, in so far as it is possible, will be fixed to serve the interests not of any particular affiliate but that of the enterprise as a whole.

(3)   The national producing firm which exports part of its factor inputs, for example, material or human capital. Like it, the MNE exports income-generating assets but, unlike it, supplies these as a package deal and maintains control over the use made of them.

Likewise, the foreign *affiliates* of MNEs also may be distinguished from indigenous firms in the countries in which they operate. They have two near relations. First, firms which import factor inputs from foreign sources, and second, branch plants of multi-location domestic firms. In the first case, while both groups of firms are dependent on foreign source for (some of) their resources, only the foreign affiliates are controlled from abroad in the use of these resources. In the second case, both firms are part of larger enterprises, and so their activities are likely to be truncated in some way or another; the difference here lies mainly in the extent to which division of labour is practicable and in the inter-country distribution of the proceeds of the output.

Although it may be argued that these differences are ones of degree rather than of kind, and arise largely because the world is divided into a number of sovereign states, they do confer a certain distinctiveness on MNEs and their affiliates, the extent and character of which will vary according to, *inter alia*, the industries and countries in which they operate and their organisational strategies. However, wherever they occur, the response of MNEs and their affiliates to the economic environment of which they are part, or to changes in that environment, will, to some extent, be different from that of their near relations.[6]

Partly because of this and partly because some of the output generated by the affiliates of multinational enterprises in one country will accrue to the owners of resources in other countries, both the international allocation of resources and the distribution of economic welfare will be affected. Since the operating objectives of affiliates will be geared primarily to those of the enterprises of which they are part, rather than those of the countries in which they operate, clashes with host governments over some aspects of their behaviour are unavoidable. These clashes are likely to be most pronounced *inter alia* the more a country pursues a policy of economic autarky and hence the more the activities of MNEs are in response to market imperfections, for example, barriers to trade in goods, inappropriate exchange rates, etc., and the greater the differences in incentives and/or penalties imposed by governments which cause MNEs to shift resources, or claims to resources, across national boundaries.

III

To what extent do the distinctive characteristics of multinational enterprises necessitate modification to received economic analysis? Economic analysis is concerned with explaining the way in which resources possessed by economic agents are (or could be) used, and how the resulting output is (or could be) distributed. In so doing, it is interested both in the formulation of empirically testable hypotheses, and in advancing understanding about the relationship between economic phenomena. Economic policy deals with more normative matters. It is concerned with identifying and evaluating ways in which resources may be allocated to achieve certain goals, both economic and non-economic.

There are three main objectives that guide most policy makers in their attitudes towards the allocation of resources for which they are responsible.

These may be summarised under three heads: efficiency, equity and sovereignty.[7]

(1) *Efficiency* is concerned with the volume and composition of output produced by a community from the resources available to it, and its rate of growth over time. In the present context it is the contribution of MNEs (or their affiliates) to gross *national* output which is relevant; this is equal to gross *domestic* output, plus income earned on assets owned abroad minus income earned on foreign owned domestic assets.

(2) *Equity* (in this context) is a function of the way the proceeds from production or the rate of growth of production are distributed between the contributing factor inputs, customers and tax authorities, both within the country of production and between that country and others which provide part of the resources for the production.

(3) *Sovereignty* is a catch-all word which may be loosely defined as the ability of a country to run its own affairs and retain the maximum freedom of choice in the allocation of its resources. Within this heading, one might include such targets as economic nationalism, participation in decision taking, cultural identity and so on.

The extent to which these goals are realised will, of course, depend on the achievement of various subgoals; for example, the need to cure a balance-of-payments deficit may act as a constraint (in the short run) on maximising efficiency. Moreover, both goals and subgoals may sometimes conflict with each other. The implicit assumption of our analysis is that the behaviour of multinational enterprises is different from that of other economic agents and that this will affect the success of countries in achieving their objectives.

Clearly it is of interest to the economist to study these differences, the reasons for them and their effects on the realisation of both micro and macroeconomic objectives, but before looking into them more fully, a comment about the current state of economic analysis and the MNE may be in order. Until recently, the subject held little appeal to the academic economist and the main body of economic literature has remained substantially unaffected by it. Only in the last five or six years have articles on it begun to appear in the leading journals. This apparent lack of concern could be because economists believe that the subject matter is not sufficiently distinctive to warrant separate attention, or that the existing tools of analysis are adequate to deal with it, or even that economic analysis has little to contribute to an understanding of it.

On the other hand, it may be that economists have insufficiently appreciated either the extent of the MNE or its implications for economic analysis. We are inclined to take this latter view, or, at least, suggest there is an *a priori* case for it. Certainly, even the most cursory glance at the empirical work done on the subject makes one uneasy about its implications for received theory. Notwithstanding that much of this work has been descriptive, and most of the discussion outside academic circles has been politically oriented, traditional economic doctrines have been frequently called to task. Is this because the theories are wrong, or because they inadequately take account of the distinctive characteristics of the MNE? Or, could it be that the critics do not properly understand the theories?

IV

There are three ways in which a new institutional phenomenon might affect existing explanations of the structure of resource utilisation. The first is that existing assumptions about the behaviour of institutions may no longer be appropriate. Take, for example, the goals of business behaviour. To what extent are MNEs likely to be differently motivated than other enterprises? How far does their presence affect the goals of other economic agents including governments? For example, are consumer tastes likely to be more interdependent or cosmopolitan as a result of the closer links they make possible between people of different cultures? Will the community's welfare function be more geared towards economic nationalism? What, too, of the assumptions about the value of exogenous variables, or those one usually chooses to hold constant? Foremost among these in microeconomics are that prices are determined by the actions of independent buyers and sellers. Where the exchange of goods is between different parts of the same economic agent this latter assumption may no longer hold good. New tools of analysis may be needed to explain these prices and, hence, behaviour dependent on them.

Second, new institutions may require economic analysis to be reconstructed or extended to take account of new independent variables which might influence their behaviour. In the present context, these arise partly because the MNE introduces a new dimension to both the theory of the firm and the theory of international relations, and partly because behavioural variables which may have been previously unimportant are now important.

Third, an explanation of the relationship between variables may be affected because the *value* of variables is no longer appropriate. This does not affect analysis itself but rather the conclusions to be drawn from the analysis.

Put in simpler terms, the MNE may influence resource allocation and economic policy through affecting: (1) the goals of economic agents; (2) the means of achieving these goals, that is, the availability and efficient use of resources; and (3) the mechanism by which means are related to ends, for example, the economic system. We shall now discuss each of these from the viewpoint of the three broad aims of governments set out earlier.

(a) *Efficiency*

Most economists see no *a priori* reason to suppose that the MNE is motivated any differently from a large national enterprise.[8] The fact that the world is organised into separate sovereign states *of itself* need make no difference to the way in which firms exploit markets. However, given the fact of MNEs and that individual governments *do* operate policies to advance the economic welfare of their own citizens, the allocation of resources may be different than would occur in the absence of separate governments. These actions might be independent of the operations of multinational enterprises, but may also be affected by them. Mention might be particularly made of their impact on competition, regional and demand management policies. None of these raises new conceptual issues; they arise equally at a regional level wherever affiliates of multi-plant national companies are operating. The question as to whether the territorial extension of an enterprise's activities makes for more or less economic power, thereby affecting the efficiency of resource allocation, is a separate one.

The impact of MNEs on world output arises partly from the extent to which the enterprises are themselves more efficient, as a result of their multinationalism, and partly by the response of such companies to government policies designed to advance their own economic and social goals.[9] These policies differ widely across national boundaries. Examples include different tax rates and fiscal provisions, exchange rate policies, labour laws, differential monopoly and regional policies, import substitution and export promotion policies. Such policies, of course, affect all firms, but to the enterprise producing in more than one country they represent discriminatory treatment, and since their options, with respect to geographical resource allocation, are wider they are able to respond differently than indigenous companies.

The analogy with a spatially diversified national firm is a particularly apposite one as, by its behaviour within the framework of both regional and national policies, it can affect the disposition of economic activity both between industries and between regions. It can influence the level and rate of growth of employment and real income distribution between regions in a way which may increase the efficiency of resource usage in the region in which it operates, yet lower its actual production. It can create disturbance problems in the same way as can exogenous structural changes, and it is likely to do this more easily than a uniregional firm partly, at least, because of its wider spatial choices. As far as the government of the nation state (of which the region is part) is concerned, this may be an acceptable price to pay where it advances national economic welfare, as it is able to alleviate, in part, undesirable distributional effects by appropriate adjustment policies. Moreover, in the last resort, it has power to directly influence the locational choice of the multilocation domestic firm.

At an international level, this is not the case. There is no *a priori* presumption that the presence of (say) US affiliates in Britain will make for a higher economic welfare of the UK, even if they are more efficient than indigenous firms. One can easily imagine takeovers of UK companies by US firms that may benefit both the investor and the US economy and, indeed, the combined welfare of the US and UK economies, yet may not be in the best interests of the UK economy. The reason for this lies partly in the greater immobility of resources, particularly unskilled labour, across national boundaries than within national boundaries, and partly in the fact that there is no machinery by which the UK can share in the increased wealth accruing to the US economy, which directly arises from the employment of its own resources. In the case of a UK company taking over a firm in the north-east of England, the same thing may happen, but at least devices are open to the national government to ensure that the North-East can share in the prosperity of the country as a whole.

The identification and measurement of the international resource allocative effects of supplying markets from alternative production locations are questions which concern both location and trade economists. Is there any reason to suppose that a firm supplying the national market with only one production unit will behave very differently than one that is spatially diversified? On the other hand, there is a separate branch of economic analysis concerned with trade between nations rather than regions within a nation. As will be emphasised in Chapter 2, the analytical threshold which distinguishes the two sorts of trade is the immobility of factor inputs, while intra-country differences in the institutions and actions of governments also differentiate the determinants of external trade from those of internal trade. Presumably, the theory of capital movements, once national boundaries are crossed, should also take on a new meaning, though there seems to be no reason (at a micro level) to suppose that the determinants of international investment by enterprises are significantly different from those of domestic investment (Stevens, 1974).

Perhaps one important difference between national multiregional and international trading enterprises, on the one hand, and MNEs, on the other, revolves around the question of *ownership*. A market for a particular product may be serviced in three main ways: (1) by domestically owned firms producing within that market; (2) by imports either from (a) foreign firms or (b) the foreign affiliates of domestically owned firms; (3) by the affiliates of foreign firms producing in that market. Location theory is concerned with explaining the choice of firms between options (1) and (2b) or (2a) and (3): trade theory is largely concerned with explaining the choice between options (1) and (2a). It is only by using *both* approaches that one can appreciate why neither, by itself, is sufficient to explain the choices open to multinational enterprises. For example, how does one explain the share of a market serviced from a given location by indigenous firms and affiliates of foreign firms or by importing goods from foreign firms or affiliates? Trade theory is deficient because its assumption about the immobility of factor inputs is inappropriate. Location theory is deficient because it cannot explain why firms of different ownership vary in efficiency. Both theories fail to appreciate that where there are barriers to or imperfections in the transmission of knowledge between firms, this will tend to increase the concentration of ownership, but widen the options open to firms to service their markets. Such advantages may be *enterprise*, *industry* or *country* specific. *Enterprise*-specific advantages include access to particular markets or sources of inputs, the economies of size and integration and the possession of proprietary knowledge. *Industry*-specific advantages include those concerned with market structure and the economics of production. *Country*-specific advantages include the educational system and state policy towards research and development.[10]

These specific advantages may be a function of many factors apart from the multinationality of firms, and some, such as economies of integration, may apply to multilocation domestic enterprises. Again, however, there are some advantages which only arise if firms produce in more than one country. Sometimes these are matters of degree, for example, the extent to which an American firm in America might possess a comparative advantage over a UK firm in the UK compared with a UK firm in Birmingham over a UK firm in Southampton. Since the difference between the two locations is more pronounced in the first case, so will be the comparative advantage of their firms. Perhaps more important is the case where a firm trades with another at other than 'arm's length' prices, that is, the terms of trade that would operate in independent transactions. Although in a world context this is primarily a distributional matter, from the point of view of a particular country, it will influence its efficiency of resource usage and its share of the output produced.

Such intra-group trading, whether it be of goods, services, money or assets, at other than arm's length prices, emphasises the distinction between the international trading and the international producing firm. There are other ways in which the latter type of enterprise may have more control over its market than the former, but these are similar in kind to those available to the multiregional firm. The extent to which a multinational enterprise will wish to earn income in one country rather than in another depends very much on conditions outside its control, in particular the policies of individual governments and the international monetary system.

In his contribution to an earlier volume edited by the author, Max Corden examined the impact of the MNE on the pure theory of international trade and concludes it can be easily incorporated into its framework (Corden, 1974). *Most* of the ingredients of received theory remain —

notably, the immobility of certain productive factors, for example, land and most kinds of labour. On the other hand, because of a common ownership of factor inputs, some features immobile between independent firms across national boundaries, for example, knowledge, information and various kinds of services, become mobile in the case of the multi-national company. Moreover, because of intra-group pricing, the *terms* of trade and hence the allocation of resources and composition of trade may be different. This point has also been recognised by Baldwin (1970) and Gray (1981) who plead for a more systematic incorporation of the movement of inputs in trade theory. Several empirical studies have also shown that international investment and trade are closely linked (Bergsten, Horst and Moran, 1978; Hood and Young, 1979).

Most writers on the MNE have been concerned with both their *positive* and *normative* implications. It is, for example, well recognised that their effect on economic welfare is strongly influenced by both government policies and institutional mechanisms. Several economists have asserted that market imperfections favour MNEs more than national enterprises (Lundgren, 1974).[11] It is also clear that second best government policies lead to lower efficiency; a protectionist import policy is one example. Like other institutions, MNEs respond to economic signals; if these are inappropriate they could lower rather than raise welfare standards, and make it more, rather than less, difficult for governments to achieve their social goals.[12] By their behaviour, for good or bad, multinationals may also force governments or markets to modify established policies. An example of a beneficial impact (according to some economists at least) is the adoption of flexible exchange rates by countries following some of the financial activities of MNEs, but such companies may cause governments to take restrictionist measures with less welcome consequences and econ-omic well-being. However, in spite of recent research, we are only at the threshold of our understanding of the interactions between the behaviour of MNEs and government policy.

(b)   *Equity*

It has been suggested above that the economic welfare of individual nation states is likely to be influenced by MNEs and their affiliates by the effect they have on the distribution of income between investing and host countries. This has its parallel in international trade, where the terms of trade will determine the share of the gains from exchange accruing to the participants. Given the output created by an affiliate of an MNE, the question of its distribution between the citizens of the host nations in which the affiliate is located and those of other nations providing resources to that affiliate is of critical importance. It is, for example, possible that an affiliate may be more efficient than an indigenous firm, in the sense that its contribution to the gross *domestic* product is higher, but that all or more of this accrues to the investing country, so that gross *national* product is unchanged (or lowered). Higher efficiency of foreign affiliates does not guarantee an increase in gross national product, as it does when achieved by indigenous firms, where the issue is entirely one of distribution of the product between sectors within a nation state.

This, indeed, is a noteworthy difference between the impact of MNEs on the nation states in which they operate and those of national enterprises in the regions in which they operate. Both affect the economies of the area of their adoption, but only in the latter case is wealth created and available for distribution in a way that *all* participants might gain. Again, it is worth emphasising that the effects differ primarily because the world happens to be organised into sovereign nation states, each with its own economic and social objectives, and its ways of achieving these, which may be very different from each other.

The determination of the benefit/cost ratio for companies and countries, and the extent to which it is as high as it might be, is central to any study of the economic consequences of multinational enterprises. Rarely, of course, is the bargaining conducted in an easily identifiable way. The components of costs and benefits are many and varied, and some defy easy measurement. To the host country they include all the externalities, or spill-over effects, both positive and negative, arising from the presence of affiliates of the MNEs. This is a subject on which there has been a great deal of research, at both a macro and micro level.[13] The share of the benefits created directly by the affiliates, which is then distributed to the investing company (or other affiliates), includes not only profits, interest, royalties, technical fees and contributions to managerial and administrative overheads, but also income resulting from the intra-group exchange of goods and services at above arm's length prices charged to the affiliate.[14] In various contributions, Constantine Vaitsos has argued that the true income accruing to MNEs is often well in excess of the profits recorded, and that some countries, particularly developing countries, are paying well above their opportunity cost for the assets, goods and services provided.[15]

All governments are concerned with evaluating the contribution of resident economic agents to their economic and social goals. For income generated by national enterprises, this reduces to a question of the distribution of the proceeds between factor inputs, notably between capital and labour within the country. The share does not directly affect the size of the national income except in so far as it affects incentives. With affiliates to MNEs the situation is very different for reasons already given, which is why the bargaining process becomes all important. How far are existing models, for example, that of bilateral monopoly, relevant? It is here that economic analysis leaves much to be desired.[16] Certainly there is no direct parallel in the case of the multiregional company, nor with the international trading company, where the question of the terms of trade is the relevant one.

Perhaps it is the national company, which obtains its inputs separately from independent foreign sellers, which offers the nearest parallel. In this case the economist is interested in assessing the differential effects of control over the use of local resources, and the decision of whether or not to supply the foreign resources which is implicit in international direct investment, and the benefits and costs of this investment. What is the difference in economic terms? It is partly a question of price. In the case of licensing fees and interest on local capital negotiated by firms in the open market the price is known in advance. Even in the case of equity capital one knows the range of benefits and costs and is prepared to make a choice on this basis. However, in the case of a company whose price can be affected in so many different ways and which does not always wish to act in the way it would on an open market there is a large difference. In addition, there is the question of concentration of economic power. Investment by the large multinationals is often indivisible. An investment of £100 million by a dozen companies is very different from the same expenditure by 1,000 companies.

Because of the complexity and uncertainty surrounding the behaviour of MNEs as a result of their economic power, and because of ignorance surrounding their pricing strategy, they do seem to have established a new set of rules in the bargaining game. The bargaining options open to multi-nationals call for some reappraisal of the traditional theories of wage determination. Although one can cite illustrations of bargaining strengths and weaknesses, we are still awaiting a satisfactory theory to explain the distribution of income generated by the multinationals.

A secondary question concerns the factors influencing the distribution of income *within* a country arising from MNEs. Carlson (1974) has addressed himself to this question. Again, from the viewpoint of economic analysis, it is possible to examine these effects on the distribution of income as having been caused by different goals of MNEs, or of means to achieve these goals, or of the system in which they operate. Does one need a new theory to explain the share of the benefits accruing from the operation of affiliates to the investing company, where that company is domiciled in a different country? Possibly, in so far as the multinationals have more choice in the use of the income they earn, modification is required. There is also some evidence to suggest that their policy towards the distribution of profits may be different from that of uninational firms (Stevens, 1974). Far more important, however, is the bargaining position of the multinational company with domestic authorities. Here there is no comparable model which economic analysts can call upon.

Summarising, then, the MNE introduces a new institutional situation which may expose weaknesses in existing mechanisms of resource allocation, either at a national or international level. Where the effects of domestic economic policies of governments are confined to firms earning income within their jurisdiction, the fact that these policies may be different across national boundaries may have no effect on the international distribution of income. For companies operating in different parts of the world, this becomes an imperfection in the market system, and affects behavioural patterns, which will not necessarily be in accord with policies of governments. A national firm which operates management policies to maximise its receipts is operating in the country's best interests; but, by becoming international and pursuing the same objectives, it may find itself in conflict with the governments of one or more of the countries in which its activities are located. The fact that it is the structure of the international economic system which causes this and not any change in behaviour of the companies (whose interests only coincide with nation states in so far as it pays them so to do) does nothing to endear them to governments.

Lastly, what of the means by which MNEs achieve their ends of the optimum distribution of income? The answer in the case of efficiency lay in technology and the economies of integration and size. The answer here also lies with some of those same variables and particularly those which affect bargaining and competitive strength. Of these, size, flexibility in operation, access to information about international goods and factor markets, and sheer professional skill and adroitness in international management explain how distribution of income may be affected by additional means open to MNEs. However, sometimes the bargaining strength is on the side of nations, particularly where nations by grouping together (e.g. Organisation of Petroleum Exporting Countries, the Andean Pact countries) can evolve common strategies towards MNEs.

(c)   *Political Aspirations and Economic Sovereignty*

Positive economics takes political ends as given, but the cost and benefits of attaining political ends have economic consequences. Ultimately, a country will wish to be as politically independent as it can. This is its right. Economic nationalism is a 'good' in itself, the opportunity cost of which, like that of any other good, may be evaluated in economic terms.

Here, I would simply mention that the economist must be clear on what grounds he is making decisions which may affect the behaviour of MNEs. When a country nationalises or expropriates the assets of a foreign affiliate in its midst; when it imposes a tariff or import controls to encourage inward direct investment; when it seeks to control the movement of funds from affiliates to parent company (or vice versa); when it insists on a certain proportion of the equity capital of the affiliate being locally owned or a minimum of local representation on the board of directors; when it requires the affiliate to purchase a certain quantity of its inputs from local firms and to recruit its management from indigenous sources; when it discriminates against local subsidiaries in its purchasing policies, or in their use of local capital markets; when it insists on research and development being undertaken locally; does it pursue these and similar policies to promote higher efficiency or to achieve a more acceptable distribution of income, or because, by so doing, it is better able to control the use of its resources or achieve non-economic goals? On the first issue the economist can make a direct assessment, though, in practice, this may be an extremely difficult thing to do. On the second, he can still estimate the economic trade-off between alternative courses of action to the decision takers to make the final choice. In both cases, his role may be a valuable one in that it enables more informed and rational decisions to be taken.

V

The growth of the MNE and international production adds a new dimension to various branches of economic thought, the theory of international trade, the theory of the firm and the theory of bargaining being perhaps the most affected. Factors which appear irrelevant or insignificant for analysing the behavioural consequences of the multiregional or international trading firm take on a new meaning with the MNE. Foremost among these are the presence of intra-group pricing across national boundaries, the international allocation of resources and the distribution of the output of MNEs between the nation states in which they operate. We have also suggested that the interactions between MNEs and domestic economic policies and mechanisms create new tensions. These arise because the growth of MNEs has coincided with developments in technology, communications, patent systems and with the increasing intervention of governments in economic affairs. They are both the creatures of these circumstances and have helped fashion them. Policies or mechanisms appropriate in their absence may no longer work in their presence; they may also give rise to a completely new set of problems. The usual response of governments is to try and control the MNEs so that they behave in a way consistent with their policies and mechanisms. But sometimes a country's goals may be better served if the policies or mechanisms are themselves changed. On such normative issues the economist may be able to give important advice.

Notes: Chapter 1

1   As, for example, summarised by Hood and Young (1979).
2   For a comprehensive analysis of the various definitions of the multinational (or transnational) enterprise, see U.N. (1978).
3   See, for example, U.N. (1978) and citations in Section II of Chapter 4.
4   Particularly among some of the smaller countries, for example, Switzerland (77 per cent) Belgium (60 per cent) and Sweden (33 per cent). Of the larger European countries, the UK recorded the highest overseas production ratio of 41.3 per cent and Italy the lowest of 16.5 per cent.
5   For a further examination of these and other differences, see Chapter 9.

6   Chapters 8 and 9 take this point up further.
7   A more pragmatic classification of the objectives of countries is set out in Nau (1976).
8   See, for example, Horst (1974) and Teece (1979).
9   This point is further explored in Chapter 14.
10   These advantages are discussed in more detail in Chapter 2.
11   See also Chapter 7.
12   See Chapter 14.
13   See also Chapter 13.
14   In other cases, affiliates may be charged below arm's length prices, for example, subsidised inputs, cheap loans, machinery at knock-down prices, etc.
15   See, for example, Vaitsos (1974).
16   But here see especially Lall and Streeten (1977) and Streeten (1974).

References

Baldwin, R. E. (1970), 'International trade in inputs and outputs', *American Economic Review*, Vol. 60 (May).

Bergsten, C. F., Horst, T., and Moran, T. H. (1978), *American Multinationals and American Interests* (Washington, DC: The Brookings Institution).

Carlson, S. (1974), 'Wage determination and collective bargaining', in J. H. Dunning (ed.), *Economic Analysis and the Multinational Enterprise* (London: Allen & Unwin).

Corden, W. M. (1974), 'The theory of international trade', in J. H. Dunning (ed.), *Economic Analysis and the Multinational Enterprise* (London: Allen & Unwin).

Commission of the European Communities (1976), *Survey of Multinational Enterprises*, Vol. 1 (Brussels: the Commission).

Dunning, J. H. (ed.) (1974) *Economic Analysis and the Multinational Enterprise* (London: Allen & Unwin).

Dunning, J. H., and Pearce, R. D. (1981), *The World's Largest Industrial Enterprises* (Farnborough: Gower).

Gray, H. P. (1981), 'Towards a unified theory of international trade, international production and foreign direct investment', in J. H. Dunning and J. Black (eds), *International Capital Movements* (London: Macmillan).

Hood, N., and Young, S. (1979), *The Economics of Multinational Enterprise* (London: Longman).

Horst, T. O. (1974), 'The theory of the firm', in J. H. Dunning (ed.), *Economic Analysis and the Multinational Enterprise* (London: Allen & Unwin).

Lall, S., and Streeten, P. (1977), *Foreign Investment, Transnationals and Developing Countries* (London: Macmillan).

Lundgren, N. (1974), 'Multinational firms and economic stability', in J. S. G. Wilson and C. F. Scheffer (eds), *Multinational Enterprises, Financial and Monetary Aspects* (Leiden: Sijthoff).

Nau, H. R. (1976), *Technology Transfer and US Foreign Policy* (New York: Praeger).

Stevens, G. V. G. (1974), 'The determinants of investment', in J. H. Dunning (ed.), *Economic Analysis and the Multinational Enterprise* (London: Allen & Unwin).

Streeten, P. (1974), 'The theory of development policy', in J. H. Dunning (ed.), *Economic Analysis and the Multinational Enterprise* (London: Allen & Unwin).

Teece, D. (1979), *Technology Transfer and R & D Activities of Multinational Firms: Some Theory and Evidence*, (mimeo). Stanford University, Stanford, Calif.

UN (1978), *Transnational Corporations in World Development. A Reexamination*, E.78 II A5 (New York: United Nations Economic and Social Council).

UNIDO (1979), 'Transnational corporations and the industrialisation of developing countries', ID/CONF/4/14 6/12/79. Paper prepared for Third General Conference in New Delhi, India, 1980.

US Tariff Commission (1973), *Implications of Multinational Firms for World Trade and Investment and for US Trade and Labour* (Washington DC: US Government Printing Office).

Vaitsos, C. V. (1974), 'Income distribution and welfare considerations', in J. H. Dunning (ed.), *Economic Analysis and the Multinational Enterprise* (London: Allen & Unwin).

2

Trade, Location of Economic Activity and the Multinational Enterprise: A Search for an Eclectic Approach

I

The main task of this chapter is to discuss ways in which production financed by foreign direct investment, that is, undertaken by MNEs, has affected our thinking about the international allocation of resources and the exchange of goods and services between countries. The analysis takes as its starting point the growing convergence between the theories of international trade and production, and argues the case for an integrated approach to international economic involvement, based both on the location-specific advantages of countries and the ownership-specific advantages of enterprises. In pursuing this approach, the chapter sets out a systemic explanation of the foreign activities of enterprises in terms of their ability to internalise markets to their advantage. It concludes with a brief examination of some of the effects which the MNE is allegedly having on the spatial allocation of resources, and on the patterns of trade between countries.

We begin by looking at the received doctrine on international economic involvement. Until around 1950 this mainly consisted of a well-developed formal theory of international trade and a complementary but less well-developed theory of capital movements. With the notable exceptions of John Williams (1929)[1] and Bertil Ohlin (1933), international economists of the interwar years were less concerned with explanations of the composition of goods and factors actually traded across boundaries (and implicitly, at least, of the spatial distribution of economic activity) as with theorising on what would occur if, in the real world, certain conditions were present. The Heckscher—Ohlin model, for example, asserted that, provided certain conditions were met, countries would specialise in the production of goods

An earlier version of this chapter was published as Chapter 12 of B. Ohlin, Per Ove Hesselborn and Per Magnus Wijkman (eds), *The International Allocation of Economic Activity* (London: Macmillan, 1977).

which required relatively large inputs of resources with which they were comparatively well endowed, and would export these in exchange for others which required relatively large inputs of factors with which they were comparatively poorly endowed. The conditions included that countries had two homogeneous inputs, labour and capital, both of which were locationally immobile (i.e. they were to be *used* where they were *located*); inputs were converted into outputs by the most efficient (and internationally identical) production functions; all enterprises were price-takers, operating under conditions of atomistic competition; there were no barriers to trade and no transaction costs; and international tastes were similar.

The Heckscher–Ohlin model has been criticised in the literature on various grounds, including the unreality or inapplicability of its assumptions. Here, I would underline some of the implications of three of these assumptions: factor immobility, the identity of production functions and atomistic competition. These are, first, that all markets operate efficiently; second, there are no external economies of production or marketing; and third, information is costless and there are no barriers to trade or competition. In such a situation international trade is the only possible form of international involvement; production by one country's enterprises for a foreign market must be undertaken within the exporting country; and all enterprises have equal access to location-specific endowments.

One of the deductions of the Heckscher–Ohlin theory is that trade will equalise factor prices. Replacing the assumption of factor immobility with that of the immobility of goods, it may be shown that movements of factors also respond to differential resource endowments. This was the conclusion of the early writings of Nurkse (1933), Ohlin (1933) and Iversen (1935) which explained international (portfolio) capital movements in terms of relative factor prices, or differential interest rates. For many years trade and capital theory paralleled each other, it being accepted that, in practice, trade in goods was at least a partial substitute for trade in factors. Eventually, the two were formally integrated into the factor price equalisation theorem by Samuelson (1948) and Mundell (1957).

In the late 1950s there was a striking shift of direction in the interests of international economists brought on, *inter alia*, by the tremendous postwar changes in the form and pattern of trade and capital exports. Building on the empirical work of MacDougall (1951) and Leontief (1953 and 1956), and taking advantage of much improved statistical data, the 1960s saw the first real attempts to explain trade patterns as they were, rather than as they might be; contemporaneously, the emergence of international production as a major form of non-trade involvement was demanding an explanation.

Over the past twenty years the positive theory of international economic involvement has 'taken off'. For most of the period it comprised two quite separate strands. The first concerned explanations of trade flows. Here, contributions were mainly centred on introducing more realism into the Heckscher–Samuelson–Ohlin doctrine. Basically, there were two main approaches. The first was that of the neofactor theories, which extended the two-factor Heckscher–Samuelson–Ohlin model to embrace other location-specific endowments (notably natural resources) and differences in the *quality* of inputs, especially labour. The second group of theories was more path-breaking, as it cut at the heart of the Heckscher–Samuelson–Ohlin model by allowing for the possibility of differences in the production function of enterprises and of imperfect markets. These theories, which included the neotechnology and scale economy models, were different in kind to the neofactor theories because they introduced new explanatory variables which focused not on the specific resource endowments of countries but on the exclusive possession of certain assets by enterprises. Sometimes, in addition to, but more often as a substitute for, orthodox theories, these new hypotheses of trade flows have been exposed to various degrees of testing. Yet as Hufbauer (1970) has shown, the predictive power of the neofactor and the neotechnology theories is scarcely better than that of the crude factor proportions theory. In his own words, 'No one theory monopolises the explanation of manufacturing trade'.

The second strand of research in the 1960s centred on explaining the growth and composition of foreign direct investment, or of production financed by such investment. At first causes were sought either from orthodox location theory (witness the plethora of microeconomic field studies and more macro-oriented econometric studies) or from neoclassical investment doctrine; but for various reasons, discussed elsewhere (Dunning, 1973a), neither approach proved very helpful. More rewarding were the attempts to identify the distinctive features of foreign *direct* investment in terms of ownership advantages of foreign firms. Though the gist of this idea was contained in the writings of Southard (1931) and Dunning (1958), it was left to Stephen Hymer in his seminal PhD thesis (Hymer, 1960) to explore it in depth. Out of this approach, later refined and extended by Caves (1971, 1974a & b), several hypotheses, focusing on particular kinds of ownership advantages of MNEs, were put forward: for example, access to superior technology (Johnson, 1970), better capabilities for product differentiation (Caves, 1971), underutilisation of entrepreneurial and managerial capacity (McManus, 1972; Wolf, 1977), etc., while a more behavioural perspective was taken by Vernon and his colleagues, notably Knickerbocker (1973), who chose to emphasise the role played by defensive oligopolistic strategy. These theories, too, have been subject to some testing,[2] but again it seems clear that no single hypothesis offers a satisfactory explanation of non-trade involvement.

Though these new theories of trade and production originated quite independently of each other, by the early 1970s it was clear they were converging on, and even overlapping, each other. Though expressed differently, the same variables were being increasingly used to explain both trade and non-trade involvement. Comparable to the technological gap theory of trade was the knowledge theory of direct investment; analogous to monopolistic competitive theories of trade were theories of direct investment focused on product differentiation and multi-plant economies. Yet, with the exception of Vernon's early integration of trade and investment as different stages of the product cycle (Vernon, 1966), which took as its starting point the innovative advantages of *enterprises* in a particular country, and the later discovery of Horst (1972) that the same variable — *size* of firm — which best explained foreign investment also explained investment plus trade, no attempt was made to integrate the two forms of involvement into a single theory, although the need for this had been discerned by Baldwin (1970) and others. Nor, indeed, was there any explicit recognition that, because the decisions to trade or engage in foreign production are often alternative options to the same firm, any explanation of one must, of necessity, take account of the other.

The last decade has seen the first, albeit faltering, attempts to do just this. In a paper published in 1973, this author suggested that only by considering trade and foreign production as alternative forms of international involvement in terms of ownership and location endowments could the economic implications of the UK joining the EEC be properly evaluated (Dunning, 1973b). Seev Hirsch (1976) formalised these concepts into a model that specifies, very clearly, the conditions under which foreign markets will be serviced by alternative routes. Tom Parry (1975) applied these concepts to a study of the pharmaceutical industry; his contribution is especially noteworthy as he included licensing as a third form of economic involvement. Buckley and Dunning (1976) examined comparative US and UK trade and non-trade in these terms. Birgitta Swedenborg (1979) uses a similar approach in her analysis of the international operations of Swedish firms. In the belief that this is a helpful route towards an eclectic theory of international economic involvement, I now explore it in more detail.

II

Exactly what is to be explained? Here an important point of taxonomy arises. A country's economic involvement outside its national boundaries may be perceived in two ways. First, it may mean the extent to which its own resources, that is, those located within its boundaries, are used by economic agents (irrespective of their nationality) to produce goods or services for sale outside its boundaries; or the extent to which it imports either resources or the products of resources located in other countries. This is the interpretation of orthodox international economics; *inter alia* it implies arm's length trade in inputs and outputs. But secondly, a country's involvement may mean the extent to which its own economic agents[3] service foreign markets with goods and services, irrespective of where the resources needed to do this are located or used, and the extent to which its own economic agents are supplied goods by foreign owned firms, irrespective of where the production is undertaken. Here, a country's economic space is perceived more in terms of the markets exploited by its institutions than of its geographical boundaries.

Like the distinction between gross national product and gross domestic product[4] which of the two interpretations is the more appropriate depends on the purpose for which it is being used. But for an evaluation of the contribution of a country's international economic involvement to the economic welfare of its citizens, the second has much to commend it, particularly where inward or outward investment account for a substantial proportion of its net capital formation.

Economic involvement by one country's enterprises in another may be for purposes of supplying both foreign and home markets. Production for a particular foreign market may be wholly or partly located in the home country, in the foreign market, in a third country or in a combination of the three. Similarly, production for the home market may be serviced from a domestic or a foreign location.

The capability of a home country's enterprises to supply either a foreign or domestic market from a foreign production base depends on their possessing certain resource endowments not available to, or not utilised by, another country's enterprises. We use resource endowments in the Fisherian sense (Johnson, 1968) to mean assets capable of generating a future income stream; they include not only tangible assets, such as natural resources, manpower and capital, but intangible assets, such as knowledge, organisational and entrepreneural skills, and access to markets. Such endowments could be purely location specific to the home country, in other words they have to be used where they are located[5] but are available to all firms, or they could be ownership specific, that is, internal to the enterprise of the home country, but capable of being used with other resources in the home country or elsewhere.[6] In most cases, both location and ownership endowments affect competitiveness.

For some kinds of trade it is sufficient for the exporting country to have a location-endowment advantage over the importing country, that is, it is not *necessary* for the exporting firms to have ownership-endowment advantage over indigenous enterprises in the importing country. Much of the trade between industrialised and non-industrialised countries (which is of the Ricardian or H/O type) is of this kind. Other trade, such as that which mainly takes place between developed industrialised countries, is of high skill intensive or sophisticated consumer goods products, and is based more on the ownership advantages of the exporting firms;[7] but, observe, this presupposes that it is better to use these advantages in combination with location-specific endowments in the exporting rather than in the importing (or in a third) country. Where, however, these latter endowments favour the importing (or a third) country, foreign production will replace trade. Foreign production then implies that location-specific endowments favour a foreign country, but ownership endowments favour the home country's firms, these latter being sufficient to overcome the costs of producing in a foreign environment (Hirsch, 1976). (Again we assume that transfer costs can be considered as a negative endowment of countries other than the country of marketing.)

From this it follows that any theory that purports to explain the determinants of any one form of international economic involvement is unlikely to explain the whole; nor, where that form is one of a number of possible alternatives, will it be adequately explained unless the forces explaining these alternatives are also taken into account. One should not be surprised, then, if trade theories of the neofactor brand, based on location-specific endowments, will not normally be able to explain trade in goods based on ownership-specific endowments. But neither should one be disquieted if the neotechnology and monopolistic competitive theories of trade, based on ownership-specific endowments, are also inadequate where the *use* of such advantages is better exploited in conjunction with location-specific endowments of foreign countries.

It may be reasonably argued, however, that this latter criticism would be better directed against the way in which data on international transactions are collected and presented, and the way in which the exported ownership advantages are priced. First, trade statistics usually give details of the *gross output* of goods exported. But where exports contain a high import content, their total value may tell us little about the use made of indigenous endowments. This deficiency can only be overcome by recording exports on a domestic value-added basis. Second, trade statistics either ignore, or classify completely separately, intermediary goods, such as technology, management and organisation, which are exported in their own right. If these could be given a commodity classification, and their value added to the export of final products, then the ownership advantages of exporting enterprises would be better captured. Third, where trade takes place within the same enterprises the recorded prices may bear little resemblance to arm's length prices, and so to the value of factor inputs used. If these problems could be overcome, a combination of the neofactor, neotechnology and monopolitistic competitive theories of trade would probably explain trade patterns very well.

III

So far the multinational enterprise has not been explicitly introduced into the discussion. MNEs are companies which undertake productive activities outside the country in which they are incorporated. They are, by definition, also companies which are internationally involved. The extent to which

they engage in foreign production will depend on their comparative ownership advantages *vis-à-vis* host country firms, and the comparative location
endowments of home and foreign countries.

Unlike location-specific endowments, which are *external* to the enterprises that use them, ownership-specific endowments are *internal* to
particular enterprises. They consist of tangible and intangible resources,
including technology, which itself dictates the efficiency of resource usage.
Unlike location endowments many ownership endowments take on the
quality of public goods, that is, their marginal usage cost is zero or minimal
(hence, wherever a marginal revenue can be earned, but is not earned, they
are underutilised); and although their *origin* may be partly determined by
the industry or country characteristics of enterprises, they can be used
anywhere.

What, then, determines the ownership advantages which one country's
enterprises possess over those of another? For our purposes, we distinguish
between three kinds of advantage. The first comprises those which any
firms may have over another producing in the same location. Here, Bain's
(1956) classic work on the barriers to new competition provides the basic
answer. Such benefits may lie in the access to markets or raw materials
not available to competitors; or in size (which may both generate scale
economies and inhibit effective competition); or in an exclusive possession
of intangible assets, for example, patents, trademarks, management skills,
etc., which enable it to reach a higher level of technical or price efficiency
and/or achieve more market power. These advantages, then, stem from
size, *monopoly power*, and better *resource capability and usage*.

The second type of advantage is that which a branch plant of a national
enterprise may have over a *de novo* enterprise (or over an existing enterprise breaking into a new product area), again producing in the same
location. This arises because, while the branch plant may benefit from
many of the endowments of the parent company, for example, access to
cheaper inputs, knowledge of markets, centralised accounting procedures,
administrative experience, R & D, etc., at zero or low marginal cost, the
de novo firm will normally have to bear their full cost. The greater the
non-production overheads of the enterprise, the more pronounced this
advantage is likely to be.

The third type of advantage is that which arises specifically from the
multinationality of a company, and is an extension of the other two. The
larger the number and the greater the differences between economic
environments in which an enterprise operates, the better placed it is to
take advantage of different factor endowments and market situations. I
shall return to this point later in the chapter.

Most of these benefits, both individually and collectively, have been
used by economists to explain the participation of affiliates of MNEs in
the output of industries in host countries. However, while recognising they
are interrelated, there have been few explicit attempts to explain either the

basis of the interrelationship or why the more marketable of the advantages are not sold directly to *other* firms. In consequence, not only has one of the fundamental attributes of MNEs been largely overlooked, but so also has the basis for much of the concern about the present international economic order. The substance of our thesis is not, in itself, new; it is more a reinterpretation and extension of an idea first formulated by Coase in 1937, and more recently resurrected in the literature by Arrow (1969, 1975), Williamson (1971, 1975, 1979), Alchian and Demsetz (1972), Furobotn and Pejovich (1972), McManus (1972), Baumann (1975), Brown (1976), Magee (1977a, b) and, perhaps most systematically of all, by Buckley and Casson (1976).[8]

The thesis is that the international competitiveness of a country's products is attributable not only to the possession of superior resources and, in some cases, the necessity of its enterprises but also to the desire and ability of those enterprises to internalise the advantages resulting from this possession; *and* that servicing a foreign market through foreign production confers unique benefits of this kind. Where, for example, enterprises choose to replace, or not to use, the mechanism of the market, but instead allocate resources by their own control procedures, not only do they gain but, depending on the reason for internalisation, others (notably their customers and suppliers prior to *vertical* integration, and their competitors prior to *horizontal* integration) may lose. Internalisation is thus a powerful motive for takeovers or mergers, and a valuable tool in the strategy of oligopolists.

It has long been recognised that such gains may follow from vertical integration and, to a lesser extent, from horizontal integration of a firm's activities; and much of current antitrust legislation is designed to prevent or minimise abuses arising as a result. But much less attention has been paid to the type of internalising practised by conglomerates, or that which reflects in the internal extension of a company's activities, or that associated with the internalisation of resources, products or markets over geographical space.

Consider, for example, the areas in which the participation of MNEs, irrespective of their country of origin, is most pronounced in host countries. These include export-oriented primary goods sectors requiring large amounts of capital, for example, aluminium, oil, copper and/or those faced with substantial barriers to foreign marketing and distribution, for example, bananas, pineapples, coffee, etc.; technologically advanced manufacturing industries or those supplying branded consumer products with a high income elasticity of demand and subject to the economies of large-scale production; capital or skill intensive service industries, such as insurance, banking and large-scale construction; and activities in which the spatial integration of inputs, products or markets is essential to efficiency, for example, airlines, hotels, etc. All of these not only require endowments in which MNEs have a comparative advantage, and which are difficult to acquire by *de novo* entrants, but, more pertinent to our argument, they are all sectors in which there is a pronounced propensity of firms to internalise activities, particularly across national boundaries.

What, then, are these incentives of firms to internalise activities? Basically they are to avoid the disadvantages or capitalise on the advantages of imperfections or disequilibria in external mechanisms of resource allocation.[9] These mechanisms are mostly of two kinds − the price system and public authority fiat. Where markets are perfectly competitive, the co-ordinating of interdependent activities cannot be improved upon; once imperfections arise or can be exploited through internalisation, this becomes a possibility.

Market imperfections may be both structural and cognitive. Uncertainty over future market conditions in the absence of competitive future markets, or about government policies, is another kind of imperfection. *Structural imperfections* arise where there are barriers to competition and economic rents are earned; where transaction costs are high; or where the economies of interdependent activities cannot be fully captured. *Cognitive imperfections* arise wherever information about the product or service being marketed is not readily available, or is costly to acquire. The cost of *uncertainty* may be gauged by the risk premium required to discount it, which may differ quite significantly between firms. From the buyer's viewpoint, market imperfections to avoid include uncertainty over the availability and price of essential supplies, and lack of control over their delivery timing and quality. From the seller's viewpoint, the propensity to internalise will be greatest where the market does not permit price discrimination; where the costs of enforcing property rights and controlling information flows are high; where the output produced is of more value to the seller than the buyer is willing to pay (again, possibly because of ignorance on the part of the buyer),[10] or, in the case of selling outlets, where the seller, to protect his reputation, wishes to ensure a certain quality of service, including after-sales maintenance. For both groups of firms, and for those considering horizontal integration, the possession of underutilised resources, particularly entrepreneurial and organisational capacity, which may be used at low marginal cost to produce products complementary to those currently being supplied, also fosters internalisation.

At the same time, to benefit from some of these advantages an enterprise must be of sufficient size. This prompts firms to engage in product diversification or integration, which, in turn, increases their opportunities to profit from other internalising practices such as cross-subsidisation of costs, predatory pricing, etc. One suspects that many of the advantages of conglomerate mergers are of this kind; and it cannot be a coincidence that, in recent years, takeovers and mergers have been concentrated in areas in which advantages of internalisation are most pronounced.[11]

Public intervention in the allocation of resources may also encourage enterprises to internalise activities. Many policy instruments of governments, however justified in the pursuance of macroeconomic (and other) goals, may create distortions in the allocation of resources which enterprises may seek to exploit or protect themselves against. Some of these provoke reactions from all enterprises; others from only those which operate across national boundaries.

Here the analysis will be confined to two kinds of government intervention especially relevant to the behaviour of MNEs. The first concerns the production and marketing of public goods, which are not only characterised by their zero marginal cost, but by the fact that their value to the owner may hinge on the extent to which others also possess them. Under these circumstances, an orthodox perfect market is impossible, unless the purchaser relies on the seller to withhold the sale of a good to other buyers, or not to price it lower.

Some commodities and services produced by private enterprises also have the characteristics of public goods. The major example is technology — an intermediary good which embraces all kinds of knowledge embodied in both human and non-human capital (Johnson, 1970). The significance of technology in the modern world economy needs no elaboration: it is the main engine of development, a leading determinant of both absolute and relative living standards, and a controlling factor in the spatial allocation of resources. Its phenomenal growth since the Second World War, especially in the field of information and communications technology, has undoubtedly facilitated the internationalisation of firms, just as the railroad, telegraph and telephone helped the creation of national enterprises a century ago.[12]

It is my contention that the need both to generate innovations and ideas and to retain exclusive right to their use has been one of the main inducements for enterprises to internalise their activities in the last two decades. Governments have encouraged this by extensively subsidising R & D, continuing to endorse the patent system and by recognising that, in some industries, if the benefits of technological advances are to be fully exploited, not only may it be necessary to restrict the number of producers, but that enterprises should be free to internalise their knowledge-producing with their knowledge-consuming activities. Even without the intervention of governments, technology possesses many of the attributes for internalising (or not externalising) markets. At the time of its production, it is the sole possession of the innovator, who naturally wishes to exploit it most profitably; it is costly and takes time to produce but there is no future market in it; it is often difficult for a potential buyer to value as its usefulness can only be determined after it has been purchased. Yet often, for its efficient exploitation, it needs complementary or back-up resources. These qualities apply particularly to the kind of knowledge which *cannot* be patented, for example, financial systems, organisational skills, marketing expertise, management experience and so on.

The second example of government intervention is particularly relevant to the operations of MNEs. It both encourages such enterprises to inter- nalise existing activities and to engage in new activities which offer the possibility of internalising gains. It arises because of different economic policies of national governments which often lead to distortions in the international allocation of resources. Assume, for example, that an MNE wishes to maximise its post-tax profits and that corporate tax rates differ between countries. One way it can reduce its total tax burden is to capital- ise on its intra-group transactions by manipulating its transfer prices so as to record the highest profits in the lowest tax areas. Other things being equal, the more internal transactions the company engages in the greater its opportunities for doing this — hence, in the case of MNEs, the added impetus to engage in a global strategy and to practise product or process specialisation within its organisation.

The MNE has other reasons for internalising its operations across boundaries (Rugman, 1980). These include the desire to minimise the risk and/or costs of fluctuating exchange rates; to cushion the adverse effects of government legislation or policy, for example, in respect to dividend remittances; to be able to take advantage of differential interest rates and 'leads' and 'lags' in intra-group payments; and to adjust the distribution of its short-term assets between different currency areas. Some of these benefits of internalisation are now being eroded by government surveil- lance over transfer pricing and by the tendency for contractual arrange- ments between foreign and indigenous firms to replace equity investments of the former.

How far MNEs actually *do* manipulate intra-group prices to transfer income across national boundaries is still a matter for empirical research; so far the evidence collected is partial and impressionistic. Suffice to say there are many reasons why an MNE may wish to take advantage of such opportunities (Lall, 1973), and that however vigilant the tax authorities may be in some areas, for example, the pricing of intangible assets, the difficulty of (1) estimating the extent to which a transfer of goods or ser- vices has taken place, and (2) assigning a value to them, is a very real one.

It has been illustrated, at some length, why firms, and MNEs in partic- ular, gain from internalising their activities, especially in respect of the production and marketing of technology. Another sector in which MNEs are particularly active is the capital intensive, resource based industries. Here, all the traditional reasons for vertical integration hold good, in addition to those which result from multinationality *per se*; the classic example is the oil industry. They imply, for the most part, a vertical division of activity of firms, though the operations may be horizontal as well, where similar products are produced. Here, too, the impetus to inter- nalise transactions (as opposed to engaging in contractual arrangements) in the case of international vertical integration is likely to be greater than in the case of domestic vertical integration.

It must not be forgotten, however, that there are costs as well as benefits to internalising economic activities; for an examination of these see Coase (1937) and Buckley and Casson (1976). As markets become less imperfect the net gains of internalisation are reduced. The move towards externalising the marketing of many raw materials, partly stimulated by the actions of governments, testifies to this. In his study of UK direct investment overseas, Reddaway (1968) found that only 4 per cent of the output of UK plantation and mining affiliates, originally set up to supply the investing firms, was now directly imported by them.

It can be concluded, therefore, that the ownership advantages of firms stem from their exclusive possession and use of certain kinds of assets. Very often, enterprises acquire these rights by internalising those previously distributed by the market or public fiat, or by not externalising those which they originate themselves. This will only be profitable in imperfect market conditions, and where it is thought the co-ordinating and synergising properties of the firm to allocate resources are superior to those of markets or public fiat. It is possible to identify the source of such imperfections, both within countries and internationally, and to point to the types of activities which offer the greatest gains from internalisation. Of these, the production and marketing of intangible assets and of essential location-specific resouces are the two most important. Both happen to be areas in which MNEs are particularly involved; the fact that the ownership advantages are exploited by foreign production is partly explained by location-specific endowments of the foreign country, and partly by certain ownership advantages which accrue only when a firm produces outside its national boundaries.[13]

IV

What is the link between the above discussion and other explanations of international involvement? Simply this. The neotechnology theories of trade and the knowledge theories of direct investment both emphasise the possession of superior technology as an explanation of both trade and production. The monopolistic competitive theories concentrate on some aspect of arm's length imperfect competition as the explanation for trade and investment.

It is my contention that the two approaches should be treated as complementary aspects of an eclectic theory of international involvement, which should embrace not only the product but also the factor and intermediary goods markets, and should acknowledge that the ownership advantages arise not only from the exclusive possession of certain assets, but from the ability of firms to internalise these assets to protect themselves against the failure of markets (including the consequences of this failure for competitors' behaviour) and government fiat over the rest of their activities. Because it relates to the way in which the enterprise co-ordinates its activities, this approach may be called a *systemic* theory of ownership advantages, applied to both trade and international production.[14] In favouring such an approach admittedly I may be in danger of being accused of eclectic taxonomy. I also acknowledge the interdependence between technology, imperfect competition and the internalisation process, and that it is not always easy to separate cause and effect.

But in the search for a composite measure of ownership advantage a systemic approach has something to commend it. Empirically, there can be little doubt of the increase in the vertical and horizontal integration of firms and of market and product diversification, which has enabled firms to benefit from the internalisation of their activities. This is demonstrated both by the increase in the concentration of enterprises in industrial economies in the postwar period and by the growing importance of the pre- and post-production activities of firms. Other data suggest that about one-half of all exports of MNEs are intra-group in character.

More generally, the eclectic model can be perceived as a general theory of international production in so far as it provides an analytical framework for explaining all forms of such production. This, however, is not to assert that particular forms of international production are to be explained by the *same* ownership, location or internalisation characteristics. This is clearly not the case, and it is readily accepted that different types of international production may call for quite different explanations. But our contention is that these should be regarded as complementary, rather than alternative, interpretations of MNE activity and of the eclectic paradigm. For this reason, I have no difficulty in reconciling seemingly competing theories within this paradigm, as, more often than not, they are seeking to explain different things.

What, then, is the positive value of the eclectic theory of international production? The theory suggests that, given the distribution of location-specific endowments, enterprises which have the greatest opportunities for and derive the most from, internalising activities will be the most competitive in foreign markets.[15] *Inter alia* these advantages will differ according to industry, country and enterprise characteristics. Hence, the ownership advantages of Japanese iron and steel firms over South Korean iron and steel firms will be very different from those of UK tobacco firms over Brazilian tobacco firms or US computer firms over French computer firms. Enterprises will engage in the type of internalisation most suited to the factor combinations, market situations and government policies with which they are faced. For example, the systemic theory would suggest not only that research intensive industries would tend to be more multinational than other industries, but that internalisation to secure foreign based raw materials would be greater for enterprises from economies which have few indigenous materials than those which are self-sufficient; that the most efficient MNEs will exploit the most profitable foreign markets – compare, for example, the US and UK choice of investment outlets (Stopford, 1976); that the participation of foreign affiliates is likely to be greatest in those sectors of host countries where there are substantial economies of *enterprise* size. This theory is consistent with Horst's conclusion (1972) that most of the explanatory variables of foreign direct investment can be captured in the size of enterprise; indeed, one would normally expect size and the propensity to internalise to be very closely correlated, and MNEs to be better equipped to spread risks than national multiproduct firms.

What does the eclectic theory predict that the other theories of international production do not? Taking the theories as a group, probably very little, except in so far as the independent variables fail to capture the advantages of internalisation. Indeed, it could be argued that this theory is less an alternative theory of ownership advantages of enterprises than one which pinpoints the essential and common characteristics of each of the traditional explanations. There is, however, one difference of substance. The eclectic approach would argue that it is not the possession of technology *per se* which gives an enterprise selling goods embodying that technology to foreign markets (irrespective of where they are produced) an edge over its competitors, but the advantage of internalising that technology, rather than selling it to a foreign producer for the production of those goods. It is not the orthodox type of monopoly advantages which give the enterprise an edge over its rivals − actual or potential − but the advantages which accrue through internalisation, for example, transfer price manipulation, security of supplies and markets, and control over use of intermediate goods. It is not surplus entrepreneurial resources *per se* which lead to foreign direct investment, but the ability of enterprises to combine these resources with others to take advantage of the economies of production of joint products.

In other words, without the incentive to internalise the production and/or sale of technology, foreign investment in technology-based industries would give way to licensing agreements and/or to the outright sale of knowledge on a contractual basis. Without the incentive to internalise market imperfections there would be much less reason to engage in vertical or horizontal integration, and again transactions would take place between independent firms. This, it could be argued, is the distinctiveness of this approach.

V

So far the discussion has concentrated on the ownership endowments of its enterprises as an explanation of a country's international competitiveness, whatever the form of the involvement. It has been argued that, although the advantages are enterprise specific, the fact that these may differ according to nationality of enterprise suggests that such advantages, though endogenous to the individual firms at that time, are not independent of their industrial structure, or of the general economic and institutional environment of which they are part. For example, US government science and education policy may be a key variable in explaining the technological lead of US firms in many industries, while, as Vernon (1974) has pointed out, innovations respond to factor endowment and market needs, which also influence the likely advantages of internalising those innovations. The institutional arrangements by which innovations are rewarded are no less relevant.

But these country or industry variables affecting ownership advantages are not the same as the location specific endowments referred to earlier. With this interpretation, these comprise three components: the resources which can only be *used* by enterprises in the locations in which they are sited, unavoidable or non-transferable costs such as taxes, government constraints on dividend remission, etc., and the costs of shipping products from the country of production to the country of marketing.

Each of these elements has received extensive attention in the literature of location theory, which usually assumes ownership endowments as the same between firms, and seeks to explain *where* they are exploited. Our concern here is a different one. Put in question form it is: given the ownership endowments, is the location of production by MNEs likely to be different from that of non-MNEs? The systemic theory suggests that it is, and for three reasons. First, there may be particular internalising economies resulting from the friction of geographical space. Second, the location-specific endowments, which offer the greatest potential for internalisation, are not distributed evenly between countries.[16] Third, where there are differences in the market imperfections or government policies of countries, then MNEs might be influenced by the extent to which they take advantage of these imperfections by internalising their operations.

In elaboration of these points, four observations can be made. First, various studies have underlined the advantages of co-ordinating R & D activities of MNEs (Ronstadt, 1977; Fischer and Behrman, 1979; Lall, 1979) and centralising them in or near the markets which stimulate such activities (Michalet, 1973; Creamer, 1976). In the case of US-based MNEs, this suggests, that for most kinds of R & D, both ownership and location endowments work in favour of a home R & D base.[17] In the case of MNEs from smaller home markets this tendency may not be so pronounced. By contrast, because the advantages of internalisation are generally much less, it may be profitable to spatially disperse some kinds of manufacturing activities, especially where the production processes involved have become standardised (Vernon, 1974).

Second, an MNE which produces in different market environments may well seek to co-ordinate its activities differently. The degree of uncertainty over local consumer tastes, future market conditions and government policy certainly varies between countries. For example, the less imperfect is the market for technology, the less likely is an enterprise to market technology based products itself. Compare, for example, the role of foreign pharmaceutical companies in Italy, which does not recognise patent protection on drugs, with that of such companies in almost any other European country. By contrast, in some developing countries, MNEs may be reluctant to license local firms because they feel that the complementary technology is insufficient to ensure the quality control they need.[18]

Third, and perhaps most important, is the advantage that a diversified earnings base provides for an MNE to exploit differential imperfections in national or international markets and/or currency areas (Aliber, 1970), *inter alia*, through transfer-price manipulation; the use of leads and lags in intra-group transactions; the acquisition and monitoring of information; and the extension of benefits enjoyed by multi-plant national firms at an international level. These are some of the (potential) advantages of internalisation afforded by international production, compared with international trade.

Fourth, there is the drive towards international production as part of oligopolistic behaviour (Knickerbocker, 1973; Flowers, 1976; Graham, 1978). This is really a territorial extension of domestic strategy, and does not pose any new conceptual problems (but, see Vernon, 1974). Again, however, in so far as a company perceives its foreign interests to be part of a global strategy, rather than as an independent entity, the internalising advantages may be crucial to the locational decision of both leaders and followers.

VI

In the light of the above analysis, what might one expect the impact of the MNE to be on location of production, the international diffusion or transfer of technology and trade patterns?

There are many different views about the effect of MNEs on the international distribution of resources. Partly, these reflect differences in the perspective one takes, for example, that of a particular country or region, or that of all countries; or of the goals one is seeking to promote. We shall confine ourselves to economic issues viewed in a global context from two main viewpoints. The first is that MNEs promote a more efficient distribution of resources since, by internalising imperfect markets, they are able to overcome distortions in the economic system such as barriers to the transfer of technology, import controls and inappropriately valued exchange rates. Moreover, in a world of uncertainty and information imperfections, their more efficient scanning and monitoring processes, and their flexibility to respond better to market signals, is a useful competitive stimulus. In short, this view extols the MNE as an integrating force in the world economy, surmounting national barriers, circumventing high transaction costs and improving the allocating of resources.

The second view asserts that, far from overcoming market imperfections, the MNEs are themselves a major distorting force in resource allocation; this is partly because they operate mostly in oligopolistic markets and partly because of their ability to bypass market mechanisms and/or government regulations (Hymer, 1970). As a result, it is argued, they engage in restrictive practices, raise barriers to entry and, by their internalisation and centralisation of decision taking, adversely affect the efficiency of resource allocation between countries. Far from promoting competition, the co-ordination of activities by entrepreneurs freezes existing production patterns, encourages agglomeration and makes it more difficult for countries to exploit their dynamic comparative advantages. Since MNEs *do* exert monopoly power, it is legitimate (on the lines of the optimum tariff argument) for home or host countries to impose restrictions on their activities.

The truth, in so far as it is possible to generalise, is obviously somewhere between these two extremes, with the balance steering one way or another according to (1) the efficiency of the resource allocative mechanism prior to the entrance of the MNEs and (2) the market conditions under which MNEs compete — which will vary *inter alia* according to industry and country.

But there are certain effects of MNEs, however they may be interpreted, which do seem to have been reasonably well established in the literature, and we will now touch on three of these.

(1)   In some instances, MNEs have been an integrating force and have taken advantage of existing factor endowments, thus promoting the more efficient use of resources. The best example is where mobile resources of capital and technology are transferred from a capital- and technology-rich country and combined with immobile resources of labour and/or materials in labour- and materials-rich countries, thereby helping these countries to exploit their dynamic comparative advantage. Other examples include what is currently happening in Europe as a result of the EEC, namely, that the MNEs are rationalising their activities to take advantage of the economies of specialisation. This is a slow process but no different, in principle, to the behaviour of multiregional (national) enterprises in the USA, which may well be one of the explanations of the greater specialisation in the US than within the EEC, as demonstrated by Hufbauer and Chilas (1974).

(2)   There is some evidence of a spatial specialisation of the activities of MNEs and, in particular, the centralisation of R & D activities in the home country. Something over 90 per cent of the R & D activities of

Swedish and US MNEs is undertaken in their home countries, and the proportion is probably not very different for most of the other leading investors. Hymer suggests that MNEs are encouraging the specialisation of activities, not for technological as much as organisational or strategic reasons, most of which enhance the incentive to internalise R & D in the home country. But it does not necessarily follow that, without MNEs, the distribution of innovative activities would have been any the less centralised. R & D among Japanese and European enterprises has certainly been stimulated by the competition from US MNEs. The impact on the UK pharmaceutical and semiconductor industries are classic examples (Tilton, 1971; Lake, 1976). In the LDCs, because of the lack of indigenous competitors, the Hymer hypothesis probably holds more weight, though even here there are examples of MNEs setting up specialised R & D facilities (Behrman and Fischer, 1980).[19]

(3)   In any analysis of the impact of MNEs on trade and location it is useful to distinguish between the different motives for foreign direct investment. Kojima (1978), for example, has distinguished between trade-oriented and anti-trade-oriented activities of MNEs. He suggests that current Swedish and Japanese investments are mainly made in areas in which the home countries are losing a comparative advantage and host countries are gaining it. These have been of two kinds; one to exploit natural resources not available indigenously, and the other to switch labour intensive activities from high labour cost to low labour cost locations. On the other hand, Kojima asserts that many foreign investments by US firms have been made to protect an oligopolistic position in world markets and in response to trade barriers, and have transferred activities from which they have a comparative advantage to where they have a disadvantage. Such investments, he claims, are anti-trade oriented and run against the principles of comparative advantage. Kojima cites here the extensive US foreign investments in the capital and technologically intensive industries.

The border between transferring a comparative advantage and creating a new one is a narrow one, and the Kojima distinction between trade-generating and trade-destroying investments is not altogether convincing. Moreover, his approach tends to be a static one and is couched in terms of first-best solutions. It also fails to consider vertical specialisation *within* industrial sectors. Assuming technology (as an intermediate good) can be sold for a competitive price between independent parties, one might reasonably expect non-skilled labour intensive operations of high technology industries to be transplanted to those areas which possess such labour in abundance, and countries with an abundance of materials to utilise such materials with technology developed by nations which have a limited amount of materials. The Japanese and US patterns may be complementary to each other; their ownership and locational advantages may reflect country-specific characteristics.[20] Evidence collected about the trading patterns of US MNEs (Lipsey and Weiss, 1973) supports this view. The imports of US MNEs tend to be more capital intensive than those of other US firms, mainly because of the ability of MNEs to export capital and technology to undertake the labour intensive production processes of a capital intensive product in low labour cost areas.

From a normative viewpoint, the point of greater interest is the extent to which technology transfer through the co-ordination of the firm is preferable to that of the market, but, on this subject, there has been only limited research (Arrow, 1969; Williamson, 1979; Teece, 1979). Yet this, as has been suggested, is a crucial issue, which both helps explain the growth of the MNEs (relative to non-MNEs) and their effect on the spatial distribution of economic activity. Assuming perfectly competitive markets are not generally feasible (nor, from viewpoints other than economic efficiency, necessarily desirable), under what circumstances is it preferable for the resource allocative process to be decided upon by markets or governments, however imperfect they may be, and under what circumstances by the internal governance of MNEs? For there is no *a priori* reason to suppose one form of resource allocation is preferable to the other. In remedying the imperfections and alleged distorting behaviour of MNEs, should not as much attention be given to removing some of the distortions of the environment in which they operate, so that they have less incentive to internalise their activities? To give a recent example, the replacement of fixed by flexible rates has decisively reduced the impetus for MNEs to engage in speculative or protective currency movements across boundaries. The candidate most in need of attention at the moment is technology. It is here that the present system of rewards and penalties leaves so much to be desired (Johnson, 1970) and it is here that both the incentive to internalise by MNEs *and* the potential for distorting behaviour on their part in exploiting the benefits of that internalisation arise.

In the last resort, however, we must acknowledge that it is not efficiency, and certainly not efficiency viewed from a global standpoint, that is the standard by which the relative merits of internalisation of MNEs and imperfect markets of allocating resources is likely to be assessed. It is the effects of such patterns of resource allocation on the distribution of income between or within nations; on the relative economic powers of countries or of different groups of asset owners; on the sovereignty of one country to manage its own affairs. It is these matters which are at the centre of the arena of public debate at the moment; and it is on such criteria as these that the actions of MNEs are judged.

Some countries facing the choice offered above have clearly preferred to buy their resources in imperfect markets than through MNEs (Japan is the obvious example), while many LDCs are increasingly seeking to depackage the package of resources provided by MNEs in the belief that they can externalise the internal economies. Within the advanced countries the non-market route is generally accepted. But here, too, there are murmurings of concern, articulated not only in such polemics as *The Global Reach* (Barnet and Muller, 1974) but in research studies done at the Brookings Institution (Bergsten, Horst and Moran, 1978) and by Peggy Musgrave (1975) on the effect of the (internalising) advantages of international production on the domestic economic power of US corporations.

This particular area of the debate on the role of MNEs in trade and the transfer of technology and the location of production is still in its infancy. It is an area hazardous and not altogether attractive for the academic economist; the issues are controversial; the concepts are elusive; the data are not easily subject to quantitative manipulation and appraisal; and the standard of debate is often low. But, intellectually, it presents a great challenge, offering much scope for the collaboration not only of economists of different specialities and persuasions, but between economists and researchers from other disciplines. For these reasons alone, it deserves to attract our ablest minds.

Notes: Chapter 2

1   The following observation by Williams (1929) about industries which had expanded beyond their political frontiers is of especial interest to our discussion.

> They represent in some cases the projection by one country into others of its capital, technique, special knowledge along the lines of an industry and its market, as against the obvious alternative of home employment in other lines. They represent, in other cases, an international assembling of capital and management for world enterprises ramifying into many countries. They suggest very strikingly an organic inter-connection of international trade, movement of productive factors, transport and market organisation.

2   For further details see Chapter 3. p. 48.
3   Mainly enterprises: by a country's enterprises is meant those whose head offices are legally incorporated in that country.
4   Gross domestic product = incomes earned from domestic resources; gross national product = gross national product + income earned from assets abroad less income paid to foreigners on domestic assets.
5   Proximity to the point of sale may be treated as a location-specific endowment for these purposes; distance (implying transport and other transfer costs) is thus considered as a negative endowment.
6   See Lall (1980) for a discussion on the extent to which ownership specific advantages are mobile, that is, transferable across national boundaries.
7   For an elaboration of the complementarity between the neofactor and neotechnology theories of trade, see Hirsch (1974).
8   One of the most recent and stimulating contributions on these lines is contained in Swedenborg (1979). For a general reappraisal on the literature on internalisation see Rugman (1980), Calvet (1980) and Teece (1981).
9   To avoid being subject to imperfections of markets when they are the weaker party to an exchange but to capitalise on imperfections when they are the stronger party.

10   Such as particularly applies in the case of transactions involving non-standard technology or information, and which are infrequent and conducted under uncertainty.
11   For a recent study of the applicability of the eclectic theory and the markets and hierarchies paradigm to the acquisition activity of foreign firms in Canada and that of domestic firms in the USA see Calvet (1980).
12   The transition from regional to national railroads in the nineteenth and early twentieth century was paralleled by the transition from national to multi-national airlines after the Second World War.
13   We have not the space to deal with the role of internalisation in prompting other forms of foreign direct investment; in some cases, the co-ordinating advantages of the firm clearly transcends that of the market for technological reasons, such as airlines; in others it is more to do with controlling information among inter-dependent activities, such as advertising, and tourism; or as a form of oligopol-istic strategy. In many cases, an investment based on technological innovation has managed to create its own barriers to entry through economies of size.
14   Licensing and other forms of contractual arrangements of intermediate products.
15   The points made in this paragraph are extended and set out in a rather different way in Table 3.1 and Table 4.2.
16   This point is elaborated in Chapter 4.
17   Lall (1979) suggests that in cases where major technological efforts on products and processes are not crucially linked to each other, international experience and cost advantages tend to promote greater reliance on foreign R & D. By con-trast, in those sectors where innovation centres around product development and testing it is much more difficult to separate any major part of R & D activity from the main markets and centre of decision taking. Michalet (1973), on the other hand, distinguishes between a specialised and imitative R & D strategy of MNEs, while Ronstadt (1977) adopts a more functional approach arguing that different types of R & D have different location needs. In a study of the over-seas R & D activities of fifty-five US-based MNEs, Mansfield, Teece and Romeo (1979) found that such activities were increasing relative to those in the USA and were concentrated on product and process improvements and modifications rather than the discovery of new products and processes. The authors argued that one important reason – at least in the 1960s and early 1970s – for foreign R & D activities was that the cost of R & D inputs was considerably lower in Japan, Europe and Canada than in the USA.
18   See Chapter 5.
19   Mainly in material processing or product adaptation to meet specialised local needs. Behrman and Fischer (1980) note that US enterprises have some R & D facilities in Hong Kong, Argentina, Colombia, Egypt, Philippines and Taiwan, whereas Argentina, Hong Kong and Singapore are among developing countries attracting such activities by European MNEs.
20   This point is further explored in Chapter 4. Here it is worth pointing out that vertical foreign direct investment often precedes horizontal foreign direct invest-ment (as it did in the UK and USA) and that the pattern of new Japanese investment in the late 1970s resembles much more that traditional US kind than it did in the 1960s.

References

Alchian, A., and Demsetz, H. (1972), 'Production, information costs and economic organisation', *American Economic Review*, Vol. 62 (December).
Aliber, R. (1970), 'A theory of foreign direct investment', in C. P. Kindle-berger (ed.), *The International Corporation* (Cambridge, Mass.: MIT Press).

Arrow, K. J. (1969), 'The organisation of economic activity: issues pertinent to the choice of market and non market considerations', in Joint Economic Committee, *The Analysis and Evaluation of Public Expenditures: the PPB System* (Washington, DC: US Government Printing Office).

Arrow, K. J. (1975), 'Vertical integration and communication', *Bell Journal of Economics*, Vol. 5, no. 1 (Spring).

Bain, J. S. (1956), *Barriers to New Competition* (Cambridge, Mass.: Harvard University Press).

Baldwin, R. E. (1970), 'International trade in inputs and outputs', *American Economic Review*, Vol. 60 (May).

Barnet, R. J., and Muller, R. E. (1974), *The Global Reach* (New York: Simon and Schuster).

Baumann, H. (1975), 'Merger theory, property rights and the pattern of US direct investment in Canada', *Weltwirtschaftliches Archiv*, Vol. 111, no. 4.

Bergsten, E. F., Horst, T., and Moran, T. E. (1978), *American Multinationals and American Interests* (Washington, DC: Brookings Institution).

Behrman, J. N., and Fischer, W. A. (1980), *Overseas R and D Activities of Transnational Corporations* (Cambridge, Mass.: Oelgeschlager, Gunn and Hain).

Brown, W. B. (1976), 'Islands of conscious power: MNCs in the theory of the firm', *MSU Business Topics* (Summer).

Buckley, P. J., and Dunning, J. H. (1976), 'The industrial structure of US direct investment in the UK', *Journal of International Business Studies*, Vol. 7 (Summer).

Buckley, P. J., and Casson, M. (1976), *The Future of the Multinational Enterprise* (London: Macmillan).

Calvet, A. L. (1980), 'Markets and hierarchies: towards a theory of international business', PhD thesis, Sloane School of Management, Cambridge, Mass.

Caves, R. E. (1971), 'Industrial corporations: the industrial economics of foreign investment', *Economica*, Vol. 38 (February).

Caves, R. E. (1974a), 'Causes of direct investment: foreign firms' shares in Canadian and United Kingdom manufacturing industries', *Review of Economics and Statistics*, Vol. 56 (August).

Caves, R. E. (1974b), 'Industrial organisation', in J. H. Dunning (ed.), *Economic Analysis and the Multinational Enterprise* (London: Allen & Unwin).

Coase, R. H. (1937), 'The nature of the firm', *Economica*, Vol. 4 (November).

Creamer, D. (1976), *Overseas Research and Development by US Multinationals 1966–75* (New York: The Conference Board).

Davidson, W. H., and McFetridge, D. G. (1980), *International Technology Transactions and the Theory of the Firm* (mimeo).

Dunning, J. H. (1958), *American Investment in British Manufacturing Industry* (London: Allen & Unwin).

Dunning, J. H. (1973a), 'The determinants of international production', *Oxford Economic Papers*, Vol. 25 (November).

Dunning, J. H. (1973b), 'The location of international firms in an enlarged EEC: an exploratory paper', Manchester Statistical Society.

Fischer, W. A., and Behrman, J. N. (1979), 'The co-ordination of foreign R and D activities by transnational corporations', *Journal of International Business Studies*, Vol. 10 (Winter).

Flowers, E. B. (1976), 'Oligopolistic reaction in European and Canadian direct investment in the US', *Journal of International Business Studies*, Vol. 7 (Fall/Winter).

Furubotn, E. G., and Pejovich, S. (1972), 'Property rights and economic theory: a survey of recent literature', *Journal of Economic Issues*, Vol. 6 (December).

Graham, E. M. (1978), 'Transatlantic investment by multinational firms: a rivalistic phenomenon', *Journal of Post Keynesian Economics*, Vol. 1 (Fall).

Hirsch, S. (1974), 'Capital and technology confronting the neo-factor proportions and neo-technology accounts of international trade', *Weltwirtschaftliches Archiv*, Vol. 110, No. 4.

Hirsch, S. (1976), 'An international trade and investment theory of the firm', *Oxford Economic Papers*, Vol. 28 (July).

Horst, T. (1972), 'Firm and industry determinants of the decision to invest abroad: an empirical study', *Review of Economics and Statistics*, Vol. 54 (August).

Hufbauer, G. C. (1970), 'The impact of national characteristics and technology on the commodity composition of trade in manufactured goods', in R. Vernon (ed.), *The Technology Factor in International Trade* (New York: Columbia University Press).

Hufbauer, G. C., and Chilas, J. G. (1974), 'Specialisation by industrial countries: extent and consequences', in H. Giersch (ed.), *The International Division of Labour: Problems and Perspectives* (Tubingen: Mohr).

Hymer, S. (1960), 'The international operations of national firms: a study of direct investment', unpublished doctoral thesis, MIT.

Hymer, S. (1970), 'The multinational corporation and the law of uneven development', in J. Bhagwati (ed.), *Economics and World Order* (New York: World Law Fund).

Iversen, C. (1935), *Aspects of International Capital Movements* (London and Copenhagen: Levin and Munksgaard).

Johnson, H. (1968), *Comparative Cost and Commercial Policy Theory for a Developing World Economy* (Stockholm: Almquist and Wiksell).

Johnson, H. (1970), 'The efficiency and welfare implications of the international corporation', in C. P. Kindleberger (ed.), *The International Corporation* (Cambridge, Mass.: MIT Press).

Knickerbocker, P. T. (1973), *Oligopolistic Reaction and the Multinational Enterprise* (Cambridge, Mass.: Harvard University Press).

Kojima, K. (1978), *Direct Foreign Investment* (London: Croom Helm).

Lake, A. (1976), *Transnational Activity and Market Entry in the Semiconductor Industry* and *Foreign Competition and the UK Pharmaceutical Industry* (National Bureau of Economic Research: New York, Working Papers Nos 126 and 155).

Lall, S. (1973), 'Transfer pricing by multinational manufacturing firms',

Oxford Bulletin of Economics and Statistics, Vol. 35 (August).

Lall, S. (1979), 'The international allocation of research activity by US multinations', *Oxford Bulletin of Economics and Statistics*, Vol. 41 (November).

Lall, S. (1980), 'Monopolistic advantages and foreign involvement by US manufacturing industry', *Oxford Economic Papers*, Vol. 32 (March).

Leontief, W. (1953), 'Domestic production and foreign trade; the American captial position re-examined', *Proceedings of the American Philosophical Society*, Vol. 97.

Leontief, W. (1956), 'Factor proportions and the structure of American trade; further theoretical and empirical analysis', *Review of Economics and Statistics*, Vol. 38.

Lipsey, R. E., and Weiss, M. Y. (1973), 'Multinational firms and the factor intensity of trade', National Bureau of Economic Research Working Paper 8.

MacDougall, G. D. A. (1951), 'British and American exports. A study suggested by the theory of comparative costs, Part I', *Economic Journal*, Vol. 61.

MacDougall, G. D. A. (1952), 'British and American exports. A study suggested by the theory of comparative costs, Part II', *Economic Journal*, Vol. 62.

McManus, J. C. (1972), 'The theory of the multinational firm', in G. Pacquet (ed.), *The Multinational Firm and the Nation State* (Toronto: Collier-Macmillan).

Magee, S. P. (1977a), 'Multinational corporations, the industry technology cycle and development', *Journal of World Trade Law*, Vol. XI (July/August).

Magee, S. P. (1977b), 'Technology and the appropriability theory of the multinational corporation', in J. Bhagwati (ed.), *The New International Economic Order* (Cambridge, Mass.: MIT Press).

Mansfield, E., Teece, D., and Romeo, A. (1979), 'Overseas research and development by US based firms, *Economica*, Vol. 46 (May).

Michalet, C. (1973), 'Multinational enterprises and the transfer of technology', unpublished paper for OECD, DAS/SPR/73.64.

Muller, R. (1975), 'Global corporations and national stabilisation policy: the need for social planning', *Journal of Economic Issues*, Vol. 9 (June).

Mundell, R. A. (1957), 'International trade and factor mobility', *American Economic Review*, Vol. 47 (June).

Musgrave, P. B. (1975), *Direct Investment Abroad and the Multinationals: Effects on the US Economy*. Prepared for the use of the Sub-Committee on Multinational Corporations of the Committee on Foreign Relations, US Senate, August (Washington, DC: US Government Printing Office).

Nurkse, R. (1933), 'Causes and effects of capital movements', reprinted in J. H. Dunning, *International Investment* (Harmondsworth: Penguin Readings, 1972).

Ohlin, B. (1933), *Interregional and International Trade* (Cambridge, Mass.: Harvard University Press, rev. edn. 1967).

Orr, D. (1973), 'Foreign control and foreign penetration in Canadian manufacturing industries', unpublished manuscript.

Owen, R. F. (1979), *Inter-Industry Determinants of Foreign Direct Invest-*

ment. *A Perspective Emphasising the Canadian Experience*, Working Papers in International Economics, Princeton University (May).

Parry, T. G. (1975), 'The international location of production: studies in the trade and non-trade servicing of international markets by multinational manufacturing enterprise', PhD Thesis, University of London.

Parry, T. G. (1980), *The Multinational Enterprise: International Investment and Host Country Impacts* (Greenwich, Conn.: JAI Press).

Reddaway, N. B., Potter, S. T., and Taylor, C. T. (1968), *The Effects of UK Direct Investment Overseas* (Cambridge: Cambridge University Press).

Ronstadt, R. (1977), *Research and Development Abroad by US Multinationals* (New York: Praeger).

Rugman, A. M. (1980), 'Internalisation as a general theory of foreign direct investment. A reappraisal of the literature', *Weltwirtschaftliches Archiv*, Vol. 116, no. 2.

Samuelson, P. (1948), 'International trade and equalisation of factor prices', *Economic Journal*, Vol. 58 (June).

Southard, F. A. (1931), *American Industry in Europe* (Boston: Houghton Mifflin).

Stopford, J. (1976), 'Changing perspectives on investment of British manufacturing multinationals', *Journal of International Business Studies*, Vol. 7 (Fall/Winter).

Swedenborg, B. (1979), *The Multinational Operations of Swedish Firms: An Analysis of Determinants of Effects* (Stockholm: Almquist and Wiksell).

Teece, D. J. (1979), *Technology transfer and R & D Activities of Multinational Firms: Some Theory and Evidence* (mimeo), Stanford University (November).

Teece, D. J. (1981), 'The multinational enterprise: market failure and market power considerations', *Share Management Review*, Vol. 22, no. 3.

Tilton, J. E. (1971), *International Diffusion of Technology: The Case of Semi-conductors* (Washington, DC: The Brookings Institution).

Vernon, R. (1966), 'International investment and international trade in the product cycle', *Quarterly Journal of Economics*, Vol. 80 (May).

Vernon, R. (1974), 'The location of economic activity', in J. H. Dunning (ed.), *Economic Analysis and the Multinational Enterprise* (London: Allen & Unwin).

Williams, J. H. (1929), 'The theory of international trade reconsidered', *Economic Journal*, Vol. 39 (June).

Williamson, O. E. (1971), 'The vertical integration of production market failure considerations', *American Economic Review*, Vol. 61 (May).

Williamson, O. E. (1975), *Markets and Hierarchies: Analysis and Antitrust Implications* (New York: The Free Press).

Williamson, O. E. (1979), 'Transaction-cost economics: the governance of contractual relations', *Journal of Law and Economics*, Vol. 22 (October).

Wolf, B. M. (1977), 'Industrial diversification and internationalisation: some empirical evidence', *Journal of Industrial Economics*, Vol. 26 (December).

3

Trade, Location of Economic Activity and the Multinational Enterprise: Some Empirical Tests

I

There is now a concensus of opinion that the propensity of an enterprise to engage in international production, that is, production financed by foreign direct investment, rests on three main determinants: first, the extent to which it possesses (or can acquire, on more favourable terms) assets[1] which its competitors (or potential competitors) do not possess; second, on how far it is possible, and in its best interests, to lease these assets to other firms, or make use of them itself; and third, on whether it is more profitable to exploit these assets in conjunction with the indigenous resources of foreign countries or with those of the home country. The more the ownership-specific advantages possessed by an enterprise, the greater the inducement to internalise them, and the wider the attractions of a foreign rather than a home country production base, the greater the likelihood that an enterprise will engage in international direct investment.

A national firm supplying its own market has various avenues for growth. It can diversify horizontally or laterally into new product lines, or vertically (i.e. upstream or downstream) into new activities, including the production of knowledge; it can acquire existing enterprises; or it can exploit foreign markets. When it makes good economic sense to choose the last route (which may also embrace one or more of the others), the enterprise becomes an international enterprise. However, for it to be able to produce alongside indigenous firms domiciled in these markets, it must possess additional ownership advantages sufficient to outweigh the costs of servicing an unfamiliar and/or distant environment (Hirsch, 1976).

An enterprise is an integrated and co-ordinated unit of decision taking,

This chapter is based on an article which first appeared in the *Journal of International Business*, vol. XL, no. 1 (Spring/Summer 1980). I am much indebted to Professor Guy Landry, of Brandon University, Winnipeg, who was responsible for most of the computational work behind the tables and who assisted in writing the first draft of pages 52–66.

the function of which is to transform, by the process of production, valuable inputs into more valuable outputs. The boundaries of an enterprise extend to where it no longer has control over the use of such inputs, or the assets from which they are derived.[2] In the present context, it is helpful to distinguish between two kinds of assets. The first are those which are available, on the same terms, to all firms whatever their size or nationality, but which are specific in their origin to particular locations, and have to be used in those locations. These include not only Ricardian type assets, viz. natural resources, most kinds of labour and proximity to markets,[3] but also the social, legal and commercial environment in which the endowments are used, market structure, and government legislation and policies. In classical and neoclassical trade theories, differences in the possession of these endowments between countries entirely explain the willingness and the ability of enterprises to become international,[4] but since all firms, whatever their nationality of ownership, are assumed to have full and free access to them there are no advantages to be gained from foreign production.

The second type of asset is that which an enterprise may create for itself (e.g. certain types of knowledge, organisation and human skills) or can purchase from other institutions, but which, in so doing, it acquires some proprietary right of use. Such ownership-specific assets may take the form of a legally protected right, or of a commercial monopoly, or they may arise from the size diversity or technical characteristics of firms, for example, economies of joint production and/or marketing and surplus entrepreneurial capacity (Kojima, 1978).

The essential feature about this second type of asset is that although its *origin* may be linked to location-specific endowments, its *use* may not be so confined. This can be explained as follows. The ability of enterprises to acquire ownership endowments is clearly not unrelated to the endowments specific to the countries in which they operate, and particularly their country of origin. Otherwise, there would be no reason why the structure of foreign production of firms of different nationalities should be different. But as Chapter 4 shows, this is so. Such differences as these can only be explained by an examination of the characteristics of the countries in which the MNEs operate, and especially those of the home country, which normally give rise to the ownership advantages in the first place. Raymond Vernon's product cycle theory was among the first to use this approach from the viewpoint of the activities of US MNEs (Vernon, 1966). More recently Birgitta Swedenborg (1979) has extended and applied it to a study of Swedish, US and UK direct foreign investment. It is also implicit in Aliber's thesis (Aliber, 1970) that differences in the capitalisation rates for firms of different nationality explain much of foreign direct investment, because while these rates may be largely determined by country-specific factors, they create an asset which only firms of a particular nationality are able to exploit.[5]

There is one final strand to the eclectic theory of international production. The possession of ownership advantages determines *which* firms will supply a particular foreign market, whereas the pattern of location endowments explains whether the firm will supply that market by exports (trade), or by local production (non-trade). But why does a firm choose to use the ownership advantages itself to exploit a foreign market — whatever route it chooses — rather than sell or lease these advantages to a firm located in that market to exploit? The answer — as set out at some length in the previous chapter[6] — is that it does so wherever it is in the firm's interests to internalise the use of its ownership-specific endowments rather than lease or sell these to other firms or where by the act of internalising an external contractual relationship, for example, by a takeover, a firm is able to use these assets better than can the acquired firm.

The matrix set out in Table 3.1 attempts to relate, in an encapsulated form, the main types of activities in which MNEs tend to be involved to the three main determinants of the extent and form of international involvement. Such a table may be used as a starting point for an examination of the industrial and geographical distribution of foreign direct investment. It will be noted that, as part of the explanation of ownership advantages, the possession of country endowments is also introduced, as these will influence the geographical origin of such investment.

II

Broadly speaking, there have been five approaches to testing the theory of international production. The first has attempted to explain the causes of direct foreign investment by examining its industrial composition from the viewpoint of individual home countries (almost exclusively the USA) and host countries (notably Canada, the UK and Australia). A common thread running through all these studies[7] is that they have sought to explain the pattern of foreign direct investment in terms of ownership advantages of MNEs. The second approach has been to look at the form of international economic involvement, and to identify the determinants of whether foreign markets are exploited by trade or non-trade routes.[8] The third has combined the two approaches by examining both the level and composition of international involvement, in terms of ownership and locational characteristics.[9] The fourth approach has been to extend the first three to incorporate the internalisation thesis,[10] and the fifth has been to relate the ownership endowments of firms to those of home countries (Vernon, 1966; Swedenborg, 1979; Lall, 1980). The empirical contribution of this chapter is primarily of the third kind but with the issues of the fourth very much in mind.

From both a technical and motivational standpoint these strands of research have much in common. Each uses, with varying degrees of

Table 3.1 Types of International Production: Some Determining Factors

Types of International Production	Ownership Advantages (The 'why' of MNC activity)	Location Advantages (The 'where' of production)	Internalisation Advantages (The 'how' of involvement)	Illustration of types of activity which favour MNEs
1 Resource based	Capital, technology, access to markets	Possession of resources	To ensure stability of oil supply at right price. Control of markets	Oil, copper, tin, zinc, bauxite, bananas, pineapples, cocoa, tea
2 Import substituting manufacturing	Capital, technology, management and organisational skills; surplus R & D and other capacity. Trade marks.	Material and labour costs, markets, government policy (e.g. with respect to barrier to imports, investment incentives, etc.)	Wish to exploit technology advantages, high transaction or information costs, buyer uncertainty, etc.	Computers, pharmaceuticals; motor vehicles, cigarettes
3 Rationalised specialisation (a) of products (b) of processes	As above, but also access to markets	(a) Economies of product specialisation and concentration (b) Low labour costs, incentives to local production by host governments	(a) As type 2 plus gains from interdependent activities (b) The economies of vertical integration	(a) Motor vehicles, electrical appliances, agricultural machinery (b) Consumer electronics, textiles and clothing, cameras, etc.
4 Trade and distribution	Products to distribute	Local markets. Need to be near customers. Aftersales servicing, etc.	Need to ensure sales outlets and to protect company's name	A variety of goods, particularly those requiring close consumer contact
5 Ancillary services	Access to markets (in the case of other foreign investors)	Markets	Broadly as for types 2 and 4	Insurance; banking and consultancy services
6 Miscellaneous	Variety – but include geographical diversification (e.g. airlines and hotels)	Markets	Various (see above)	Various kinds (a) Portfolio investment in properties (b) Where spatial linkages essential, e.g. airlines and hotels

sophistication, multiple regression analysis to test explanations about the relationship between various measures of international involvement and a variety of explanatory variables. Each, too, is beset by the same kind of methodological and statistical problems, notably the establishment of operationally testable hypotheses, data limitations and multicollinearity between the individual variables. From a motivational standpoint, with one exception (Knickerbocker, 1973), all the studies assume either that enterprises are profit maximisers or that their behaviour is not inconsistent with that which might be expected from a profit maximising firm.

Turning now to an empirical testing of the two hypotheses implicit in the eclectic theory of international production, we concentrate on only two forms of international economic involvement, viz. exports and production, which are assumed to be alternative to each other in servicing foreign markets.[11]

The data used are those covering the foreign activities of US MNEs in manufacturing industry as published by the US Tariff Commission (1973). In particular, interest is centred on the involvement of US firms in seven countries and in fourteen manufacturing industries. The Commission published data for two years, 1966 and 1970, but we shall confine ourselves to an analysis of the 1970 data as set out in Table 3.2. The two basic hypotheses to be tested are:

H1   The competitive advantage of a country's enterprises in servicing foreign markets is determined both by the ownership advantages of these enterprises, relative to those of enterprises of other nationalities, and the location advantages of the countries in which they produce, relative to those of other countries.

H2   The *form* of the involvement, or participation, will essentially depend on the relative attractiveness and/or production of the endowments of the home and host countries.[12]

It is also contended that the gains to be derived from internalising activities, which would otherwise be allocated by markets or government fiat, make up an important part of ownership advantages and, in some cases, of location advantages as well.

Concerning H1, the dependent variable is taken to be the share of the output of a particular industry (IS) in a particular country supplied by exports (X) plus local production (AS) of US-owned firms,[13] that is, $AS + X/IS$. These components can, of course, be considered separately, but in this hypothesis, we wish to exclude location-specific variables influencing the form of involvement. This dependent variable is noted as DV1.

The two components of international involvement may be considered separately. The share of the affiliates' sales of total output in the host

Table 3.2 US Affiliate Sales, US Exports and Total Industry Sales in Seven Countries, 1970 ($b)

	Canada AS	X	IS	United Kingdom AS	X	IS	France AS	X	IS	West Germany AS	X	IS	Belgium–Luxembourg AS	X	IS	Mexico AS	X	IS	Brazil AS	X	IS	Total AS	X	IS
1 Food products	2220	98	8532	1054	56	10294	473	7	17137	634	33	15583	121	9	2415	487	16	5773	107	8	3947	5096	227	63681
2 Paper and allied products	1503	118	3840	141	118	2763	183	61	2161	69	103	3474	96	27	496	121	52	525	65	9	504	2180	488	13763
3 Chemicals and allied products	2124	554	2490	1918	226	9356	971	107	8190	963	215	13888	654	220	1357	764	171	3888	623	146	3325	8017	1639	42494
4 Rubber products	613	146	628	373	22	1185	119	24	1854	211	36	1972	79	13	96	108	19	267	175	9	363	1678	269	6365
5 Primary and fabricated metals	1964	631	6877	804	237	7905	208	167	10750	1821	228	25280	252	81	3989	749	95	1981	262	83	2209	6060	1522	58991
6 Non-electric machinery	2222	1837	2778	2496	578	11862	1439	395	10581	1742	508	16529	429	221	1059	208	367	330	304	247	895	8840	4153	44034
7 Electrical machinery	1822	603	2213	1607	221	8961	514	136	6059	876	237	13888	425	52	993	478	195	919	246	49	1014	5968	1493	34047
8 Transportation equipment	5600	2430	6222	3430	211	12645	936	180	12086	3250	261	12843	275	139	1523	567	239	1261	1171	88	1792	15229	3548	48372
9 Textiles and apparel	532	168	3281	77	46	10275	21	13	8220	100	29	10470	207	54	2002	66	41	1969	124	10	2405	1127	361	38622
10 Lumber, wood and furniture	1322	91	2632	35	22	2763	15	4	3135	33	25	4475	0	2	478	5	16	316	5	1	705	1415	161	14504
11 Printing and publishing	176	153	1516	125	29	5003	51	4	4320	35	6	2589	5	2	390	6	9	396	4	4	429	401	207	14643
12 Stone, clay and glass	406	140	1260	242	14	3818	252	13	2897	239	20	6043	45	7	727	191	19	725	76	5	821	1451	218	16291
13 Instruments	563	219	626	739	101	1321	399	48	1976	406	90	1608	15	21	33	76	42	—a	91	26	—a	2289	547	5564
14 Other manufacturing	567	135	1916	3205	53	10541	35	36	3122	409	63	7282	5	44	1093	411	38	645	128	9	630	4760	378	25229
Total	21636	7323	44811	16246	1934	98692	5616	1195	92488	10788	1854	135924	2603	892	16651	4236	1319	18995	3381	694	19039	64511	15211	426600

a Not available.
Source: US Tariff Commission (1973).

country (*AS/IS*) is noted as DV2 and the share of exports from the USA of that output (*X/IS*) as DV3; DV2 and DV3 can be similarly derived to obtain comparative advantage indices.

Concerning H2, the dependent variable (DV4) is defined as $X/IS \div AS/IS$ (or simply X/AS); in other words, it is the ratio between exploiting a particular market by exports from the USA relative to local production by US affiliates in the country of marketing. The higher this ratio, the more the USA is favoured as a location for production, relative to the country in which the goods are being sold (or being exported from). It should be emphasised that, for the purposes of this exercise, it is assumed that the market can only be supplied from these two locations.

III

We now turn to a statistical testing of the two main hypotheses.

(a)   *The dependent variables: Hypothesis 1 – The international competitive hypothesis*

The overall involvement index reflects both location- and ownership-specific advantages. The explanation of the foreign production ratio lies in identifying and measuring ownership advantages (as the location of production is assumed to be the same for all firms), and that of the export ratio in identifying both location and ownership advantages. In examining the export ratio, one naturally turns to trade type theories for guidance. Here, as we have seen, the neofactor and neotechnology theories suggest that trade is related both to resource endowments and factor costs, and to certain ownership variables, notably technology and scale economies. But no attempt, to my knowledge, has been made to explain shares of a particular industry's sales accounted for by foreign imports.[14] In discussing the determinants of foreign production, one should be solely concerned with ownership advantages. Yet the fact that trade and production are often related to each other suggests that these advantages may also be associated with location-specific endowments.[15] Explanations of foreign production that ignore the latter specific advantages are thus likely to be inadequate.

The share of a particular industry's output supplied by foreign affiliates is determined by the competitive advantages of the affiliates and the relative attractions of the host country as a production base. It is likely to be greatest where the barriers to entry facing indigenous producers *and* exports from the home (and other countries) are highest. Trade is similarly determined, except that it will flourish where barriers to exports are low and where barriers to entry to all producers in the host country are high. International involvement is determined simply by the competitive advantage of the investing and exporting firms *vis-à-vis* indigenous and other foreign companies.

In symbolic terms:

DV1 $$AS + X/IS = f(C)$$

where C is the international competitive advantage

DV2 $$AS/IS = f(C, X/AS)$$

and

DV3 $$X/IS = f(C, X/AS)$$

(b) *The dependent variables: Hypothesis 2 – The location hypothesis*
This is simple and straightforward. To produce a particular good, an enterprise will choose that location which best advances its overall goals. The interface between received location theory and the MNE is a relatively unexplored territory, but a good start has been made by Vernon (1974). In principle, there is no reason to suppose a national multi-location firm would behave very differently if its activities were in a different country. New variables, for example, exchange risks, differences in taxation rates, and policies of host governments towards inward direct investment, may need to be incorporated, but this can be done without too much difficulty.

The location hypothesis is solely concerned with country-specific variables affecting (1) the size and character of markets[16] and (2) production and transfer costs, though, as we have seen, these may have a special impact on MNEs because of their ability to internalise the costs and benefits of some of the differences that exist between countries.

DV4 $$X/AS = f(L)$$

where L is the locational advantage of the home country.

(c) *The independent variables: Hypothesis 1*
How does one assess the competitive advantage of firms of one nationality over those of another – both in particular industries and countries? This essentially reduces to a question of (1) allocative, technical and scale efficiency, (2) product range and quality, and (3) market power. Since we are concerned with inter-industry comparisons, allocative efficiency, that is, of resources between industries, may be discounted. However, goals may differ between firms, as may the competence of firms to achieve these goals. For example, the greater the innovative ability of an enterprise, the greater its resourcefulness, and the more talented its managerial and labour force, the higher its market share is likely to be. Similarly, the advantages of size, of being part of a larger organisation and of being able to internalise external economies will affect a firm's competitive strength, independently of the location of its activities.

Some of these variables, of course, reflect industry- or country-specific characteristics of firms. Governments, for example, can and do influence the extent to which there is an adequate labour force to draw upon, the promotion of new technologies, the role of advertising in fostering product differentiation, and so on. These factors are acknowledged and will be considered explicitly in Chapter 4.

It may be helpful to break H1 down into two sub-hypotheses. The first is:

H1$_a$ Given the export participation ratio (X/IS), the foreign production participation ratio (AS/IS) will be highest in those industries where the comparative advantage of foreign (meaning US here) firms, is greatest *vis-à-vis* indigenous firms.

In principle, many of these advantages may be captured in a catch-all measure, viz. the comparative productivity of US firms and host country firms or some proxy for integration, for example, percentage of net to gross output. The comparative advantage of US firms is presumably highest where their relative productivity and/or value-added ratio is highest and, therefore, in those cases, the affiliate penetration ratio should be highest. In practice, difficulties in measuring productivity and identifying internalising economies makes both measures of doubtful applicability.

H1$_b$ Given the production participation ratio (AS/IS) the export penetration participation ratio (X/IS) will be highest in those industries where the national resource endowments of the USA is greatest in comparison to those of other countries, and where barriers to trade are minimal.

The contribution of trade theory to these determinants of location-specific advantages has been examined in terms of comparative cost advantages. Location theory approaches export success more in terms of differences in absolute production costs and the costs of traversing space. Artificial barriers to trade include those imposed by governments or imperfect markets. An incentive to export may also result from the inability of a host country's firms to effectively compete, due to the absence of a market sufficiently large to yield economies of scale in production.

(d)   *The independent variables: Hypothesis 2*
Like H1$_b$, the second hypothesis appears to be best explained by the theories of trade and location. Among the relative costs that play an important part in determining the location choice are those of labour and material inputs. The former is particularly critical in this study as it is limited to manufacturing industries where horizontal direct investment is the rule. This is in contrast to the situation in resource industries where vertical direct investment plays a much greater role. By the same token, labour productivity and its growth will be important elements in determining the real value of labour.

Production costs may also be closely related to the scale of plant which can be built. Market size will therefore be relevant. So also will rates of growth of the markets involved, as these will determine the extent to which economies of scale may be exploited in the future.

(e) *The choice of independent variables for this exercise*
Table 3.3 lists some of the variables which might be considered as proxies for ownership- and location-specific advantages. Also identified, with an asterisk, are those which might also be used as indices of internalisation advantages.[17] Some of these are very similar to each other, but not all can be used for this particular exercise, partly because we are concerned with explaining patterns of involvement by *industries* rather than by *firms*, and partly because of data constraints.

It will also be noted that for some variables listed, data are required for host countries; in others, for the home country, or for both host and home countries. Where only the home country is involved, then location advantages become irrelevant and one cannot use the data to determine both industry and country participation ratios. But the main constraint has been the paucity of good data about *host* countries which seriously inhibits testing both hypotheses for the seven countries considered separately. An exercise has also been conducted omitting the two LDCs, partly because there is less confidence in the data for these two countries, and partly in order to use a tariff variable, data for which were not available for Mexico and Brazil.

Ultimately, the independent variables were chosen and then used to test both hypotheses. Data on each relate to 1970, or nearest year, except where otherwise stated. The data for these variables were mainly extracted from the US Tariff Commission Study, except for those on imports which were obtained from the OECD Commodity Trade Statistics Series C and tariffs and from a Political and Economic Planning publication (1962).

A schematisation of variables follows:

For the Seven-Country exercise

(1) Ownership-specific variables
   (a) SER — skilled employment ratio, viz. the ratio of salaried employees to production employees for all firms in the host countries;
   (b) AHC — average hourly compensation of all employees in the host countries (1a and 1b are both measures of human capital intensity);
   (c) RSM — relative sales per man (an efficiency index) viz. the sales per man year of firms in the USA divided by sales per many year of firms (including the affiliates of US firms) in the host countries;
   (d) GRSPM — growth in sales per man of all firms (in the host country) 1966/70.

Table 3.3   *Identifying the Main Ownership and Location Advantages[a]*

Determinants	By Industry and/or Country
Ownership Advantages: Specific Determinants	

1 *Access to Productive Knowledge*

    (a) Skilled (professional and technical)/
         unskilled labour ratio*   Home cf. host firms

    (b) R & D as percentage of sales*   Home cf. host firms

2 *Economics of the Firm*

    (a) Size of enterprise*   Home firms

    (b) Relative size of enterprises   (Average) Home cf. host firms

    (c) Number of non-production to all workers*
         or wage bill of non-production to all
         workers *or* non-production[b] costs/total
         costs* (gross output) *or* R & D plus
         advertising costs to total costs (or sales)*   Home firms

    (d) Capital/Labour ratio   Home firms

3 *Opportunities for Investment*

    (a) Size of local market   (Industry) sales of host firms

    (b) Size of local market plus exports   (Industry) sales of host firms

4 *Diversification Indices[c]*

    (a) Average number of countries MNEs
         operate in* or   Home firms

    (b) % of foreign/total production of home
         firms*   Home firms

    (c) % of intra-group exports to total
         exports of MNEs*   Home firms

    (d) Number of product groups in which
         parent companies produce *or* % of
         output of main product group to all
         output*   Home firms

    (e) % of shipments from multi-plant
         enterprises to total shipments (in
         home country)*   Home firms

5 *Market Concentration*

    (a) Percentage of output of industry
         accounted for by x largest firms   Home firms

6 *Efficiency*

    (a) Wage costs (per man hour) of   Foreign affiliates as % of
         production workers   home firms

7 *Resource Availability*

    (a) % of main material(s) imported*   Either import/export ratio of
                                  home firms *or* % imports to
                                  total consumption

    (b) % of main material(s) used in   % of main matrial costs to
         production process   gross output

8 *Product differentiation*
    Advertising/sales ratio   Home firms

Table 3.3 (*cont*)

Determinants	By Industry and/or Country
9 *Oligopolistic Behaviour* Entry Concentration Index Knickerbocker PhD thesis	Home firms in host countries

Ownership Advantages: General Determinants

1 *Productivity* Net output or sales per man	1 Home firms cf. host firms 2 Foreign affiliates cf. host firms
2 *Profitability* Profits/assets or sales	1 Home firms cf. host firms 2 Foreign affiliates cf. host firms
3 *Growth* Increase in sales	1 Home firms cf. host firms 2 Foreign affiliates cf. host firms

Location Advantages: Specific Determinants

1 *Production Costs* (a) Wages per man hour	Home firms cf. host firms
(b) Energy costs (e.g. electricity or oil)	Home firms cf. host firms
(c) Material costs (cost of major inputs; or commodity price indices for main materials) *or* some index of resource availability	Home firms cf. host firms
(d) Tax rates (including, where possible, tax allowances)*	Home firms cf. host firms
(e) Average number of countries MNEs operating in	Home firms only
2 *Transfer Costs* (a) Transport costs	Home-host country
(b) Tariffs	Host country
(c) Non-tariff barriers	Host country
3 *General* (a) Political risks	Host country

Location Advantages: General Determinants

1 *Productivity* (a) Production costs per man *or* (b) Net output or sales per man	Home firms cf. foreign affiliates
2 *Profitability* Profits/assets or sales	Home firms cf. foreign affiliates
3 *Growth* Increase in sales	Home firms cf. foreign affiliates

a Internalizing advantages marked with an asterisk.

b Non-production = pre- + post-direct production costs.

c (a)–(d) specific to MNEs; (e) general to multi-plant enterprises.

The predicted sign for each of these variables for each of the hypotheses is positive, but their significance is likely to be greater for H1 than H2. US firms will invest in those industries and countries in which they have the greatest technological advantage and where their productivity *vis-à-vis* local firms is the highest.

(2)   Location-specific variables
    (a) XMR – the export/import ratio, measured by the ratio of value of exports to value of imports of *host* countries (as a measure of a country's ability to produce particular products);
    (b) RMS – relative market size, viz. value of industry sales in the USA divided by value of industry sales in the host countries;
    (c) RW – relative wages, viz. average hourly compensation (in particular industries) in the USA divided by average hourly compensation in the host countries for all employees (an often quoted cost determinant of foreign production);
    (d) RES – relative export shares of USA and host countries – another measure of country performance;
    (e) CMG – comparative market growth of USA (domestic industry local sales plus imports) and host countries 1966/70.
The predicted signs of these variables vary. In the case of RES it is positive, but in the case of XMR, RMS and CMG it is negative. It might also be expected that these variables would be most often used to support hypothesis H2.

(3)   General performance indicators
    (a) AVNIS – the average ratio of net income to sales of all firms in different industries and countries for 1966 and 1970;
    (b) MG – market growth (domestic industry local sales plus imports) in host countries 1966/70.
The predicted sign of AVNIS is negative for H1 but positive for H2, that for MG is positive for all hypotheses.

The Five Advanced Countries
As above, but with an additional location-specific variable.
    (f) TR – average tariffs measured on a country and industry basis.
The predicted sign of this variable is negative for DV4.

Such a large number of independent variables invites problems associated with multicollinearity. These problems were compounded when the two different groups of independent variables were tested against the 'wrong' dependent variables as well, in order to determine if the general hypotheses were too restrictive. It was therefore decided to correlate separately each of the independent variables to the dependent variables (DV1–4) to determine which ones appeared worthy of further statistical investigation. Only those that approached significance at a 95 per cent level were incorporated into multivariate form.

The large number of equations tested, given four dependent variables and twelve independent variables, also sharply increased the possibility of chance significance. Because of this, any value below the 99 per cent significance should be treated with caution.

IV

(a) Statistical Results – Case A: The Seven Countries

These countries vary quite considerably in income levels, economic structure, political ideologies, culture and proximity to the USA and the extent to which they themselves spawn MNEs which compete in international markets with US-based MNEs. It would not be surprising to find that different factors explain the absolute and relative success of US exports and affiliate production in these countries when tested individually; here, however, we are concerned with factors which explain export and affiliate success in the seven countries *as a group*, and which can, perhaps, be regarded as 'worldwide' determinants of such success.

H1(DV1–3). Table 3.4 summarises the more significant results of the regression analyses. The explanatory variables presented were extracted from the bivariate analysis and a series of multivariate equations constructed from them. For each of the variants of H1, most of the variation in the share of US firms in the output of countries can be put down to two or three variables, with the best results coming from the overall international competitiveness index (DV1). Since we are dealing with ninety-eight observations, the explanatory power of the three variants of the hypothesis is encouraging. All the signs (apart from that of RW) are consistent and in the right direction.

The equations reveal that the main advantage of US firms is revealed in one location-specific variable, viz. relative market size (RMS), and one ownership-specific variable, viz. the skilled employment ratio (SER). It has also been suggested (see Table 3.4) that this latter ratio may be used as a proxy for internalising advantages. Both are consistently significant at the 'double asterisk', that is, 99 per cent level for each of the dependent variables. The other ownership variables, which are significant at this level for DV1 and DV3, are the productivity index, viz. relative sales per man (RSM), and average hourly compensation (AHC). Two location variables, viz. wage differentials (RW) and net income per sales (AVNIS), are also significant for the same two dependent variables, but only at the 95 per cent level. For DV2, no variables, other than RMS and SER, were significant, although average hourly compensation (AHC) came closest. This last variable appears to be collinear with SER; this is not unexpected, as higher salaries are usually obtained by more highly skilled non-production employees.

Table 3.4 Determinants of Participation Ratios of US MNEs in Seven Countries, 1970

	Constant	AVNIS	RMS	SER	AHC	RW	RES	CGS	$R(R^2)$
(1) DV1 ($AS + X/IS$)									
1.1	0.060		−0.991 (4.058)**	1.133 (4.993)**					0.546 (0.298)
1.2	−0.068		−1.137 (4.831)**	1.007 (4.613)**			0.375 (3.422)**		0.613 (0.376)
1.3	−0.051		−1.219 (4.759)**	0.910 (3.652)**	0.027 (0.815)		0.279 (1.728)		0.617 (0.380)
1.4	0.002	−0.002 (2.474)**	−1.155 (4.635)**	0.732 (2.987)**	0.161 (2.603)*	−0.777 (2.615)*	0.494 (2.880)*		0.673 (0.452)
1.5	−0.028	−0.002 (2.365)*	−1.136 (4.519)**	0.809 (2.994)**	0.131 (1.735)	−0.648 (1.840)	0.480 (2.765)**	0.0065 (0.683)	0.675 (0.455)
(2) DV2 (AS/IS)									
2.1	0.018		−0.580 (3.459)	0.497 (3.192)**					0.430 (0.185)
2.2	0.0026		−0.693 (3.829)**	0.374 (2.164)*	0.026 (1.585)				0.454 (0.206)
2.3	0.016	−0.0009 (1.151)	−0.717 (3.942)**	0.388 (2.129)**	0.025 (1.522)				0.466 (0.217)
2.4	0.028	−0.0010 (1.260)	−0.669 (3.545)**	0.295 (1.597)	0.084 (1.801)	−0.322 (1.438)	0.072 (0.599)		0.485 (0.235)
(3) DV3 (X/IS)									
3.1	0.078		−1.571 (4.372)**	1.631 (4.883)**					0.553 (0.306)
3.2	−0.079		−1.750 (4.957)**	1.476 (4.510)**			0.459 (2.792)**		0.599 (0.359)
3.3	0.022		−1.987 (5.265)**	1.177 (3.260)**	0.095 (2.803)**				0.599 (0.359)
3.4	0.030	−0.0038 (2.271)*	−1.824 (4.856)**	1.027 (2.780)**	0.245 (2.627)*	−1.098 (2.454)*	0.566 (2.190)*		0.657 (0.432)

* Significant at the 95 per cent level.
** Significant at the 99 per cent level.

Table 3.5 Determinants of Export/Local Production Ratios of US MNEs in Seven Countries, 1970

	Constant	XMR	AVNIS	RMS	RSM	GRSPM	R/R^2
	(4) DV4 (X/AS)						
4.1	0.308	−0.101 (3.301)**	0.043 (7.256)**				0.601 (0.362)
4.2	0.042	−0.101 (3.363)**	0.043 (7.277)**			0.0085 (1.942)	0.622 (0.386)
4.3	0.103	−0.099 (3.210)**	0.042 (7.007)**	−0.561 (0.600)		0.0084 (1.896)	0.624 (0.389)
4.4	0.100	−0.100 (3.287)**	0.042 (7.101)**		−0.0000048 (0.441)	0.0090 (1.983)	0.623 (0.388)

** Significant at 99 per cent level.

These same relationships were also run using the 1966 data and much the same results obtained, with the exception that the 1966 profit variable (net income to sales AVNIS) is never quite significant.

H2(DV4). The results obtained from this hypothesis set out in Table 3.5 are quite different from those of H1. Two variables, viz. the export/import ratio (XMR) and net income to sales (AVNIS), are consistently significant at the 99 per cent level, and explain nearly 60 per cent of the variation in the location ratio. Growth of relative sales per man (GRSPM) comes very close but is never quite significant. The results for 1966 were virtually the same as for 1970.

(b)   *Statistical Results – Case B: The Five Advanced Countries*
Quite early in the study, it was decided to run the data with Mexico and Brazil excluded. Although to a certain extent, each country exercises its own unique set of influences on the involvement of foreign firms, there is something to be said for separating Mexico and Brazil from the five other countries. Historically, LDCs have produced relatively more raw materials and semi-finished manufactures and less of finished products for world markets than the developed countries. And, as we have seen, investment in resource based industries is often based on very different considerations than investment in manufacturing. Mexico and Brazil, in spite of recent rates of rapid industrial growth, are still sufficiently different in their stages of development to justify separate treatment.

H1(DV1–3). The results are presented in Table 3.6. In all equations one ownership variable, viz. the skilled employment ratio (SER), and two location variables, viz. relative market shares (RMS) and average hourly compensation (AHC), are consistently significant at the 99 per cent level. These three variables clearly have some influence on both US trade and affiliate success in each of the five countries. Relative export shares (RES) and relative wages (RW) appear significant at the 95 per cent (and in one case at the 99 per cent) level in some of the equations of DV2 and DV3, but only where there are few independent variables regressed together. This suggests that these latter two location variables exert some influence on the competitiveness of US trade but not on that of foreign production.

The tariff variable (T) appears to be a significant explanation of the overall involvement of US firms in the five countries. In combination with the three universally successful variables above (RMS, SER and AHC) it yielded an R^2 of 0.577 which is quite satisfactory.

The data for 1966 suggest much the same results, with the exception that, in some combinations, involving four or less independent variables, RS and RW also become significant as an explanation of DV1. This rather weakens the argument, based on the 1970 data, that these two have an

Table 3.6 Determinants of Participation Ratios of US MNEs in Five Advanced Countries, 1970

	Constant	AVNIS	RMS	SER	AHC	RW	RES	SPM	T	R(R²)
(1) DV1 (AS + X/IS)										
1.1	0.058		-0.990 (3.323)**	1.162 (4.445)**						0.587 (0.343)
1.2	0.0956	-0.0028 (1.884)	1.084 (3.653)**	1.137 (4.425)**						0.614 (0.377)
1.3	-0.014	-0.0026 (1.791)	-1.015 (3.522)**	1.289 (2.373)**					0.010 (2.373)*	0.653 (0.427)
1.4	0.470	-0.0019 (1.482)	-0.9234 (3.660)**	0.872 (3.608)**	0.152 (4.609)**				0.014 (3.486)	0.755 (0.570)
1.5	-0.436	-0.0022 (1.688)	-0.912 (3.576)**	0.891 (3.409)**	0.173 (2.844)**	-0.318 (0.942)	0.202 (0.943)		0.013 (3.330)**	0.760 (0.577)
(2) DV2 (AS/IS)										
2.1	0.0125		-0.540 (3.595)**	0.506 (3.841)**						0.566 (0.321)
2.2	-0.096		-0.522 (3.675)**	0.334 (2.438)**	0.056 (3.007)**					0.634 (0.403)
2.3	-0.055	-0.0010 (1.346)	-0.539 (3.727)**	0.339 (2.291)*	0.077 (2.254)*	-0.274 (1.426)	0.148 (1.225)			0.657 (0.432)
2.4	-0.051	-0.0012 (1.609)	-0.545 (3.845)**	0.391 (2.648)*	0.099 (2.787)**	-0.390 (1.969)	0.283 (2.059)	-0.0000043 (1.900)		0.681 (0.464)
(3) DV3 (X/IS)										
3.1	0.070		-1.530 (3.771)	1.669 (4.686)**						0.617 (0.381)
3.2	0.307		-1.467 (4.007)**	1.071 (3.031)**	0.194 (4.051)**					0.710 (0.504)
3.3	-0.314		-1.466 (3.830)**	1.464 (4.282)**		0.695 (3.079)*				0.677 (0.459)
3.4	-0.250	-0.0030 (1.616)	-1.570 (4.275)**	1.070 (3.064)**	0.185 (3.903)**					0.723 (0.523)
3.5	-0.206	-0.0037 (1.938)	-1.536 (4.072)**	1.137 (3.016)**	0.221 (2.532)*	-0.627 (1.280)	0.438 (1.422)			0.735 (0.540)

* Significant at 95 per cent level.   ** Significant at 99 per cent level.

influence on trade, but not on foreign production. But probably they are only marginally significant in all three cases. For both years, 1966 and 1970, when the number of independent variables is increased, these two variables become less significant, which suggests that the added variables capture the significant influences duplicated in RS and RW. There appears, for example, to be a fair amount of collinearity between RW and AHC and between RS and SPM. For 1970, the correlation coefficients (at the seven-country level) between these variables are 0.944 and 0.705, respectively.

As may be seen in Table 3.7, quite different variables explain most of the form of penetration than those which explain H1. The profitability ratio (AVNIS) and the growth in sales per man (GRSPM) are consistently significant, the former at extremely high levels of significance and the latter at either 99 per cent or 95 per cent levels of significance. These two alone explain more than half the variance in the location ratio. Other variables which are occasionally significant are three location specific variables: relative export shares (RES), relative wage costs (RW) and comparative market growth (CMG). They are only significant in small groups, however, which suggests an overlap between many of these variables. Equation 4 of DV4 is a good example where relative wage costs (RW) and relative export shares (RES) are both significant at a 95 per cent level and where the R^2 is 0.587.

The data for 1966 yield similar results with country or industry (rather than ownership) differences in profitability (AVNIS) and growth in sales per man (GRSPM) (an ownership variable) being rather more significant. But in this case (market share) MG becomes marginally significant in combination with GRSPM. None of the labour cost and productivity variables is significant.

Comparing Case A and Case B
Excluding Mexico and Brazil, the seven-country analysis produced some noticeable differences in the results of the statistical analysis. This section deals with a few of these and speculates on the reasons for them.

First the general level of the R^2s rises quite noticeably. This suggests that the independent variables used were more relevant in explaining export and affiliate success in the more homogenous advanced countries than in Mexico and Brazil. Running the regressions excluding Canada suggests even higher R^2s could have been obtained.[18]

Second, considering the data for 1966 as well as 1970, differences in wage costs (RW) and export shares (RS) tend to be more significant in explaining H1(DV2) in the seven-country than in the five-country case. Perhaps these variables are too similar over different industries in the industrialised countries, and, not until the widely different figures for Mexico and Brazil are included, is their influence clearly indicated.

Third, AHC differences are significant in the compensation of the five-

Table 3.7   Determinants of Export/Local Production Ratios of US MNEs in Five Advanced Countries, 1970

	Constant	AVNIS	AHC	RW	RSM	RES	CMG	GRSPM	MG	T	R(R²)
(4) DV4 (X/AS)											
4.1	-0.251	0.050 (7.953)**						0.012 (2.206)*			0.717 (0.515)
4.2	-0.130	0.050 (7.857)**						0.025 (2.942)**	-1.309 (1.967)		0.736 (0.542)
4.3	1.777	0.050 (8.119)**			-0.000045 (2.510)*		-3.517 (2.845)**	0.013 (2.515)**			0.755 (0.570)
4.4	0.508	0.044 (7.150)**		-2.548 (2.657)*		1.803 (2.174)*		0.024 (2.914)**	-1.240 (1.928)		0.766 (0.587)
4.5	1.492	0.046 (7.325)**		-1.509 (1.289)	-0.000043 (1.906)	1.647 (1.645)	-2.534 (1.694)	0.012 (2.316)*			0.767 (0.588)
4.6	1.277	0.045 (7.159)**		-1.760 (1.486)	-0.000030 (1.212)	1.605 (1.608)	-1.848 (1.159)	0.021 (2.361)*	-0.864 (1.210)		0.773 (0.598)
4.7	1.603	0.045 (7.086)**	0.249 (0.859)	-2.516 (1.703)	-0.000045 (1.483)	1.672 (1.666)	-2.598 (1.427)	0.022 (2.436)*	-1.004 (1.367)		0.776 (0.602)
4.8	1.521	0.045 (7.082)**	0.307 (1.008)	-2.430 (1.630)	-0.000050 (1.600)	1.483 (1.415)	-3.002 (1.555)	0.023 (2.499)*	-0.964 (1.303)	0.012 (0.656)	0.778 (0.605)

 * Significant at the 95 per cent level.
** Significant at the 99 per cent level.

country but not in the seven-country case for H2(DV4). This result is difficult to interpret. It may be due to less reliable figures on hourly compensation in Mexico and Brazil than in the other countries; or to a vastly different labour force structure which influences the extent to which local firms can compete successfully against imports in different ways.

Fourth, in the case of H1(DV1), there are virtually no differences between Cases A and B. There is one major difference between the two cases involving DV4, viz. the export/import ratio (XMR) is significant with the larger group but not with the smaller. This may be interpreted to mean that the export potential of an industry may be more important in a less developed economy in determining the form of penetration. The negative sign implies that US firms in those industries will tend to establish affiliates rather than export to the less developed countries, and perhaps even export some portion of their output. This is consistent with both the product cycle model's last stage and the growth of export-platform investments in some developing countries, including Mexico.

Appendix 3.1: Note on Methodology

The statistical analysis was restricted to common linear regression analysis and was carried out by Guy Landry at the University of Reading Computing Centre. Initially, single variable regressions with each of the independent variables and for each dependent variable were run. The purpose was to choose potentially useful explanatory variables from the number available. As a result of this a few variables were dropped because they either indicated no explanatory value or appeared less useful than very similar variables which were retained.

The next step involved multiple regressions. As explained in the body of this chapter, the independent variables were divided into three categories:

(1)   the *ownership*-specific variables: SER, AHC, RSM, and GRSPM. These are variables suggested by industrial organisation theory.
(2)   the *country*-specific variables: XMR, RMS, RW, RES, and CMG. These are mostly suggested by trade and location theory.
(3)   the general performance indicatiors: AVNIS and MG.

For each of the dependent variables, various combinations of the independent variables in each category were subjected to regression analysis. The most significant results are those shown in the tables. The purpose of this step was to determine which independent variables in each category best explained the dependent variables. Next, these same variables were analysed, but with the categories grouped in different combinations. Once again the tables reveal the results. These particular equations should reveal the explanatory power of various combinations of the independent variables chosen from two or all of three categories.

The values in parentheses are the *t*-values: those marked by a single asterisk are significant at the 95 per cent level, while those marked by two asterisks are significant at the 99 per cent level.

The last column of each table gives the values of the coefficient of determination.

Appendix 3.2: List of Industries (and Concordance)

	BEA Code	SIC Code	SITC Code		
1 Food products	410	20	013	047	062
			023	048	092
			024	053	099
			032	055	111
			046	061	112
2 Paper and allied products	420	26	64		
			251		
3 Chemical and allied products	430	28	5		
4 Rubber	440	30	231.2		
			62		
			893		
5 Primary and fabricated metals	450	33	67		
			68		
			69		
			812.3		
6 Non-electrical machinery	460	35	71		
7 Electrical machinery	470	36	72		
8 Transportation equipment	480	37	73		
9 Textiles and apparel	491	22	65		
		23	84		
			266		
10 Lumber, wood and furniture	492	24	63		
		25	243		
			82		
11 Printing and publishing	493	27	892		
12 Stone, clay, and glass products	495	32	66		
			−667		
13 Instruments	496	38	86		
			−863		
14 Ordnance, leather, tobacco,	494	19	122	891	
and other manufacturing	497	21	61	894	
	498	31	667	895	
	499	39	81	897	
			−812.3	899	
			83	951.0	
			85		

Appendix 3.3: Statistical Sources

Dependent Variables
The dependent variables of the analysis are described in the text and are all ratios based on the following four variables.
1   AS — Affiliate Sales: foreign sales of all affiliates of US MNEs, by industry and by country. From US Tariff Commission (USTC)(1973), p. 372.
2   X — Exports: exports from USA, by countries receiving and by industry. From USTC Study, p. 384.
3   ASX (or AS + X) — Affiliate Sales plus Exports: the sum of the above two.
4   IS — Industry Sales: sales (production) by all firms, by industry and by country. From USTC Study, pp. 693—706.

Independent Variables
A. By industry, for all seven selected countries.
1   SER — Skilled Employment Ratio: the ratio of salaried employment to total (salaried plus production) employment for all firms. Derived from USTC Study, pp. 693—706.
2   AHC — Average Hourly Compensation: estimate average hourly compensation of all employees. Fom pp. 724—5 of USTC Study.
3   AVNIS — Net Income to Sales: the ratio of net income (after foreign income tax) to sales of affiliates of US MNEs. Derived from USTC Study, pp. 446—52. Unlike the case of most of the other variables where the data is for 1970, this refers to an average of 1966 and 1970.
4   XMR — Export—Import Ratio: the ratio of exports to imports. Derived from USTC Study, p. 377 (for exports) and OECD, Series C, Commodity Trade (for imports).
5   RES — Relative Export Share: a Balassa-type measure of export performance, based on data from USTC Study, p. 377.
6   RSM — Relative Sales per Man: estimated sales per man in the host country/estimated sales per man in the USA, for all employees. Derived from USTC Study, pp. 748—9.
7   RW — Relative Wages: estimated average hourly compensation in the host country/estimated average hourly compensation in the USA, for all employees. Derived from USTC Study, pp. 724—5.
8   GRSPM — Growth in Sales Per Man, 1966—1970. Based on USTC Study, pp. 748—9.
9   RMS — Relative Market Size: industry sales in the host country/industry sales in the USA. Based on USTC Study, pp. 691—706.
10 CMG — Comparative Market Growth, 1966—1970. Market growth in the host country/market growth in the USA. The market is here defined as industry sales plus imports. Based on USTC Study, pp. 691—706 (for industry sales) and OECD, Series C, Commity Trade (for imports).
11 MG — Market Growth rate, 1966—1970. The market is here defined as industry sales plus imports. Based on USTC Study, pp. 693—706 (for industry sales) and OECD, Series C, Commity Trade (for imports).

B. By industry, for the industrialised five countries.
1   TR — Tariffs: average tariff rates in effect, 1958. Based on Political and Economic Planning (1962).

Notes: Chapter 3

1   Throughout this chapter, 'assets', 'endowments' and 'resources' are used interchangeably, and in the Fisherian sense, to mean 'anything capable of generating a future income stream'. See also Chapter 2, pp. 41.

2   Thus a firm of one nationality may *own* assets but sell the right of their *use* to firms of another nationality, for example, by engaging in portfolio investment or international licensing; where it owns them, but uses them itself in another country, then it engages in foreign direct investment, that is, it becomes a MNE.

3   In this chapter, distance from foreign markets is treated as a negative location-specific endowment.

4   Moreover, since perfect competition and identical production functions between firms were two of the assumptions underlying the theories, they were not interested in explaining the international activities of firms — only of countries.

5   That is, an advantage which is country specific *in origin* becomes an ownership-specific advantage *in use*.

6   See also Chapters 4 and 5. For a succinct review of the literature on the theory of internalisation, see Rugman (1980).

7   Among these one might mention particularly those of Vaupel (1971) and Horst (1972a, b, 1975) (in this latter paper the author explicitly acknowledges the importance of internalising advantages). The study of Wolf (1977) is also particularly pertinent to explaining why firms choose to engage in foreign direct investment rather than other forms of growth. Writers doing research on host country data include Orr (1973), Baumann (1975), Caves (1974), Buckley and Dunning (1976), Lall (1979), Owen (1979), Parry (1980) and Papandreou (1980).

8   See here particularly the work of Hirsch (1976), Buckley and Pearce (1979), Hawkins and Webbinek (1976), Parry (1975, 1976), Buckley and Davies (1979) and Buckley and Casson (1981). The question of the extent to which trade and foreign investment substitute for each other has been very well explored by Lipsey and Weiss (1973, 1976a, b), Cornell (1973) and Horst (1974).

9   There has been only limited empirical testing of this approach. The Hirsch contribution (Hirsch, 1976) is again very relevant. See also Dunning and Buckley (1977).

10 Here the work of Buckley and Casson (1976) is especially relevant.

11 The complications of this assumption will be dealt with later in this chapter. See also Horst (1974).

12 We extract from the possibility that firms might supply foreign markets from third locations.

13 Consumption figures would have been more appropriate but these were not available.

14 But see Dunning and Buckley (1977).

15 In other words, some ownership advantages are not independent of the location of production.

16 Which *inter alia* may be affected by competitors' behaviour.

17 For a different approach to the measurement of these advantages see Buckley and Casson (1976).

18 This was not actually done because to do so would have substantially reduced the degrees of freedom.

References

Aliber, R. Z. (1970), 'A theory of foreign direct investment', in C. P. Kindleberger (ed.), *The International Corporation* (Cambridge, Mass.: MIT Press).

Baumann, H. (1975), 'Merger theory, property rights and the pattern of US direct investment in Canada', *Weltwirtschaftliches Archiv*, Vol. 111, no. 4.

Buckley, P. J., and Casson, M. C. (1976), *The Future of the Multinational Enterprise* (London: Macmillan).

Buckley, P. J., and Casson, M. C. (1981), 'The optimal timing of a foreign direct investment', *Economic Journal*, Vol. 91 (March).

Buckley, P. J., and Davies, H. (1979), *The Place of Licensing in the Theory and Practice of Foreign Operations*, University of Reading Discussion Papers in International Investment and Business Studies No. 47.

Buckley, P. J., and Dunning, J. H. (1976), 'The industrial structure of US direct investment in the UK', *Journal of International Business Studies*, Vol. 7, (Summer).

Buckley, P. J., and Pearce, R. D. (1979), 'Overseas production and exporting by the world's largest enterprises', *Journal of International Business Studies*, Vol. 10 (Spring).

Caves, R. E. (1974), 'The causes of direct investment: foreign firms' shares in Canadian and UK manufacturing industries', *Review of Economics and Statistics*, Vol. 56 (August).

Cornell, R. (1973), 'Trade of multinational firms and nation's comparative advantage', paper presented to a Conference on Multinational Corporations and Governments, UCLA, November 1973.

Dunning, J. H., and Buckley, P. J. (1977), 'International production and alternative models of trade', *Manchester School of Economic and Social Studies*, Vol. 45 (December).

Hawkins, R., and Webbinek, E. S. (1976), 'Theories of direct foreign investment: a survey of empirical evidence', unpublished manuscript.

Hirsch, S. (1976), 'An international trade and investment theory of the firm', *Oxford Economic Papers*, Vol. 28 (July).

Horst, T. (1972a), 'Firm and industry determinants of the decision to invest abroad: an empirical study', *Review of Economics and Statistics*, Vol. 54 (August).

Horst, T. (1972b), 'The industrial composition of US exports and subsidiary sales to the Canadian market', *American Economic Review*, Vol. 62 (March).

Horst, T. (1974), *American Exports and Foreign Direct Investments*, Harvard Institute of Economic Research Discussion Paper No. 362 (May).

Horst, T. (1975), 'American investments abroad: and domestic market power', unpublished paper (for Brookings Institution, Washington, DC).

Kojima, K. (1978), *Direct Foreign Investment* (London: Croom Helm).

Knickerbocker, F. T. (1973), *Oligopolistic Reaction and the Multinational Enterprise* (Cambridge, Mass.: Harvard University Press).

Lall, S. (1979), 'Multinationals and market structure in an open developing economy. The case of Malaysia', *Weltwirtschaftliches Archiv*, Vol. 114, no. 2.

Lall, S. (1980), 'Monopolistic advantages and foreign involvement by US manufacturing industry', *Oxford Economic Papers*, Vol. 32 (March).

Lipsey, R. E., and Weiss, M. Y. (1973), *Multinational Firms and the Factor Intensity of Trade*, National Bureau of Economic Research, New York, Working Paper No. 8.

Lipsey, R. E., and Weiss, M. Y. (1976a), *Exports and Foreign Investment in the Pharmaceutical Industry*, National Bureau of Economic Research, New York, Working Paper No. 87 (revised).

Lipsey, R. E., and Weiss, M. Y. (1976b), *Exports and Foreign Investment in Manufacturing Industries*, National Bureau of Economic Research, New York, Working Paper No. 13 (revised).

Orr, D. (1973), 'Foreign control and foreign penetration in Canadian manufacturing industries', unpublished manuscript.

Owen, R. F. (1979), *Inter-industry Determinants of Foreign Direct Investment: A Perspective Emphasising the Canadian Experience*, Working Papers in International Economics, Princeton University (May).

Papandreou, V. A. (1980), 'Multinational enterprises, market industrial structure and trade, balance in less developed countries: the case of Greece', University of Reading PhD thesis.

Parry, T. G. (1975), 'Trade and non trade performance of US manufacturing industry: "revealed" comparative advantage', *Manchester School of Economics and Social Studies*, Vol. 43 (June).

Parry, T. G. (1976), *Methods of Servicing Overseas Markets: The UK Owned Pharmaceutical Study*, University of Reading Discussion Paper (Series 2) No. 27.

Parry, T. G. (1980), *The Multinational Enterprise: International Investment and Host Country Impacts* (Greenwich, Conn.: JAI Press).

Political and Economic Planning (1962), *Atlantic Tariffs and Trade* (London: Allen & Unwin).

Rugman, A. (1980), 'Internalisation as a general theory of foreign direct investment', *Weltwirtschaftliches Archiv*, Vol. 116 (June).

Swedenborg, B. (1979), *The Multinational Operations of Swedish Firms: An Analysis of Determinants and Effects* (Stockholm: Almqvist and Wiksell International).

US Tariff Commission (1973), *Implications of Multinational Firms for World Trade and Investment and for US Trade and Labor* (Washington, DC: US Government Printing Office).

Vaupel, J. W. (1971), 'Characteristics and motivations of the US corporations which invest abroad', unpublished manuscript.

Vernon, R. (1966), 'International investment and international trade in the product cycle', *Quarterly Journal of Economics*, Vol. 80 (May).

Vernon, R. (1974), 'The location of economic activity', in J. H. Dunning (ed.), *Economic Analysis and the Multinational Enterprise* (London: Allen & Unwin).

Wolf, B. (1977), 'Industrial diversification and internationalisation: some empirical evidence', *Journal of Industrial Economics*, Vol. 26 (December).

4
Explaining Changing Patterns of International Production: In Support of the Electic Theory

I

This chapter takes as its starting point the changes in the geographical origin and industrial composition of international production (production financed by foreign direct investment) which have occurred since the early 1960s, and assesses how far the theories of foreign direct investment put forward in the 1960s, primarily to explain a US phenomenon, need to be modified. Section II briefly outlines the historical changes. Section III reiterates the case for an eclectic theory of international production which helps explain both the extent of, and the way in which domestic and foreign markets are served by, enterprises of different nationalities and the industrial and geographical composition of such activities. Section IV makes use of this theory to suggest reasons for differences in the industrial pattern of the outward direct investment by five developed countries, viz. the USA, the UK, West Germany, Japan and Sweden, in 1975. Section V draws the main conclusions.

II

(a) *In the early 1960s*
In retrospect, the pattern and form of international production in the first fifteen years after the Second World War were unique. Foreign production was dominated by one home country, the USA, and reflected the first stage in the evolution of the modern multinational enterprise (MNE). Research in the 1950s and 1960s concerned itself almost exclusively with attempting to explain the growth and industrial composition of US foreign direct investment, its location and its impact on the economies of individual host countries.[1]

This chapter was first published in *Oxford Bulletin of Economics and Statistics*, vol. 41, no. 4 (November 1980). I am particularly indebted to Birgitta Swedenborg and H. Peter Gray for stimulating comments on an earlier version of this chapter.

In 1960, the USA accounted for about three-fifths of the accumulated foreign direct investment stake of market economies.[2] The UK was responsible for one-sixth, and the rest was fairly widely dispersed among the other OECD countries. Of the new investment (including reinvested profits) between 1945 and 1960, the US share was nearer three-quarters, and of that directed to manufacturing industry, more than four-fifths.

There are many reasons why US MNEs dominated the foreign direct investment scene in this era but most of them can be placed in one of two groups: first, the huge lead built up by the USA between 1939 and 1945 in technological capacity and management and organisational expertise, and second, the advances in international transport and communications and a world shortage of dollars which made it both possible and desirable to exploit these advantages by foreign production, rather than by exports or portfolio resource movements.

Although the main features of the industrial and geographical pattern of postwar US direct investment were already apparent by the early 1960s, it was not until the publication of results of the Harvard project on the 187 leading US industrial multinations (Vaupel and Curhan, 1969, 1973) and a special study by the US Tariff Commission in 1973 that the evidence was fully documented. On the basis of these and other data, the industrial composition of US direct investment was subjected to a good deal of scrutiny *inter alia* by such researchers as Horst (1972a, b, 1974), Caves (1974a, b), Parry (1975), Hirsch (1976), Lipsey and Weiss (1976a, b), Hawkins and Webbinek (1976), Owen (1979) and Lall (1980). The picture portrayed is a fairly clear one. First, within manufacturing industry, the activities of US MNEs are mainly directed to technology intensive industries and/or to those producing differentiated high income consumer goods, and, within resource based industries, to capital and/or technology intensive industries supplying products to markets in which the investing firm has a favoured access. Second, the propensity of US MNEs to involve themselves overseas in both trade and production is most pronounced in these sectors. Third, such firms tend to account for the largest share in the output of host countries in these industries.

Rather less attention was paid to the geographical composition of US direct investment in the 1960s, except within particular regions like Western Europe.[3] But it also strongly reflected its origins – no less than 70 per cent of US investment was made in Canada and Latin America in 1950 and 64 per cent in 1959. The 1960s saw a greater surge into Europe, and by 1972 this region had replaced both Canada and Latin America as the preferred destination.[4]

During this period, US firms preferred a 100 per cent stake in their foreign affiliates, except in the case of long-established affiliates where a minority local shareholding was quite common. In 1957, 69.0 per cent of the affiliates of the largest 187 US corporations were wholly owned and another 15.2 per cent majority owned (UN, 1978). The fully owned affiliate was regarded as the normal or natural form of involvement by US firms abroad; other forms of ownership were accepted only for special reasons or under pressure from host governments. This philosophy of treating the foreign affiliate as a satellite of the parent firm also fashioned the views of economists about the determinants of international production.

(b)   *From the early 1960s to late 1970s*
Perhaps the most striking feature of the changing pattern of international production over the last fifteen years or so has been a diversification of its country of origin. As Table 4.1 shows, between 1967 and 1978 the share of the direct investment stock of the two leading home countries fell from 70.4 per cent to 56.6 per cent while that of Germany and Japan rose from 4.2 per cent to 15.9 per cent. Data from the *Fortune* leading industrial companies reveal, even more dramatically, the rise of non-US companies. In 1962, 292 (60.5 per cent) of the largest 483 industrial companies were US-owned, 51 (10.6 per cent) UK, 91[5] (18.8 per cent) other European, 29 (6.0 per cent) Japanese and 3 (0.6 per cent) were from developing countries. The corresponding figures for 1977 were US 240 (49.7 per cent), UK 40 (8.3 per cent), other European 104 (21.2 per cent), Japanese 64 (13.3 per cent) and developing countries 18 (3.7 per cent) (Dunning and Pearce, 1981).

It is worth observing that the above changes may reflect not only differences in the rate of new foreign direct investment between countries, but the differences in the rate of divestment by MNEs. Thus, the number of voluntary foreign divestments by the 500 largest US MNEs rose from 50 in 1967 (31 of them in Western Europe) to 335 in 1975 (196 of them in Western Europe); and for every two affiliates added by the 180 largest US MNEs over the same period, one had been liquidated, sold or nationalised. Divestments by UK firms rose from 39 in 1968 to 235 in 1975 (Sachdev, 1976). Data are less comprehensive for MNEs of other nationalities, but what there are suggest that while there has been an increase of divestments from both continental European and Japanese MNEs since the mid-1970s, the ratio of such divestments to new investments is still well below the US average – and, in the Japanese case, very considerably so.[6]

Changes have also occurred in both the industrial composition and geographical destination of foreign direct investment. This is partly a consequence of the first feature,[7] but the more established MNEs have also shifted their interests away from the traditional areas of investment (Canada, Latin America and the ex-colonial territories) towards some of the newly industrialised countries in South-East Asia.

As the extent of multinationality of MNEs has widened,[8] the nature of international production has changed. From investing overseas primarily to exploit natural resources for export, or to supply local markets with a similar product to those produced at home, MNEs have increasingly engaged

Table 4.1 Stock of Direct Investment Abroad of Development Market Economies, by Major Country of Origin, 1967–1978

Country of Origin	$b. at end of				Percentage distribution			
	1967	1971	1975	1978	1967	1971	1975	1978
United States	56.6	82.8	124.1	168.1	49.6	49.3	47.2	45.5
United Kingdom	17.5	23.7	30.4	41.1	15.3	14.1	11.6	11.1
Germany, Federal Republic of	3.0	7.3	16.0	31.8	2.6	4.3	6.1	8.6
Japan[a]	1.5	4.4	15.9	26.8	1.3	2.6	6.0	7.3
Switzerland	5.0	9.5	17.6	24.6	4.4	5.7	6.7	6.7
Netherlands	11.0	13.8	19.0	23.7	9.6	8.2	7.2	6.4
France	6.0	7.3	11.1	14.9	5.3	4.3	4.2	4.0
Canada	3.7	6.5	10.4	13.6	3.2	3.9	4.0	3.7
Sweden	1.7	2.4	4.4	6.0	1.5	1.4	1.7	1.6
Belgium–Luxembourg	2.0	2.4	3.6	5.4	1.8	1.4	1.4	1.5
Italy	2.1	3.0	3.3	3.3	1.8	1.8	1.3	0.9
Total above	110.1	163.1	255.8	359.3	96.5	97.0	97.3	97.3
All other (estimate)[b]	4.0	5.0	7.2	10.0	3.5	3.0	2.7	2.7
Grand total	114.1	168.1	263.0	369.3	100.0	100.0	100.0	100.0

[a] Fiscal year beginning 1 April of the year indicated on the basis of cumulative annual flows of direct investment as reported to the International Monetary Fund.

[b] Includes Austria, Denmark, Norway, Finland, Portugal, Spain, Australia, New Zealand and South Africa. For 1978: data not available for Denmark and South Africa.

Source: UN Centre on Transnational Corporations: Data provided for author.

in regional or global process and product specialisation, to take advantage of differential resource endowments, scale economies and integrated markets. Sometimes this specialisation is *horizontal*, where different final products are produced in different locations (such as practised by Philips, Ford and International Harvester in the European Economic Community); in other cases it is *vertical*, such as investment by Japanese and US MNEs in South East Asia to supply the labour intensive processes of the production of a wide range of consumer electronics, mostly for export to industrialised countries. This kind of international production is worth distinguishing in that it usually involves a centralised management strategy and control over resource allocation in the foreign affiliates and a substantial trade in intermediate and final products between different parts of the same enterprise (Helleiner and Lavergne, 1979; Lall, 1978).

Finally, in spite of the need to centralise decision taking in the integrated enterprise, important changes have been taking place in the ownership structure of international production. Data published by the UN Centre on Transnational Corporations (UN, 1978) show that the proportion of foreign affiliates established in developed countries between 1961 and 1975[9] with a 100 per cent ownership was 25.3 per cent compared with 41.1 per cent of those set up before 1960. Affiliates of MNEs from those countries which are expanding their foreign activities the fastest, viz. Japan and the developing countries, tend to be increasingly minority owned compared with those of US origin.[10]

III

Early attempts to explain foreign direct investment by use of international capital theory were soon abandoned for two main reasons. First, such investment involves the transfer of other resources than capital (technology, management, organisational and marketing skills, etc.) and it is the expected return on these, rather than on the capital *per se*, which prompts enterprises to become MNEs. Thus capital is simply a conduit for the transfer of other resources rather than the *raison d'être* for direct investment.

Second, in the case of direct investment, resources are transferred internally within the firm rather than externally between two independent parties: *de jure* control is still retained over their usage. Furthermore, without this control, resources which are transferred may not have been transferred, and the production function of the receiving firm is different from what it would otherwise be. This is essentially the difference between portfolio and direct investment.

If international capital theory could not explain international production, what could? In the 1950s and early 1960s there were two main approaches, viz. the 'why' or 'how it is possible' approach, based on industrial organisation theory, and the 'where' approach based upon location theory.[11] The former concentrated on identifying the characteristics of MNEs that gave them a net competitive advantage over other firms that might otherwise supply the same foreign markets. Though the gist of this idea was contained in the studies of Southard (1932), Barlow (1953), and Dunning (1958), it was left to Stephen Hymer, in his seminal doctoral thesis (Hymer, 1960), to refine and formalise it into a separate theory of foreign direct investment. Based on an internationalisation of Bain's notion of barriers to entry, Hymer's theory was essentially that firms undertaking foreign direct investment operated in an imperfect market environment, where it was necessary to acquire and sustain certain net advantages *vis-à-vis* firms in the countries in which they operated. The identification and evaluation of these advantages commanded much of the attention of economists in the late 1960s and early 1970s;[12] again, US data were used almost exclusively.

The second approach tried to answer the question 'Why do firms produce in one country rather than in another?' The pioneering work of Frank Southard in *American Industry in Europe* followed this approach, as did that of the authors of most of the early country case studies published between 1953 and 1970.[13] In most cases the influences on location were extracted from field study data, and, occasionally, ranked in significance.[14] Later, when more complete statistics were available, regression analysis was used to identify the main factors leading to US investment in Europe and Canada (Horst, 1972b).

For the most part, these two approaches to explaining international production evolved independently of each other, and for this reason, if no other, neither was wholly satisfactory. The industrial organisation approach did not answer *where* ownership advantages were exploited; the location theory approach did not explain *how* it was that foreign owned firms could outcompete domestic firms in supplying their own markets. Neither approach attempted to explain the dynamics of foreign investment. In this respect, the work of Raymond Vernon and his colleagues on the product cycle theory (Vernon, 1966; Wells, 1972) was of particular value, partly because it treated trade and investment as part of the same process of exploiting foreign markets, and partly because it explained this relationship in a dynamic context. To the questions 'why' and 'where', Vernon added 'when' to the theory of foreign investment. But even the Vernon theory was initially put forward to explain the growth of US manufacturing investment abroad, and in the 1960s, at least, relied exclusively on data about US corporate activity.[15]

Advances in the theories of international production over the last decade have taken four main directions. First, there have been extensions of the industrial organisation approach. These have focused on identifying and evaluating *which* of the advantages are most likely to explain patterns of foreign direct manufacturing investment by the US. Here, perhaps, the work of Caves (1971, 1974a, b) has been the most extensive, but others, notably Johnson (1970), Wolf (1977), Ozawa (1979), Lall (1980) and those listed in Section IIa above have also contributed to our understanding. Of the ownership advantages which seem to best explain such investment, superior technology and innovative capacity and product differentiation consistently appear to have the best explanatory power. Only very limited testing has been done on the industrial structure of foreign direct investment by other countries.[16]

Second, there has been a resurgence of interest on some of the financial aspects of the foreign activities of firms.[17] There have been a series of strands, but most can be classified into two groups: first, those which emphasise the imperfections of foreign exchange and capital markets, for example, Aliber (1970), and, second, those which extend portfolio theory to explain the industrial and geographical distribution of foreign activities to take account of risk diversification and the stability of earnings. Here the work of Lessard (1979) and Rugman (1979) is particularly illuminating.

Third, there has been a major new theoretical thrust in seeking an explanation for international production as an extension to the theory of the firm. This reflects a switch in attention from the act of foreign direct investment, which is now recognised as a particular form of involvement by firms outside their national boundaries, to the institution making the investment. The main approach here has been to apply the theory of market failure to explaining their foreign activities, using the principles first expounded by Coase (1937) and Penrose (1959) but later refined and extended by Arrow (1969), Alchian and Demsetz (1972) and Williamson (1975) in their analysis of information markets and the economics of transaction costs. In the later 1970s various economists, for example, McManus (1972), Brown (1976), Buckley and Casson (1976), Magee (1977), Teece (1979), Swedenborg (1979) and Calvet (1980) have sought to explain the propensity of firms to engage in foreign direct investment, rather than to license or sell their proprietary assets to foreign firms, in terms of market disequilibrium. The basic proposition is that market imperfections or failures, particularly in the buying and selling of essential inputs and outputs, as well as economies of interdependent activities, lead a firm to exploit its foreign markets by internalising the markets for these inputs and outputs.

This approach helps explain by which route a firm chooses to exploit any advantages it possesses over its foreign competitors (although the route itself may sometimes affect these advantages) — this question was largely ignored in the early literature on international production. The problem of choosing between a different set of options of servicing a foreign market was first taken up systematically by Hirsch (1976), who produced a model identifying the conditions under which a firm might exploit its ownership advantages through exports or foreign direct investment. This theme has been extended by Buckley and Davies (1979), Giddy and Rugman (1979), Lall (1980) and Buckley and Casson (1981)[18] who have also addressed themselves to the principles of choice between foreign direct investment and licensing and between exports and licensing.

It was, however, the dissatisfaction with these partial explanations of international production, and the lack of a formal model relating it either to trade or other modes of resource transfer, that led economists to favour a more *eclectic approach* to the subject. This fourth line of development draws upon and integrates three strands of economic theory to explain the ability and willingness of firms to serve markets, and the reason why they choose to exploit this advantage through foreign production rather than by domestic production,[19] exports or portfolio resource flows.[20] Its principal hypothesis is that a firm will engage in foreign direct investment if three conditions are satisfied:

(1) It possesses net ownership advantages *vis-à-vis* firms of other nationalities in serving particular markets. These ownership advantages largely take the form of the possession of intangible assets, which are, at least for a period of time, exclusive or specific to the firm possessing them.

(2) Assuming condition (1) is satisfied, it must be more beneficial to the enterprise possessing these advantages to use them itself rather than to sell or lease them to foreign firms, that is, for it to internalise its advantages through an extension of its own activities rather than externalise them through licensing and similar contracts with independent firms.

(3) Assuming conditions (1) and (2) are satisfied, it must be profitable for the enterprise to utilise these advantages in conjunction with at least some factor inputs (including natural resources) outside its home country; otherwise foreign markets would be served entirely by exports and domestic markets by domestic production.

The greater the ownership advantages of enterprises (net of any disadvantages of operating in a foreign environment) (Hirsch, 1976), the more the incentive they have to exploit these themselves. The more the economics of production and marketing favour a foreign location, the more they are likely to engage in foreign direct investment. The propensity of a particular country to engage in international production is then dependent on the extent to which its enterprises possess these advantages and the locational attractions of its endowments compared with those offered by other countries.

Table 4.2 offers a classification of some of these advantages. Industrial organisation theory mainly explains the nature of ownership advantages and is directly in the Bain tradition; however, there may be additional advantages which arise specifically from the multinationality of the firm.[21] The theory of property rights and the economics of transaction costs

Table 4.2   *The Eclectic Theory of International Production*[a]

---

(1) *Ownership-Specific Advantages* (of enterprises of one nationality, or affiliates of same, over those of another).

   (a) Which need not arise due to multinationality.

   Those due mainly to size and established position, product or process diversification, ability to take advantage of division of labour and specialisation; monopoly power, better resource capacity and usage.

   Proprietary technology, trade marks (protected by patent, etc., legislation).

   Production management, organisational, marketing systems; R & D capacity; 'bank' of human capital and experience.

   Exclusive or favoured access to inputs, e.g. labour, natural resources, finance, information.

   Ability to obtain inputs on favoured terms (due e.g. to size or monopsonistic influence).

   Exclusive or favoured access to product markets.

   Government protection (e.g. control on market entry).

   (b) Which those branch plants of established enterprises may enjoy over *de novo* firms.

   Access to capacity (administrative, managerial, R & D, marketing, etc.) of parent company at favoured prices.

   Economies of joint supply (not only in production, but in purchasing, marketing, finance, etc., arrangements).

   (c) Which specifically arise because of multinationality.

   Multinationality enhances above advantages by offering wider opportunities.

   More favoured access to and/or better knowledge about information, inputs, markets.

   Ability to take advantage of international differences in factor endowments, markets. Ability to diversify risks, e.g. in different currency areas, and to exploit differences in capitalisation ratios.

(2) *Internalisation Incentive Advantages* (i.e. to protect against or exploit market failure).

   Reduction of costs (e.g. search, negotiation, monitoring) associated with market transactions.

   To avoid costs of enforcing property rights.

   Buyer uncertainty (about nature and value of inputs, e.g. technology, being sold).

   Where market does not permit price discrimination.

   Need of seller to protect quality of products.

   To capture economies of externalities and interdependent activities (see 1(b) above).

   To compensate for absence of futures markets.

   To avoid or exploit government intervention (e.g. quotas, tariffs, price controls, tax differences, etc.).

   To control supplies and conditions of sale of inputs (including technology).

Table 4.2 (*continued*)

To control market outlets (including those which might be used by competitors).

To be able to engage in practices, e.g. cross-subsidisation, predatory pricing, etc., as a competitive (or anti-competitive) strategy.

(3) *Location-Specific Advantages*

Spatial distribution of inputs and markets.

Input prices, quality and productivity, e.g. labour, energy, materials, components, semi-finished goods.

Transport and communications costs.

Government intervention.

Control on imports (including tariff barriers), tax rates, incentives, climate for investment, political stability etc.

Infrastructure [commerical, legal, transportation].

Psychic distance (language, cultural, business, customs etc. differences).

Economies of R & D production and marketing (e.g. extent to which scale economies make for centralisation of production).

---

[a]These advantages are not independent of each other. For example, those listed in (2) may be partially dependent on how MNEs exploit those listed in (1).

explain why firms should choose to internalise these advantages. Theories of location and trade explain the factors determining the location of production.

The eclectic theory suggests that all forms of international production by all countries can be explained by reference to the above conditions. It makes no *a priori* prediction about which countries, industries or enterprises are most likely to engage in foreign direct investment, but it does hypothesise that at least some of the advantages identified in Table 4.2 will *not* be evenly spread across countries, industries and enterprises. Moreover, it accepts that such advantages are not static: ownership, internalisation and location advantages may change over time.[22] However, if country-specific characteristics are important in influencing such investment, it may be invalid to generalise from one country's experience to another. It is to this question that the next part of the chapter addresses itself.[23]

IV

Country-specific characteristics have always been the centrepiece of the theory of international trade. In the neoclassical formulation, the assumptions of immobility of factors of production between countries, identity of production functions and atomistic competition rule out the possibility of international production. No firm can have a permanent ownership advantage over another, as there are no obstacles to other firms acquiring these advantages. Trade is based entirely on differences in the level and structure of resource endowments between countries.

Neotechnology and scale theories offer a different explanation for trade in a world in which imperfect product markets and differences in the supply of technology exist. Trade may then be based, not on differences in endowments, but on differences in production functions, scale economies and consumer tastes. However, the implicit assumption of the theories seems to be that these differences are country specific rather than enterprise specific, not only in their origin but also in their use. Clearly this is not necessarily the case. The very presence of the MNE suggests that at least some ownership advantages are transferable across national boundaries. Indeed, the greater the degree of multinationality, the more likely it is that the origin of ownership advantages will not be tied to a particular location.

The extent to which a country engages in international production and the industrial composition of that production depends, first, on the structure of its economic activities[24] and, second, on the ability of its firms to generate ownership-specific advantages which are best exploited by these same firms in a foreign rather than (or in addition to) a domestic location. Before turning to an analysis of how this propensity may itself be country specific, some data are presented on the level and industrial spread of the outward direct capital stake in manufacturing industry of five developed countries in 1975. These are set out in Table 4.3. In order to be able to better interpret the differences in the industrial spread between countries, the revealed comparative advantage (RCA(A)) indices, which are reproduced in Table 4.4, have been calculated. These indices were obtained by dividing the share of a particular country's stock of the foreign investment stake in a particular industry by its share of the total stock of foreign investment for the five countries.[25] They directly parallel the Balassa indices of RCA in exports (RCA(X)) (Balassa, 1965), which were also calculated (see Table 4.5).[26]

Tables 4.3 and 4.4 suggest that the five countries fall into two main groups: the US, Sweden and West Germany with a RCA(A) in the more technology intensive industries, and Japan and the UK with a RCA(A) in the less technology intensive industries. Even a cursory examination of these data reveals that any explanation of the industrial structure of foreign direct investment based upon that of any one country in the group may not hold good for all countries. Factors affecting the ownership, location and internalisation advantages of enterprises specific to their country of origin must clearly be taken into account. It should be emphasised that the data in the tables represent the outcome of a combination of these advantages. In other words, the RCA(A) indices reflect *both* the ownership advantages of enterprises *and* the way in which these advantages can best be exploited. By themselves, such data do not allow any conclusions to be drawn as to whether a high RCA(A) is due to relatively favourable ownership advantages, to foreign direct investment being a relatively favourable way for ownership advantages to be exploited, or to a combination of

Table 4.3 Outward Direct Investment Stake of Five Industrialised Countries by Main Manufacturing Sectors, 1975

	USA ($m.)	(%)	Japan ($m.)	(%)	UK ($m.)	(%)	Sweden ($m.)	(%)	West Germany ($m.)	(%)
More Technology Intensive Sectors	38,691	69.2	1,049	39.4	6,437	43.8	1,722	71.4	8,697	71.2
Chemicals and allied products	12,609	22.6	408	15.3	3,108	21.2	245	10.2	4,046	33.1
Mechanical and instrument engineering	11,311	20.2	198	7.4	1,210	8.2	925	38.3	1,459	11.9
Electrical engineering	6,355	11.4	274	10.3	1,630	11.1	385	16.0	1,905	15.6
Transportation equipment	8,416	15.1	169	6.3	489	3.3	167	6.9	1,287	10.5
Less Technology Intensive Sectors	17,194	30.8	1,614	60.6	8,253	56.2	691	28.6	3,524	28.8
Food, drink and tobacco	4,725	8.5	149	5.6	3,947	26.9	19	0.8	759	6.2
Textiles, leather, clothing and footwear	964	1.7	591	22.2	1,038	7.1	8	0.3	497	4.1
Paper, printing and publishing	3,306	5.9	272	10.2	1,073	7.3	287	11.9	158	1.3
Primary and fabricated metals	3,662	6.6	409	15.4	602	4.1	198	8.2	1,841	15.1
Other manufacturing industries	4,537	8.1	193	7.2	1,593	10.8	179	7.4	269	2.2
All manufacturing	55,885	100.0	2,663	100.0	14,690	100.0	2,413	100.0	12,221	100.0

Source: Data compiled by Jeremy Clegg at University of Reading from a variety of government publications and from information supplied to him from various ministries and/or government departments. Although definitions of the investment stake vary slightly between countries, it basically represents the book value of the fixed assets (net of depreciation) plus current assets (net of amounts owing by the investing company less current liabilities) (net of amounts owing to investing companies) less long-term liabilities (other than to the investing company of overseas subsidiaries and branches).

Table 4.4   Revealed Comparative Advantage Index for Outward Direct Investment Stake (RCA(A)) of Five Industrialised Countries, 1970 and 1975

	USA 1970	USA 1975	Japan 1970	Japan 1975	UK 1970	UK 1975	Sweden 1970	Sweden 1975	West Germany 1970	West Germany 1975
More Technology Intensive Sectors	1.056	1.075	0.556	0.633	0.684	0.683	1.167	1.111	1.210	1.108
Chemicals and allied products	0.957	0.972	0.333	0.667	0.898	0.910	0.458	0.444	1.670	1.424
Mechanical and instrument engineering	1.146	1.178	0.444	0.433	0.439	0.479	3.000	2.259	0.620	0.698
Electrical engineering	0.899	0.947	0.667	0.867	1.193	0.928	0.958	1.333	1.370	1.302
Transportation equipment	1.253	1.256	0.889	0.533	0.176	0.275	0.292	0.593	1.000	0.878
Less Technology Intensive Sectors	0.901	0.865	1.889	1.733	1.545	1.581	0.708	0.815	0.630	0.813
Food, drink and tobacco	0.741	0.774	0.556	0.500	2.364	2.461	0.083	0.074	0.470	0.568
Textiles, leather, clothing and footwear	0.565	0.489	6.333	6.367	2.321	2.006	0.083	0.111	1.230	1.151
Paper, printing and publishing	1.029	1.020	3.778	1.767	1.080	1.263	1.750	2.074	0.230	0.223
Primary and fabricated metals	1.065	0.858	2.000	2.033	0.487	0.539	1.167	1.074	1.390	1.971
Other manufacturing industries	1.024	1.053	0.778	0.967	1.358	1.407	0.708	0.963	0.260	0.288

Source: As for Table 4.3 and comparable 1970 data.

Table 4.5   Revealed Comparative Advantage Index for Exports (RCA(X)) of Five Industrialised Countries, 1970 and 1975

	USA 1970	USA 1975	Japan 1970	Japan 1975	UK 1970	UK 1975	Sweden 1970	Sweden 1975	West Germany 1970	West Germany 1975
More Technology Intensive Sectors	1.111	1.111	0.858	0.936	0.933	0.944	0.776	0.828	1.047	1.003
Chemicals and allied products	1.150	1.076	0.676	0.693	1.000	1.111	0.466	0.534	1.146	1.169
Mechanical and instrument engineering	1.166	1.184	0.574	0.629	1.018	1.069	0.810	0.828	1.108	1.075
Electrical engineering	0.919	0.965	1.477	1.223	0.811	0.882	0.793	0.983	0.949	0.948
Transportation equipment	1.121	1.115	1.034	1.342	0.835	0.701	0.914	0.914	0.956	0.827
Less Technology Intensive Sectors	0.785	0.753	1.267	1.144	1.140	1.139	1.431	1.397	0.902	1.000
Food, drink and tobacco	1.355	1.198	0.608	0.381	1.823	1.965	0.259	0.310	0.553	0.902
Textiles, leather, clothing and footwear	0.427	0.576	1.886	1.297	1.238	1.264	0.534	0.638	1.031	1.153
Paper, printing and publishing	1.202	1.153	0.324	0.302	0.677	0.722	5.241	5.534	0.536	0.593
Primary and fabricated metals	0.664	0.538	1.483	1.693	0.963	0.778	1.190	0.793	1.041	1.121
Other manufacturing industries	0.951	0.986	0.932	0.530	1.366	1.764	1.310	1.655	0.824	0.844

Source: Data collected by Jeremy Clegg at University of Reading.

both.[27] It is, however, worth noting that there are some noticeable differences between the individual RCA(*A*) and RCA(*X*) indices, which suggests that the choice of exploiting ownership advantages, as well as the presence of such advantages, varies between countries.

(a) *Country-specific Determinants of Ownership Advantages*

Table 4.2 listed some of the advantages which MNEs are commonly thought to possess over indigenous firms in the country to which they are selling. A casual examination of these suggests that some are more applicable, not only to particular products, industries or types of firms, but also to particular home countries, than others. Let us look at the origin of such advantages and the conditions under which they are sustained and attempt to match these with the characteristics which distinguish countries from one another in their international economic involvement (using the word to cover all forms of trade and non-trade activity by their firms across national boundaries). The proposition is that home countries will have a high combined RCA, that is, RCA in exports (RCA(*X*)) *plus* international production (RCA(*A*)) *plus* portfolio resource transfers (RCA(*P*)), in those activities in which their ownership-specific advantages best match their resource endowments and market structures.[28]

There are two main ways in which this might be done. First, for each industry, we might try and identify those ownership advantages which are specific to that industry and then examine how far particular countries possess the necessary characteristics to generate and sustain these advantages. Second, we may look at the type of ownership advantages particular countries are most likely to generate and sustain, and then relate these to the resource and market requirements of particular industries. Mainly because of data constraints, this chapter explores the second way.

Table 4.6 sets out some of the possible links. It classifies ownership advantages of enterprises (which may be mobile or immobile across national boundaries) into a number of groups, which may be related to country-specific characteristics (which are immobile); these in turn, can be related to the industries whose competitive position is most likely to be affected by those advantages.

Take first, for example, the size of firm. If it can be shown that this variable is positively related to the size and structure of the markets facing the firm, it might be reasonably postulated that large markets will support large firms and thus give ownership advantages to those industries which are able to benefit from the economies of large-scale production. If there is little product diversification and/or no restraint is placed on the extent of industrial concentration, then the size of the market necessary to achieve such economies will be smaller. In some cases, large domestic markets seem to be a prerequisite for a thriving domestic industry (but not necessarily domestically owned industry); the motor vehicle industry is a classic case in point.[29] In others, by exploiting foreign markets some

Table 4.6 Links between Selected Ownership-Specific Advantages and Country-Specific Characteristics Likely to Generate and Sustain Them

Ownership-Specific Advantages	Country Characteristics Favouring Such Advantages
1 Size of firm (e.g. economies of scale, product diversification)	Large and standardised markets. Liberal attitude towards mergers, conglomerates, industrial concentration.
2 Management and organisational expertise	Availability of managerial manpower; educational and training facilities (e.g. business schools). Size of markets, etc., making for (1) above. Good R & D facilities.
3 Technological based advantages	Government support of innovation. Availability of skilled manpower and in some cases of local materials.
4 Labour and/or mature, small-scale intensive technologies	Plentiful labour supplies; good technicians. Expertise of small firm/consultancy operation.
5 Product differentiation, marketing economies	National markets with reasonably high incomes; high income elasticity of demand. Acceptance of advertising and other persuasive marketing methods. Consumer tastes and culture.
6 Access to (domestic) markets	Large markets. No government control on imports. Liberal attitude to exclusive dealing.
7 Access to, or knowledge about natural resources	Local availability of resources encourages export of that knowledge and/or processing activities. Need for raw materials not available locally for domestic industry. Accumulated experience of expertise required for resource exploitation/processing.
8 Capital availability and financial expertise	Good and reliable capital markets and professional advice.
9 As it affects various advantages above	Role of government intervention and relationship with enterprises. Incentives to create advantages.

countries manage to achieve economies of scale without a large internal market; the Swiss pharmaceutical and food processing MNEs and the Swedish and Dutch electrical appliance MNEs are good examples.

Or again, it might be reasonable to suppose that countries with an above average expenditure on research and development (as a percentage of net output) or with a highly skilled labour force will enjoy above average RCA in technology and skill intensive industries. Those with (relatively) plentiful supplies of cheap but efficient labour will enjoy RCA in labour intensive industries (or sectors of industries). Countries with an above average income per capita will have an above average RCA in consumer good industries supplying differentiated products which (at least over certain ranges of income) tend to have a high income elasticity of demand.[30]

The possession of natural resources, or the expertise in exploiting such resources, may also generate ownership advantages. Vertical expansion forwards into secondary processing abroad has prompted a good deal of foreign investment by Swedish, Australian and Canadian companies. However, other resource based investment, especially by mining companies, may be in areas in which they have no domestic experience. Here, the skills, expertise and technology relevant to identifying the location and value of particular resources and their exploitation, and access to capital and markets — often accumulated over many years in *other* foreign markets — may give such MNEs substantial advantages over *de novo* companies in new markets. Skills and proprietary assets related to particular sectors of the mining industry established over the years may, for instance, explain the success of many UK companies like Rio Tinto Zinc.[31] In such cases a body of knowledge, associated, for example, with management of large enterprises or market access, originally generated for one purpose may spread over to other lines of activity, long after the initial advantage has disappeared.

Countries may engage in resource based investment for two quite different reasons. The first arises where there are abundant domestic natural resources, which lead either to the exploitation of similar activities overseas or of secondary processing, and are prompted by the need to internalise the markets. The second arises where backward integration is undertaken to manufacture end-products to which the home economy is particularly suited, but for which local resources are inadequate. Examples of the first kind are Swedish MNEs in paper and wood products and Canadian MNEs in agricultural machinery; and of the latter, investment by Japanese MNEs in the energy and metal sectors.

More generally, the level and structure of the resource endowments of a country will affect the form of the ownership-specific advantages of its enterprises. First, it may be supposed that firms that are resident in countries which are comparatively well endowed with particular resources have an initial advantage, at least, over non-resident firms in their knowledge of such resources, their access to them and the way in which they can best be used. Second, over time, these advantages may well be expected to give rise to others in the form of new or improved production and marketing techniques, and organisational and management skills which, because of market imperfections, tend to become locked into, that is, specific to, the firms generating them, as ownership advantages. Thus, one would expect firms in countries that were comparatively well endowed with human capital to acquire comparative ownership advantages in knowledge intensive sectors, while those based in countries with plentiful supplies of unskilled or semi-skilled labour would develop comparative advantages in labour intensive sectors.[32]

The difference between the pattern of US and Japanese resource endowments in influencing the activities of the MNEs from these countries has been explored by Kojima (1978) and Ozawa (1979). Kojima argues, for example, that while the foreign activity of Japanese MNEs has been trade oriented and designed to complement Japan's comparative trading advantage — hence the major part of its foreign investment has been directed towards natural resource development and those sectors of manufacturing industry in which Japan is losing its export competitiveness — US MNEs have tended to exploit their ownership advantages in innovative and oligopolistic industries, which works against the USA's comparative advantage and is anti-trade oriented. While it is possible to exaggerate the differences between the behaviour of Japanese and US MNEs, the patterns of the two countries' investment in 1975 do support the contention that country-specific factors (of the kind just described) and the institutional framework (e.g. the market structures in which firms compete) do considerably affect the industrial composition of their foreign investments.

Government intervention is another country-specific variable which affects both the generation of ownership advantages and the economic ties between investing and recipient countries. Such involvement may be direct — through government ownership or participation of industries (it is noteworthy that the role of state-owned MNEs is increasing, especially in some of the developing countries) — or indirect, as in the case of Japan, by the creation of an industrial environment and strategy in which industry and government work closely with each other.[33] Governments may also affect several other important factors: the availability, type and quality of skilled labour available to firms through education and training policies; the level and pattern of innovation through patent and trade mark legislation; their own research and development (R & D) programmes, which may have important spin-off effects in the private sector (the space research programme of the USA is a classic example), and the financing of private R & D; growth, size and diversification of firms through competition policy; the level and direction of domestic investment, for example, between the public and private sector, through a variety of fiscal and/or monetary measures; the level and direction of foreign investment by such measures as export rebates, capital export and/or dividend remittance controls and taxes on foreign profits; and, by a whole host of macro-economic policies, the industrial climate in which firms operate.

To summarise: given the industry in which they operate, the (combined) RCA of industries of different nationalities in international markets is a function of market size, income per head, the structure of resource endowments, technological capacity, industrial concentration, resource availability or need, and government policy. Such variables include some which are commonly put forward to explain patterns of international trade[34] (Stern, 1975; Hufbauer, 1970). In a recent contribution, however, Baldwin (1979) has compared the industrial composition of US trade and direct investment: he argues that while both US (net) exports and investment are high in industries with an above average skilled/unskilled labour ratio, industry concentration ratios (which he uses as a proxy for the extent of product differentiation) are significantly positive in explaining foreign investment but not trade.

The ownership advantages of enterprises of one nationality over those of another in serving particular markets are themselves a function of which markets are being served and in which countries production is taking place. This, in turn, may reflect country-specific economic, political or cultural ties, for example, UK investment in the Commonwealth or French investment in North Africa. This is not a question of the choice of location from which to supply a particular market,[35] but one of the extent to which particular host countries have the kind of endowments that are complementary to the kind of industries in which the home country has a comparative advantage.

Much of the newly emerging foreign investment by developing countries may be explained in these terms (Lecraw, 1977; Diaz-Alejandro, 1977; Wells, 1977; Heenan and Keegan, 1979; Wells and V'Ella, 1979; Lall, 1979). Not only does India have a thriving engineering consultancy sector, Hong Kong a thriving textiles and clothing industry, Argentina a thriving meat processing and packing industry and South Korea a thriving construction industry, but there are countries whose enterprises may be able to exploit these advantages better not only than indigenous firms but also than other MNEs.[36] This could explain the tendency to invest, initially at least, in countries at close 'psychic' distance,[37] and/or at a similar or earlier stage of investment development process than themselves. A cursory look at the geographical distribution of the investment stake of the countries examined in Table 4.3 shows that the richer countries (USA, Germany and Sweden) invest proportionately more than Japan and the UK in the relatively high income countries because their RCA(A) is greatest in those industries, supplying goods most likely to be bought by those countries. The UK and Japan follow one step behind, supplying the kind of goods more likely to be bought by medium income countries. The developing countries' comparative advantage seems to be in mature, labour intensive and small-scale technologies, and in the supply of fairly standardised low income products, mainly to other Third World countries.

A difficulty in testing these hypotheses is that today's ownership advantages of enterprises may be the inheritance of yesterday's country-specific endowments. This is especially true of those associated with national resources and government policy. Further, such endowments may not give enterprises the same advantages at all points of the product and/or investment development cycle. It is possible that, as a new product becomes more standardised, ownership advantages will diminish[38] or change. For example, the USA provided a favourable environment for the commercialisation of the motor car and fostered the early dominance of US firms in this industry. Once the production process became standardised, however, it became increasingly profitable for US firms to locate production outside the US, and increasingly possible for enterprises from other countries to develop their own industries, breaking down the barriers to entry imposed by size of markets.

Furthermore, as technology becomes mature and diffused the propensity of other countries' firms to become multinational increases and concentration levels among MNEs fall (UN, 1978).[39] The data in Tables 4.4 and 4.5, which set out the changes in the RCA indices between 1970 and 1975, also point to some convergence between the investment patterns of the five countries. As an enterprise increases its degree of multinationality, the characteristics of the home country become less, and that of other countries more, important in influencing the extent and character of its ownership advantages.[40] This again suggests that there may be some kind of convergence in the RCAs of a country's international production over time as the extent of intra-industry trade and investment increases, with the most noticeable differences between the RCAs being concentrated in the industries that require unique factor endowments, which are found only in a very few countries.[41]

Finally, it is worth noting that country-specific characteristics may affect the level as well as the structure of the ownership advantages of firms. Inter-country interest rate differentials and uncertainty over exchange rates, by affecting *inter alia* the capitalisation rates of firms of different nationalities, will influence the geographical pattern of direct investment flows (particularly those involving takeovers). This is the basis of Aliber's theory of foreign direct investment (Aliber, 1970) which we find no difficulty in incorporating into our own approach.

(b) *Country-Specific Determinants of Location-Specific Advantages*
The extent to which a country's enterprises serve particular markets or serve them from one location rather than another will vary according to characteristics of home and host countries and the physical and/or 'psychic' and 'economic' distance[42] between them. Some of these will primarily affect the level rather than the structure of international production; some

will affect *which* countries are served through *which* routes; and some will affect the ease with which particular products are supplied from a domestic or a foreign base.

In explaining the overall propensity of a country to invest abroad, given the ownership-specific advantages of its enterprises described in the previous section, distances between home and host country, risk diversification and the exchange rate are perhaps the most important factors. Luostarinen (1978) has shown that the propensity of Finnish companies to engage in foreign direct investment in forty-six countries (other than Sweden), rather than in exports or portfolio resource transfers, is directly (and negatively) associated with psychic and economic distance. Risk diversification is especially significant in affecting the propensity of firms originating from countries which are themselves regarded as risky locations for MNEs (Lecraw, 1978). Over the last ten years or so, the realignment of exchange rates, and particularly the devaluation of the US dollar and the upward revaluation of the mark and yen, have caused a substantial shift in the export/foreign direct investment stock ratio (X/A) of US, German and Japanese companies.

There are also longer-term factors making for a greater (or lesser) propensity to invest overseas. These include the size of domestic markets (compare Switzerland with the USA), the geographical proximity of the home country to its main markets (compare Australia with the Netherlands), psychic distance (Japanese as compared to US investment in the UK), and, of course, the industrial structure of the investment. Abstracting from this last factor, our concern is to explain why, in the same industry, the export/foreign asset (X/A) ratio should vary between home countries.

Table 4.7 reveals the extent to which these ratios differ among the five countries in 1975. However, as the normalised RCA(X/A) ratios show, the major part of the differences, with one or two exceptions, is explained by the differences in the *average* export/assets (X/A) ratio of particular industries, due to the kind of factors mentioned above which apply to a greater or lesser extent to all sectors. The deviation is, in fact, more pronounced in the less technology intensive sectors like textiles.

In suggesting reasons for differences in the sectoral (X/A) or RCA (X/A) ratios, it is worth comparing these with the RCA ratios for both investment and exports, that is, RCA(A) and RCA(X) set out in Tables 4.5 and 4.6. Here two hypotheses might be advanced. The first is that RCA(X/A) ratios are likely to be negatively associated with the RCA ownership ratios, the reasoning being that the stronger the ownership advantages of its enterprises, the better it is able to exploit foreign markets through foreign direct investment.[43] The alternative hypothesis is that where the ownership advantage is a direct reflection of country-specific advantages of the home country, which can only exploited by production located in that country, for example, those based on natural resources, then the (X/A) ratio will be positively associated with the RCA, particularly the RCA(E) ratios.

Table 4.7 *Export/Foreign Direct Investment Stake Ratio and Revealed Comparative Indices (RCA(X/A)) of Five Industrialised Countries, 1975*

| | USA | | Japan | | UK | | Sweden | | West Germany | |
| | RCA | | RCA | | RCA | | RCA | | RCA | |
	(X/A)	(X/A)	(X/A)	(X/A)	(X/A)	(X/A)	(X/A)	(X/A)	(X/A)	(X/A)
More Technology Intensive Sectors	1.53	1.109	33.46	1.643	3.90	1.483	5.13	0.799	6.55	0.972
Chemicals and allied products	0.86	0.623	12.00	0.589	1.80	0.684	4.36	0.679	3.10	0.460
Mechanical and instrument engineering	2.07	1.500	44.21	2.171	8.71	3.312	3.57	0.556	15.51	2.301
Electrical engineering	1.23	0.891	25.27	1.241	2.18	0.829	4.15	0.646	4.28	0.635
Transportation equipment	2.05	1.486	85.92	4.220	11.10	4.221	17.14	2.670	10.61	1.574
Less Technology Intensive Sectors	1.04	0.754	11.84	0.582	1.64	0.624	9.65	1.503	7.20	1.068
Food, drink and tobacco	0.55	0.399	3.86	0.190	0.54	0.205	7.11	1.107	2.72	0.404
Textiles, leather, clothing and footwear	2.57	1.862	6.60	0.324	2.61	0.992	65.45	10.195	10.61	1.574
Paper, printing and publishing	0.90	0.652	2.01	0.099	0.87	0.331	10.06	1.567	10.34	1.534
Primary and fabricated metals	1.55	1.123	30.62	1.504	6.78	2.578	8.57	1.335	6.83	1.013
Other manufacturing industries	0.92	0.667	8.14	0.400	2.34	0.890	7.86	1.224	14.13	2.096
All manufacturing	1.38	1.000	20.36	1.000	2.63	1.000	6.42	1.000	6.74	1.000

Source: As for Tables 4.3 and 4.5.

A = DFI carried out by industry from host nation in

X = Exports

The data in Tables 4.5, 4.6 and 4.7 suggest that the former hypothesis possesses greater validity. Countries with the highest RCA(X/A) ratios tend to be those with the lowest RCA(A) or (X) ratios. This is very clearly shown in the case of transport equipment, chemicals and textile industries. In other sectors, either the RCA(A) or (X) advantages (but not both) are inversely related to the RCA(X/A) ratios. In electrical equipment, Japan has the highest (X/A) and lowest RCA(A), but it has the highest RCA(X) ratio; the same is true for Japan's motor vehicle industry.[44] In other cases, both ownership and location advantages favour the home country. The two most clear-cut cases are paper, printing and publishing, where the RCA(A) and (X) ratios are both associated with a high RCA(X/A) ratio; and food, drink and tobacco, where Japan combines a low RCA(X/A) ratio with low RCA ratios.

These varying relationships suggest that country-specific characteristics, by affecting the structure of economic activity, may also influence a country's propensity to engage in foreign direct investment. In particular, countries whose comparative advantages rest on the abundance of natural resources are less likely to be important foreign investors than those whose advantages rest on more transferable assets, for example, managerial skills, technology, product differentiation (Lall, 1980).

Differences in the (X/A) ratios between countries are, in general, likely to be highest when the variables affecting location-specific advantages vary significantly between countries. For example, in sectors where transport costs are important, distances between home and host countries and the number of countries served are clearly likely to influence the (X/A) ratio. Similarly, in industries where economies of scale or labour costs are significant,[45] country-specific characteristics are again likely to exert an important influence on the method of serving foreign markets. The general principle for evaluating the significance of these elements is then, first, to identify the variables likely to affect the (X/A) ratio; second, to analyse the particular country-specific variables that affect these, and, third, to identify which countries possess these and in what form. Table 4.8 illustrates, with examples, this kind of procedure.

As with ownership-specific advantages, country-specific determinants of location advantages may change over time. There is an initial constraint to invest overseas associated with overcoming the barriers of physical and psychic distance mentioned by Hirsch (1976) and Luostarinen (1978). Once these have been surmounted, there is much less resistance to increases in foreign production. For example, the language and cultural barriers facing the establishment of Japanese affiliates in Western Europe are considerable, but as these are overcome one would expect much less resistance to increases in this form of involvement in the future. The product cycle thesis also suggests how, within a particular industry, the (X/A) ratio may change over time. Country-specific factors may influence the stages of a production process and/or the type of rationalised product specialisation

Table 4.8 Links between Selected Location-Specific Factors and Country-Specific Characteristics likely to Affect Them

1 *Production costs*	
Labour costs/productivity	Obviously greatest difference between developed and developing host countries.
Extent to which economies of scale are possible	Size and character of markets.
Nature of production process	Factor proportions/markets in home country.
2 *Movement costs*	
Transport costs	Distance between home and host country great, therefore likely to impede countries which are of above average distances from main markets.
Psychic distance	Where cultures, customs, language etc. different, barriers to setting up production units likely to be greater (Luostarinen, 1978) cf. Japan and US firms in Western Europe.
3 *Government intervention*	
Tariff barriers	May be country-specific in character, e.g. EEC tariffs for non EEC investors.
Taxation	Varies between countries. Also affected by double taxation agreements etc.
General environment for foreign involvement	Political, economic, etc., ties between governments of countries.
Incentives, policies towards foreign direct investment	Again will considerably vary between host countries and sometimes home countries treated differently. Also attitudes towards outward investment may differ between home countries.
4 *Risk factors*	
(a) general propensity for foreign investment	Environment of home and all foreign countries.
(b) geographical distribution	Cf. risk in host countries to which *particular* home countries most likely to invest.

engaged in at home and abroad. Both of these may affect the (X/A) ratio, especially where there is a substantial amount of intra-firm trade.[46] On the other hand, shifts in the relative labour costs between countries might cause (X/A) ratios to change. Countries which are at different stages of the investment development cycle might also be expected to have different (X/A) ratios.

Identifying the determinants of overall (X/A) ratios and seeing how far particular countries possess these, and then examining how far they are due to a different industrial structure of activity, is a different way of proceeding. Data set out in Chapter 5 confirm there are marked variations in both outward and inward direct investment by countries with similar incomes per capita, which might partly be explained by differences in the country-specific chacteristics. Thus countries with low labour costs and/or natural resources tend to have an above average inward investment because of their locational attractions, while rich industrialised countries have an above average outward direct investment, because their factor endowments favour mobile ownership advantages. These advantages, because of *inter alia* high domestic labour costs and barriers to exports, are best exploited in foreign countries. This approach, coupled with the one just described, may help us to understand newly developing patterns of international production.

(c)   *Country-Specific Internalisation Advantages*
Market failure causes enterprises to internalise transactions in intangible assets or goods which otherwise would be externalised. As before, we may first identify the reasons for firms to internalise their international production, then establish how these are related to country characteristics, and finally relate these to the countries likely to possess them.

The market mechanism may be replaced by administrative fiat for six possible reasons;[47] (1) to avoid or reduce transaction and negotiating costs; (2) the fact that, owing to the lack of knowledge or inefficiency on the part of the buying firm, it is unwilling or unable to pay the selling firm a price that will be sufficient to compensate it for not internalising the transaction; (3) to gain advantage over one's competitor through controlling the supply of inputs, product or production strategy and the access to markets; (4) to exploit, or protect oneself against, the consequences of government intervention, for example, by taxation and other actions, which may otherwise place the firm in a less favourable position (the ability of a firm to engage in transfer pricing is one such example); (5) to protect the property rights of the owning firm, *inter alia* by avoiding misrepresentation by the sellers of one's product, and/or ensuring product quality and after-sales maintenance and servicing; (6) to make better use of capacity or overheads to gain advantage of size, joint production, integration and/or diversification (one of the main reasons for takeovers and mergers (Baumann, 1975; Calvet, 1980).

Such propensities to internalise vary between industries. This helps to explain why the transference of ownership advantages sometimes takes place by licensing or other contractual routes, and sometimes by foreign direct investment (Buckley and Davies, 1979; Giddy and Rugman, 1979). The willingness of some firms to set up joint ventures rather than wholly-owned subsidiaries shows that some externalisation is worthwhile because of gains reaped through joint internalisation, or that the bargaining power of the investing company (*vis-à-vis* the host country or partner firm) is insufficient for it to insist upon a 100 per cent equity interest. There are also firm-specific factors to be taken into account. There are suggestions that as an enterprise grows larger and becomes more diversified the more its ownership advantages take the form of those which cannot be transferred to other enterprises, for example, economies of scale and intra-firm integration (Kojima, 1978). Buckley and Casson (1976) have shown that internalisation advantages tend to be greatest in technology intensive sectors and in those engaging in backward resource integration, while Lall (1978) has made a useful distinction between market failure in commodity and information markets in his analysis of the determinants of intra-firm trade. Telesio (1979) concludes that the propensity of firms to licence rather than engage in foreign direct investment is positively correlated with investment in R & D and the level of product diversification, and negatively associated with size and the degree of experience of a company in foreign operations.[48]

But why should this type of advantage vary according to the country of the investing firm? Basically, because both market failure and government intervention are, to some extent, country specific. Take, for example, the markets for primary commodities, finance and technology. In some countries, particularly small developing countries, these are highly imperfect – if they exist at all; in others, for example, the USA and the UK, they are highly sophisticated.[49] The hierarchical structure of firms will also be related to government policy towards mergers and industrial concentration. Differences between the policies of host governments towards the extent and modality of involvement by foreign firms may affect MNEs from some home countries more than others. And, as we noted earlier, the philosophy of MNEs from Japan and the developing countries towards joint ventures and non-equity arrangements seems to be generally more flexible than that of US MNEs.

Chapter 2 illustrated cases of MNEs internalising activities to circumvent, counteract or take advantage of government fiat,[50] which, in part at least, is country specific. Thus one might predict that the incentive for MNEs to manipulate transfer prices would be least where, among other things, tax rates, import controls and non-tariff barriers were comparable between the countries where they operate, exchange rates were stable, or where governments were strong enough to prevent firms from exploiting this channel. The explanation for the preference of UK firms to invest in, rather than licence to firms in the least developed countries is largely explained by the higher transaction costs and greater difficulty in the protection of property rights experienced by them in those countries.[51]

While some of these differences are general to all industries, for example, transfer pricing, the *extent* to which they can be taken advantage of may vary according to industry. Some pressure for internalisation may be industry specific. For example, adequate quality control and the provision of efficient after-sales maintenance is a more important competitive advantage in some industries than others; and countries which have an RCA in these industries may also have a higher foreign direct investment/ licensing ratio. Patent and trademark legislation may also affect the method of exploiting ownership advantages in research and advertising intensive industries. Finally, not all ownership advantages are marketable and/or transferable across countries; in such cases, direct investment and exports are the only two routes of international involvement open to an enterprise.

In concluding this section, it may be interesting to explore the relevance of the eclectic theory to explaining the sharp increase in UK direct investment in the USA since 1976.[52] Here, the dramatic rise in the (dollar) exchange rate of sterling, from under $1.60 in mid-1976 to $2.25 in mid-1979, increased the location advantages of supplying the US market from a US rather than a UK base, while the accompanying rise in UK relative to US interest rates, and their consequential impact on capitalisation ratios, benefited UK- relative to US-based enterprises. Because of imperfections in the capital market, these changes, coupled with the uncertainty over future exchange and interest rates, lowered US stock market prices relative to UK stock market prices and encouraged the flow of capital into the USA (cf. the reverse situation in the 1950s and 1960s). By acquiring US firms, UK enterprises internalised their ownership-specific advantages. The continued rise in the value of the pound and interest rates in the UK further stimulated this movement of funds in 1980; the acquisition of (US) Howard Johnson by the (UK) Imperial Tobacco Group is just one case in point. This explanation fits in very well with the Aliber theory of foreign direct investment (Aliber, 1970) which, it is worth recalling, is mainly interested in explaining deviations around the trend of such investment between two countries in different currency areas.[53]

V

A country's international economic involvement comprises the sum of the activities by its enterprises in trade in goods, assets and money and in outward direct investment. Enterprises engage in production abroad whenever they possess net competitive advantages over firms of other nationalities which can best be exploited by foreign rather than domestic production, and which are more profitable to internalise than to sell or lease to other enterprises. It is possible to identify these advantages (and any corresponding disadvantages), all of which arise from some imperfections in product or factor markets, physical or psychic distance between countries or government intervention. These net advantages are not, however, evenly spread over industries, countries and enterprises. In this chapter, we have mainly been concerned with suggesting reasons why the industrial spread of foreign direct investment may vary between home countries. A full explanation of the pattern of international production must, of course, rest on identifying industry- and firm-specific characteristics making for ownership, location and internalisation advantages: the eclectic theory offers a useful tool-kit for doing this.

The growth of the modern MNE may be explained in terms of the growth of ownership advantages of enterprises. Particularly in knowledge and resource intensive industries, the spread of production abroad has been caused by the desire to exploit these advantages internally rather than through the market (the nineteenth century route) and the shift in locational advantages (due *inter alia* to a reduction in transport and communication costs, an increase in the size of foreign markets, and import barriers imposed by host governments) towards foreign production. The predominance of US-owned MNEs in the 1950s and 1960s reflected the fact that the USA was particularly well favoured with the endowments necessary to generate the ownership advantages emerging at that time. In part, its enterprises found it more profitable to internalise their advantages rather than sell them to foreign firms; and, in part, locational forces (especially the shortage of dollars in the 1950s and the overvaluation of the dollar in the 1960s) favoured the exploitation of these advantages outside the USA.

Since the early 1960s, the relative position of the USA as a source of international direct investment has declined. Initially the UK, then the continental European countries and the Japanese, and most recently of all, some of the less developed countries, increased their propensity to engage in foreign production. This reflects both the increasing international competitiveness of their firms and the need to exploit the changes in the comparative advantage of their resource endowments.

It will be some time before the developing countries become important as suppliers of direct investment capital, but a few are beginning to make their mark. This is noticeable in the more industrialised developing countries, which are beginning to invest according to their country-specific advantages in the poorer (but not poorest) developing economies. There may be special reasons why firms from such economies – and those from developed peripheral areas like Australia – have advantages over firms from larger countries like the USA and UK. Certainly they tend to be smaller, more adaptable and often more welcome than the giant MNEs from the powerful industrialised nations.[54] In some cases, the advantages are natural resource based (e.g. Tunisian date processing plants in Southern France). In others it is skill based, sometimes with protection and/or encouragement given by home governments.[55] In others still, it is based on knowledge of a particular market, for example, Singapore firms operating in Malaysia to serve the local Chinese community by making noodles and pickles (Lall, 1979).

The chances are that there will be much more cross-hauling of international investment and more joint ventures or quasi-contractual resource flows. If governments attempt to 'unpackage' the activities of MNEs, or if technology becomes more standardised, then contractual ventures will take the place of foreign production and the traditional MNE may become less important. If, on the other hand, technical progress accelerates and intra-firm communication networks continue to improve; if the distribution of innovation continues to be uneven across countries, and if the world moves towards closer economic interdependence rather than away from it, then international production will remain the dominant form of the foreign activities of enterprises.

Notes: Chapter 4

1   For example, of Mexico (Barlow, 1953; Faynzylber and Tarrago, 1976), UK (Dunning, 1958), India (Kidron, 1965), Norway (Stonehill, 1965), Australia (Brash, 1966), Canada (Safarian, 1966), Singapore (Hughes and You Pol Seng, 1969), France (Johnstone, 1965), New Zealand (Deane, 1970), The Netherlands (Stubenitsky, 1970), Taiwan (Schreiber, 1970).
2   Estimates derived from data published in the IMF Balance of Payments Yearbook.
3   See, for example, the work of d'Arge (1969), Scaperlanda and Mauer (1969) and Krause (1972).
4   In 1959, 18 per cent of the US direct capital stake was in Europe, 34 per cent in Canada and 30 per cent in Latin America and the Caribbean. By 1972, the respective proportions were 33 per cent, 27 per cent and 18 per cent.
5   Excluding Anglo-Dutch and Anglo-Italian companies.
6   For a recent summary of research done on foreign divestment see Boddewyn (1979).
7   For example, at the end of 1975, some 74.6 per cent of Japan's manufacturing investment was concentrated in the developing countries compared with 17.3 per cent of US investment and 20.0 per cent of West German investment (Ozawa, 1979).
8   As shown *inter alia* by the percentage of assets, sales or employment accounted for by foreign affiliates of the world's largest industrial companies (UN, 1978; Dunning and Pearce, 1981). Other figures quoted by Franko (1978) show that the number of US companies among the world's top twelve declined in all industry groups except aerospace between 1959 and 1976.
9   1970 in the case of non-US MNEs.
10   Table III of UN (1978), p. 229. In 1975, minority ownership accounted for 43.9 per cent of Japanese overseas ventures, compared with 8 per cent of US-based multinationals (Ozawa, 1979).
11   These and other approaches are described at some length in Dunning (1973).

12   For a review of these approaches see especially Caves (1974a, b).

13   See those listed in note 1.

14   For further details see Dunning (1973).

15   For Vernon's later views on the value of the product cycle theory as an explanation of other types of foreign investment, and of non-US investment, see Vernon (1974) and (1979).

16   Geroski (1976) has done some work on explaining UK foreign direct investment, Juhl (1979) on explaining German investment, and Swedenborg (1979) on explaining the foreign activities of Swedish MNEs in these terms.

17   Described *inter alia* in Dunning (1973) and Stevens (1974).

18   The Buckley and Casson contribution analyses the foreign market servicing decision of firms in terms of the costs of servicing that market, demand conditions in the market, and its actual and perspective growth.

19   Meaning in this case domestic production in place of imports from a firm's foreign affiliates.

20   Defined as flows of factor inputs, for example, management, capital and technology between independent economic agents at arm's-length prices.

21   See Chapter 2.

22   This proposition is explored in Chapter 5.

23   Here we are entirely concerned with *home* country characteristics. For an incorporation of host country characteristics into a model of foreign market servicing see Buckley and Casson (1981).

24   This is because, as we have seen, the propensity of firms to undertake foreign direct investment is itself, in part, activity or industry specific. See, for example, Caves (1971).

25   Symbolically, where K = capital stock, i = a particular industry, j = a particular country, a = total manufacturing industry and t = all five countries, the RCA of the ith industry in the jth country is $(K_{ij}/K_{it})/(K_{aj}/K_{at})$.

26   See also Parry's estimate of the non-trade performance indices of US manufacturing in six foreign markets (Parry, 1975).

27   Reference to the data in Tables 4.4 and 4.5 suggests that where the RCA(A) and RCA(X) indices for a particular country are both greater or less than 1.000, the comparative ownership advantage (or disadvantage) of that country is clear cut; where one is greater than 1 and the other is less, then the ownership advantage (disadvantage) may be at least partially dependent on the particular route of exploiting the advantage (disadvantage).

28   In this Chapter I illustrate arguments by reference only to data on the RCA(A), RCA(X) and X/E ratios. The foreign direct investment stock is taken as proxy of a country's enterprises' foreign production.

29   Compare the RCA(A) for transportation equipment of 1.293 for the USA with 0.603 for Sweden. The low ratio for Japan reflects the propensity of Japanese motor vehicle manufacturers to exploit their ownership advantages by exporting rather than by direct investment. The RCA(X) for the Japanese transportation equipment industry in 1975 was 1.337, higher than that of any other country.

30   Advertising is related to degree of product differentiation, which is a form of discretionary spending and is positively related to income levels.

31   And more recently that of Australian mining companies in the Pacific and Far East (McKern, 1976).

32   One recent interesting example is South Korea, whose large construction firms not only invest capital and technology in the Middle East but export the labour for such building projects as well.

33   Ozawa (1979) notes that the Japanese government has sometimes assisted Japanese firms, threatened by competition from developing countries, to set up off-shore manufacturing units in these countries. In terms of the eclectic theory, this suggests a subsidisation of the investing firms' ownership-specific advantages.

34   It will be observed that these variables are not independent of each other. For example, the industrial distribution of R & D expenditure may be closely related both to government policy and to the natural and human resource endowments of the country.

35   Svedberg (1980), for example, has argued that the higher profitability of UK direct investment in the British colonies, compared with that in other countries, during the colonial era may well have been influenced by acts of discrimination against non-UK investors.

36   For example, in 1978, three of the fifty largest constructional companies in the world were from South Korea and five from other developing countries.

37   For a definition of 'psychic' distance see note 42.

38   The most obvious example is where a patent expires.

39   Concentration ratios have generally fallen most in industries in which technological progress has been the least, for example, rubber tyres, motor vehicles and some branches of the chemical industry. Note too that the share of Japanese and developing country MNEs is greatest in these sectors.

40   Indeed one of the main benefits claimed for the MNE is that it can draw upon such a variety of country-specific advantages and hence take the fullest benefit of the international division of labour.

41   To this extent, the evolution of a country's foreign direct investment patterns may well follow that of its trade patterns, with investment being initially based on differences in factor endowments but later, if and when countries become industrialised, technology gaps or intra-industry investment become more important.

42   The concept of 'psychic' distance has been particularly developed by the Swedish economists (Hornell and Vahlne, 1972). It refers to 'circumstances which prevent or restrain the flow of goods and/or payments between business and market'. It depends on differences in the level of development between the home country and foreign market, in their levels of education, language, culture, customs, and legal and commercial systems. More recently some Finnish economists (Luostarinen, 1978) have added a third component of distance, viz. 'economic' distance – the inverse of the economic 'pull' of a particular market, for example, as measured in terms of GNP or growth of GNP.

43   This is because the ownership advantages required for foreign production are likely to be greater than those required for exporting (Hirsch, 1976) and that multinationality itself adds to the ownership advantages of firms.

44   One of the reasons for the high (X/A) ratio of this industry is the low cost of Japanese steel.

45   It should be noted that production methods in a particular industry may themselves vary between countries and hence, too, may the economies of local production and exports. For example, *ceteris paribus* the more factor endowments favour labour intensive methods of production the lower the optimum size of the plant may be and the greater the incentive to decentralise production at an earlier output than in the case of the size threshold for capital intensive methods of production. This could explain why firms in some industries from developing countries that invest abroad may be smaller than European or US firms.

46   The influence of intra-firm trade in the (X/A) ratio is likely to be an industry- or firm-specific determinant (Lall, 1978), it being highest (for this reason) in those MNEs whose affiliates buy in a substantial proportion of their materials, parts and components from their parent companies, or which engage in international product or process specialisation, for example, in the motor vehicles industry. In general, country-specific characteristics are unlikely to be important, except in so far as countries may be at different stages of international marketing programmes, for example, the Japanese compared with the US motor vehicles industry in Western Europe.

47   For a more extended discussion of these reasons, see Casson (1979).
48   For a useful discussion of a firm's alternative ownership strategies see Robinson (1978).
49   The development of international commodity and futures markets over the last century explains much of the *divestment* by UK companies in several primary goods sectors, for example, tea, rubber, sugar, etc.
50   See pages 28 ff.
51   Direct investment by less technologically advanced countries in more technologically advanced countries is sometimes prompted by a desire to acquire (internalise) ownership-specific advantages, which will improve the competitiveness of the investing enterprise.
52   Between the end of 1973 and 1976 the UK direct capital stake in the USA rose from $5,403 million to $5,802 million – an increase of 10.7 per cent; in the following three years it rose to $9.391, that is, by 61.9 per cent.
53   Whereas most industrial organisation and locational theories are more concerned with explaining the trend.
54   In the case of Australia, it has been suggested by Parry (1979) that the Australian experience in scaling down and adaptation of imported technology from the US and UK to meet the needs of the Australian economic environment gives Australian enterprises (including the affiliates of foreign MNEs) an ownership specific advantage in exporting such technology to less developed countries.
55   As in the case of the protection given to the domestic acquisition and learning of basic design, engineering and process technology by the Indian government which has helped establish their own MNEs in these areas (Lall, 1979).

References

Aliber, R. Z. (1970), 'A theory of foreign direct investment', in C. P. Kindleberger (ed.), *The International Corporation* (Cambridge, Mass.: MIT Press).

Alchian, A., and Demetsz, H. (1972), 'Production, information costs and economic organisation', *American Economic Review*, vol. 62 (December).

Arrow, K. (1969), 'The organization of economic activity: issues pertinent to the choice of market and non-market considerations', in Joint Economic Committee, *The Analysis and Evaluation of Public Expenditure: the PPB System* (Washington, DC: US Government Printing Office).

Balassa, B. (1965), 'Trade liberalization and "revealed" comparative advantage', *The Manchester School of Economic and Social Studies*, vol. 33 (June).

Baldwin, R. E. (1979), 'Determinants of trade and foreign investment: further evidence', *Review of Economics and Statistics*, vol. 61 (February).

Barlow, E. R. (1953), *Management of Foreign Manufacturing Subsidiaries* (Cambridge, Mass.: Harvard University Press).

Baumann, H. (1975), 'The determinants of the pattern of foreign direct investment: some hypotheses reconsidered', *Weltwirtschaftliches Archiv*, vol. 111, no. 4.

Boddewyn, J. J. (1979), 'Foreign divestment: magnitude and factors', *Journal of International Business*, vol. 10 (Spring/Summer).

Brash, D. (1966), *American Investment in Australian Industry* (Canberra: Australian University Press).

Brown, W. G. (1976), 'Islands of conscious power: MNCs in the theory of the firm', *MSU Business Topics* (Summer).

Buckley, P. J., and Casson, M. C. (1976), *The Future of the Multinational Enterprise* (London: Macmillan).

Buckley, P. J., and Casson, M. C. (1981), 'The optimal timing of a foreign direct investment', *Economic Journal*, vol. 91 (March).

Buckley, P. J., and Davies, H. (1979), *The Place of Licensing in the Theory and Practice of Foreign Operations*, University of Reading Discussion Papers in International Investment and Business Studies No. 47.

Calvet, A. L. (1980), *Markets and Hierarchies: Towards a Theory of the Multinational Enterprise*, unpublished doctoral dissertation, MIT.

Casson, M. C. (1979), *Alternatives to the Multinational Enterprise* (London: Macmillan).

Caves, R. E. (1971), 'International corporations: the industrial economics of foreign investment', *Economica*, vol. 38 (February).

Caves, R. E. (1974a), 'Multinational firms, competition and productivity in host country markets', *Economica*, vol. 41 (May).

Caves, R. E. (1974b), 'The causes of direct investment: foreign firms' shares in Canadian and UK manufacturing industries', *Review of Economics and Statistics*, vol. 56 (August).

Chung, W. K., and Fouch, G. G. (1980), 'Foreign direct investment in the United States in 1979', *Survey of Current Business*, vol. 60 (August).

Coase, R. (1937), 'The nature of the firm', *Economica*, vol. 4 (November).

D'Arge, R. (1969), 'Notes on customs unions and foreign direct investment', *Economic Journal*, vol. 79 (June).

Deane, R. S. (1970), *Foreign Investment in New Zealand Manufacturing* (Wellington: Sweet & Maxwell).

Diaz-Alejandro, C. F. (1977), 'Foreign direct investment by Latin Americans', in T. Agmon and C. P. Kindleberger (eds), *Multinationals from Small Countries* (Cambridge, Mass.: MIT Press).

Dunning, J. H. (1958), *American Investment in British Manufacturing Industry* (London: Allen & Unwin) (reprinted by Arno Press, New York, 1976).

Dunning, J. H. (1973), 'The determinants of international production', *Oxford Economic Papers*, vol. 25 (November).

Dunning, J. H., and Pearce, R. D. (1981), *The World's Largest Industrial Enterprises* (Farnborough: Gower).

Faynzylber, F., and Tarrago, T. (1976), *Las Empresas Transnaccionales* (Mexico City: Fondo de Cultura Economica).

Franko, L. G. (1978), 'Multinationals: the end of US dominance', *Harvard Business Review* (November and December).

Geroski, P. A. (1976), *An Industry Characteristics Analysis of UK Direct Investment*, Warwick Economic Research Papers, No. 85.

Giddy, I., and Rugman, A. (1979), 'A model of foreign direct investment trade and licensing', unpublished manuscript.

Hawkins, R., and Webbinek, E. S. (1976), 'Theories of direct foreign investment: a survey of empirical evidence', unpublished manuscript.

Helleiner, G. K., and Lavergne, R. (1979), 'Intra-firm trade and industrial exports to the US', *Oxford Bulletin of Economics and Statistics*, vol. 41 (November).

Heenan, D. A., and Keegan, W. J. (1979), 'The rise of Third World multi-nationals', *Harvard Business Review* (Jan–Feb).

Hirsch, S. (1976), 'An international trade and investment theory of the firm', *Oxford Economic Papers*, vol. 28 (July).

Hornell, E., and Vahlne, J. E. (1972), 'The deciding factors in the choice of subsidiary sales company as a channel for exports', *Acta Universitatis Usaliensis*, No. 6.

Horst, T. (1972a), 'Firm and industry determinants of the decision to invest abroad: an empirical study', *Review of Economics and Statistics*, vol. 54 (August).

Horst, T. (1972b), 'The industrial composition of US exports and sub-sidiary sales to the Canadian market', *American Economic Review*, vol. 62 (March).

Horst, T. (1974), *American Exports and Foreign Direct Investments*, Harvard Institute of Economic Research, Discussion Paper 362 (May).

Hufbauer, G. C. (1970), 'The impact of national characteristics and tech-nology on the commodity composition of trade in manufactured goods', in R. Vernon (ed.), *The Technology Factory in International Trade* (New York: Columbia University Press).

Hughes, H., and You Pol Seng (1969), *Foreign Investment and the Indus-trialisation of Singapore* (Canberra: Australian National University Press).

Hymer, S. (1960), 'The international operations of national firms: a study of direct investment', doctoral dissertation, MIT.

Johnson, H. (1970), 'The efficiency and welfare implications of the inter-national corporation', in C. P. Kindleberger (ed.), *The International Corporation* (Cambridge, Mass.: MIT Press).

Johnstone, A. W. (1965), *United States Investment in France* (Cambridge, Mass.: MIT Press).

Juhl, P. (1979), 'On the sectoral patterns of West German manufacturing investment in less developed countries: the impact of firm size, factor intensities and protection, *Weltwirtschaftliches Archiv*, vol. 115, no. 3.

Kidron, M. (1965), *Foreign Investments in India* (London: Oxford Univer-sity Press).

Kojima, K. (1978), *Direct Foreign Investment* (London: Croom Helm).

Krause, L. R. (1972), *European Economic Integration and the US* (Wash-ington, DC: Brookings Institution).

Lall, S. (1978), 'The pattern of intra-firm exports by US multinationals', *Oxford Bulletin of Economics and Statistics*, vol. 40 (August).

Lall, S. (1979), 'Developing countries as exporters of technology: a pre-liminary analysis', in H. Giersch (ed.), *International Development and Resource Transfer* (Tübingen: Mohr).

Lall, S. (1980), 'Monopolistic advantages and foreign involvement by US manufacturing industry', *Oxford Economic Papers*, vol. 32 (March).

Lecraw, D. (1977), 'Direct investment by firms from less developed coun-tries', *Oxford Economic Papers*, vol. 29 (August).

Lessard, D. R. (1979), 'Transfer prices, taxes and financial markets', in R. Hawkins (ed.), *The Economic Effects of Multinational Corporations* (Greenwich, Conn.: JAI Press).

Lipsey, R. E., and Weiss, M. Y. (1973), *Multinational Firms and the Factor Intensity of Trade*, National Bureau of Economic Research, New York, Working Paper No. 8.

Lipsey, R. E., and Weiss, M. Y. (1976a), *Exports and Foreign Investment in the Pharmaceutical Industry*, National Bureau of Economic Research, New York, Working Paper No. 87 (revised).

Lipsey, R. E., and Weiss, M. Y. (1976b), *Exports and Foreign Investment in Manufacturing Industries*, National Bureau of Economic Research, New York, Working Paper No. 13 (revised).

Luostarinen, R. (1978), *The Impact of Physical, Cultural and Economic Distance on the Geographical Structure of the Internationalization Pattern of the Firm*, Helsinki School of Economics, FIBO Working Paper No. 1978/2.

McKern, R. B. (1976), *Multinational Enterprise and Natural Resources* (Sydney: McGraw-Hill).

McManus, J. F. (1972), 'The theory of the multinational firm', in G. Paquet (ed.), *The Multinational Firm and the National State* (Toronto: Collier-Macmillan).

Magee, S. P. (1977), 'Information and the multinational corporation: an appropriability theory of direct foreign investment', in J. N. Bhagwati (ed.), *The New International Economic Order* (Cambridge, Mass.: MIT Press).

Owen, R. F. (1979), *Inter-industry Determinants of Foreign Direct Investment: A Perspective Emphasising the Canadian Experience*, Working Papers in International Economics, Princeton University (May).

Ozawa, T. (1979), 'International investment and industrial structure: new theoretcal implications from the Japanese experience', *Oxford Economic Papers*, vol. 31 (March).

Parry, T. G. (1975), 'Trade and non-trade performance of US manufacturing industry: "revealed" comparative advantage', *Manchester School of Economics and Social Studies*, vol. 43 (June).

Parry, T. G. (1979), 'The multinational enterprise and two-stage technology transfer to developing nations', paper prepared for Conference on Third World Multinational Corporations, East/West Centre, Honolulu, September.

Penrose, E. (1958), *The Theory of the Growth of the Firm* (Oxford: Basil Blackwell) (rev. edn published 1979).

Robinson, R. D. (1978), *International Business Management* (Hinsdale, Ill.: The Dryden Press).

Rugman, A. (1979), *International Diversification and the Multinational Enterprise* (Lexington, Mass.: Lexington Books).

Sachdev, J. C. (1976), 'A framework for the planning of divestment policies for multinational companies', PhD thesis, University of Manchester Institute of Science and Technology.

Safarian, A. E. (1966), *Foreign Ownership of Canadian Industry* (Toronto: McGraw-Hill).

Schreiber, J. C. (1970), *US Corporate Investment in Taiwan* (New York: Dunellen).

Scaperlanda, S., and Mauer, L. J. (1969), 'The determinants of US direct investment in the EEC', *American Economic Review*, vol. 59.

Southard, F. A. (1932), *American Industry in Europe* (New York: Houghton Mifflin).

Stern, R. M. (1975), 'Testing trade theories', in P. B. Kenen (ed.), *International Trade and Finance* (London: Cambridge University Press).

Stevens, G. V. (1974), 'Determinants of investment', in J. H. Dunning (ed.), *Economic Analysis and the Multinational Enterprise* (London: Allen & Unwin).

Stonehill, A. (1965), *Foreign Ownership in Norwegian Enterprises* (Oslo: Central Bureau of Statistics).

Stubenitsky, F. (1970), *American Direct Investment in Netherlands Industry* (Rotterdam: Rotterdam University Press).

Svedberg, P. (1981), 'Colonialism and foreign direct investment profitability', in J. H. Dunning and J. Black· (eds), *International Investment and Capital Movements* (London: Macmillan).

Swedenborg, B. (1979), *The Multinational Operations of Swedish Firms. An Analysis of Determinants and Effects* (Stockholm: Almquist and Wiksell).

Teece, D. (1979), *Technology Transfer and R and D Activities of Multinational Firms: Some Theory and Evidence*, mimeo, Stanford University.

Telesio, P. (1979), *Technology Licensing and Multinational Enterprises* (New York: Praejer).

UN (1978), *Transnational Corporations in World Development. A Reexamination*, E.78 II A.5 (New York: Economic and Social Council).

US Tariff Commission (1973), *Implications of Multinational Firms for World Trade and Investment and for US Trade and Industry* (Washington, DC: US Government Printing Office).

Vaupel, J. W., and Curhan, J. P. (1969), *The Making of Multinational Enterprise* (Cambridge, Mass.: Harvard Business School).

Vaupel, J. W., and Curhan, J. P. (1973), *The World's Multinational Enterprises* (Cambridge, Mass.: Harvard Business School).

Vernon, R. (1974), 'The location of economic activity', in J. H. Dunning (ed.), *Economic Analysis and the Multinational Enterprise* (London: Allen & Unwin).

Vernon, R. (1966), 'International investment and international trade in the product cycle', *Quarterly Journal of Economics*, vol. 80 (May).

Vernon, R. (1979), 'The product cycle hypothesis in a new international environment', *Oxford Bulletin of Economics and Statistics*, vol. 41 (November).

Wells, L. (ed.) (1972), *The Product Life Cycle and International Trade* (Cambridge, Mass.: Harvard University Press).

Wells, L. (1977), 'The internationalisation of firms from the developing countries', in T. Agmon and C. P. Kindleberger (eds), *Multinationals from Small Countries* (Cambridge, Mass.: MIT Press).

Wells, L. T., and V'Ella, W. (1979), 'Developing country investors and Indonesia', *Bulletin of Indonesian Economic Studies*, vol. 15 (March).

Williamson, O. E. (1975), *Markets and Hierarchies* (New York: Free Press).

Wolf, B. (1977), 'Industrial diversification and internationalization: some empirical evidence', *Journal of Industrial Economics*, vol. 26 (December).

5

Explaining the International Direct Investment Position of Countries: Towards a Dynamic or Developmental Approach

I

This chapter explores the proposition that a country's international direct investment position, and changes in that position, may be usefully explained by the eclectic theory of international production. Using data on the direct investment flows (or changes in the direct capital stock) of some sixty-seven countries, over the period 1967–78, it also suggests that there is a systematic relationship between the determinants of those flows and the stage and structure of a country's economic development.

II

A country's net international direct investment position is the sum of the direct investment by its own enterprises[1] outside its national boundaries minus the direct investment of foreign owned enterprises within its boundaries.[2]

The eclectic theory suggests that this position, whether one is concerned with the stock of accumulated investment, that is, the direct capital stock, or changes in the stock over time, is determined by three sets of factors. The first is the extent to which its own enterprises possess, or can gain access to, assets or rights which foreign enterprises do not posses or to which they cannot gain access, at least on such favourable terms. Such assets are called ownership-specific advantages[3] in so far as they are

First published in *Weltwirtschaftliches Archiv*, vol. 117, no. 1 (1981), this chapter draws upon some ideas from a paper by the author, Dr Peter Buckley and Mr R. D. Pearce, presented at a Conference of the Association of International Business in Manchester in 1978. The concept of the investment development cycle is also explored in a chapter, by the author, in K. Kumar (ed.), *Multinationals from Third World Countries* (Cambridge, Mass.: MIT Press, 1980).

assumed to be exclusive to the enterprise that owns them, and at least some of them are likely to be transferable (i.e. mobile) across national boundaries (Lall, 1980). The second is whether the enterprises possessing the assets perceive it to be in their best interests to internalise their use or sell this right (but not the assets themselves[4]) to enterprises located in other countries; such internalising advantages reflect the perceived efficiency of multinational hierarchies, compared with market mechanisms, as asset administrators and allocators.[5] The third factor determining international production is the extent to which enterprises find it profitable to locate any part of their production facilities outside their home countries; this will depend on the attractions of location-specific endowments, that is, those which are not transferable or mobile across national boundaries and offered by the home, as compared with a foreign, country.

The generalised predictions of the eclectic theory are straightforward. At any given moment of time, the more a country's enterprises possess ownership-specific advantages, relative to enterprises of other nationalities, the greater the incentive they have to internalise rather than externalise their use; and the more they find it in their interest to exploit them from a foreign location, the more they (and the country as a whole) are likely to engage in international production.[6] By the same token, a country is likely to attract investment by foreign enterprises when the reverse conditions apply. Similarly the theory can be expressed in a dynamic context;[7] changes in the outward or inward investment position of a particular country can be explained in terms of changes in the ownership and internalisation advantages of its enterprises, relative to those of other nationalities, and/or changes in its location-specific endowments, relative to those of other countries, as perceived by its own and foreign enterprises.

A good deal of work has been done on identifying the origin and nature of these ownership–location–internalisation (OLI) advantages, and the conditions under which they are most likely to exist: some of these were set out in Table 4.2 in the previous chapter.

This approach to the theory of international production has been called eclectic for three main reasons. First, it draws on each of the three main lines of explanation which have emerged over the past twenty or so years;[8] second, it is relevant to all types of foreign direct investment; third, and perhaps of most interest, it embraces the three main vehicles of foreign involvement by enterprises, viz. direct investment, exports and contractual resource transfers, e.g. licensing, technical assistance, management and franchising agreements, and suggests which route of exploitation is likely to be preferred. In the case of each modality, the possession of ownership advantages is a necessary prerequisite for foreign involvement.[9] But the presence of internalisation advantages suggests that enterprises will exploit these advantages by way of exports or foreign direct investment rather than by contractual resource exchanges; whereas the equity

Table 5.1   *Alternative Routes of Servicing Markets*

		Advantages	Ownership	Internalisation	(Foreign) Location
Route of Servicing Market		Foreign direct investment	Yes	Yes	Yes
		Exports	Yes	Yes	No
		Contractual resource transfers	Yes	No	No

investment route, rather than exports, will be chosen where locational advantages favour a foreign rather than a domestic production base. The matrix in Table 5.1 summarises the conditions underlying these choices.

Although the three strands in the explanation of international production interact with each other, conceptually there is something to be said for considering them separately. Certainly the location and mode of foreign involvement are two quite independent decisions which a firm has to take, while, by itself, no one strand is both a necessary and a sufficient condition to explain international production. Take, for example, the distinction between ownership and internalisation advantages. Ownership advantages may be internally generated (e.g. through product diversification or innovations) or acquired by enterprises. If acquired, for example, by way of a purchase (be it domestic or foreign) of another enterprise, the presumption is that this act will add to the acquiring firm's ownership advantages *vis-à-vis* those of its competitors (including the acquired firm).[10]

It is convenient to distinguish between two kinds of ownership advantages. The first is that which may generate income whether its use is externalised or internalised; most patents and trademarks, and some management marketing, financial and organisational assets fall into this category. The second is that which can only be realised if it is internalised within the firm, that is, not saleable to other firms. This includes the genuine joint economies of hierarchical activities, for example, product and process integration, the spreading of managerial and technological capacity, the reduction in transaction costs and the gains arising from asset, product or market diversification. Quite a lot of international backward and forward integration is designed to capture the benefits of internalisation as well as to secure exclusive access to inputs and markets.

There is some reason for supposing that the greater the diversification practised by an MNE, the higher the proportion of ownership advantages attributable to internalisation gains (or more correctly the capitalisation of such gains[11]) is likely to be. To this extent, the internalisation paradigm may be more helpful in explaining degrees of multinationality than discrete acts of foreign direct investment.[12] But, except where foreign investment is undertaken to acquire ownership advantages which can only be reaped if they are exploited within the acquiring firm, the two kinds of advantages are quite distinct and should be analysed separately from each other.

In seeking to test the eclectic theory of international production, economists have found it useful to distinguish three structural determinants, viz. those which are specific to particular *countries*, to particular *types of activities* (or industries) and to particular *firms* or *enterprises*. In other words, the propensity of enterprises of a particular nationality to engage in foreign production will vary according to the economic, *et al.*, characteristics of their home countries and the country(ies) in which they propose to invest, the range and type of products (including intermediate products) they intend to produce, and their underlying management and organisational strategies (which *inter alia* may be affected by their size and attitude to risk diversification). Again, as is illustrated in Table 5.2, these characteristics can be readily identified.

Combining the data in Tables 4.2 and 5.2 gives the framework of the eclectic theory that explains each of the main types of foreign direct investment. As can be seen, it is a very general theory. Up to now, most empirical tests of it have been directed to explaining either the industrial composition of a particular country's outward or inward direct investment (or capital stake)[13] or the determinants of the location of that investment.[14] Much less work has so far been done on explaining the country-specific characteristics of the geographical origin of inward direct investment, and none, to my knowledge, on the determinants of the balance between such investment flows. Apart from the product cycle literature, the dynamics of foreign direct investment have been largely ignored while, viewed from a global standpoint, scant attention has been paid to the interaction between the international investment position of a country and its stage and character of economic development.

This chapter should be taken as a starting point in correcting some of these lacunae. I have taken as the variables to be explained the average annual outward, inward and net outward direct investment flows of countries (including reinvested profits and intra-company transfers[15]) for the period 1967–75.[16] Data on the *flow* rather than on the *stock* of foreign direct investment were used because the main source, the IMF *Balance of Payments Yearbook*, provides statistics on both inward and outward investment flows, while the main sources of comparative stock data, viz. the OECD and UN Centre on Transnational Corporations, do not. Information is available for sixty-seven countries over this period, although in the case of a number of countries it had to be supplemented by data from other sources, especially where IMF statistics did not take account of reinvested profits.

Table 5.2 Some Illustrations of how OLI Characteristics may vary according to Structural Variables

OLI Characteristics \ Structural Variables	Country Home – Host	Industry	Firm
Ownership	Factor endowments (e.g. resources and skilled labour), market size and character. Government policy towards innovation, protection of proprietary rights, competition and industrial structure. Government controls on inward direct investment.	Degree of product or process technological intensity. Nature of innovations. Extent of product differentiation. Production economics (e.g. if there are economies of scale). Importance of favoured access to inputs and/or markets.	Size, extent of production, process or market diversification. Extent to which enterprise is innovative or marketing-oriented, or values security and/or stability, e.g. in sources of inputs, markets, etc. Extent to which there are economies of joint production.
Internalisation	Government intervention and extent to which policies encourage MNEs to internalise transactions, e.g. transfer pricing. Government policy towards mergers. Differences in market structures between countries, e.g. with respect to transaction costs, enforcement of contracts, buyer uncertainty, etc. Adequacy of technological, educational, communications, etc., infrastructure in host countries and ability to absorb contractual resource transfers.	Extent to which vertical or horizontal integration is possible/desirable, e.g. need to control sourcing of inputs or markets. Extent to which internalising advantages can be captured in contractual agreements (c.f. early and later stages of product cycle). Use made of ownership advantages. Cf. IBM with Unilever type operation. Extent to which local firms have complementary advantages to those of foreign firms. Extent to which opportunities for output specialisation and international division of labour exist.	Organisational and control procedures of enterprise. Attitudes to growth and diversification (e.g. the boundaries of a firm's activities. Attitudes towards sub-contracting – contractual ventures, e.g. licensing, franchising, technical assistance agreements, etc. Extent to which control procedures can be built into contractual agreements. Type of transactions undertaken, e.g. the degree of uncertainty or idiosyncrasy attached to technology transfers. The frequency with which transactions occur.
Location	Physical and psychic distance between countries. Government intervention (tariffs, quotas, taxes, assistance to foreign investors or to own MNEs, e.g. Japanese government's financial aid to Japanese firms investing in South East Asian labour intensive industries).	Origin and distribution of immobile resources. Transport costs of intermediate and final good products. Industry-specific tariff and non-tariff barriers. Nature of competition between firms in industry. Can functions of activities of industry be split? Significance of 'sensitive' locational variables, e.g. tax incentives, % energy and labour costs.	Management strategy towards foreign involvement. Age and experience of foreign involvement (position of enterprise in product cycle, etc.). Psychic distance variables (culture, language, legal and commercial framework). Attitudes towards centralisation of certain functions, e.g. R & D, regional office and market allocation, etc. Geographical structure of asset portfolio and attitude to risk diversification.

Table 5.3   Direct Investment Flows per Capita 1967–78 and GNP per Capita 1971

GNP	Investment (annual average) ($)						
	Weighted Average [a]			Unweighted Average [b]		Net Outward	
	1967–75			1967–75			
	Outward	Inward	Net Outward	Outward	Inward	1967–75	1976–78
1 $4,000 and over	33.0	16.3	16.7	24.8	30.3	−5.5	7.9
2 $2,500 to $3,999	20.0	15.7	4.3	20.8	31.4	−10.6	−7.6
3 $1,000 to $2,499	3.2	12.9	−9.7	1.2	39.6	−37.4	−32.6
4 $500 to $999	0.4	8.6	−8.2	0.4	21.8	−21.4	−14.4
5 $400 to $499	0.2	7.4	−7.2	0.2	9.0	−8.8	−7.1
6 $300 to $399	0.2	3.2	−3.0	0.1	3.7	−3.6	−3.2
7 $125 to $299	0	3.1	−3.1	0	1.9	−1.9	−2.9
8 Less than $125	0	0.5	−0.5	0	1.3	−1.3	−1.6

[a] Weighted average – obtained by summing outward/inward/net outward investment flows for the x countries in the group and dividing by the population of the x countries. This gives a country with a large population a dominating influence on the result for an income group, for example, the USA in the over $4,000 group. (GNP per capita data from UN *Statistical Year Book*.)

[b] Unweighted average – obtained by (1) calculating outward/inward/net outward flow per capita separately for each of the x countries in an income group; (2) summing these separate results; (3) dividing by x.

Source: IMF with adjustments, in some cases, by author to allow for reinvested profits and/or expropriation of foreign investments over period 1967–75.

III

As an initial proposition (and it is not difficult to find reasons to support this)[17] let us suppose that a country's international investment position is related to the value of its gross national product (GNP) — both variables being normalised by size of population. Table 5.3 sets out a frequency distribution between gross outward (GOI), gross inward (GII) and net

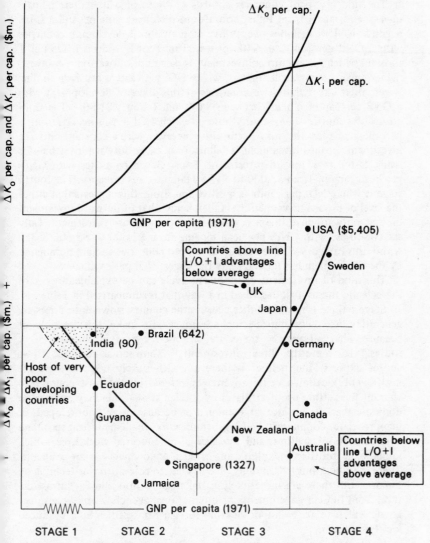

Figure 5.1.   *(N.B. These diagrams are not drawn to scale)*

outward investment flows (NOI) averaged for the period 1967–75,[18] and the GNP per capita in 1971 for sixty-seven countries.[19] Illustrated diagrammatically (see Figure 5.1) these data suggest that, after a 'threshold' GNP per capita has been reached, further increases are associated with rising GOI and GII, but that the shape of the NOI curve takes a U, or J shaped, form. It would also appear that countries may be classified into four main groups corresponding to four stages of development.

The first group of countries consists of those in which there is little inward and, apart from India, no outward direct investment, and a small negative NOI; it includes twenty-five of the poorest developing countries with a GNP per capita of $400 or less. The second group is made up of those in which inward direct investment is rising but outward direct investment remains very small, that is, where NOI is negative but is becoming larger; there are twenty-five countries at this stage of development with a GNP per capita ranging between $400 and (about) $1,500. The third group of countries consists of those in which NOI is still negative but is becoming smaller; this may occur either because, with a constant outward investment, inward investment is falling, or because outward investment is rising faster than inward investment. Some eleven countries with GNPs per head ranging from $2,000 to $4,750 fall into this category. The fourth stage is where NOI per capita is positive and rising; this suggests that either the level of inward investment has fallen below that of outward investment or that outward investment is rising faster than inward investment. Only six countries, with GNPs per head ranging from $2,600 to $5,600,[20] fall within this category.[21] They are all developed countries and are dominated by the USA, which has far and away the largest NOI per capita.

This kind of investment development cycle can be explained by use of the eclectic theory just described in a way that is summarised in Table 5.4. In Stage 1 there is no GOI either because the country's own enterprises are generating no ownership-specific advantages to make this possible or because what advantages there are, are best exploited through other routes, viz. minority direct investment,[22] contractual resource flows and/or exports. But neither is there any GII, simply because there are insufficient location-specific advantages offered by the host country to warrant the setting up of affiliates by foreign firms. This may be because domestic markets are not large enough or because of an undeveloped, or inappropriate, commercial and legal framework, inadequate transport and communication facilities, and the lack of an educated workforce, which inhibits the profitable exploitation of such endowments as are available. There may be a limited amount of arm's length capital and/or technology imports, but these are more likely to take the form of aid for infrastructure, from foreign governments or international agencies, while consumer goods will tend to be imported from foreign firms rather than produced locally by them.

In Stage 2, inward direct investment begins to become commercially

Table 5.4   *Inward and Outward Direct Investment and Stages of Economic Development*

		Inward Investment		Outward Investment
Stage 1	Of	Substantial	Od	Virtually none
	I	Substantial	I	Not applicable
	Ld	Few	Lf	Not applicable
Stage 2	Of	Substantial	Od	Few
	I	Probably declining	I	Few and specialised
	Ld	Increasing	Lf	Beginning to emerge
Stage 3	Of	Declining/more specialised	Od	Increasing
	I	Probably increasing	I	Still limited
	Ld	Declining	Lf	Increasing
Stage 4	Of	Declining and/or more specialised	Of	Increasing
	I	Substantial	I	Increasing
	Ld	Declining	Lf	Increasing

Key to symbols:
O = ownership advantages   f = foreign
L = location advantages   d = domestic
I = internalisation advantages

viable as domestic markets increase and the variable costs of servicing those markets are reduced (Buckley and Casson, 1981). At this point, it is helpful to distinguish between the main forms of foreign direct investment. Import-substituting manufacturing investment, aimed at replacing or supplementing consumer and capital good imports (and often stimulated by host governments imposing barriers to imports), will be initially attracted to well populated, developing industrialising countries, for example, Brazil, India, Malaysia, etc. (Lecraw, 1977; Wells, 1977). On the other hand, investment to exploit national resources, for example, petroleum, raw materials and foodstuffs, mainly for export markets, is likely to wait upon the provision of adequate transport and communications facilities; while rationalised investment designed to take advantage of cheap and productive unskilled or semi-skilled labour will flow as soon as a well motivated and educated labour force (at secondary school level) is available. However, it seems generally agreed that an essential locational characteristic for all kinds of GII is a congenial investment climate and an adequate legal and commercial framework (Root and Ahmed, 1978). At this stage, most transfers of resources are likely to be internalised within the transferring firm — except where host governments insist otherwise. This may be to overcome or reduce supply instabilities, or because of the lack of local, technological, managerial, organisational and marketing capacity.[23] Also, since information, commodity and capital markets (including futures markets) are extremely imperfect, if they exist at all, transaction and negotiating costs associated with contractual relationships are likely to be very high indeed. As in Stage 1, outward direct investment remains small, simply because indigenous enterprises have not yet generated sufficient ownership advantages of their own to overcome the initial barriers of foreign production. However, even at this stage there may be some foreign direct investment in neighbouring territories, for example, within Africa and Latin America, or that designed to acquire foreign technology or buy an entry into foreign markets; and also some exporting of the kind which may eventually lead to import-substituting investment.

Stage 3 is a particularly interesting one, as net inward investment per capita now starts to fall. This could be because, as they move through the technology cycle (Magee, 1977), the original ownership advantages of foreign investors become eroded;[24] or because indigenous firms, stimulated *inter alia* by larger markets, the presence of foreign affiliates and/or assisted by host governments, improve their competitive capacity; or because outward investment is now rising as indigenous firms develop their own comparative ownership advantages, which they find it best to exploit through foreign direct investment.[25] This stage may mark the beginning of a country's international direct investment specialisation, in which it seeks to attract inward direct investment in those sectors in which its comparative location advantages are strongest, but the comparative ownership advantages of its enterprises are weakest; while it urges its own enterprises to invest abroad in those sectors where their comparative ownership advantages are strongest but their comparative location advantages are weakest.

Again, much will depend on both host government policies and the characteristics of the direct investment. This is the stage of development in which host governments are likely to encourage a fuller integration of foreign affiliates into their economies; for example, subsidiaries in mineral exploitation will be pressed to undertake more of their secondary processing locally while those in import-substituting or export platform activities will be persuaded to establish linkages with local enterprises. Moreover, as indigenous firms become more competitive, one would expect the ownership advantages of foreign firms in the mature or standard technology sectors to be whittled away.[26] On the other hand, these advantages may be replaced by others as new activities, in which MNEs have even more pronounced ownership advantages, develop. And since it is in the technologically more advanced sectors that MNEs are most prone to internalise their activities,[27] and, indeed, to gain ownership advantages through internalisation,[28] any tendency towards more licensing and other forms of contractual resource transfer in the sectors originally invested in by MNEs will be more than counteracted.[29]

In Stage 4, a country is a net outward investor, that is, its investment flows abroad exceed those of foreign owned firms in its own country. This reflects strong ownership advantages of its firms and/or an increasing propensity to exploit these advantages internally from a foreign rather than a domestic location. The tendency towards more internalisation is again related to the growing size and geographical diversification of home country MNEs, and to take advantage of regional or global product and process specialisation.[30] At the same time companies, especially from the industrialised economies, are increasingly being induced to exploit their ownership advantages from a foreign location, partly because of rising domestic labour costs and lower rates of productivity growth (often associated with high levels of economic development), partly by the pressure to obtain additional resources (including some types of labour) to help sustain their international competitive position in world markets, and partly to overcome increasing barriers to trade in the kind of goods exported by these countries. Again, depending on the amount of specialisation, GOI may be associated with substantial or little GII. For example, the (second) point of zero NOI could mean that the country engages in no inward or outward investment, that is, is self-sufficient in its investment, or that it has a sizeable outward investment which is balanced by an equally sizeable inward investment.

The interpretation of the investment—development cycle just outlined is based on cross-sectional country data. It suggests that a country's international investment position is related to its level of development as measured by its GNP per capita.[31] However, a proper test of this proposition would require an examination of time series data for individual countries over quite a long period. Unfortunately, except in the case of a few developed countries, data are not available to do this, but casual empiricism does lend some support to the idea of an investment—development cycle. Certainly the USA fits neatly into this pattern as do most continental European countries and Japan; of the developing countries there are some, for example, Nigeria, Indonesia and Kenya, which over the last fifteen years have emerged from the first to second stage; while others, including some of the newly industrialised developing countries (NICs), for example, Hong Kong, Singapore, South Korea, Brazil and Mexico, appear to be moving quickly from the second to the third stage.

IV

The previous paragraphs have suggested that the relationship between a country's international direct position and its GNP per capita may be explained in terms of the extent to which its enterprises, relative to those of other nationalities, possess ownership-specific advantages, which are best exploited within these enterprises, and the locational attractions of that country, relative to others, as a site for productive activities. At the same time, a more detailed inspection of the data reveals that there are considerable variations between the outward and inward investment position of countries at a particular stage of development. It will be argued that these differences may also be explained by reference to the eclectic theory of international production.

Again, let us consider Figure 5.1. On this diagram, we illustrate the kind of relationship between NOI and GNP suggested by Table 5.3. But the diagram also shows that the variations around this line at any particular GNP (or ranges of GNPs) per capita (we have shown four stages on the diagram) are as great or are greater than the variations between levels of development. For example, the UK and New Zealand had about the same GNP per capita in 1971; but the former was a substantial net outward investor while the latter was a substantial net inward investor. On the other hand, Australia, with a GNP per capita of $4,099, had an identical (negative) NOI per capita, as did Jamaica with a GNP per capita of $890. Why too, at similar income levels, is Korea already becoming a sizeable outward investor, while Paraguay or Jordan are not?

The first and most obvious explanation for these deviations is that they reflect differences in the economic structure of countries. The distinction used by most development economists,[32] which parallels fairly closely the main types of foreign direct investment, is between mainly industrialising or industrialised countries and resource rich countries. Table 5.5 and Figure 5.2 trace out two possible investment–development paths (around the average development path illustrated in Figure 5.1). The data show that industrialising or industrialised countries[33] record consistently higher GOIs and NOIs per capita but lower GIIs per capita at any given income level than do the resource rich countries, and that for the higher income groups the differences are very marked indeed.

Table 5.5   *Direct Investment Flows per Capita and GNP per Capita 1967–75 by Economic Structure of Countries*

	GNP per capita (1971) ($m.)	Investment (ΔK_o or ΔK_i) per capita (annual average) ($)					
		(1) Industrialised/ Industrialising Countries			(2) Resource Rich Countries		
		Outward	Inward	Net	Outward	Inward	Net
1	$4,000 and over	32.1	14.9	17.2	17.5	45.7	−28.2
2	$2,500 to $3,999	25.8	29.6	−3.8	8.4	34.7	−26.3
3	$1,000 to $2,499 (a)[a]	2.3	11.5	−9.2	neg	69.4	−69.4
	(b)[b]	1.0	43.9	−42.9			
4	$500 to $999	0.1	16.0	−15.9	0.4	26.2	−25.8
5	$400 to $499	neg	5.5	−5.5	0.1	10.2	−10.1
6	$300 to $399	0.1	2.5	−2.4	neg	6.7	−6.7
7	$125 to $299	neg	1.1	−1.1	neg	3.4	−3.4
8	Less than $125	neg	1.1	−1.1	neg	1.7	−1.7

[a] 3(a) Comprising countries mainly producing manufactured goods for domestic markets.

[b] 3(b) Comprising countries mainly producing manufactured goods for export markets, for example, Hong Kong, Singapore and Taiwan.

Source: As for Table 5.3.

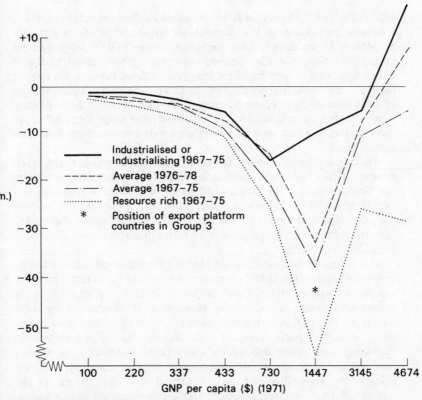

Figure 5.2.   *(N.B. This diagram is not drawn to scale)*

How then are such differences to be explained? The eclectic theory suggests that countries with NOIs above the average possess characteristics such as to generate *above* average ownership advantages for their enterprises, and/or *above* average incentives to internalise these advantages, coupled with *below* average location advantages.[34] In such circumstances foreign MNEs are either less able or less willing to invest in those countries, while domestic companies prefer to exploit their growing competitive and/or internalisation advantages from a foreign rather than a domestic production base. By contrast, the features of countries which record NOIs below the average are such as to generate *below* average ownership advantages for their enterprises, and/or below average incentives for them to internalise these advantages, coupled with above average location-specific advantages, such as to encourage inward and discourage outward investment.

Of course, it is not quite as straightforward as this. The NOI line represents the difference between GOI and GII. Therefore, it follows that deviations around this line may be due to deviations around an average

GOI and/or GII.[35] In turn, such deviations may reflect the extent to which a country participates in the international division of labour of activities by MNEs. As has already been suggested, a zero NOI in Stage 3 could mean that a country neither imports nor exports direct capital; or that it does a great deal of both but there is an exact balance between the two. In the latter case, countries would tend to exploit the ownership advantages of their own MNEs in economic sectors in which they had a competitive edge *vis-à-vis* foreign firms, and import those (via foreign based MNEs) in those sectors in which their own companies were comparatively disadvantaged.

While it is possible to identify the OLI advantages which might determine the NOI of countries, because of differences in economic structure, and hence in the type of outward and inward investment of countries, it is exceedingly difficult to present a generalised test of the eclectic theory in the sense of pinpointing the particular OLI advantages and/or the balance between them, which might explain all forms of international production in and by all countries.

This is mainly because different kinds of foreign investment tend to be associated with different OLI characteristics.[36] Take for example location-specific advantages. Here, most empirical research suggests that while import-substituting manufacturing investment is determined by such factors as the size and structure of the local market, host government policy towards imports, transport costs, and the strategy of enterprises in exploiting their ownership-specific advantages, investment in primary products and rationalised manufacturing is more governed by such variables as the availability and cost of natural resources, the extent and quality of the local technological and communications infrastructure, taxes and incentives, the proximity of the leading export markets and the extent to which trade (including trade in intermediary products) is free between home and host countries, and between host countries in which foreign affiliates of MNEs are located.[37]

Similarly, while each type of international production implies the presence of some ownership-specific advantages on the part of the investing firms, these differ in both kind and extent. In the case of import-substituting manufacturing investment (which normally replicates part or all of the range of products produced by the affiliate's parent company), technology, trade marks, management and organisational and marketing skills make up the ownership advantages. With vertically or horizontally integrated investments there are additional ownership advantages, which arise uniquely from internalisation economies (notably those of joint production) which cannot be transferred to other firms; in addition, access to markets, the economies of large-scale production and the ability of MNEs to better exploit differences in factor endowments and markets are likely to be more important than in the case of import-substituting investments.

Finally, the propensity of enterprises to internalise the use of their intangible assets will also differ according to type of investment, partly for the reasons just mentioned, and partly because, where the option between internalising and externalising advantages does exist, the net benefit of each route may differ considerably according to the nature of the advantage and the extent to which the market is capable of providing the advantaged firm an economic rent at least equal to what it may earn by internalising the transaction.

Using this kind of approach, then, it is possible to suggest a number of propositions about the causes of deviation of countries above or below the NOI line. From the viewpoint, first, of GII, one might hypothesise that countries with the same GNP per capita, which are (1) rich in natural and/ or human resources, (2) have a large home market, (3) offer a congenial environment to inward investment, (4) have a well-developed infrastructure, and an acceptable legal and/or commercial framework, and yet (5) whose indigenous firms are not able (or do not choose) to generate the kind of ownership advantages to enable them to successfully compete with foreign enterprises, will be those that will record an above average inward investment; whereas those that do not share these characteristics, where competition from indigenous firms is strong, or where host governments control inward direct investment, will record a below average inward investment.

From the viewpoint of GOI one would expect countries to engage in above average outward investment, where their firms generate strong ownership advantages but where it is profitable (or less risky) for them to utilise these advantages in foreign countries. One might then predict that countries which, at a given GNP per capita, were mainly industrialised, yet whose internal markets offered only limited opportunities for domestic growth, whose indigenous and location-specific resources were costly or inefficient, whose general economic and political climate of all kinds of investment was unfavourable and whose governments assisted their less competitive industries to invest in more congenial environments,[38] would generate above average outward investment; while those whose prosperity rested more on immobile resource endowments (e.g. minerals, raw materials and foodstuffs) would generate less than average outward investment.

What does the above analysis imply for the investment—development cycle? There are two ways in which one might take the deviations in NOI per capita at any given income level into account. The first is to classify countries according to the different kinds of investment they tend to attract or generate, and then to relate this variable to GNP; the second is to replace GNP as an explanatory variable by a variable, or set of variables, which reflects the OLI characteristics that might determine NOI, and relate these to NOI per capita.

Analytically, the second is the more attractive of the two alternatives as variations in GNP can themselves be interpreted in terms of differences in the ability of countries to generate the kind of characteristics embraced by the eclectic theory. Pragmatically, the first has some merit as, by distinguishing between different types of investment, one is automatically distinguishing between different types of OLI advantages *at a given stage* of economic development. What remains then is the relationship NOI and the kind of NOI characteristics which are proxied by levels of GNP.[39]

This chapter adopts a two-stage approach. First, some descriptive data are presented on the relationship between selected OLI characteristics and groups of countries classified both by GNP and economic structure (as set out in Table 5.3). Then for the more formal statistical testing, the sixty-seven countries are regrouped by cluster analysis, and, for each cluster, multiple regression analysis is used to identify the more significant OLI variables explaining the investment flows of the constituent countries.

V

Since this approach is macro-oriented, the search for operationally testable OLI variables concentrates on those that are likely to be of the broadest applicability.[40] A reading of the literature, and particularly an article written by Root and Ahmed in 1978, which used multiple discriminant analysis to identify the most important location-specific variables influencing foreign direct manufacturing investment in developing countries, and work by industrial organisation economists (as described in Chapters 3 and 4) in pinpointing the main ownership-specific variables, suggests that there is now a reasonable consensus of opinion about the more significant explanatory variables that should be incorporated in any general cross-sectional country model of international production. It is when one comes to pinpointing operationally testable proxies for internalisation advantages that one runs into difficulties. This is partly because some of these advantages are themselves embodied in ownership advantages, but mostly because the various forms of market failure and/or administrative fiat are extremely difficult to quantify, particularly at a country level. Because of this, a kind of revealed advantage approach[40] has been adopted and variables chosen that seem likely to be associated with internalisation. Three possible proxies will be examined: (1) the ratio of imports plus exports to total sales of foreign affiliates (arguing that the more an affiliate engaged in trade, the more likely it is to gain from the kind of advantages associated with the international division of labour), (2) the ratio of (internalised) intra-group to all imports and exports of MNE affiliates and (3) the percentage of all foreign earnings derived from transfers of technology derived from non-affiliated companies (in the form of royalties and fees). Data limitations force us to confine ourselves to a modified version of (1) and

(3) using US and UK data. As far as (2) is concerned, there are some regional and country data in respect of US MNEs which help corroborate the other two sets of data.

The OLI variables chosen for consideration are set out at the end of Table 5.6. These comprise two ownership variables, two internalisation variables and six location variables. Also included are two structural variables, viz. size of population and share of primary products plus tourism receipts of total trade.

It should be noted that while the eclectic theory would generally predict a positive relationship between location advantages and inward investment and a negative relationship between location advantages and outward investment; and a positive relationship between ownership advantages and outward investment and a negative relationship between ownership advantages and inward investment,[41] it is the *balance* between O, L and I advantages that will affect the propensity of a country to be a net inward or net outward investor. As has already been suggested, a zero NOI could either mean sizeable O and I advantages are evenly balanced by sizeable L advantages or that the country has very few advantages of any kind.

The data on the OLI variables are presented in Table 5.6. Taking first GOI, this appears to be strongly associated with $O(1)$ and $O(2)$, with any substantial amounts of outward investment being restricted to countries whose most educated and trained workers account for 10 per cent or more of the population and whose R & D expenditure is normally 1.6 per cent or more.[42] In the case of the location variables, the picture is mixed. For any given $L(1)$, there is some suggestion that outward investment per capita is greater in industrialised than resource rich countries, but, other than this, for Groups 1–3 the value of $L(1)$ remains about the same, while thereafter it is positively associated with outward investment. It seems that there is a generally positive association between average earnings $(L(2a))$ and outward investment; but a generally negative association between growth in industrial output and such flows, at least for countries comprising Groups 1–4. For most of the other locational variables, the association is in the reverse direction to what one might expect, but it is believed this primarily reflects their 'pull' on inward investment rather than their 'push' to outward investment.[43] $L(5)$, the taxation variable, suggests the right relationship, viz. that higher taxation is associated with more outward investment but below Group 4 countries, although the tax incidence continues to fall (at least until Group 6), there is no effect on outward investment (one exception is India). There is some reason to suppose that above average outward investment is associated with (an average of) the two indices of internalisation used, but the relationship is not as clear as one would like. Finally, there seems no obvious relationship between population size and the propensity to engage in outward investment; looking at individual data, of the twelve countries with an average outward

Table 5.6 Net Outward Direct Investment and Indicators of OLI-Specific Advantages and Economic Structure 1967–75; Countries grouped by GNP per Capita

Countries (GNP per capita)	Investment per capita[a] Outward	Inward	Net	O(1) (%)	O(2) (%)	L(1) ($m.)	L(2a) ($)	L(2b) ($)	L(3) (%)	L(4) (%)	L(5) (%)	I(1) (%)	I(2) (%)	L(1)/O(1)	S(1) mln.	S(2) (%)
(averages for countries in each group)																
(a) Developed Countries																
Group 1: $4,000 and over																
I	32.1	14.9	17.2	18.4	2.1	111.5	2.80	3.8	75.7	72.2	34.5	40.9	23.0	0.48	92.1	15.8
R	17.5	45.7	−28.2	15.7	1.2	382.7	2.78	4.4	74.7	70.6	34.4	26.7	18.4	1.66	13.1	36.9
A	24.8	30.3	−5.5	17.0	1.7	221.5	2.79	4.9	75.2	71.4	34.3	33.8	20.7	1.07	52.6	26.4
Group 2: $2,500–$3,999																
I	25.8	29.6	−3.8	13.8	2.1	112.8	1.77	5.1	71.4	71.8	32.5	39.3	34.2	0.58	45.4	17.9
R	8.4	34.7	−26.3	13.9	0.9	355.8	1.77	4.2	72.8	69.5	36.3	37.9	17.0	1.74	6.9	37.8
A	20.8	31.4	−10.6	13.8	1.6	220.8	1.77	4.7	74.4	66.7	34.2	38.7	25.8	1.24	45.4	25.4
(b) Developing Countries[b]																
Group 3: $1,000–$2,499																
I	2.3	11.5	−9.2	10.5	1.3	113.6	1.00	6.4	52.0	59.4	25.0	35.8	14.2	0.63	28.8	36.6
E	1.0	43.9	−42.9	8.3	0.4	98.7	0.30	11.2	70.7	57.2	15.5	43.9	nsa	0.77	7.2	8.5
R	neg	69.4	−69.4	8.5	0.3	384.8	0.75	nsa	54.0	36.0	22.8	38.0	30.9	3.26	4.0	66.5
A	1.2	38.6	−37.4	9.3	0.6	190.8	0.69	7.2	57.7	51.8	21.5	38.0	22.5	1.40	14.9	40.1
Group 4: $500–$999																
I	0.1	16.0	−15.9	9.5	0.4	66.0	0.68	8.7	nsa	34.7	22.1	nsa	12.9	0.64	39.8	47.8
R	0.4	26.2	−25.8	8.9	0.2	173.8	0.60	7.6	nsa	38.7	11.1	nsa	50.6	1.33	1.5	102.9
A	0.2	21.6	−21.4	9.1	0.3	126.1	0.63	8.1	55.3	36.4	16.4	30.9	28.0	0.95	18.5	78.4
Group 5: $400–$499																
I	neg	5.5	−5.5	6.3	0.3	43.8	0.50	8.0	nsa	32.0	23.1			0.50	9.6	55.3
R	0.1	10.2	−10.1	5.0	0.7	91.0	0.44	7.1	nsa	25.4	17.6			1.13	5.9	65.5
A	0.1	8.9	−8.8	5.4	0.6	77.5	0.47	7.7	47.6	27.3	21.5			0.95	6.9	62.8
Group 6: $300–$399																
I[c]	0.1	2.5	−2.4	4.4	0.5	18.0	0.34	10.3	nsa	34.7	15.0			0.49	12.4	55.5
R	neg	6.7	−6.7	5.4	0.3	68.1	0.32	17.9	nsa	24.8	18.3			0.61	4.2	53.1
A	0.1	3.7	−3.6	4.7	0.4	37.4	0.33	9.6	50.7	31.9	16.1			0.54	10.1	54.4

For Groups 5 and 6 the I(1) and I(2) columns are bracketed together with values 31.3[d] and 9.3[b].

Group 7: $125–$299

I	neg	1.1	4.1	0.6	27.2	0.33	8.1	46.4	18.6	nsa		0.64	13.8	63.5
R	neg	3.4	2.9	0.6	31.0	0.29	5.5	42.5	18.7	nsa		0.77	23.1	53.9
A	neg	1.9	3.7	0.6	28.6	0.31	6.4	45.1	18.6	21.1	29.0[e]	0.68	16.9	60.3

Group 8: Under $125

I	neg	1.1	2.9	0.3	6.5	0.16	7.8	38.1	13.7	nsa		0.19	130.5	57.1
R	neg	1.7	1.2	0.3	10.6	0.18	9.9	nk	6.1	nsa		0.57	3.8	61.5
A	neg	1.3	2.4	0.3	8.1	0.17	8.6	38.1	11.1	24.3	34.8[e]	0.38	79.7	59.3

a Annual average.
b Includes two developed countries, viz. Spain and Italy.
c Includes one export platform country, viz. Korea.
d Average for Groups 5 and 6.
e Average for Groups 7 and 8.

I = Industrialised or industrialising; R = Resource rich; E = Export platform; A = Average (see Table 5.3).
nsa = not separately available; nk = not known.

Key to Headings of Table 5.6 and Sources

O(1) Stock of human capital, measured by percentage of professional, technical, administrative and managerial workers to total workforce in 1973 or nearest year (ILO Yearbook of Labour Statistics).

O(2) Expenditure on research and development (R & D), as percentage of GNP in 1973 or nearest year (UNESCO Statistical Yearbook).

L(1) Natural resource endowments, measured by exports of primary products plus tourism receipts, per capita in 1973 or nearest year (UN Statistical Year Book and IMF Balance of Payments Yearbook).

L(2)(a) Average earnings per hour in manufacturing industry in 1971. (Business International, 7 and 14 December, 1973).

L(2)(b) Growth of manufacturing (or industrial) output; average growth 1960–77 (World Bank: World Development Report 1979).

L(3) BERI Environmental Risk Index; average 1972–76 (100.0 represents a no risk situation) (BERI – unpublished data).

L(4) Infrastructure index; average of two percentages: (1) percentage of urban to total population (average 1960 and 1975) and (b) percentage of secondary school children in appropriate age group (average 1960 and 1975) (World Bank: World Development Report, 1978).

L(5) Tax burden; average of two percentages: (a) (realised) corporate income tax rates, 1968 (Kopits, IMF Staff Papers, November 1976) and (b) percentage of all taxes to GNP, 1969–71 (Tait, Grätzand, Eichengreen, IMF Staff Papers, March 1979; OECD Revenue Statistics of OECD Member Countries 1965–1975).

I(1) Internalisation(1); royalties, management and other fees received by UK enterprises from foreign unaffiliated firms as percentage of fees received by UK enterprises from foreign affiliated and unaffiliated firms, 1974 (UK Business Monitor M4, 1977 edition).

I(2) Internalisation(2); the percentage of exports of US foreign affiliates in manufacturing industry, 1974 (US Survey of Current Business, May 1976).

S(1) Population (UN Statistical Year Book).

S(2) The exports of primary products plus tourism receipts as percentage of total visible exports in 1973 (UN Statistical Year Book and IMF Balance of Payments Yearbook.

S(3) See Table 5.7. GNP per capita.

L(1)/O(1) L(1) ÷ O(1), each set of data being normalised by the highest value in the series.

investment of more than $10 per capita, five had populations of more than fifty million, and five of less than twenty-two million.

As far as GII is concerned, the influence of the L(1) variable seems pretty convincing, both between groups of countries and between industrialised or industrialising and resource rich countries. For the rest, it is useful to distinguish between the first five and last three groups of countries. It seems for there to be any sizeable inward investment (per capita) certain locational advantages must be present. These include a BERI index of at least 50.0 and a combined educational/urbanisation infrastructure ratio of at least 30.0. The only countries which do not meet these minimum requirements are very large industrialised countries, for example, India and Indonesia, and one resource (oil) rich country, viz. Nigeria. And as the penultimate column of Table 5.6 suggests, along with GNP per capita, the size of population seems to be as important a factor influencing inward investment in industrialised countries as the availability of natural resources is in influencing such investment into resource rich countries.

It has been said that the NOI ratio should reflect the *balance* of OLI advantages, rather than the *extent* of them. In general, as set out in Table 5.6 we have the kind of OLI relationships which are consistent with the U- or J-shaped investment development pattern. For industrialised countries in Groups 1 and 2, a *positive* NOI is generally associated with strong locational advantages pulling investment in, which are outweighed by stronger locational disadvantages and/or ownership and internalisation advantages pushing investment out. For resource rich Groups 1 and 2 countries and for industrialised Group 3 countries, this relationship is reversed; fairly strong ownership plus internalisation advantages of domestic enterprises are offset by strong locational advantages which encourage them and foreign based companies to exploit indigenous endowments. Beyond this point, as income levels fall, OLI advantages lessen, but with ownership advantages falling faster than locational advantages until, at an income level of around $400 per capita, in all except highly populated countries, locational advantages are below the threshold necessary to attract any inward investment. Here, minimal O and L advantages are balanced as finely as they are when countries move from Stage 3 to Stage 4 in the development cycle.

There is no single variable which may be used as a proxy for the balance of OLI variables — if for no other reason than the values of these variables are differently denominated. However, as a very rough approximation of such a balance (and no more than this), for each country O(1) and L(1) data were recalculated as index numbers, expressing the highest O(1) and L(1) values as 100; the adjusted L(1) was then divided by the adjusted O(1) figure, and the ratio correlated with the NOI ratio. For the sixty-seven countries the rank correlation coefficient worked out at -0.62; when five countries, which appeared markedly out of line with the rest, were removed the coefficient improved very considerably to -0.77.

VI

We now turn to the more formal statistical testing of the relationship between direct investment flows, OLI characteristics and selected structural variables.[44] Taking GOI, GII and NOI as the dependent variables, we first sought, by use of multiple regression analysis, to identify which of the OLI variables listed on page 127 best explained the direct investment flows of countries. We did this by means of a stepwise inclusion of variables in the computation of ordinary least square coefficients using a double criterion: a significance level of at least 10 per cent for the coefficient and a correlation tolerance of 70 per cent with the other independent variables. A selection of those variables with the best explanatory power is set out in Table 5.7.

The results are disappointing in two respects. First, the sign of the coefficient of the human capital variable $O(1)$ in equation (2) is unexpected, and second, a plot of residual against predicted values indicated a probable presence of heteroscedasticity for more than half the regression equations. This led us to believe that the specification of the equations needed refining. However, we suspected that it was the differences in economic structures among countries that weakened the explanatory power of the variables rather than the choice of variables themselves. This being so, we first distinguished between industrialised or industrialising countries and resource rich countries. However, the same problems that we faced earlier continued to affect the results, so we turned to a second option which was to perform an automatic classification of the countries by means of cluster analysis.

To do this, the technique of correspondence analysis[45] was used. This is a type of factoring, analogous to the principal component method of factoring, but designed to permit the comparison of variables and objects in the same factorial space.[46] In this instance, the variables were the OLI characteristics, the investment flows and the structural variables, and the objects the sixty-seven countries. The results showed that, as expected, the factors explaining the largest amount of variance were those representing GNP per capita and NOI per capita. Looking at the factorial space they depicted, and eliminating those variables and countries with correlation coefficients of less than 10 per cent with both factorial axes, we were able to identify three distinct clusters of countries and associated variables which exhibited homogeneous characteristics within each cluster.

To further check this procedure, a discriminant analysis was performed on those remaining countries and variables before applying the regression methodology to the clusters formed. In Table 5.8 the results show that the clusters are indeed natural and distinct.

The countries in each cluster were closely allied to the development stages (rather than to economic structure) described earlier in this chapter. The first group of sixteen countries broadly comprised those in which

Table 5.7   Relationship between Investment Flows, OLI Variables and Economic Structure of Countries

| | Dependent Variables | | | | Independent Variables | | | | | | | | | |
	GOI	GII	NOI	Constant	L(1)/O(1)	S(2) ECSTR	S(3) GNP	O(1)	O(2)	L(1)	$\bar{R}^2$	F	DW	N[c]	H
(1)	•			-6.349							0.52	35.7***	1.9**	33	*[d]
(2)		•		-0.108				0.290 (0.43)	17.784 (5.97)***[b]	0.103 (4.16)***	0.44	13.5***	2.4**	33	*
(3)			•	-7.661					11.874 (2.28)**	-0.081 (3.45)***	0.29	7.4***	2.3**	33	*
(4)	•			-2.716			-0.006 (8.67)***				0.53	75.2***	2.1**	67	*
(5)		•		8.707			-0.007 (3.56)***				0.15	12.7***	1.4	67	*
(6)			•	5.350	27.981 (9.31)***	-0.246 (3.56)***					0.57	44.2***	1.8**	67	*
(7)			•	8.725	-23.550 (7.44)***						0.45	55.4***	1.8**	67	
(8)	•			-3.545			-0.007 (6.41)***				0.49	41.2***	2.1**	43	*
(9)			•	-5.066			-0.006 (3.10)***				0.34	11.9***	2.2**	43	

Significance: ** at the 5 per cent level.
              *** at the 1 per cent level.

[a] The broken-line box indicates the variables that were given to the stepwise procedure. A missing coefficient means that the variable did not meet the criterion. The OLI variables, as well as the structural variables, not represented on this table did not meet the criterion.

[b] The number in brackets represents the t statistic value.

[c] Number of observations.

[d] The star under H indicates the probable presence of heteroscedastic disturbances.

Table 5.8   *Classification of Clusters Tested by Discriminant Analysis*

Actual Cluster	No. of cases	Predicted cluster membership		
		1	2	3
Cluster 1	16	16	0	0
		100.0%	0.0%	0.0%
Cluster 2	15	0	14	1
		0.0%	93.3%	6.7%
Cluster 3	20	0	1	19
		0.0%	5.0%	95.0%

Percentage of cases correctly classified: 96.08 per cent
F test $= 2.94$***[a]
t test $= 9.31$***[b]

*** shows significance at the 1 per cent level.
[a] The F statistic tests the discriminating power of the variables. Here we reject the hypothesis that the clusters' individual centres are positioned with the over-all centre.
[b] This t statistic was used by Mosteller and Bush (1954) to test the hypothesis that the classification obtained from experiment was not better than a chance classification. Here we reject this hypothesis with a high degree of confidence.

there was some outward investment (GOI); these include most of the developed and a few developing countries. The second group comprised fifteen countries which had a considerable inward investment (GII), but little or no GOI, that is, they were all associated with a substantially negative NOI. The third group was made up of twenty very poor developing countries, which attracted only a small amount of inward investment.

This analysis of clustering also identified distinct sets of O, L and I variables within each country cluster, and these variables were used to perform the regression methodology used earlier. The results are set out in Table 5.9.[47] Here it can be quite clearly seen that while the O(1) advantage dominates the explanation for GOI, the balance of O(1) and L(1) advantages dominates the explanation for NOI of group 1 countries; L advantages, in particular the availability of natural resources, L(1), and degree of urbanisation, L(4a), affect GII and NOI of group 2 countries; while in group 3 countries only L(1) is at all significant. However, it may be noted, as far as this last group of countries is concerned, that the urbanisation index L(4a), which is highly significant as an explanation of GII in group 2 countries, is not a significant variable. This is because (as was suggested on page 128) it is only after the index has risen above 30.0 per cent that foreign companies seriously consider investing in the country.

VII

For the rest of this chapter, I would like to return briefly to some more analytical issues. It was argued earlier that to understand the relationship

Table 5.9 Relationship between GII, GOI and NOI and Selected O and L Variables Classified by Three Groups of Countries

	Dependent Variables			Independent Variables[a]										
Countries	GOI	GII	NOI	Constant	L(1)/O(1)	O(1)	L(1)	L(2b)	L(4a)	L(5)	$\bar{R}^2$	F	DW	No. of observations
Cluster 1														
(1)	•			44.559						−1.507 (2.20)**	0.37	5.41**	2.6**	16
(2)			•	12.401	−19.772 (2.37)**	2.653 (2.55)**b					0.23	5.62**	2.1**	16
Cluster 2														
(3)		•		2.941			0.138 (5.53)***	−2.030 (2.33)**	0.336 (3.09)***		0.78	18.03***	1.9***	15
(4)			•	−0.149			−0.147 (4.98)***				0.63	24.82***	1.6***	15
Cluster 3														
(5)		•		0.813			0.054 (2.16)**				0.16	4.66**	1.4***	20
(6)			•	−0.786			−0.055 (2.18)**				0.17	4.77**	1.5***	20

Significance: ** at the 5 per cent level.
               *** at the 1 per cent level.

[a] The OLI variables, as well as the structural variables not represented here, did not meet the criterion.
[b] The number in parentheses represents the *t* statistic value.

between a country's international investment position and its economic development not only requires a time series rather than a cross-sectional approach, but that development should be viewed in a relative rather than an absolute economic context.

As to the former point, there has been little use of the eclectic model to explain changes in a country's international direct investment position, though the next chapter attempts to do this for the UK for the period 1962 to 1977. But the data set out in Table 5.10 do seem to corroborate the idea of an investment—development cycle of countries. As far as the newly emerging foreign investors from developing countries are concerned, each of the five countries, for which IMF data are available, exhibits a clear trend towards a higher outward/inward investment ratio. Separate data on inward and outward investment suggest that this is primarily because outward investment has risen rather than because inward investment has fallen. *Inter alia*, this is shown by the fact that outward *plus* inward investment per capita has been rising. This, in turn, implies that it has been the rising *ownership* rather than falling *location* advantages of these countries which have been responsible for the changing ratio. The identification and evaluation of these advantages, which are linked to the structure of industry and the strategy of firms, both of which (particularly the former) are affected by the resource endowments of the country, government policy and market size, is a matter for further research.

On the latter point, it is clear that since the NOI for all countries taken together must be zero (i.e. the positive NOI of some countries must equal the negative NOI of others) not all countries will be able to reach the final stage of the investment—development cycle.[48] The eclectic theory predicts neither whether countries will move from Stage 1 through to Stage 4, nor what might subsequently happen to countries currently with the highest income levels.[49] What it does suggest, however, is that, if and when countries advance their relative economic status, the consequential changes in their OLI characteristics will affect their NOI position.[50] The implication of this is that, over time, as average living standards in the world rise, the curve depicted in Figure 5.1 will shift towards the right. Alternatively, normalising each country's GNP per capita by a world average, while the shape of the curve may remain more or less the same, the position of individual countries, on or around the curve, may shift to the left or right. Finally it is interesting to speculate on the nature of the curve in relation to the vertical axis (which reflects the amount and dispersion of GOI and GII). What happens when more countries become outward investors? What if there is a convergence in ownership- and location-specific advantages? What if investment flows follow the pattern of trade flows, and the proportion of intra-industry investment rises? Will the curve then become shallower, that is, more 'saucer' shape than that revealed by the 1967–75 data? These are all fascinating issues, worthy of scholarly investigation.

Table 5.10　*Inward and Outward Direct Investment Flows for Selected Countries: Mid-1960s–1978*

Countries	Annual average ($m.)		
	(a) Inward	*(b)* Outward	$\dfrac{(b)}{(a)}$ %
Brazil			
1978	1,606	102	6.4
1975–77	1,555	135	8.7
1972–74	1,100	45	4.1
1969–71	403	10	2.5
1966–69	161	0	0
South Korea			
1978	71	24	33.8
1975–77	91	13	14.3
1972–74	84	9	10.7
1969–71	50	2	3.3
1966–68	11	0	0
Singapore			
1978	337	24	7.1
1975–77	453	7	1.5
1972–74	333	3	0.9
1969–71	82	1	1.2
1967–68	30	0	0
Columbia			
1978	60	12	20.0
1975–77	37	11	29.8
1972–74	24	3	12.5
1969–71	47	4	8.5
1967–68	46	2	4.3
Malaysia			
1978	476	22	4.6
1975–77	318	9	2.8
1972–74	241	5	2.1
1969–71	91	2	2.2
1967–68	37	0	0
Germany			
1978	1,320	2,880	218.2
1975–77	1,193	2,050	171.8
1972–74	1,867	1,473	78.9
1969–71	745	878	117.9
1967–68	691	415	60.0
Japan			
1978	n.k.	1,870	–
1975–77	103	1,520	1,475.7
1972–74	97	1,273	1,312.4

Table 5.10 (*continued*)

Countries	(a) Inward	(b) Outward	$\frac{(b)}{(a)}$ %
1969–71	125	307	407.2
1967–68	61	172	282.0
1964–66	52	79	153.2

Source: IMF, *Balance of Payments Year Book.*

VIII

Let us briefly recapitulate on the main thesis of this chapter.

(1)   A country's propensity to engage in foreign direct investment and/or be invested in by foreign enterprises rests upon:
  (a)   the extent to which its enterprises (relative to enterprises of other nationalities) possess net ownership advantages;
  (b)   Whether it pays these enterprises to internalise these advantages or leave them (through the market) to other enterprises to exploit;[51]
  (c)   whether it is profitable for enterprises to locate their production units in the home country or a foreign country.

(2)   It is possible to identify the nature of these advantages by reference to:
  (a)   industrial organisation theory,
  (b)   location theory,
  (c)   the theory of the firm.

(3)   The extent to which one country's enterprises possess the capacity and willingness to produce abroad will *inter alia* depend on:
  (a)   country,
  (b)   industry,
  (c)   enterprise-specific factors.

These factors, particularly (a) and (b), are clearly interlinked, but given (a) and (b), the advantages described above will differ between enterprises; given (a) and (c), they will differ between industries; given (b) and (c) they will differ between countries.

(4)   Countries vary in their propensity to engage in foreign direct investment or be invested in, because of their different:
  (a)   level and structure of resource endowments,
  (b)   size and character of markets,
  (c)   government policies (e.g. towards foreign direct investment, innovation, industrial concentration, etc.).

These differences will reflect themselves in the extent and kind of *ownership* and *internalisation* advantages which firms of different nationalities possess, *location* advantages which different countries possess and *inter alia* the industrial spread of their outward and inward direct investment and capital stake.

(5)   There is some evidence to suggest that the forces determining the level of inward and outward direct investment and the balance between the two are linked to a country's stage of development, and that it is reasonable to think of a four-stage investment development process or cycle, in which, after the first stage of little inward or outward investment, inward investment rises. This is eventually followed by a third stage when outward investment begins to rise and/or inward investment falls, but NOI is still negative, and finally NOI becomes positive. The developing countries now emerging as outward investors are entering into the third stage.

(6)   At any particular stage of development, countries may differ from each other in their international investment involvement and structures. The deviations from the 'average' NOI can be explained by different country-specific characteristics, reflected in the possession of ownership, location and internalisation advantages set out above. The significant difference between the investment paths of industrialising and resource rich countries bear this point out.

(7)   The eclectic theory may also be used to explain changes in the outward/inward investment (or capital stake) ratio of a particular country over time, either in the short or medium term or in the long run. In the case of one industrialised country, the UK, a rising outward/inward direct capital stake in manufacturing industry between 1960 and 1976 reflected both rising ownership advantages on the part of UK firms and falling location advantages on the part of the UK as a site for production. One suspects that in the more recent past, for example, since around 1975, the falling outward/inward investment stake of the USA has reflected the opposite combination of forces. In the case of the five developing countries chosen for illustration, the rising outward/inward investment primarily reflects the rising ownership advantages of their own enterprises *vis-à-vis* those of other countries. Here, it should be noted that ownership-specific advantages, for example, size of firm, may also account for part of these advantages as may the geographical distribution of the investment.[52]

(8)   Any attempt to forecast the future of NOI by *developing* countries must then rest on the answer to the following question — to what extent do the specific endowment, market and environmental characteristics of developing countries, taken either as a group or individually, generate ownership advantages for its enterprises *relative* to those generated by developing countries which are best exploited by foreign direct investment rather than by exports or contractual resource transfers? Anything which generates such advantages which favour the particular characterisation of developing countries will aid

their foreign investment; anything which does not favour these characteristics will inhibit it.

(9) The future of NOI of *developed* countries will rest more on their *relative* economic status, which is both reflected in and determined by the balance of their OLI advantages. Much depends, on the one hand, on their ability to create and sustain technological and human capital advantages (which become exploited by their firms) and, on the other, the character of the comparative advantage of their immobile resource endowments.

(10) The empirical part of the chapter has confined itself to an examination of inward and outward investment flows. A complete explanatory model of the kind described would need data on exports and imports and on contractual resource flows since investment flows reflect both the ownership advantages of firms *and* the way in which these are exploited. A change in either or both may affect the timing and nature of both the investment—development cycle described in this chapter and the position of a particular country at a point in the cycle.

Appendix 5.1: List of Countries Included in Sample

Group 1   Sweden, USA, Canada, Denmark, Australia, Germany.
Group 2   Norway, France, Belgium and Luxembourg, Netherlands, Finland, Austria, UK, Japan, New Zealand.
Group 3   Israel, Italy, Spain, Gabon, Trinidad and Tobago, Venezuela, Taiwan, Singapore, Hong Kong, Argentina.
Group 4   Jamaica, Panama, Barbados, Costa Rica, Brazil, Malaysia, Nicaragua, Malta, Mexico.
Group 5   Dominican Republic, Ivory Coast, Algeria, Tunisia, Guyana, Peru, Guatemala.
Group 6   Columbia, Ecuador, Paraguay, El Salvador, Honduras, Jordan, South Korea.
Group 7   Ghana, Morocco, Senegal, Bolivia, Nigeria, Sierra Leone, Uganda, Phillipines, Kenya.
Group 8   Haiti, Indonesia, Zaire, Niger, Benin, Malawi, Chad, Ethiopia, Pakistan, India.

Notes: Chapter 5

1   Strictly speaking that of all economic agents, that is, enterprises, individuals and governments.
2   We shall eschew the difficult problem of defining the boundaries between a portfolio and direct investment by taking the IMF definition that a direct investment implies some control of decision taking in the 'invested in' enterprise by the 'investing enterprise'.
3   Sometimes called firm-specific advantages; the reason for our preferred nomenclature will be clear as the argument progresses.
4   This distinction is important; once the assets are sold, then the enterprise disposes of its ownership advantages altogether.
5   For example, in terms of maximising the NPV of the expected income flows from the assets.

6   Strictly speaking, the decision as to whether or not to engage in (or increase) international production should be kept separate from that of whether or not to engage in (or increase) foreign direct investment. But for the purposes of this paper, we are not concerned with the finance of international production. We use investment data as a proxy for international production data as the latter are not available on a country by country basis.

7   See Section III.

8   That is, those based respectively on industrial organisation, location and market failure theory. For further details see Chapters 2 and 3; also Rugman (1980).

9   Even when an enterprise is acquiring another for defensive reasons (e.g. as is the case for some Japanese foreign investment), the presumption is that the acquiring firm has some ownership advantages which it wants to protect; hence it is willing to offer a price that will encourage the acquired firm to sell. In some cases, the home government may assist its own firms in this kind of investment (Ozawa, 1979).

10   That is, that the NPV of the asset acquired is perceived to be greater by the acquiring than by the acquired firm.

11   See an interesting chapter in Kojima (1978) in which a distinction is made between genuine economies of scale (arising from internalisation) and pseudo-economies. These latter simply benefit the internalising firm (in the form of additional economic rent) and essentially originate because of the enhanced monopoly power which the firm gains from them. The former consist of the kind of economies of scale which may exist under competitive conditions and which advance efficiency.

12   In a recent paper, Rugman (1980) argues that 'existing theories of foreign direct investment are basically subsets of the general theory of internalisation'. The present author prefers to think of the eclectic theory as the paradigm, with internalisation being a subset of this general theory.

13   See Chapter 3.

14   See especially Root and Ahmed (1978).

15   Obviously, for a variety of reasons to do with both the valuation and interpretation of direct investment, these data should be regarded as approximate rather than precise values.

16   I have excluded most developing countries, which have been involved in substantial expropriation or nationalisation programmes over the period 1967–75, and also all tax haven countries.

17   See, for example, Chenery (1977), Bornschier (1978, 1979) and UN (1978).

18   We have chosen to express our data in terms of average investment flows; it would have been possible, and produced exactly the same inter-country patterns, to have taken the aggregate investment flows over the period in question, which, in most cases, is long enough for the flow to be a reasonably good proxy of the stock of investment at the end of the period.

19   A list of these is set out in Appendix 5.1.

20   Note that the income ranges covered by countries whose investment behaviour is classified in groups 3 and 4 overlap. This suggests that, especially in these later stages, investment behaviour cannot be fully explained by GNP per capita. As we shall see, the eclectic theory aspires to explain these exceptional cases as well as the more normal cases.

21   In the period 1976–78, this number had increased to nine.

22   This indeed is the main form of involvement of Third World MNEs, as in most cases they have neither the financial capital nor the complete package of ownership advantages for them to 'go it alone' in their foreign ventures.

23   Reasons not dissimilar to those explaining why, in the early stages of the product cycle, firms prefer to locate their production units near their centres of innovation. Later, as the scale and efficiency of production increases, it may become profitable to locate it elsewhere (Vernon, 1974).

24 An obvious example being the expiry of a patent.
25 Especially if they perceive that supplying foreign markets from a foreign location is likely to involve them in less risk than supplying them from a domestic location. It does not seem unreasonable to suppose that *ceteris paribus* the more risky a particular country is thought to be as a location for inward investment, the more likely its own firms will be prompted to exploit foreign markets from a foreign production base.
26 This, of course, may lead to divestment, or partial divestment, by such firms. According to Wilson (1978), the propensity to disinvest is greatest in those industries producing mature, homogenous products under near competitive conditions, and least in those industries supplying high technology and/or differentiated products. Location-specific factors – notably government attitudes towards foreign direct investment – are also frequently cited by business men as reasons for divestment.
27 Dunning and Pearce (1981) have shown that in 1977, whereas only 5.9 per cent of the exports of the parent companies of the leading MNEs in low research intensity industries were internalised, the proportions for medium and high research intensity industries were 36.9 per cent and 50.0 per cent respectively.
28 That is, advantages of a non-transferable kind, for example, economies of joint production, of product, process market or financial integration, etc.
29 In addition, there is some evidence to suggest that the more multinational an enterprise is the more likely it is to internalise resource transfers (Dunning and Pearce, 1981).
30 The Dunning and Pearce study shows that internal exports from parent companies of MNEs whose foreign production/worldwide production ratio exceeds 1:8 averaged 48 per cent in 1977; those whose ratio was less than 1:8 averaged 6 per cent.
31 Both absolute and relative to that of other countries. This normalisation would help to explain how a country's net outward investment ratio may decrease as its GNP per capita increases, if the GNP of its major competitors was increasing at a faster rate.
32 See, for example, Chenery and Taylor (1968) and Chenery (1977, 1979).
33 Apart from Italy and Spain the industrialised countries were all classified in Groups 1 and 2. All industrialising countries were classified in Groups 3 to 8.
34 It is important to distinguish between location advantages which help generate ownership-specific advantages (i.e. a favourable climate to innovation and the accumulation of knowledge and financial capital) and those which affect the economics of production and marketing.
35 By the same token, a country with an average NOI could be deviating from the norm in both its outward and inward investment, but the two deviations cancel themselves out.
36 Some of these have been set out in Table 3.1, p. 49.
37 This applies equally to vertically integrated investment, for example, as shown by the impact of export processing zones, and to horizontal investments, for example, the impact of the EEC on the rationalisation of investments by companies like Ford, Philips and Honeywell within this free trade area.
38 As in the case of some Japanese investments. See Ozawa (1979).
39 A mixture of the two approaches is possible, by distinguishing between the main types of investment and then relating the NOIs to OLI characteristics.
40 Another alternative is to evaluate the advantages of internalisation by studying the kinds of situations (e.g. industries and firms) in which fdi is likely to yield the best results (e.g. in terms of maximising net present value (NPV)) *vis-à-vis* the market (e.g. the licensing route). See, for example, Giddy and Rugman (1979).
41 Internalisation advantages make for both outward and inward investment, depending on whether it is the domestic or foreign MNEs which possess the

ownership advantages, and also the extent to which market failure is more pronounced in the home or in the host country.

42   Canada is one exception. With an R & D, as a percentage of GNP, of 1 per cent in 1971, she had the fifth largest outward investment per capita over the 1967–75 period.

43   Also that some variables may 'push' and 'pull' at the same time. For example high earnings per head may reflect high costs (a 'push' factor), but also high spending power (a 'pull' factor).

44   I am most grateful to Mr D. Depelteau of the Ecole des Hautes Etudes Commerciales, University of Montreal, for his most valuable computing assistance, and for introducing me to the concept of correspondence analysis. A fuller version of the results presented below is published as *Explaining the International Investment Position of Countries: A Statistical Analysis* in Ecole des Hautes Etudes Commerciales (University of Montreal), Les Cahiers du CETAI (Research Paper Series, October 1981).

45   For details of this technique see M. O. Hill, 'Correspondence analysis: a neglected multivariate method', *Applied Statistics*, vol. 23, no. 3 (1974).

46   Two elements distinguish correspondence analysis from other measures of variance. First is its treatment of distance. Whereas conventional analyses of variance (i.e. regression and other factoring methods) use the deviation to the mean as a measure of distance, correspondence analysis uses a chi-square measure of distance to depict the position of both the objects and the variable with respect to the global centre of gravity of the data. Second is the coding of the data into binary form; this procedure amounts to breaking down a variable into subvariables and then assigning a value to one of them – to indicate its belonging to the original observation – and to the rest the value of 0.

47   At this stage, we are confident we have homoscedastic, normally distributed disturbances. There is however one wrong sign, that of the coefficient of the rate of increase in industrial output, $L(2b)$, in equation (3). It can be explained by the presence of three particular countries, viz. Hong Kong, Barbados and Jamaica, in the sample, whose large inward investment biased the covariance between the two variables. Removing these three countries from the sample results in a *positive* correlation between GII and $L(2b)$ of 0.60.

48   Any more than all firms reach the final stage of the product cycle.

49   The extent to which fdi itself influences patterns of economic development is a subject for further research.

50   Again this chapter has not explored the mechanism of such changes, for example, how far is a rising (declining) advantage brought about by a devaluation (revaluation) of the exchange rate.

51   Foreign firms in the case of outward resource flows; domestic firms in the case of inward resource flows.

52   For example, due to such factors as geographical and/or psychic distance, cultural, political and economic ties, etc. Note that the geographical distribution of foreign investment of LDCs is very different from that of most developed countries. This reflects *inter alia* that the ownership/internalisation advantage of one country's enterprises over those of another may vary considerably according to the destination of the investment. See also Stopford's explanation of the geographical composition of UK direct investment (Stopford, 1976).

References

Bornschier, V. (1978), *Multinational Corporations in the World Economy and National Development*, Zurich, Sociologisches Institut der Universitat No. 32.

Buckley, P. J., and Casson, M. (1981), 'The optimal timing of a foreign direct investment', *Economic Journal*, vol. 91 (March), no. 48.

Chenery, H. B., and Taylor, L. (1968), 'Development patterns among countries and over time', *Review of Economics and Statistics*, vol. 50 (November).

Chenery, H. B. (1977), 'Transnational growth and world industrialisation', in B. Ohlin, P. O. Hesselborn and P. J. Wisjkman (eds), *The International Allocation of Economic Activity* (London: Macmillan).

Chenery, H. B. (1979), *Structural Change and Development Policy* (Washington, DC: The World Bank).

Dunning, J. H., and Pearce, R. D. (1981), *The World's Largest Industrial Enterprises* (Farnborough: Gower).

Giddy, I. H., and Rugman, A. M. (1979), *A Model of Trade, Foreign Direct Investment and Licensing*, Graduate School of Business, Columbia University, Research Working Paper No. 274A.

Kojima, J. (1978), 'Giant multinational corporations: merits and defects', *Hitotsubashi, Journal of Economics*, vol. 18, no. 2.

Lall, S. (1980), 'Monopolistic advantages and foreign involvement by US manufacturing industry', *Oxford Economic Papers*, vol. 32 (March).

Lecraw, D. (1977), 'Direct investment by firms from less developed countries', *Oxford Economic Papers*, vol. 29 (August).

Magee, S. P. (1977), 'Multinational corporations, the industry technology cycle and development', *Journal of World Trade Law*, vol. XI (July/August).

Mosteller, F., and Bush, R. R. (1954), 'Selective quantitative techniques', in G. Lindsay (ed.), *Handbook of Social Psychology*, vol. 1 (Reading, Mass.: Addison-Wesley).

Ozawa, T. (1979), 'International investment and industrial structure: new theoretical implications from the Japanese experience', *Oxford Economic Papers*, vol. 31 (March).

Root, F., and Ahmed, A. A. (1978), 'The influence of policy instruments on manufacturing direct investment in developing countries', *Journal of International Business Studies*, vol. 9 (Winter).

Rugman, A. M. (1980), 'Internalisation: the general theory of foreign direct investment', *Weltwirtschaftliches Archiv*, vol. 116, no. 2.

Stopford, J. M. (1976), 'Changing perspectives on investment by British manufacturing multinationals', *Journal of International Business Studies*, vol. 7 (Fall/Winter).

UN (1978), *Transnational Corporations in World Development: A Re-examination* (New York: UN Economic and Social Council), E.78 II A5.

Vernon, R. (1974), 'The location of economic activity', in J. H. Dunning (ed.), *Economic Analysis and the Multinational Enterprise* (London: Allen & Unwin).

Wells, L. T. (1977), 'The internationalisation of firms from the developing countries', in T. Agmon and C. P. Kindleberger (eds), *Multinationals from Small Countries* (Cambridge, Mass.: MIT Press).

Wilson, B. D. (1978), *Foreign Disinvestments: Friend or Foe*, Graduate School of Business Administration, University of Virginia, Working Paper DSWP-78-08.

6

The UK's International Direct Investment Position in the Mid-1970s

I

Little has been written about the UK's international investment position since the Reddaway report on the effects of UK direct investment overseas, which was published in 1968 (Reddaway *et al.*, 1968) and the Steuer report on foreign direct investment in the UK, which was published in 1973 (Steuer *et al.*, 1973), both of which dealt with the situation in the decade ending in the mid-1960s. Since that time, quite significant changes in the level and composition of outward and inward direct investment flows have occurred, and also in the balance between the two, particularly as between economic sectors and regions. The centre of interest concerning the consequences of such capital movements has also shifted. With the coming on stream of North Sea oil, concern over the balance-of-payments effects of outward investment has lessened, but, as domestic unemployment has risen, so has anxiety over the possible loss of jobs which such investment might cause. Disquiet about the questionable business practices of some British and foreign owned multinational enterprises, the involvement of UK firms in politically unacceptable régimes, and the threats of some foreign based companies not to invest further in the UK because of the unco-operative policies of labour unions has intensified over the last decade.

The focus of this chapter is, however, more general. Its underlying thesis is that trends in UK inward and outward direct investment, and the balance between them, are a reflection of changes in the international competitive position of UK-owned firms and the locational attractions of the UK as a production base. An increase in outward investment may suggest either that UK firms have improved their competitive position, *vis-à-vis* firms of other nationalities, or that the locational attractions of producing abroad as opposed to in the UK have improved. On the other hand, an increase in investment by foreign firms in the UK could mean that they were penetrating UK markets at the expense of UK competitors, or that the economic environment for production in the UK was becoming more

This chapter is a revised and amplified version of an article (of the same title) published in *Lloyds Bank Review* (April, 1979).

attractive relative to that of other countries. I accept, straight away, that international investment flows are not the same thing as foreign capital formation by MNEs which, in the context of this chapter, is our primary interest. Net asset growth by MNEs may be financed from domestic or foreign sources; by the same token, a rise (fall) in outward or inward investment might take the place of local financing and this need not affect international capital formation.

Because they believe that direct investment is an 'inadequate measure of net asset growth', Beenstock and Willcocks (1980) attempt to circumvent this deficiency by relating gross domestic capital formation in the UK to external profit rates. I am by no means persuaded that the data (such as exist) necessitate such a drastic procedure,[1] particularly as the conclusions of the authors and that of Beenstock (1980) are not very different from those set out in this chapter. In any case, capital formation data are not available in the detail of direct investment data and until they are, with the caveat expressed above, we have to make the best use we can of the latter.[2]

II

In line with the terminology used in previous chapters, we distinguish between two possible reasons for international investment flows by referring to the ownership-specific advantages of firms and the location-specific advantages of countries. Ownership advantages include all those competitive strengths which a firm of one nationality may have over that of another nationality, when both are producing in the same location. These strengths may vary over time, but, at any given moment, they are unique to particular firms; however, within an enterprise, many are transferable across national boundaries, that is, they do not have to be used where they originate. Location advantages refer to the facilities which a particular country may offer to a firm to set up a production unit there, rather than in another country. While these facilities are specific to a particular location and immobile across national boundaries, they are available to firms of all nationalities. They include not only all natural resources and most kinds of labour, but institutional and other factors, for example, industrial structure, size of markets, taxes and subsidies, import controls and transport costs from country of production to country of marketing.

The international competitive position of the UK depends upon the extent to which it possesses these two sets of advantages. The ability of the firms located in the UK to export reflects the ownership advantages of such firms and the fact that it is profitable to exploit these from production outlets in the UK. By the same token, imported goods suggest that foreign firms have such an advantage over UK firms which is best used in a foreign location. Where, however, UK firms have a competitive edge over foreign firms, which they find profitable to exploit from a foreign rather than a domestic location, then outward foreign investment will occur. Similarly, the penetration of UK production by foreign affiliates suggests that these firms possess advantages over UK firms but that the UK is preferred as a production base to other countries.

This chapter first traces the trends in the UK's international position between the early 1960s and mid-1970s. Second, it suggests the extent to which these changes reflect an improvement (or deterioration) in the ownership advantages of UK firms or an improvement (or deterioration) in the location advantages of the United Kingdom. Third, it examines some of the implications of these trends for the UK's economic welfare and for economic policy towards inward and outward investment.

III

But, first, does it matter whether a country's enterprises engage in foreign production as if it is a net outward or inward direct investor. A country's economic prosperity rests mainly on the extent and quality of its resources and any others it can acquire, and its ability to transform those resources into end-products and market them. The output produced by these resources – the gross *national* product – is equal to the output derived from all the resources used in the country, *less* any payments made to foreigners for resources imported, *plus* the income earned on resources exported, which are used in conjunction with the resources of other countries. In the national accounts, this is equal to gross domestic product plus (or minus) net investment income earned overseas. To the extent that inward and outward direct investment (and/or capital formation by MNEs) affect both the level of resources available to the country and the extent to which indigenous resources are used (and the efficiency of their use), then it is relevant to examine whether the investment is at its optimum level and properly directed.

It is admitted that *a priori* it may be very difficult to identify the optimum level or balance of international investment and/or capital formation. This will vary *inter alia* according to a country's level of economic development, its structure of resources, its social objectives and so on. Indeed, as Chapter 5 has shown, there is some evidence of a correlation between a country's stage of development and its propensity to be a net outward investor. Historically, too, those countries which possess a lead in management and technology – the main ownership-specific advantages – have been those which have been the leading foreign investors, for example, the UK in the nineteenth century and the USA for much of the twentieth century.

Basically, of course, the same is true of trade. Although it may be difficult to generalise on the appropriate level of trade, one can identify the conditions under which trade is desirable, and one should be able to do the same for direct investment, which in many cases is a substitute for trade. The principle of comparative (trading) advantage asserts that countries should export those goods which require resources in which they are comparatively well endowed and import goods which require resources in which they are comparatively poorly endowed. Similarly, one might suggest that a country's firms should be encouraged to invest overseas to produce products which require resources in which they have a comparative ownership advantage but the investing country has a comparative location disadvantage, while inward investment should be directed to producing goods which require resources in which the recipient country has a comparative location advantage but in which its own firms have a comparative ownership disadvantage.

In the real world, of course, there are a host of distortions to the free movement of goods and resources caused by both the market disequilibrium and government intervention. Moreover, the political economy of international investment is different from that of trade. In trade, the final decision of what is produced, and where it is produced, is taken within the exporting or importing country; in international investment, decisions may be taken outside the country in which they are implemented and their effect chiefly felt. This introduces questions of sovereignty and control which, while acknowledging their importance, will not be considered in this chapter.[3]

IV

(a) *Central Statistical Office Data*

At the end of 1979 the book value of the net assets owned by UK companies abroad (K_o) was £25,497 million, some £6,640 million more than the book value of the net assets in the UK owned by foreign companies (K_i). Along with the USA, the UK continues to be the leading net creditor in the world on long-term capital account; indeed, apart from the period around the Second World War, the UK has remained a net foreign creditor since the mid-nineteenth century.

Table 6.1 shows that between 1962 and 1979 UK firms invested £20,627 million abroad, while foreign companies invested £16,727 million in the UK. Over this period, the growth of the outward capital stake lagged behind that of the inward capital stake; taking 1962 as 100, the index of growth of the former was 523.6 and that of the latter was 885.3. As a result, the ratio between the outward and inward capital stake has fallen from 2.29 in 1962 to 1.35 in 1979. The data are only marginally affected when revaluation and exchange rate movements are excluded.[4]

Table 6.2 sets out some indicators of the significance of outward and inward direct investment to the UK economy. As a proportion of the UK's gross national product (GNP), the combined inward and outward capital

Table 6.1   The UK's Direct International Stake Position 1962–79

	Outward capital stake (K_o) £m.		Inward capital stake (K_i) £m.		$\dfrac{Col\ 1}{Col\ 3}$	$\dfrac{Col\ 2}{Col\ 4}$
	A	B	A	B	A	B
1962	4,870		2,130		2.29	
1969	8,300		4,245		1.96	
1970	8,800		4,885		1.80	
1971	9,130		5,570		1.64	
1972	9,970		6,245		1.60	
1973	11,850	11,850	7,585	7,585	1.56	
1974	13,380	13,723	9,635	9,346	1.39	1.47
1975	15,040	14,954	11,130	10,656	1.35	1.40
1976	18,320	17,362	11,700	12,193	1.57	1.42
1977	19,240	19,589	14,901	14,560	1.29	1.35
1978	21,751	22,940	16,600	16,551	1.31	1.39
1979	25,497	28,453	18,857	19,102	1.35	1.49

A = Capital stake figures *inclusive* of revaluation, exchange rate movements and other changes.

B = Capital stake figures *exclusive* of revaluation, exchange rate movements and other changes.

Source: UK Balance of Payments 1980 (Central Statistical Office, 1978 and 1980). Data refers to direct investment plus investment by oil companies.

Table 6.2   The Significance of Outward and Inward Investment for the UK Economy: Selected Indicators, 1962–78

	As a % of GNP				As a % of Company Capital Formation in UK		Earnings of K_o and K_i as % of UK Company Earnings		As a % of trade	
	K_o	K_i	I_o	I_i	I_o	I_i	π_o	π_i	I_o/X	I_i/M
1962	19.3	8.4					8.1	4.0		
1964	19.1	8.7					7.9	4.5		
1966	19.2	9.2					9.5	4.5		
1967	20.8	9.8	2.66	1.07	69.4	28.0	10.6	5.4	12.6	4.8
1968	20.7	10.3	1.26	1.19	29.0	33.2	13.0	7.5	5.3	4.8
1969	21.2	10.8	1.56	0.96	30.3	18.7	13.6	7.3	6.1	3.8
1970	20.5	11.0	1.30	1.22	25.2	26.1	14.1	8.9	4.9	4.7
1971	18.9	11.0	0.73	1.29	16.1	30.0	11.9	6.5	2.8	5.2
1972	19.4	11.6	2.44	0.73	58.3	17.3	13.7	9.9	9.9	2.9
1973	18.1	10.6	1.36	2.63	24.9	48.0	18.2	8.8	5.0	8.8
1974	17.8	11.8	2.17	2.72	38.6	48.3	19.2	7.9	7.0	7.3
1975	16.1	12.9	2.05	1.50	45.4	33.3	21.8	8.4	6.2	4.8
1976	17.1	11.3	3.01	0.52	79.6	13.9	25.8	11.1	9.4	1.6
1977	15.6	11.7	0.73	2.55	20.4	71.0	16.2	9.4	2.1	7.6
1978	15.2	11.6	1.76	1.19	39.0	26.4	14.3	9.7	5.3	3.7

Source: K and I data from Table 6.1 (Series A). All other data from CSO National Income Blue Book, various issues.

stake $(K_o + K_i)$ has ranged from around 28 per cent at the beginning and end of the period to a peak of 32 per cent in 1969. The relative significance of the inward capital stake has risen fairly consistently throughout the years covered by the table; the outward capital stake, while increasing marginally in the 1960s, dropped back in the 1970s, and in the years 1975–78 was lower than at any time in the past sixteen years.

An examination of investment (i.e. change in capital stake, ΔK or I) data reveals fairly sizeable annual fluctuations, but Table 6.2 confirms that, relative to GNP and net fixed capital formation by companies in the UK, both inward and outward investment reached their peak in the mid-1970s, and that, as a proportion of all profits earned in the UK, earnings of UK firms abroad and foreign affiliates in the UK have both doubled since the early 1960s. In the period 1974–8, UK companies earned nearly one fifth of all their profits from foreign operations, while of the profits earned in the UK foreign firms accounted for 9 per cent.

The final columns in Table 6.2 relate inward investment to imports (M) (as these may be alternatives to servicing the UK market by foreign firms) and outward investment to exports (X) (as these may be alternative ways for UK firms and foreign affiliates in the UK to service foreign markets). They show that, apart from the early 1970s, inward investment and imports have more or less kept pace with one another, but that, 1977 apart, outward investment has grown more than exports since 1973.

(b)   *The Department of Industry Data*

The first step in disaggregation is to extract, from the data presented in Tables 6.1 and 6.2, those of oil for outward and inward investment and those of oil and insurance for inward investment.[5] The remaining activities embrace those covered by the Department of Industry in their annual investment enquiries.[6] However, because of problems of definition and valuation, banking and insurance activities are exluded from the Department's periodic surveys of the book value of the foreign capital stake owned by UK companies and the net assets owned by foreign firms in the UK.[7]

The redirection of interest of British firms, between 1962 and 1978, away from the rest of the world, that is, developing countries, towards Western Europe is strikingly seen in Tables 6.3 and 6.4. On the other hand, all regions apart from North America have increased their share of the inward capital stake since 1971. The most substantial increases in the outward/inward capital stake ratios have occurred in the case of Switzerland, Italy, Germany, and USA; the ratio has fallen in the case of France, Australia and most parts of the developing world.

The next step is to classify investments by their broad types[8] which, up to a point, is quite easy to do. To the data on oil investments published by the Bank of England we may add investments in mining and agriculture,

Table 6.3 Distribution of UK Outward and Inward Direct Capital Stake by Broad Geographical Area, 1962–78 (£m.)

	Western Europe		North America		Other Developed Countries		Rest of the World		All Countries	
(a) Outward Capital Stake (K_o) (£m. and %)										
1962	455.4	13.4	785.3	23.1	922.9	27.1	1,241.4	36.5	3,405.0	100.0
1965	647.3	15.4	919.0	21.8	1,259.1	29.9	1,384.6	32.9	4,210.0	100.0
1968	984.7	17.6	1,286.9	23.0	1,722.6	30.8	1,591.1	28.5	5,585.3	100.0
1971	1,461.5	21.9	1,465.7	20.0	1,984.7	29.8	1,755.0	26.3	6,666.9	100.0
1974	2,866.6	27.5	2,271.6	21.8	3,138.2	30.0	2,159.4	20.7	10,435.8	100.0
1978	5,954.5	31.0	5,017.5	26.1	4,446.2	23.1	3,796.7	19.8	19,214.8	100.0
(b) Inward Capital Stake (K_i) (£m. and %)										
1962	298.8	20.9	1,085.7	75.9	32.7	2.3	12.5	0.9	1,429.7	100.0
1965	397.0	19.9	1,546.7	77.3	20.5	1.0	35.7	1.8	1,999.9	100.0
1968	594.3	21.8	2,054.8	75.3	48.6	1.8	30.3	1.1	2,728.0	100.0
1971	891.6	23.4	2,718.7	71.2	156.5	4.1	50.2	1.3	3,817.0	100.0
1974	1,882.1	28.7	4,070.0	62.0	302.9	4.6	312.2	4.8	6,567.2	100.0
1978	3,253.8	29.7	6,982.6	63.8	468.8	4.3	244.0	2.2	10,949.2	100.0

Source: British Business, 27 February 1981.

Table 6.4   *Geographical Distribution of Outward and Inward Direct Capital Stake 1971 and 1978 (£m.)*

	(K_o)		(K_i)		(K_o/K_i)	
	1971	1978	1971	1978	1971	1978
Western Europe	1,461.5	5,954.5	891.6	3,253.8	1.64	1.83
EEC	985.2	4,544.4	472.9	2,031.9	2.08	2.24
of which:						
France	247.5	823.1	80.4	493.0	3.08	1.67
German Federal						
Republic	305.7	1,437.7	59.8	251.8	5.11	5.71
Italy	93.0	282.4	74.0	128.5	1.26	2.20
EFTA	190.1	1,050.4	409.3	1,219.5	0.27	0.86
of which						
Sweden	38.4	169.0	75.8	296.4	0.51	0.57
Switzerland	53.4	630.1	280.4	789.4	0.19	0.80
North America	1,465.7	5,017.5	2,718.7	6,982.6	0.54	0.72
of which:						
Canada	671.0	1,255.9	270.7	466.8	2.48	2.69
US	794.7	3,761.6	2,448.0	6,515.8	0.32	0.38
Other Developed						
Countries	1,984.7	4,446.2	156.5	468.8	12.68	9.48
of which:						
Australia	1,137.5	2,622.5	29.2	141.1	39.0	18.59
South Africa	651.7	n.a.	108.4	333.4	6.01	–
Rest of the World	1,755.0	3,796.7	50.2	244.0	35.0	15.56
Africa	594.9	1,325.4	nsa[a]	nsa	–[b]	–
of which:						
Kenya	60.5	178.2	nsa	nsa	–	–
Nigeria	155.6	479.1	nsa	nsa	–	–
Asia	707.5	1,486.2	11.9	157.0	59.45	9.47
of which:						
Hong Kong	47.4	302.5	nsa	nsa	–	–
India	289.8	346.6	nsa	nsa	–	–
Malaysia	195.7	316.8	nsa	nsa	–	–
Latin America and						
Caribbean	488.5	997.9	38.9	128.5	12.56	7.77
of which:						
Argentina	58.4	107.2	nsa	nsa	–	–
Brazil	79.5	610.4	nsa	nsa	–	–
Other Countries	−35.9	−11.8	−0.6	−41.5[c]	–	–
World	6,666.9	19,214.8	3,817.0	10,949.2	1.75	1.75

[a] nsa: not separately available.

[b] – : dashes indicate information insufficient to calculate.

[c] including Africa.

Source: As for Table 6.3.

arguing that this group of investments are all of the resource based kind. Beyond this point, it becomes more difficult. Obviously some manufacturing investments, particularly those in the chemical, metal and food processing sectors may also be influenced by the presence of the local raw materials, foodstuffs or minerals which they use. However, because of the classification adopted by the Department of Industry, there is no means of identifying how much. But, in the developing countries in particular, it is likely to account for quite a substantial proportion of UK activities in the food, drink and tobacco sectors.

The other two kinds of manufacturing investment referred to in Chapter 3 were of the import-substituting and rationalised kind. Again, there is no way the data enable the two to be separated. We do know, however, the main industries and countries or regions in which the latter type of investment is most prominent.[9] As a rough approximation (and, because there is so little UK rationalised investment, this is all that is needed), we can (arbitrarily) take one-half of the investment in the electrical and mechanical engineering sectors and all the investment in textiles, clothing and footwear in Hong Kong, Singapore, Mexico, Far East countries (other than the Indian subcontinent, Malaysia and Thailand) and Southern Europe. The balance is assumed to consist of import-substituting investments.

Of the tertiary investments, it may be assumed that investments in distributive trades are export promoting, while those in transport, communications, shipping, finance and insurance are primarily (though not exclusively) ancillary to other foreign investments. The rest consists of a 'rag-bag' of activities which include building and construction, a genuine direct investment, and property owning and managing, which may be a direct investment, for example hotel management, or a portfolio investment – and various other activities.

It was suggested in Chapter 4 that the motives, forms and effects of the activities of MNEs may differ according to their country of origin and the location of their involvement. After a general review of the data we shall concentrate our attention on investment flows of one main type (import-substituting manufacturing) and between the UK and one main region (Western Europe), as it is here that the greatest complementarity between the determinants of inward and outward capital flows reveals itself, and where the data are most helpful to our understanding of Britain's international competitive situation.

Table 6.5 sets out data on the UK outward and inward stake in 1962 and 1974 and the estimated capital stake for 1976[10] classified by main type of investment and geographical areas. The following points may be highlighted:

(1)   The proportion of the K_o stake accounted for by manufacturing and the distributive trades has increased from 65.9 per cent in 1965 to 76.1 per cent in 1976. Over the same period, the share of resource

Table 6.5   *Distribution of Outward and Inward Direct Capital Stake by Economic Sector 1965–76*

| | Outward Capital Stake (K_o) | | | | | |
| | 1965 | | 1971 | | 1976 | |
	(£m.)	*(%)*	*(£m.)*	*(%)*	*(£m.)*	*(%)*
Primary products	636.1	15.1	1,001.1	15.0	1,226.4	9.2
Manufacturing	2,103.4	50.0	3,934.3	59.0	7,842.8	58.8
Distributive trades	671.1	15.9	876.4	13.1	2,304.4	17.3
Other non-manufacturing activities	799.4	19.0	855.1	12.8	1,946.7	14.6
All activities	4,210.0	100.0	6,666.9	100.0	13,320.3	100.0
	Inward Capital Stake (K_i)					
Manufacturing	1,629.4	81.5	3,180.2	83.3	5,524.4	70.6
Distributive trades	242.8	12.1	392.6	10.3	840.1	10.7
Other activities	107.8	5.4	244.2	6.4	1,456.7	18.6
All activities	1,999.9	100.0	3,817.0	100.0	7,821.2	100.0

Source: Department of Industry, *Business Monitor* M4, various editions. *British Business*, 27 February 1981.

N.B. For all activities, the K_o figure for 1978 was £19,214.8m and for manufacturing industry it was £12,147.9m (63.2%). The corresponding figures for K_i were £10,949.2m, £8,118.7m and 74.2%.

based activities fell from 15.1 per cent to 9.2 per cent. Due primarily to expropriation or the voluntary withdrawal of assets by UK firms, the most dramatic fall occurred in developing countries;[11] on the other hand, new mining ventures in North America and Australia enabled the developed world to maintain its share of such investments around 8 per cent.

(2)   The industrial distribution of inward investment has become considerably more diversified over the years, chiefly because of the substantial capital inflow into North Sea Oil. North American (mainly US) firms have tended to dominate this sector, as they have continued to do so within manufacturing industry. But in the service industries there has been a sizeable UK investment in the 1970s by some developing countries, especially in property management and development, distribution and financial activities.

(3)   The ratio between the outward and inward capital stake (the K_o/K_i ratio) in manufacturing industry was generally stable in the 1960s but it rose sharply in the 1970s, especially to and from Western Europe.[11a] In the oil sector, between 1971 and 1976, the K_o/K_i ratio fell from 1.34 to 0.90, while in trade and distribution the trend of the ratio, while sharply upwards in the early 1960s, dropped after 1968, except in the case of developing countries and, since 1971, North America. Some of the most remarkable falls in the K_o/K_i ratio have occurred in the other service industries.

Some of these trends are more dramatically highlighted by changes in the ratio between outward and inward investment (the I_o/I_i ratio). But because annual figures are considerably influenced by the acquisitions of share capital in a particular year, which tend to involve large sums of money and which are erratic, three yearly averages have been taken over the period 1960–74 and two yearly averages in the subsequent four year period. Table 6.6 presents some relevant statistics. Here, one sees most clearly the faster rate of manufacturing investment by British firms abroad than by foreign firms in the UK, in the 1970s up to 1976, since when this trend appears to have been reversed. In 1975, for the first time since 1960, there was more UK manufacturing investment in North America than there was North American manufacturing investment in the UK. In the early 1970s, British firms were investing in Western Europe at three times the rate of Western Europeans investing in the UK. By contrast, the rate of growth of primary product and service investments, outside trade and distribution by foreign companies in the UK has exceeded that by UK firms overseas, the I_o/I_i ratio falling from 3.06 in 1960–62 to 2.26 in 1977–78. In the distributive trades sector, the I_o/I_i ratio has generally increased, except as between the UK and Western Europe, where it has fallen.

(c) *The Picture Within Manufacturing Industry*
Until 1971, there were no detailed data on the industrial composition of outward manufacturing investment. Table 6.7 sets out the distribution of manufacturing net assets owned by UK firms abroad and foreign firms in the UK at that date, and that of the new investment between the end of 1971 and the end of 1976.[12] It also classifies sectors according to whether they may be broadly described as more technology intensive (MTI) and less technology intensive (LTI).[13]

The following conclusions may be drawn from this table:

(1) UK direct investment abroad is primarily concentrated in the less technology intensive (LTI) industries while foreign direct investment in the UK is primarily concentrated in the more technology intensive (MTI) industries. In 1971 57.5 per cent of the UK capital stake abroad was within the former group, as was 50.8 per cent of the new investment in the following seven years; the balance, 42.5 per cent and 49.2 per cent, was in the MTI industries. The corresponding figures for the inward capital stake and new investment were 31.1 per cent and 30.9 per cent and 68.9 per cent and 69.1 per cent. In one MTI industry, viz. chemicals, UK firms have consistently invested abroad proportionately more than foreign firms have invested in the UK, while in one LTI sector, that is, food, drink and tobacco, foreign firms have increased their share of inward investment faster than UK firms have increased their share of outward investment. It is,

Table 6.6 Distribution of Outward and Inward Investment by Geographical Area and Sector of Economic Activity 1960–78

Annual average	All Areas (£m.) I_o	I_i	I_o/I_i	Western Europe (£m.) I_o	I_i	I_o/I_i	North America (£m.) I_o	I_i	I_o/I_i
				Investment in all activities					
1960–62	228.3	167.0	1.37	38.5	23.2	1.66	34.3	136.3	0.21
1963–65	269.0	173.0	1.55	52.5	29.6	1.77	32.3	144.6	0.22
1966–68	322.3	213.0	1.51	66.9	48.1	1.39	86.7	152.3	0.57
1969–71	590.2	372.6	1.58	196.6	63.9	3.08	143.2	254.1	0.56
1972–74	1,311.0	656.0	2.00	458.7	151.6	3.03	384.8	375.8	1.02
1975–76	1,601.3	618.0	2.59	441.6	183.0	2.41	437.2	339.1	1.29
1977–78	2,092.2	1,248.8	1.68	690.1	417.5	1.65	668.2	716.5	0.93
				Manufacturing investment					
1960–62	119.2	132.7	0.89	24.9	13.8	1.81	16.3	116.5	0.14
1963–65	130.5	135.1	0.97	20.4	21.5	0.95	15.2	111.9	0.14
1966–68	169.4	166.4	1.02	33.1	36.5	0.91	37.0	129.1	0.29
1969–71	328.8	274.7	1.20	126.9	42.7	2.97	78.1	216.9	0.36
1972–74	670.7	382.4	1.75	222.7	68.6	3.26	213.1	298.7	0.71
1975–76	912.8	411.9	2.22	234.2	90.6	2.59	316.8	305.0	1.04
1977–78	1,110.7	848.6	1.31	357.8	200.2	1.79	402.1	648.4	0.62

Distributive trades

Period									
1960–62	37.0	15.7	2.35	6.4	2.8	4.48	3.8	13.2	0.29
1963–65	55.9	23.3	2.40	22.1	4.4	4.64	11.5	15.4	0.75
1966–68	55.8	20.5	2.72	25.2	6.3	4.00	10.6	9.9	1.07
1969–71	106.7	39.3	2.71	38.2	11.2	3.41	13.1	6.6	1.98
1972–74	205.3	77.9	2.64	113.0	31.4	3.60	26.3	26.8	0.98
1975–76	262.5	−11.9	nc	109.9	26.8	4.10	51.0	−2.6	nc
1977–78	428.9	155.2	2.76	173.5	75.3	2.30	86.3	18.0	4.78

Other activities

Period									
1960–62	56.9	18.6	3.06	6.7	6.5	1.04	14.1	5.5	2.56
1963–65	57.3	14.4	3.98	9.7	3.8	2.55	5.5	17.2	0.32
1966–68	61.3	26.4	2.32	13.7	3.3	4.15	39.1	13.3	2.94
1969–71	117.7	57.3	2.05	23.5	10.6	2.22	50.7	26.4	1.92
1972–74	353.5	195.8	1.81	104.7	56.6	1.85	124.5	50.3	2.48
1975–76	355.1	218.0	1.63	91.9	65.6	1.40	47.8	36.7	1.30
1977–78	552.6	245.0	2.26	158.8	142.0	1.12	179.8	50.1	3.59

nc = not computable.
Source: As for Table 6.5.

Table 6.7 *Distribution within Manufacturing Industry of UK Net Assets and Investment Abroad and Foreign Net Assets and Investment in UK*

	1971				1972–78			
	K_o (£m.)	(%)	K_i (£m.)	(%)	I_o (£m.)	(%)	I_i (£m.)	(%)
More technology intensive sectors	1,672.8	42.5	2,191.1	68.9	2,983.9	49.2	2,535.4	69.1
Chemicals and allied manufactures	683.9	17.4	460.4	14.5	1,665.7	27.5	768.7	21.0
Mechanical and instrument engineering	263.4	6.7	684.4	21.5	553.9	9.1	1,027.1	28.0
Electrical engineering	498.0	12.7	466.4	14.7	569.0	9.4	339.9	9.2
Motor Vehicles	93.4	2.4	385.3	12.1	85.9	1.4	314.5	8.6
Rubber	134.1	3.4	194.6	6.1	109.4	1.8	85.2	2.3
Less technology intensive sectors	2,261.6	57.5	989.1	31.1	3,075.3	50.8	1,132.6	30.9
Food, drink and tobacco	1,104.2	28.1	391.9	12.3	1,671.0	27.6	497.8	13.6
Metal manufacture	142.7	3.6	258.6	8.1	178.5	2.9	71.9	2.0
Textiles, leather, clothing and footwear	298.6	7.6	30.9	1.0	267.7	4.4	34.2	0.9
Paper, printing and publishing	261.5	6.7	2.5	2.9	268.9	4.4	226.5	6.2
Other manufacturing	454.6	11.6	215.2	6.8	689.2	11.3	302.2	8.2
Total manufacturing industries	3,934.4	100.0	3,180.2	100.0	6,059.2	100.0	3,668.0	100.0

Source: As for Table 6.5.

Table 6.8 Ratio between Net Assets Owned by UK Firms Abroad and Foreign Firms in UK (1971) and between Outward and Inward Investment (1972–8)

	Western Europe		North America		All areas	
	K_o/K_i 1971	I_o/I_i 1972–8	K_o/K_i 1971	I_o/I_i 1972–8	K_o/K_i 1971	I_o/I_i 1972–8
More technology intensive sectors	0.75	2.13	0.22	0.48	0.76	1.18
Chemicals and allied manufactures	1.25	2.76	0.67	1.12	1.49	2.17
Mechanical and instrument engineering	1.25	1.79	0.05	0.24	0.38	0.54
Electrical engineering	0.41	6.66	0.38	0.55	1.07	1.67
Motor vehicles	1.94	1.16	0.03	0.01	0.24	0.27
Rubber	0.20	1.41	0.65	6.67	0.69	1.28
Less technology intensive sectors	2.08	2.67	0.83	1.34	2.29	2.72
Food, drink and tobacco	2.29	4.73	1.19	1.92	2.82	3.36
Metal manufacture	0.81	–	–	–	0.55	2.48
Textiles, leather, clothing, and footwear	3.11	–	–	–	9.66	7.83
Paper, printing and publishing	1.48	0.88	2.10	1.10	2.83	1.19
Other manufacturing	2.44	2.28	0.36	1.02	2.11	2.28
Total manufacturing industries	1.07	2.36	0.42	0.74	1.24	1.65

– Included in Other manufacturing.

Source: As for table 6.5.

however, in the mechanical engineering and vehicles industries, on the one hand, and the textiles and printing industries, on the other, that the differences in the structure of inward and outward investment are most clearly revealed, particularly over the 1972–78 period.[14]

(2)   The above observations are confirmed by an examination of the K_o/K_i ratios for 1971 and I_o/I_i ratios for 1972–78. Table 6.8 shows that for all areas, in all MTI sectors and all but two of the LTI sectors the I_o/I_i ratio is higher than the K_o/K_i ratio; for Western Europe and North America the increase in the I_o/I_i ratio is particularly pronounced. The data also suggest that there were important changes in the industrial and regional composition of investment during the 1970s. For all manufacturing industry, the I_o/I_i ratio for 1972–78 was 1.65 compared with a K_o/K_i ratio of 1.24 in 1971. But, for the MTI sectors, the corresponding ratios for UK investment to and from Western Europe were 2.13 and 0.75; while in the case of trans-Atlantic flows, the ratio for the LTI industries rose from 0.83 to 1.34. From being a net importer of capital from North America, the UK has become a net exporter of capital to North America. Only in the case of 'Other Developed Countries' and 'Rest of the World' did inward investment increase more rapidly than outward investment between 1972 and 1978.

(3)   As a broad generalisation, the most noticeable rises in the ratios since 1971 have occurred in the industries in which K_o/K_i ratios were the lowest in 1971 (cf. e.g. motor vehicles and metal products with textiles, leather and clothing, and food, drink and tobacco).

V

How far can one explain the data just described, using the model of international production earlier put forward? Put another way: To what extent can one account for differences in the K_o/K_i or I_o/I_i ratios

(1)   between the UK and different countries,
(2)   between different industries, and
(3)   between years in the same country and/or industry, in terms of differences or changes in
        (a) the *ownership* advantages of UK firms (cf. those of non-UK firms) and
        (b) the *location* advantages of the UK (cf. those of other countries)?

It must be admitted that *a priori* there is no way of assessing whether a rising K_o/K_i or I_o/I_i ratio reflects an improvement in the competitiveness of UK firms or a deterioration of the competitiveness of UK resource endowments, or some combination of the two. Yet clearly, from a policy framing viewpoint, this is one of the most crucial distinctions which needs to be made. Is capital leaving the UK because UK entrepreneurs, managers, and the technological capabilities of UK firms are better (or becoming better) than their continental, US, Japanese, etc., counterparts? Or is it because UK firms are finding they have to produce in an economic environment which is becoming less congenial compared to that offered by other countries? Is the rate of increase in foreign capital entering the UK falling because foreign affiliates are less able to compete effectively with UK firms? Or is it because the foreign firms can make a higher profit by producing outside rather than in the UK?

The rest of this Chapter offers some hints about the likely role played by these two variables in influencing changes in the UK's manufacturing I_o/I_i ratio over the last ten years or so. In doing so it takes as an index of the change in the ownership advantage of UK firms that of the profitability of such firms relative to that of non-UK firms producing in the same country or group of countries; and as indices of change in the UK's location advantage two measures, viz. (1) the change in the profitability of UK and US-owned firms producing in the UK, relative to that of the same firms producing in other countries, and (2) the change in the UK export/ import of manufactured goods (X/M) ratio.[15]

More specifically, and putting the two sets of indices together, we examine the following proposition.

Differences (or changes) in the K_o/K_i or I_o/I_i ratios reflect differences (or changes) in the profitability of UK firms relative to that of non-UK firms; and differences (or changes) in the profitability of UK (or other) firms producing in the UK, relative to the profitability of the same firms in other countries, or differences in the UK export/import of goods ratio.

This proposition will now be tested by an examination of (1) changes in the UK's manufacturing I_o/I_i ratio between 1960 and 1977 and (2) differences in the K_o/K_i and I_o/I_i ratios between particular industries and/or regions in 1971–73 and 1974–76.

Table 6.9 relates changes in the I_o/I_i ratio for all manufacturing industry between the UK and the rest of the world and the UK and Western Europe for selected years for the period 1960 to 1977 to changes in the indices of ownership and location advantages just set out.

A cursory examination of the table suggests a positive association between the growth of I_o/I_i ratio and an improvement in the competitiveness of UK firms and a weakening of the competitive advantage of the UK as a production base. A rise in UK outward investment relative to inward investment has generally coincided with declining location profitability ratios (L_A and L_B) and X/M ratios and an increase in UK ownership

Table 6.9 UK Foreign Investment Ratios in Manufacturing Industry, Ownership and Location Specific Advantages, 1961–77

	All countries						Western Europe					
	I_o/I_i	O_A	O_B	L_A	L_B	X/M	I_o/I_i	O_A	O_B	L_A	L_B	X/M
1961–62	0.93	0.73	1.11	1.21	0.86	2.09	1.84	0.67	na	1.13	0.81	1.55
1963–64	1.01	0.79	0.91	1.10	1.05	1.90	0.94	0.55	na	1.65	1.03	1.52
1965–66	0.97	0.82	0.82	0.91	1.05	1.80	1.49	0.67	1.27	1.25	1.13	1.39
1967–68	1.10	0.92	0.78	0.86	0.99	1.49	0.77	0.92	1.18	1.00	1.09	1.19
1969–70	1.26	0.82	0.76	0.73	0.74	1.49	2.32	0.84	1.21	0.61	0.68	1.30
1971–72	1.34	0.78	0.93	0.93	0.80	1.45	3.76	0.73	1.25	0.88	0.74	1.15
1973–74	1.80	0.82	0.87	0.64	0.66	1.16	3.62	0.74	1.53	0.67	0.61	0.93
1975–76	2.21	1.03	0.97	0.60	0.42	1.26	2.48	0.81	1.33	0.70	0.40	0.97
1977	1.15	0.85	0.74	1.00	0.86	1.25	1.36	0.67	1.18	1.08	0.76	1.00

na: not available.

Sources: Business Monitor M3 (various editions), Business Monitor M4 (various editions), US Dept. of Commerce Survey of Current Business (various editions) and US Balance of Payments (various editions).

Key to notations:

I_o = outward investment.

I_i = inward investment.

O_A = All countries – Rate of return on total UK overseas direct investment (excluding North America) in manufacturing divided by rate of return on US overseas direct investment (excluding Canada and UK) in manufacturing.

O_A = Western Europe – Rate of return on UK direct investment in Western Europe in manufacturing divided by rate of return of US investment in Western Europe (excluding UK) in manufacturing.

O_B = All countries – Rate of return on domestic manufacturing investment in UK divided by rate of return on all foreign direct investment in UK manufacturing.

O_B = Western Europe – Rate of return on domestic manufacturing investment in UK divided by rate of return of Western European investment in UK manufacturing.

L_A = All countries – Rate of return on domestic manufacturing investment in UK divided by rate of return of total UK overseas direct investment in manufacturing.

L_A = Western Europe – Rate of return on domestic manufacturing investment in UK divided by rate of return on UK manufacturing investment in Western Europe.

L_B = All countries – Rate of return on US direct investment in manufacturing in the UK divided by rate of return on US direct investment in manufacturing in the rest of the world excluding Canada.

L_B = Western Europe – Rate of return of US direct investment in manufacturing in the UK divided by rate of return on US direct investment in the rest of Western Europe.

X/M = All countries – Total UK manufacturing exports divided by total UK manufacturing imports.

X/M = Western Europe – UK manufacturing exports to Western Europe divided by UK manufacturing imports from Western Europe.

For further definition of rates of return see footnotes to Table 6.12, p. 169.

profitability ratios (O_A and O_B). *Inter alia* the data show that, while in the fifteen years up to 1975–76, the I_o/I_i ratio for all countries doubled, and the profitability of UK relative to US direct investment in foreign countries has risen by two-thirds, both location profitability measures fell by two-thirds and the X/M ratio by a third.

For Western Europe, a similar though less decisive pattern holds. The I_o/I_i ratio increased between the early 1960s and early 1970s. This coincided with a fall in the $X(\text{WE})/M(\text{WE})$ ratio of 30 per cent, a halving of the location profitability ratio and a substantial improvement in the performance of UK firms relative to that of their competitors.

The table offers rather different explanations for the changes in the I_o/I_i ratio in the 1960s and 1970s. In the 1960s, the fall in the ratio by about one-half coincided with a halving of the location profitability ratios and a substantial fall in the X/M ratio. The competitive advantage of UK firms improved by a lesser extent, viz. about 18 per cent. In the 1970s while there continued to be a decline in the attractiveness of a UK location, the main explanation for the rise in the I_o/I_i ratio appeared to be the improvement in the ownership advantages of UK firms – though it declined again in 1977.

The data for Western Europe are less conclusive. In the first half of the 1960s, the I_o/I_i ratio fell; this was consistent with a rise in the location profitability ratios and a fall in the ownership profitability ratios. From about 1965 onwards, the I_o/I_i ratio rose markedly; however, this appears to be mainly a reflection of a decline in the location profitability ratios rather than any improvement in the performance of UK firms. This is a significant finding as one suspects that investment by UK firms in Western Europe is the most likely to be substitutable for investment in the UK.

Other evidence also tends to corroborate these findings. For example, since 1965, the increase in the value of manufacturing imports into the UK has consistently exceeded the increase in the foreign capital stake in UK manufacturing industry. In 1965 Western Europe firms exported $3\frac{1}{2}$ times the value of their capital stake in the UK; ten years later this ratio had risen to nearly 7. Similarly, up to the early 1970s, UK manufacturing exports to industrial countries lagged behind the growth of the UK capital stake in foreign manufacturing industry. Since 1973 there has been a reversal of this trend but, even so, the ratio of UK manufacturing exports to Western Europe to the UK outward capital stake has fallen from 5.27 in 1965 to 4.20 in 1975. This suggests that over the last decade or so UK firms have tended to exploit the European market more by the setting up or expansion of production units than by exports. On the Continent, however, European firms have tended to exploit the UK market by exports rather than by the setting up or expansion of production units in the UK. In other parts of the world, where exports and foreign production are less likely to be substitutes for each other, the ratio of UK exports to manufacturing investment increased from $2\frac{1}{2}$ to 3 between 1965 and 1975.

VI

Data on the ratios just discussed for the main manufacturing sectors in 1971–73 and 1974–76 are set out in Table 6.10. It can be seen that they broadly support the explanations for the UK international investment position offered earlier. In particular, the industries with the lowest K_o/K_i ratio in both years, viz. mechanical engineering and motor vehicles, had among the lowest ownership profitability ratios and the highest location profitability ratios, that is, UK firms perform comparatively badly relative to non-UK firms, but profits in UK industry compare relatively favourably to those earned in other countries. On the other hand, British firms generally do much better in the more traditional sectors, notably food, drink and tobacco, textiles, and paper and publishing, while the overall UK competitive environment is less congenial. In the case of chemicals the ownership advantage ratios would suggest a rather lower K_o/K_i ratio than that actually revealed, while in electrical engineering the location advantage ratios favour production in the UK; in both cases, however, there are factors working in the opposite direction.[16]

Since 1971, the more technology intensive (MTI) sectors have shown the greatest rate of increase in the I_o/I_i ratio; apart from chemicals these sectors have also shown the most pronounced fall in the E/M ratio.[17] The experience with changes in the profitability of UK firms at home and abroad has been mixed, while such data that are available on changes in the performance of UK firms relative to US firms suggest that the most substantial improvements have taken place in the MTI sectors.

Other data, published in *Business Monitor*[18] suggest that throughout the 1970s there was an increase in both the UK export/sales[19] ratio and the import penetration ratio.[20] This has been especially pronounced in the case of products in industries where intra-industry trade is above average, which are also those in which MNEs tend to be most concentrated (Panic, 1980). *Inter alia* this reflects the growth of rationalised investment by US MNEs in Western Europe, and the entry of Japan as a powerful international competitor. For it is in those sectors where US investment in Europe relative to that in the UK, and the Japanese impact, has made itself most noticeably felt that the E/M ratio has fallen the most in the 1970s.

To summarise, then, the data set out in Tables 6.9 and 6.10 seem to point to one important generalisation about the UK's international competitive situation. Since, in the last decade and a half, UK firms have been improving their performance relative to firms of other nationalities in world markets, the greater part of the UK's poor international performance must be laid at the door of the deterioration in the location advantages of the UK relative to those of other countries. This conclusion supports the contention of those writers who argue that the British 'disease' or 'predicament' is primarily due to factors specific to the UK economic environment, rather than any lack of technological expertise or failure on the part

Table 6.10 Some Determinants of Foreign Capital and Investment Ratios Classified by Industry 1971–3 and 1974–6

	K_o/K_i (1971)	1971–73		X/M 1971	I_o/I_i (1972/6)	1974–76		X/M 1975
		O_A	L_A			O_A	L_A	
More technology intensive sectors								
Chemicals and allied manufactures	1.49	0.64	0.77	1.26	2.52	0.60	0.57	1.36
Mechanical and instrument engineering	0.38	0.56	0.71	1.99	0.51	0.50	0.51	1.67
Electrical engineering	1.07	0.79	0.75	1.68	2.13	1.01	0.90	1.41
Motor vehicles	0.24	0.82	0.71	3.63	0.79	1[1]	1	2.00
Rubber	0.69	nsa	nsa	3.18	1.38	nsa	nsa	2.29
Less technology intensive sectors								
Food, drink and tobacco	2.82	0.64	0.56	0.75	3.12	0.67	0.44	0.62
Metal manufacture	0.55	3.13	0.60	1.34	3.22	1.43	0.72	0.91
Textiles, leather, clothing and footwear	9.66	4.29	1.09	1.08	7.50	2[2]	0.75	0.80
Paper, printing and publishing	2.83	0.93	1.00	0.61	2.44	0.96	0.62	0.56
Other manufacturing	2.11	1.33	0.97	2.21	1.77	0.80	0.59	1.21
Total manufacturing industries	1.24	0.84	0.80	1.56	1.95	0.91	0.57	1.21

[1] Both figures negative.
[2] One figure negative.
nsa = not separately available.
Source: as for Table 6.9.

of British management.[21] It also corroborates the findings of two studies of US industry in the UK published in the mid-1970s (Dunning, 1976; Lincoln, 1975). In explaining the falling share of new US investment in Western Europe directed to the UK, both reports stressed that in spite of the liberal attitude of the UK government towards foreign investment the availability of satisfactory labour, of attractive investment incentives and a congenial working and living environment, the concern of prospective investors over inflation, the perceived lack of long-range government policy on taxes and nationalisation, industrial unrest, the restrictive practices of trade unions, a social system which produced a disincentive to work, and the better growth prospects of most other European countries militated against the UK as a production base. Since these reports were published, the depreciation of the pound, a lower rate of inflation, an improved balance-of-payments situation and a clearer indication from the government about its long-term industrial strategy have done much to revive the confidence of both foreign and domestic investors, but low growth rates and discouraging labour attitudes continue to act as a locational disincentive.

VII

The final issue to be touched upon concerns the effect of outward and inward investment flows on the structure of resource allocation within the UK and by UK firms. We shall confine ourselves entirely to two questions: Do outward and inward investment flows raise or lower the UK's gross national product? and What effect do these flows have on the structure of economic activity in the UK?

Earlier, it was suggested that the structural benefits of international benefits should parallel those of trade which arise primarily from the specialisation of a country's economic activities in those areas which involve the use of (immobile) resources in which it is comparatively well endowed. In the case of international investment, however, since at least some ownership advantages are mobile across national boundaries, one also has to consider what is the best use a country can make of its own enterprises' resources, both inside and outside its boundaries, and those of foreign companies along with its own resources within its national boundaries.

As a general principle, a country which is seeking to maximise its gross national product, or rate of economic growth, should invest abroad in those sectors in which its enterprises have a comparative ownership advantage but which its location-specific endowments are comparatively unsuited to supply. It should encourage inward investment in those sectors in which foreign firms have a comparative ownership advantage but supply products which its immobile resources are comparatively well suited to provide.[22]

This proposition may be tested by looking at both the profitability and structure of UK outward, inward and domestic investment in manufacturing industry. It is assumed that each of these forms of investment is a substitute for the other but that at all times the UK economy is operating at a full employment level.[23] It is also assumed that there are no feedback effects on the domestic profitability on UK domestic activity as a result of their foreign investments and none on the parent companies of foreign affiliates as a result of their investment in the UK.

Table 6.11 sets out details of the profitability of UK outward and inward investment in manufacturing industry and that of investment of all firms in UK manufacturing industry for the period 1960–77, while Table 6.12 presents average performance data for selected industries for the periods 1971–73 and 1974–76. Table 6.11 confirms very clearly the main conclusions of the previous section, viz. that the profitability of UK firms abroad has been rising relative to that of UK firms in the UK, while that of foreign firms in the UK has been falling relative to UK firms in the UK. By the mid-1970s, even the social return of UK domestic investment (i.e. the private return *before* tax) was hardly greater than the return on foreign investment.[24]

Suppose now that there was no international investment in these years, but that the gap in activity would have been made up by additional domestic investment. Then as Table 6.13 sets out, by multiplying the net assets owned by UK firms abroad and those of foreign firms in the UK by the profitability of the UK investment by UK firms (column 1), and deducting the result from the actual profits earned on inward and outward investment, it is possible to obtain a crude first-stage estimate of the net gain or loss to the UK's gross national product. We can also calculate what part of the gain or loss is due to outward investment and what part to inward investment.[25]

The data in Table 6.13 suggest that, from the mid-1960s to the mid-1970s, the profitability of both foreign investment by UK firms and investment in the UK by foreign firms has consistently exceeded that of domestic investment by UK firms, with net gains ranging from £12 million in 1963–65 to £408 million in 1975–77. However, in the 1960s the main gain to the UK economy arose from the higher profitability of inward investment. By the mid-1970s, it was outward investment which was responsible for the greater part of the benefits. Table 6.12 also shows that, in the earlier period, it was the more technology intensive (MTI) sectors which seemed to gain most from inward investment while the less technology intensive (LTI) sectors gained most from outward investment. By the mid-1970s, such a distribution of benefits was no longer as clear cut, as UK firms abroad out-performed foreign firms in the UK in the chemicals and electrical engineering sectors.

To what extent do these gains suggest that international investment flows improve the efficiency of resource allocation in the UK? For this

Table 6.11 Profitability of UK and Foreign Firms in UK Manufacturing Industry and of UK Firms in Foreign Manufacturing Industry 1960–77

	UK domestic firms		UK firms abroad			Foreign firms in UK		
	(1) Private Rate of Return	(2) Social Rate of Return	(3) Western Europe	(4) North America	(5) All Areas	(6) Western Europe	(7) North America	(8) All Areas
1960	11.5	16.0	8.1	5.8	8.0			11.7
1965	9.1	13.1	6.1	10.3	9.0	7.1	12.6	11.8
1966	7.3	11.4	7.2	10.0	9.0	5.8	8.9	8.4
1967	7.2	11.5	5.8	8.0	7.9	6.0	8.8	8.3
1968	7.9	13.1	10.6	9.5	9.8	6.9	12.6	11.4
1969	7.4	12.4	11.6	8.4	10.0	5.7	10.5	9.3
1970	7.0	10.8	12.0	7.7	9.9	6.3	11.0	9.9
1971	8.3	12.4	9.5	8.3	9.2	6.1	9.6	8.8
1972	10.4	14.8	11.8	9.7	10.7	9.2	11.7	11.3
1973	8.9	15.9	16.0	13.4	14.5	7.7	14.2	12.7
1974	8.3	15.3	10.6	14.0	12.3	4.4	9.2	8.0
1975	6.6	13.0	9.2	12.4	11.8	4.4	6.3	5.9
1976	9.0	17.0	13.0	13.0	14.1	7.8	12.2	11.0
1977	10.6	17.5	9.8	9.3	10.6	9.0	16.4	14.3

Profits net of tax and depreciation as a percentage of net assets.

Source: National Income Blue Book; Business Monitor (M4) various issues. Profitability is as defined in Table 6.9. The social rate of return is the profitability of domestic investment gross of tax.

Table 6.12 Profitability of UK Overseas Direct Investment, Foreign Investment in UK, and UK Domestic Firms 1971–3 and 1974–6

		UK Outward Investment[a]					Foreign Investment in UK[a]			UK Domestic Firms[b]	
		Western Europe	North America	Other Developed Countries	Rest of World	Total	Western Europe	North America	Total	Unadjusted[c]	Adjusted[c]
More technology intensive sectors	1974–76	15.6	16.4	13.3	16.8	15.0	4.9	10.8	9.6	9.9	9.4
	1971–73	13.3	8.5	9.3	12.4	10.7	8.9	14.1	12.9	9.4	10.8
Chemicals and allied products	1974–76	14.8	17.1	18.5	20.4	17.2	3.8	6.8	5.9	11.8	9.8
	1971–73	8.9	10.4	12.7	15.5	11.2	8.5	12.7	11.0	9.3	8.6
Mechanical engineering	1974–76	17.3	16.3	11.8	17.3	14.6	10.5	15.5	14.8	9.5	7.4
	1971–73	18.6	5.3	8.1	12.5	11.8	9.8	15.8	15.1	9.2	8.4
Electrical engineering	1974–76	12.4	13.7	11.2	8.9	11.5	1.4	13.3	10.2	10.6	10.3
	1971–73	11.7	5.9	8.5	6.3	8.2	9.1	16.4	13.9	10.3	11.0
Motors	1974–76	18.5	2.1	-2.3	17.1	8.7	4.8	-1.0	-0.9	-0.3	nsa
	1971–73	25.2	11.2	-0.9	17.2	10.3	1.5	9.1	8.9	7.3	nsa
Less technology intensive sectors	1974–76	9.2	13.9	12.3	17.5	13.0	6.9	7.6	7.4	8.8	6.8
	1971–73	12.5	11.6	12.0	14.0	12.4	6.4	8.5	7.9	10.0	9.1
Food, drink, tobacco	1974–76	12.0	18.4	14.0	18.3	15.6	9.9	10.5	10.3	9.1	7.9
	1971–73	14.6	15.8	14.8	14.1	14.9	6.9	14.4	13.1	10.0	8.4
Metal manufacture	1974–76	-9.1	11.8	10.7	14.9	9.1	5.4	4.2	4.6	7.2	6.6
	1971–73	4.1	7.2	13.7	22.9	12.1	8.5	0.9	2.3	8.2	7.2
Textiles, clothing, leather and footwear	1974–76	9.5	9.0	13.8	13.9	11.2	-15.1	-8.1	-8.5	8.4	7.6
	1971–73	12.8	10.2	10.3	9.6	10.6	4.0	0.2	2.7	11.4	11.6
Paper, printing and publishing	1974–76	11.3	10.9	9.2	20.2	11.2	9.2	5.7	7.2	8.0	7.9
	1971–73	7.4	7.3	9.4	16.1	8.7	11.1	7.6	9.5	8.8	8.8
Other manufacturing	1974–76	5.3	9.2	11.8	16.9	10.6	7.1	8.2	7.9	9.1	6.3
	1971–73	9.6	6.8	8.8	13.9	9.8	5.1	8.6	7.1	10.4	9.5

Total manufacturing	1974–76	11.8	14.6	12.7	17.1	13.6	5.8	9.5	8.6	9.2	7.8
	1971–73	12.4	10.5	10.4	13.4	11.5	7.7	11.8	10.9	9.7	9.2
All industry	1974–76	12.9	14.0	14.5	22.0	15.6	7.6	11.5	10.3	9.0	6.1
	1971–73	13.1	13.7	12.6	14.3	13.3	8.2	13.2	11.9	10.2	9.0

[a] For outward and inward investment rate of return is calculated from *Business Monitor* M4 data and is defined as profits divided by net assets, where profits include unremitted profits as well as those remitted to the parent, and are measured after deducting provisions made for depreciation of fixed assets and after provision for overseas tax on outward earnings and UK tax on inward earnings.

[b] For UK domestic firms rate of return is calculated from *Business Monitor* M3 data and is defined as net income less total tax divided by net assets, where net income is gross trading profit (net of short-term interest) plus investment and other revenue income and prior year adjustments other than tax, less hire of plant and machinery and depreciation provisions.

[c] Figures for UK domestic firms are based on the *Business Monitor* M3 coverage of listed UK companies. These companies are predominantly UK controlled. Thus in 1975 94.3 per cent of listed companies in manufacturing plus distribution (manufacturing only figures were not available) were UK controlled. The figures, however, while excluding UK 'companies operating mainly overseas' included the overseas operations of other UK companies. This overseas component, judging by the proportion of the companies' total tax paid overseas (20 per cent in 1976 and 27 per cent in 1975 for manufacturing), is significant. In the first column no attempt is made to adjust for this overseas component. However, in the second column, from the *Business Monitor* M3 data on assets and profits (i.e. including the domestic UK and overseas operations of the companies) the *Business Monitor* M4 data on UK companies overseas operations have been subtracted. Though there are a number of deficiencies to this process (which are most likely to operate in the direction of exaggerating actual differences in rate of return, rather than providing misleading results) it is a useful way of getting close to isolating the results of UK controlled firms' domestic operations.

Source: As for Table 6.11.

Table 6.13 Estimated Gains and Losses to UK as a Result of Outward and Inward Investment

	UK Domestic Firms		UK Firms Abroad			Foreign Firms in UK			Columns (5) + (8)	(8) as % of (9)
	π after tax (1)	π before tax (2)	$\bar{K}_o$ (3)	π after tax (4)	£m. gain or loss[a] (5)	$\bar{K}_i$ (6)	π after tax (7)	£m. gain or loss[a] (8)	(9)	(10)
1963–65	9.4	13.1	1973.7	8.9	−9.8	1392.2	11.0	22.2	12.4	179.0
1966–68	7.5	12.0	2523.9	8.9	35.3	1946.2	9.4	36.9	72.2	51.1
1969–71	7.6	11.9	3439.3	9.7	72.2	2721.6	9.3	46.3	118.5	39.1
1972–74	9.2	15.3	4975.8	12.6	169.2	3940.2	10.7	59.1	238.3	25.9
1975–77	8.7	15.8	8740.8	12.2	305.9	6011.6	10.4	102.1	408.0	25.0

[a] For explanation see text.
Source: Data derived from Table 6.11.

to be so, it is necessary to show that the profitability of outward investment is highest in activities where the ownership profitability surpasses
that of foreign firms, but where the location profitability ratio least favours
the UK. By contrast, inward investment should be concentrated in those
industries in which the ownership profitability ratio favours foreign firms
and the location profitability ratio favours the UK.

While this hypothesis has not been fully tested, the information set out
earlier in Table 6.10 does tend to support rather than refute it. Industries
which have an above average ownership profitability ratio and below average location profitability and/or export/import ratio also tend to be those
which have an above average I_o/I_i ratio. Industries which have a below
average ownership profitability and above average location profitability
and/or export/import ratio tend to have a lower than average foreign
investment ratio. Examples of the first group include textiles, paper,
printing and publishing, and metal manufacturing: and of the second,
chemicals, motor vehicles, mechanical and instrument engineering, and
electrical engineering. The main exceptions to the rule are the food, drink
and tobacco industries but this may reflect the very different product
compositions of UK outward and inward investment as much as anything
else.

VIII

While this chapter has not attempted a comprehensive analysis of the causes
and effects of UK inward and outward investment, it has pinpointed a
number of features which policy makers would do well to consider. Four
of these stand out. First, although, for all sectors, the UK outward/inward
capital stake has fallen over the last two decades, for that on which the
future of the UK's international competitive position so much depends,
viz. manufacturing industry, it has risen considerably. Second, the explanation for this trend is to be found partly in the improved international
competitive position of UK owned firms, and partly in the increasing
tendency of such firms to supply overseas markets — particularly in Western
Europe — from production outlets outside the UK. By the same token,
foreign, particularly Western European, firms have tended to exploit the
UK market by imports rather than by inward direct investment. Third, assuming that the capital invested by UK firms invested overseas would not
have been invested at home, then the gains to gross national product from
outward and inward investment have increased over the period, with the
contribution from outward investment becoming increasingly more significant. Fourth, the evidence suggests that international investment flows
have improved the structure of resource allocation in the UK economy.
Foreign firms in the UK tend to be concentrated in the more dynamic
and technologically advanced sectors of the UK economy, while UK firms

have exploited their advantages in the less technology intensive industries by investing overseas.

All these conclusions support the continuation of a basically liberal policy towards outward and inward investment by the British government. Indeed, it may be there is less justification for the imposition of investment controls than at the time of the Reddaway and Steuer reports, partly because the UK location profitability ratio has fallen and partly because the balance-of-payments constraints are less pressing than they once were. On the other hand, as suggested at the beginning of this chapter, the concern that, by replacing domestic investment, foreign investment has had an adverse effect on UK jobs and economic growth has become more pronounced. My answer to this argument is that if the reasons for the rising foreign investment ratio set out here are correct, the best way for the government to reverse this trend is to focus its attention on improving the locational attractions for UK and foreign producers. What it should not do is anything that might damage the ownership advantages of UK firms. And this is precisely what controls on outward investment would do, as their main effects would be to cut back on the overseas markets of UK firms. Given the UK location advantages, such markets can be served only by foreign production.

A final comment concerns the relationship between ownership and location advantages. This chapter has treated them as if they were independent of each other. While, at a given moment of time, this may be so, over a period of time this is clearly not the case. The ability of firms to undertake research and development and the incentives for them to do so will be influenced by a country's science, technology and educational policy, while the ability of a firm to benefit from economies of size may rest on market size and structure.[26] The ownership advantages of Japanese firms today cannot be separated from the industrial strategy of the Japanese government in the 1950s and 1960s. UK foreign investment policy should then be designed in a wider context of international competitive strategy that will seek to identify and stimulate the ownership advantages of UK firms, and improve the locational attractions of the UK. If this is done, then international investment, along with international trade, can play its proper role in improving resource allocation in the UK and the efficiency of its industries.

Appendix 6.1: Statistical sources on UK international direct investment

The most carefully prepared time series of the UK outward and inward direct capital stake and international investment flows is contained in the Central Statistical Office's publication *UK Balance of Payments 1967–77* (1978 and subsequent editions published in 1979 and 1980). Tables 12.1 and 12.2 of this former publication present the relevant details, including, since the end of 1973, estimates of that part of the increase in foreign assets and liabilities accounted for by revaluation, exchange rate and other changes. An earlier edition of this publication (*UK Balance of Payments, 1965–75*) also gave estimates of such changes for the period 1963–73 as a whole. Of the increase in the outward capital stake recorded in Table 6.1 of this chapter such changes accounted for £815 million (or approximately 20 per cent); of the increase in the inward capital stake they accounted for £155 million (or just over 5 per cent).

The most comprehensive industrial and geographical breakdown of the annual foreign direct investment by UK firms and foreign direct investment by foreign firms in the UK is contained in the annual publication of the Business Statistics Office, *Business Monitor* (M4) *Overseas Transactions*: the latest data relate to the year 1977. The most recent periodic *Census of Overseas Assets* of UK firms abroad and of foreign firms in the UK is for the year 1974 and was published in 1976 but provisional data for 1978 were published in *Business Monitor*, 27 February 1981. Previous censuses were taken for the years 1971, 1968 and 1965.

Preliminary estimates of the UK's international direct investment position for any particular year and revised estimates for previous years are published in *Business Monitor*.

Details of the UK's international portfolio investment position are set out in the *UK Balance of Payments 1969–79* (1980) and the *Bank of England Quarterly Bulletin* (June, 1980).

Notes: Chapter 6

1   For example, evaluating the determinants of the foreign activities of US firms by use of plant and equipment expenditure of US affiliates and direct investment by US firms gives broadly the same results.

2   Both sets of data are imperfect measures of the activities of MNEs in so far as they are partial input measures. Far better (and the preferred procedure in this book) is to take value of output (ideally value-added) as a measure of such activity.

3   These questions are explored in some detail in Chapters 13 and 14.

4   See the Appendix to this chapter on page 172.

5   Excluding insurance for outward investment for 1962 also.

6   The results of these were first published in *British Business* (formerly *Trade and Industry*) and then subsequently in *Business Monitor* (M4).

7   Capital stake is defined as the book value of fixed assets (net of depreciation) plus current assets (net of amounts owing by the investing company) less current liabilities (net of amounts owing to the investing companies) less long-term liabilities (other than to the investing company) of overseas subsidiaries and branches.

8   For example, as set out in Chapter 3, page 48. For an analysis of the motives for UK foreign direct investment see Houston and Dunning (1976) and Morgan (1979).

9   See, for example, various essays on intra-industry and intra-firm trade in Giersch (1979).

10   Based upon the actual capital stake for 1974 plus net investment in 1975 and 1976. At the time of completing this Chapter, no sectoral breakdown of the direct capital stake was available for 1978.

11   Where the share dropped from 29.3 per cent in 1962 to 15.2 per cent in 1976.

11a By 1978, the world ratio had risen to 1.50, that for Western Europe to 2.34 and that for North America to 0.64.

12 Defined as the value of net assets in 1974 minus those in 1971, plus the value of new investment in 1975 and 1976.

13 MTI industries spent at least 2 per cent of their net output on research and development in 1974; LTI industries spent a lower percentage. It is accepted that, within these industries, there were wide variations in this proxy for technological intensity.

14 This is a finding consistent with that of Van Den Bulke *et al*. (1979) in their study of divestment by MNEs in Europe in the early 1970s.

15 It being argued that an increase (decrease) in the ratio indicates the UK endowments are becoming more (less) attractive to those of competitor countries.

16 For more details of the comparative profitability of UK and US firms and of UK firms at home and abroad in the 1950s and 1960s see Dunning (1970).

17 Panic (1980) notes that during the period 1971–78, particularly in the latter half, the E/X ratio declined most in goods produced by sectors in which foreign participation was higher than average for manufacturing industry.

18 Particularly M10 *Overseas Trade Analysed in Terms of Industries* and MQ12 *Import Penetration and Export Sales Ratios for Manufacturing Industry*.

19 The ratio of exports to manufacturers' total sales.

20 The ratio of imports to total home demand.

21 See, for example, the study by Hood and Young (1980) of US manufacturing affiliates in Scotland. The authors also cite the conservatism of management in corporate headquarters as a contributory factor to poor industrial relations. See, too, Allen (1976) and Phelps Brown (1977).

22 Note that one is talking in terms of comparative advantage. It is possible that UK firms and the UK may both have an absolute advantage over other firms and countries in the production of one or more commodities. If there were only one commodity being produced, then there would be no outward or inward investment. Once one considers two or more commodities then even if the mobile and immobile resources of the UK were superior to those of other countries, both trade and international investment are likely to be beneficial.

23 This is a crucial assumption. One would clearly get very different results from the contribution of international investment if one assumed that without inward investment there would be unemployed resources in the UK, or in the absence of outward investment, there would be no effect on capital formation in the UK.

24 It is assumed that the private and social rates of return on foreign investment are broadly the same, as the tax paid on the earnings of the foreign investment accrues mainly to host governments.

25 It should be emphasised that this is only the starting point to calculating the costs and benefits of international investment. But since we are primarily interested in the allocative effects of such investment, they are sufficient for our purposes.

26 For further details see Chapter 4.

References

Allen, G. C. (1976), *The British Disease* (London: Institute of Economic Affairs).

Beenstock, M. (1980), *Finance and International Direct Investment in the United Kingdom*, London Business School Economic Forecasting Unit, Discussion Paper No. 81 (July).

Beenstock, M., and Willcocks, P. (1980), *Capital Formation in a Small Open Economy*, London Business School Economic Forecasting Unit, Discussion Paper No. 73 (March).

Business Statistics Office (various dates), *Business Monitor* M4, M10 and M12Q (London: HMSO).

Central Statistical Office (1978), *UK Balance of Payments 1967–77* (London: HMSO).

Dunning, J. H. (1970), *Studies in International Investment* (London: Allen & Unwin).

Dunning, J. H. (1976), *US Industry in the UK* (London: Wilton House).

Giersch, H. (ed.) (1979), *On the Economics of Inter Industry Trade* Tubingen: Mohr).

Hood, N., and Young, S. (1980), *European Development Strategies of US-Owned Manufacturing Companies Located in Scotland* (Edinburgh: HMSO).

Houston, T., and Dunning, J. H. (1976), *UK Industry Abroad* (London: Financial Times).

Lincoln, R. A. (1975), *US Direct Investment in the UK* (London: Economist Intelligence Unit), QER Special No. 23.

Morgan, A. (1978), 'Foreign manufacturing by UK firms', in F. Blackaby (ed.), *De-Industrialisation* (London: Heinemann).

Panic, M. (1980), 'UK manufacturing industry: international integration and trade performance', *Bank of England Quarterly Bulletin* (March).

Phelps Brown, A. (1977), 'What is the British predicament?', *Three Banks Review* (December).

Reddaway, W. B., Potter, S. T., and Taylor, C. T. (1968), *The Effects of UK Direct Investment Overseas* (Cambridge: Cambridge University Press).

Steuer, M. D. *et al.* (1973), *The Impact of Foreign Direct Investment in the United Kingdom* (London: HMSO).

Van Den Bulke, D., Boddewyn, J. J., Martens, B., and Klemmer, P. (1979), *Investment and Divestment Policies of Multinational Corporations in Europe* (Farnborough: Saxon House).

PART TWO

7

Multinational Enterprises, Market Structure, Economic Power and Industrial Policy

I

It has long been recognised that both the efficiency of resource allocation and the distribution of economic welfare are strongly influenced by the structure of the markets in which enterprises buy and sell goods and services, and their conduct and performance within these markets. Up to now, however, most of the standard texts and readings on the subject,[1] have confined their analysis to the behaviour of firms in the context of a closed economy and have largely ignored the phenomenon of international production, that is, the production, across national boundaries, of goods and services financed by foreign direct investment. In view of the internationalisation of production in many sectors and the dominant role of MNEs in these sectors, this omission is a little surprising.[2]

This chapter describes and analyses the interaction between MNEs, or their affiliates, and the market structures in which they operate. It will concern itself with the distinctive behaviour of these firms, and their reactions to policies of governments designed to promote the kind of structure they think will best meet their economic and social goals.

These interests are linked. The way in which firms organise themselves to produce and sell goods and services embraces *inter alia* the number and size of firms supplying similar products; the relative efficacy of markets or hierarchies as means of co-ordinating economic activities; the conditions of entry facing potential buyers and sellers; the technology of production and marketing; the characteristics and diversity of the products supplied; and the spatial deployment of markets and production units.

This last point is worth elaborating in the present context. Where a market consists of a large group of firms, each manufacturing the same product in a single location and selling it to one market, the strategy and

---

This chapter is a revised and expanded version of an article first published in *Journal of World Trade Law* (Nov./Dec. 1974).

options of individual sellers will be simple and straightforward. If the British market for detergents is serviced by fifty indigenous firms, each more or less the same size and supplying an identical product from a single plant, then both the market structure and the behavioural options open to firms are readily identified. Suppose, however, that one of the fifty firms now produces another commodity, for example, a new kind of toilet soap, under monopolistic conditions; another begins to export detergents to France; a third is bought out by a US company; a fourth sets up a branch factory elsewhere in the UK (also to supply detergents); a fifth merges with its main British supplier of raw materials; and a sixth is taken over by a foreign conglomerate. The number of firms producing detergents in the United Kingdom is unchanged, as may be the demand conditions for detergents, but the behavioural pattern of six firms, at least, may be very different.[3]

In this chapter we shall be concerned with the effects of one particular form of hierarchical diversification, viz. the operation of production units, under common ownership, across national boundaries. We shall concentrate our interest on the markets supplied by the affiliates of MNEs. The impact of multinationality may be both direct or first-stage, through the entry of an affiliate of an MNE on the structure of the market; and indirect or second-stage, through the consequences of the distinctive conduct and performance of the affiliates of MNEs on other economic agents.

The argument proceeds in the following way. Section II considers the effects on the received theory of industrial market structure[4] of incorporating a situation in which, first, markets and, second, production units are internationally diversified. Section III outlines some distinctive features of the MNE and distinguishes between two groups of MNE affiliates, viz. the independent and interdependent affiliates. Section IV examines the likely impact of these features on market form and behaviour. Section V considers possible policies that governments might introduce, where the consequences of the operations of foreign affiliates are different from those of indigenous firms. Section VI looks briefly at the empirical evidence surrounding these issues from the viewpoint of the affiliates of US MNEs in the UK.

II

A Closed Economy

(a)   *Single product, single plant firms*

In a closed economy, all the output of firms is sold to consumers in that economy, who also purchase all their goods from these same firms. There is no spatial separation of production units and markets. For any product, it is possible to construct demand functions for each consumer and, by aggregation, obtain a market demand function. Where there is perfect competition among sellers, a market supply function can be similarly derived and an equilibrium price struck. In other market situations this is not possible, as supply and price are not independent of each other.

For our purposes, however, all that needs to be identified are the factors leading to any particular market structure. These include the technical properties of the product being supplied; the ownership and locational patterns of firms; and inter-firm differences in efficiency, reflecting technological, price or scale considerations, and/or transport and other movement costs. Government intervention also has to be considered. Since all consumers are assumed to be price takers, the limits to the growth of the output are easily determined.

(b)   *Multi-plant and multi-product firms*
Assume, now, firms have the option of producing the same product in more than one location, or of producing more than one product from the same location. What are the consequences of these forms of diversification on market structure? Spatial diversification of single product firms will not normally influence the size distribution of *firms* except in so far as such diversification affects efficiency; but, clearly, the size distribution of *establishments* may be affected. Moreover, the size of any one particular establishment will understate its competitive power, wherever there are economies associated with the spatial diversification of plants and the size of firms. The individual conduct of these plants may also differ *because* they are part of a larger organisation.

Where firms produce different products (or processes) either in the same or different locations, market form is affected in two ways. First, an opportunity is created to concentrate the output of particular products in different plants; if this is done, it will affect the size structure of plants, depending on any one plant's share in the total output. Second, their strategy of behaviour may be modified; this has long since been acknowledged in the case of products jointly supplied, but it can also apply whenever product diversification enlarges a firm's options. In other words, like multi-plant firms, multi-product firms are able to advance their competitive position *vis-à-vis* specialist producers. While this may not affect directly the size or product structure of firms in the short run, over time, it could well do so.

When multi-product firms are also multi-plant, a further choice becomes available. This is to specialise products or production processes, either vertically or horizontally, between plants. This may clearly affect the size distribution of plants in the industry. It will also influence their behaviour *vis-à-vis* single product or process firms, which are limited and cannot take the advantages of economies of integration where these exist. The multi-product, multi-plant firm will then affect market structure; and the behaviour of the individual affiliates may differ from that of indigenous firms.

An Open Economy. Stage I

Suppose next that the market for any given product can be supplied by firms producing outside the market and that firms located in the market can export part of their output. No longer need domestic production be equal to domestic consumption. Neither will the market structure facing domestic firms necessarily reflect either the economic strength of particular producers or the extent to which they are faced with domestic competition. Thus, concentration ratios of domestic firms may be high while at the same time competition from imports is strong; alternatively, the output sold by such firms to the domestic market might be a small proportion of their total output.

The introduction of diversified international outlets immediately complicates the concept of the market area. On the demand side, at one extreme, it may embrace each and every market to which firms supply at all; at the other, simply the local market. On the supply side, it may include the total production of all firms supplying either the total or home market or just that of the domestic firms. As governments are usually concerned with the economic welfare of their own citizens, we shall concentrate on the consequences of international trade on domestic consumers and firms.

What is the likely effect on market structure of territorial diversification of this kind? There is no simple *a priori* answer to this question. Consider first the widening of markets of domestic firms. Whether the number of firms or concentration ratios increases or falls depends on *which* firms supply the exports. If the export propensity is greater among the largest firms, then concentration ratios may increase; if it is greater among smaller firms, it might decrease. Now consider imports. If imports are substantial, then concentration ratios of domestic firms will tell us little about the market structure in which they compete. Initially, as a result of import competition, one would suppose that the market structure would become more competitive and the number of firms would increase, though, subsequently, depending on the competitive advantages of the two groups, and the reaction of domestic firms, they might fall.

A similar analysis may be applied to other aspects of market structure. Product diversity and/or differentiation are likely to increase as new and different markets are serviced and as existing outlets are serviced from sources previously supplying different markets. However, the extent to which domestic firms can penetrate foreign markets, and foreign firms the domestic market is likely to depend more on the barriers of entry facing *de novo* firms. These include transport costs, import controls, non-tariff barriers and consumer resistance to foreign products. As the market widens, these obstacles tend to increase; but a larger market may also allow more efficient production techniques which may add to the barriers facing *de novo* firms. Moreover, depending on the extent to which a firm is multi-product or multi-plant, market diversification might encourage vertical, horizontal or conglomerate integration.

International diversification of markets may also affect the behaviour of firms. It may, for example, cause a firm to modify its goals, perhaps because of the new risks involved, for example, with respect to exchange rates. It may affect its performance relative to that of its competitors, particularly if there are economies of size and market diversification. It will almost certainly widen its options of behaviour. Once an enterprise diversifies its markets, its sales to any one market may be substituted for those of another, and hence its elasticity of supply to that market is raised. Immediately, too, a firm can choose to exploit a particular market to gain advantages of economies of scale for the firm as a whole, even though that market *per se* is not profitable. It can engage in devices to increase its market share not available — or available to the same extent — to local firms, for example, cross-subsidisation and predatory pricing[5] (Telser, 1966). These options (some of which may be open to firms practising other forms of diversification) suggest that the share of output of a firm supplied to any one market may not be a good indicator of its competitive strength; and that its behaviour in that market will be influenced by its performance in *all* markets.

An Open Economy. Stage II

Stage II of international spatial diversification occurs when firms diversify not only their markets across national boundaries, but their production facilities as well. Output in a particular country may now be supplied both by home based and foreign based establishments; the combined output is sold both to that market and abroad; and the amount sold to the domestic market plus imports comprises the total goods marketed locally. On the other hand, part of the production of firms will be located outside their country of origin. This, coupled with their domestic production (which might be sold locally or exported), makes up their total output. There need be no spatial relationship whatsoever between the production of a particular good or service and its consumption.

In such circumstances, the boundaries of a market become even more difficult to delineate. Again, the precise frame of reference is important. From the viewpoint of customers within a particular country, it is the structure of the firms supplying their needs which is relevant. The difficulty is that, because the behaviour of these firms may be influenced partly by their *ownership* and partly by the *location* of their production units, any given structure — in terms of range of products produced, number and size of firms, processes of production, barriers to entry, etc. —

may produce different results between one group of firms and another. The first stage of openness in trade introduced firms of a different nationality of ownership into the market; the second stage involves both this *and* the operation of international production units, with all the consequences of branch plant activity.

The distinctiveness of the MNE has already been discussed in a previous chapter. Here, we would simply observe that, compared with imports from the parent company, local production by foreign affiliates will affect existing domestic concentration ratios, increasing or decreasing them according to the relative size of the foreign affiliates. But, because the affiliates are part of larger enterprises, their share of the local output may inadequately reflect their competitive power. On the other hand, foreign production by domestic companies, relative to exports, will affect the concentration ratio, inasmuch as, if the largest firms substitute production for exports, it will be reduced, while if their smaller competitors do so, it will increase. Again, however, the economic strength of the firms will be understated by domestic concentration ratios.

From the customer's viewpoint, it is mainly a question of how his demands are serviced. Thus, a substitution of local production for imports may affect the form of competition and the types of products produced, but it will not dramatically change unless, as a result of local production, the future market structure is affected. But the strategy of firms has altered, due either (or both) to changes in their ownership or location of production. Again, the totality of a firm's operations affects structure as much as the extent of its participation in a particular market (cf., for example, the role of Nestles, Philips or SKF in domestic and foreign markets). Sometimes, too, imports of a country may originate from the foreign affiliates of its domestic companies.

We can conclude that as an enterprise diversifies its activities, whether it be its markets, its products, its processes or the location of its production units, its impact on the structure of any *one* of the markets it serves will be modified. Its main advantages over specialist firms stem from its diversity of operations and the wider options these allow. The affiliate of a multi-plant firm may score over a single plant indigenous firm because it is part of a larger organisation; moreover, a multi-plant firm is able to take advantage of the different cost and/or demand structures of particular locations. A multi-product firm is often able to switch resources from one type of production to another; a firm selling to diversified markets makes it possible for such a firm to meet changing demand conditions in that market by reallocating its supply.

Likewise, a firm engaging in international production is in a position to affect the structure of the market it serves and also the conduct within these markets. Very often, the MNE, because it is large, is diversified in each of these respects, and its impact on local market structure arises from these characteristics. But although the principles of diversification by international production are similar to other forms of diversification, their effects on market structure are distinctive. The reasons for this will now be explored.

III

Chapter 1 has observed the similarities and differences between MNEs and multi-location domestic enterprises. To host countries, the difference between an affiliate of a foreign owned MNE and an indigenous firm may be considered under two headings:

(1) the *branch plant* effect (how do the activities of *part* of one firm compare with that of the whole of another?);
(2) the *ownership* effect (how far does an affiliate of an indigenous enterprise behave differently from one owned by a foreign enterprise?).

Similarly, the distinctive effects of international production need to be identified. From the viewpoint of *host* countries, market structure and the performance of firms are important as they affect the efficiency of resource allocation and the distribution of the net output (value added) among the participating agents of production, consumers and government. In the case of national enterprises, the entire proceeds help to swell the gross *national* product, but with affiliates of MNEs part of the value added will accrue to residents of the investing country. This part represents a loss to the gross national product of the host country, and is essentially a price paid for the resources (e.g. capital, knowledge, trademarks, entrepreneurship, etc.) provided by the MNE. *Inter alia*, the theory of industrial organisation is concerned with factors determining the conditions of sale between buyers and sellers. Applied to the behaviour of MNEs and their affiliates, it is interested in the conditions of sale of the resources supplied by MNEs to host countries, as determined by

(1) the benefits accruing from these sales and their contribution to gross *domestic* product;
(2) the price paid for the benefits, both by way of profits, interest, dividends, royalties, fees, etc., remitted by the affiliates, and of disguised payments, for example, other than arm's length prices, paid for various goods and services.[6]

To assess the costs and benefits of foreign direct investment would take us outside the scope of this chapter,[7] but, in so far as MNEs by their ability to influence market structure and behaviour may also affect the distribution of the value added created by them between host and home countries, this is of direct interest to economic welfare. It might be no less appropriate to consider some of the control or sovereignty issues surrounding the domination of an industry by foreign firms.

With these things in mind, let us look at the effects of international production in countries which are *host* to the affiliates of MNEs.[8]

To aid discussion, let us concentrate on two types of affiliates of MNEs, viz. those which operate largely *independently* of the rest of the enterprise of which they are part, and those which are *interdependent* on the rest of the enterprise of which they are part. Clearly, in practice, no hard and fast line can be drawn between these types of affiliates; there is a continuum of degrees of independence ranging from zero to complete. But, basically, an *independent* affiliate is one which has a substantial degree of autonomy over its own resource usage, and whose contribution to the investing enterprise may be measured by the income earned or remitted on the assets invested. To the affiliate, the value of being a member of the MNE consists, on the one hand, of access to knowledge and expertise, in excess of that which an independent firm of the same size could acquire (at the same cost) and, on the other, of access to centralised facilities, for example, technical, administrative and managerial, provided by the parent company or other affiliates for the group as a whole. For both these benefits it is assumed the independent affiliate will pay the marginal cost of supply. While these latter gains essentially derive from its being part of a larger organisation, that is, the *branch plant* effect, the former arise from its being part of a foreign firm, that is, the *ownership* effect. Compared to a group of independently owned companies, the main advantages of common *and* foreign ownership are contained in these elements.

The *interdependent* affiliate is one whose operations are largely determined by the common strategy of the multinational hierarchy of which it is part (Calvet, 1980). Usually, it has little autonomy of choice on such matters as its product range, the amount and type of investment, markets, sources of inputs, location of production units, etc.; decisions about these are taken centrally with the interests of the whole enterprise in mind. This immediately suggests that decisions *may* be differently motivated in the two types of affiliates. The product and/or process ranges of the interdependent affiliate are likely to be more specialised and integrated than those of the independent affiliate; and there is often a great deal of intragroup trade. Product strategy will be planned to take full account of the international differences in input costs and productivity, as will the markets served, research and development and sourcing of inputs. Where appropriate, purchasing will be centralised to gain the economies of bulk buying; and the parent company is also likely to have control over capital expenditure, the financing of investment and the management of the liquid assets of the group.

The interdependent affiliate is, of course, not unique to the MNE; branch operations of multi-location domestic firms may also be centrally controlled. The special character of interdependent multinational affiliates arises because of the differences in the economic characteristics *between* nations, over and above those that exist between regions *within* a nation. Foremost among these are:

(1)   differences in demand and cost structures (cf. labour costs in Southern Italy or Pakistan with New York State, and, say, Texas or Wyoming with New York State), which make international specialisation relatively more attractive;[9]

(2)   differences in (a) micro-cost or profit directed inducements (or penalties) offered by host governments and (b) their macro-economic goals and efficiency in achieving these goals;

(3)   uncertainties surround (a) policies of foreign governments and (b) movements in exchange rates.

These latter two factors will also affect the way in which MNEs treat their affiliates as agents in securing their objectives, for example, by recording income in countries with low rate of taxes, hard exchange rates, liberal policies towards dividend remission and political stability. By affecting the distribution of the value added from affiliates between host and home countries, MNEs may also influence the host government's attitude towards them. But both market considerations and the role of governments towards companies can be better taken advantage of by affiliates of MNEs than by local companies, because of the wider options of the former.[10]

The above argument suggests that the market structure emerging from the operations of the affiliates of MNEs, particularly interdependent affiliates, may better conform to the principle of international division of labour than that of national firms. The exceptions are (1) where prices in particular markets do not reflect world prices (Little and Mirrlees, 1969), (2) where there are restrictions on the transference of certain assets or property, for example, knowledge or trademarks across boundaries, and (3) where there is imperfect competition between MNEs. Similarly, behaviour by affiliates of MNEs will be oriented towards the goals of parent companies, which, since production is internationally diversified,[11] may well lead to a different level and composition of products or processes *and* a different distribution of the benefits of such activities than those that would arise from a multi-plant national firm or international trading firm. However, while the strategy of MNEs based on maximising their global profits will, depending on the extent of the constraints mentioned above, generally advance world real output, there is no guarantee that the distribution of this output, or the cultural or sociological spill-over effects on host countries, will advance national goals. The behaviour of affiliates of MNEs may also be constrained by unwelcome extra-territorial policies of *home* governments.

The foregoing analysis suggests a number of propositions concerning the impact of MNEs on market structure and behaviour, and sheds light on the industrial and geographical spread of their activities. Why is it, for example, that MNEs of a particular geographical origin tend to be concentrated in sectors of activity with a particular type of market structure? Why is it that the MNEs or their affiliates in these sectors possess distinct behavioural characteristics?

Earlier chapters have asserted that the industrial distribution of MNEs can be explained using the eclectic theory of international production.[12] In the context of the present chapter, this approach would suggest that MNEs would be concentrated in those sectors where structural or cognitive market imperfections prompt firms to internalise transactions. Since the choice between market and hierarchical activities is, to some extent at least, influenced by country-specific factors, it follows that the sectors in which MNEs predominate may also be country specific.[13] Thus the Japanese government's protection of the domestic iron and steel industry may favour more MNEs (and other large firms) in that industry than in the USA, where market forces have a freer rein. But generally *within* a particular country, sectors which are marked by high concentration ratios, product differentiation and barriers to entry tend to be those in which there is some degree of market disequilibrium, which both generates and attracts MNEs and other large firms. Such research which has been undertaken on the market structure of *home* country MNEs, notably those of US, UK and Swedish origin, all point to this conclusion.[14]

Turning to the structure of markets facing the affiliates of MNEs in host countries, we see a similar pattern to that just described, with both industry- and country-specific factors influencing the degree and form of foreign participation. For example, most empirical findings suggest that the affiliates of MNEs tend to be concentrated in industrial sectors characterised by a high degree of concentration. Typical among these is a study by Newfarmer and Mueller (1975) of the affiliates of MNEs in Mexico and Brazil. In Mexico, the authors found that, in 1970, 61 per cent of MNE production was sold in markets where the largest four plants accounted for 50 per cent or more of the markets' total sales. In Brazil, in those industries where three of the four leading firms are affiliates of MNEs, the plant concentration ratio in 1968 was 54 per cent. In those industries in which the four leading plants are Brazilian owned the average concentration ratio was 39 per cent. In Canada, in 1972 some 52.5 per cent of the value added of foreign subsidiaries was in industries with concentration ratios above 50 per cent (Statistics Canada, 1978) whereas in Australia (Parry, 1978), Guatemala (Willmore, 1976) and Malaysia (Lall, 1979) the correlation between foreign presence and industrial concentration has been shown to be positive and statistically significant.[15] By contrast, in the UK both Steuer *et al.* (1973) and Globerman (1979) found only a weak association between these two variables. Further details in respect of the participation of US affiliates in UK industry are set out in Table 7.1.

These and other studies also reveal that the affiliates of MNEs are likely to be concentrated in industries characterised by above average product differentiation (Caves, 1974b; Owen, 1979) and product diversity (Wolf, 1977; Statistics Canada, 1978; Parry, 1978). They also tend to be larger in size than their indigenous competitors (in similar sectors) (Dunning, 1976; Statistics Canada, 1978), particularly in technology or knowledge intensive sectors and those in which economies of *firm* size are of above average significance (Horst, 1972; Dunning and Buckley, 1977; Bergsten, Horst and Moran, 1978). There is also some evidence that an increasing proportion of the foreign direct investment of US MNEs is being directed to conglomerate activities rather than to advance the horizontal or vertical specialisation and/or integration of the investing firm (Kopits, 1979).[16]

IV

What next of differences in behavioural patterns and impact on industrial structure of MNEs or their affiliates *within* particular industries? What does the foregoing analysis suggest? How far will the structural features of an industry in which the MNEs produce be reflected in the industries of the affiliates? To tackle these and similar questions, let us examine some of the possible consequences of the entry of a foreign affiliate on the existing market structure and behaviour. We shall consider both the first stage and second stage impact on market structure.

First Stage Impact

(a) *Number and size of firms*
The first question is whether entry is accomplished by the purchase of, or merger with, an existing producer or by the establishment of a green field venture, and, where the former, the position of the existing firm in the market structure. Second, one has to consider what would have happened to the existing market structure in the absence of foreign investment. The effect of a takeover on an ailing firm, which would otherwise have been acquired by a domestic company or gone out of business, may be quite different from that of an acquisition of a thriving business. One also wishes to identify the reasons for the takeover; is the affiliate intended to supply domestic markets in place of imports, or to supply foreign markets previously serviced from other countries? Or is the takeover prompted by the desire of the acquiring company to reduce competition?

Most empirical studies (e.g. Rosenbluth, 1970; Stubenitsky, 1970; Deane, 1971; Horst, 1972; Steuer *et al.*, 1973; Willmore, 1976; Statistics Canada, 1978; Parry, 1980) assert that foreign affiliates, on average, are considerably larger than their indigenous competitors. Caves (1974a) suggests that a major explanation for this might be their access to scale

Table 7.1   Estimated Share of Production of US Affiliates and Market Structure in UK Manufacturing Industry

	Industrial Concentration[a] (1968)		
Share of Market (1973)	High (Employment or net output concentration ratio of 67%	Medium (Concentration ratios of 34–66%	Low (Concentration ratios of 33% or under)
Dominant (over 50%)	Breakfast cereals Cinematic films Commercial vehicles Computers Condensed milk Detergents Dog and cat foods Motor vehicles Pens and pencils Photocopying equipment Printing and typesetting machinery Sewing machines Vacuum cleaners	Construction equipment Office machinery Pens, pencils, crayons, etc. Portable power tools Toilet preparations and perfumery	
Substantial (30–50%)	Abrasives Coffee and coffee essence Lifts and escalators Petroleum products Potato crisps Razor blades and safety razors Rubber tyres Soups	Agricultural machinery Boilers Cameras Foundation garments Measuring and control instruments Safes, locks, latches, etc.	

Fairly important (15−29%)	Starch Washing machines Watches and clocks	Chemicals (general) Greetings cards Mining machinery Ophthalmic instruments Refrigeration machinery	Heating and ventilation apparatus Pumps, valves and compressors
	Cigarettes Man-made fibres Polishes Precious metals refining Synthetic resins (thermoplastics) Telegraph and telephone apparatus		

[a] Proportion of sales of products accounted for by the five largest enterprises.
Source: *Census of Production 1968*, Vol. 13 (London: Business Statistics Office), Table 5, p. 98, and J. H. Dunning, *US Industry in Britain* (London: Wilton House, 1976).

economies. Because of their wider options, MNEs are less likely than *de novo* domestic firms to set up affiliates of *below optimum* size. On the other hand, because they tend to operate in oligopolistic industries, and adopt follow-my-leader tactics, the number of *plants* in an industry may be too large to permit maximum efficiency (Kindleberger, 1969).[17] This has been particularly the case in Canada — where, for example, three-fifths of a group of 165 foreign affiliates reported their unit costs were typically higher than those of their parent plant (Safarian, 1969) — in Australia (Brash, 1966; Parry, 1974) and in several developing countries (Behrman, 1972; Vaitsos, 1974), for example, in the motor vehicle, petrochemical and pharmaceutical industries.

The evidence on the effects of MNEs on industrial concentration in host countries is mixed. In the case of Malaysia, Guatemala, Mexico, Brazil and Pakistan foreign direct investment appears to have led to an increase in seller concentration; but in the UK, Australia and Canada there is little or no correlation between the increase in concentration ratios and degree of foreign participation.[18] Using data from the Harvard Multinational Enterprise project, Knickerbocker (1976) found that industries in which 'no more than one or two' multinational manufacturing subsidiaries of US firms operated in 1950 usually contained five or more rival affiliates in 1970; and that there was a negative association between the number of MNE affiliates set up in the USA, West Germany, France and Italy between 1960 and 1970 and the change in the four-firm concentration ratio in these countries over this period.[19]

(b) *Product and process structure*
This will vary *inter alia* according to strategy of the investing firm and the role of the affiliate in this strategy. If the parent company is larger, and produces a wider range of products than the average indigenous firm and the affiliate duplicates these, then product differentiation may increase; on the other hand, if product rationalisation follows a takeover the reverse may happen.

Again, much depends on the original motive for the foreign investment, and the ease at which products currently imported can be bought from other plants of the enterprise. Because the parent company is domiciled elsewhere, however, one would expect affiliates to be rather more truncated in their operations than in the case of independent firms and, in this respect at least, for the spatial activities of MNEs to conform to the principle of comparative advantage. *Ceteris paribus*, one would expect rather less product differentiation and rather more product or process specialisation in interdependent than in independent affiliates. In the case of process specialisation it is possible that no country in which the MNE operates supplies the complete product, for example, IBM in Europe. Empirical studies (Eastman and Stykolt, 1967; Horst, 1972; Statistics Canada, 1978), in general, support the contention that the presence of

MNEs tends to increase product differentiation and promotional behaviour in host countries. Almost certainly the range of products produced by MNEs, as a whole, is greater than it would have been had their foreign markets been served by exports.

(c) *Barriers to competition*

It is difficult to generalise about the effect of the establishment of a foreign affiliate on barriers to entry or competition. On the one hand, because it has the resources to overcome entry barriers, an MNE may help lessen market imperfections, for example, by opening up new markets, sources of inputs, access to patents, trademarks, etc. On the other hand, some of the advantages of the foreign affiliate arise because it enters the local market in a truncated form, capitalising on the economies of scale that stem from the centralising functions which would otherwise have to be undertaken by a *de novo* indigenous firm (Caves, 1974a). This is likely to create new barriers for potential entrants, with the exception, perhaps, of other MNEs (Knickerbocker, 1976).

Other obstacles may be created by the strategy of the investing firm. If, for example, the affiliate is restricted in its activities, for example, with respect to products produced, R & D, exports, use of technology and trademarks, etc., to meet the global strategy of the foreign enterprise of which it is part, then, in the event of an entry by takeover barriers to competition may be raised. Finally, in the case of vertically integrated investments, it may become more difficult for *de novo* firms to acquire their inputs or establish new markets.[20]

(d) *Economic power and control*

With an independent affiliate, this again depends on the form of new investment. In the case of a takeover, the shift of ownership introduces a new source of economic power to the acquired firm, which, depending on its previous competitive position, may weaken or strengthen competition in the industry. The power will be greater with the size and market position of the investing firm, and, if used, will show itself in the behavioural tactics of the affiliate and in the reactions of competitive firms. It may also raise barriers to entry by making potential newcomers less able and more hesitant to compete.

Though the market power of an interdependent affiliate, relative to its indigenous competitors, might be less (simply because it is likely to be truncated in its activities, e.g. with respect to R & D), that of the parent company is more likely to be used to protect or advance the position of the affiliate than where its affiliates pursue an independent economic strategy. This is especially likely in the case of vertically integrated resource based and technology intensive industries. It is the impact of this kind of foreign direct investment on market structure which many developing, and smaller developed, countries are most concerned about.[21]

Second Stage Impact

(a)   *Behaviour of foreign affiliates*
The long-term impact on market structure will depend on the behaviour or conduct of the foreign affiliate; compared with that of a *de novo* indigenous firm, and the reactions of other firms, both indigenous and other foreign affiliates, to its presence or behaviour. We outline first how the behaviour of the affiliate may be distinctive, and then its effect on structure.

(i) *Efficiency effects*. It has been suggested that foreign affiliates, whether independent or interdependent, may possess certain advantages over local firms, which arise partly from their possession of certain non-transferable income generating assets, and partly because, as part of a larger enterprise, they are better geared to benefit from the international division of labour.[22] Where such gains are reinvested by the firm in cost-reducing techniques, product innovation, more intensive marketing, etc., or are passed on to the consumer in the form of lower prices, one would expect, over time, a new affiliate's share of the market to increase; this, except in the case of a takeover of a leading indigenous firm, will tend to lower concentration. Where an MNE invests to overcome tariffs, some of these gains may still be realised where the price of the locally produced product is lower than imports. But the gains will normally be less than the price of imports, net of tariffs, and may indeed be negative. The same result may occur where an affiliate is subsidised by other parts of the organisation of which it is part.

(ii) *Product and process structure*. Here we assume that the affiliate will behave differently than an indigenous firm, by producing a different range of products or engaging in process specialisation *because* it is part of an MNE. This arises partly through the branch plant effect, mentioned earlier, and partly because of its international character. Compared with an affiliate of a multilocation domestic firm, the resources involved in providing services on behalf of the group, for example, top level administration, management, finance, research and development, etc., will tend to be done *outside* the host country. This might lead to centralisation of higher order activities. Such spatial specialisation may well advance the goals of the parent company but, depending on the comparative advantage of resources offered by the countries in which the MNE operates, the activities of the local affiliate, cf. indigenous firms, may be dramatically different. Depending too on the types of markets served, the competitive position of the local industry in world markets may improve or deteriorate.

MNEs may create more or fewer linkages with domestic corporations in the countries in which they operate than their indigenous competitors. One of the frequent complaints of developing countries is that, all to frequently, the affiliates of MNEs engaged in the exploitation of raw materials export their secondary processing activities to the industrialised countries while in the manufacturing sector they make insufficient use of local sub-contractors. Some facts on both these issues are contained in two United Nations documents (UNIDO, 1978; UN, 1980). Both stress the role of host government policy in influencing the behaviour of MNEs in the disposition of product and process activities, particularly in their provision of the appropriate technological and educational infrastructure. More generally, however, there seems little doubt that MNEs can and do influence the international division of labour and resource allocation both within and between the countries in which they operate.

(iii) *Competitive tactics*. Compared with those practised by an indigenous firm, these may be different partly because the affiliate is part of a larger enterprise and partly because of its foreign ownership. On the first point, it is possible for it to draw upon the market power of the rest of the enterprise to assist it in its marketing strategy. This it can do by various devices which may have nothing to do with efficiency. These include predatory pricing,[23] use of 'deep pocket' advantages to promote non-price competition, tying arrangements, subsidising costs (e.g. of research and development), willingness to accept below normal profits or dividends, transfer price manipulation, etc.

Most of these devices are practised by conglomerates of all kinds and are not always against the public interest (Weston, 1973). However, there are two main differences in the case of MNEs.

First, because an MNE operates in a variety of economic and political environments, each with its particular advantages and disadvantages, it can better exploit these techniques; some — for instance, the manipulation of transfer prices — are largely (but not exclusively) unique to it. Second, whatever the effects on the distribution of the benefits arising from the operation of national companies, they are retained within the country of production; with the affiliates of the MNE, however, part of the benefits will accrue to the investing enterprise.

Of course, there are various practices of the parent company that will affect the long run prosperity of its affiliates, even though they may have no direct bearing on their day-to-day behaviour. Such practices, for instance, the management of international money and the allocation of export markets, may benefit the enterprise of which the affiliate is part, but not always the affiliate itself, or the country in which it operates. In some cases, too, the policies of home governments may affect the competitive position of affiliates.

Here, we are particularly concerned with competitive tactics which affect market structure. As a general proposition, one might expect that affiliates of MNEs will engage in more non-price competition than indigenous firms in the same industry. This is partly because the type and/or range of products of the parent company are likely to be different from those of firms in the host country and partly because part of the advantage of MNEs tends to lie in their possession of assets which encourage product differentiation (Caves, 1974a). This is confirmed by their above average expenditures both on innovative activities and on advertising to differentiate established products from those of their competitors.

To what extent, however, are such practices against the interests of the host economy, that is, in the sense they inhibit the achievement of its national goals? Here we distinguish between two kinds of practices.

(1) Practices undertaken by affiliates of MNEs that would normally be regarded as restrictive when undertaken by individual national firms, or by groups of independent firms of different nationality.

(2) Practices that would not normally be regarded as restrictive when undertaken by the above firms but when undertaken by an MNE may be so regarded.

(1) These include the whole gamut of practices of firms, which lead to lower efficiency, higher costs, inferior quality goods, unfair competition, increased barriers to entry, wasteful advertising, excessive product differentiation, and so on. They arise largely because the market structure, in at least one area of a firm's operations, allows it to earn above competitive profits in this area; these profits can then 'buy' these practices, any or all of which can either help to protect the firm's established market position or to force out its competitors, or to enable it to operate at less than maximum efficiency. Once identified, such conduct in MNEs or their affiliates can be dealt with in exactly the same way as when practised by national firms; the only difficulty is that the usual criteria by which the performance and behaviour of indigenous firms is evaluated is not necessarily appropriate in the case of affiliates of MNEs.

(2) These are more important in our present context. They do, however, pose two difficulties. One is to discover whether the practices are, in fact, restrictive; the other is to evaluate them in the light of the *total* effects of the affiliate's operations. Normally the practices in this category are restrictive only in so far as particular nations believe they gain less from the activities of affiliates than they should do. Among such practices are the territorial allocation of markets supplied by the affiliates, standardised pricing, limitations on use of technology, patents and trademarks, control over sourcing of inputs, and intra-corporate transfer pricing at other than arm's length prices.

Within a nation state, such actions on the part of multi-regional firms may not be thought restrictive, because the product of their activities is still retained domestically. But once they are engaged in across national boundaries, they take on a very different complexion. Yet, the fact remains that such behaviour often arises because of distortions in the international price structure of goods and services, which may inhibit the efficient division of labour, or because of differences in the incentives given by countries to MNEs to produce or market goods, or to earn income within their boundaries. It also reflects the efficiency of international economic institutions and policies, for example, the international patent, taxation and monetary systems. Some of the concerns of host countries towards MNEs could in fact be removed by the rationalisation or harmonisation of certain national economic policies and institutions.

But if it is right that governments should accept the legitimacy of the conduct of MNEs, these enterprises must accept that similar patterns of behaviour may produce different effects in different situations. Control of exports of an affiliate by the parent company may have the same effect as a barrier to market entry; control over the sourcing of inputs bought by affiliates may not always operate in the best interests of the affiliate; control over research and development activities may be a barrier of entry to innovation or to the development of local skills; control over trademarks and/or prices may be a barrier to competition; control over product or process strategy may inhibit a country developing an independent industry.[24]

All these practices are the stock in trade of MNEs whose affiliates are interdependent and geared to a common strategy. One cannot generalise on their effects on market structure; much will depend on the competitive position of the affiliates. But they undoubtedly add a greater element of flexibility to the behaviour of MNEs.

(b)   *Reaction of other firms*

Up to this point, we have been considering the distinctive behaviour of affiliates of MNEs. Consider now the consequences of this conduct. Two in particular may be singled out: first, the reaction of competitors of the MNE *outside* the host country; second, the reaction of indigenous firms *within* the host country. As to the first group of firms, the existing market structure is the crucial variable. If competitive firms in the investing country feel they can only protect their market position by 'follow my leader' tactics then, depending on form of entry and type of competition, while the share of production accounted for by foreign firms might increase, the concentration ratio might fall.

Perhaps, more to the point, is the effect on the size structure of firms in the industry and degree of capacity used. In research and/or capital intensive industries, where the market is small and the competitive structure of the investing country is duplicated, then no firm might be able to produce at its optimum level or range of output. This has certainly happened in Canada, Australia, New Zealand (Deane, 1971; Brash, 1972; Government of Canada, 1972; Parry, 1974), some of the smaller European economies and in many of the less developed countries.[25] Again, it is possible that, at one and the same time, concentration ratios and excess capacity may be increased. This is especially likely to follow from *defensive* investment, for example, investment induced by a tariff or other protective devices, or where the foreign affiliate fails to adapt its product or process technology to meet the local resource and market needs (Baranson, 1969).

Put rather differently, the influx of foreign firms could be accompanied by excessive product differentiation and proliferation of small-scale plants; in these circumstances, it might have been preferable if some of the affiliates, at least, had production agreements to manufacture each other's products under licence, even though they might be marketed separately.[26] In some cases, anti-trust legislation of the *home* country may thwart an efficient market structure, particularly where this can only be accomplished by a rationalisation of affiliates or a merger between them and local firms.

The reaction of domestic firms again will depend on their structure, efficiency and competitive strategy. Where scale economies are unimportant, the presence of foreign companies may stimulate competitors and an improved market structure may be attained. Where there are scale economies, then effective competition may only be possible through mergers or takeovers of indigenous firms which will tend to increase the concentration ratio. In the past, inward investment has had both effects. In the UK, for example, the reaction of the retailing business to Woolworths and that of Wilkinson Sword to Gillette are examples of the first case; that of Morris and Austin and later BMC and Leyland to Ford and Vauxhall is an example of the latter. Sometimes, indigenous firms may be driven out of business (e.g. in the UK typewriter and motor vehicle industries) while sometimes they respond by product or process diversification (e.g. in the electrical equipment industry). Again, much depends on the host government's policy, the causes of the penetration by foreign firms and its likely consequences.

Can one, then, generalise as to the likely effects of the entry of foreign affiliates into an industry? Can one predict the consequences according to types of MNEs or industries in which they are operating, or government policies pursued? Can one formulate testable hypotheses of how structure will be affected? Are affiliates likely to engage in restrictive practices more or less than indigenous firms? What should be the appropriate policy of governments once such practices are identified? Assuming a basically neutral government policy to foreign investment in general, one can, perhaps, put forward the following propositions:

(1)   *Ceteris paribus* the more multinational it is, the better an MNE is able to take advantage of a change in the economic environment facing any one of its operating units.

(2)   In practice, this will most affect behaviour of interdependent affiliates whenever there are advantages of horizontal specilisation or vertical or conglomerate integration. (Both these propositions concern the ability of the firm to take advantage of the international division of labour. Some industries will spawn independent affiliates,

and others interdependent affiliates. Also relevant is the geographical origin of the MNE and the countries which are host to its affiliates.)

(3) As production in industries becomes international, so do market structures. In particular, industries which are oligopolistic in domestic markets tend to duplicate this structure abroad (Knickerbocker, 1973). Conspicuous cases of this include the oil, motor vehicles, tyre, computer, pharmaceutical, non-ferrous metals and electrical equipment industries.[27]

(4) Affiliates of MNEs gain their economic power relative to indigenous firms (of a similar size and diversification to themselves) by being part of a larger and international organisation. The greater the diversification of MNEs relative to indigenous firms, the more the possibility arises that the affiliate will engage in competitive tactics other than would arise if it were an independent firm.

(5) The behaviour of the MNE is partly in response to differential government policies, which will influence its ability and/or willingness to operate or earn profits in different countries. Because of these differential policies they have a greater inducement to switch resources around.

(6) The concern of host governments towards affiliates of MNEs stems from the way they affect both resource allocation and the distribution of the proceeds of the finished output. This distribution may also affect market structure in the future.[28]

(7) In some cases, affiliates might engage in excessive product differentiation, not always adjusting their range of output or technology of production to smaller markets. The market structure of investing firms is often exported; in circumstances of capital intensive firms operating in oligopolistic markets, this might result in overcapacity.

(8) Once established, affiliates of MNEs may be able to create barriers to entry to *de novo* firms by dint of the control of their parent company over markets, sources of inputs and other competitive (or anticompetitive) strategies.

V

We now consider possible policies aimed at achieving the market structure which authorities believe will best meet their economic and social goals.[29] Once it is established that the behaviour of affiliates of MNEs is different from that of indigenous companies, what, if any, change in policy is required on the part of host governments?

Unilateral Policies

We shall consider, first, *unilateral* type policies of host governments. These will be directed towards advancing economic and social objectives, and it is by these criteria that the effects of inward direct investment will be judged. Sometimes, the achievement of goals may be in conflict with each other: thus foreign affiliates may be more efficient than indigenous competitors, but may worsen the balance of payments or exacerbate inflation. In taking action to remedy these effects, care must be taken lest this is accomplished at the expense of more fundamental goals. In the last resort, the effects of MNEs on market structures cannot be evaluated in isolation from their other consequences.

The second point concerns the assumptions about the efficiency of broader macroeconomic policies. It is possible, at least, that the contribution of MNEs to national governments is inhibited by inappropriate or misguided government policies. Firms respond to economic signals. If their behaviour is unacceptable, this could be because the signals are wrongly set. For example, exchange rate policies, competition policies, import protection and/or substitution policies, employment policies, fiscal and monetary policies, regional policies, all induce certain reactions by firms. In certain circumstances, policies that may be appropriate in dealing with national firms may be inappropriate in dealing with MNEs. Whether, in the light of the overall effects of MNEs, governments change their policies or cause the MNEs to alter their behaviour depends on which cause of action is thought to best meet their primary goals. But there is no *a priori* reason to suppose that one rather than the other is correct. In other cases, the policies (or the machinery to administer them) may have been inappropriate in the first place; history is littered with examples of second, or third best, or simply bad government policies. Here, there is some evidence to suggest that MNEs are better placed to benefit from these policies than are indigenous firms.[30] Modify the policies, and part of the problem of governments will disappear.

The third point concerns the effectiveness of existing institutions or markets to allocate resources effectively. It is perhaps worth recalling that the MNE largely owes its existence to the imperfection of microeconomic markets. *Defensive* investment is largely prompted by artificially created barriers to trade; *aggressive* investment often relies on the ownership of knowledge and/or markets being the exclusive property of the investing firm, at least over a certain time period. And, as has been said, much investment takes place among oligopolists, with behaviour related specifically to this form of market distortion. Anything that helps to reduce these imperfections may aid economic welfare.

Among the general policies of host governments which affect market structure and behaviour, some are specifically directed to this end; others incidentally affect it. Of the latter, two kinds might be mentioned. One relates to industrial policy as a whole and basically concerns itself with the allocation of resources between industrial sectors, for example, which sorts of industry should a country be encouraged to develop? How much diversification or specialisation should there be? (Behrman, 1972). These are the sorts of problem with which the regional blocs like the EEC, the Latin American Free Trade Area and the Andean Group are currently grappling. Industrial policy does have implications for affiliates of MNEs since (1) the viable size and structure of an industry will both affect and be affected by the size of its constituent firms and their product strategy, and (2) the component of foreign ownership will vary between industries.

The second type of policy relates to the market structure of particular industries, which is framed to encourage both economic efficiency and an equitable distribution of the proceeds between agents of production and consumers within particular industries. There may be other goals, for example, ensuring an adequate choice of products without excessive differentiation; encouraging a healthy sector of small firms; seeing that the greater part of production remains in the hands of indigenous firms, and so on. It may be felt that such decisions could be left to private enterprise in a competitive situation, and where social and private costs and benefits do not diverge a great deal. In some cases, however, this will not be so, and governments may wish to modify the behaviour of firms.

It is not the purpose of this chapter either to describe or to evaluate the ways in which governments might seek to achieve their objectives. Suffice to say that in market economies and in a *static* context most industrial policies tend to be directed to (1) promoting effective competition, (2) where, for technological or other reasons, perfect competition cannot exist, to creating a market structure that will ensure that resources are allocated as nearly as possible as if it did exist, and (3) in both (1) and (2) maximising the net *social* benefits of actions of firms.

In a *dynamic* situation there are the more difficult problems of allocating the right amount of investment in growth and the financing of innovation and the production of knowledge. Currently, most governments not only protect firms which produce commercial knowledge from competitors, gaining the benefits without payment; they also actively finance research and development.

When MNEs are introduced into the picture, then, depending on the distinctiveness of their behaviour, more specific policies may be required. These are usually of two kinds. First, governments might direct action to foreign firms by means of *persuasive* or *mandatory* policies to affect either the conditions of entry or their behaviour once they are established. On entry, certain assurances or constraints might be required of firms both as to the form of their activity and their conduct: some will be to directly affect market structure, and some the ability of MNEs for avoiding taxation by transfer price manipulation. Still other forms of behaviour might be conditioned by extra-territorial policies of home governments, for example, anti-trust legislation; here unilateral policies will be inadequate and the difficulties can only be resolved by agreements or negotiations between governments.

Governments possess various options to rid themselves of these kinds of practices, or to mitigate their impact. Most of them involve a cost to firms, in so far as they consider it in their own interests to engage in them. Whether or not firms are prepared to accept the costs without altering their behaviour depends on whether or not they are earning above normal profits. If they are forced to modify their conduct, this may have both direct and indirect consequences on the achievement of the primary goals of governments, and it is in this light that all policies must be looked at.

The second approach of governments is to control the activities of foreign firms, or the distribution of the value added produced by them, by encouraging more indigenous competition. Thus local firms may be favoured with government contracts or fiscal incentives; they may be helped to improve their efficiency, subsidised in their research and development, supported in management training schemes, advised on export markets, prompted to rationalise their activities by merger, product specialisation, and so on. In some cases such policies may be justified, even in the absence of foreign investment; in others, much will depend on the extent to which the strong position of the foreign affiliates is due to their higher efficiency (or that of the enterprises of which they are part) or to their monopoly power (particularly that part associated with multi-nationality). If the former, action should be confined to gaining a larger share of the economic rent of the affiliates: if the latter, to improving their efficiency. In any event, any form of permanent protection *per se* to domestic producers may, on *economic* grounds, be difficult to justify.

Finally, in the context of the present discussions, it is necessary to look into alternatives open both to governments and MNEs. Clearly, governments want to know if the affiliates of MNEs are contributing as much as they might do to their economic and social goals; they also want to know the cost of obtaining the benefits they confer by alternative routes, for example, borrowing capital, licensing know-how, buying management, freeing imports, etc. Assuming that these benefits cannot be more cheaply obtained, then the aim must be to minimise the economic rent earned by affiliates. This may be accomplished by various routes, each of which has its costs and benefits (Streeten, 1974).

Bilateral, Regional and Multilateral Policies

In some cases, individual countries may not be able to take effective measures to achieve their goals. Their domestic markets may be too small to allow the countervailing power to large firms in the form of new competition. This is where a harmonisation of procedure policies and legislation between countries enters the picture. Sometimes agreements need to be negotiated and disputes adjudicated at an inter-government level; in these cases unilateral policies are obviously no longer adequate (Behrman, 1970). Various suggestions have been made of the ways in which anti-trust standards towards MNEs may be harmonised (Wertheimer, 1971; Timberg, 1973) but any kind of international convention, much less any uniformity of legislation, seems a long way off. Some progress has, however, been made in various UN bodies.[31] At a regional level, both in the EEC and, to a lesser extent, in LAFTA and the Andean Group, we are seeing the emergence of a concerted policy towards competition and restrictive practices, but again progress is slow, and, even where this may lead to a more efficient allocation of resources by MNEs, it brings with it its own distributional and non-economic problems. Finally, included in the OECD guidelines, are several clauses covering industrial corporate behaviour; and complaints about MNEs breaking the spirit or the letter of these guidelines have already been brought before the Committee of International Investments and Multinational Enterprises.[32]

VI

In these concluding pages, we will examine how far the propositions so far formulated help us to understand the impact of US affiliates of US enterprises on UK market structure and the conduct of indigenous firms.

Market Structure

(a) *Size of firms*
In a study on the impact of foreign direct investment and on the UK economy conducted in the 1960s, Max Steuer and his colleagues concluded that foreign firms in the UK had not significantly affected the size structure of British industry, and that there was no evidence that in the industries in which they were most strongly represented concentration ratios were increasing faster than the average (Steuer *et al.*, 1973).

Some later work, conducted by the present author on US affiliates in the UK, confirms and extends these findings (Dunning, 1976; Globerman, 1979). In 1973 affiliates of US firms were, on average, larger than their indigenous competitors and slightly more concentrated in their size structure. As Figure 7.1 shows, the proportion of employment accounted for by the largest US affiliates has increased since 1939; on the other hand, there is no reason to suppose that US investment has led to higher concentration ratios, except perhaps in the motor vehicles industry. In some sectors, US affiliates have increased their share of the market, yet concentration ratios have fallen, for example, pharmaceuticals, industrial instruments. In others, retaliatory measures by British competitors have reduced their share, yet concentration ratios have risen, for example, potato crisps, toilet tissues, foundation garments.

Occasionally, inward US investment has added to the problem of

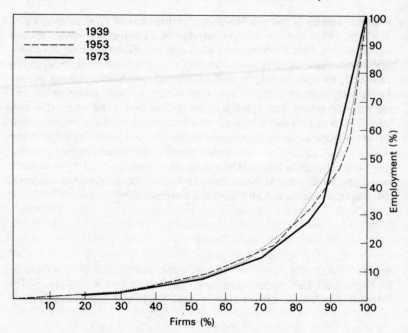

Figure 7.1. *Lorenz Curves of Employment in US Affiliates in UK Manufacturing Industry 1939, 1953, 1973*

over-capacity in British industry due to follow-my-leader tactics of the investing firms. This was the case of aluminium semi-manufacturers,[33] pharmaceuticals, man-made fibres and banking in the 1960s. Often these are industries in which there are sizeable economies of scale for the firm but not for individual production units. In general, US affiliates have injected more competition into the British economy, as in the detergents, tobacco and hotel industries, but, in a few cases, an early position of market domination has been maintained, for example, Champion Sparking Plugs in the sparking plug industry and Kodak in the film processing industry. In its evidence to the Monopolies Commission in 1966, Kodak asserted that its position arose primarily from the benefits of scale economies but the Commission concluded that tariff protection was a no less important factor.

(b)   *Mergers involving US firms*
About one-quarter of US manufacturing affiliates in Britain originated through a takeove of, or merger with, a British company. Since 1960 about a score of cases involving foreign firms have been referred either to the Monopolies Commission[34] or to the Industrial Reorganisation Corporation (IRC):[35] all but one have been allowed, and all but the large ones

unconditionally. Perhaps most welcome among these have been those involving a British firm in economic difficulty where an acquisition, by providing hope of revival, has protected the competitiveness of the industry. Such was the situation when Chrysler invested in Rootes in 1966, a takeover that was not even referred to the Monopolies Commission. Another interesting case was the acquisition of Smiths Food Group, producers of potato crisps, by General Mills in 1967. Earlier, hints had been given that a takeover of Smiths by Imperial Tobacco would not have been well received by the Commission. It was hoped that the acquisition would provide additional competition to Imperial which already had an entrenched market position through its Golden Wonder brand.[36]

Other examples of purchases of British companies by US firms which have strengthened their competitive position include American Tobacco's acquisition of Gallahers in 1968[37] (*contra* Imperial Tobacco); the purchase by Revlon of Berk Pharmaceuticals in 1971 (*contra* Roche); and the acquisition of Lansil, a small firm producing cellulosic fibres in 1962 by Chemstrand (*contra* Courtaulds). An example of a takeover which failed to resuscitate an ailing UK firm was Litton's purchase of Imperial Typewriter Company in 1966.

During its lifetime the IRC, set up by the Labour government in 1966 to aid the restructuring of British industry,[38] also encouraged mergers involving foreign firms. These included support for the purchase of Worthington Simpson, a pump company, by a US concern in preference to a large Scottish company.

(c) *Mergers involving British firms*

There have been several examples of mergers of British companies in retaliation to the presence of US subsidiaries. Most of these have been *horizontal* mergers – the most famous perhaps being the merger between BMC and Leyland to counteract competition from the US car affiliates, and of a group of British computer and industrial instrument firms to form International Computers Ltd to curb the domination of the US computer companies, particularly IBM. In both cases, financial support was given by the IRC or the Ministry of Technology. The Corporation also supported *vertical* mergers. Again, the car industry, in the form of the merger of Pressed Steel and BMC in 1966, offers the best example. Pressed Steel was worried lest Chrysler-Rootes, which had previously been one of its leading customers, should decide to buy its car bodies from elsewhere or produce them itself; moreover, BMC wanted to protect its own source of supply. In recommending the merger should be allowed, the Monopolies Commission observed that there was some advantage in Pressed Steel being taken over by a British rather than by a foreign company.

(d) *Product differentiation*

Two reports of the Monopolies Commission dealing respectively with detergents (1966d) and breakfast cereals (1973a), had something to say about the effect of US affiliates on product differentiation. In neither case was price considered an effective weapon of competition.

The ready-to-eat breakfast cereal market, except for one British firm, is dominated by North American affiliates, and competition is found to be largely in marketing techniques. When, five years earlier, the Price Commission (1978a) investigated a leading firm in the industry it concluded that 'no change of substance has occurred since 1973 to affect the competitive situation within this industry. Development of retailers' own brands, which appeared, at that time, to be a possible source from which price competition might emerge, has been contained at a modest level. Competition still tends to operate through the promotion of existing products and the introduction of new ones rather than through price' (para. 4.7).

In detergents, the major share of the market is held by one foreign owned and one domestic multinational company. In investigating this latter duopoly, the Monopolies Commission criticised both firms' advertising and promotion policies on the grounds that they acted as a barrier to entry of producers and were wasteful expenditure, thus supporting high profits.[39] Both the firms in the duopoly were investigated later by the Price Commission (1978c, 1978d) which recognised 'that strong competition between major retailers, combined with the emergence of their own brand products and the growing price consciousness of the consumer, are starting to produce real competition within the soaps and detergents market. As a result, advertising by manufacturers now plays a less important part in maintaining their sales than promotion by temporary price offers' (1978d, para. 5.9; see also paras 3.6, 3.19, 3.20, 3.58, 3.59). The Price Commission (1978d, para. 3.34) also drew attention to the longer-term potential for increased competition in the industry through new entrants. These could either be existing detergent manufacturers from other countries or the diversification into detergents by firms already established in the UK. The existence of such potential entrants, the Commission suggested, might already be constraining the behaviour of the duopolists.

Nevertheless, there are probably many industries where the generally established high levels of promotional and marketing expenditure represent major barriers to entry. In such cases, only firms already estabished in other geographical and/or product markets are likely to be able to assemble the finance and expertise to effectively enter a market where product differentiation is a crucial factor. This was exemplified by the successful, but more expensive than expected, entry into the UK toothpaste market by Procter and Gamble with its *Crest* product in the mid-1970s (Price Commission, 1978e, paras 2.11, 3.19, 5.19, 6.6). It should be recorded, however, that the Price Commission did suggest that, during the 1970s, media costs in the toothpaste industry declined somewhat in real terms and that there was some growth in price competition, especially in the form of 'temporary price reductions' (1978e, para. 6.7).

Behaviour

Evidence is fragmentary on the behaviour of US affiliates in the UK. Their performance and growth records have generally outshone those of their competitors, though the profitability gap appears to have narrowed in the 1970s (Dunning, 1976).[40] Part of this higher profitability now seems to have been due to the ability of the pioneering US affiliates to earn high economic rents, due both to a lack of competition and to parent protection, for example, in the pharmaceutical industry (Sainsbury, 1967), and also to the undercharging by parent companies for research and overhead services.

Some of the earlier reports of the Monopolies Commission involving US affiliates asserted that this latter benefit was one of the most substantial which might arise from US direct investment in the UK.[41] On the other hand, it appears that, in several cases, these benefits were not passed on to the British consumer. Among the US affiliates charged by the Commission with monopolistic or quasi-monopolistic pricing were Champion Sparking Plugs, Kodak and Procter and Gamble. Of Champion, for example, the Commission said 'it is an efficient company whose main fault has been to reserve for itself too high a proportion of the rewards of efficiency'.[42]

There is little reason to suppose that the UK has suffered as a result of export restrictions imposed by foreign MNEs. Indeed, US affiliates, in general, export a higher proportion of their output than their competitors, even when normalised for size and industrial structure of firm. This could change in the future as one of the original motives for investment, the shortage of dollars, no longer applies. Moreover, there are many more foreign production bases of US MNEs than there once were. As firms seek to integrate their European activities, much will depend on the UK's competitive ability.[43] For example, the effect on UK exports of permitting the US company Fruehauf to take full control of its UK joint venture Crane Fruehauf was a major concern of the Monopolies Commission during its investigation of the proposed merger. An important reason for this interest was Fruehauf's proposal to set up 'Fruehauf Europe' to integrate and rationalise its European marketing and sourcing (Monopolies Commission, 1977, paras 85, 86, 87, 106, 108, 283, 420).

Data on research and development suggest that US affiliates undertake at least as much (as a proportion of their sales) as their indigenous competitors (US Tariff Commission, 1973). In the UK 180 of the 270 leading US affiliates had local research and development laboratories in 1970. Two years earlier, the affiliates that reported research and development activities claimed that they made 7,789 products not produced by their parent companies in the USA. But resources are oriented towards adapting existing knowledge to meet the ends of the local market. In general, the MNE has probably speeded up the international diffusion of new technology (Mansfield, 1974),[44] but whether it adds to the technological viability of countries host to its affiliates is less certain. There are exceptions in the UK, where some fundamental research is done. Cases have been reported on the transfer back to the United States of research and development activities (Dunning and Steuer, 1969), but these are very few and far between. The question of research and development has frequently come up in merger discussions involving foreign firms. In the discussion of the proposed takeover of the British Amalgamated Dental Company by Dentists Supply Company of New York in 1968, the company confirmed that the research establishments would continue in existence (Monopolies Commission, 1966c).

The pricing behaviour of affiliates of MNEs has been touched upon in various reports of the Monopolies Commission or Prices and Incomes Board (see those already quoted and Prices and Incomes Board, 1968, 1969).

The Monopolies Commission (1977, paras 285, 389) also believed it likely that the pricing policy of Crane Fruehauf would be changed by Fruehauf were it to gain full control of the company. Perhaps of greatest interest, however, is the report dealing with the supply of Chlordiazepoxide and Diazepan (Monopolies Commission, 1973b). In this case, it was calculated that in the period between 1966 and 1972 the Swiss-owned company Hoffman-La Roche earned 76 per cent of its income from its British affiliate Roche Products Ltd in the form of a high transfer price charged for the raw material imported by the affiliate from its parent company; and that, if this amount was added to the actual profits recorded by the British affiliate, the return on capital employed earned would have been over 70 per cent.

How widespread such transfer pricing manipulations are is difficult to say.[45] Neither do such manipulations always work against the interests of the UK. The underpricing of insulators bought from the parent company of Champion Sparking Plugs in the 1950s helped to swell the profits of the affiliate. In the case of butyl rubber, produced by Esso Chemical Ltd (a US affiliate), which buys most of its main raw material, isobutylene, from the Esso Petroleum Company, the company informed the Prices and Incomes Board that the transfer price was less than if the material had been bought on the open market, and, from other sources, the Board confirmed that this was so.

Policy

The policy of the UK government has been generally liberal and non-discriminatory towards foreign affiliates of MNEs once they are established in the UK.[46] Prior to the entry of larger firms, by way of a takeover or merger, certain restrictions are sometimes required, but it is difficult to see how these could be enforced. Only very rarely have takeovers been disallowed, and in the past most controls and/or requirements have related to the need to preserve foreign exchange.[47]

This is not to say that the British government has been neutral towards the effects of foreign controlled companies on market structure, and especially the growing participation of foreign companies in certain sectors. But the response has mainly been to encourage countervailing power and general competition, rather than to curb the activities of foreign affiliates. However, it is highly likely that some potential US bidders for British companies have been frightened off at an early stage by the likelihood that the bid would be referred to the Monopolies Commission (Kanter and Sugerman, 1970).

The most noticeable recognition by the Labour government (1964–70) of the possible impact of foreign affiliates on British industrial and market structures was in the setting up of the IRC in 1966, to encourage the reorganisation of industry and to promote or assist the establishment of development of any industrial enterprise. From the start, it was inclined to look favourably on mergers involving foreign firms.

The IRC recognises the potential importance of mergers across national boundaries and growing role played by the ME in the principal markets of the world. An improvement in the structure of British industry is, at the present time, the IRC's principal task, but there is no doubt that the IRC will increasingly have to consider supporting schemes designed to create industrial groupings on an international scale.

During its life, the IRC's activities were involved with three groups of industries:

(1) Those whose production technology was such that the minimum viable size of plant was very large indeed and getting larger, for example, computers, airframes, some chemical installations, and telecommunications. For the UK to remain competitive in world markets, its units had to be large and efficient. But in all of the industries quoted, prior to the appearance of the IRC, the leading firms were smaller than their most prominent US competitors.

(2) Fragmented industries in which there were a large number of small companies using obsolete equipment, or inefficient management and facing bankruptcy. Included in this group were cotton and wool textiles, machine tools, paper and board and many engineering sectors.

(3) Industries requiring special attention, for example, strategic industries. Among these was the ball and roller bearing industry referred to the IRC in 1968. In that year, total production of bearings was

£70m. of which £15m. was exported. There were six major manufacturers, three of which were wholly owned foreign affiliates, that is, Skefco Ball Bearing Company (a Swedish firm), British Timken (US) and Fafnir (US). For technological reasons the IRC felt that rationalisation should be encouraged to advance export markets. It decided, however, against allowing further participation by SKF on the grounds, first, that this particular MNE, acting in the interest of its own efficiency, might well find it advantageous to rationalise its production methods, locate its R & D, buy its raw materials and machine tools and direct its marketing policy in a way that would not necessarily benefit the British economy, and, second, if the deal were allowed, in due course there was a genuine possibility that eventually there might be no viable British-owned company in the industry.

For the most part, however, the IRC was more concerned with helping British companies to compete more effectively against large foreign companies in international markets. This was most clearly seen in the electrical and electronics industry. In 1967, the IRC supported the merger between Elliott Automation and English Electric to form AEI, Britain's largest electrical firm, and in the following year between General Electric and AEI to create the General Electric–English Electric Company. The rationale of this latter merger was to provide more effective competition to the giant US firm ITT (and its British subsidiary Standard Telephones and Cables) in international markets. It also helped pave the way, later in 1968, for the formation of International Computers Ltd (ICL), which brought together International Computers and Tabulators (ICT), the major British computer firm, the data processing interests of English Electric, investment and future co-operation of Plessey, and $36 million of government support.[48] This important reorganisation created the largest non-American computer group in the world and provided a direct challenge to the power of IBM (Kanter and Sugerman, 1970).

One criticism of the approach adopted by the Monopolies Commission in its investigations of the performance and behaviour of US and other foreign affiliates is that it has tended to use the same criteria of evaluation as it has used for indigenous firms. In no case, to our knowledge, has the Commission examined the performance and conduct of the affiliate in the context of that of the group as a whole, or treated foreign affiliates differently from indigenous firms. In consequence, it has never considered the relationship between profitability and payments made for centralised research, development and administrative facilities. Neither has it studied the activities of the parent company or other affiliates in as much as their behaviour may well influence the conduct and performance of the British affiliate (Hodges, 1974).

The Price Commission, however, has interested itself in these matters.

For example, in its report on a leading foreign affiliate in the starch indus- try – CPC (UK) Ltd (1978b, paras 4.14 and 4.15) it makes use of various performance and efficiency indices to compare the Manchester CPC plant with its other European and US plants.

Again, it does not appear that the Commission has much interested itself in the problem of intra-group transactions at other than arm's-length prices. In the case of the Roche enquiry, for example (Monopolies Com- mission, 1973b), while the Commission recommended that the prices of the two main products supplied by the British affiliate of the Swiss com- pany, viz. librium and valium, should be reduced, it did not tackle the transfer-pricing problem (which had been the cause of the high profits originating from the affiliates in the first place) directly. Indeed, only a few countries (e.g. the USA) have a clear-cut policy in the important area of the operations of MNEs.

The Price Commission does seem to have made a practice of collecting evidence on the internal transactions of MNEs it has investigated (e.g. 1978d, paras 4.24–4.26 and 1978b, paras 5.22–5.24).

It is also noteworthy that none of the early Monopoly Commission or Prices and Incomes Board reports, dealing with industries in which US affiliates are well represented, had anything to say about the explicit or implicit control of export markets exerted by the parent companies. This practice has created considerable concern in many other countries[49] but, like the transfer pricing issue, provoked little reaction in the UK, possibly because the export performance of US affiliates in the UK compares favourably with that of the indigenous competitors. As has been noted earlier, the Monopolies Commission report on the proposed merger between Fruehauf and Crane Fruehauf showed much more concern with this and other aspects of the behaviour of MNEs (Monopolies Commission, 1977).

VII

Conclusions

A country's reaction to the effects of affiliates of MNEs on its industrial and competitive policy will vary according to the nature of the impact, the structure and potential structure of the market, its bargaining position with foreign firms, and its ability to extract the highest efficiency and maximum economic rent from the affiliates. In some industries, and in some countries, the impact of foreign affiliates will be small; their presence and practices may be easily absorbed. In other cases the impact may be dramatic, due either to the structure of the industry or to differences in behaviour which host governments are unable to tolerate.

Policies will vary according to the ability of governments and the chances of success. In the UK there has been more success in promoting countervailing power to foreign affiliates than in most continental European countries; a more intelligent general policy towards monopolies and restrictive practices might also explain success. There may be less reason for the company to engage in transfer pricing in some countries or adversely affect market shares. Much depends on comparative fiscal policies and competitive position (not least the valuation of currency); again, behaviour reflects government policy.

In their policies towards MNEs, it is important that host governments should look at the whole enterprise of which the affiliate is part; they have to assess their total contribution and the effects of a change in policy on that contribution. They need also to evaluate alternative ways of acquiring the benefits which foreign investment may bring. They should ensure that, in the light of the presence of foreign affiliates, their general macroeconomic policies are consistent with the national good. In this connection there is fairly widespread agreement among economists that the tariff policy of developed countries and import substitution policies of less developed countries in general inhibit the efficient allocation of resources by MNEs.

Having said all this, it must be admitted that the normal behaviour of affiliates may not always be in the host country's best interests; and that the power of government to control operations, apart from nationalising them, is limited by their knowledge, size and bargaining strength, and by their ability to promote effective competition. Here, the role of direct negotiation and affiliates becomes more important. In smaller or less prosperous countries this may be difficult, which is why combined action (e.g. the Andean Pact, Organisation of Petroleum Exporting Countries, etc.) is being sought as an alternative, though often takeovers or mergers involving immediate neighbours are less popular than those between domestic and foreign firms.

Notes: Chapter 7

1 See, for example, Bain (1968), Scherer (1971), Yamey (1973) and Williamson (1975).
2 With the exception of the work of Caves (1971, 1974a) and some scholars working in the field of foreign direct investment, for example, Steuer *et al.* (1973) and Parry (1980).
3 One firm is now multi-product, a second is multi-market, a third is multi-national, a forth is multi-plant, a fifth is multi-process and a sixth is part of a conglomerate; because of this the options for strategy in the British detergent market, for example, in investment, pricing, marketing and location policies are widened.
4 The textbooks usually identify three key determinants of market structure (viewed from the perspective of a participating firm), viz. (1) the level of market concentration, (2) the relative market position of the individual firm and (3) the barriers facing new competitors wishing to enter the market. It is the interaction between the MNE and these variables with which this chapter will be particularly concerned. See also Connor and Mueller (1977) and Newfarmer and Mueller (1975).

5   Made possible by what Kojima (1978) calls 'pseudo' economies of scale, that is, those captured entirely by the firm practising such economies.

6   In theory, these payments may be negative, and in exceptional circumstances may exceed the direct price paid.

7   See Chapter 13.

8   Of course, the welfare of the home country may also be considerably affected by the extent to which its own firms are multinational. See, for example, Chapter 12.

9   In this connection, see an interesting paper by Hufbauer and Chilas (1974).

10 Although governments may introduce discriminatory policies against the affiliates of MNEs which might nullify these advantages.

11 Although domestic MNEs will also have wider options than domestic non-MNEs.

12 Especially Chapter 2.

13 See Chapter 4.

14 See, for example, Parry (1975), Lall (1980), Houston and Dunning (1976) and Swedenborg (1979).

15 Other studies on the relationship between foreign participation and concentration include Rosenbluth (1970), Rhader (1973), Steuer *et al.* (1973), Ghosh (1975), Buckley and Dunning (1976), Gorecki (1976) and Evans (1977).

16 For a discussion of the implications of conglomerate internalisation by MNEs, see Kojima (1978). For an analysis of the relationship between size of firm and the economies of internalisation see *inter alia* Buckley and Casson (1976), Teece (1979) and Calvet (1980).

17 A quote from the recent US Tariff Commission (1973) report is particularly relevant here.

> The entry and subsequent activity of a single large US MNE is frequently beneficial to all and may not disrupt local markets, but the fact is that several US MNEs often enter all at once. This simultaneous entry into an area of market opportunity is characteristic of oligopolistic competition in the USA in which the competing large enterprises employ similar methods of analysing and exploiting new investment opportunities. One of their primary objectives is to maintain their share of the market, with the result that they tend to respond quickly to each other's strategic moves. This has happened in aluminium, tyres, hotels, synthetic fibres, and agricultural machinery. It may result in over capacity, labour shortages, and higher wage levels.

18 See particularly Steuer *et al.* (1973).

19 For the USA the correlation coefficient was -0.21 and for the three European countries -0.25. Both coefficients were significant at the 5 per cent level.

20 The aluminium industry is a classic case. On the other hand, Vernon (1968) believes that the trend to vertical integration might be decelerated by governments intruding into the affairs of MNEs.

21 This issue is explored in detail in Newfarmer and Mueller (1975) and Connor and Mueller (1977). For a study of the market power of MNEs in the electrical industry see Newfarmer (1978).

22 Which explains why most country and industry studies reveal that foreign affiliates record a higher total or labour productivity than their indigenous counterparts. For a survey of some of the field studies of the 1970s, see Parry (1980).

23 A classic example of the 1920s was the American Tobacco Corporation's attempt to get control of the cigarette market in Puerto Rico by lowering the price of Lucky Strike cigarettes from 18 to 12 cents. The losses resulting from the price cut were covered by profits earned elsewhere in the enterprise.

24   But, as we have already seen, these practices can operate in the reverse way; affiliates can overcome as well as create barriers.

25   Parry's study of the chemical industry in Australia is particularly illuminating in this connection. In Europe, over-capacity in the aluminium industry in the 1960s owed much to the activities of American affiliates. For a discussion of the role of MNEs in affecting the structure of the computer and pharmaceutical industries in the OECD area, see Michalet (1980) and Dunning, Burstall and Lake (1981).

26   As, for example, in the case of some of the tyre companies.

27   For an examination of the market structure of companies engaged in world production see Vernon (1977) and Dunning and Pearce (1981).

28   It also affects the way in which international division of labour mentioned in (1) and (2) affects a country.

29   This section should be read in conjunction with Chapter 14.

30   Here we are referring to general policies not those designed specifically to affect the behaviour of MNEs.

31   Notably UNCTAD, in the formulation of guidelines to governments of developing countries in their dealings with MNEs (UNCTAD, 1973), and the UN Centre on Transnational Corporations in the preparation of a code of conduct for TNCs, which will embrace a section on competition and restrictive practices.

32   Cases in which MNEs have been involved include Continental Can (1973), Commercial Solvents (1974), United Brands (1978) and Hoffman-La Roche (1979). For further details see Robinson (1979).

33   For further details see Prices and Incomes Board (1967).

34   Any foreign takeover affecting more than one-third of the market or exceeding £5m. must be approved by the Department of Trade and Industry. If in doubt, the Department may refer the case to the Monopolies Commission.

35   This represents less than 10 per cent of all cases so referred.

36   Examples of this type of acquisition, or part acquisition, by foreign firms of continental European companies include the General Electric's purchase of Machine Bull in France and that of Lepper (the third ranking German chemical company) by a Swedish enterprise. On the other hand, the French government prevented the American purchase of a textile company, preferring to see it go bankrupt rather than fall into US hands (Behrman, 1970).

37   This was an interesting acquisition, as it is believed the prime reason for the American company's bid was to prevent another US company from gaining this foothold in the UK market.

38   But disbanded in 1970.

39   In the words of the Commission: 'The crux of the public interest issues was in the way in which competition in advertising had displaced competition in price and how to increase the area of price competition' (see Monopolies Commision, 1966d).

40   See also Chapter 5.

41   See particularly Monopolies Commission (1963, 1966b, c, d).

42   Monopolies Commission (1963, para. 1005).

43   See Chapter 5.

44   This was accepted by the Monopolies Commission in their investigation into the British film processing and sparking plug industries.

45   For a general review of the transfer pricing issue see Lall (1973) and Plasschaert (1979).

46   The UK is signatory to the OECD Guidelines on Behaviour for MNEs which urges host governments to give equal treatment to domestic and foreign owned enterprises.

47   For the present position see *Britain. An Official Handbook* (London: HMSO, 1980).

48 Giving the government a 10 per cent holding in the new company. For further details of the work of the IRC, see references at end of this chapter.
49 See, for example, various UNCTAD publications, but notably UNCTAD (1973).

References

Arndt, H. (1973), 'Multinational corporations and economic power', in G. Bertin (ed.), *La Croissance de la Grande Firme Multinationale* (Paris: Centre National de la Recherche Scientifique).

Bain, J. (1968), *Industrial Organisation* (New York: Wiley).

Baranson, J. (1969), *Industrial Technologies for Developing Economies* (New York: Praeger).

Behrman, J. (1970), *National Interests and the Multinational Enterprise* (Englewood Cliffs, NJ: Prentice-Hall).

Behrman, J. (1972), *The Role of International Companies in Latin America: Autos and Petrochemicals* (Lexington, Mass.: Lexington Books).

Bergsten, C. F., Horst, T., and Moran, T. H. (1978), *American Multinationals and American Interests* (Washington, DC: Brookings Institute).

Brash, D. T. (1966), *American Investment in Australian Industry* (Sydney: Australian National University Press).

Buckley, P. J., and Casson, M. (1976), *The Future of the Multinational Enterprise* (London: Macmillan).

Buckley, P. J., and Dunning, J. H. (1976), 'The industrial structure of US direct investment in the UK', *Journal of International Business*, vol. VII (Fall/Winter).

Calvet, A. L. (1980), 'Markets and Hierarchies. Towards a Theory of International Business', PhD thesis, Sloan School of Management, Boston, Mass.

Caves, R. E. (1971), 'International corporations: the industrial economics of foreign investment', *Economica*, vol. 38 (February).

Caves, R. E. (1974a), 'The multinational enterprise and the theory of industrial organisation', in J. H. Dunning (ed.), *Economic Analysis and the Multinational Enterprise* (London: Allen & Unwin).

Caves, R. E. (1974b), 'Causes of foreign investment: foreign firms' shares in Canadian and UK manufacturing industries', *Review of Economics and Statistics*, vol. 56 (August).

Connor, J. M., and Mueller, W. F. (1977), *Market Power and Profitability of Multinational Corporations in Brazil and Mexico*, Report to the Sub-Committee on Foreign Economic Policy of the Committee on Foreign Relations, US Senate (Washington, DC: Government Printing Office).

Deane, R. S. (1971), *Foreign Investment in New Zealand Manufacturing* (London: Sweet & Maxwell).

Dunning, J. H. (1976), *United States Industry in Britain* (London: Wilton House).

Dunning, J. H., and Buckley, P. J. (1977), 'International production and alternative models of trade', *Manchester School of Economic and Social Studies*, vol. XLIV (December).

Dunning, J. H., Burstall, M., and Lake, A. (1981), *Multinational Enter-*

prises, *Governments and Technology: The Pharmaceutical Industry* (Paris: OECD).

Dunning, J. H., and Pearce, R. D. (1980), *The World's Largest Industrial Enterprises* (Farnborough: Gower Press).

Dunning, J. H., and Steuer, M. (1969), 'The effects of US direct investment on British technology', *Moorgate and Wall Street* (Autumn).

Eastman, H. C., and Stykolt, S. (1967), *The Tariff and Competition in Canada* (London: Macmillan).

Evans, P. B. (1977), 'Direct investment and industrial concentration', *Journal of Development Studies*, vol. 13 (July).

Ghosh, A. (1975), 'Concentration and growth of Indian industries 1948–68', *Journal of Industrial Economics*, vol. XXIII, no. 3 (March).

Globerman, S. (1979), 'A note on foreign ownership and market structure in the United Kingdom', *Applied Economics*, vol. II, no. 1 (March).

Gorecki, P. (1976), 'The determinants of entry by domestic and foreign enterprises in Canadian manufacturing industries: some comments and empirical results', *Review of Economics and Statistics*, vol. 58 (November).

Government of Canada (1972), *Foreign Direct Investment in Canada* (The Gray Report) (Ottawa: Government Printing Office).

Hodges, M. R. (1974), *Multinational Corporations and National Governments: A Case Study of the UK Experience 1964–70* (Lexington, Mass.: Heath).

Horst, T. O. (1972), 'Firm and industry determinants of the decision to invest abroad: an empirical study', *Review of Economics and Statistics*, vol. 14 (August).

Houston, T., and Dunning, J. H. (1976), *UK Industry Abroad* (London: Financial Times).

Hufbauer, G. C., and Chilas, J. G. (1974), 'Specialisation by industrial countries: extent and consequences', in H. Giersch (ed.), *The International Division of Labour: Problems and Perspectives* (Tubingen: Mohr).

Industrial Reorganisation Corporation (1968) 1st Report and Accounts. December 1966 to March 1968.

Industrial Reorganisation Corporation (1969) 2nd Report and Accounts. March 1968 to March 1969.

Industrial Reorganisation Corporation (1970) 3rd Report and Accounts. March 1969 to March 1970.

Industrial Reorganisation Corporation (1971) 4th Report and Accounts. April 1970 to April 1971.

Johns, B. L. (1967), 'Private overseas investments in Australia: profitability and motivation', *Economic Record*, vol. 43 (June).

Kanter, A. B., and Sugerman, S. O. (1970), 'British anti-trust response to the American business invasion', *Stanford Law Review*, vol. 22, no. 3.

Kindleberger, C. P. (1969), *American Business Abroad* (New Haven, Conn., and London: Yale University Press).

Knickerbocker, F. T. (1973), *Oligopolistic Reaction and the Multinational Enterprise* (Cambridge, Mass.: Harvard University Press).

Knickerbocker, F. T. (1976), *Market Structure and Market Power*

Consequences of Foreign Direct Investment by Multinational Corporations (Washington, DC: Center for Multinational Studies), Occasional Paper No. 8.

Kopits, G. (1979), 'Multinational conglomerate diversification', *Economic Internationale*, vol. XXXII, no. 1 (February).

Kojima, K. (1978), *Direct Foreign Investment* (London: Croom Helm).

Lall, S. (1973), 'Transfer pricing by multinational manufacturing firms', *Bulletin of Economics and Statistics*, vol. 35 (August).

Lall, S. (1979), 'Multinationals and market structure in an open developing economy. The case of Malaysia', *Weltwirtschaftliches Archiv*, vol. 115, no. 2.

Lall, S. (1980), 'Monopolistic advantages and foreign involvement by US manufacturing industry', *Oxford Economic Papers*, vol. 32, no. 1 (March).

Little, I. M. O., and Mirrlees, J. A. (1969), *Manual of Industrial Project Analysis in Developing Countries* (Paris: OECD).

Mansfield, E. (1974), 'Technology and the multinational enterprise', in J. H. Dunning (ed.), *Economic Analysis and the Multinational Enterprise* (London: Allen & Unwin).

Michalet, C. (1980), *MNEs in the Computer Industry and Their Impact on National Scientific and Technological Policy* (Paris: OECD).

Monopolies Commission (1963), *A Report on the Supply of Electrical Equipment for Mechanically Propelled Land Vehicles*.

Monopolies Commission (1966a), *BMC and Pressed Steel*, Report on the Merger.

Monopolies Commission (1966b), *A Report on the Supply and Processing of Colour Film*.

Monopolies Commission (1966c), *Dental Manufacturing Co. Ltd or Dentists Supply Co. of New York and Amalgamated Dental Co. Ltd*, Report on the Proposed Merger.

Monopolies Commission (1966d), *A Report on the Supply of Household Detergents*.

Monopolies Commission (1968), *A Report on the Supply of Man Made Cellulosic Rubber*.

Monopolies Commission (1973a), *A Report on the Supply of Ready Cooked Breakfast Cereal Foods*.

Monopolies Commission (1973b), *A Report on the Supply of Chlordiazepoxide and Diazepan*.

Monopolies Commission (1977), *The Fruehauf Corporation and Crane Fruehauf Ltd. – A Report on the Proposed Merger*.

Newfarmer, R. S. (1978), *The International Market Power of Transnational Corporations*, UNCTAD/ST/MD/13.

Newfarmer, R. S., and Mueller, W. F. (1975), *Multinational Corporations in Brazil and Mexico, Structural Sources of Economic and Non-Economic Power*, Report to the Sub-Committee on Multinational Corporations of the Committee on Foreign Relations, US Senate (Washington, DC: US Government Printing Office).

Owen, R. F. (1979), *Inter-industry Determinants of Foreign Direct Investment, A Perspective Emphasising the Canadian Experience*, Working Papers in International Economics, Princeton University (May).

Parry, T. G. (1974), 'Plant size, capacity utilisation and economic efficiency: Foreign investment in the Australian chemical industry', *Economic Record*, vol. 50 (June).

Parry, T. G. (1978), 'Structure and performance in Australian manufacturing with special reference to foreign owned enterprises', in W. Kasper and T. G. Parry (eds), *Growth Trade and Structural Change in an Open Australian Economy* (Kensington, Australia: Centre for Applied Economic Records).

Parry, T. G. (1980), *The Effects of Foreign Direct Investment on Host Countries* (Greenwich, Conn.: JAI Press).

Plasschaert, S. (1979), *Transfer Pricing and Multinational Corporations* (Farnborough, Hampshire: Saxon House).

Price Commission (1978a), *Weetabix Ltd. – Cereal and Muesli Products*.

Price Commission (1978b), *CPC (United Kingdom) Ltd. – Increases in the Prices of Maize Starch, Glucose Syrups, Starch-Derived and Glucose-Derived Products*.

Price Commission (1978c), *Lever Brothers Ltd. – Soaps, Detergents and Related Products*.

Price Commission (1978d), *Procter and Gamble Ltd. – Soaps and Detergents*.

Price Commission (1978e), *Prices, Costs and Margins in the Production and Distribution of Toothpaste*.

Prices and Incomes Board (1967), No. 39, *Costs and Prices of Aluminium Semi Manufactures*, Cmnd 3378.

Prices and Incomes Board (1968), No. 66, *Price of Butyl Rubber*, Cmnd 3626.

Prices and Incomes Board (1969), No. 100, *Synthetic Organic Dyestuffs and Organic Pigments Prices*, Cmnd 3895.

Rhader, G. M. (1973), 'Some aspects of direct foreign private investment in Pakistan', *Pakistan Development Review*, vol. 12, no. 1 (Spring).

Robinson, J. (1979), *Multinationals in the 1980s* (Brussels: European News Agency).

Rosenbluth, G. (1970), 'The relation between foreign control and concentration in Canadian industry', *Canadian Journal of Economics*, vol. 3 (February).

Rowthorn, R. (1970), *International Big Business* (Cambridge: Cambridge University Press).

Safarian, A. E. (1966), *Foreign Ownership of Canadian Industry* (New York: McGraw Hill).

Safarian, A. E. (1969), *The Performance of US Firms in Canada*, Canadian–American Committee.

Sainsbury Committee (1969), *Report of the Committee of Enquiry into the Relationship of the Pharmaceutical Industry with the National Health Service, 1965–7*.

Scherer, F. M. (1971), *Industrial Market Structure and Economic Performance* (Chicago: Rand McNally).

Statistics Canada (1978), *Structural Aspects of Domestic and Foreign Control in the Manufacturing Mining and Forestry Industries* (Ottawa: Ministry of Industry Trade and Commerce).

Steuer, M. *et al.* (1973), *The Impact of Foreign Direct Investment on the United Kingdom* (London: HMSO).

Streeten, P. P. (1974), 'The theory of development policy', in J. H. Dunning (ed.), *Economic Analysis and the Multinational Enterprise* (London: Allen & Unwin).

Stubenitsky, F. (1970), *American Direct Investment in the Netherlands Industry* (Rotterdam: Rotterdam University Press).

Swann, D., and Lees, D. (1973), *Anti-Trust Policy in Europe*, EAG Business Research Study (London: Financial Times).

Swedenborg, B. (1979), *The Multinational Operations of Swedish Firms, An Analysis of Determinants and Effects* (Stockholm: Almqvist & Wiksell).

Teece, D. (1979), *Technology Transfer and R and D Activities of Multinational Firms: Some Theory and Evidence*, mimeo., Stanford University.

Telser, G. (1966), 'Cut throat competition and the long purse', *Journal of Law and Economics*, vol. 9 (October).

Timberg, S. (1973), 'An international anti-trust convention', in M. Ariga, ed. *International Conference on International Economy and Competition Policy: Papers and Reports* (Tokyo: Council of Tokyo Conference).

UN (1980), *Transnational Corporation Linkages in Developing Countries* (New York: UN Centre on Transnational Corporations).

UNCTAD (1973), *Report of Expert Group on Restrictive Business Practices in Relation to Trade and Development of Developing Countries*, TD/B/C2/119 (April).

UNIDO (1978), *Transnational Corporations and the Processing of Raw Materials: Impact on Developing Countries*. Report prepared by UN Centre on Transnational Corporations for 12th Session of Industrial Development Board, Vienna, May 1978, ID/B/209.

United States Tariff Commission (1973), *Implications of Multinational Firms for World Trade and Investment and for US Trade and Labour*, Report to Committee on Finance, US Senate (Washington, DC: US Government Printing Office).

Vaitsos, C. (1974), *Intercountry Income Distribution and Transnational Enterprises* (Oxford: Oxford University Press).

Vernon, R. (1968), 'Anti-trust and international business', *Harvard Business Review* (September/October).

Vernon, R. (1977), *Storm over Multinationals* (Cambridge, Mass.: Harvard University Press).

Wertheimer, H. W. (1971), 'The international firm and international aspects of policies on mergers', in J. B. Heath (ed.), *International Conference on Monopolies, Mergers and Restrictive Practices* (London: HMSO).

Weston, J. F. (1973), 'Conglomerate firms', in B. Yamey (ed.), *Economics of Industrial Structure* (Harmondsworth: Penguin).

Willmore, L. (1976), 'Direct foreign investment in Central American manufacturing', *World Development*, vol. 4, no. 6.

Williamson, O. E. (1975), *Markets and Hierarchies: Analysis and Anti-*

Trust Implications (New York: The Free Press).

Wolf, B. (1977), 'Industrial diversification and internationalisation', *Journal of Industrial Economics*, vol. 26 (December).

Yamey, B. S. (ed.) (1973), *Economics of Industrial Structure* (Harmondsworth: Penguin).

8

Multinational Enterprises and Domestic Capital Formation

I

This chapter will be mainly concerned with the impact of MNEs on the generation of real capital formation and on the application of macro-economic policy in countries which are hosts to their affiliates.

We have chosen to focus attention on the capital formation of MNEs for two reasons. The first is that the long-term economic effects of their activities derive from their control of all the resources in their possession, irrespective of how, and from where, these are obtained. In the last two decades, the proportion of foreign capital formation of MNEs from all leading industrialised countries financed from direct investment inflows has steadily fallen and in the mid-1970s was around 20 per cent. In the period 1957–60, the proportion of plant and equipment expenditures by US foreign manufacturing affiliates financed by US savings was 35 per cent, by 1967–70 had fallen to 22 per cent, and by 1975–78 to 11 per cent. However much foreign direct investment may act as a catalyst to the recipient country's capital formation, and whatever the short-term significance of financial flows for the balance of payments may be, the twenty years up to 1970 of increasing controls on capital movements (Cairncross, 1973), imposed by both home and host countries, have coincided with the most rapid growth of the foreign activities of national firms. This suggests that the real distinctiveness of MNEs to host countries lies in the 'foreignness' not of their capital, but of other resources, including managerial control.

The second reason is allied to the first. If there is a single feature which sets apart direct from portfolio capital flows, it is that the former is almost always part of a package of income-generating assets made available to the borrowing country but over which the supplier continues to

This chapter is a revised and expanded version of a paper first published in *Manchester School of Economic and Social Studies*, vol. 38 (September 1973) and in J. S. G. Wilson and C. F. Scheffer (eds), *Multinational Enterprises – Financial and Monetary Aspects* (Leiden: Sijthoff, 1974).

Table 8.1 Estimated Cumulative Funds of US-owned Affiliates Abroad, 1966–70

	Amounts ($b.)			% of total sources/uses		
	All industries	All manufacturing	Other	All industries	All manufacturing	Other
Sources of funds:						
Depreciation, depletion, and related charges	26.0	13.9	12.1	20	26	16
Net income of affiliates after taxes	42.1	14.8	27.3	32	27	36
Net affiliate borrowing outside the United States[a]	34.1	18.7	15.4	26	35	20
Net capital flow from parents to affiliates	21.3	6.5	14.8	16	12	20
Unallocated[b]	6.2	0	6.2	6	0	8
Total sources	129.7	53.9	75.8	100	100	100
Uses of funds:						
Investment in new plant and equipment	51.2	24.8	26.4	39	46	35
Remittances of dividends and[c] branch profits to parents	21.3	6.1	15.2	16	11	20
Increase in non-fixed assets	57.2	23.0	34.2	44	43	45
Total uses	129.7	53.9	75.8	100	100	100

a Net of borrowings used to liquidate liabilities to foreigners, and excluding foreign borrowing by parents.

b A principal item here consists of sales, retirements and similar disposals of fixed assets – the remaining component of internally generated funds besides retained earnings and depreciation/depletion charges. The cumulative value of this item, comparable to the $6.2 billion 'unallocated' amount shown, is conservatively estimated at $4.0 billion. Allocation of this amount has not been made because data are not available for its two components: sales of fixed assets, the net proceeds of which should have appeared in the income statements as extraordinary income (non-operating income), and ordinary write-offs (retirements), which are not reflected in net income. The former of these components, to the extent that it has importance, already is reflected in the 'net income' source of funds. The latter, however, cannot be specifically identified and allocated.

c Excludes estimated interest remittances to parents. While relevant for measuring balance-of-payments flows, interest remittances are entered as costs in income statements, with the result that these remittances should already be reflected in the 'net income' source of funds above, as deductions from that source.

Sources: US Tariff Commission (1973).

Based on data for 1966 and 1970 supplied by US Department of Commerce, Bureau of Economic Analysis, International Investment Division; and supplemented by information from *Survey of Current Business*, September 1971 and October 1971.

exercise control, while the latter simply consists of loanable funds or savings.[1] Indeed, it is the other ingredients of the package (technology, management, entrepreneurship, access to markets, etc.) which make direct investment so welcome to host countries, and enable foreign affiliates to compete effectively with indigenous firms. This being so, there is much to be said for adopting Irving Fisher's interpretation of capital as any income-generating assets, and investments as anything which augments these assets. When related to the activities of MNEs, capital then consists of all forms of assets which are capable of generating a flow of income; *inter alia* these include the stock of material assets, of productive knowledge and of human skills. Again, while the way in which the latter two components are financed may be important in analysing their effects on the economy in which they are used, for example, whether management expertise is imported or locally supplied, it is the total capital formation with which we shall be concerned.

The discussion proceeds in the following way. Section II examines some determinants of capital formation by MNEs and their affiliates. Section III discusses the effects of government policy in host countries on the capital expenditure by foreign affiliates. Section IV is concerned with some broad macroeconomic implications and with the consequences of activities of MNEs in three areas of particular interest to national and international economic policy.[2]

II

There are various approaches to this subject, and that which one chooses depends largely on the precise question one is seeking to answer. The first approach we shall consider in this chapter is that of the international economist who is primarily interested in capital *flows*. Here one takes the standard models of international *portfolio* capital flows, which relate the supply of funds to interest-rate differentials (or changes in interest rates) or to the yields of real investment (or changes in yields), both appropriately discounted for risk, and then attempts to see how far these can explain the foreign direct investment by, or capital formation of, MNEs.[3] The answer is that, very often, they cannot, partly because the value of a direct investment is assessed by its long-term contribution to the investing enterprise *as a whole*, of which the earnings of a particular affiliate may be an unimportant part, for example, as in the case of some horizontally or vertically integrated or conglomerate investments, and partly because one of the basic determinants of foreign direct investment is the expectation that affiliates will out-perform indigenous companies in host countries. This suggests that while long-term portfolio capital will normally move across national boundaries to those sectors in the borrowing country that have a higher yield than their counterparts in the lending country, direct investment will flow to those sectors of the host country in which the investing country has a competitive, innovatory, managerial or marketing advantage, but which can produce or partly produce goods more cheaply than can the investing country. Much of the work of economists concerned with direct investment has been directed to identifying and evaluating the form of these advantages and the reasons for them. We shall return to this point later.

The second approach is more micro-oriented and stems from the theory of investment behaviour of *firms*. There are two variants of this approach. The first, which represents the main stream of research to date, has been to extend models of the domestic investment behaviour of firms to explain either the capital formation of the affiliates of MNEs or that part of it financed by the investing firm.[4] Most of the empirical work has been based upon data of the plant and equipment expenditure of US affiliates abroad, or that part of their total investment financed from US sources, including the reinvested profits of the affiliates. The second variant has received very little attention in the literature. It concerns the extent to which models of investment behaviour by indigenous firms can be used to explain the behaviour of investment by foreign affiliates in similar industries.

(a) The capital formation of MNEs

Broadly speaking, there have been two variants of the first type of study – the *investing* country approach. The first is illustrated by the work of Stevens (1969, 1974), Severn (1971), Popkin (1965) and other writers.[5] Severn, for example, used a neoclassical, two-country model (the USA and the rest of the world) to explain both differences in the specification of domestic and foreign investment functions of firms, and the distribution of corporate funds between home and foreign uses. He concluded that, subject to a liquidity constraint, the accelerator type models gave the best answers in both cases. He also found that MNEs allocated funds without reference to national boundaries and that, eliminating factors common to both foreign and domestic investment, the two were at least partially substitutable for each other and interrelated through the financing mechanism. Popkin, in his study of United States manufacturing affiliates (1965), also asserted that the relative profit rates and other financial variables were more important than market structure and technological variables in explaining variations in their investment behaviour. Stevens (1971), using similar data, and an extension of the Modigliani–Miller (1958) theorem, derived equations which *inter alia* related plant and equipment expenditure to the maximisation of the market value of firms, and also financial flows to the same goal and that of exchange loss minimisation. He found that all equations explained past data quite well.

Most of the research just mentioned accepts that there are certain determinants of the foreign capital formation of MNEs which are unique to such firms, and the second group of studies has attempted to identify these to explain the growth of US direct investment in Western Europe since the mid-1950s. The writings of Bandera and White (1968), d'Arge (1969), Scaperlanda (1967), Wallis (1968), Scaperlanda and Mauer (1969) and Krause (1972) are examples of this approach. Most of these, using either time series or cross-sectional data, relate either absolute values of United States investment (or capital stake) to profit rates, size of markets, growth of markets, tariff rates and some kind of trend and/or slope shifting variable; the Bandera and White study included an international liquidity variable. The cross-sectional studies very clearly show that the capital stake of United States affiliates has risen most in those countries which have recorded fastest rates of growth of GNP, with profitability and other variables, including tariffs, the formation of the EEC being of secondary importance.[6,7] The time series data lend support to these conclusions particularly when the capital stake is taken as the dependent variable (Bandera and White, 1968). Again, in all cases, the market variable showed up better than the profit rate.

As an explanation of the distribution of investment by MNEs between home and foreign activities where these are independent of each other, these studies are generally acceptable; where, however, their activities are interrelated and part of an international strategy they are less convincing. This is because they tend both to assume the goals of affiliates are synonymous with those of the investing firms, and to focus attention on the income stream of the former, rather than that of the latter of which they are part. The profit variable is a key example. Assuming the aim of investment by MNEs is to maximise their post-tax profits, it does not follow that this objective will be achieved by maximising profits of each and every affiliate. There are three main reasons for this. The first is that where tax rates are different between countries, a £'s worth of income earned in a high tax country is worth less than the same income earned in a low tax country. The second is wherever the activities of one part of the MNE affect the profits earned by another part, the profits of the first part will understate or overstate its contribution to the group; export-replacing investment is a case in point. The third is that profits may inadequately measure the worth of affiliates, such as where investment leads to the feedback of technical knowhow, or gives access to markets and/or raw materials, or where income is remitted in other forms, for example, interest, royalties, fees, etc., or via intra-group transactions at above or below arm's-length prices.

These possibilities are most obvious in the case of integrated or conglomerate MNEs as they have more opportunity for shifting income from the place where it is earned to where it is taxed the least. Investment by US companies in Taiwan or South Korea to supply the US market with TV sets is not motivated by the size of the Taiwan or South Korean market; this is no less true of the vertical specialisation by IBM in the

European market or the auto companies in the Latin American market. But, in principle, the issue arises not primarily because a firm is multinational but because it is multi-plant, and it is difficult to identify goals of plants without reference to those of the firm of which they are part.

The above discussion suggests that the determinants of capital flows or capital formation is as much a question of location theory as corporate investment theory. For while the latter may help to establish the *level* of investment (for this is primarily a question of the marginal efficiency of capital, related to size of market and structure of input prices and productivity), the former is necessary to explain where that investment is located, that is, its geographical distribution.[8]

(b)   *The capital formation of the affiliates of MNEs*

This brings us to the second variant of the approach to micro-investment studies. From the viewpoint of the policy of *host* countries towards foreign investment, it is less important to know the differences in the factors influencing the behaviour of MNEs at home and abroad, or between MNEs and indigenous firms in *investing* countries, than those which influence the behaviour of affiliates of MNEs in host countries *vis-à-vis* those of their indigenous competitors.

Received theory suggests that the level of real corporate investment is a function of the cost and availability of loanable funds and the marginal efficiency of capital. In turn, the marginal efficiency of capital is determined *inter alia* by the productivity of the investing firms, the prices of inputs, other than loanable funds, the market for the products the investment helps to produce, and taxes and incentives. Similarly, changes in capital stock will be governed by the sensitivity of investment to changes in the values of these variables, and the extent of these changes. Host governments, through their ability to affect both the conditions under which loanable funds are supplied and the marginal efficiency of capital of firms, for example, by fiscal or exchange rate policy, can obviously influence capital formation and its financing. But to what extent is the marginal efficiency of capital of affiliates of MNEs or the price they have to pay for loanable funds likely to be different from that of indigenous firms?

A report prepared by the US Tariff Commission (1973) has shown that, relative to national enterprises, US MNEs tend to concentrate in research intensive industries, in those with diversified product structures and above average advertising budgets, and in those which export an above average proportion of their output.[9] Similarly, relative to indigenous firms, the affiliates of multinational enterprises tend to be most active in these same industries, particularly where the locational advantages of production favour the host country. In a study of American affiliates in forty UK industries, it was found that their participation ratios[10] varied from 84.6 per cent to 0.7 per cent around an average of 12.1 per cent (Dunning,

1976). In general, the higher the ratio, the greater the distinctive advantages of the affiliates relative to indigenous firms.

Previous chapters have shown that MNEs tend to be most dominant in those sectors characterised by market imperfections and market failure, which afford such firms ownership and/or internalisation advantages over and above those of non-MNEs in the countries in which they operate. We have also seen that such advantages may take various forms: a better product, superior technology or management, access to inputs at lower (or subsidised) prices, and the economies of synergistic activities, better knowledge of world capital markets and financial institutions, the ability to acquire loanable funds, both from other parts of the organisation or from external markets at a lower composite cost, and the facility to circumvent credit rationing in any one country, *inter alia* by adjustment of retained earnings in its affiliates and transfer price manipulation (Hawkins, 1978).[11]

The market for the goods produced by affiliates may be wider than that of domestic companies, although this will partly depend on the extent to which they are allowed to exploit these markets by their parent companies. Where barriers to trade are negligible or where it is more efficient to supply the market from elsewhere, the opportunity cost of a local investment may be high; where barriers are high, and production advantages favour the host country, local production will be preferred to imports.

The extent and share of capital formation in a particular country or industry by MNEs thus depends, first, on their comparative advantage (*vis-à-vis* indigenous firms) in acquiring those inputs (including knowledge) necessary to produce the output in question, and, second, on the comparative advantage of their affiliates in that country (*vis-à-vis* their parent companies or other affiliates) to undertake the production or part of the production process. These conditions also explain the growth of such investment, although as the participation of foreign firms increases, so it is likely will the barriers to entry facing indigenous firms.

The level of capital formation by multinational enterprises in any one country will also be related to the *type* of operations which it is desired to exploit. Even for an MNE operating independent affiliates, the choice is rarely between producing the whole of the output of a particular product from one location or another, but between producing an increase in output from one location or another. It is the capital formation necessary to produce this extra output which is in question, and this, unless costs are sharply increasing, will be less than the capital formation per unit of product because of certain fixed costs, incurred on behalf of the group, which are located elsewhere, usually at the group's headquarters. On the other hand, an MNE might choose to concentrate some of its group activities in a particular location. Several US firms, for example, have centralised their European R & D activities in a single European country; while cities like London, Paris, Honolulu, Coral Gables have attracted regional office functions of MNEs (Heenan, 1977).

In between, there will be a whole spectrum of activities that will be determined by locational factors and the logistics of MNEs. An inter-dependent MNE which specialises vertically or horizontally will engage in the capital formation appropriate to that activity to which it is best suited. These activities will not necessarily be substitutes for imports. They will be conducted on the ordinary principles of location theory, that is, given the level of demand, a profit maximising firm will choose a location which will minimise total costs. *Inter alia* this would suggest that MNEs should concentrate labour intensive activities in areas of labour availability and/or low labour costs, and technology intensive activities in areas of technology availability and/or low technological costs. The extent of government pressure on the activities of firms, movement costs including tariffs, and competitors' behaviour may also be significant. But the evidence on the location of production and other activities of MNEs does seem to support this proposition.

The effects of capital formation by the affiliates of MNEs on particular industrial sectors has not received much attention in the literature, but one would suppose that these are not very different from those of the national multi-plant firm in a regional context. In general, one would expect a rather more concentrated output, in terms of ownership of assets, than would have occurred in their absence; this concentration tends to be associated with a greater capital intensity and more opportunity for the territorial specialisation of product and processes. In response to a situation which reflects the free play of market resources, the mobility of capital leads to higher efficiency; where it is the result of imperfections, for example, import controls, non-tariff barriers, differential taxes, etc., this may not be the case.

III

Having outlined some of the main factors which will determine the share of capital formation in particular countries or industries accounted for by affiliates of foreign MNEs we now consider the extent to which their response to changes in the value of these factors will be different from that of indigenous firms.[12] To narrow our discussion, we shall focus attention on three areas of any host government's policy, viz., monetary, fiscal and exchange rate policy, and we shall further distinguish between two effects of a change in policy, the first being the initial responsiveness of affiliates and the second the effect on their competitive position.

Since we have suggested that affiliates of MNEs *do* possess distinctive characteristics *vis-à-vis* indigenous firms, there is a strong presumption that their reactions to changes in policies affecting their investment behaviour will be different. But in what way? Will they be more or less responsive to, for example, movements in interest rates, changes in corporation tax, regional subsidies, capital grants and so on? Let us consider these questions in relation to four major ways in which affiliates of MNEs differ from indigenous firms, after normalising for structural differences, for example, capacity utilisation, size and industrial composition; these are:

(1)   their activities will be determined by what is best not for themselves but for the enterprise of which they are part;

(2)   their operations will almost certainly be truncated to some degree or another;

(3)   they have access to the resources, notably knowledge and managerial expertise, well beyond those which they can generate themselves, and usually at lower or subsidised cost;

(4)   because they operate in different national markets, their opportunities for obtaining factor inputs, and in particular labour, finance capital and technology, and their access to markets are that much greater, as are those for transferring intermediate products across national boundaries *within* the firm.

With these points in mind consider, first, the possible effects on the capital formation of affiliates of MNEs of an increase in the rate of interest on loanable funds in the host country. Will they react more or less noticeably than indigenous firms? It is difficult to give a generalised answer, as there are forces working in both directions. On the one hand, affiliates may find it easier than indigenous firms to obtain capital from other sources outside the host country (e.g. from their parent companies or the Eurodollar market). This suggests that while they will by *more* interest responsive in their demand for loanable funds from sources, in the host country they will be *less* interest responsive in their capital formation. Their sensitivity will also be less where the elasticity of substitution between capital and other inputs is less than that of indigenous firms (and there is reason to suppose this may be so in capital intensive industries) or the elasticity of demand for their finished products is lower. In this latter case, it is the nature of the export market which is crucial; here one might suppose that, because of their specialised character, intragroup exports would have a relatively inelastic demand, while independent exports might be more or less responsive, depending on the structure of the markets served.

On the other hand, what of the opportunities for supplying the market from alternative locations? A rise in domestic interest rates in one country adds to the cost of production in that country relative to elsewhere. This reduces the attraction of the first country as a locational base. An indigenous company may have little option but to produce in that country; a foreign based MNE may be less constrained. Where capital is mobile across the exchanges it is unlikely to use this option; where this is not the case, or affiliates adopt an 'every tub on its own bottom' type financial policy, then a capital intensive firm, faced with a high elasticity of demand for its finished product, may well respond to an increase in interest rates by switching its investment elsewhere, in which case the policy will be more effective than in the case of indigenous firms.

Depending on the balance of these forces, affiliates of MNEs are likely to increase or lower their market share of capital formation relatively to indigenous companies. Our impression is that in the UK at least, they have strengthened their competitive position, mainly due to the greater opportunities for obtaining capital from other sources at times of domestic credit restraint, and that on other grounds, too, their interest sensitivity (in respect of capital formation) is less than that of indigenous firms.

Table 8.2 illustrates some possible effects of other types of domestic policy measures intended either to induce or curtail the level of capital spending or to affect its pattern. Most of these operate through making it more or less costly for firms to borrow money; but the input of others is *via* their effect on the demand for the finished product. Exchange rate changes, in general, have had wider purposes in view.

How far will affiliates of MNEs react differently to such changes, compared with indigenous firms? The incidence of a change in corporation tax cannot easily be shifted by indigenous firms; but by various devices (e.g. by transfer price manipulation, including prices charged for services of intra-group transactions) affiliates may be able to shift the earnings of pre-tax income from the higher tax country to elsewhere where tax rates are lower. Alternatively, they may be better placed to convert their equity into debt capital. On the other hand, since net profits after tax have now been reduced relative to those which might be earned in other locations, an affiliate might be tempted to shift new investment (or even existing investment) elsewhere.[13]

Most empirical studies on the response of MNEs or their affiliates to tax changes relate to such decision variables as dividends, direct investment flows, transfer prices, etc. (Kopits, 1976). One US study, however (Horst, 1977), has estimated that the elimination or deferral of US taxes or replacing foreign tax credit by a simple deduction, while likely to substantially reduce net capital outflow, would have only a minimal effect on the location of real investment by MNEs between the USA and other countries.[14] We know of no studies that have attempted to compare the responses of foreign affiliates and indigenous firms to taxation changes.

This same flexibility makes affiliates more sensitive to changes in investment incentives of one kind or another. Several surveys (Dunning and Yannapoulos, 1973) have emphasised the importance of financial inducements by countries, or regions within countries, as important factors influencing the location of new US manufacturing affiliates in Western Europe in the 1960s, and in so far as the options open to MNEs are more than those open to national firms, one would expect a greater sensitivity to such inducements. This would certainly seem to have been believed by some of the less prosperous regions in Europe — notably Ireland and

Table 8.2 Response of Affiliates of Multinational Enterprises, relative to those of Indigenous Firms, to Selected Changes in Policy on Capital Spending

	Elasticity of substitution		Likely effect on total costs	Location of new investment	Elasticity of demand for product		Net effect on affiliates (vis-à-vis indigenous firms)
	Capital from other sources	Other factor inputs			Intra-group trade (cf. all exports)	Other	
(a) Monetary policy							
Increase in rate of interest	More, leading to less effect on capital formation	?	less	more	less	?	more
Reduction in availability of credit	"	less	less	more	less	less	more
(b) Fiscal policy							
Increase in corporation tax	no effect	?	?	more	less	?	?
Increase in consumer credit (in UK)	no effect	more	?	?	no effect	?	?
Increase in investment allowances	no effect	more	more	more	less	?	more
(c) Exchange rate policy							
Pre-devaluation	more	more	?	more	more	?	more
Post-devaluation	more	more	less	more	less	?	less

Belgium — who have made extensive use of fiscal incentives to attract new foreign capital, and with some success.[15] In the 1970s, with the growing integration of US MNE affiliates in Europe, such incentives seem to have become less important. In some developing countries, particularly those which compete for export oriented manufacturing investments of foreign based MNEs, government assistance in the form of grants, tax free holidays, duty free imports and tariff production continue to be of some importance.[16] To the extent that affiliates tend to be more capital intensive than indigenous firms, capital grants will benefit them more; on the other hand, regional employment premiums may have the opposite effect.[17]

Efforts to stimulate or retard investment by operating on consumers' expenditure may also have discriminatory effects. As a group, MNEs tend to supply products with a relatively high income elasticity of demand, and there is some evidence that their profits are more susceptible to cyclical fluctuations than those of indigenous companies. On the other hand, since they often export a higher proportion of their output, an increase in domestic spending will have rather less effect. The consequences on capital spending of an exchange rate change may be less marked than with indigenous firms, as a fairly substantial percentage of both imports and exports of affiliates tend to be intra-group, and hence price inelastic. Moreover, MNEs tend to operate in oligopolistic markets in which prices are often insensitive; and where world markets are divided between individual affiliates, the opportunities of any one affiliate for exploiting hierarchical advantages might be blunted. At the same time, this inelasticity would emphasise that affiliates, particularly those of integrated concerns, are *more* susceptible to changes in economic conditions *outside* the host country, including policy changes of other governments, than are indigenous firms.

Other aspects of the comparative responsiveness of the affiliates of MNEs and locally owned competitors to changes in the economic environment have been discussed by McAleese and Counahan (1979). They conclude, from a study of the behaviour of foreign affiliates in the Irish Republic, that, during a period of recession from 1973 to 1977, there was no evidence to suggest that the employment loss in the foreign affiliates was noticeably different from that of their domestic counterparts. On the other hand, Ashcroft and Ingram (1978) have argued that there is some reason to suppose that foreign affiliates in the UK mechanical engineering industry do adapt, either their choice of production technology or their choice of location, to changes in the local economic environment more readily than their indigenous competitors.

One of the reasons for a differential response between MNEs and indigenous firms lies in the greater ability of MNEs to take advantage of internalised decision taking. This is particularly so in respect of their financial behaviour and their capability to shift funds and profits across national boundaries. Although such internalising devices may have no direct bearing on capital formation, indirectly they do so by affecting the balance of location advantages between countries, the valuation of particular projects[18] and the risks attached to alternative spreads of geographical and/or industrial diversification (Rugman, 1979).

Further support for the differences in the capital spending patterns of US foreign affiliates and indigenous firms is presented by Hawkins and Macaluso (1977) and Hawkins (1978). Of the six developed countries considered, there were 'very positive indications that US multinational firms are able to avoid restrictive monetary policies in host countries' in the case of Germany, Japan and the UK. 'Positive but less persuasive evidence' was found for Canada and France and no evidence for Germany. They also found that MNEs utilised their superior financial flexibility in adjusting their sourcing of funds in the case of Belgium, France and West Germany, but there was no verification of this in the case of Japan and the UK and only slight evidence in the case of Canada.

We conclude that the level and structure of capital formation of affiliates in particular industries in host countries will be different from that of indigenous firms for various reasons, which *inter alia* are to do with differences in product composition and efficiency, the extent of vertical or horizontal integration, and to opportunities to move money, goods and services across national boundaries. These factors explain why the shape of investment functions will differ from those of indigenous firms and that the nature and/or extent of this difference will depend on the type of policy instruments introduced. Some of the macro-implications of these differences will be explored in the final section of this chapter.

IV

The *total* capital formation of a country depends very much on the national economic management policy pursued by the government. But MNEs do have some impact on the formation and direction of this policy and its success. This they can achieve in two ways: first, by the way in which their capital is financed and, in particular, the extent to which it is obtained from outside the country of expenditure; second, by the indirect or multiplier effects of capital formation by MNEs on the capital formation of suppliers, competitors and customers.

Again, there are no generalised answers to these questions. Apart from the extent to which there is capacity of capital and labour at the time the initial investment is being made, whether capital formation by MNEs augments a country's stock of capital will vary with circumstances. Most import-substituting production will increase the demand for indigenous capital goods as the new output need not replace domestic output; by contrast, if inward investment (however financed) is spent on imports of equipment, domestic capital formation may be less than it might be. The implications of an investment to finance a takeover are different from those of setting up a greenfield venture; an investment to supply a completely new product will have a different effect than one to replace an existing product. According to from which source capital is obtained, and how it is spent, the implications for planned savings and planned investment will be different.

Such data as are available suggest that MNEs and their affiliates are concentrated in capital intensive industries or in industries supplying branded products; that in these industries their affiliates' operations tend to be more capital intensive than those of indigenous firms; and that, initially, their products neither replace imports nor are destined for markets that otherwise would be served by other parts of the organisation. The proportion of imports of capital equipment varies between industries, but it is not noticeably higher than that of indigenous firms. On the other hand, the import of human and knowledge capital is almost certainly greater than that of indigenous firms.

Concerning the influence on the *supply* of capital, we have already said that only a small proportion of the capital formation of UK and US MNEs is funded from capital imports; the greater part is self-financed through depreciation and profits. The balance is borrowed locally or internationally, noticeably from the Euro-dollar market. In terms of the *demand* for funds, the impact is fairly small, but this may have repercussions. Multinational enterprises have almost certainly increased the demand for indigenous knowledge or human skills in the countries in which they operate and, in some cases, this has affected the price for such inputs. As to the spillover effects of the presence of MNEs on capital formation, much depends on the proportion of purchases bought locally and the extent to which capacity is being used efficiently. Competitors and sub-contractors are stimulated wherever foreign firms bring higher price, technical or scale efficiency. These 'linkage' effects will be spread over time, as indeed will be the 'technological' multiplier (Quinn, 1968). This reinforces the normal Keynesian multiplier effect and results from the improvement in productivity made possible by new innovations.

The other main effect on other capital formation arises from the character of the operations of affiliates of MNEs. Here the argument is sometimes put that foreign firms do not create income generating assets of the right kind and that they may even reduce a country's ability to create income for itself by forcing it to rent capital. This is directed particularly to knowledge capital. There are two versions of this contention. One is that foreign firms somehow prevent host countries from developing their true economic potential; this is a variant of the infant industry argument, but arises out of the monopoly power and control over resource allocation which MNEs are alleged to possess over (*de novo*) local competitors. It suggests that the system for the dissemination of knowledge is not that which maximises dynamic comparative advantage.

The second version is based on the assertion that either the country does not get a fair distribution of the output created by the operations of MNEs or it prefers to be in control of its income-generating ability, even if this should result in a lower income than it might earn as a hirer of capital.

V

There are certain features about capital flows of MNEs common to those of all capital movements. In a world free of imperfections, capital movements between independent lenders and borrowers perform the same function as movements in goods and services and will lead to a more efficient allocation of the world's resources and increase real output. The same applies to capital formation, given the appropriate macroeconomic conditions. On the other hand, we have argued that capital movements and formation by MNEs are differently generated from those of portfolio investment, and chiefly arise not because the recipient country is short of savings but of the other ingredients of the package of factor inputs which MNEs provide. To the extent that there are costs to the transmission of productive knowledge, MNEs, by helping to produce domestically goods which would otherwise have to be imported at a higher price, are *ceteris paribus* increasing allocative efficiency. Whether or not this could be better dealt with by devising alternative methods of compensating the producers of knowledge is another matter. Moreover, to the extent that MNEs help countries to develop their full economic potential, they may be fulfilling the principle of comparative advantage. Certainly, too, by their ability to buy inputs more cheaply and by their access to wider markets than those available to indigenous firms, they may again make for a more efficient deployment of resources.[19]

The issues become more complicated in other than static competitive conditions and where MNEs are involved. While tariff barriers might induce portfolio capital movements which could either mitigate or increase the adverse effects of the barriers, the effects are even more uncertain with direct investment, where the tariff might induce the mobility of human capital and productive knowledge as well. On the other hand, where a tariff is imposed to counteract monopoly power to or encourage the more efficient deployment of resources, which in the long run conform to dynamic comparative advantage, then the operations of MNEs (which are essentially concerned with private rather than social ends and cannot be expected to invest in developmental infrastructure) might be to the advantage of host countries. Similarly, differential fiscal penalties or incentives will not only have the usual effects on the flows of capital between independent parties; they will also cause multinational enterprises, which engage in intra-company trade, to practise tax deferral or tax avoidance devices, which may or may not improve allocative efficiency, but will certainly have implications for the distribution of income. A fixed exchange rate, like any other price pegging device, will also induce a different type of response from MNEs than from portfolio investors, especially again where substantial intra-group transactions make it possible for firms to shift funds across national boundaries to suit their needs. Finally, the whole gamut of national government controls, except those which are designed to cure market imperfections, will cause a more marked reaction by MNEs and, again, these may not always be in the same direction as in the case of portfolio investors.

It is far beyond the scope of this chapter to examine all the effects of the capital formation of multinational enterprises. For the remaining space available I propose to concentrate on three areas of interest: (1) national economic management, (2) inflation and (3) distribution of income.

(a)   *National economic management*
Perhaps the most widespread argument used by governments against MNEs or their affiliates is that they make the task of economic management more difficult. The complaints are most vocal from insulated and socialist-type economies or from countries where foreign firms have a substantial share of the capital formation in key industries; and they are directed particularly to large MNEs which are interdependent in their operations, and engage in substantial intra-group trading.

The reason for this concern is little different in principle from any other form of openness to which an economy might be subject, be it international trade or the integration of financial markets. Openness implies interdependence both of economic fortune and disaster. Where an economy can easily and speedily adjust to such openness, the costs involved might not be great; but rarely is this the case today, and the costs of interdependence may be substantial.

In discussing the effects of capital movements on national economic management, it is important to distinguish between the cause of these movements, that is, whether they are endogenous or exogenous, and whether they are in response to movements in interest rates or in expectancy of higher profits (Johnson, 1966). Most of the standard analysis of the effects of capital movements has been to explain these in terms of response to or in anticipation of interest rate changes. Here it is generally accepted that international capital movements weaken domestic monetary policy under fixed exchange rates, although, by the same token, they may help to cure a short-run balance-of-payments situation. To protect their sovereignty, governments may take various measures ranging from outright prohibition of capital movements (usually exports but sometimes imports) to controlling access by foreign firms to domestic capital markets, or imposing special reserve requirements, to manipulating interest rates to make capital movements less worthwhile.

Many of these problems do not arise with flexible exchange rates but, even here, capital movements generated by the expectation of higher profits may reduce the leverage of monetary policy over income and employment, and, in many cases, much depends on the reactions of borrowers and lenders to changes in the interest rate, for example, whether they expect any change to be permanent or not. On the other hand, a high mobility of portfolio investment, under fixed exchange rates, may increase the effectiveness of fiscal policy, as capital flows tend to eliminate the adverse monetary effects of fiscal policy and to reduce the change in foreign exchange reserves. Under flexible exchange rates, as shown by the experience of Canada in the 1950s (Caves and Reuber, 1971), fiscal policy can be undermined.

Similarly, free capital movements may affect exchange rate policy (Cooper, 1971). In the short run, this is demonstrated primarily by the extent of currency speculation in anticipation of exchange rate changes. In the long run, while exchange risk might inhibit capital flows, Aliber (1970) has shown that in a multiple currency system, this can work to increase the flow of foreign investment, particularly where a higher capitalisation rate is applied to an income earned by a foreign firm than by an indigenous firm. No less important is the effect such flows might have on monetary integration and feasible currency areas. Corden (1972) has suggested that such flows can only help solve the internal and external balance simultaneously in the short run. While monetary integration may end destabilising short-term capital movements, if the exchange rates of the countries within the area, relative to those outside, become more rigid, then destabilising capital movements could increase.

How does the introduction of the MNE affect these conclusions? Much of what has been said presupposes the existence of an international capital market. MNEs have most certainly enlarged this market in the last two decades, particularly the Eurodollar market, which has helped to finance a good deal of the expansion of such companies in Europe. This, indeed, has been an important source of external funds to MNEs as well as an outlet for European savings. At the same time, the existence of such a market, coupled with the particular ability and incentive of MNEs to speedily take advantage of it — especially those that engage in international monetary management procedures — has considerably reduced the effectiveness of the monetary policies of individual European countries. This has meant that while, almost certainly, the growth of the international capital market has aided long-run economic development, it may have weakened the efforts of national governments to maintain short-term monetary stability; moreover, because of their easier access to the Eurodollar market, multinational enterprises, both domestic and foreign-owned, have been given additional competitive edge over national enterprises, and this has enabled them further to increase their penetration of the local market.

But the main impact of the MNEs arises from their income mobility of capital and from their ability over indigenous firms to engage in internal transactions across national boundaries. Theoretically, the effects of income mobility of capital are rather different from those of interest-mobile capital (Johnson, 1966). The former eases national economic management under a fixed exchange rate system, using either monetary or fiscal measures, but reduces the leverage under a floating rate system. More practically, the role of MNEs is shown in a variety of ways. First, because they tend to export more than indigenous firms, fiscal policy is likely to affect their total activities rather less than might otherwise be the case. Second, because the transactions are internal to the company, the possibility of shifting funds from high tax to low tax countries for hedging or speculative purposes are that much greater, through the use of leads and lags. This latter flexibility (which has been demonstrated at various times in recent years) has most certainly led to pressure on weak exchange rates. The fact that this is a perfectly normal and reasonable thing for MNEs (or any enterprises) to do, and is a direct reflection of the way in which the international monetary system is organised, does nothing to endear them to governments. For authorities committed to the fixed exchange rates, this can be very disturbing, particularly when one remembers that the liquid assets controlled by multinational enterprises and similar institutions, estimated, in the mid 1970s, to be three times the total world gold and currency reserves,[20] reflects *not* the cash flow which originates from abroad but that of their operations.

Governments can and do respond to the activities of MNEs in the areas just discussed in a number of ways, including the substitution of floating for fixed exchange rates. But, as Maynard (1974) has suggested, MNEs may themselves reduce the effectiveness of such flexibility as their activities may affect the size of the feasible currency area. For this depends on whether or not an economy, by varying its exchange rate, can bring about the necessary changes in relative prices without employment and output being adversely affected; in other words, whether or not real wages (but not money wages) are flexible in a downward direction. It may be argued that MNEs, prompted *inter alia* by the international action of trade unions, are reducing the likelihood of this being achieved by their gradual adoption of harmonised wage settlements. In consequence, any devaluation would encourage unions to press for an increase in money wages, which, if this led, through the wage transfer mechanism, to an increase in wages throughout the economy, would offset the benefits of devaluation and violate the propositions of the feasible currency area. The net result would be a failure to cure unemployment, and an encouragement to countries to consider monetary integration, and so increase the feasible currency area.

(b) *Inflation*[21]

In an essay published in 1968, A. J. Brown argued that the long-term effects of international capital flows on inflation could not be generalised, and that everything depended on the amounts of investment in the national and regional economies and on the balance between the amounts of capital formation directed in the world towards increasing capacities to produce goods of flexible and rigid prices, respectively. Moreover, at a macro level, it is possible to argue that MNEs (like other institutions) can only affect the policies pursued by governments towards inflation but cannot be held responsible for inflation.

Nevertheless, the impact of MNEs on cost-push inflation and the response this generates from trade unions are interesting phenomena. It has sometimes been argued that foreign affiliates contribute to regional inflation by their propensity to pay higher wages to attract labour; it is not difficult to extend this to the national level. If this is the case, why is it so? Is it a feature of multinationalism itself or the structure of MNEs? In most cases it is part of both. MNEs (and their affiliates) tend to be concentrated in capital intensive industries and their productivity is above average. Because of this, they can afford to pay above average wages, and may be willing to do so to avoid the high cost of industrial unrest or strikes. But this, in itself, will not necessarily lead to higher wages being paid, unless a wage transfer mechanism is operating. This, in turn, will depend *inter alia* on the way in which wage agreements are negotiated, for example, industry-wide agreements are more likely to be related to average profits in an industry, etc., while plant bargaining agreements are related more to the ability to pay of the most productive firms. The spread of this type of bargaining technique by US MNEs has made it more likely that firms competing with their affiliates will ask for the wages paid by them.

More to the point is that the trade unions negotiating with MNEs might themselves try and press for wage parity on an international scale. In these circumstances, and where competition in the goods market is oligopolistic, the goods supplied have a low price elasticity of demand and the wage transference mechanism may easily cross national boundaries. A low price elasticity of demand, of course, implies that there is little import competition or that the prices of imports have also risen. In most industries in which MNEs are operating there is a substantial trade in goods. But where there are sympathetic movements in wages, both between production units in the same firm across national boundaries and between firms in the same industry within national boundaries, the consumer is no longer protected and prices will rise.

As yet, little empirical research has been done on the wage transfer mechanism and the rôle played by MNEs in it. But various pieces of evidence are coming to light which tend to support the hypothesis outlined above. This is partly a structural phenomenon. In the 1960s, for example, wages increased most in advanced industrial countries in those industries in which MNEs were most strongly concentrated. In these same industries, too, US affiliates tend to pay higher wages than indigenous firms, while between countries wages tend to be less dispersed than the average. Worker cohesion is strongest and trades unions are the most active where MNEs are concentrated — the motor and chemical industries are cases in point; while, because of the effects on the rest of the enterprise, affiliates can less afford industrial unrest or strikes than indigenous producers. Such facts as these suggest that, in a fully employed economy, capital formation by foreign owned companies may have more inflationary implications than that of their indigenous competitors; although domestic MNEs may cause similar anxieties. It is one further example of the effects on the openness of an economy, where the pressures of costs are internationally transmitted. At the very least, it results in a redistribution of income towards those who work in MNEs away from the rest of the community; at worst, it could result in the twin evils of inflation and unemployment being more difficult to contain. Once again, it has implications for the way in which governments manage the economy for the form and content of national economic planning.

(c)   *Distribution of income*

A final, and very brief, comment about the distribution of income arising from the activities of MNEs. Received theory suggests normal capital flows will raise the marginal product of labour in recipient countries and lower it in investing countries. Owners of capital will be affected in the opposite way. This model, however, is hardly appropriate to capital movements generated by MNEs, one of the main results of which is to raise the level of the marginal productivity in host countries, which may benefit both labour *and* capital and, in so far as resources *are* more effectively allocated, raise the level of factor productivity in the investing country.

A more interesting question concerns the distribution of the costs and benefits arising from the operations of MNEs *between* host and investing countries, assuming these can be assessed accurately. In theory, it is possible to draw up a balance sheet of costs and benefits of capital formation by MNEs in a particular country, both to MNEs and to host countries. One could, for example, imagine a cost (dividends remitted, royalties and fees, etc.) beyond which host countries would not be prepared to pay for the benefits; this would depend on the alternatives open to them to obtain these benefits. Similarly, one can envisage a price (in the form of forgone profits, etc.) which the investing company is not prepared to pay to the host country, which, again, will depend on the opportunities it forgoes from investing elsewhere. The price finally agreed will depend *inter alia* on the bargaining strength of the two parties, and their knowledge of the opportunities open to the other. In practice, costs and benefits are difficult to compute, but recently, research by Vaitsos (1974) has suggested that the benefits to both parties are more substantial than is commonly thought.

Even the above calculation does not get to the root of the sharing problem. An analogy might help here. A multi-locational domestic UK enterprise might decide to shut down a factory in the north-west of England and transfer production to the south-east because it is economic so to do. This clearly has certain social consequences; let us assume, however, that this will result in an increase in allocative efficiency and a marked shift in the distribution of income to the south-east. Since the UK government has a responsibility for the economic welfare of the north-west, it is likely to take action to assist the people in that area to find jobs either by moving to the more prosperous south-east or encouraging new activity in the north-west; if necessary, it can use part of the increased income generated by the company moving to the south-east to do this. In other words, the country as whole, out of increased wealth created, may be able to compensate, in part at least, those who have been adversely affected by the (efficient) action of a private company.

There is no device which can compensate for similar type actions of the MNEs. If a US company closes its Welsh factory to transfer production to the USA, the UK government can use the devices of regional policy to help compensate for this. But the contribution of output of the company has been transferred to the USA. A supra-national authority might devise a fiscal system which in some way would compensate for this or at least assist the adjustment to a new pattern of resource allocation. Alternatively, if there were complete mobility of all resources across national boundaries, the readjustment problem would be much easier to deal with.

Again, it may be argued this is not a new problem and that free international trade is constantly causing adjustment problems, and that no one suggests that this should result in some distribution of income from nations that gain to those that lose. But here the nature of the problem is different because affiliates of MNEs are much more part of the fabric of the countries in which they operate, and are able to exert more control over decision taking.

VI

The impact of capital flows generated by MNEs differs from that of portfolio investment due to the fact that the former is primarily a vehicle for moving a package of resources, within the same enterprises, across national boundaries, while the latter is a vehicle for transferring savings between independent lenders and borrowers. This not only affects immediately the determinants of investment of MNEs compared with other firms in the *investing* country, but of the capital formation by affiliates of MNEs compared with indigenous companies in the host countries. A further difference arises from the ability of MNEs to take advantage of differences in input prices and availability and markets throughout the world, and to trade goods and services internally as well as capital. This leads to different types of operations of affiliates of non-resident enterprises, which range from truncated production to a commitment covering a wide range of activities on a world scale.

The effects of the capital formation reflect the operations of the affiliates of foreign firms and of their group. While portfolio investment is essentially interest- (or money capital) mobile, investment by MNEs is essentially income-mobile, income here being the total benefits received by the investing group. The precise impact will vary according to the type of MNE and government policies pursued. The general conclusion of the final section, in which we briefly examined the impact of MNEs on national economic management, inflation and the distribution of income was that their effects were parallel to those of a free movement in capital and in goods, viz. that domestic management policies became more difficult to achieve the greater the openness of the economy. But because MNEs were so much more involved in international transactions than national firms and a substantial part of these were intra-group; because they were among the world's largest and most powerful financial institutions; and because they operated in a world comprised of sovereign states each with different fiscal, monetary and exchange rate policies designed to meet its own particular objectives, the clash between such firms and national governments was the more dramatically expressed.

None of the alternatives suggested to resolve this dilemma and the balance between equity and efficiency are without cost. Unilateral or multilateral controls over MNEs, the abandonment of national sovereignty to world economic forces, the integration of nations to create an environment offering countervailing power to multinational enterprises but one in which they can operate freely, have all been suggested. But the extent to which any or all of these are possible may depend on how far countries are prepared to abrogate their authority in monetary or fiscal matters and this in the end may be the most crucial question of all.[22]

Notes: Chapter 8

1 For an application of this distinction to nineteenth century UK foreign investment, see Houston and Dunning (1976) and Svedberg (1978).
2 In the original version of this chapter there was an additional section on the distinctive features of MNEs, which has already been covered in Chapter 1 of this book.
3 For a discussion of alternative theories of international capital movements, see Branson and Hill (1971). For a discussion of the impact of changes in external, relative to domestic, interest rates on UK inward and outward investment see Boatwright and Renton (1975), Beenstock and Bell (1979) and Beenstock and Willcocks (1980). All these studies suggest that such changes have only a small impact on capital flows. By contrast, Beenstock and Willcocks argue that the net asset formation of *all* firms in the UK is influenced by such differences in interest rates and that this is partly accounted for by the behaviour of UK and foreign based MNEs.
4 Sometimes, too, comparisons are made between MNEs and firms engaged only in domestic activities. See Parker (1974) and Houston and Dunning (1976).

5   These are summarised by Stevens (1974). See, too, J. H. Dunning (1973) from which the following two paragraphs are derived.

6   An exception is that of Krause (1968) who argues that there is some relationship between indices of plant and equipment expenditure by US firms in the EEC in different industries and the common external tariff.

7   On the impact of the EEC opinions differ somewhat: compare, for example, the approach of Scaperlanda (1967) and d'Arge (1969).

8   Indeed, the techniques for appraising alternative investment projects can easily be applied to appraising the same investment project in alternative locations.

9   See also Vaupel (1971) and Parry (1975).

10 Defined as the share of the gross output of a particular industry accounted for by US affiliates.

11 Because of the truncated activities of the affiliates.

12 See also Chapter 15.

13 There is some evidence to suggest that corporate tax rates do affect the geographical location of investments (see Mellors, 1973).

14 Kopits (1976), in summarising Horst's work, estimates arc elasticities of −6.8 for net capital flow, +0.3 for parent real investment and −0.6 for subsidiary real investment.

15 One estimate by the EEC suggests that 50 per cent of the increase in manufacturing output in the least developed regions of Ireland in the early and mid-1970s came from export oriented foreign companies. See Hood and Young (1980).

16 See, for example, Riedel (1975), Reuber (1973) and Kagawuchi (1978).

17 These points are expanded in Chapter 9.

18 For a discussion of some financial reasons why a project valuation may be different for an MNE compared with a local firm see Lessard (1979). For an incorporation of exchange risk into the model see Aliber (1970).

19 Assuming they are allowed to exploit these markets.

20 As observed by the US Tariff Commission (1973, p. 539), 'A movement of a mere 1 per cent of these assets in response to exchange rate weakness or strength is quite sufficient to produce a first class international financial crisis.'

21 Some of the points covered in this section are elaborated on in Chapter 10.

22 See also Chapter 14.

Appendix 8.1

Summary of shares of plant and equipment spending by US-owned multinational corporations in gross fixed capital formation in the manufacturing industries of seven key countries, 1966 and 1970

Industry description	Plant and equipment spending by multinational corporations as percentage of gross fixed capital formation							Aggregate for all seven countries		
	UK	France	W. Germany	Belgium–Luxembourg	Canada	Mexico	Brazil[b]	P & E spending by MNEs ($m.)	GFCF[f] ($m.)	P & E as % of GFCF[g]
1966										
All manufacturing	16.3	4.3	9.2	17.0	42.7	6.7	12.4	3,014	22,407	13
Food	4.6	1.9	1.4	n.a.[a]	22.5	2.7	n.a.[a]	109[c]	2,670[c]	4
Chemicals	15.8	1.9	5.1	23.3	86.6	20.8	16.8	561	4,348	12
Primary and fabricated metals	11.3	1.7	1.8			4.0	n.a.[a]	195[d]	8,579[d]	20
Machinery	21.5	15.4	19.4	19.3	64.0	5.3	50.8	748		
Transportation equipment	47.6	8.8	37.8			3.1	28.2	831		
All other manufacturing	11.6	1.0	1.1	10.6	23.6	0.2	6.7	570	6,810	8
1970										
All manufacturing	20.9	5.8	12.3	14.1	32.2	9.3	18.3	4,152	29,739	13
Food	4.4	0.9	2.0	n.a.[a]	23.5	3.1	11.1	163[e]	4,030[e]	4
Chemicals	17.9	2.1	10.4	24.9	68.1	10.7	27.4	691	5,155	13
Primary and fabricated metals	21.1	1.0	8.4			8.3	11.9	457		
Machinery	29.0	23.3	27.8	12.0	57.8	13.9	57.1	1,292	11,482	22
Transportation equipment	45.5	9.8	27.8			17.9	25.6	870		
All other manufacturing	18.2	2.8	2.7	10.8	20.5	13.0	5.9	679	9,072	7

[a] Included in 'all other industries'.
[b] Figures for 1970 are based on 1969 data for GFCF.
[c] Excludes food processing in Belgium-Luxembourg and Brazil. Figures for these countries are included in 'all other manufacturing'.
[d] Excludes primary metals and fabricated metals in Brazil. These figures are included in 'all other manufacturing'.
[e] Excludes food processing in Belgium-Luxembourg, for which the relevant data are included in 'all other manufacturing'.
[f] 'Gross fixed capital formation'.
[g] Plant and equipment expenditures as percentage of gross fixed capital formation.
Source: US Tariff Commission (1973).

References

Aliber, R. Z. (1970), 'A theory of direct investment', in C. P. Kindleberger (ed.), *The International Corporation* (Cambridge, Mass.: MIT Press).

Arge, R. d' (1969), 'Notes on customs unions and foreign direct investment', *Economic Journal*, vol. 74.

Ashcroft, B., and Ingham, K. P. D. (1978), *The Response of MNC Subsidiaries and Indigenous Companies to Regional Policy: The Effect of Company Adaptation*, Department of Economics, University of Strathclyde, Discussion Paper 78/4.

Bandera, V. N., and White, J. J. (1968), 'US direct investment and domestic markets in Europe', *Economica International*, vol. 21.

Beenstock, M., and Bell, S. R. (1979), 'A quarterly econometric model of the capital account in the UK balance of payments', *Manchester School of Economic and Social Studies*, vol. XLIV (March).

Beenstock, M., and Willcocks, P. (1980), *Capital Formation in a Small Open Economy*, London Business School, Economic Forecasting Unit, Discussion Paper No. 73 (March).

Boatright, B. D., and Renton, G. A. (1975), 'An analysis of UK inflows and outflows of foreign direct investment', *Review of Economics and Statistics* (November).

Branson, W. H., and Hill, R. D. (1971), *Capital Movements in the OECD Area* (Paris: OECD).

Brown, A. J. (1968), 'Capital movements and inflation', in J. Adler (ed.) *Capital Movements and Economic Development* (London: Macmillan).

Cairncross, A. K. (1973), *Control over International Capital Movements* (Washington, DC: Brookings Institute), Staff Paper.

Caves, R., and Reuber, G. (1971), *Capital Transfers and Economic Policy in Canada 1951/62* (Cambridge, Mass.: Harvard University Press).

Cooper, R. N. (1971), 'Towards an international capital market', in C. P. Kindleberger and A. Shonfield, *North American and Western European Economic Policies* (London: Macmillan).

Corden, M. (1972), *Monetary Integration*, Essays in International Finance No. 93, Princeton University.

Dunning, J. H. (1973), 'The determinants of international production', *Oxford Economic Papers*, vol. 25 (November).

Dunning, J. H. (1976), *US Industry in Britain* (London: Wilton House).

Dunning, J. H., and Yannapoulos, G. (1973), 'The fiscal factor in the location of affiliates of multinational enterprises', in *Vers Une Politique Fiscale Européene à l'égard des Enterprises Multinationales*, Centre de Recherches Interdisciplinaires Droit-Economie, Louvain.

Hawkins, R. G., and Macaluso, D. (1977), 'The avoidance of restrictive monetary policies in host countries by multinational firms', *Journal of Money Credit and Banking*, vol. IX (November).

Hawkins, R. G. (1978), 'Cyclical investment behaviour of indigenous firms and US affiliates', in M. Ghertman and J. Leontadies (eds), *European Research in International Business* (Amsterdam: North Holland).

Heenan, D. A. (1977), 'Global cities of tomorrow', *Harvard Business Review* (May/June).

Hood, N., and Young, S. (1980), *European Development Strategies of US Owned Manufacturing Companies Located in Scotland* (Edinburgh: HMSO).

Horst, T. (1977), 'American taxation of multinational firms', *American Economic Review*, vol. 67 (June).

Houston, T., and Dunning, J. H. (1976), *UK Industry Abroad* (London: The Financial Times).

Johnson, H. G. (1966), 'International capital movement and economic policy', in I. Bagiotti (ed.), *Essays in Honour of Marco Fanno*, Padora.

Kagawuchi, W. B. (1978), *The Role of Japanese Firms in the Manufactured Exports of Developing Countries*, mimeo, World Bank.

Kopits, G. (1976), 'Taxation and multinational firm behaviour: a critical survey', *IMF Staff Papers*, vol. XXIII, no. 3 (November).

Krause, L. R. (1968), *European Economic Integration and the US* (Washington, DC: The Brookings Institution).

Lessard, D. R. (1979), 'Transfer prices, taxes and financial markets', in R. G. Hawkins (ed.), *The Economic Effects of Multinational Corporations* (Greenwich, Conn.: JAI Press).

McAleese, D., and Counahan, M. (1979), '"Stickers" or "snatchers"? Employment in transnational corporations during the recession', *Oxford Bulletin of Economics and Statistics*, vol. 41 (November).

Manser, W. A. P. (1973), *The Financial Role of Multinational Enterprises* (London: International Chamber of Commerce).

Maynard, G. W. (1974), 'The multinational enterprise and monetary policy', in J. H. Dunning (ed.), *Economic Analysis and the Multinational Enterprise* (London: Allen & Unwin).

Mellors, J. (1973), *International Tax Differentials and the Location of Overseas Direct Investment: A Pilot Study*, University of Reading, Discussion Papers in International Investment and Business Studies No. 4.

Modigliani, F., and Miller, M. (1958), 'The cost of capital, corporation finance and the theory of investment', *American Economic Review*, vol. 48 (June).

Parker, J. E. S. (1974), *The Economics of Innovation* (London: Longman).

Parry, T. G. (1975), *Forms of International Production and Home Industry Characteristics*, University of Reading Discussion Papers in International Investment and Business Studies No. 19 (April).

Popkin, J. (1956), 'Interfirm differences in direct investment behaviour of US manufacturers', unpublished doctoral dissertation, University of Pennsylvania.

Quinn, J. B. (1968), *The Role of Science and Technology in Economic Development* (Paris: UNESCO).

Reuber, G. (1973), *Private Foreign Investment in Development* (Oxford: Clarendon Press).

Riedel, H. (1975), 'The nature and determinant of export oriented direct foreign investment in a developing country. A case study of Taiwan', *Weltwirtschaftliches Archiv*, vol. III (September).

Rugman, A. (1979), *International Diversification and the Multinational Enterprise* (Lexington, Mass.: Lexington Books).

Scaperlanda, A. E. (1967), 'The EEC and US foreign investment: some empirical evidence', *Economic Journal*, vol. 77 (March).

Scaperlanda, A. E., and Mauer, L. J. (1969), 'The determinants of US direct investment in the EEC', *American Economic Review*, vol. 59 (September).

Severn, A. J. (1971), 'Investment and financial behaviour of American investors in manufacturing industry', in F. Machlup, L. Tarshis and W. Salant (eds), *International Mobility and the Movement of Capital* (Universities National Bureau of Economic Research and Washington, DC: Brookings Institution).

Stevens, G. V. (1969), 'Fixed investment expenditure of foreign manufacturing affiliates in US firms: theoretical models and empirical evidence', *Yale Economic Essays*, vol. 9.

Stevens, G. V. (1974), 'The multinational enterprise and the determinants of investment', in J. H. Dunning (ed.), *Economic Analysis and the Multinational Enterprise* (London: Allen & Unwin).

Svedberg, P. (1978), 'The portfolio-direct composition of private foreign investment in 1914 revisited, *Economic Journal*, vol. 88 (December).

US Tariff Commission (1973), *Implications of Multinational Firms for World Trade and Investment and for US Trade and Investment*. Report for Committee on Finance of US Senate (Washington, DC: US Government Printing Office).

Vaitsos, C. (1974), 'Inter-country income distribution and trans-national corporations', in J. H. Dunning (ed.), *Economic Analysis and the Multinational Enterprise* (London: Allen & Unwin).

Vaupel, J. W. (1971), 'Characteristics and motivations of the US corporations which manufacture abroad, paper presented to meeting of participatory members of the Atlantic Institute, Paris.

Wallis, K. F. (1968), 'Notes on Scaperlanda's article', *Economic Journal*, vol. 73 (September).

9

Multinational Enterprises, Locational Strategies and Regional Development

I

It is generally recognised that the choice of sites of foreign based enterprises will be dominated by locational considerations that are different from those affecting similar choices of national enterprises (Vernon, 1974). What is not clear both from the existing literature and the available statistical evidence is whether the investment location decisions of MNEs tend to strengthen the agglomeration tendencies prevailing in the spatial structure of the market economies. Blackbourn (1974) finds that foreign based enterprises, and especially American enterprises in Europe, have an obvious preference for the developed areas of heavy industrial concentration. He argues that unfamiliarity with national market conditions drives managers of MNEs to select apparently safe locations among potential sites so that they can reduce uncertainty and eliminate unacceptable risks. Another writer (Klemmer, 1979) has argued that MNEs tend to prefer existing areas of industrial concentration as part of a locational strategy of loss minimisation in the event of a commercial failure. The probability of such a failure is thought to be higher in an unfamiliar environment. Central locations offer a reasonable chance of speedily selling premises and capital equipment with minimum loss. However, observing the locational patterns of European MNEs investing in the US economy, Faith (1972, ch. 8) found a heavy concentration of direct investment of these MNEs in areas of labour surpluses and with a recent history of industrial development.

Other writers believe that the locational strategies of foreign owned enterprises diminish the effectiveness of government regional policies — policies which are designed precisely to reduce regional unemployment and income disparities. Holland (1973, 1975, 1976) argues that the impact

This chapter is a revised version of a paper first published in *Regional Studies*, vol. 10 (1976). I am most grateful to Mr Yannopoulos for his collaboration in making the amendments to this paper.

of regional policies is diminished either because the effect of regional labour subsidies is reduced (due to the access of MNEs to low cost foreign labour or because the effect of regional capital incentives is reduced through the capacity of MNEs to charge their local affiliates high import prices from subsidiaries in low tax countries) or because government authorities, faced with companies able to site their plants in alternative locations outside the national economy, are often forced to relax controls like the IDCs. However, evidence from other sources presents a different picture. The 1968 report of the then Board of Trade (Howard, 1968) on the movement of manufacturing industry in the UK shows that over the twenty years' period 1945—65 foreign based companies moving plants in the UK had a much higher propensity to locate these plants within the development areas than British companies establishing new plants or moving existing ones to locations outside the region of their original expansion. As Table 9.1 reveals, of the total moves originating from the UK (excluding inter-regional ones) only about 49 per cent were directed to locations within the development areas (comprising Scotland, Wales, the northern region of England and Northern Ireland). When movements originating from abroad are examined, one sees that slightly less than 55 per cent of them were directed to development areas. The picture does not change if one concentrates on the distribution of employment generated by the mobile plants rather than the distribution of the number of moves.

It is interesting to note (see figs. between brackets in Table 9.1) that during the five-year period 1960—65, which corresponds with the beginnings of a more active regional policy in the UK, the percentage of movements originating from abroad and destined to development areas remained at about the same level as for the whole period, whereas the corresponding percentage of movements originating from the UK only and destined to the development areas declined. Thus if no subsidiaries of foreign based MNEs were establishing plants in the UK during that period, the concentration of production and employment in the developed, non-assisted areas would have been more pronounced.

Further analysis for the post-1965 period has produced additional evidence of a continuous shift in the geographical distribution of overseas-controlled manufacturing employment towards the peripheral regions of the UK. Between 1963 and 1971 the share of all overseas controlled employment found in the core region of the South-East declined from 51 per cent to 41 per cent (Dicken and Lloyd, 1976). The geographical pattern of the redistribution of jobs resulting from employment changes by foreign firms between 1963 and 1971 was compared by Watts (1979) to the corresponding pattern generated from employment changes by British owned firms. He found that the South-East region accounted for 95 per cent of the net loss of jobs by foreign firms compared to only 35 per cent of the net employment losses over the same period by British owned firms. This suggests that foreign firms have moved their growth out of the

Table 9.1 *Regional Distribution of Industrial Moves in UK, 1945–65*

	UK	Region of Destination Development areas	Development areas as % of total UK moves
A. *Movements originating from UK only* (excluding intra-regional moves)			
No. of moves	1521	743	48.8 (44.1)[a]
Employment (thousands)	466.1	248.4	53.3 (47.3)
B. *Movements originating from abroad*			
No. of moves	258	141	54.7 (54.0)
Employment (thousands)	108.5	69.4	64.0 (63.9)

[a] Numbers in parentheses refer to the sub-period 1960–65.
Source: Howard (1968).

Table 9.2   *Regional Distribution of Foreign Production Units according to Starting Year: Belgium*

Province	Before 1945	1945–57	1958–63	1964–68
Brabant	38	44	17	12
Antwerp	19	25	26	20
Eastern Flanders	14	13	20	18
Limbourg	4	6	19	22
Hainaut	10	4	5	12
Liege	10	6	5	7
Western Flanders	3	2	8	6
Namur	3	1	0	2
Luxembourg	0	0	0	2
Belgium	100	100	100	100

Source: van den Bulcke (1971).

South-East at a rate much faster than UK firms. Two of the more depressed development areas of the UK, viz. Scotland and Northern Ireland, accounted for more than half the net gains of foreign firms but experienced about 4 per cent of the net losses of UK firms. The pattern for the other development areas of the UK is less clear but, overall, a careful comparison of the geographical characteristics of the redistribution of employment by UK and foreign firms, during the period 1963–71, strongly suggests that foreign firms showed a bias in favour of locations in assisted areas.

That MNEs are influenced by regional policy incentives when selecting locations within a foreign country can also be seen from a set of Belgian data found in Van Den Bulke (1971). From this data it is possible to compare the regional distribution of the production units of MNEs located in Belgium at different points in time that correspond to periods characterised by different policy approaches to regional development (Table 9.2). Before the enactment of the first Expansion Law in 1959, regional development in Belgium was more or less directed by market forces. The introduction of a first set of regional policy instruments in 1959 was followed by the enactment of a second Expansion Law in 1966 offering stronger incentives. As can be seen from Table 9.2, there has been a noticeable change since 1959 in the regional distribution of foreign production units in favour of the assisted areas in the problem regions of Hainaut, Eastern Flanders and Limbourg. For example, the less developed Province of Limbourg, which during 1945–65 received 6 per cent of all new production units of foreign subsidiaries, increased its share to 22 per cent during the period 1964–68. Commenting on the Belgian experience, de Jons (1972) argues that the attraction of regional incentives offered by the Expansion Laws of 1959 and 1966 has had only limited success as foreign affiliates have been attracted predominantly to only two of the provinces covered by the Expansion Laws (Limbourg and East Flanders). However,

Table 9.3 *Regional Distribution of Grant-Aided Manufacturing Plants Established in Ireland 1960–73*

Organisational structure	Nationality	% located in development areas
Branch	MNE	58.9
	Irish	48.9
Independent	MNE	59.7
	Irish	40.0

Source: O'Farrell (1980), p. 143.

since the Belgian Expansion Laws cover a broad area of the country which includes subregions with differences in their locational disadvantages, it is not surprising that there were only certain areas, that is, the intra-marginal regions, that attracted the largest share of foreign direct investment.

The Irish evidence on the locational pattern of foreign and indigenous plants over the period 1960–73 presents considerable interest. As Table 9.3 shows, overseas firms (both branch plants and independent companies) established a higher proportion of their plants in Ireland's designated development areas than the indigenous Irish ones. Even when appropriate statistical controls are carried out to take account of the interaction effects between market orientation and nationality (O'Farrell, 1980), the analysis of the locational pattern at the assisted/non-assisted area level confirms that (1) foreign plants marketing in the UK and located in towns below 5,000 population (i.e. about 25 per cent of all grant-aided plants during 1960–73) revealed a significantly greater tendency to establish in the peripheral development areas than indigenous Irish ones and (2) foreign plants other than those under (1) have been at least as likely to locate in the development areas as indigenous ones.

Furthermore, according to the report of the US Tariff Commission (1973), incentives for regional development exert an important influence on an MNE's choice of location within a foreign country. The Commission estimates that approximately 50 per cent of all investments by American MNEs in Europe during the postwar period were located in the assisted areas of the European countries, and explains this relatively high percentage by the fact that 'US companies have been much more alert than European companies in discovering how to take advantage of such depressed area incentives'.

More significant, however, is the evidence presented in the British inquiry into location attitudes (House of Commons Papers, 1974) which covered 69 per cent of all moves in the UK that involved the opening up of a manufacturing plant in a new location in a new subregion during 1964–67. Regional policy incentives were regarded as a major factor influencing location choice by 51 per cent of overseas owned firms compared to 39 per cent of all firms. Survey evidence from other countries is reviewed in Yannopoulos (1980).

The significance of policy incentives is, however, challenged in a study on the location of manufacturing establishments in Holland by Kemper and de Smidt (1980). In this study, the authors divided the period 1945–72 into two sub-periods; the first, 1945–58, was characterised by the lack of an active regional policy while the second, 1959–72, was characterised by an active regional policy. The geographical distributions of foreign manufacturing establishments for the two subperiods were then compared to see whether they differed in a significant way. The application of the Kalmogorov–Smirnof test indicates that the highest deviation between the two spatial distributions is below the critical value at the 0.10 level of significance. On the basis of this test, Kemper and de Smidt concluded that the Dutch regional policy did not contribute in a decisive manner in shifting the regional distribution of foreign establishments in the Netherlands. However, as these authors point out, there is a clear contrast between the Dutch (and also German) experience, where the development regions have attracted a relatively minor share of foreign direct investment, and the experience of Britain, Ireland, Belgium and possibly France where foreign direct investment is over-represented in these regions.

It can be argued that while MNEs tend to favour peripheral, assisted areas when opening up new manufacturing plants they may equally be biased against such locations when confronted with decisions to close already existing plants. Not much work has been done in testing this additional hypothesis with the exception of the analysis of industrial closures in Ireland during 1960–73 by O'Farrell (1976). This analysis shows that closure rates of grant-aided manufacturing plants operating in Ireland are independent of nationality.

II

The contradictory views often found in the literature dealing with the impact of MNEs on regional disequilibria can be explained either by the inadequacy of the available statistical information for meaningful comparisons with national enterprises or by the fact that MNEs are, all too often, treated as a homogeneous group without due regard to differences in their structural and organisational characteristics.

In this chapter an attempt is made to clarify this issue and to show how differences in enterprise structures and strategies can influence locational choices. The starting point of the analysis is that the size of the effective subsidy required to induce a multiplant firm (either national or multinational) to set production units in less preferable locations depends on a number of product-related and enterprise-related variables (Moody and Smith, 1975). It is necessary to look through a list of such variables in order to establish their influence on the degree of responsiveness of a multiplant firm to regional development incentives. In order to do this, in the third section of the chapter an analytical framework for assessing the microeconomic effectiveness of regional subsidies is developed. Then we must examine to what extent the structural and organisational character-istics of MNEs are such as to induce them to respond to regional subsidies differently from a multilocation domestic enterprise (MLDE). We find that in a number of instances an MNE will tend to be more responsive than an MLDE to certain types of regional incentives, while in other cases the opposite is true. Finally, we examine how multinationality as such and the fact that a local subsidiary is part of an enterprise with a global strategy will influence the choice of location within a national economy.

The evaluation of the spatial impact of overseas investment is concerned with either investment for the establishment of new facilities or the growth of existing MNE plants within a country. In other words, the spatial im-pact of that process of enterprise internationalisation that takes place through takeover, purchase or participation is ignored. In the latter case the spatial impact of foreign direct investment will be determined by the regional distribution of plants eligible for takeover or purchase (Klemmer, 1979).

III

Areas designated as development or assisted regions are usually considered as inferior locations, and plants established in these areas may be faced with higher costs of production for a variety of reasons. These include poor accessibility to major suppliers or major markets and higher transport and communications costs (including communications with the parent plant). Moreover, the existence of surplus resources (and, in particular, labour) does not necessarily confer locational advantages to development areas. Given the nature of collective bargaining and trade union practices, money wage rates in assisted areas may not be very different from those in non-assisted areas. With a lower quality labour force, or one that must be trained at additional cost, the labour cost per unit of output in the development areas may be higher than that in non-assisted regions.[1] Financial, fiscal and other incentives, offered through regional policies, can thus be considered as compensating for higher costs of production associated with inferior locations. But, to be effective as regional policy instruments, such incentives have to provide positive (net) advantages to locations within the assisted areas. The importance of such incentives then depends on whether their size compares favourably with inter-regional differentials in total costs.

Following Thoman (1973) we define a break-even subsidy as a subsidy (or the present value of a stream of subsidies over time) that will enable a plant located in an assisted area to be fully compensated for all cost disadvantages associated with such a location. Regional policy incentives can then be designated as 'effective' if the subsidy equivalent of such incentives exceeds the break-even subsidy sufficiently to compensate for any uncertainty associated with either the unknown environment in which the plant will be established or a sudden discontinuation of the system of incentives consequential upon changes in government policy. There is thus a difference between the *break-even* subsidy (which just compensates for cost differentials between alternative locations) and a *required* subsidy, which compensates not only for cost differentials but also for the appropriate degree of uncertainty about the continuation of the subsidy for the period the firm deems essential.

From what has been written so far, it is clear that we are here concerned with the 'microeconomic' effectiveness of regional subsidies as distinct from their 'macroeconomic' effectiveness. By 'microeconomic' effectiveness is meant the impact of the regional incentives on the locational decision of the *individual* firm. 'Macroeconomic' effectiveness, that is, the impact of the subsidies on regional development, depends not only on how these subsidies affect the locational decision of a single plant, but also on (1) the number, scale and nature of the firms that are induced to move to the assisted areas, (2) the secondary development that these firms attract through their inter-industry linkages and external economies and (3) the extent of overbidding by other regions.

To determine the size of cost differences between assisted and non-assisted areas, all differences in labour costs, in transport and marketing costs (both of raw materials and final products) and in management communication costs[2] must be taken into account. Assuming that the number of workers employed, the quantities of raw materials and final products to be moved around and the number of contacts between different levels of management are the same, irrespective of whether the plant is located in an assisted or a non-assisted area, then the size of the break-even subsidy will be affected by (1) differences in unit labour costs, (2) differences in unit transport costs and (3) differences in communications costs per management contact. Sometimes in cases where the parent plant is located in a non-assisted area, the establishment of a new plant in the same area will involve practically zero management communication costs. Also the number of units to be transported may be far fewer and the freight costs per unit of either raw materials or finished products or both may be practically zero for a certain proportion of the inputs and/or the outputs of the plant. In such cases, when comparing operating costs between an assisted and a non-assisted location, it is assumed that the number of units to be transported or the number of management contacts needed is the same. However, for some, the unit costs will be zero in a non-assisted location if either the source of raw materials or the market or the higher echelons of management are located in the non-assisted area.

By far more difficult to justify is the assumed quality in the number of

workers employed irrespective of whether the location of the plant producing a given level of output is in an assisted or non-assisted area. If
labour costs per unit of output are higher in the development areas than in
the non-assisted regions then in order to maintain a given level of output
and employment one must additionally assume that the amount of co-
operating non-labour factors, other than raw materials or management
inputs, should appropriately adjust.

Another assumption implicit in the approach used in this chapter is that
the choice of location will not affect significantly the size of the market
area surrounding the centre of production. This may not be true for some
products and will certainly not be true in cases of substantial variations in
demand density distributions over space (Nelson, 1972).

On the basis of the assumptions so far made the size of the break-even
subsidy can be defined as:

$$S_t = \sum_{t=1}^{n} \left[\frac{L_t(W_t^* - W_t) + L_t(N_t^* - N_t) + M_t(r_t^* - r_t) + T_t(C_t^* - C_t)}{(1 + i)^t} \right]$$

where:

S = amount of break-even subsidy
L = output (measured in physical units)
M = number of units to be transported (either of raw materials or final products)
T = number of contracts between different echelons of management
W = efficiency wages (i.e. wages/output)
r = freight costs per unit transported
C = communication costs per management contact
n = life time of project
t = time period
i = discount rate (cost of capital rate)
$*$ = refers to assisted (development) areas

Once the size of the break-even subsidy is established, a calculation of
the subsidy equivalent of the various regional policy incentives will show
how far such incentives compensate effectively for the higher operating
costs of inferior locations, given the degree of uncertainty that the investing firm is prepared to accept.[3] The subsidy equivalent of an incentive will
depend on the characteristics of the enterprise which are critically related
to that incentive. An enterprise with a high capital to labour ratio will
find investment grants more attractive than an enterprise with a lower
degree of capital intensity, whereas an enterprise with a preference for a
low equity to debt ratio will find an incentive based on interest rate subsidisation more attractive than an enterprise with a preference for a high
equity to debt ratio.

The above formulation of the problem enables us to see the reasons why the responsiveness of the MNE to regional policy incentives may differ from that of an MLDE. Given the unique characteristics of the MNE it is possible, as is argued below, that both the size of the break-even subsidy may be smaller and/or the size of the subsidy equivalent of the actual incentives offered may be larger in the case of an MNE than in the case of an MLDE. But first, it is essential to establish what are the factors that influence the general effectiveness (as defined above) of the various regional policy incentives. The effectiveness of such incentives will depend on a number of variables that influence (1) the size of the break-even subsidy or (2) the size of the present value of the actual subsidies or, finally, (3) the amount by which (2) must exceed (1) in order to compensate the firm for any degree of uncertainty that it attaches to operating from a subsidised location.

The variables that influence (1)–(3) above can be classified into two broad groups: *product*-related and *enterprise*-related. Product-related variables are those characteristics of the product that will influence the size of the break-even subsidy or the size of the subsidies that an enterprise locating in an assisted area is entitled to receive. Enterprise-related variables are those characteristics of the enterprise that crucially affect its responsiveness to regional policy incentives. As a OECD report (1973) puts it, each of the various types of regional policy incentives available 'will have quite different effects on the balance sheets of individual firms according to their structure and the relative importance of the various elements within it.'

The product related variables include:

(1)   the skill and/or capital intensity of the production process;
(2)   the extent to which this process is subject to economies of scale;
(3)   the physical characteristics of the product, for example, the bulk or weight to value added ratio;
(4)   the age and/or uniqueness of the product.

(a)   *Skill and/or capital intensity*
The skill intensity of the production process is likely to influence the size of the break-even subsidy, whereas the capital intensity may influence the size of the subsidy equivalent of incentives. If the incentive is capital based (e.g. capital grants), then the higher the capital intensity of production, the greater will be the size of the subsidy equivalent of the incentives offered. If the regional policy incentives are labour based (e.g. the regional employment premium) the opposite will hold.

This is supported by some of the results of an intensive survey (Donaldson, 1966) of thirty-four new firms with foreign participation that started operations in Ireland between 1958 and 1964. Nine of these firms stated firmly that they would not have invested without government assistance (consisting mainly of grants and tax exemptions). Compared with the rest of the firms which gave either inconclusive answers (ten) or considered such assistance of no importance, the nine firms were the most capital intensive in the sample. In Belgium, however, where grants are very rarely used by firms locating in development areas, a positive but rather small correlation was found between an industry's propensity to invest in regional development areas[4] and its labour intensiveness (Thoman, 1973). In general, the microeconomic effectiveness of operational grants which relate to labour will depend on the relative importance of wage costs.

The differential in unit labour costs between an assisted and non-assisted location is likely to be higher (for a given size of labour force) the higher is the ratio of skilled to non-skilled employees, assuming a lower investment in human capital and similar money wage rates in the assisted areas. Obviously, if there exist inter-regional differentials in money wage rates, then the importance of this variable will be reduced since such differentials will tend to diminish the discrepancies in efficiency wages.

(b) *Economies of scale at the plant level*
The tendency to decentralise production activities in response to regional policy incentives will be stronger where the economies of scale at the plant level are small in relation to the size of the market surrounding the firm's (regional) centre of production. This factor probably explains the tendency, observed in the Belgian study referred to above, for the propensity to invest in regional development areas to decline as the size of investment increases.

(c) *Freight costs*
The higher the freight costs for a product in relation to its value added, the more the likelihood that this plant will locate itself near either the source of its materials or its markets. Material or market orientation is the characteristic of industries manufacturing such transport sensitive products. Since the most important consuming regions are likely to be the non-assisted areas, such a high ratio will tend to work against an assisted area location. On the other hand, if the freight costs are a low proportion of total costs, assisted area locations will become attractive at a lower level of a break-even subsidy. It follows too that export oriented firms which produce goods with comparatively low ratios of bulk to value added will tend to be more sensitive to regional subsidies than other firms serving the national market only. Examining evidence from the less developed countries, Reuber (1973) concluded that export oriented foreign affiliates were more sensitive than national market oriented affiliates to fiscal incentives. Contrary to Reuber's findings, however, the Belgian study quoted earlier found no significant association between propensity to invest in regional development areas and export orientation.

(d) *New versus standardised products*

In its initial phase of marketing, the development of a new product requires quick and close communications between the marketing and the R & D department of the enterprise, as well as between designers and manufacturers. Consequently, in the initial stages of the development of a new product there will be a tendency to locate production facilities near the innovative centre of the enterprise (Vernon, 1974). These innovative centres are rarely to be found in assisted regions. However, the emergence of research parks in development areas (e.g. the IBM research unit in Peterlee) indicates that some decentralisation of more basic R & D activities is feasible.

IV

Several major enterprise characteristics can be identified as influencing either the size of the break-even subsidy or the subsidy equivalent of the regional policy incentives. These include:

(1) internal organisation of the enterprise;
(2) extent of vertical integration of the firm;
(3) motivation of investment;
(4) size of the firm: company planning tends to be more systematic in large corporations;
(5) the firm's ratio of capital equipment to total capital, which influences the subsidy equivalent of a system of differential depreciation allowances;
(6) the equity debt ratio, which will determine the relative effectiveness of interest-rate subsidies.

(a) *International organisation of the enterprise*

In a spatially dispersed multiplant firm the balance between centralising and decentralising decisions is crucial in determining the cost of delays in management contacts, particularly those involving face-to-face contacts Thorngren, 1970). The British postwar experience in industrial mobility has shown that an important factor constraining the establishment of new plants or branches in the peripheral regions has been distance from the firm's original location. Part of the reason for this is the fact that personal contacts between headquarters and plant level management required longer journeys. Keeble (1970) has shown that distance from established areas of production (e.g. the South-East and Midlands) is one of the major factors explaining the spatial variations in the patterns of industrial movements to the peripheral regions between 1945 and 1965. The need for frequent personal contacts and consultations between different levels of management depends on the degree of centralisation of the corporate administrative structure. Companies that have succeeded in developing a modern decentralised, multi-divisional corporate structure (Chandler, 1962) will be less constrained in new plant location decisions by the cost of management communications. For such companies, the size of the break-even subsidy required will be lower.

With its factors of production relatively more mobile, an enterprise with a multidivisional structure is in a position to take more decisively into account, in its plant location decisions, the various incentives available in development areas.

(b) *Extent of vertical integration*
Quite often a lack of subcontracting facilities in the assisted areas imposes a considerable strain on the operation of production units located there. In the case of a vertically integrated firm, this may not be such a serious disadvantage since the local plant can draw upon other producing units of the parent firm. Thus, the degree of uncertainty from unsuitable or unreliable subcontracting facilities is considerably reduced. This tends to increase the attractiveness of the regional policy incentives for vertically integrated firms.

(c) *Motivation of investment*
It is important to distinguish between investment in new plant and equipment motivated by rate of return considerations and that motivated by strategic considerations. If the ultimate motive is to improve the firm's overall rate of return, that is, if the firm is anxious to improve or protect its price competitiveness then investment location decisions will be based on factors relating to costs and the reliability of production (Reuber, 1973). In this case regional policy incentives will exert an influence on location decisions, provided their subsidy equivalent sufficiently exceeds the amount of the break-even subsidy to compensate for a given degree of uncertainty. Evidence from Belgium (Thoman, 1973) shows that firms which have tended to invest most in the country's development areas are those which are concentrated in the low profit industries of Belgium. On the other hand, investment motivated by long-run strategic considerations (such as defence of existing markets against encroachment by competitors, or a desire to maintain a position in raw material sources, and/or to induce a country to a long-run commitment to a particular type of technology) will tend to be less sensitive to regional policy incentives. Strategic investment is associated with mature oligopolies (Vernon, 1971, 1974). In industries characterised by that particular market structure plant location decisions can hardly be affected by fiscal or financial incentives.

(d) *Size of the firm*
By and large, large firms engage in more systematic planning than smaller firms. Indeed, as Galbraith argues, it is this ability to plan systematically

that confers a distinct advantage to firms of large size. The larger, multiplant enterprises have been dominant in manufacturing movement in Britain in the postwar period (Keeble, 1970). A large firm, with a more effective department for gathering and processing information, will have a lower (marginal) cost of scanning in site selection (Otterbeck, 1973).

The ability to engage in more extensive search procedures is just one manifestation of a more general ability of adaptation that large firms have when confronted with different conditions in a new location. This means that the larger firm has a better capacity (1) to adjust its production technology through a more systematic search procedure for appropriate techniques, (2) to restructure its linkage patterns and (3) to engage in a process of continuous retraining of its workers and its managerial staff (Ashcroft and Ingham, 1979).

From another viewpoint, the subsidy equivalent of certain incentives may be larger for larger firms. The effectiveness, for example, of reduced interest rates on state loans available to firms investing in assisted areas will depend on the ability of the firm to raise such a loan. Since small firms find it harder to raise loans, they cannot always take advantage of such an incentive. A large firm, with its extensive use of corporate planning techniques, is not handicapped in this way.

As it has been pointed out by Groo (1971), the process of site search and selection abroad 'requires deeper research, more negotiations and more alternatives . . . from the start of the search to completion of the facility is a longer process abroad than in the (country of the parent company)'. The large firm is both equipped to better handle the 'hidden traps' of site search and selection abroad and to bear more easily the additional cost of this longer search process.

(e)   *Ratio of capital equipment to total capital assets*
This ratio will affect the subsidy equivalent of differential depreciation allowances, which in practice constitute a widely used form of relief from direct taxes on profits. This is not to say that this ratio is the only determinant of the subsidy equivalent of this type of incentive; other factors include the length of life of the asset (Scholefield and Franks, 1972). The OECD (1973) doubts the effectiveness of regionally differentiated depreciation allowances, which, it argues, act only marginally on a firm's profitability, given the tax treatment of the cost of capital equipment.

(f)   *Equity to debt ratio*
This is another enterprise-specific characteristic which influences the size of the subsidy equivalent of incentive schemes based on interest rate subsidisation. A firm that adopts a low equity to debt ratio will tend to be more responsive to interest rate subsidies compared to a firm that keeps a high equity to debt ratio.

The above list of enterprise-related variables does not necessarily exhaust all the characteristics which affect the size of the subsidy equivalent of the various incentives. Take, for example, the case of an incentive based on duty-free imports of certain raw materials or components. A firm which does not import any raw materials or components that enjoy remission of custom duties does not obviously benefit from such an incentive scheme (OECD, 1973).

V

Previous chapters have suggested that MNEs possess a number of ownership and hierarchial attributes which are distinct from those of the indigenous firms. It is thus relevant to ask how far MNEs differ from MLDEs, in their response to regional policy incentives. Apart from differences in *structural* characteristics, *multinationality* as such may produce different patterns of response to regional incentives. Characteristics that will produce higher responsiveness include:

(1) A concentration of affiliates in the production of commodities requiring a high ratio of unskilled to skilled employees. In such types of production the differential in efficiency wages between assisted and non-assisted areas will tend to be small. Other things being equal, the size of the required subsidy will then be smaller. According to a US study (de La Torre, Stobaugh and Telesio, 1973) the jobs created in the USA within firms investing abroad are more heavily skewed towards the higher skill levels than are jobs in other firms. It seems then that the foreign investment process involves the shifting of lower skill jobs from the parent to the subsidiary.

(2) Existing evidence tends to show that the capital intensity of affiliates of MNEs is higher than that of indigenous firms. This will make them more responsive to capital subsidies. Experience with regional policies in Western Europe clearly shows that capital subsidies have been the most preferred form of incentives. Such incentives are thus invariably non-neutral as between MNEs and MLDEs. Writers like Helleiner (1973) have shown that in the 1960s there emerged 'the development of specialised labour intensive activities or processes within vertically integrated international manufacturing industries'. However, most of these specialised processes or activities are not located in the industrialised countries practising regional policies. As has already been mentioned, an analysis of Belgian data revealed only a small positive correlation between labour intensity and propensity to locate in an assisted area.

(3) As foreign production is often a substitute for exports, it is understandable that the affiliates of MNEs should concentrate more than MLDEs in the production of goods with relatively low bulk or weight

ratio to value added, thereby making the assisted area attractive as a place for affiliate location at a lower level of a break-even subsidy. As a British report emphasised (Steuer *et al*., 1973) 'foreign direct investment is more concentrated in light manufacturing and science based industries (where) there is a high ratio of value of products to transport cost'.

(4)   Manufacturing affiliates of MNEs usually produce 'standardised' commodities (Vernon, 1974). As it was pointed out earlier the location of production units engaged in the manufacture of such products is not tied up to a few innovative centres.

(5)   Many MNEs have internal organisations based on the multidivisional form of enterprise, with all the advantages that this brings in factor mobility and reduced costs of management communications. Hence such enterprises will be more responsive to advantages available through regional development policies. But, equally important, the multidivisional structure and the organisational logistics of the MNE enable it to take simultaneous advantage of a variety of fiscal incentives. This would suggest that a MNE can benefit from labour cost subsidies by locating its labour intensive activities in areas where labour costs are reduced by such incentives (e.g. regional employment premium) and its capital intensive activities in areas where capital grants and subventions reduce the cost of capital. 'Multi-sourcing' is a distinct feature of the economics of location of the MNE. As Adam (1971) has noted, the concern of the MNE is not only in deciding whether to supply a market from within or from outside but also in 'selecting the best sources and alternatives to supply the firm's home and international markets'. On the other hand, it may be argued that 'multi-sourcing' and a much more expanded set of alternative locations from which to choose (particularly locations in developing countries) may reduce the pull effect of some regional incentives on MNEs. If locations like Taiwan or Hong Kong or the Philippines are included together with the assisted areas in the set of alternative locations for the labour intensive processes of a MNE, it is clear that labour subsidies have to be very high indeed in order to close the gap between the labour costs of a British assisted area and the foreign labour costs (Holland, 1973). On the contrary, MLDEs will tend to pay more attention to labour subsidies available in assisted areas because they do not have access to locations in developing countries with relatively lower labour costs.

Of course, there are differences among the various groups of MNEs regarding the degree of management decentralisation. This may explain sometimes contrasting patterns of spatial distribution by MNEs of different nationalities. It is usually accepted that US MNEs have a more decentralised management structure than continental or Japanese MNEs. Such differences suggest a higher degree of locational mobility. Taking this factor into account, it is not difficult to explain, for example, why US foreign direct investment in Germany is more dispersed and more represented in problem areas whereas foreign direct investment of Swiss and Dutch origin is concentrated in the adjoining border regions (Klemmer, 1979). It seems that in this case the location of foreign direct investment has been influenced by the direction of the head office or parent plant (Ray, 1965). By adopting the policy of locating their plants in Germany in the adjoining border regions, the Swiss and Dutch MNEs succeeded in setting up their new plants near the chief market in the foreign country on the side facing corporate headquarters.

(6) The extent of the vertical integration prevailing in the majority of MNEs also ensures more flexibility in locational decisions, as the constraint from lack of local subcontracting facilities in assisted areas may not be so severe. By extending the scope of its operations to many countries the MNE reduces its locational dependence on transport costs and local suppliers of inputs.

(7) Large size has been mentioned as an important determinant of the firm's responsiveness to regional incentives. Multinational firms are usually larger than non-multinational firms. Indeed, research on the determinants of foreign direct investment has demonstrated (Horst, 1972) that 'once interindustry differences are washed out, the only influence (on direct investment) of any separate significance is firm size'.

(8) One aspect of the financial strategies of the MNEs is the relatively low equity to debt ratio of their affiliates. Various studies of American MNEs (e.g. US Tariff Commission, 1973, p. 420) show that, in the late 60s and 70s, net affiliate borrowing outside the USA constituted a substantial proportion of the sources of funds available to the MNE subsidiaries. This particular ownership-specific characteristic will tend to make MNEs more responsive than indigenous firms to incentives like interest rate subsidies. Such incentives are widely used, for example, in Belgium. Another structural characteristic mentioned earlier was the ratio of capital equipment to total capital. Without further information it is difficult to say how far there exist substantial differences between MNEs and MLDEs with respect to this characteristic.

There are, however, other structural characteristics of the MNE which will tend to work in the opposite direction:

(1) Certain characteristics of MNEs such as their relatively higher degree

of research intensity and their above average advertising budgets will tend to make the locational requirements of *certain* of their functions less flexible, for example, those dependent on the availability of white collar workers, information, proximity to mass media, etc. However, such constraints will affect the location of non-production facilities and of the production units of new products. Plant location decisions for standardised products, that is, the products in which subsidiaries specialise, are not seriously affected by such considerations.

(2)   Scale economies are probably more important for MNEs than for MLDEs. But some of the more significant of these scale factors, for example, proprietary knowledge within the firm, are space free in the sense that they can be used in combination with other factors in many different locations rather than in the initial place of the firm's growth.

(3)   Direct investment is often viewed as a function of imperfect competition and market failure. This leads many authors to conclude that strategic considerations will be dominant in the choice of subsidiary location rather than rate of return considerations. Indeed, under such market conditions, investment location decisions have to be analysed within the chessboard world of oligopolists (Vernon, 1974).

However, one important barrier to entry which gives rise to imperfect markets is the existence of proprietary knowledge within the firm. Indeed, foreign direct investment is particularly active among the research intensive industries. Research has shown (Severn and Lawrence, 1974) that profitability of foreign direct investment is associated with R & D rather than with direct investment itself. Foreign direct investment raises the expected return to research activity. Investors in research intensive manufacturing activities know that the availability of foreign as well as domestic investment causes the marginal efficiency of R & D expenditure to be higher than it would have been if they operated in a closed economy. This means that in such research intensive industries, the internal rate of return on foreign direct investment will exceed the actual average rates of return in the host countries. So the fact that the capital may flow from countries with high rates of return to countries where the actual rates of return are lower cannot be taken as an indication that foreign direct investment has been motivated by strategic rather than rate of return considerations.

VI

What now of the influence that multinationality as such exerts on locational choices? We suggest that the influence would make MNEs both more and less responsive to regional incentives.

(1) MNEs have no particular commitments to specific regions of a country whereas MLDEs are often characterised by inertia to move from the region of their initial development. A foreign firm may have fewer preconceived ideas about regional development areas. As Cameron and Clark (1966) reported the (then) BOT was more successful in interesting overseas companies (rather than British) in Scottish locations.

It could be equally maintained (and indeed it has been by Ashcroft and Ingham, 1979) that an MNE is also freer from preconceived and deeply entrenched notions of appropriate technology. As Solomon and Forsyth (1977) have shown MNEs seem to be more able to adapt to the prevailing relative prices and efficiencies in the developing areas. Thus the locational efficiency of the MNEs seems to be superior to that of the indigenous firm.

(2) The alien status of affiliates of MNEs makes them more liable to pressure in the negotiations which often precede the establishment of a subsidiary. To demonstrate more responsiveness to regional incentives reflecting national priorities concerning a country's economic development is one way of establishing better relations with government agencies and of reducing the political risks involved in investing in another country. For example, Univac (Sperry Rand) stated in evidence before the Trade and Industry Sub-committee of the House of Commons Expenditure Committee that they became committed to a decision to go to a development area of the United Kingdom right from the outset following their early discussions with the Department of Trade and Industry (Minutes of Evidence, Session, 1972–73, December 1972).

(3) The MNE has usually more freedom in shifting its tax burden. It will not only possess the option of shifting the tax burden forwards (on the product) or backwards (e.g. on labour) *within* the country in which it operates but also *between* countries through its financing and transfer pricing policies. Thus, in addition to the possibility of intra-country shifting open to both MLDEs and MNEs, there exists also the possibility of inter-country shifting open only to the MNE. This additional ability reduces the uncertainty surrounding the MNE regarding changes in regional policies during the lifetime of an investment project, since a reduction in incentives can be taken as equivalent to an increase in profits taxes. This additional tax burden can then be shifted in the ways mentioned above.

Transfer pricing may offer additional advantages to an MNE which intends to use regional incentive schemes. Suppose that the main regional incentives are investment grants, calculated on the basis of the value of investment in plant and equipment. Suppose too that an MNE through transfer pricing in intra-group trade in capital goods can overprice this equipment (assuming zero tariffs on capital goods imports). In such a case it will receive larger grants than an MLDE locating in the same assisted area but purchasing its capital equipment at arm's length prices.

If export subsidies are part of a regional incentive scheme, then, provided such exports are connected with intra-company trade, the MNE may increase these subsidies through appropriate transfer pricing policies (Lall, 1973, p. 125).

(4)   Other aspects of multinationality may work towards less responsiveness to regional incentives. Affiliates of MNEs may be controlled in their behaviour by the policies of host governments. For example, if access to the local capital market is restricted then the availability of, say, interest rate subsidies in assisted areas is of no value to the subsidiary affected by these restrictions. The behaviour of affiliates of MNEs may also be controlled by their parent companies. However, it is doubtful whether the choice of location within a country is strictly controlled by the head office. Local management is usually consulted on such decisions and it is rarely overruled by the head office (Groo, 1971). It seems that the sequential process involved in the locational decision is usually split between head offices and local management in such a way that it allows the former to have the final say on the choice of the broad geographical area within which the MNE will start new operations and the latter to have considerable freedom on the choice of a specific location within a national economy (McNee, 1974).

VII

This chapter has demonstrated that the impact of the locational strategies of MNEs on regional disequilibria will depend on

(1)   the extent to which the locational characteristics of the depressed regions (labour availability, lower rents, etc.) match the locational requirements of the planned new developments of MNEs;

(2)   the extent to which MNEs respond more than MLDEs to regional incentives;

(3)   the extent to which MNEs are more amenable than MLDEs to pressure or persuasion by national governments.

The fact that differences exist in the locational strategies of MNEs and MLDEs does not necessarily imply that the strategies of the former will intensify in a predictable manner the regional imbalances within countries. On the contrary, this chapter has shown that elements of enterprise structure and strategy interact in so many different ways that it is not possible to take any dogmatic position regarding the influence of the locational strategies of MNEs on regional disequilibria within countries.

Notes: Chapter 9

1   Cameron and Clark (1966, p. 196) argued that money wage differentials may still arise because plants in assisted areas respond with a lag to money wage rises that are first negotiated in the (non-assisted) areas of labour shortages. It is doubtful, however, whether these savings in money wages adequately compensate for the lower output per worker.

2   Differences in agglomeration economies are taken into account in this approach because they will affect either the level of efficiency wages (e.g. lack of a pool of trained labour will tend to push up efficiency wages given nationally negotiated money wage rates) or the transport costs per unit of inputs or output, or the magnitude of the management communications costs.

3   Methods of calculating the subsidy equivalent of the various incentives usually offered through regional policies can be found in Thoman (1973, pp. 94–101) or in Moody and Smith (1975).

4   The (average) propensity to invest in assisted areas is defined as the ratio of the new plants established in development areas to the total number of plants set up within an industry in a given country.

References

Adam, G. (1971), 'New trends in international business: worldwide sourcing and dedomiciling', *Acta Oeconomica*, vol. 7, nos. 3–4.

Ashcroft, B., and Ingham, K. P. D. (1979), 'Company adaptation and the response to regional policy: a comparative analysis of the MNC subsidiaries and indigenous companies', *Regional Studies*, vol. 13, no. 1.

Blackbourn, A. (1974), 'The spatial behaviour of American firms in Western Europe', in Ian F. G. Hamilton (ed.), *Spatial Perspectives on Industrial Organisation and Decision Making* (New York: Wiley).

Cameron, G. C., and Clark, D. D. (1966), *Industrial Movement and the Regional Problem*, University of Glasgow Social and Economic Studies, Occasional Papers No. 5 (Edinburgh: Oliver and Boyd).

Chandler, A. D., Jr. (1962), *Strategy and Structure, Chapters in the History of the American Industrial Enterprise* (Cambridge, Mass.: MIT Press).

Dicken, P., and Lloyd, P. (1976), 'Geographical perspectives on United States investment in the United Kingdom', *Environment and Planning*, A, vol. 8, no. 6.

Donaldson, L. (1966), *Development Planning in Ireland* (New York: Praeger).

Faith, N. (1972), *The Infiltrators, The European Business Invasion of America* (London: E. P. Dutton).

Groo, E. (1971), 'Choosing foreign locations: one company's experience', *Columbia Journal of World Business*, vol. 6 (Sept./Oct.), pp. 71–8.

Helleiner, G. K. (1973), 'Manufactured exports from less developed countries and multinational firms', *Economic Journal*, vol. 83 (March).

Holland, S. (1973), 'Multinational companies and a selective regional policy', House of Commons Expenditure Committee (Trade and Industry Subcommittee), *Minutes of Evidence. Session 1972–73* (London: HMSO).

Holland, S. (1975), *The Socialist Challenge* (London: Quartet Books).

Holland, S. (1976), *The Regional Problem* (London: Macmillan).

Horst, T. (1972), 'Firm and industry determinants of the decision to invest abroad', *Review of Economics and Statistics*, vol. 54 (August).

House of Commons Papers (1974), Expenditure Committee (Trade and Industry Sub-committee), *Regional Development Incentives, Minutes of Evidence* (from July 1973), Appendices and Index, Session 30 October 1973–8 February 1974, vol. VI, 85–I (London: HMSO).

Howard, R. S. (1968), *The Movement of Manufacturing Industry in the United Kingdom: 1945–65* (Board of Trade) (London: HMSO).

Jong, H. W. de (1972), 'Multinational enterprise in the Low Countries', paper presented at the CNRS International Symposium on the Growth of the Large Multinational Corporations (mimeo.).

Keeble, D. E. (1970), 'The movement of manufacturing industry – comments', *Regional Studies*, vol. 4. no. 3.

Kemper, N. J., and de Smidt, M. (1980), 'Foreign manufacturing establishments in the Netherlands', *Tijdschrift voor Econ. en Soc. Geographie*, vol. 71, no. 1.

Klemmer, P. (1979), 'The regional impact of multinational corporations', in D. van den Bulcke *et al.* (eds), *Investment and Divestment Policies of Multinational Corporations in Europe* (Farnborough: Saxon House).

Lall, S. (1973), 'Transfer-pricing by multinational manufacturing firms', *Oxford Bulletin of Economics and Statistics*, vol. 35 (August).

McNee, R. B. (1974), 'A systems approach of understanding the geographic behaviour of organisations, especially large corporations', in I. F. G. Hamilton (ed.), *Spatial Perspectives on Industrial Organisation and Decision Making* (New York: Wiley), Ch. 2.

Moody, T., and Smith, K. G. D. (1975), 'Some problems in the evaluation of subsidies to British manufacturing industry', *Oxford Economic Papers*, vol. 27 (July).

Nelson, R. G. (1972), 'Economies of scale and market size', *Land Economics*, vol. 48 (August).

OECD (1973), *Issues of Regional Policy* (A report prepared by A. Emmanuel) (Paris: OECD).

O'Farrell, P. N. (1976), 'An analysis of industrial closures: Irish experience 1960–73', *Regional Studies*, vol. 10, no. 4.

O'Farrell, P. N. (1980), 'Multinational enterprises and regional development: Irish evidence', *Regional Studies*, vol. 14.

Otterbeck, L. (1973), 'Multinational companies and international site selections', *Skandinavisca Enskilda Banken Quarterly Review*, vol. 3, no. 3.

Ray, D. M. (1965), *Market Potential and Economic Shadow* (Chicago: Chicago University Press).

Reuber, G. L. (1973), *Private Foreign Investment in Development* (London: Oxford University Press).

Scholefield, H. H., and Franks, J. R. (1972), 'Investment incentives and regional policies', *National Westminster Bank Quarterly Review* (February).

Severn, A. K., and Laurence, M. L. (1974), 'Direct investment, research intensity and profitability, *Journal of Financial Quantitative Analysis*, vol. 9 (March).

Solomon, R. F., and Forsyth, D. J. C. (1977), 'Substitution of labour for capital in the foreign sector: some further evidence, *Economic Journal*, vol. 87 (June).

Steuer, M. D. *et al.* (1973), *The Impact of Foreign Direct Investment on the UK* (Department of Trade and Industry) (London: HMSO).

Thoman, Richard D. (1973), *Foreign Investment and Regional Development. The Theory and Practice of Investment Incentives with a Case Study of Belgium* (New York: Praeger).

Thorngren, B. (1970), 'How do contact systems affect regional development?', *Environment and Planning*, no. 2.

Torre, J. de la, Stobaugh, R. B., and Telesio, P. (1973), *US Multinational Enterprises and Changes in the Skill Composition of US Employment* (mineo.).

US Tariff Commission (1973),*Implication of Multinational Firms for World Trade and Investment and for US Trade and Labour* (Washington, DC: US Government Printing Office).

Van Der Bulcke, D. (1971), *Les Enterprises Etrangeres dans l'Industrie Belge, Aspects Generaux, Regionaux et Economiques* (Gand: Office Belge pour l'Accroissement de la Productivite).

Vernon, R. (1971), *Sovereignty at Bay: The Multinational Spread of US Enterprise* (London: Longman).

Vernon, R. (1974), 'Location of Economic Activity', in J. H. Dunning (ed.), *The Multinational Enterprise and Economic Analysis* (London: Allen & Unwin), Ch. 3.

Watts, H. D. (1979), 'Large firms, multinationals, and regional development: some new evidence from the United Kingdom', *Environment and Planning*, A, vol. 11, no. 1.

Yannopoulos, G. (1980), 'Location of affiliates: fiscal factors in the MNC's choice', in *Ten Years of Multinational Business, The Main Issues For and About Multinational Enterprise Today* (London: Economist Intelligence Unit Special Report No. 79.

10

Employee Compensation in US Multinationals and Indigenous Firms: An Exploratory Micro/Macro Analysis

I

The operation of MNEs in the labour markets of different countries has aroused considerable interest in the comparison of wage payments made by parent companies and non-MNEs within the former's home economy, and between foreign affiliates, compared both with the parent company and with other firms in the host countries in which they operate. This interest has been increased by recent trade union activity in respect of MNEs, which has centred on demands for uniformity of wage and fringe benefits for similar jobs as well as the harmonisation of working conditions.[1] The demands have so far been voiced most strongly with respect to plants of the same firm *within* a particular country, but, with the emergence of an international trade union movement, pressure for parity wages and conditions of work is increasingly being felt at an international level. In addition, fears that the operation of MNEs in the labour market of particular countries may contribute to inflation have stimulated further concern about the movements of comparative earnings.

The purpose of this chapter is to analyse the evidence about certain characteristics of US manufacturing MNEs and their affiliates in the labour market; to offer an explanation of these characteristics; and to attempt to assess whether the wage policies of MNEs have contributed to inflation in the period 1966 to 1970. The paper is divided into three sections. Section I continues with a description of the data used in the analysis. In Section II, comparisons are made between the employee compensation of US parent MNEs, their affiliates in host countries, non-MNEs in the USA and the indigenous firms in host countries. Some possible explanations of the patterns observed are then tested. Section III takes up some macroeconomic questions and explores some hypotheses about the extent to which multinational firms have contributed to inflation through their operations in the labour market.

This chapter is a revised version of a paper first published (with Eleanor Morgan) in *British Journal of Industrial Relations*, vol. XVIII, no. 2 (July 1980).

The Data

The main source of data for this analysis is the Report of the United States Tariff Commission (1973) which provides information about the activities of the US multinational enterprises for two benchmark years, 1966 and 1970. The 1966 data in this report were taken from a census of all known US-based MNEs covering some 3,400 US parent companies and about 23,000 majority-owned foreign affiliates. The 1970 data used by the Tariff Commission were compiled from a sample survey of 298 US parent companies and their 5,237 majority owned foreign affiliates, as conducted by the Bureau of Economic Analysis (BEA).

In the present study, attention is concentrated on the experience of a sample of seven countries using data for both 1966 and 1970.[2] Six of these countries, viz. the UK, Canada, Mexico, France, Belgium—Luxembourg, and West Germany, were host to US firms and, between them, accounted for three-fifths of the book value of US foreign direct investment in manufacturing industry in 1970; the seventh was the US itself.[3] These countries, which together form a substantial part of the industrialised world outside the centrally planned economies, have all experienced inflation in the postwar period which accelerated substantially in the late 1960s. The industrial classification of manufacturing activities, used by the Tariff Commission and set out in Appendix 1, has been adopted.

Definitions and sources of all the variables used in this analysis are given in Appendix 2. Wages are defined throughout as average hourly compensation per employee (the total wage bill divided by the number of hours worked per man per year). These estimates vary in accuracy, as the Tariff Commission Report emphasises, and the possible variation in accuracy between those recorded for all firms and for MNEs is $0.30 per employee.[4] Of the seven countries considered in this chapter the probable errors in the estimates are greatest for Mexico, less for the European countries and least for the USA and Canada. However, there is no reason to suspect that the estimates are systematically biased, and while the results must be interpreted carefully, it is believed that the figures are sufficiently accurate to reflect general trends and reveal any substantial differences in wage payments.

II

(a) *Comparisons of Employee Compensation*

Many problems arise in the attempt to make accurate comparisons of wage payments. Ideally, one would wish to measure the difference between the total real remuneration (including fringe benefits) made to workers performing identical tasks in different firms and countries. However, difficulties occur, both in evaluating the comparability of jobs in particular occupations, and in calculating the value of non-monetary benefits

274 *International Production and the Multinational Enterprise*

received in addition to wages. When payments to workers in different countries are being considered, further problems arise with converting them into a common unit of measurement. Although exchange rates are often used for this purpose, such rates do not always accurately reflect the real value of money of different countries, and detailed statistics on consumption patterns and prices would need to take this into account.[5] The lack of data, particularly with regard to the operations of MNEs, means that exact comparisons cannot be made, and conclusions based on such limited statistics as are available must be treated cautiously.

Despite the difficulties, several studies have attempted to establish the differences in the wage payments made by MNEs and by other firms.[6] For example, an analysis of a sample of 500 US affiliates in Britain in 1973 (Dunning, 1976) concluded the US affiliates tended to pay higher than average wages, as measured by differences in the yearly wage bill per capita. Later data, derived from the Census of Production for 1975 confirmed this but suggested that, in most industries, the differences were within 10 per cent (Stopford, 1979). In developing countries, a study by Mason (1973) established that in most industries foreign affiliates paid more than local firms in the Philippines[7] and Mexico, a conclusion also reached by Langdon (1975) for Kenya, Sourrouille (1976) for Argentina, Jo (1976) for South Korea, Iyanda and Bello (1979) for Nigeria and Possas (1979) for Brazil. On the other hand, Cohen (1975) found that local firms paid higher wages in Singapore than foreign firms, while in Taiwan no clear pattern emerged. In Latin America, US MNEs paid annual wages between 1.4 and 2.1 times those of indigenous firms in 1966, while in India and Pakistan the ratios were respectively 2.4 and 2.6 (Sabolo and Trajtenberg, 1976). In Greek manufacturing industry Papandreou (1980) estimated that, while in 1973 foreign affiliates paid higher *salaries* than domestic employers, differences in average *wages* per head between the two groups of firms were not statistically significant.[8]

Perhaps the most detailed comparative study of wage payments of MNEs and non-MNEs to date has been that conducted by the US Tariff Commission. The data embrace the total yearly payroll costs (i.e. earnings) per employee of a sample of 298 firms and their 5,237 majority-owned foreign affiliates in 1966 and 1970. Comparisons of domestic payroll costs per employee of the MNEs and of all US firms for all industries showed that the payroll costs of MNEs were significantly above the national average, mainly because of the heavier weight of manufacturing in the MNE sample, where payroll costs per capita tended to be relatively high. Mixed results were shown for the different industries, and it was suggested that this was due partly to differences in the distribution of activity within the industrial groupings, and partly to other influences affecting wages, including technical efficiency, profitability and the rate of company expansion.

Payroll costs per employee of the foreign affiliates were universally much lower than those of the US parents, and in manufacturing, the payroll costs per capita of the foreign affiliates exceeded the average paid in the same host country.

The next part of this section provides a more detailed analysis of the wages paid by US MNEs and non-MNEs engaged in manufacturing industry in the USA and in six host countries. The results of exploratory tests of possible explanations of the differences observed are then presented. The data on hourly compensation, classified by country and industry, which forms the basis of the analysis, are presented in Tables 10.1 and 10.2, while Tables 10.3 and 10.4 set out some estimates of the dispersion of wages as measured by the standard deviation.

(b) *US parent companies compared with non-MNEs in the USA*

(i) *Average hourly compensation.* The weighted average hourly compensation per employee paid by parent companies for the twelve sample industries combined was significantly greater than the average wages paid by other firms in the USA, both in 1966, when it was $0.79 or 24 per cent higher, and in 1970 when it was $1.24 or 32 per cent higher.[9] As Tables 10.1 and 10.2 show, the only industries in which MNEs paid less than average wages were transportation equipment (1966), the paper and allied industry (1970) and other manufacturing (in both 1966 and 1970).

The tendency of MNEs to pay higher wages than the average can be partly attributed to their concentration in high wage industries. In 1966, 87 per cent of their total employment of MNE parents was in industries where non-MNEs paid above average wages; the corresponding figure for 1970 was 75 per cent. The extent to which the wage differential was due to the different industrial structure of MNEs and non-MNEs was estimated by recalculating the mean wage of the parent companies using the distribution of employment in the non-MNEs as weights. In 1966 the mean normalised for these structural differences was $3.57, suggesting that 42 per cent of the difference previously noted may be attributed to differences in industrial structure, but it was still significantly different from the non-MNEs. The corresponding mean for 1970 was $4.48; in that year 45 per cent of the difference observed was due to structural effects but again the normalised mean wages paid by MNEs were significantly higher than those paid by non-MNEs.

Between 1966 and 1970, the increase in hourly compensation was greater for the MNEs than non-MNEs in the USA; average wages rose by $1.13 (an increase of 7 per cent a year) compared with a $0.68 rise for the other firms, which represents an annual increase of 5 per cent. An estimated 48 per cent of the differential was due to the differences in industrial structure as the MNEs tended to be concentrated in the industries where wages were increasing most rapidly, and the remaining 52 per cent to other factors. The picture for the industries taken separately is less clear

Table 10.1 Estimated Average Hourly Compensation paid to all Employees by Multinational and Indigenous Firms[a] in 1966 ($)

Industry	Canada		United Kingdom		Belgium-Luxembourg		France		West Germany		Mexico		All excluding USA		USA		All countries	
	M	I	M	I	M	I	M	I	M	I	M	I	M	I	M	I	M	I
All industries	(2.50)[b] 2.74[c]	2.37	(1.48)[b] 1.46[c]	1.71	(1.51)[b] 1.62	1.59	(1.58)[b] 1.75[c]	1.67	(1.85)[b] 1.94[b]	1.88	(1.00)[b] 0.99[c]	0.58	(1.63)[b] 1.95[c] (1.77)[b]	1.70	(3.57)[b] 4.03[c]	3.24	(2.23)[b] 3.57[c] (2.00)[b]	2.18
Chemicals	2.90	2.08	1.40	1.99	1.80	2.17	2.10	2.14	2.10	2.21	1.10	0.82	1.95 (1.75)	1.95	4.10	3.75	3.64[c] (2.80)[b]	2.13
Rubber	2.60	2.06	1.40	1.56	1.60	1.73	1.90	1.84	2.10	1.95	1.20	0.72	2.08[c] (1.65)[b]	1.73	3.70	3.34	3.20[c] (2.39)[b]	2.60
Machinery except electrical	2.80	2.24	1.40	1.67	1.70	1.74	1.70	1.80	1.90	1.88	1.20	0.49	1.84[c] (1.64)[b]	1.77	4.30	3.63	3.59[c] (2.25)	2.29
Electrical machinery	2.50	2.50	1.30	1.69	1.50	1.90	1.80	1.86	1.90	1.99	0.90	0.53	1.81 (1.84)	1.83	3.90	3.33	3.47[c] (2.06)[b]	2.23
Transportation equipment	3.10	2.59	1.70	1.68	1.60	1.92	1.80	1.86	2.10	2.18	1.30	0.66	2.18[c] (1.69)[b]	1.83	4.20	5.46	3.84[c] (2.61)[b]	2.17
Instruments	2.60	1.78	1.50	1.70	1.60	2.20	1.70	1.81	1.80	1.95	na	na	1.78 (1.41)	1.83	4.50	3.21	3.65 (2.12)	2.29
Food	2.40	1.97	1.50	1.80	1.50	1.68	1.40	1.44	1.60	1.49	0.70	0.42	1.74[c] (1.82)[b]	1.42	3.30	3.14	2.77[c] (2.59)[b]	2.06
Paper and allied industry	2.90	2.70	1.80	1.80	1.60	1.59	1.50	1.57	1.80	1.62	1.10	0.72	2.59[c] (1.69)[b]	1.74	3.80	3.29	3.50[c] (2.56)	2.35
Primary and fabricated metals	2.90	2.65	1.30	1.63	1.60	1.70	1.50	1.69	1.90	2.00	0.90	0.74	1.99 (1.45)	1.82	4.10	3.78	3.72[c] (1.91)[b]	2.53
Textiles and apparel	2.10	2.45	1.60	1.72	1.30	1.18	1.20	1.32	1.60	1.42	0.70	0.55	1.65[c] (1.75)	1.47	2.70	2.33	2.44[c] (2.36)[b]	1.79
Stone, clay and glass	2.40	2.44	1.30	1.58	1.60	1.61	1.80	1.60	1.80	2.21	0.80	0.59	1.86 (1.53)[b]	1.76	4.10	3.11	3.66[c] (2.04)[b]	2.13
Other	2.00	2.12	1.50	1.67	1.30	1.26	1.40	1.69	1.70	1.66	1.00	0.65	1.70	1.66	3.00	3.32	2.71[c]	2.23

[a] M = Affiliates of MNEs outside the USA with parent companies in the USA.
I = Indigenous firms outside the USA and non-MNEs in the USA.
( ) Figures shown in parentheses are normalised mean wages in MNEs.
[b] Wages in MNEs normalised for industry structure, significantly different from wages in indigenous firms.
[c] Wages in MNEs weighted by employment which are significantly different from wages in indigenous firms.
Source: US Tariff Commission (1973).

Table 10.2 Estimated Average Hourly Compensation paid to all Employees by Multinational and Indigenous Firms[a] in 1970 ($)

Industry	Canada M	Canada I	United Kingdom M	United Kingdom I	Belgium–Luxembourg M	Belgium–Luxembourg I	France M	France I	West Germany M	West Germany I	Mexico M	Mexico I	All countries excluding USA M	All countries excluding USA I	USA M	USA I	All countries M	All countries I
All industries	(3.52)[b] 3.90[c]	3.44	(1.77)[b] 1.82[c]	1.95	(2.14)[b] 2.22	2.26	(2.22)[b] 2.50[c]	2.58	(2.83)[b] 3.07[c]	2.91	(1.15)[b] 1.17[c]	0.74	(2.23)[b] 2.60[c]	2.37	(4.48)[b] 5.16[c]	3.92	(2.91)[b] 4.51[c]	2.84
Chemicals	4.00	3.97	1.70	2.26	2.70	2.95	2.70	3.02	3.20	3.53	1.60	1.09	(2.50)[b] 2.61[c]	2.77	5.10	4.54	(2.73)[b] 4.55[c]	2.93
Rubber	4.10	2.98	1.80	1.96	2.00	2.81	2.20	2.60	2.60	2.68	1.40	1.24	(2.23)[b] 2.52	2.41	4.60	4.07	(3.57)[b] 3.72[c]	3.35
Machinery except electrical	4.20	5.04	1.80	1.88	2.40	2.50	2.90	3.26	3.40	2.87	1.50	0.49	(2.66)[b] 2.67[c]	2.57	5.70	4.33	(3.49)[b] 4.69[c]	3.05
Electrical machinery	3.70	3.68	1.60	1.98	2.20	2.78	2.60	3.94	3.10	3.08	1.10	0.52	(2.45)[b] 2.51[c]	2.76	5.30	3.46	(3.11)[b] 4.71[c]	2.92
Transportation equipment	4.40	4.26	2.30	2.08	2.60	2.64	2.50	2.54	3.40	3.44	1.50	0.89	(2.66)[b] 3.10[c]	2.56	5.50	4.48	(2.82)[b] 4.99[c]	2.67
Instruments	3.50	4.65	1.70	2.11	2.30	2.90	3.00	3.26	3.00	2.87	na	na	(2.61)[b] 2.50[c]	2.77	5.80	3.26	(3.55)[b] 4.89[c]	2.92
Food	3.30	3.17	1.80	2.04	1.80	2.41	1.70	2.01	2.10	2.27	1.00	0.59	(1.78)[b] 2.27[c]	1.87	4.10	3.96	(2.60) 3.41[c]	2.62
Paper and allied industry	4.40	3.82	1.60	2.02	2.00	2.26	2.00	2.27	2.40	2.50	1.20	1.35	(2.22)[b] 3.39[c]	2.39	4.10	4.51	(2.93)[b] 3.9[c]	3.18
Primary and fabricated metals	4.00	4.09	1.40	1.82	2.50	2.37	2.00	2.34	2.60	3.10	1.10	0.77	(2.25)[b] 2.39[c]	2.60	5.10	4.61	(3.30) 4.48[c]	3.34
Textiles and apparel	2.60	2.41	1.80	1.88	1.70	1.61	1.80	1.87	2.10	2.18	1.10	0.68	(1.85) 2.07[c]	1.86	3.20	2.89	(2.36)[b] 2.90[c]	2.25
Stone, clay and glass	3.50	3.79	1.40	1.77	2.20	2.22	2.00	2.29	3.20	3.31	0.80	0.79	(2.19)[b] 2.33	2.40	4.90	3.98	(2.61)[b] 4.28[c]	2.82
Other	3.20	3.14	1.70	1.86	1.60	1.69	1.50	2.28	2.40	2.49	0.80	1.48	(1.87)[b] 1.80[c]	2.10	4.00	4.20	(2.59)[b] 3.09[c]	2.82

[a] M = Affiliates of MNEs outside the USA with parent companies in the USA.
  I = Indigenous firms outside the USA and non-MNEs in the USA.
[b] ( ) Figures shown in parentheses are normalised mean wages in MNEs.
[c] Wages in MNEs normalised for industry structure significantly different from wages in indigenous firms.
[d] Wages in MNEs weighted by employment, which are significantly different from wages in indigenous firms.
Source: US Tariff Commission (1973).

Table 10.3   *The Dispersion of Employee Compensation^a of Multinational and Indigenous Firms in 1966 and 1970*

Country	1966 M	I	1970 M	I
Canada	0.29	0.27	0.47	0.67
United Kingdom	0.15	0.09	0.27	0.12
Belgium, Luxembourg	0.10	0.30	0.31	0.43
France	0.16	0.23	0.39	0.61
West Germany	0.15	0.26	0.41	0.42
Mexico	0.20	0.14	0.28	0.21
All countries excluding United States	0.59	0.32	0.91	0.61
United States	0.33	0.60	0.56	0.62
All countries including United States	0.90	0.76	1.21	0.88

^{a}As measured by the Standard Deviation.
Source: US Tariff Commission (1973).

cut; the differences tended to be small although substantially greater wage increases were shown in non-MNE firms in the paper industry.

(ii) *The dispersion of average hourly compensation.* Table 10.3 reveals that in 1966, the wages paid by MNEs in the USA were significantly less dispersed between industries than those of non-MNEs. In 1970, the wages of MNEs were significantly less dispersed than those of non-MNEs, although more dispersed than in 1966. The dispersion of MNEs' wages increased substantially over the period, while the dispersion of wage payments by other firms rose only slightly.

(c)   *US affiliates in host countries compared with indigenous firms*

(i) *Average hourly compensation.* The average hourly compensation paid by US affiliates in the six host countries for all industries combined was significantly higher than that paid by indigenous firms in both 1966 and 1970; in 1966 the average wage paid by affiliates was $1.95 compared with the $1.70 paid by indigenous firms, and in 1970 it was $2.60 compared with $2.37 for indigenous firms.

Significant differences in the wages paid by US affiliates and indigenous firms emerged in five of the six host countries; generally, the foreign affiliates paid more, with the exception of the UK (in 1966 and 1970),[10] and France in 1970. Differences in wage payment by nationality of firm were not significant in Belgium–Luxembourg, where the US affiliates paid slightly more in 1966, but less than indigenous firms in 1970.

The results for the industries separately are more mixed. In five of the twelve industries, viz. food, paper, textiles, non-electrical machinery and transport equipment, the wages paid by the affiliates of MNEs were significantly higher than domestic firms in both 1966 and 1970. In the rubber industry wages were significantly higher in 1966, but by 1970 the difference was insignificant. In no industry in 1966 were wage payments by affiliates significantly below those of indigenous firms, but, by 1970, the picture had changed with indigenous firms paying significantly more in five industries – chemicals, electrical machinery, primary and fabricated metals, instruments and other manufacturing.

The growth of average wages over the period 1966–70 for all industries and all countries seems to have been greater in indigenous firms than in US affiliates, with an overall increase of $0.67 or 10 per cent a year as compared with the $0.65 rise (8 per cent annually) shown by the affiliates. The growth rates shown by the countries individually are mixed. The wages of indigenous firms have increased rather more rapidly in percentage terms in Canada, Belgium–Luxembourg, France and Mexico, but the reverse was the case in the United Kingdom and West Germany. Only in Canada was the absolute difference large enough not to have arisen from estimation errors. The growth of wages appears to have been greater in the indigenous firms for each industry taken separately, with the exception of transport equipment and textiles and apparel, but only for 'other manufacturing' was the difference substantially significant.

To what extent do these results reflect the different distribution of industrial activity between foreign affiliates and indigenous firms? When the mean wage of the affiliates for all countries and industries was recalculated with industrial distribution of employment in the indigenous firms as weights, it emerged that the affiliates would have paid lower wages than the indigenous firms on average for all industries and countries combined in both 1966 and 1970 if the structure of their activity had been the same. In 1966 the average wage paid by the affiliates, normalised for industrial structure, was $1.63, $0.07 less than other firms, and it was $2.23 (or $0.14 less than the indigenous firms) in 1970. However, the growth rate of wages in indigenous firms between 1966 and 1970 still appeared to be only marginally higher than for the US affiliates.

Turning to the individual countries, the affiliates still paid significantly more in Canada and in Mexico in both years after normalising for differences in employment structure. As before, the US affiliates in the UK paid significantly less than the indigenous firms, but now this was also true of such affiliates in France, Belgium, Luxembourg and West Germany.

The individual industries were also investigated after a similar adjustment had been made for differences in the *country* composition of their employment structure. This correction showed that the tendency of foreign affiliates to pay more in particular industries was due partly to the differences in employment patterns by country of the two types of firm. Where differences were significant, it generally appeared that the indigenous firms had higher mean wages than the MNEs; indigenous firms paid significantly more in five industries in both years, viz. primary and

Table 10.4   *The Dispersion of Employee Compensation^a of Multinational and Indigenous Firms in 1966 and 1970*

	1966				1970			
	M		I		M		I	
Industry	A	B	A	B	A	B	A	B
Chemicals	0.70	0.94	0.45	0.68	0.96	1.13	0.82	0.93
Rubber	0.57	0.81	0.26	0.82	1.02	1.23	0.38	0.86
Non-electrical machinery	0.56	1.15	0.16	0.85	0.94	1.52	0.63	0.95
Electrical machinery	0.53	0.87	0.27	0.71	0.89	1.21	0.82	0.77
Transport equipment	0.61	0.81	0.31	1.10	0.86	1.06	0.69	0.80
Instruments	0.40	1.28	0.11	0.65	0.75	1.53	0.48	0.46
Food	0.60	0.82	0.53	0.93	0.82	1.02	0.71	1.15
Paper and allied industry	0.57	0.60	0.39	0.82	1.27	0.69	0.57	1.12
Primary and fabricated metals	0.79	0.88	0.34	0.98	1.06	1.25	0.73	1.13
Textiles and apparel	0.43	0.50	0.38	0.51	0.47	0.56	0.40	0.59
Stone, clay and glass	0.53	0.92	0.45	0.71	1.04	1.21	0.83	0.99
Other manufacturing	0.28	0.56	0.18	0.80	0.76	1.19	0.35	1.03
All industries	0.20	0.32	0.17	0.23	0.36	0.54	0.35	0.35

^a As measured by the Standard Deviation.
A Excluding USA.
B Including USA.
Source: US Tariff Commission (1973).

fabricated metals, chemicals, other manufacturing, electrical machinery and instruments. The wages paid by indigenous firms were significantly higher in non-electrical machinery manufacturing in 1966, and in food, paper and allied industry, stone clay and glass and rubber in 1970. Only in the paper industry in 1966 and non-electrical machinery and transport equipment in 1970, did affiliates pay significantly more than indigenous firms.

The picture of comparative growth rates, by country, was little altered by the correction for different industrial structures, except for Belgium, where the percentage growth rates for the two types of firm now appeared to be exactly the same. Most industries conformed to the overall pattern with indigenous firms recording a faster growth in per capita wages than foreign affiliates: the exceptions were in non-electrical machinery, transport equipment, textiles and apparel and instrument manufacturing where the foreign affiliates recorded marginally larger percentage increases in wages.

(ii) *The dispersion of average hourly compensation.* As Table 10.3 shows, wages of the US affiliates in host countries were significantly more dispersed by country than those of indigenous firms in both 1966 and 1970. The same was true by country industry (see Table 10.4), while the dispersion increased over the period in both types of firms. When the dispersion of wages was examined for individual countries, it was found that some did not follow this overall pattern; thus the wages of affiliates exhibited less variation in Canada (in 1970) and in France, Belgium and West Germany in both years. However, the findings for the industries considered separately are consistent with the overall result. Each country showed increases in the relative wage dispersion, and every industry followed this pattern.

In 1966 the differences in the dispersion of wages across countries between affiliates and indigenous firms were significant for each individual industry except textiles; while in 1970, the differences for individual countries across industries were significant, except for West Germany.[11]

(d) *US parent companies compared with affiliates in host countries*

(i) *Average hourly compensation.* Parent companies in the USA paid significantly more than their foreign affiliates in both 1966 and 1970; in 1966 the average hourly compensation for US affiliates was $1.95 compared with $4.03 paid by the parent companies, and in 1970 the respective figures were $2.60 and $5.16. Each of the countries conformed to this pattern in both years.

The percentage growth of average wages paid by US affiliates over the four-year period, was greater than that paid by their parent companies, with growth rates of 33 per cent ($0.65) compared with 28 per cent ($1.13) in the parent firms. Percentage growth rates were higher for the affiliates in each industry, with the exception of 'other' manufacturing, but the experience of individual countries was mixed, with affiliates in the UK, France and Mexico showing growth rates which were slower than average in percentage terms.

(e) *US parent companies and affiliates in host countries compared with non-MNEs in the USA and indigenous firms in host countries*

(i) *Average hourly compensation.* US MNEs and their affiliates appeared to pay significantly higher wages than non-MNEs in both 1966 and 1970. In 1966 the average wage paid by all MNEs was $3.57, 64 per cent more than the non-MNEs; by 1970 the average wage paid by all MNEs was $4.51, a difference of 59 per cent. This result held for all industries separately and the differences were all significant. The growth rate of wages was greater in the non-MNEs in percentage terms (30 per cent compared with 26 per cent) although the MNEs showed the greater absolute increases.

These results are, in large part, due to the large amount of employment by the US firms, for as we have seen (Section IId) parent companies paid substantially more than non-MNEs in the USA whereas the affiliates only paid slightly more than the indigenous firms in host countries. The extent to which the results were due to the different structure of employment was estimated by recalculating the mean wage of the MNEs and their affiliates weighted by the distribution of employment in the non-MNEs. In 1966 the normalised mean wage of the MNEs was $2.23 and it was $2.91 four years later, showing that a substantial portion of the differences previously observed was due to broad differences in structural character- istics, although the normalised mean wage of the MNEs was still signifi- cantly higher than wages paid by non-MNEs in the USA and indigenous firms in both 1966 and 1970.

When the mean wage of MNEs, normalised for country composition, was calculated for individual industries, the previous results were again modified substantially. Although in seven industries (transport equipment, instruments, paper, textiles, stone, rubber and non-electrical machinery) MNEs still paid significantly higher wages in both years, there were now two industries in which non-MNEs paid more. These were chemicals (in 1966 and 1970) and other manufacturing (in 1966).

(ii) *The dispersion of average hourly compensation.* The dispersion of wages paid by the MNEs was significantly more than for non-MNEs in both 1966 and 1970 for all countries and industries taken together. This was the pattern in each industry in 1966 with the exception of rubber, transport equipment, textiles and apparel, food, paper and allied industry, primary and fabricated metals and other manufacturing, and in 1970 with three exceptions — food, paper and allied, and textiles and apparel. All the differences in dispersion were significant except for textiles in 1966 and 1970 and rubber in 1966 (according to a one-tailed F test at the 5 per cent level).

III

There has been little previous work on the explanation of differences in wage payments by MNEs and other firms, as was noted above. There is, however, a substantial literature concerned with the determinants of average earnings and changes in earnings, both by industry in particular countries and across countries.[12] These statistical studies have tended to adopt an *ad hoc* approach whereby various explanatory variables are hypothesised and then tested, either by simple correlation or regression analysis. The relationships estimated vary from study to study and none of the models has been generally accepted. In view of this, it may be useful to briefly summarise the main explanations which have been advanced of differences in inter-industry and inter-country wage pay- ments, before investigating the ways in which the multinationality of firms might also exert an influence.

The reasons most commonly advanced to explain differences in hourly wage payments in different firms and industries[13] in a perfectly competitive market include the skill mix of the labour force and the productivity of individual workers, differences in working conditions and other non-monetary rewards, the type of payments system, and the amount of over-time and shift working. Of course, labour markets are not perfectly competitive, and so some of the differences in wages are due to market imperfections. These include sex differentials in wage payments, the existence of regional labour markets, the nature and strength of the bargaining power of workers, or labour of trade unions, and the existence of state intervention, as well as the market power of firms and other aspects of market structure. Some of these influences are more important in explaining differences between firms while others primarily affect inter-industry variations in wages. *Inter alia* this depends partly on whether wages are negotiated at the plant level or covered by industry wide agreements. For example, in the UK, and to a significant extent in other European countries, wages are determined by industry wide collective bargaining, whereas in the US company wage bargaining at a firm level is the usual practice.

Some of the influences mentioned above (such as skill mix of the labour force) might also vary systematically according to the country of operation, and thus may enter into the explanation of inter-country differences in wage payments. Several additional factors which become variable in cross-country comparisons can also be distinguished, including the socio-, legal and cultural environment, the stage of development, the extent of international trade, the type of industrial relations system and aggregate policies pursued by the government.

Let us now explore the ways in which the multinationality of firms might affect the wage payments of their employees by taking some examples. In host countries, the operation of foreign affiliates in the labour market may be affected by a number of influences, including differences in bargaining practices imported from the country of origin, the presence of expatriate personnel leading to pressure for parity in working conditions and wage payments with the parent company, differences in knowledge of the local labour market, easier access to modern technology affecting the skill mix of the labour force and ability to pay, and the effects of the firm's multinationality on the market power of firms and unions (such as the ability to shift production to different countries). For reasons such as these, which arise purely from the multinational character of the company, differences may occur between wages paid by MNEs and other firms.

In an industry comprising both affiliates of MNEs and indigenous firms, one might expect the former to be the wage leaders. This is partly because foreign affiliates are likely to be more productive than their local competitors and partly because where they are part of an integrated MNE, their interdependence makes them more vulnerable, that is, increases the cost of labour disruptions;[14] at the same time it may also help them to better absorb wage increases.

Following the above analysis, the influences which determine the patterns of wage payments observed previously are viewed as falling into three main groups, namely, *industry*-specific, *country*-specific and *firm*- (or ownership-) specific factors. However, besides these main effects, there may also be interaction effects caused by the combination of any two of the main influences. These interaction effects may be distinguished from the main effects and are analysed separately. For example, if a firm is in an industry which is expanding very rapidly, is highly productive and profitable, and is also located in a country which offers conditions favourable to the payment of high wages, the two may interact in such a way that part of the average wage payments should be attributed to an 'industry—country effect'. A firm may pay higher wages because it is multinational and located in a country where all companies tend to pay labour well and this may show up as a 'firm—country' effect. Finally, an 'industry—firm' interaction suggests that factors leading to differences in wage payments between multinational and indigenous firms apply more to some industries than others.

(a)   *Analysis of Variance*

I have chosen to test the influences of the three main effects and the interaction effects on wage payments by the use of variance analysis as this technique allows the analysis of measurements which depend on several kinds of influences operating simultaneously. Essentially, what this technique does is to separate the total sum of the squared deviations and the degrees of freedom of a population of estimates into the component effects. The accuracy of the estimate of the variance obtained in this way depends on whether the means of the effects are the same. The F distribution of variance ratios is used to test which effects have a significant influence, that is, to identify those groups whose means are, in fact, different.

The analysis of variance, reported in Tables 10.5 and 10.6, shows that country-specific factors are by far the most important in explaining the variation in wage levels in 1966 and 1970, and that industry-specific factors are highly significant. It is therefore necessary to examine wage patterns for the countries and industries separately, rather than analysing aggregate figures which would tend to conceal these sources of variation. Firm-specific factors are also significant when the US parent companies and non-MNEs are included (Table 10.6), and in 1970 for the firms in the sample of host countries (Table 10.5).

These findings, however, must be interpreted in the light of the results for interactive effects. The interaction between firm- and country-specific factors was highly significant in all cases, showing that the difference in wages paid by MNEs and other firms varied according to the country in which they operated. The industry and country interaction was also significant at the same level throughout, indicating that the wages paid in

Table 10.5 *Explanatory Power and Significance of Country, Industry and Firm Factors shown by an Analysis of the Variance of Wages in Six Host Countries*

Factor	Percentage of variation explained	F Statistic	Degrees of freedom		Significance (%)
1966					
Industry	6.4	9.71	11	53	1
Country	79.2	263.00	5	53	1
Firm	0.1	1.26	1	53	—
Industry—country	6.2	1.87	55	53	1
Industry—firm	0.6	0.88	11	53	—
Country—firm	4.3	14.40	5	53	1
Residual	3.2				
1970					
Industry	9.8	15.10	11	53	1
Country	76.9	261.00	5	53	1
Firm	0.5	6.54	1	53	5
Industry—country	7.8	2.43	55	53	1
Industry—firm	0.5	0.89	11	53	—
Country—firm	1.4	4.81	5	53	1
Residual	3.1				

Source: Data derived from Tables 10.1 and 10.2.

Table 10.6 *Explanatory Power and Significance of Country, Industry and Firm Factors shown by an Analysis of the Variance of Wages in Seven Countries including the USA*

Factor	Percentage of variation explained	F Statistic	Degrees of freedom		Significance (%)
1966					
Industry	4.5	9.95	11	64	1
Country	85.9	349.00	6	64	1
Firm	0.2	4.18	1	64	5
Industry—country	4.8	1.76	66	64	5
Industry—firm	0.3	0.69	11	64	—
Country—firm	3.0	7.12	6	64	1
Residual	1.3				
1970					
Industry	7.5	12.70	11	64	1
Country	80.9	252.00	6	64	1
Firm	0.0	0.02	1	64	—
Industry—country	5.3	1.49	66	64	5
Industry—firm	0.4	0.67	11	64	—
Country—firm	2.5	7.93	6	64	1
Residual	3.4				

Source: Data derived from Tables 10.1 and 10.2.

different industries varied according to the country of operation. The industry–firm interaction was significant at a 5 per cent level in the case of the seven-country analysis for 1970 but otherwise it was insignificant.

(b)   *Analysis of variance excluding first Mexico and then the UK*

The analysis of variance was rerun excluding Mexico to see whether country-specific factors would still be most important when only European host countries and Canada were included in the analysis. The results were much as before. Country-specific factors were still the most powerful determinant of wage variations, although the percentage of variation explained by them was reduced from 79.2 per cent to 61.8 per cent in 1966 and from 76.9 per cent to 64.7 per cent in 1970. By contrast the explanatory power of industry-specific factors increased from 6.4 per cent to 12.9 per cent in 1966, and from 9.8 per cent to 17.7 per cent in 1970. Firm-specific factors were significant at the 1 per cent level for 1970 at which date they explained 1.6 per cent of the variations; they were insignificant for 1966. The results shown for the interactive effects were less consistent than for the six host countries; in particular, both results for 1970 showed the country–firm interaction as insignificant. When the UK instead of Mexico was excluded,[15] the percentage of variations explained by country-specific factors increased slightly compared with the original results, as did that of industry-specific factors. The importance of firm-specific factors also increased more (from 0.2 per cent to 0.5 per cent) and became significant at the 5 per cent level. Interaction effects, on the other hand, were less significant and explained a smaller proportion of the variation.[16]

What are the explanations for the differences in wage structure set out in Tables 10.1 and 10.2? A number of possible determinants are discussed in the following paragraphs where the relationships between average wages (weighted by employment) and various explanatory variables are examined. The evidence is analysed by country, by industry and in particular countries and industries and as between two groups of firms, viz. US affiliates (both excluding and including the US parent companies) and between MNEs and non-MNEs (exluding and including US parent companies and non-MNEs in the USA).[17]

Simple correlations were used to test the relationships rather than multiple regression analysis primarily because of data limitations. The statistical problems are acute even when examining the cause of wage differentials within a particular country[18] but they are compounded many times when the comparisons are cross-country and between firms of different nationality of ownership.[19]

Two other difficulties were encountered in this exploratory analysis. The first was the well-known problem of causality; a significant correlation tells nothing of the causation between wages and the related variable. The second was the small number of observations which may affect reliability of the statistical tests of significance.

IV

(a)   *Wages of US MNEs both excluding and including the wages of parent companies*

(i)   *Productivity.* Productivity was taken as a proxy for the ability to pay the workforce different wage rates; it was hypothesised that the most productive firms would tend to pay the highest wages and that wages would increase most in firms where productivity was increasing the most rapidly. The relationship between productivity and wages in 1966 and 1970 and between changes in productivity and changes in wages from 1966 to 1970 was tested using total sales per person employed (S/N) as a measure of labour productivity.[20]

The inter-country variation in wages was found to be positively related to S/N in both 1966 and 1970, in accordance with hypothesis, and the relationship was significant in 1970 ($r = 0.77$ for the six host countries, $r = 0.74$ with the US parent companies included). The relationship was weak but positive for all the countries individually with the exception of the US in 1970. The inter-industry variation of wages and S/N were not significantly related; the correlation coefficient was positive when the US was excluded from the analysis and negative when the parent companies were included. However, the industries individually showed a consistent positive association between S/N and wages in both years (with the exception of the rubber industry, excluding the US in 1970) and the relationship was significant in the food, chemicals, primary and fabricated metals, non-electrical machinery and stone, clay and glass industries.

The correlation between the percentage change in wages and changes in S/N over the period 1966–70 was weak but positive for all countries combined both including and excluding the parent companies, but the coefficients for individual countries exhibited instability of sign. Individual industries consistently showed a positive relation between changes in wages and in S/N and the result was significant in the case of food, chemicals, primary and fabricated metals, electrical and non-electrical machinery manufacturing. Contrary to expectations, the relationship was positive for all industries combined when the US parent companies were included, but negative when they were excluded.

(ii)   *Profitability.* It was expected that differences in profit rates – another proxy for the capacity of companies to pay different wage rates – might play an important part in the explanation of differences in wage levels, and that a relationship might emerge between changes in profit rates and in wages. These relationships were examined using two alternative measures of profitability: the profit/net assets (P/A) ratio and the profit/ sales (P/S) ratio. As comparable data on the profits of the US parent companies were not readily available, the results only refer to the affiliates in the six host countries.

When the inter-country variation in wage levels was related to either measure of profits a weak positive association emerged in 1966 and a weak negative association in 1970. The results for individual countries were mixed and significant only in Germany where the industries paying the highest wages appear to have been the least profitable. The relationship between inter-industry variation in wages and profitability was not significant, and was unstable in sign, as were the results for the countries individually. The host countries in which the affiliates appeared to have experienced the largest wage increases tended to be those where profitablility was increasing relatively slowly, a finding which was significant when P/A was used as the proxy for profitability. However, the individual countries presented a mixed picture, and, in France, increases in wages and increases in profitability were significantly and positively related, in contrast to the overall result.

(iii)   *Growth*. High wages may be paid to attract workers into rapidly expanding industrial activities, as part of the competitive process. Two proxies for growth, the percentage growth in sales $(\dot{S})$ and the percentage growth in employment $(\dot{E})$, were used to investigate whether the fastest growing firms in 1966–70 paid the most in 1966 and 1970 and to establish to what extent they tended to be the firms which increased their employee compensation the most rapidly during the period.

An examination of the inter-country variation of wages and growth in 1966 and 1970 showed that the firms that paid the most tended to grow relatively slowly both in terms of sales and employment. When growth was measured with $\dot{S}$ as a proxy, the coefficients of correlation for the US affiliates were $r = 0.58$ in 1966 and $r = -0.48$ in 1970 and these increased to $r = -0.65$ and $r = -0.54$, respectively, when wages were related to $\dot{E}$. The countries taken separately usually showed a negative relationship, but the only significant result was for Canada in 1970. The inter-industry relationship between wages and growth was consistently negative and was significant when growth was measured by $\dot{E}$ whether the US parents were included or excluded $(r = 0.76$ and $r = -0.74$, respectively). The individual industries usually conformed to the overall pattern but the only significant result was for stone, clay and glass manufacturing.

The increase in wages tended to be negatively associated with growth for all countries together but the relationship between inter-industry variation of wages showed a consistently positive relationship between wage change and growth, which was strong for the six host countries in terms of sales and significant in terms of employment $(r = 0.80)$. Results for the separate industries were mixed, and the only significant result was for instrument manufacturing where the coefficient was positive.

(iv) *Capital Intensity.* A proxy for capital intensity was introduced for a number of reasons. First, it may affect the bargaining power of workers, as trade union membership tends to be greater in more capital intensive industries and a strike will be more costly for an employer here than in a labour intensive industry. Second, capital intensity may also act as a proxy for firm or plant size. This is important as firm and plant size have been shown to exert a significant influence on wage levels and it is not possible to measure plant size directly using these data. Third, it has been suggested that capital intensity may also be used as a surrogate for labour quality as capital intensive technology often requires more skilled people to service it.

It was therefore hypothesised that the firms which were the most capital intensive would tend to pay the highest wages. This hypothesis, together with the relationship between changes in wages and changes in capital intensity, was investigated using net assets per employee (A/N) as a measure of capital intensity. Data were not available for MNEs in the USA and indigenous firms in host countries, and so the results reported refer to the affiliates in the six host countries.

Examination of the inter-country variation in wages showed a positive but insignificant relationship between A/N and wages per capita[21] in both 1966 and 1970, a result which held when the countries were examined individually. A positive and significant association was shown by the analysis of inter-industry variation in both years, although the results for the industries were mixed and seldom significant.

(v) *Technology.* It was hypothesised that firms in industries with advanced technologies would tend to pay higher wages and grant larger wage increases than other firms. This was investigated by dividing the twelve industries into two groups, viz. the more technology intensive (MTI) industries which were taken to include chemicals, rubber, non-electrical and electrical machinery, transport equipment and instrument manufacturing, and the less technology intensive industries (LTI) including food, paper and allied industry, primary and fabricated metals, stone, clay and glass, textiles and other manufacturing. The weighted average wage in 1966 and 1970 and the change in wages over the period were compared for the two groups to see whether any substantial differences emerged. The mean wage paid by US affiliates in the host countries was very similar for the two groups in 1966, but in 1970 affiliates in the MTIs paid more. When the US parent companies were included the differences were significant in both years; the mean wages for firms in the MTIs were $3.66 in 1966 and $4.76 in 1970 compared with $3.32 and $3.90, respectively, for firms in the LTIs. Increases in wages were also greater for the firms in MTIs both for affiliates in the host countries and for US companies.

(b)   *Wages of US affiliates and indigenous firms (both excluding and including the US parent companies and non-MNEs in the USA)*
These differences were examined by correlating ratios for each variable constructed with the value of employee compensation for MNE firms in the numerator and that for the other firms in the denominator.

(i)   *Productivity.* It was hypothesised that the wages paid by the MNEs would tend to be higher than other firms when their productivity was relatively high. This proposition was tested by correlating the wages paid by the US affiliates, as a proportion of the wages paid by indigenous firms in host countries, to the ratio of their labour productivities, S/N, in 1966 and 1970 and subsequently it was tested with the US parent companies and non-MNEs in the USA included in the analysis.

Analysis of the inter-country variation in relative wages yielded weak but positive correlation coefficients in both 1966 and 1970, in accordance with expectations. The correlation coefficients for the countries individually were generally insignificant and had unstable signs, but, in the cases where the result was significant (Mexico in 1966), the coefficient was of the right sign. The relationships for the industries taken together were all insignificant and negative, except in 1966 when the US parent companies and non-MNEs were excluded ($r = 0.28$). Only for non-electrical goods, both including and excluding the USA, transport equipment (1966) and primary and fabricated metals (1970, when the USA was excluded) were the results significant, and here the signs were all positive.

It was expected that wages would have increased relatively faster in MNEs than in indigenous firms where productivity was also increasing more rapidly between 1966 and 1970. The relationship was positive for all countries taken together (0.65) excluding the US parent companies and non-MNEs, and (0.66) when they were included, although no country, individually, showed a significant relationship. The correlation was very low for all industries taken together and was only positive when the US was included, as was the case previously when changes in wages paid by the MNEs was considered.[22] The only significant results were found in primary and fabricated metals where the relationships were positive.

(ii)   *Growth.* The data also permitted a test of the relationship between the level and growth of wages paid by MNEs and non-MNEs and their changes in size. Again two proxies for growth in size were used, namely, the growth of total sales ($\dot{S}$) and the growth of employment ($\dot{E}$).

Examination of the inter-country variation of relative wages and growth yielded no significant results and the signs were unstable; neither were the coefficients significant in any of the countries taken separately. The relationship between the inter-industry wage levels and in growth were consistently positive but never achieved significance.

The association between $\dot{S}$ or $\dot{E}$ and the growth of wages was low for both inter-country and inter-industry variations and the coefficients were usually negative. The individual countries and industries showed mixed results but they were significant in the rubber industry where the relationship was positive.

(iii) *Market Structure.* Several arguments have been put forward by economists to suggest the existence of a positive relationship between industrial market power and wage levels (Hart and Clarke, 1978). For example, it is hypothesised that where firms earn a monopoly rent they will find it easier to absorb wage payments from that rent or take advantage of their market positions to pass on wage increases to consumers. In addition, large oligopolistic firms may pursue a non-profit maximising strategy and be tempted to pay high wages to secure a 'quiet life', or public recognition as a good employer. Moreover, it is often the case that such firms are faced by strong labour unions who bargain away part of this rent (Dunning and Stilwell, 1978). Previous statistical studies, both in the UK and USA, have found industrial concentration to be a proxy for market power and to be highly correlated with inter-industry wage differences.[23] However, the concentration variable became insignificant in these studies once the size of plant was included as an additional independent variable in multiple regression analyses. These results are difficult to interpret owing to the collinearity between plant size and concentration.

In this study, four firm concentration ratios in the USA for 1966 were taken as a proxy for market power and these were found to be positively related to wage levels paid by all firms in the USA in both 1966 and 1970. The results were highly significant ($r = 0.78$ for 1966 and $r = 0.82$ in 1970), in accordance with previous work. Empirical evidence has shown that MNEs tend to be most active in oligopolistic industries,[24] and this was also supported by our data: US concentration ratios were positively correlated with the percentage share of MNE sales in the USA and with the share of MNE and affiliate sales in all countries by industry in 1966. Both coefficients were significant ($r = 0.78$ and 0.75). Unfortunately, the data did not permit a test of how far differences in wages paid within a particular industry by MNEs and non-MNEs were due to differences in market share or other aspects of firm structure; neither was it possible to test the influence of relative *plant* size of MNEs and non-MNEs on wage levels.

(iv) *Trade Union Power.* A number of previous studies have supported the hypothesis that differences in trade union activity between industries are a significant source of inter-industry variation in earnings within particular countries.[25] Although cross-country analyses have paid less attention to trade union bargaining power, a study by R. L. Thomas (1976) showed that the percentage of the labour force which is unionised does exert a significant influence on the growth rate of wages.

In the present context, if trade unions are more active in industries in which the MNEs are concentrated than in other industries, one might expect higher wage payments or wage increases in MNEs than non-MNEs, *ceteris paribus*. Trade union activity in the USA (measured by the percentage of workers in the USA in establishments where the majority of workers were under collective bargaining agreements) was found to be positively correlated with the representation of MNEs in all firm sales in the USA and with the share of MNEs and their affiliates in total sales in all countries by industry, but these relationships were insignificant.[26]

(v)   *Interdependence of activities within MNEs.* It has already been seen[27] that it is difficult to construct a separately identifiable variable to measure the extent to which MNEs internalise their decision taking and the interdependence between the activities of affiliates and parent companies. One proxy sometimes used is the extent of intra-firm trade, it being assumed that the higher the percentage of exports of MNEs which are intra-group, that is, internalised, the more this reflects an integrated product or process structure within the different plants of the MNEs. Using this measure (for 1970) in respect of the industries identified in Table 10.2,[28] and relating it to the differences in the average hourly compensation paid to employees of MNE affiliates and indigenous firms in all the countries considered gives a rank correlation of only $+0.18$; using rather different data (Dunning, 1976) and relating wage differentials of US and indigenous firms in the UK (in 1970) to the same series of intra-group exports gives a higher correlation of $+0.39$ (or $+0.57$ excluding non-electrical machinery). It should be observed that other studies, for example, Buckley and Pearce (1979), have revealed a close association between research intensity and intra-group exports.

That there is not a closer association between the degree of interdependence of MNEs and differences in wage payments may not only be due to data imperfections. In some of the sectors where there are wage differentials the indigenous firms are themselves MNEs; while in others, countervailing the vulnerability of MNEs is their bargaining strength and flexibility *vis-à-vis* organised labour.[29]

(vi)   *Other possible explanations.* There are not sufficient data to permit a test of how far differences in other industry or country characteristics are associated with the wages and rate of changes of wages in MNEs and non-MNEs. Moreover, it must be remembered that the patterns observed may be due to non-economic factors such as differences in the characteristics of the labour force — for example, differences in skill mix, age structure, numbers of male/female, part-time/full-time and shift workers would all be expected to exert an influence. Although the ILO study cited earlier has assmbled some fragmentary evidence of the division between salaried employees and wage earners in MNEs and non-MNEs in general, the data are not sufficiently detailed to take these possibilities into account.[30]

V

The similarity of experiences with rates of inflation since 1960 in many different countries has attracted much attention, and has led to the suggestion that with growing international interdependence, inflation is being transmitted from country to country. Various ways in which inflation might be spread internationally have been identified, and of these perhaps the most widely discussed has been the working of the monetary mechanism. Other possibilities include general demand pressure, international demonstration effects, the development of international trade unions and the activities of MNEs.

This section of the chapter is concerned with the role played by MNEs in recent inflation, and specifically with the suggestion that MNEs may have contributed to international inflation through their operations in the labour market. The possible influence of MNEs on inflation may occur through the 'wage transference mechanism', which involves the transmission of wage pressure from sectors of the economy where productivity is high and increasing to other sectors where productivity is lower and increasing more slowly. Only since 1970 has this issue received any detailed discussion in the literature and there has been very little empirical work in the area.[31]

The approach to the subject presented here is an exploratory one; several hypotheses are suggested concerning the activities of MNEs, which might be expected to hold if a wage transference mechanism is at work within an international framework and then these propositions are tested in so far as data permit.

Table 10.7 sets out details of increases in wages in manufacturing industry and consumer prices between 1966 and 1970. *Inter alia* it reveals that of the countries in this sample, the UK experienced the largest increases in consumer prices, with a price rise totalling 20.3 per cent, while the average increase in prices of all countries during the period was 16.4 per cent.

Table 10.7 *Average Hourly Compensation in Manufacturing Industry and Percentage Increase in Consumer Prices, 1966–70*

Country	Wages	Prices
United States	24.9	19.6
United Kingdom	14.7	20.3
West Germany	54.4	10.0
Mexico	32.2	14.9
Belgium–Luxembourg	39.3	13.1
France	48.2	20.7
Canada	50.4	16.5
All countries	29.6	16.4

Source: Wages – US Tariff Commission (1973).
Prices – *International Financial Statistics*, vol. 26 (1973).

Wage increases in all countries except the UK outstripped price increases by a considerable margin[32] with the greatest gain in real wages occurring in Germany and France.

(a) The propositions

(i) *Employee compensation within affiliates of MNEs in particular industries would be less geographically dispersed than that within indigenous firms.* The dispersion of employee compensation was examined by industry for MNEs and indigenous firms in 1966 and 1970. As Table 10.4 shows, there is no evidence to support this hypothesis if US parent companies are excluded from the analysis. Employee compensation was less dispersed among affiliates of MNEs in all industries in both 1966 and 1970. When the US parent companies were included, however, some of the results were more consistent with the hypothesis. The dispersion of employee compensation in affiliates and their parent companies was less in seven industries in 1966 with the exception of chemicals, non-electrical and electrical machinery, instruments, and stone, clay and glass, and in 1970 the hypothesis is supported by the results in three of the twelve sectors, viz. food, paper and textiles.

(ii) *The dispersion of employee compensation in those industries in which the MNEs are strongly represented would be less than those in which they are weakly represented.* The standard deviation was used to measure the dispersion of employee compensation in all firms and the representation of MNEs was measured by the proportion of MNE sales to total sales. When the relationship between the dispersion of employee compensation among all firms in host countries by industry and MNE representation was examined, the correlation was found to be of the right sign but insignificant in both 1966 and 1970. However, when the MNE parents were included in the analysis the relationship, contrary to hypothesis, became positive and significant in both years (1966, $r = 0.81$; 1970, $r = 0.71$).

(iii) *Over time there would be a greater tendency for the dispersion of employee compensation to be reduced or to increase less in the case of industries dominated by MNEs than in other industries.* Contrary to this hypothesis, there was an insignificant positive relationship between the percentage change in the wage dispersion of all firms by industry in the host countries between 1966 and 1970 and the importance of MNE sales in total sales in 1966 ($r = 0.40$). When the USA was included in the analysis, the relationship was negative but insignificant. Similarly there was a negative but weak relationship between the importance of MNEs in 1966 and the change in dispersion of wages by industry, whether the USA was excluded or not.

The dispersion of employee compensation among MNEs showed a smaller percentage increase (or greater decrease) than indigenous firms in

seven of the twelve sample industries, viz. chemicals, primary and fabricated metals, non-electrical machinery, electrical machinery, transport, stone and instruments. The increase was the same in the food industry but greater for MNEs in the remaining three sectors. However, when
the USA was included there were only three industries in which the
MNE dispersion increased less (stone) or decreased more (chemicals and
textiles).

(iv) *The countries in which the affiliates of MNEs are most strongly
represented would tend to increase their wages the most over time. This
tendency should be particularly true for those countries in which wages
are below average.* The wages in countries in which the MNEs were
strongly represented showed no consistent tendency to increase their
wages the most over time. The correlation coefficient between the
percentage increase in wages in all firms and the share of MNEs in total sales was 0.22 for the host countries and -0.34 when the USA was
included. Nor was there any tendency for an increasing representation
of MNEs to be associated with largest increase in wages. The countries
with below average wages in 1966 were the UK, France, Belgium/Luxem-
bourg and Mexico, but an inspection of the data reveals that the level
of wages in that year together with the representation of MNEs did not
relate closely to the changes in the wages of all firms between 1966 and
1970.

(v) *The general index of retail prices may rise faster in those countries/
industries where MNEs (or their affiliates) are most represented, and/or
the prices of products produced by MNEs or their affiliates will rise faster
than others.* Aggregate data of retail prices by country were obtained but
figures for individual industrial sectors and separately for MNEs and indigenous firms have not been found.

Correlation analysis showed no significant relationship between the increase in retail prices by country and either the representation of MNEs in
1966 or the increase in MNE representation between 1966 and 1970 ($r =$
0.19 and 0.15, respectively). When the USA was excluded, the results were
still insignificant.

It is true that increased productivity may act as a deflator to price increases. Evidence on price behaviour in MNEs is very limited. However,
there is evidence from the behaviour of unit value indices of the net output of sectors which have high productivity growth that in the majority of
cases prices are not cut by a significant percentage of productivity gains
(Eatwell, Llewellyn and Tarling, 1974).

Data concerning *wholesale* prices for ten industrial sub-sectors in the
USA (excluding instruments and other manufacturing) related to the share
of MNEs in US sales and to the share of MNEs and their affiliates to total
sales were insignificant in both cases.

VI

The purpose of this chapter has been to set out some facts about the employee compensation paid by MNEs in a number of countries and to suggest reasons for the variation observed between these and the differences from the hourly wages paid by indigenous firms. The latter part of the paper has also attempted to test various hypotheses which might shed some light on whether the wage policies of MNEs contributed towards the international transmission of inflation and/or made the anti-inflationary policies of national governments more difficult to achieve in the period between 1966 and 1970.

The consensus of the evidence set out is that, normalising for industry and country differences, MNEs do, in general, pay higher wages than indigenous firms, but that the margin of difference is not as great as is sometimes alleged. The analysis of variance confirmed that the nationality of ownership of firms has a separate influence on wage payments, quite apart from the industrial activity concerned and the country of operation. It also suggested the existence of some interaction between these elements, in particular, showing that the difference in wages paid by MNEs and other firms tends to vary according to the country considered. Attempts to explain the differences in employee compensation by a number of economic variables yielded mixed results, but it would seem that differences in employee compensation are more significantly related to the value of net output per employee than any other cause. To what extent such productivity differences reflect differences in the efficiency of resource allocation and to what extent they reflect other factors (e.g. greater monopoly power and transfer price manipulation) one cannot say. However, there is reason to suppose that such differences are more pronounced in countries and/or industries in which there is less competition, or more opportunity for transfer pricing. Better data are needed before further analysis can be carried out, but in conclusion it is worth considering some of the more general policy implications.

We have seen that there is some support for the proposition that MNEs are wage leaders in the industries in which they are represented (Enderwick, 1978) and that, because of their ability to pay higher than average wages in their industry, they may affect the wages offered by their competitors. The 15 per cent wage settlement at the Ford Motor Company UK in the autumn of 1978 when the government guideline for wage increases was 5 per cent is a classic case in point. However, the fact that British Leyland workers accepted a much lower percentage increase when the productivity of their company was considerably less than that of Ford's suggests that, even in oligopolistic industries where trade union power is strong, market forces may still exert a powerful influence.

Moreover, in the UK at least, the difference in average wage payments between foreign and domestically controlled firms is not as great as that in productivity (Stopford, 1980). To this extent, at least, foreign firms can hardly be accused of inflationary wage bargaining.

If MNEs do have an impact on the climate of wage bargaining, it is partly a reflection of their better capacity to pay higher than average wages and partly due to the fact that, within the industries in which they are most strongly represented, the market structure is oligopolistic and there are powerful labour unions which tend to be multinational in scope and organisation. This often gives workers in such firms and industries a privileged position *vis-à-vis* both workers in other industries and consumers. It may also be true that MNEs use their economic muscle in order to recruit labour in short supply, but this is likely to have a regional rather than a national impact on wage inflation.

At the same time, anti-inflationary policies of governments may be made more difficult by the presence of affiliates of MNEs, particularly where wage bargaining is conducted at an industry level. On the one hand, a rigid incomes policy penalises workers in efficient firms; on the other, to allow firms to break such guidelines may set a precedent (as it did in the UK in the winter of 1978–79) for higher wage claims than the community can afford. Where free collective bargaining is coupled with strict monetary control, inflation may be kept in check, but this may only be achieved at the cost of a substantial increase in unemployment and a weakened competitive position of indigenous firms. Here other policies, such as those towards mergers and restrictive practices, must enter the government's calculation.

In developing countries, the effect of MNEs is dramatically highlighted. Where affiliates of MNEs are replicating the production methods of their parent companies and productivity is similar, profits earned by the MNE affiliates are likely to be extremely high if they pay competitive wages. Yet to pay these workers comparable wages to those received by their labour force in developed countries would put MNE wages way out of line with the rest of the local community and create a small enclave of high-income earners. A solution to this problem, suggested by a UN Study Group in 1974,[33] is that the excess profits should be siphoned off through appropriate fiscal measures and allocated to assist development in general or the welfare of labour as a whole, rather than simply benefiting those who happen to be employed by MNEs. Alternatively, where the production of MNEs is sold almost exclusively to the local market, price controls may be sufficient to prevent excessive profits and lower prices may contribute to raising the real incomes of the population. However, this latter measure may simply result in more demand for the output of the MNE at the expense of local competitors, which may not be the government's intention.

Some of these problems are simply a reflection of the impact of MNEs on the distribution of income between countries and between different sectors within economies. This may not matter a great deal within a country as by the use of appropriate fiscal or monetary measures national governments can take the necessary compensatory action. But across national boundaries there is no international mechanism for such control, or for ensuring that the resulting distribution of income is not the result of imperfect market forces, including inappropriate price fixing. While trade unions claim they are in a position to exert some countervailing power to MNEs and to prevent MNEs from adversely affecting their workers, there is no guarantee that the other workers or the rest of the community will not be penalised or that they will obtain their full share of the benefits.

The issues raised in this section are not unique to MNEs, but they are more likely to be manifested in their extreme form where MNEs are present. By dint of their size, flexibility and, in many cases, their efficiency, MNEs are likely to be able to afford to pay higher wages than the average indigenous firm; this is most likely to be the case in the least developed countries. Economic theory would suggest that more resources will flow to MNEs, whether attracted by higher wages on the supply side or more recruitment on the demand side, spurred on by higher profits; from a policy viewpoint, this would also seem to be desirable, unless the capacity of MNEs to earn a higher net output per unit of labour is the result of the exercise of monopoly power. Clearly, labour unions want to maximise the economic rent of their members at the expense of other stakeholders. At a micro level, this is purely a question of the distribution between shareholders, management, consumers and labour; if, however, this causes reverberations on wage claims both at an intra-industry (or intra-regional) and an inter-industry (or inter-regional) level, the macro implications could be considerable. The government then has to consider a set of trade-offs. A rigid wages policy can only work in an economy if there are few differences in productivity between firms, or if some way can be found of siphoning excessive profits made by efficient firms without discouraging a redistribution of resources into efficient sectors. Rarely are these conditions met, and the presence of affiliates of MNEs makes it less, rather than more, likely that they will be.

In such situations there are three main options open to a government; first, if it is fully dedicated to an incomes policy, the role of MNEs in that economy may need to be reappraised; second, at the other extreme, an incomes policy may have to be abandoned. The third route, though practically the most difficult, is theoretically the most appealing; and that is to devise an economically viable mechanism in consultation with all the relevant parties by which the major benefits of the activities of MNEs could be gained but the distribution of these benefits would be arranged in such a way as to advance both anti-inflationary and income distribution policies, and to safeguard the right of unions. Few, if any, governments have seriously attempted to follow this route.

Appendix 10.1

The Classification of Manufacturing Activity by SIC Code

Industrial Activity	SIC Code
All manufacturing	D, excluding 29
Food	20
Paper and allied products	26
Chemicals	28
Rubber	30
Primary and fabricated metals	33, 34
Machinery except electrical	35
Electrical machinery	36
Transportation equipment	37
Textiles and apparel	22, 23
Stone, clay and glass	32
Instruments	38
Other	19, 21, 31, 39

Note: The sectors Lumber wood and paper (SIC 24, 25) and Printing and publishing (SIC 27) were excluded from this study because of the lack of data.

Appendix 10.2

Data Sources

Statistics for non-MNEs in the USA and indigenous firms in host countries were derived from data for all firms and MNEs given in the Tariff Commission Report, which was the main statistical source for the analysis.

(i)	Variables derived from Tariff Commission Tables	Tables
	Average hourly compensation	A1–16, 20–23, 42
	Sales	A44–57
	Employment	A19–33
	Sales per employee	A44–57, A19–33
	Employee compensation	A105–118
	Profits (= net income after depreciation and foreign income taxes)	A10–16
(ii)	Variables derived from other sources	
	Consumer price indices	International financial statistics
	Concentration	Shepherd (1970)
	Trade union activity	Marshall (1968)
	Net assets	Supplementary information provided by US Tariff Commission on request

Notes: Chapter 10

1   For a discussion of recent trade union activity in this direction see ILO (1973).

2   The Tariff Commission focuses on eight countries, but Brazil was excluded here due to lack of data.

3   Tariff Commission *Report*, p. 404, Table 6. These countries accounted for an estimated \$1,892m. of a world total of \$30,915m. US-owned foreign net fixed assets in manufacturing industry in 1970.

4   This total possible variation between wages in all firms and MNEs can be classified into estimate errors (\$0.10 per employee for both MNEs and all firms) and rounding errors (\$0.05 also for both groups of firms).

5   For a fuller discussion of these problems, see ILO (1956).

6   For a useful summary of these, see ILO (1976).

7   Also confirmed by Tanchoco-Subido (1979).

8   The difficulty with all of these studies is to identify the extent to which any differences observed in the wages paid by MNE affiliates (compared to indigenous firms) is ascribed to their foreign ownership as such, or to other attributes of the affiliates, for example, size, product mix, skill composition, location (within a country) and so on. Moreover, comparisons are generally made in terms of money wage rates rather than total employee benefit, which includes fringe benefits, job security, etc.

9   The differences between means were tested for statistical significance. It must be noted, however, that some of the differences which emerged as significant according to a two-tailed test lie within the possible range of data error.

10   These data are not easily reconcileable with those of other sources (see particularly Dunning, 1976).

11   Measured by a one-tailed F test at the 5 per cent level.

12   See Scherer (1971) for a useful summary of the US studies, and Wabe and Leech (1978).

13   For simplicity this analysis is presented in terms of wage levels. It could be re-written in terms of changes in wages. Certain factors would be less important in a time series analysis as they could reasonably be assumed constant over a certain period of time.

14   An exception may be where indigenous firms are themselves MNEs. The relationship between interdependence and wage leadership is explored by Enderwick (1978) using a wage adjustment model of Addison and Burton (1978). Steuer and Gennard (1971) suggest that the lower propensity to strike action in foreign affiliates in the UK (compared to indigenous firms), in spite of factors making more industrial disputes, is explained by higher financial inducements to forestall industrial conflict.

15   This was done purely because of the apparent inconsistencies between the Tariff Commission data on the relative wages of MNEs and non-MNEs and that of other sources.

16   Details of the variance analysis are available from the authors on request.

17   The firms in the USA were excluded or included in inter-country comparisons simply by varying the number of observations; for industry comparisons, different means were calculated according to whether the US observations were excluded or included.

18   Wabe and Leech (1978).

19   One possibility which we considered was an analysis in terms of equations explaining the ratio of MNE wages to indigenous firms' wages by a country dummy (to take account of the country factors which are obviously important, but difficult for which to derive proxies), and by various other independent variables representing industry influences, all expressed as ratios of MNE wages divided by indigenous or non-MNE wages. This did not prove possible because of the problems of data collection for indigenous firms.

20   There are problems with using the value of sales as the numerator in a proxy measure of productivity. Besides the more familiar one that gross output may not be an accurate reflection of value added, distortions may arise from the monopoly rents imputed in the prices of the corresponding goods and services produced. For example, high productivity estimates for foreign affiliates may be due to higher prices. However, when productivity is taken primarily as an indicator of ability to pay higher wages, this measurement problem is not serious.

21   Which is really relating assets to total wages as both variables are divided throughout by employment.

22   See page 280–281.

23   For the United States see Masters (1969) and Haworth and Rasmussen (1971). Two UK studies yielding similar conclusions are Sawyer (1973) and Hood and Rees (1974).

24   See Chapter 7.

25   See, for example, Pencavel (1974), Mulvey (1976) and Hart and Clarke (1978).

26   This relationship was tested for nine industrial sectors for which data on trade union activity were available and excluded rubber, electrical machinery and other manufacturing.

27   Chapters 3 and 5.

28   Derived from US Tariff Commission data; see also Buckley and Casson (1976).

29   Including the choice of locating new investments.

30   ILO (1973).

31   For a discussion of the theory see Maynard (1974). For some empirical work which links the overall rate of increase of money wages to the rate of increase of productivity in those sectors with fastest productivity growth see Eatwell, Llewellyn and Tarling (1974) and Thomas (1976).

32   There appears to be an inconsistency between the wage increases recorded by the US Tariff Commission and the Department of Employment's (then Ministry of Labour) figure, for the same period.

33   United Nations, *The Impact of Multinational Enterprises on Economic Development and International Relations* (New York: UN Economic and Social Council, 1974).

References

Addison, J. T., and Burton, J. (1978), 'Wage adjustment processes: a synthetic treatment', *British Journal of Industrial Relations*, vol. 16, no. 2.

Buckley, P. J., and Pearce, R. D. (1979), 'Overseas production and exporting by large enterprises', *Journal of International Business Studies*, vol. 10 (Spring/Summer).

Buckley, P. J., and Casson, M. (1976), *The Future of the Multinational Enterprise* (London: Macmillan).

Cohen, B. I. (1975), *Multinational Firms and Asian Exports* (New Haven and London: Yale University Press).

Dunning, J. H. (1976), *US Industry in Britain* (London: Wilton House).

Dunning, J. H., and Stilwell, F. J. B. (1978), 'Theories of business behaviour and the distribution of surplus profits', *Kyklos*, vol. 31, no. 4.

Eatwell, J., Llewellyn, J. and Tarling, R. (1974), 'Money wage inflation in industrial countries', *Review of Economic Studies*, vol. 44 (October).

Enderwick, P. (1978), *A Model of the Wage Leadership Potential of Foreign Owned Firms in UK Manufacturing Industry 1960–1975* (mimeo).

Gennard, J. (1972), *Multinational Corporations and British Labour. A Review of Attitudes and Responses* (London: British North American Committee).

Hart, P. E., and Clarke, R. (1978), *Profit, Margins, Wages and Oligopoly*, University of Reading, Discussion Papers in Economics, Series A, No. 108 (November).

Haworth, C. T., and Rasmussen, D. W. (1971), 'Human capital and inter-industry wages in manufacturing', *Review of Economics and Statistics*, vol. 53 (November).

Hood, W., and Rees, R. D. (1974), 'Inter-industry wage levels in UK manufacturing', *Manchester School of Social and Economic Studies*, vol. 42 (June).

ILO (1956), *International Comparisons of Real Wages: A Study of Methods, Studies and Reports*, New Series No. 45 (Geneva: International Labour Office).

ILO (1973), *Multinational Enterprises and Social Policy* (Geneva: International Labour Office).

Iyanda, O., and Bello, J. A. (1979), *Employment Effects of Multinational Enterprises in Nigeria*, Research on Employment Effects of Multinational Enterprises, Working Paper No. 10 (Geneva: International Labour Office).

Jo, Sung-Hwan (1976), *The Impact of Multinational Firms on Employment and Incomes; the Case Study of South Korea*, ILO Working Papers, World Employment Programme Research (July) (Geneva: International Labour Office).

Langdon, S. (1975), 'Multinational corporations in the political economy of Kenya', PhD thesis, University of Sussex.

Marshall, R. (1968), 'The development of organised labour', *Monthly Labour Review* (March).

Mason, R. H. (1973), 'Some observations on the choice of technology by multinational firms in developing countries', *Review of Economics and Statistics*, vol. 55 (August).

Masters, S. H. (1969), 'An inter-industry analysis of wages and plant size', *Review of Economics and Statistics*, vol. 51 (August).

Maynard, G. W. (1974), 'Monetary policy', in J. H. Dunning (ed.), *Economic Analysis and the Multinational Enterprise* (London: Allen & Unwin).

Mulvey, C. (1976), 'Collective agreements and relative earnings in UK manufacturing in 1973', *Economica*, vol. 43 (November).

Papandreou, V. A. (1980), 'Multinational enterprises, market industrial structure and trade balance in host less developed countries: the case of Greece', PhD thesis, University of Reading.

Pencavel, J. (1974), 'Relative wages and trade unions in the United Kingdom', *Economica*, vol. 41 (May).

Possas, M. L. (1979), *Employment Effects of Multinational Enterprises in Brazil*, Research on Employment Effects of Multinational Enterprises, Working Paper No. 7 (Geneva: International Labour Office).

Sabolo, Y., and Trajtenberg, R. (1976), *The Impact of Transnational Enterprises in the Developing Countries* (Geneva: International Labour Office).

Sawyer, M. C. (1973), 'The earnings of manual workers: a cross section analysis', *Scottish Journal of Political Economy*, vol. 20 (June).

Scherer, F. M. (1971), *Industrial Market Structure and Economic Performance* (Chicago: Rand McNally).

Shepherd, W. G. (1970), *Market Power and Economic Welfare* (New York: Random House).

Sourrouille, J. V. (1976), *The Impact of Transnational Enterprises on Employment and Income: The Case of Argentina*, ILO Working Papers, World Employers Programme Research (December) (Geneva: International Labour Office).

Steuer, M. D., and Gennard, J. (1971), 'Industrial relations, labour disputes and labour utilisation in foreign owned firms in the United Kingdom', in J. H. Dunning (ed.), *The Multinational Enterprise* (London: Allen & Unwin).

Stopford, J. M. (1979), *Employment Effects of Multinational Enterprises in the United Kingdom*, Research on Employment Effects of Multinational Enterprises, Working Paper No. 5 (Geneva: International Labour Office).

Tanchoco-Subido, C. (1979), *Employment Effects of Multinational Enterprises in the Philippines*, Research on Employment Effects of Multinational Enterprises, Working Paper No. 11 (Geneva: International Labour Office).

Thomas, R. L. (1976), 'Money wage inflation in industrial countries: an alternative explanation', *Review of Economic Studies*, vol. 43, no. 135 (October).

US Tariff Commission (1973), *Implications of Multinational Firms for World Trade and Investment and for US Trade and Labour* (Washington, D.C.: US Government Printing Office).

Wabe, J. S., and Leech, D. (1978), 'Relative earnings in UK manufacturing: a reconsideration of the evidence', *Economic Journal*, vol. 88 (June).

11

Multinational Enterprises and Trade Flows of Developing Countries

I

In this chapter, we shall take as axiomatic the efforts of the developing countries to formulate policies suited to improving their dynamic comparative advantage. We shall ignore political objectives and constraints, although it is accepted that these, and particularly the desire for economic sovereignty and autonomy in decision taking, may be of overriding importance.

In considering the dynamics of trade and development, two aspects might be considered: first, the extent to which trade, through permitting increased specialisation, enables the production frontiers of participating countries to be extended; second, the extent to which the exogenous growth of resources affects the comparative advantage of countries, and hence their trade and development. Using a comparative static model, classical theory had something to say about both these questions, but its main emphasis lay in explaining a reallocation in resources due to changes in the quantity or price of factor inputs. This was because it assumed that advances in technology initiated by one country would be instantaneously and freely available to others. Information was treated as a free good rather than a scarce input. In these circumstances, there were no obstacles to a country attaining its potential comparative advantage.

Such an approach is no longer acceptable. In the world of the second half of the twentieth century, not only are advances in productive knowledge, that is, technology, a much more important vehicle of economic development than they once were; it is also quite clear that such knowledge is neither immediately nor freely transferred across national boundaries. From this three things follow: first, production functions may differ between countries – at least temporarily; second, countries may not always be able to exploit their potential comparative advantage; and third, because technology is often the specific property of enterprises, the possibility of these enterprises exploiting their advantages by producing outside their own boundaries becomes a reality.[1]

This chapter is based upon an article with the same title published in *World Development*, vol. 2, no. 2 (1974) and a chapter in P. P. Streeten (ed.), *Trade Strategies for Development* (London: Macmillan).

Some modern theories of trade flows have attempted to incorporate changes in technology into their analysis. Both the technological gap and product cycle theories,[2] which implicitly assume that information and technology are costly and take as axiomatic a lag in their transmission between countries, examine some of the ways in which products and processes innovated in one country may subsequently become more efficiently produced in others. However, they both fall short as complete explanations of trade flows; neither do they help us to understand the root causes of trade. They are in no sense (nor do they claim to be) normative theories, and hence take us very little of the way in evolving an appropriate trade strategy for a developing world. Partly, this is because they do not sufficiently take account of the foreign direct investment of enterprises, an understanding of which, as we have seen, lies more in the theories of industrial organisation and market failure.

It is clear, then, that, in imperfectly competitive conditions, there is no hidden hand which guarantees that all countries will optimise their dynamic comparative advantage, still less an equitable distribution of the benefits of trade. This being so, it is understandable that countries which believe themselves to be losers from the economics of interdependence should wish to take action to protect their interests. For the purposes of this discussion, it may be helpful to think of the developing countries as pursuing economic strategies aimed at overcoming barriers to entry into lines of economic activity in which they perceive their comparative advantage to lie if international factor and product markets were perfect. We believe that these barriers are generally greater for developing countries than for developed countries, although there is no necessary relationship between the height of the obstacles and the policies which should be undertaken. *Inter alia* these will depend on the cost of overcoming the barriers, in relation to other forms of resource allocation.

Generally speaking, most developing countries see their best chance for prosperity in industrialisation; they also view their greatest impediments in this direction. These are put down to imperfections in world market structures and political constraints; far from reflecting the principle of comparative dynamic advance, it is asserted that the existing system of trade militates against it. To overcome these disadvantages, some protection or aid to industrialisation is believed necessary, geared either to the import replacement of manufactured goods or to the encouragement of manufacturing exports. In the short run, assuming full employment and balance-of-payments equilibrium, the structure of both manufacturing imports and exports might be out of balance, as well as the level of trade. Without knowledge of the actual situation, there is no *a priori* reason to suppose policy will increase or reduce the share of foreign trade in the national output. In the long run, with the aim of increasing the growth of industrial output, there is a strong presumption that the share of both exports and imports will rise. Most industrialisation policies of developing countries aim either to complement export earnings or to replace part of those derived from primary production.

In purely resource allocative terms, the argument for import replacement is that the importing country is paying too high a price for its import of goods, in the sense that if the resources now used to earn the necessary foreign exchange were used to produce the goods internally they could, in the long run, at least, do so at lower cost. The case for export promotion is the converse of this; it asserts that the exporting country could earn foreign exchange for exports which would enable it to import a greater quantity of goods than the resources now allocated to exports could have produced in other activities.

Once one drops the full employment assumption, a new situation emerges. Here, it is argued that the income or output potential of developing countries is retarded because they cannot improve their production functions; in Keynesian terms, both supply and demand functions are constrained by an underutilisation of resources caused by an inability to exploit dynamic comparative advantage. If this is so, then anything which promotes demand for unused resources or removes bottlenecks in obtaining foreign resources will have both the normal multiplier effect and, through the improvement of production functions, linkage effects and other external economies, a technological spill-over effect as well. In other words, growth will occur through a better use of existing resources and the employment of unemployed resources, although the origin of such growth will be brought about by improved resource allocation.

In practice, neither import substitution nor export promotion will necessarily lead to an improvement in allocative efficiency or growth; particularly where policy is geared to political goals, or is implemented inefficiently by an indiscriminate use of import controls. Again, in the short run, such devices might be acceptable – and developing countries are not alone in the implementation of such policies (it is doubtful if the restrictionist policies of the UK or US governments towards outward investment in the late 1960s could be justified in terms of resource allocative efficiency). For our purposes, however, we shall assume the primary objective is economic development, and that policy towards trade is geared to this end and assessed solely by its contribution to it.

II

There are some obstacles to economic development which can only be overcome by the appropriate domestic policies of developing countries and/or by changing attitudes and motivations of economic agents. Others, of which agricultural protectionism is the most obvious example, reflect the policies of the developed countries. Similarly, there are some constraints about which it might be impossible to do anything, simply because of the supply inelasticity of resources. Here we are concerned with obstacles to development of developing countries which arise because they are unable to take advantage of the resources they do possess, due either to difficulties in obtaining complementary resources (supply-oriented barriers) or of the markets necessary to make production worthwhile (demand-oriented barriers). It is further assumed that these barriers are the result of forces hindering the efficient allocation of resources; in other words, the price which developing countries have to pay to obtain these resources or entry to markets, in some sense, is too high.

The supply-oriented barriers can be conveniently discussed in terms of one factor input, namely, capital. Harry Johnson (1969) has distinguished between three kinds of capital: material capital, for example, plant, equipment and buildings, etc.; human capital — essentially the stock of manpower from which the services of labour flow, the quality of which is a function *inter alia* of innate ability, education, training and motivation; and productive knowledge (information and technology) which, given the factor inputs as defined in the traditional sense, will determine the form of the production function, that is, the technical efficiency of firms. Now, as far as the first two kinds of capital are concerned, developing countries may be able to hire these at a price which (discounted for risk) is, by and large, the reflection of market forces. It is true that some price discrimination may exist against developing countries in the same way as small firms may be discriminated against,[3] and some monopolistic pricing may occur. But assuming that the inputs can be used productively, there is no real barrier to acquiring them.

The situation is somewhat different in respect of productive knowledge for two main reasons. First, part of this asset is, in practice, neither produced nor distributed under the principles governing the allocation of resources in a private enterprise economy. This obviously applies to most knowledge to do with the defence industry, for which the State is often producer and consumer; the criteria for evaluating such information and technology differ and the normal rules do not apply, except, perhaps, to the efficiency of the actual production process. Second, and more relevant in the present context, within the private sector the production of commercially viable knowledge is, in most cases, only thought worthwhile if its results remain, at least for some time, the exclusive possession of the innovating firm.

The reason for this highlights a characteristic of productive knowledge; it is costly to produce, but once produced and incorporated in a marketable product or process, it can often be very easily assimilated by other firms. Hence, society has introduced the patent system, the purpose of which is to ensure that investment in the innovatory process can earn a return at least equivalent to that on any other expendable asset. But such protection inescapably creates a barrier on the free transfer of knowledge and its acquisition by other firms.

Of course, not all knowledge, once created, is expensive to acquire. Many of the findings of fundamental research are published in the scientific and professional journals. Often, firms are prepared to sell information to other producers, for example, through licensing, though there may be restrictive conditions attached to this. Technology may be embodied in goods; in other cases it may be easily imitated and disseminated. The extent to which any enterprise can acquire and benefit from knowledge to improve its competitive position will depend on (1) whether the knowledge is saleable, (2) the conditions of sale and (3) whether the firms can make use of (or effectively absorb) such knowledge. To give an example, the knowledge of how to produce motor cars using fully automated methods is of little use to a specialist producer of racing cars. Likewise, the extent to which a country can obtain and benefit from knowledge produced by another will be influenced by similar criteria (cf. the Japanese and German ways of acquiring foreign know-how). It has been suggested that the argument of the developing countries is that the price they have to pay for information and technology is too high or they are inhibited in obtaining it. But without some form of external help, it cannot be domestically produced either. At first sight, this is a variant of the infant industry argument; in fact, it is more akin to the optimal tariff argument against monopolistic pricing.

I have illustrated one important supply-oriented barrier. There are, of course, others. Firms in developing countries may not have access to raw materials or other inputs bought from firms outside their boundaries, or where they do, they may have to pay more than the competitive price for them; this could put them at a disadvantage *vis-à-vis* their larger foreign competitors. Once again, we have an example of monopolistic pricing in the first case and the economies of size and integration in the second. This latter might be construed as an advantage which, in practice, only occurs in an imperfectly competitive situation (where such economies are only profitable within an oligopolistic market structure); the difficulty is that part of the production process might best be undertaken by a developing country, but it cannot afford to do this because of high setting-up costs. Nor may it be convenient for the integrated firms to subcontract or license local producers. But, in so far as size of established producers impedes the development of potentially more efficient competitors, then, again, some kind of protection against foreign competition might be needed, particularly where barriers to entry are high.

Developing countries might also be faced with demand-oriented barriers, and once more the principle of comparative advantage assumes the absence of such barriers. Nevertheless, they apply within industries within countries and, for obvious reasons, are greater across national boundaries. Again, an independent firm seeking outlets in an industry controlled by integrated competitors might find these difficult to acquire. Obvious cases in the UK include new outlets in the petroleum and brewing industries.

This is another variant of imperfect competition and is a genuine impediment, as also where there are high costs of market entry.

Summarising, countries, like firms, may have to face barriers to entry into new lines of economic activity. Where these reflect the result of competitive forces, then on *economic grounds* there may be little justification for a protectionist policy. Where they do not, the argument for an optimum tariff (or its equivalent) may be valid. All these arise either because of the monopolistic behaviour on the part of individual firms or groups of firms, or even countries, or because of the size of established producers and/or the indivisibility of production processes. Examples of the obstacles include the difficulties in obtaining enterprise-specific knowledge, or other inputs, or markets held by firms to which access can be denied. The latter type of barrier arises from the size and integration of existing producers; the argument is not against size as such, but that in some of the processes undertaken by large firms in industrialised countries, which cannot be separated from the rest of their operations, it is possible that developing countries might have the advantage. But they cannot exercise this because firms are not willing to release their control over these processes or relocate them in developing countries. Integration or internalisation is an enterprise-specific advantage.

III

Part of the difficulty of developing countries wishing to establish new activities or patterns of trade lies in the fact that the established producers of the goods in the developed countries, operating largely within a private enterprise framework, have a certain control over the availability and/or conditions of sale of inputs and markets, which is accepted (and in some cases fostered) by the system in which they operate. The reason why it is accepted is due largely to the protection which consumers in countries have from the competition between large firms. This is not the case with potential competitors in developing countries. It follows that if there was some way of embracing developing countries into the operational network of the established producers of developed countries, at least some of these barriers might be overcome. It has been suggested that this is precisely where the MNE comes into the picture.

How far can the MNE break down barriers facing developing countries and help them achieve their goal of maximising comparative dynamic advantage? And what are the costs of it so doing?

We have seen that the MNE is a product of market imperfection and/or failure and that, within any prospective profit or growth situation, it operates most vigorously in those areas where the obstacles to exploiting the market by other means, or by competitors, are greatest. The obstacles are of two kinds. The first is that imposed by countries which are host to foreign investment or imported goods, which may cause firms in exporting countries to exploit the market by undertaking local production units in them rather than exporting to them; much of defensive foreign direct investment originates in this way. The second takes the form of ownership specific advantages which firms in investing countries possess over firms in host countries, which enable them to produce in these latter countries under the equivalent of a tariff barrier. Of these, we have suggested that access to technology markets and to the economies of internalisation are among the most important.[4] With this protection – which is sometimes temporary – firms might aggressively exploit foreign markets, and earn profits sufficient to overcome the disadvantages of producing in foreign markets.

An examination of the industrial structure of the leading MNEs confirms that they tend to be concentrated in industries in which the barriers of entry to new producers are among the highest, and the share of the local output in the industries of host countries reflects their advantages of overcoming these barriers *vis-à-vis* indigenous firms (UN, 1978). Moreover, even within the countries in which they operate, MNEs may choose to be selective in the products they produce or processes in which they engage; in this respect, a foreign affiliate is like any other branch plant of an enterprise whose main activities are located elsewhere. To compete effectively, competitors may have to set up a completely new organisation; in other words, the barriers to entry are measured not by the activities of the branch plant but those of the entire organisation of which it is part.

This, indeed, is a most substantial advantage which an established knowledge-intensive firm has over its potential competitors in new markets. The setting up of a new range of manufacturing facilities by such a firm may require little new investment in information, technology or organisation; the marginal costs of these items will be considerably lower than their average total cost to newly established firms. (This *inter alia* explains why the administrative costs to sales ratio of foreign subsidiaries in countries often tends to be lower than their indigenous competitors.) In other words, wherever capital costs external to any particular operation of a firm but internal to the firm are high, the barriers to entry to new producers are that much greater, and hence also the profitability of international production. This is a further reason why international investment tends to be concentrated in research intensive industries. Put another way, where the advantages of size of firms are most marked, then the more MNEs will stand to gain, partly because they are large, but also because of their advantages over domestic firms mentioned earlier (Kojima, 1978).

Technological and market forces in advanced countries are causing output to be more concentrated and making it more difficult for completely new firms to enter the market. This might not matter too much in countries where there are several large existing firms already competing with each other. But in countries seeking to develop a new industry from scratch, it may impose insuperable barriers for indigenous entrants and thus freeze the comparative advantage of existing producers built on these barriers. In this situation, it is the very firms responsible for the barriers which, in part, help to overcome them by establishing local manufacturing facilities. In doing so, however, they enhance their own economic strength as, once they are producing in developing countries, they make entry of local competitors more difficult.

Having suggested the origin of direct manufacturing investment in developing countries one now has to look at its possible consequences for resource allocation. For our purposes, we are interested in identifying characteristics of MNEs or their affiliates which make their impact on trade flows different from that which might be expected from indigenous firms. It is generally agreed that the main benefit inward direct investment can bring to a host country is the surmounting of barriers to access to its foreign resources and the provision of these resources more cheaply than would otherwise be the case. At one and the same time, it can offer a package deal of a superior production technology, managerial skills and marketing methods, of access to markets in inputs and outputs which it has accumulated over the years, and of being part of an organisation which may be benefiting from economies of scale and integration. Some of these benefits will remain specific only to the affiliates; others, through linkages with local firms, may permeate the economy, that is, there will be external economies. The character of these has been fully investigated in the literature.

The unique problems of inward direct investment cannot easily be separated from its advantages. Partly these arise because the goals of MNEs are different from those of developing countries, and, because of this, their contribution to development is, at best, likely to be partial and uneven; and partly because the control exerted over the behaviour of an affiliate by the enterprise which owns it, and over the sharing of the benefits which arise from it, may not be in the best interests of the host countries. Not always will particular decisions taken by Detroit or London or Amsterdam be of benefit to individual developing countries, or as much benefit as they would like; it would be surprising if they were. For, just as a MNE can open markets to developing countries, it can also shut them off or inhibit their growth. It can control (or attempt to control): the sourcing of its inputs in a way that the host country might not approve; the type of output and the terms on which goods and services are exchanged between members of the group; dividend policies and the pattern and rate of growth of new investment; the employment and/or training of indigenous labour; the transfer of technology or technological capacity; the extent to which it moves funds across national boundaries, and so on. All of these may affect resource allocation and trade flows. Again, all have been extensively examined in the literature.[5]

The extent to which these characteristics of inward direct investment are demonstrated is dependent on a host of factors, not least the economic environment of the host country. But the net outcome of the activities of foreign affiliates will be a sharing of costs and benefits between the host country and the rest of the enterprise, depending *inter alia* on the bargaining strength of the two parties. This, in itself, raises a whole set of interesting issues which are not new in principle, but which pose new problems. Compare, for example, the operations of a MNE with those of a multiregional national enterprise. The behaviour of the latter will have distributive effects throughout the regions in which it produces, such that some regions may gain and others may lose. But in the last resort, it is the national government which has responsibility for the welfare of the regions under its authority and it can take the appropriate action to protect the well-being of any region adversely affected by the decision of companies headquartered in other regions. In other words, it is a supraregional authority, responsible for ensuring that private economic agents do not cause an inequitable sharing of costs and benefits among regions. A moment's reflection shows that there is no corresponding international mechanism to ensure that the actions of MNEs do not result in an inequitable sharing of costs and benefits. And the weaker the nations participating the less likely they are to get a fair share. In the absence of any supranational authority, individual nation states take unilateral action.

It will be observed that in so far as the decisions of MNEs conform to principles of dynamic comparative advantage, all countries stand to gain – including developing countries. The question is entirely one of the distribution of the gains. But the trouble is that the development process generated by MNEs is not only motivated differently from the goals of developing countries in which they operate but it is very often in response to an imperfectly competitive environment. Obvious examples of imperfections are differences in tax rates and fixed exchange rates; both, while not affecting the behaviour of indigenous firms, may greatly affect the conduct of MNEs, and not always in the ways in which host countries might like. Moreover, in some ways an MNE may act like a country. It has fixed assets in different parts of the world and wishes to protect the interests of these assets. The extent to which a Brazilian subsidiary is permitted to export to other parts of Latin America may depend upon the proportion of capacity utilised in the Mexico plant. A purely domestic firm would not be faced with this kind of 'protectionism'.

IV

In recent years, especial attention has been paid to the impact of MNEs (or their affiliates) on the economic structure of home and host countries, and the trading relationship between them. It has been argued by some economists that the cross-country specialisation and division of labour implemented by MNEs not only reflects the international economic order fashioned at Bretton Woods and Havana after the Second World War, but itself contributes towards the maintenance of such an order by impeding a restructuring of the comparative advantage of countries. Thus by concentrating R & D activities in the home countries, but by using their technological and/or internalising advantages to outcompete competitors in host developing countries, it is alleged that MNEs impede developing countries in their efforts to build their own scientific and technological capacity. This not only creates 'dependencia' between the satellite production units and the parent company; it affects the long-term disposition of resources and markets between countries. It also impinges upon trade both in intermediary technology and finished products; with MNEs controlling the type of technology transferred, the origin of inputs and the destination of output, not primarily from the interests of individual countries in which they are located, but from that of their global strategy. Moreover, it is in this kind of integrated operation that intra-group trade is likely to dominate, the terms of which are dictated not by market forces but by the impact on the MNEs' total profitability.

In Chapter 2 reference was made to Professor Kojima's distinction between 'trade oriented' and 'anti-trade' oriented foreign direct investments.[6] Basically, Kojima defends MNEs when they distribute their activities across national boundaries in accordance with the principles of comparative advantage, but attacks them when, in engaging in defensive oligopolistic tactics, they cause a resource reallocation against this principle. While he thus approves of Japanese textile companies investing in South Korea, on the basis that because of rising labour costs Japan's comparative advantage is shifting away from labour intensive activities, he is more critical of US electronic companies transferring technological capacity to developing countries, on the basis that it is still to the USA's long-term comparative advantage to retain such capacity at home.

As far as the developing countries are concerned, while accepting the Kojima philosophy as a stage in the development process, most (and particularly the resource rich and rapidly industrialising developing countries) are fearful lest they might become *permanent* 'hewers of wood and drawers of water' to the industrialised nations. Even those desiring full economic interdependence with the rest of the world are seeking to identify their long-term comparative advantage and then to ensure that this is promoted as speedily as possible. The fact that this goal − or the timing of the progress towards that goal − may not be consistent with the strategies of the MNEs is the crux of the dilemma. This, along with the fact that MNEs do not operate within a competitive environment, but, by their very presence may frustrate any effective alternative to them, has caused some governments to be extremely sceptical of their long-term benefits.

Another area where MNEs may affect trade flows is through their purchasing and marketing policies. It is often alleged that affiliates of MNEs in both primary and secondary sectors import a higher proportion of their capital equipment than do their indigenous competitors, while those in assembly manufacturing import a larger proportion of their current inputs, for example, materials, parts and semi-finished products. Similarly it is suggested that such affiliates in the primary product sectors export a higher proportion of their output of minerals, raw materials and agricultural products than do domestic companies, who either process these goods themselves or sell them to local producers to process. A rather different assertion is that MNE manufacturing affiliates (particularly in the finished goods sectors) either export less than their indigenous competitors or less than they would do if they were not part of an integrated network of activities.

The evidence on all these issues is very mixed and few generalisations seem possible. What does seem highly probable though is that differences in the evaluating of costs and benefits between MNEs and host nations do affect the 'timing' of the initiation and/or cessation of particular activities by MNEs; while according to the extent of market imperfections, on the one hand, and government intervention (for good or bad), on the other, there may be a lasting difference between the actual contribution of MNEs and that perceived as 'first best' by governments.

It would also seem that differences between the behaviour of MNE affiliates and indigenous firms which are specifically the result of the former being part of a multinational network are frequently exaggerated. A recent study published by the UNCTC (1981) of backward linkages via subcontracting in the automobile industry in India revealed that the main determinant of linkage creation was host government policy; and that there was little difference in the local content of the foreign domestic auto firms in the late 1960s. A comparison of the proportion of items subcontracted in India, Morocco and Peru, however, revealed substantial differences which were largely put down to country-specific factors and/or the stage of development of the automobile industry. Another UN study on the international hotel industry (UNCTC, 1981) came to a similar conclusion about the local content of purchases by hotels. Given the size and grade of hotel, there were few differences between the procurement policies of hotels associated with MNEs and those which were not.

Location- rather than ownership-specific factors also explain a lot of the differences in the propensity of primary producers to engage in local secondary processing, prior to exporting (at a considerably higher local value added) the finished product. However, here, it does seem that the strategy of MNEs may differ from that of indigenous firms in several ways, particularly if it already has processing plants in other parts of the world. A study prepared by the UN Centre on Transnational Corporations for UNIDO in 1978 (UNIDO, 1978), while acknowledging the role of governments in developing countries in increasing local mineral processing over the past two decades, and the economic attractions of developing countries for downstream operations,[7] emphasised there are still powerful inducements for

MNEs to concentrate such processing in the developed countries. These include economies of scale, a well-developed infrastructure, discriminatory import tariffs which favour imports of non-processed goods, and the tendency of many MNEs to be risk averse and to preseve a maximum flexibility in their sourcing policies. In this respect MNEs, because of differences in perception and structure, do behave differently than locally owned firms and have a different impact on trade flows.

Research findings on the impact of MNEs on trade in manufactured goods are somewhat mixed. Studies by Hughes and You (1969) and Cohen (1975) are fairly typical of those concerned with foreign investment in South East Asia. Primarily motivated to take advantage of plentiful supplies of cheap and well-motivated unskilled and semi-skilled labour, such offshore affiliates of MNEs usually record above average exports and imports that do their local competitors. The same is true in most Latin American countries, although here, as in India, most foreign direct investment has been directed to import substitution (Nayyar, 1978). Exceptions include offshore assembling operations in Mexico to benefit from the usage of the US Tariff Schedules (Items 807.00 and 806.30) and those affiliates, for example, in the motor vehicles and electrical equipment industries, involved in complementation agreements within the Latin American Free Trade Area.

In a major study for UNCTAD, which covered foreign direct investment in six developing countries, Lall and Streeten (1978) found that country- and industry-specific factors were far more important than the nationality of firms in influencing trade flows, but again most of the investment they considered was import substituting and most affiliates were not part of a global strategy. The studies like those of Hufbauer and Adler (1968) and Reddaway *et al.* (1968) also stressed the importance of the alternative situation assumed in the absence of foreign investment in analysing the total balance of payments effects of foreign direct investment.[8] Taking a rather different approach, Reuber (1974) suggested that the percentage of purchases made from indigenous firms is significantly and negatively correlated to the percentage of foreign ownership but that, apart from exports to the home country of investor, there was no evidence of any positive relationship between export propensity and degree of foreign ownership. Blam and Hawkins (1975), on the other hand, in an analysis of capital and trade performance of thirty developing countries have argued that, compared with other forms of capital inflows, including aid and locally financed capital, foreign direct investment is associated with the highest export and import propensities, and is likely to have the most positive effect on the export/import balance.

What does seem to be strongly suggested by all the studies is that the 'internalisation' component of the ownership characteristics associated with foreign direct investment is likely to be a key variable affecting the impact of such investment on trade flows. It is not surprising, then, that scholars such as Helleiner (1973, 1979), Helleiner and Lavergne (1980) and Vaitsos (1979) have paid especial attention to the infra-firm trade of MNEs and their affiliates. Such trade has been of increasing importance both in the context of MNE related activities and from the viewpoint of countries in which the activities are located. In 1977, related party imports accounted for 48.4 per cent of all imports in the USA (Helleiner, 1979) whereas in 1970, 66 per cent of the manufactured exports of majority owned affiliates of US firms went to their parent companies or other affiliates. In the early 1970s around 30 per cent of UK, Swedish and Belgian exports and three-fifths of Canadian exports were on an intra-firm basis (UN, 1978; UNCTAD, 1978). A German study (Holtus *et al.*, 1974) showed that in 1971 43 per cent of the exports of twenty-seven West German MNEs that accounted for 35 per cent of that country's manufacturing exports went to their foreign affiliates.

In earlier chapters,[9] intra-firm trade was used as a proxy for the internalising advantages of MNEs. Both Lall (1978) and Helleiner (1979) have attempted to explain intra-firm trade in terms of particular ownership advantages possessed by MNEs. Lall found that US intra-firm trade was highest in those sectors characterised by scale economies, high R & D expenditure as a proportion of sales, and a dummy variable for the US value-added tariff provisions. Helleiner, examining the determinants of US related imports, found that size of firm, wages and R & D expenditures were the best predictors. Firm size, R & D intensity and country-specific factors were also shown to be significant explanatory variables of intra-firm exports of a sample of 156 of the world's largest industrial companies in 1972 (Buckley and Pearce, 1979).

In Chapter 5, it was argued that the propensity of firms to internalise their foreign operations and the extent to which internalising itself contributed towards an MNE's strength in world markets were related to stages of a country's economic development, the reasons for MNE involvement, and the geographical and product diversity of an MNE's operation. The implication of this suggestion is that intra-firm trade — and hence the distinctive impact of MNEs on trade flows — is likely to be the most pronounced where they are large, where they practice horizontal or vertical specialisation, where they operate in a large number of countries and where market failure makes it worthwhile (*via* transfer pricing and other similar devices) for them to eschew arm's length trading transactions. It is not difficult to identify the kind of developing countries which might generate this kind of trade, and hence where the impact of the MNE *qua* MNE (as opposed to other modalities of international technology and information flows) is likely to be the most marked. Empirical research, however, has some way to go before it fully captures these variables in any explanatory models. Certainly, none of the studies mentioned above has been successful in avoiding the problem of multicollinearity not only between the independent variables, but between these and the dependent variables when each is used as explanatory variables in other regression equations.

V

Any discussion of intra-firm trade inevitably leads one on to the question of intra-firm pricing and how this may be different from arm's length pricing. To the extent that these differences reflect market failure or disequilibrium, MNEs may affect the value of trade flows without affecting the volume and/or composition of such flows.[10] In an effort to protect or improve their balance of payments, many developing countries are acutely aware of the incentives which MNEs may have to underprice their exports and overprice their imports, and hence to reduce their contribution to this particular policy goal. However fragmentary and specific the evidence may be,[11] it is difficult to dispute that where they perceive it to be in their best interests and where they are allowed so to do MNEs will engage in other than arm's length pricing in their intra-group transactions. Using 1969 data, Muller and Morgenstern (1974) have argued that, although large US affiliates in Latin America export more than their indigenous counterparts, their exports would have been even higher (by something like $427 million to the other Latin American countries) if they had been conducted at arm's length prices. Another study by Roumeliotis (1977) found that in Greece overpricing of imports and underpricing exports was fairly common among the foreign affiliates studied.[12] On the other hand, research by the present author (Dunning, 1977) suggests that most of the intra-group exports of UK affiliates in developing countries were of commodities which were commonly traded between independent firms and an arm's length price could be easily established. It was also clear that the MNEs themselves believed that they were exporting the same or a higher amount of exports than an indigenous firm of the same size or product structure might do, but that country and industry factors were the main determinants of the trade flows of their affiliates.

One final aspect of the specific impact of MNEs, particularly integrated MNEs, on trade flows concerns the control exerted over the sourcing of inputs and amount and destination of exports. We touched upon these matters in Chapter 7 in so far as they may be considered (at least by the countries most affected) a restrictive practice. The evidence that such control, however much it may be legitimate on commercial grounds, may work against the trading interests of host countries in particular sectors is very persuasive.[13] However, there is a danger that the framework of analysis is too narrow and that attention would be better directed to the longer-term impact of MNEs on economic structure and to the trade generated by such a structure. Thus, it may be that exports are less than they might otherwise be in one sector, but more than they might otherwise be in another. The real question – which brings us back to the starting point of this chapter – is whether the international allocation of resources prompted by MNEs is, or is not, in the best interests of individual host countries. Unfortunately, this is not a question which can be settled on economic grounds alone, as world efficiency is not the sole, or even the main, criterion by which nation states judge the success of their economic policies. But a clearer identification of goals of governments and a willingness to approach the role of MNEs from a longer-term resource allocative viewpoint rather than from that of individual sectors or specific problem areas is to be encouraged if policy prescriptions are not to be counterproductive to what they are intended to achieve.[14]

Notes: Chapter 11

1   See Section III.
2   For references see Chapter 2.
3   On the other hand, developing countries may be treated more favourably than industrialised countries, for example, by some Arab oil countries in the pricing of loan capital.
4   For an analysis of the relationship between these advantages and foreign investment in developing countries see Chapter 5.
5   See particularly Lall and Streeten (1978) and UN (1978).
6   See particularly page 38.
7   Notably reduced transport and energy costs and an abundant supply of cheap labour.
8   See especially Chapters 8 and 9 of Lall and Streeten (1978).
9   See particularly Chapters 5 and 10.
10 Though in many instances, both will be.
11 As reviewed, for example, in Plasschaert (1979) and UNCTAD (1977).
12 In about one-half of eighty-four import cases studied in the metallurgical, chemical and pharmaceutical sectors 'substantial' overpricing was detected. In the export sector underinvoicing of a sample of major minerals traded by MNEs ranged from 8.3 per cent to 16.9 per cent.
13 See, for example, a range of UNCTAD studies and in particular UNCTAD (1972, 1975).
14 This point is further taken up in Chapter 13. For a more general analysis of the role of MNEs in the economic integration of developing countries see Vaitsos (1979).

References

Blam, Y., and Hawkins, R. G. (1975), *Forms of Foreign Investment and the External Trade of Developing Countries*, University of Reading Discussion Papers in International Investment and Business Studies (January).

Buckley, P. J., and Pearce, R. D. (1979), 'Overseas production and exporting by the world's largest enterprises', *Journal of International Business Studies*, vol. 10, no. 1 (Spring/Summer).

Cohen, B. I. (1975), *Multinational Firms and Asian Exports* (New Haven, Conn., and London: Yale University Press).

Dunning, J. H. (1977), *United Kingdom Transnational Enterprises in Manufacturing and Resource Based Industries and Trade Flows of Developing Countries*, Geneva, UNCTAD/ST/MD 8.

Helleiner, G. K. (1973), 'Manufactured exports from less developed countries and multinational firms', *Economic Journal*, vol. 83, no. 329 (March).

Helleiner, G. K. (1979), 'Transnational corporations and trade structure: the role of intra-firm trade', in H. Giersch (ed.), *On the Economics of Intra-Industry Trade* (Tubingen: Mohr).

Helleiner, G. K., and Lavergne, R. (1980), 'Intra-firm trade and industrial exports to the United States', *Oxford Bulletin of Economics and Statistics*, vol. 41, no. 4 (November).

Holtus, M. *et al.* (1974), *Die Auslandstaetigket der Deutscher Multinationalen Unternehmen*, Hamburg HWAA-Institut Report No. 31.

Hufbauer, G. C., and Adler, F. M. (1968), *Overseas Manufacturing Investment and the Balance of Payments* (Washington, DC: US Treasury Department).

Hughes, H., and You, Poh Seng (eds) (1969), *Foreign Investment and Industrialisation in Singapore* (Canberra: Australian National University Press).

Johnson, H. (1969), *Comparative Cost and Commercial Policy Theory for a Developing World Economy* (Stockholm: Almquist & Wiksell).

Kojima, K. (1978), *Direct Foreign Investment* (London: Croom Helm).

Lall, S. (1978), 'The pattern of intra-firm exports by US multinationals', *Oxford Bulletin of Economics and Statistics*, vol. 40, no. 3 (August).

Lall, S., and Streeten, P. P. (1978), *Foreign Investment, Transnationals and Developing Countries* (London: Macmillan).

Muller, R., and Morgenstern, R. D. (1974), 'Multinational corporations and balance of payments imports in LDCs. An econometric analysis of export pricing behaviour', *Kyklos*, vol. XXVII, no. 2.

Nayyar, D. (1978), 'Transnational corporations and manufactured exports from poor countries', *Economic Journal*, vol. 88, no. 349 (March).

Plasschaert, R. F. (1979), *Transfer Pricing and Multinational Corporations* (Farnborough: Saxon House).

Reddaway, W. B. *et al.* (1968), *Effects of UK Direct Investment Overseas* (Cambridge: Cambridge University Press).

Reuber, G. L. (1974), *Private Foreign Investment in Development* (Oxford: Clarendon Press).

Roumeliotis, P. (1977), 'La politique des prix d'importation et d'exportation des entreprises multinationales en Grece', *Revue Tiers Monde* (April–June).

UN (1978), *Transnational Corporations and World Development: A Re-Examination* (New York: United Nations Economic and Social Council), Sales No. E.78 II A5.

UNCTAD (1972), *Restrictive Business Practices: The Operations of Multinational Enterprises in Developing Countries* (Geneva and New York: UN).

UNCTAD (1975), *Major Issues Arising from the Transfer of Technology to Developing Countries* (Geneva and New York: UN), Sales No. E.75 II D2.

UNCTAD (1977), *Dominant Positions of Market Power of Transnational Corporations. Use of Transfer Pricing Mechanism* (Geneva: UN), ST/MO/6/Rev.1.

UNCTAD (1978), *Transnational Corporations and Expansion of Trade in Manufactures and Semi-Manufactures*, Report by Secretariat for Trade and Development Board. Committee on Manufactures (Geneva: UN), TD/B/C 2/197 (16 March).

UNCTC (1980), *Transnational Corporations: Linkages in Developing Countries* (New York: UN) (to be published).

UNCTC (1981), *Transnational Corporations in the International Tourist Industy* (New York: UN) (to be published).

UNIDO (1978), 'Transnational corporations and the processing of raw materials. Impact on developing countries', report prepared by UNCTC for 12th Session of Industrial Conference Board ID/B/209 (April).

Vaitsos, C. V. (1979), *Regional Integration Cum/Versus Corporate Integration* (mimeo).

12

The Consequences of International Transfer of Technology by MNEs: Some Home Country Implications

I

In the past two decades, a good deal of attention has been focused on the consequences of the international transfer of technology (and other resources) on recipient or host countries.[1] But it has only been since the mid-1970s that some of the implications of this transfer for the sending or home countries have been seriously discussed. This has been prompted primarily by a growing sense of concern, articulated by politicians, businessmen and academics alike, that the industrialised developed world − as represented mainly by the OECD countries − is either benefiting insufficiently from the export of technology or technological capacity,[2] or being adversely affected by it. That these concerns are being expressed at a time when host countries, particularly developing countries, are taking action to control the amount and form of technological imports and to tilt the terms of trade in their favour has led some observers to be pessimistic about the prospects for the international transfer of technology, at least as between North and South. From a time in the mid-1950s, when the exchange of technology was generally thought to be a positive sum game, with both exporting and importing nations benefiting, the mid-1970s, by contrast, were producing situations in which both parties perceived themselves to be worse off as a result of the transfer. Though *prima facie* implausible, such a result is theoretically feasible, particularly where the parties to the exchange aim to maximise relative rather than absolute economic gains, and/or have different political or cultural perceptions.

Apart from inter-government grants and loans, the main institution for the transmission of resources in the postwar period has been the multinational enterprise operating through a network of wholly majority owned foreign affiliates.[3] In such cases the transfer of technology is internalised

This is a revised version of a chapter by the author first published in T. Sagafi-Nejad, R. W. Moxon and H. V. Perlmutter (eds), *Technology Transfer Control Systems: Issues, Perspectives and Implications* (Elmsford, NY: Pergamon Press, 1981).

in the sense that there is no change in its *ownership*, and the transferor continues to exercise a *de jure* direction over the use made of the resources. It is the nature and effects of this control, and the fact that technology is transmitted as part of a package of resources, that distinguishes this vehicle of transference from that of arm's length exchange between independent sellers and buyers. It is the identification and evaluation of the consequences which arise from the transfer and dissemination of technology by MNEs that is the subject of this chapter. The presentation proceeds as follows. First, the main causes of concern, expressed by home countries, about technology exports to host countries will be described. Second, the extent and pattern of these exports over the last two decades and the role of MNEs in promoting them are summarised. Third, the effects these have had on the economic goals of home countries are considered. Fourth, there will be a discussion of some of the policies pursued by home governments and those which might be pursued to further technology transfer by their own MNEs.

II

The immediate interest of most policy makers in industrialised countries (EICs)[4] in the effects of technology exports by their own MNEs stems from a slowing down of international economic growth, a downswing in technological innovation, rising domestic unemployment, stagnant industrial productivity and widespread inflation; all of which are viewed as symptoms of a decline in international competitiveness. Such concern has been most often voiced in Sweden, the USA and the UK, the three EICs which have experienced the most dramatic fall in their share of world trade in manufactured goods and *relative* industrial status *vis-à-vis* both other industrialised countries and the rest of the world.[5]

Coincidental, and partly related to these trends, has been the increasing effort of developing countries to shift the balance of economic and industrial power from the North to the South. Illustrated by the philosophy and intent of the New International Economic Order, and the Lima Declaration of UNIDO in 1975 which *inter alia* aims to increase the share of world industrial production by developing countries to 25 per cent by the year 2000, attempts by such countries to pursue a policy of rapid industrialisation are taken as signals by the EICs that the order of economic interdependence, fashioned at Bretton Woods and Havana, is no longer acceptable, and that some developing countries — particularly the so-called newly industrialised countries (NICs) — are a force to be reckoned with. Taken together with the expansion of alternative sources of technology, for example, from Eastern Europe, the established industrial powers fear not only an erosion of their industrial hegemony but an undermining of their economic structures.

This might not matter so much within a framework of nations at similar stages of economic development and a common political ideology, such as broadly exists within the OECD. But outside it, for the most part, that is not the case. The political perceptions and economic philosophy of many developing countries anxious to acquire technology, are sufficiently divergent from those of most technology exporting countries as to make the latter worried lest the added economic leverage which the technology brings might be used to the detriment of their strategic and other aspirations. Here, as has been pointed out by Hawkins and Gladwin (1981), a conflict may arise between humanitarian, economic and political goals of the home countries. The matter is further complicated by the effects which some kinds of non-commercial technology transfers or sharing may have on the home country's commercial technological capacity. The export of weapons by the USA may help support innovation in the military aircraft and missile industries, with consequential spill-over effects on the domestic aerospace and electronics industries. Just as the cut-back in the US space research programme has reduced the flow of commercially useful technology, so any retrenchment of defence spending, including arms exports to friendly nations, could have similar effects.

While no commentator would go as far as ascribing all of the current economic difficulties of the EICs to the growing competitive strength of some developing countries, and still less to the transfer of technology by MNEs to these countries, some, most noticeably Baranson (1979), Gilpin (1975) and some of the labour unions, assign it a major role, at least from a US perspective. There are two main thrusts to this allegation. The first is that MNEs, by engaging in foreign direct investment, have diverted their energies away from technology innovating activities in their home countries. It is pointed out that between 1968 and 1976 the percentage of money spent on R & D in the USA slipped from 2.8 per cent of GNP to 2.25 per cent and that, whereas in the early 1960s the USA accounted for 75 per cent of the world's industrial R & D, by the late 1970s this proportion had fallen to about one-half.

The second (and main) charge against technological exports is that they improve the international competitiveness of firms in the recipient country at the expense of firms in the sending country. Thus, while over the last twenty years the USA has led the world in the export of technology in semi-conductor electronics, between 1965 and 1978 the US trade balance of electronics and communications equipment (excluding computers) continually deteriorated (Meyer, 1978). This, in turn (so the argument goes), erodes the market base of the technology exporting firms and makes the costs of R & D more difficult to recoup. In the case of labour intensive industries, the effect is more dramatically and immediately felt on domestic employment. In the context of North/South technology transfers, the debate has been less to do with falling export shares in the EICs and more with increasing import competition faced by them; none the less, it is a variant of the 'we want to sell more milk and fewer cows' type of argument.[6]

These, then, are some of the main concerns currently felt to a greater or lesser degree by all developed countries. How far are they justified? How far can they be attributed to the activities of MNEs? What, if anything, can be done about them?

III

We take, as a starting point, the proposition that firms will only transfer proprietary technology if they believe it to their overall benefit. Where a firm sells or leases technology to other firms, it is presumed that the terms and conditions of the exchange will fully compensate it for the opportunity costs of supplying that technology (Graham, 1978; Root, 1981). In some cases a transfer will only take place subject to the fulfilment of restrictive constraints on the part of the transferee. Thus, a licence to exploit a patent may only be granted on the understanding that the licensee will only market the good embodying the technology in his own country; or if certain production methods and material specifications are adhered to; or if a satisfactory standard of maintenance and after-sales servicing is guaranteed; or if specific tie-in arrangements are accepted. Where a firm is transferring the technology to one of its own affiliates, then, subject to the regulations and policies of the host governments, it has full and continuing control over its use. *A priori*, one may presume that, from the transferring firm's viewpoint, in the short and medium run, at least, the transfer is expected to be beneficial. In the long run the matter is less certain, as it is possible that, as a result of the competitive stimulus from foreign direct investment, indigenous firms may become technologically more progressive and out-compete the foreign affiliate.[7]

Depending on whether its sale is internalised or externalised, there are various gains to the transferor from the transfer. To the firm selling under contract, these primarily comprise the revenue it receives from the sale of technology. As long as the marginal revenue exceeds the marginal opportunity costs[8] (including externalities) of supplying the technology, the firm will find the transfer worthwhile. In practice, for many firms selling technology that would have been produced in any case for use by the firm at home, the costs reduce to the marginal negotiating and transaction costs; in other instances and for technology supplying specialists in particular, for example, construction contractors, project engineers, systems analysts, petrochemical consultants, etc., the resource costs of producing the technology are relevant (Graham, 1978; Teece, 1977). To the MNE, transferring (or sharing) technology by the direct investment route is frequently the preferred means of capturing the full economic rent of the technology and unique ownership advantages transferred with it.[9] The gains from the transfer are those which accrue to the enterprise as a whole; they include not only the profits earned on the capital invested, but all the other benefits which arise from foreign production, including the securing of new markets which help spread the R & D and other overhead costs of the parent company, thus helping the MNE to maintain and extend its competitive strength.

But MNEs may also transfer technological capacity and, by so doing, advance the ability of the recipient country to produce technology for itself. This may be done either because it is cheaper to set up new R & D facilities abroad, rather than expand facilities in the home country; or because there are some kinds of R & D best done in the host country; or because differences in factor endowments and/or markets enable it to specialise in particular kinds of R & D in different countries. Examples include R & D into tropical diseases by pharmaceutical companies in tropical locations; new methods of cultivating or blending tea and tobacco in tea and tobacco producing regions; and research into labour intensive production technologies, for example, for the production of motor vehicles, machine tools and processed foods in low labour cost countries. Again, quite apart from the efforts of host governments to attract such technological capacity, TNCs will tend to locate their R & D activities in countries which they think will best advance their own interests.

Excepting, then, cases of business misjudgement, to suggest that a home country may not benefit from an export of technology by its firms is to suggest the social opportunity costs of such exports transfer exceed the private opportunity costs. That this may be so, one only has to look at the different goals between MNEs and home countries. MNEs are primarily interested in making profits independently of where these profits are earned. They will consequently engage in foreign production and transfer the necessary technology with this objective in mind. Investing countries, on the other hand, are interested in the activities of MNE affiliates from a wider perspective; their goals include the growth of GNP, maintaining full employment, controlling inflation, building up indigenous technological capacity, promoting the most efficient structure of resource allocation, and so on. There is no presumption that, in achieving their own objectives, firms will necessarily be advancing those of their home countries.

At the same time, it would be wrong to judge the macroeconomic consequences of a transfer of technology by a MNE by its microeconomic opportunity costs, *or* to attribute such costs to the MNE. Let me give a simple example. Suppose that, as a result of the transfer of technology by their parent companies, US affiliates in South Korea are able to outcompete domestic producers in the supply of black and white television to the US market, and that jobs are displaced in the US television set industry. Suppose also that those made unemployed do not find other work. Then the immediate gains to the USA of the transfer of technology will be the profits, net of foreign tax, earned by the foreign affiliates and any reduction in the price of television sets passed on to the US consumers, while the opportunity cost will be any loss in the gross domestic product caused by the unemployment. To the MNE, on the other hand, the effect of the transfer may be higher sales and profits than otherwise would have been possible.

It is obvious that this conclusion *may* be entirely false. It may be quite wrong to attribute any fall in domestic employment to a foreign capital outflow simply because, in its absence, the investment might have been undertaken by other firms, which would not only have resulted in the same fall in domestic jobs and output but the US economy would have lost the profits which otherwise would have been earned by its own TNC. Moreover, the resulting unemployment may only be temporary and, over time, the labour displaced may be employed in more productive activities, either in the same firm, or elsewhere in the economy, so raising rather than lowering the gross domestic product.

The word 'may' has been used throughout the previous paragraph because, whatever the theoretical validity of the argument, the actual effects may be very different. For a host of reasons, labour displaced by a transfer of technology may not be easily re-employed and the costs of adjustment assistance may more than outweigh the benefits; while the argument that the recipient economy will obtain the technology it needs in any event and out-compete US producers cuts little ice with those who argue that this can be counteracted by import controls.

All this, of course, approaches the question from a microeconomic standpoint. But, depending on their consequences on the host countries, it is not only the costs and benefits of the investing firm which have to be taken into account. Studies carried out in the UK and USA[10] suggest that the main beneficiaries of outward direct investment are often the suppliers of capital equipment and intermediary products to the foreign affiliates.[11] All, or part, of these exports would have been lost without the foreign investment, as investment by firms of other nationalities would have led to these goods being bought from their home countries. On the other hand, the extra output abroad may not only replace domestic output by the investing MNE but that of its domestic competitors as well.[12] Again, the effects depend critically on the assumptions made about what would have happened, in both the home and host countries, in the absence of such a transfer of technology and as a consequence of it.

It is worth observing that in the neoclassical literature, and assuming full employment is maintained in both home and host countries and there are no market distortions, a transfer or dissemination of technology between countries will increase world real output as, by raising both allocative and technical efficiency, it pushes out the world's production frontier. Moreover, the model suggests that both technology exporting and importing countries will benefit, although some redeployment of resources may be necessary. The difficulty of using this model in the current context is that the assumptions underlying it do not necessarily hold good. MNEs do not normally transfer technology in a competitive market situation; neither are governments able to ensure that, come what may, full employment is always achieved. Moreover, the welfare functions of countries embrace goals, other than the maximisation of output, which could be adversely affected by the transfer of technology. However, even if policy makers are forced to deal with second or third best solutions, the principle of the neoclassical model may still be relevant. It may be that the transfer of technology is not as beneficial to the home country as it could be precisely because of market distortions. In such an event, rather than control the outflow of technology, policy might be better directed to removing the distortions.

So far, much of this argument has implied that the technology being transferred by MNEs will be used to produce competitive goods to those produced by the transferring firm or country. With investment designed to substitute for exports — so called import-substituting investment by the recipient country — a lot of technology will be of this kind. But even here experience has shown that where a foreign affiliate is set up to produce one line of goods, its presence may stimulate the imports of other lines of goods from the home firm or country; this has proved to be especially common in the case of firms producing consumer goods, for example, TV sets, motor vehicles, man-made textiles, processed food products, cosmetics and pharmaceuticals.

With other kinds of foreign activity, technology may be used to produce complementary, or even quite unrelated, goods to those produced by the transferring firm or country.[13] In such cases, output and employment in the home country may be increased and its technology base strengthened. Investment by MNEs in trade and distributive activities is of this kind: while it may improve the marketing competence of recipient firms, it may directly increase the exports of goods from the home country. Investment in building and construction, capital equipment and energy ventures,[14] and by chemical and engineering consultancies may have the same effect. In other words, a disembodied transfer of technology may give rise to the transfer of technology embodied in goods. It is, of course, a moot point how far technology *is* transferred through goods, but, for the purposes of this analysis, we shall treat such exports as a benefit to the home firm and country.

The transfer of technology through international vertical backward integration by MNEs in resource based industries may also result in a spin-off in technological capacity in the home country, depending on the extent to which secondary processing activities are undertaken in host or home countries. Even if there is a transfer of expansion of technological capacity, imports of capital equipment are likely to take place and these are more likely to be obtained from the home than from other countries. In some service industries, for example, banking and international tourism, similar externalities are likely.

Finally, there are multiplier effects of the income generated from the transfer of technology, whatever its kind. In the nineteenth century, these yielded substantial benefits to the UK economy. Rising incomes of recipient countries generated by the exports of British capital and expertise provided markets for UK manufactured goods which helped to finance new investment and, through the economies of firm size, reduce the prices of goods supplied to home markets. Although there is no economy currently as internationally dominant as the UK once was, depending on the domestic value added of foreign affiliates and the recipient country's marginal propensity to import from the investing country, gains may accrue to the latter. Work done by Hufbauer and Adler (1968) suggests that, for the US economy, these consequences are often significant.

It must be admitted that some of the effects on the home country ascribed to the transfer of technology by MNEs would be better ascribed to foreign direct investment in general. Our defence of the present approach is that the unique ingredient of most kinds of foreign direct investment *is* technology, be it the technology of product, materials production, management, organisation or marketing. Without this component, direct investment would become portfolio investment. The main incentive for a firm to internalise the flow of resources across national boundaries is to capture the full economic rent on the package of technological ingredients which are specific to it. It is no coincidence that MNEs tend to dominate in industries supplying products with a high technological content and that, because of the benefits from internalisation, they are the main producers and transmitters of technology.[15]

Nevertheless, accepting that the focus of interest is often on the effects of transfer of technology *per se*, it is reasonable to look at the extent to which MNEs do transfer technology across national boundaries, and see how this affects the host country and what are the short- and medium-term repercussions on the exporting countries. The previous paragraphs have suggested certain principles which will determine these effects. These include, first, the market conditions in which the transfer of technology takes place; second, the form of technological transfer and, in particular, whether it is likely to complement or substitute that produced at home; third, the strategies of the investing or technological exporting firms; and fourth, the goals of home and host governments, and the policies pursued by them to achieve these goals.

IV

(a)   *The role of MNEs*

What then has been the extent and significance of technological transfer by MNEs to developing countries?

The most widely published indicator of the extent of foreign involvement by MNEs is value of outward direct investment. Figures published by the United Nations (UN, 1978) show that at the end of 1976, the cumulative value of direct investment by MNEs of all nationalities was $287 billion.[16] Between 1967 and 1976 foreign direct investment stock increased by an average of 11.7 per cent per annum and, in the latter year, accounted for 6.9 per cent of the GNP of DAC countries.[17] In the mid-1970s, the value of international production exceeded that in international trade. In the case of the USA, the foreign direct capital stake to export of goods ratio, in the early 1970s, was 4:1; for the UK it was just over 2:1 (UN, 1973).

In 1976 about 95 per cent of the foreign investment stake was owned by MNEs from developed countries, and about three-quarters of this was located in the developed countries. The latter ratio has steadily increased since 1967, when it was 69 per cent. Receipts from technology exports to developing countries from some leading OECD countries[18] increased by 15 per cent a year during the 1970s; in 1978 they stood at $2 billion, 17.9 per cent of the flow of foreign direct investment. However, these technology exports represented only one-fifth of all such efforts from these same OECD countries; moreover, this ratio has also steadily declined from a quarter in the late 1960s[19] (OECD, 1977). These data suggest that technology exported by OECD MNEs is primarily to other OECD countries and not to developing countries. It is also worth observing that investment flows, particularly in recent years, have become more symmetrical among the OECD countries. Whereas in the late 1950s the USA was, by far and away, the dominant capital exporter, with all European countries and Japan importing more capital than they exported, the last decade has seen the rate of foreign direct investment in the USA growing much faster than that of foreign investment by the USA.[20] Since, like trade, inward and outward direct investment flows are not entirely unrelated to each other, the critics of outward technology flows would do well to take account of the possible effects of controlling such flows on inward direct investment.[21]

As recipients of foreign direct investment and technology,[22] developing countries may be divided into a number of fairly distinct groups. First, there are the OPEC countries which, in 1975, accounted for 23 per cent of the foreign capital stake in developing countries, and whose imports of technology were heavily biased towards petroleum and petroleum related activities. Second, tax haven countries accounted for a further 13 per cent; here there was little, if any, technological transfer. Third, there are the mainly industrialising countries of which eleven accounted for 42 per cent of the total foreign capital stake in 1975. These included the larger and newly industrialised countries (NICs)[23] whose imports of technology were largely directed to the manufacturing sector.[24] Fourth, there is a mixed bag of developing countries which mainly attract foreign capital and technology to specialised resource sectors and to fairly standardised import substituting manufacturing activities. By area, Latin America and the

Table 12.1   Participation Rates of MNE Affiliates in Manufacturing Sector of Selected Developing Countries

| | % of all firms | | | | Total Manufacturing Exports | |
	Sales	Assets	Employment	Exports	1976 ($m.)	1976 ÷ 1965 value
Latin America						
Argentina	31.0 (1972)		11.0 (1972)	At least 30% (1969)	975.5	12.0
Brazil	49.0 (1974)	29.0 (1974)		39.9 (1973)	2,192.3	21.0
Chile	20.0 (1964)				118.7 (1974)	7.2[a]
Columbia				27.7 (1973)	383.6	11.4
Mexico	28.0 (1970)			35.0 (1973)	2,089.9	14.0
Peru	46.0 (1969)				51.8 (1974)	4.2[b]
Asia						
Hong Kong			10.8 (1971)	10.0 (1973)	7,859.3	7.9
India	13.0 (1973)			6.2 (1973)	2,802.7	3.5
Korea, Republic of				15.0 (1972)	6,746.8	65.0
Malaysia	50.0 (1971)			28.1 (1971)	798.5	11.8
Pakistan				8.0 (1973)	677.2	3.6
Singapore			30.0 (1968)	75.0 (1972)	2,920.3	9.7
Taiwan				15.5 (1973)	6,921.0	37.1
Thailand			8.9 (1970)		510.6	42.2
Africa						
Nigeria	70.0 (1968)				18.4	2.2
Ghana	50.0 (1974)				8.8 (1975)	1.8[c]

Southern Europe and Middle East					
Greece	35.1 (1973)	28.2 (1973)	62.3 (1973)	1,252.3	28.7
Israel		41.2 (1972)	28.0 (1976)	1,854.7	6.7
Spain	11.0 (1974)		32.3 (1973)	6,025.2	15.8
Turkey		41.0 (1974)	3.0 (1973)	465.7	42.7

a 1965–74.
b 1966–74.
c 1965–75.

Source: Sales and Employment from UN (1978, Table III.54, p. 263) (NB footnote and sources to table). Exports from J. B. Donges and L. Muller-Ohlsen (1978); for Argentina, from Nayyar (1978); for Greece, from University of Reading, PhD thesis prepared by V. Papandreou.
Value of total manufacturing exports by country and increase since 1965 from Keesing (1978a, Annex B).

Caribbean accounted for about one-half of the total foreign investment in developing countries in 1972 and Africa and Asia for one-fifth each. For manufacturing industry alone, the respective proportions were 67 per cent, 12 per cent and 19 per cent (UN, 1978).[25]

How important are the affiliates of MNEs to the economies of developing countries? Tables 12.1 and 12.2 set out some details of the shares of foreign affiliates in the manufacturing sector of a sample of developing countries. They reveal that their contribution is, in general, considerably more important in Latin America than in Asia;[26] details on African countries are too scant to be reliable, although in some, for example, Nigeria, Kenya and Ghana, their participation is known to be significant. The data also show that the degree of MNE participation is negatively associated with the host country's contribution to total manufacturing exports and/or increase in manufacturing exports.[27]

Interesting as these data may be, more relevant to our present theme is the effect that the transfer of technology by MNEs may have on the *structure* of industry in developing countries. In this connection, a report published by the UN Centre on Transnational Corporations (UN, 1979) reveals that within manufacturing industry, the pattern of involvement by TNCs in developing countries is very similar to that in developed countries. There are differences *between* countries within the developing world, and particularly among the NICs, but, as Table 12.3 sets out, in both groups of countries MNEs play their most important role in those sectors characterised either by above average technological intensity or product differentiation, for example, the chemical, engineering, motor vehicles and food, drink and tobacco industries. By contrast, indigenous firms in both groups of countries dominate in labour intensive industries producing goods which require fairly standardised technology, for example, textiles, wearing apparel and leather products.

The importance of foreign affiliates of MNEs in high and medium technology industries suggests that the transfer of technology by MNEs by this route has helped to build up these sectors in these countries. However, there are some notable country differences. In Singapore, for example, foreign corporations account for 47 per cent of the assets in the textiles and clothing industry. Though lower, the figures are also significant in other South East Asian countries, notably Taiwan and South Korea. Japanese companies are known to have a particular strength in the textiles industry. In 1975, their share of all foreign direct investment in this industry was more than three times their average share of foreign direct investments in developing countries;[28] however, part of the explanation for the Japanese involvement is their strength in the man-made fibres sector[29] which is more appropriately classified to the chemical industry.[30]

(b) *Types of foreign investment and the nature of technology transfer*
It would be unwise to read too much into the kind of data just presented.

Table 12.2   *Ranking of Countries in Selected Developing Countries according to Degree of MNE Penetration in Manufacturing Industry and Export Performance*

Degree of TNC penetration	Developing Countries	Exports A^a	B^b
I *High*	Brazil	4.9	21.0
	Ghana	0.0	1.8
	Greece	2.8	28.7
	Malaysia	1.8	11.8
	Nigeria	0.0	2.2
	Peru	0.1	4.2
	Singapore	6.5	9.7
		16.2	13.3
II *Medium*	Argentina	2.2	12.0
	Chile	0.3	7.2
	Columbia	0.8	11.4
	Mexico	4.7	14.0
	Israel	4.2	6.7
	Spain	13.5	15.8
		25.6	12.2
III *Low*	Hong Kong	17.6	7.9
	India	6.3	3.5
	Pakistan	1.5	3.6
	Korea	15.1	65.0
	Taiwan	15.5	37.1
	Thailand	1.1	42.1
	Turkey	1.0	42.7
		58.2	11.3

[a] A: Share of total manufacturing exports from developing countries listed (1976 or nearest date).
[b] B: 1976 (or nearest date) ÷ 1965 manufacturing exports.
Source: as for Table 12.1.

One important deficiency is that the contribution of the foreign affiliates of MNEs is usually expressed in terms of gross sales rather than local value added. By itself, this may tell us nothing about the extent and form of the production undertaken nor about the imported technology content. The pharmaceutical industry provides a good illustration. There is very little R & D in pharmaceuticals done in developing countries by MNEs, and in only a few of the larger NICs are pharmaceutical chemicals produced in any quantities. By far the greater part of the value added created by foreign affiliates of MNEs consists of labour intensive formula or dosage preparations and the packaging of the final product. It could well be that

Table 12.3   Ranking of Industries in Developed and Developing Countries, according to Degree of MNE Penetration and Export Performance[a]

Degree of MNE Penetration	Developed Countries	Developing Countries	Exports A[b]	B[c]
I *High*	Petroleum processing	Petroleum processing	ni	ni
	Electrical machinery	Rubber	nsa	nsa
	Transportation equipment	Electrical machinery	15.7	14.7
	Instruments	Transportation equipment	2.3	8.5
	Chemical products (pharmaceutical products and petrochemicals)	Instruments	nsa	nsa
	Rubber products	Chemical products (pharmaceutical products and petrochemicals)	7.5	2.4
		Non-electrical machinery	4.0	7.8
	Non-electrical machinery	Food (incl. beverages and tobacco)	ni	ni
			29.5	6.2
II *Medium*	Fabricated metal products	Primary metals	3.6	4.6
	Primary metals	Fabricated metal products	4.9	7.2
	Food (incl. beverages and tobacco)	Construction materials (stone, clay, cement, etc.)	3.2	2.2
	Paper and paper products	Printing and publishing	nsa	nsa
	Printing and publishing	Textile	13.6	3.3
	Construction materials (stone, clay, cement, etc.)	Miscellaneous manufactures	11.0	4.3
			36.3	3.6
III *Low*	Textile	Wearing apparel	21.8	6.4
	Wearing apparel	Wood, wood products and furniture	5.3	6.5
	Wood, wood products and furniture	Leather and leather products	6.9	5.9
			34.0	6.3

[a] The developed countries are: Australia, Austria, Canada, the Federal Republic of Germany, France, Japan, Sweden and the United Kingdom. The developing countries are: Argentina, Brazil, Hong Kong, India, Mexico, Singapore and Turkey.

[b] A: Share of the total manufacturing imports from developing by developed countries in 1974.

[c] B: 1974 ÷ 1967 exports.

ni = not included.

nsa = not separately available.

Source: Degree of MNE penetration from UN (1979). Export data from Keesing (1978a, Table 27).

Table 12.4 US Related-Party Imports as a Percentage of Total Imports of Selected Manufactured Products from Selected Newly Industrialising Countries, 1977

	Textiles 65[a]	Non-electric machinery 71[a]	Electric machinery 72[a]	Clothing 84[a]	Footwear 85[a]	Scientific instruments 86[a]	Total Manufacturing
Israel	18.9	32.8	62.9	14.0	0.0	13.0	18.2
Portugal	2.8	24.7	78.4	0.4	0.2	82.5	12.5
Greece	3.7	52.2	99.1	5.0	0.8	2.2	7.8
Ireland	36.3	78.5	77.8	8.3	42.2	91.7	59.0
Spain	1.5	36.3	32.6	3.7	10.1	7.8	24.1
Yugoslavia	0.1	14.0	2.0	2.3	2.2	3.6	4.9
Argentina	0.5	39.1	76.1	2.9	0.8	10.0	9.2
Brazil	9.2	59.9	95.3	18.0	0.5	38.4	38.4
Colombia	1.5	16.8	3.9	15.7	81.2	87.8	14.1
Mexico	9.6	87.8	95.6	68.0	60.9	93.6	71.0
Taiwan	13.1	19.3	58.1	1.2	3.1	67.1	20.5
Hong Kong	4.9	68.5	43.4	3.4	3.6	30.4	18.1
India	6.1	30.5	58.7	15.8	6.1	16.7	10.1
South Korea	5.5	64.2	67.3	7.1	1.8	12.1	19.7
Malaysia	0.2	83.2	97.0	1.9	0.0	91.9	87.9
Philippines	28.9	69.7	31.7	53.4	0.0	27.0	47.5
Singapore	4.3	90.5	97.0	0.5	0.0	85.3	83.3
(Haiti)	2.9	33.7	36.5	24.8	77.2	97.9	28.4
Total All Developing Countries	7.8	63.5	75.2	11.5	4.4	51.2	37.0

[a] SITC category.
Source: G. K. Helleiner (1979), mimeo, derived from US Commerce Department Data.

within the sectors dominated by MNEs the operations actually carried out in developing countries are labour intensive, while in the developed countries they may be capital or technology intensive.

Much, of course, will depend on the type of foreign investment undertaken, its position in the product cycle and policies of host governments. Import-substituting activities normally start with simple finishing operations to a product which is mainly made elsewhere, and gradually work backwards to other, and technologically more intensive, manufacturing stages. By contrast, investment in resource based industries may start with extractive activities but later extend forwards to secondary processing operations. Investments intended to take advantage of cheap and abundant supplies of semi-skilled labour may initially be directed to labour intensive production processes and later embrace the more capital or technology intensive processes. Nevertheless, though the particular processes undertaken by MNEs may not be technology intensive, the final output produced may be classified to an industry normally regarded as such. Technology aids the use of all factor endowments; but it does not necessarily make for a more technology intensive industrial structure.

As far as the transfer of technological capacity is concerned, data on US MNEs show that of the R & D undertaken by them, only 8 per cent was undertaken outside the USA in 1970 and only 0.5 per cent in developing countries. Most of this was concentrated in a small number of industrial branches that have a high level of product differentiation in consumer products or specific requirements for adaptation to local conditions or production factors (OECD, 1981).[31] Other estimates suggest that the developing countries only account for 2 per cent of the world R & D compared with 12 per cent of world manufacturing production and 10 per cent of manufacturing exports. MNEs may also advance foreign technological capacity by training programmes and skill development. OECD studies (OECD, 1981) suggest this has been quite important in some industries, for example, rubber tyres, petrochemicals, pharmaceuticals, constructional engineering and hotels, but in others, for example, video equipment, the development of indigenous skills, at least in South East Asia, has been largely due to local efforts.

The conclusion suggested by these data is that although MNEs may transfer most of their technology within industries classified as high or medium technology intensive, in some cases, at least in developing countries, the technology will be used to improve the efficiency of labour intensive processes of production rather than to promote the development of technology intensive sectors. This is most likely to occur in the so called high technology industries in which some form of international specialisation of products or processes is practiced, and where intra-firm transactions also tend to be concentrated.

(c) *The nature of competition between developed and developing countries*
Table 12.5, which is derived from a study done for the ILO (Sabolo and

Trajtenberg, 1976), sets out the breakdown of activities of foreign affiliates of MNEs in developing regions in 1970; *inter alia* it reveals that resource based and local market oriented investments were far more important than labour oriented investments in three of the major regions lists. In Asia (which included India) labour oriented activities were of equal importance with the other two groups; the evidence suggests that, in the 1970s, they have become considerably more significant.

For the purposes of our analysis, this distinction is an important one. Not only may the *raison d'être* for foreign direct investment be very different but so might its consequences on the home country. Though there is some concern about the effects of technology exports induced by all kinds of foreign direct investment, most recent attention has been directed to the labour intensive, offshore activities of MNEs. It seems to be accepted that, as far as foreign investment designed to serve local markets is concerned, it is not often a real substitute for exports. Import controls, non-tariff barriers, availability of local materials, transport costs, the need to be near customers, and the behaviour of competitors often combine to make the transfer of technology, through direct investment, a *necessary* condition for supplying the local market. Moreover, since the type of technology required for this may be available from other MNEs the cost of *not* supplying the market may be to lose it to a rival.

With investment in labour intensive processes or products designed to supply markets outside the host country, and particularly those presently supplied by the home country, the attitude is less accommodating. Here it is asserted that, in the absence of this investment, the competition to the investing country would not (or need not) have been so great, for two reasons: first, the technology required to mount the investment in the host country is unlikely to be as standardised as in the import-substituting case; and second, because the home country can always protect its own industries from foreign competition generated by another country's MNEs. But what role have MNEs played in these industries?

In 1974 Nayyar (1978) estimated that MNEs accounted for 15 per cent

Table 12.5   *Breakdown of Foreign Direct Investments in Developing Regions by Broad Type 1970*

Region	Type of investment (%)			All investments	
	Raw material oriented	Local market oriented	Labour oriented	(%)	(US$m.)
Southern Europe	19	62	19	6.3	2.6
Africa	60	34	6	19.4	7.9
Latin America	33	62	5	51.1	20.8
Middle East	91	9	–	8.8	3.6
Asia	30	36	34	14.4	5.8
Total (US$m.)	17.0	19.6	4.0	–	40.7
Overall distribution (%)	42	48	10	100	100

Source: Sabolo and Trajtenberg (1976).

of the manufacturing exports of developing countries. At that time, ten developing countries accounted for nearly four-fifths of imports of manufactured goods by developed from developing countries. Five of these countries, Hong Kong, Singapore, South Korea, Brazil and Mexico, along with Greece, Portugal, Spain, Turkey and Yugoslavia are among the NICs whose share in the total imports of manufactures to OECD countries increased from 2.5 per cent in 1963 to more than 8 per cent in 1977. The NICs have also recorded a faster than average rate of growth in industrial production; by 1976 they were responsible for about 9 per cent of the market economy production compared with 5 per cent in 1963. Nevertheless, of the fifty top exports of manufactured products in 1976, which accounted for about 80 per cent of the exports of these countries, MNEs were actively involved in only about one-quarter. These included those most competitive to those produced in OECD countries, for example, textiles, clothing and leather goods.[32] The one sector in which MNEs do tend to dominate is electrical machinery and consumer electronics, the exports of which rose by 46 per cent between 1967 and 1974 (Plesch, 1978).[33] Even so, this does not mean that MNEs have had no influence in the extent and direction of exports – far from it; MNE subcontracting and buying groups, particularly those of Japanese origin, have played a decisive role[34] even though the production is in the hands of indigenous firms. Moreover, a high proportion of exports of MNEs from NICs tend to be internalised. Data compiled by Helleiner (1979) set out in Table 12.4 suggest that in the newer industries, in which NICs are beginning to gain an important stake in world trade, US-related party imports – mainly from US affiliates to their parent companies – account for the major proportion of all imports.

The UK Case. Let us illustrate this general point by relating the percentage of total UK imports, originating from the NICs,[35] to the extent of MNE involvement in particular industries as set out in Table 12.2. In 1977 imports from NICs accounted for 10 per cent of all imports of manufactured goods or 3 per cent of total supplies to the UK market.[36] Of these imports, those involving products from industries with a low MNE penetration[37] accounted for 40 per cent; those with a medium MNE penetration for 35 per cent, and those with a high MNE penetration for 25 per cent. A crude estimate of the percentage of these imports actually produced by MNEs would be 10–12 per cent. The percentage of UK imports originating from the NICs varied from 57.5 per cent in the case of clothing, 47.5 per cent in travel goods, handbags, etc., and 43.1 per cent in footwear to 2.2 per cent in transport equipment, 6.8 per cent in instruments and photographic equipment and 8.6 per cent in electrical machinery. Some 21.0 per cent of imported radio sets and 9.1 per cent of TV sets came from the NICs, 30.3 per cent of watches and 4.5 per cent of cameras.[38]

V

The previous paragraphs have made four main points:

(1)   The greater part of the direct investment by MNEs in developing countries has been directed towards import substitution and re-source based activities, with the exception of Southern Europe and South East Asia, where it has also been directed to production of labour intensive products and/or labour intensive processes or high or medium technology products.

(2)   Much of this investment has been prompted by a shift in the lo-cational advantages of production from the developed to the devel-oping countries, such that if MNEs of developed countries had (individually) responded by not investing they would have lost all or most of these markets.

(3)   Until the mid-1970s, most of the growth of manufacturing exports from NICs was in industries in which MNEs did not generally play a dominant role. Moreover, the revealed comparative advantage (RCA) of developing countries has improved most significantly in sectors in which the degree of MNE penetration is low.[39] Exceptions include electrical machinery and photographic supplies. In other words, a substantial part of the increasing import competition from these countries has little or nothing to do with technology transfer by MNEs.[40]

(4)   There are some suggestions that, in the 1980s, because of the impact of MNEs in restructuring the trade flows of developing countries in the newer industrial sectors, the role of MNEs will become more important.

We now turn to some of the implications of these facts for the EICs. First, from the viewpoint of international resource allocation, the transfer of technology by MNEs has had mixed effects. Where it has been prompted by import controls imposed by host countries, apart from those justified by the optimum tariff and infant industry arguments, it is likely to have had less beneficial effects than the exports. Where this has been coupled with MNEs acting as oligopolists and undertaking investment to advance product differentiation or to protect market shares, the result has almost certainly been a misuse of resource allocation. We have already referred to Professor Kojima's argument (Kojima, 1978) that much of US foreign investment in technology intensive industries has been of an anti-trade kind, and operates to the disadvantage of both host and home countries.[41] In this present context, we feel that the Kojima criticism would be better directed to the activities of MNEs *within* the EICs, as a much smaller per-centage of such activities in the developing countries is undertaken for defensive oligopolistic reasons. On the other hand, investment by MNEs to

take advantage of resource or labour cost differentials has probably benefited the allocation of resources as it has freed the flow of technology
which might otherwise not have taken place, or taken place to the same
extent. Professor Kojima regards the technology exported by MNEs to
promote this kind of activity as trade promoting and in accord with the
principle of comparative advantage.

From the viewpoint of individual home countries, the crucial questions
are:

(1) What would have happened had not the technology been exported?
(2) What effects can be attributed to it?
(3) What is the reaction of investing firms and home countries to these
     effects?

Let us now briefly look at the three types of activities by MNEs in turn.

(a) *Investment to supply the local market*
For firms of one nationality to supply foreign markets they must have
some competitive or *ownership* advantage over local or other foreign firms.
If they choose to supply that market from a local production base rather
than by exports, then it is assumed this is because *location* advantages
favour the host rather than the home country. The product cycle theory
of investment suggests there is a natural progression from exports to
foreign production. Thomas Horst (1974) has estimated that in the early
stages of foreign production by US firms, US exports increase along with
the production; eventually, however, as production becomes established,
exports decline. But his calculations make no assumption as to what would
have happened had the production not taken place. Other research suggests
that, in those cases where it is realistic to assume the foreign investment
substitutes for domestic (or other foreign) investment in the host country,
it may permit exports to be higher than they otherwise would have been
(Reddaway *et al.*, 1968; Hufbauer and Adler, 1968).

Earlier we described some of the ways in which exports of the home
country might be directly increased or reduced as a result of an internalised
transfer of technology. There are other less obvious, but no less important,
effects on the home country. For example, an expansion of the market for
a firm's products may bring with it economies of increased size, and the
spreading of organisation and administrative overheads and R & D expenditure. Where there are pressures on the firm's domestic operations, production abroad may release capacity for more productive use at home.
There may be technological feedback from the affiliate to the parent
company, especially where investment is made in a more advanced industrial country. Firms may be better able to take advantage of the geographical diversification of their activities in their purchasing arrangements, fund
raising and management recruitment. By having their assets spread over

many countries and denominated in different currencies, they can better cover their risks; they can take advantage of leads and lags, protect themselves against exchange rate changes, engage in transfer price manipulation, and so on. As a consequence of the transfer (or sharing) of the technology of production, the investing enterprise almost always strengthens its technology of information and choice and, in some cases, its technological capacity as well. Companies such as Philips of Eindhoven provide an excellent example of how domestic capacity released as a result of investment in developing countries may be used to produce new or upgraded lines and/or be given over to technologically more advanced or complex production processes (Graham, 1978).

(b) *Resource based investment*
The purpose of this investment is usually to supply the home firm or country and other countries with resources. The technology required for exploration, extraction and processing, together with the large amount of capital needs required, gives MNEs ownership advantages over domestic competitors in a number of industries (UN, 1979). Here there is no substitution between foreign and domestic investment; the transfer is of technology to increase or protect the existing supply of minerals or materials, hopefully on improved terms. Moreover, it may also strengthen the technological capacity of home companies in engineering, chemical design and consultancy and maintenance work.

In some cases, technology transfer to promote secondary processing activities may be at the expense of secondary processing in domestic markets. Again, it may be that the firm has little choice but to locate or relocate the processing operations in host countries in response to the policies pursued by their governments. But the basic equation is the relationship between social and private opportunity costs. The amount or kind of technology transferred may be too high because foreign direct investment confers lower net benefits from a social rather than a private viewpoint.

(c) *Export platform investment*
We have suggested that it is the transfer of technology associated with this kind of investment which is likely to have the most effect on domestic employment as it is concentrated in labour intensive activities. Unlike import-substituting investment, where if an MNE wishes to supply a foreign market it must produce in that market, firms do have options on the location of their export platform investments.

There are two forms of this kind of investment. The one is to produce complete goods and/or services which require substantial inputs of labour. Here the advantages of specialisation and division of labour would seem to dictate that MNEs should concentrate their production of labour or (natural) resource intensive goods in labour and resource rich countries;

and capital or technology intensive goods in countries that are rich in capital and technology.

The second kind of export platform investment is in labour intensive parts of a production process for sale in world markets, the capital or technology intensive part of the production being produced in the capital or technology rich countries. Again, this conforms to the principle of the international division of labour, except in so far as the action is prompted by distorted markets or government policies.

Perhaps the reason why this kind of investment is strongly criticised is that the critics believe that, without it, the adverse effects on domestic employment can more easily be arrested. The fact that if the home country's MNEs did not invest other firms would do so, and compete the home firms out of the market, cuts no ice, because it is also argued that this can be prevented by import controls. The fact that consumers may have to pay a higher price for their products and that domestic firms will earn lower profits is regarded as an acceptable price to pay for minimising unemployment. But, to repeat an earlier point, it is not the transfer of technology by MNEs *per se* which is the root of the difficulty, but the general dissemination of technology from both developed and socialist countries to developing countries, coupled with free trade.

VI

One of the main conclusions of an earlier section of this chapter was that in the manufacturing sectors which are most likely to generate adverse effects on the EICs from the transfer of technology to developing countries, and particularly the NICs, the role of MNEs (*qua* MNEs) was not generally a significant one. Such advantages as they did possess were mainly in the marketing of goods in the industrialised countries; hence the presence of multinational buying groups, trading companies and joint ventures with local firms. The major exception seemed to be where the technology was ownership specific and where it could only be advantageously exploited within the same firm, rather than, for example, by licensing or subcontracting. In such cases, the MNEs remained the chief vehicle for transfer of technology and the main cause of concern to the home economies.

Yet, even in the industries which are the most highly penetrated by MNEs, their role is a decreasing one in the more rapidly developing NICs in South East Asia. Moreover, unlike the dominance of US MNEs in Latin America and UK MNEs in many of the Commonwealth developing countries, the geographical parentage of foreign direct investment in South East Asia is more widely diffused. This means that not only is the impact of any one home country's MNEs likely to be less significant, but the opportunity cost of any one country not investing in these areas is correspondingly greater.

But it is not only through equity investments that MNEs may transfer technology. Following the example of Japan, many South East Asian NICs are using a variety of non-equity routes to attract foreign technology. These include not only straightforward licensing agreements and management contracts, but a whole variety of other forms, involving various institutions, for example, local firms, host governments, international agencies, consortia of MNEs, etc. (UN, 1979; Baranson, 1979). As a consequence, not only are an increasing number of manufacturing MNEs setting up international project, consultancy and advisory divisions to deal with external technology sales, especially to the NICs, Middle East and Eastern European countries, but consultancy firms in project design and evaluation, industrial and chemical engineering and managerial systems are mushrooming. Indeed, it seems likely that the growth of some NICs, notably South Korea and Taiwan, will rest more on their ability to induce externalised technology flows and technological capacity than to attract foreign direct investment. To the EICs, the relative benefits of consultancy contracts are less clear cut. While a firm like Dunlop-Pirelli argues that had not its projects division sold know-how kits on tyre factory design, construction and operation to NICs and Eastern European countries, other tyre companies would have done so, it admits that, in the long run, the EICs may not benefit as much as had their MNEs been directly involved.[42]

In the case of the transfer of petrochemicals know-how, the possible clash of interests is more serious. The specialist contractors are primarily concerned with selling knowledge of how to construct and operate a chemical plant and market its end products. Their interests are served by an increasing output of petrochemicals, and they will do what they can to assist potential buyers to obtain the necessary finance from sources like the World Bank. The petrochemical producers, on the other hand, will only invest in developing countries if they believe they can make a reasonable profit from selling the output they produce, and they will only normally wish to transfer knowledge on plant construction and operation if they believe that their own ability to sell petrochemicals in third markets is not adversely affected. Many petrochemical producers consider that whenever there is a surplus of petrochemical capacity in developing countries, it is this, aided and abetted by the transfer of technology and capital from developed countries, that is forcing down the price of petrochemical products to uncompetitive levels. The situation is further aggravated wherever host governments subsidise production and/or dump petrochemicals on the world market.

The problem just described is not confined to the petrochemicals industry; it has shown itself in the mining industry, noticeably copper mining (Dunning, 1979) and several other branches of manufacturing industry. It results in a genuine conflict of interests between the suppliers and the *existing* producers of end products using that technology, and is often exacerbated by the policies of host governments wishing to develop their own industries and break into the international market. It is the export of technology through specialised consultants which home governments need to be more perturbed about than the transfer of technology through their own manufacturing MNEs, whose interests, at least in this instance, coincide with those of their governments. On the other hand, this is not something which an individual EIC can attempt to curb without even greater loss to itself. It involves some kind of international stabilisation agreement to prevent excessive technology flows from causing instabilities in the output and prices of essential commodities.

We have said that, at a microlevel, any adverse effects which a transfer of technology may have on the investing firm's capacity may provoke various responses, ranging from a cut-back in domestic capacity to a restructuring of production into new product and process lines. Where the latter is successfully achieved, then, in effect, the firm has borne its own adjustment costs. Where it is not able to do this, unemployment results. We have suggested this is most likely to be the case in labour intensive declining industries; although, even in expanding industries, restructuring is likely to take place towards more technology or capital intensive products or processes. Here it is worth observing that most of the sectors in which MNEs have been prominent in the NICs, particularly of the export platform kind, are those in which technological change has been the most rapid and the effects on production processes, products and labour requirements has been the most pronounced.[43] This has been most obvious in the computer and consumer electronics sectors. Take a company like Philips of Eindhoven. Employment in the complex of plants located at Eindhoven hardly changed between 1965 and 1978, yet real output doubled. Over the same period, Philips' employment in the developing countries increased by 125 per cent. The company claims that technical development in the field of audio and video equipment, and particularly the technology of micro-electronics and computerisation, has caused a major restructuring of its worldwide operations from which both the company and the Netherlands has benefited. Be that as it may, it is certainly true that today's leaders in the consumer electronic industries are also those which have been active in their foreign activities. The reluctance of UK companies to engage in such investment may well have weakened rather than strengthened the position of the UK electronics industry in world markets.

The most obvious problems of technology exports occur in industries whose domestic markets are static or declining, where there is little product or process innovation, where output is specialised and where production methods are labour intensive. The textile and clothing industry is the one most typically cited. In Western Europe it is estimated that 400,000 people, or one-sixth of the labour force, have lost their jobs because of import competition from Asian and North African factories, where wages range from one-half to one-twentieth of those in Germany or Belgium.[44] Between 1970 and 1976, exports from the NICs rose sixfold, and it has only been as a result of the multi-fibre agreement that imports since 1977 have slowed down. At the same time, the anti-protectionist lobby argues that the developed countries have more to lose from protectionism than developing countries because the rate of growth of exports from the developed to the developing countries is greater than that from the developing to the developed countries.

Very often, the problem of these declining industries – like those of the basic industries in the UK after the First World War – is highlighted by the fact that they tend to be located in the less prosperous regions of the home economies and use the type of labour which cannot easily find alternative employment or be retrained. The new jobs being created require different skills to those which they replace. In such cases structural unemployment persists. The EEC Commission estimates that more than 1.6 million jobs in Europe are at risk as a result of import competition from developing countries. In the UK, it is reckoned by the Foreign and Commonwealth Office that, between 1970 and 1975, some 47,500 jobs were lost as a result of import competition from developing countries, three-quarters of which are in the textiles and clothing industry; and that over the following ten years the gross displacement of labour could be four times that amount. Though even this latter figure is around 10 per cent of the total amount of UK unemployment in 1978, it is of concern because it is likely to affect particular regions and types of workers very severely indeed.[45]

That this is an age old problem, and is the inevitable result of the emergence of newly industrialising economies, is of little comfort to those adversely affected. Neither is the fact that MNEs are not often actively involved in the industries. The fear is that import competition from a comparatively few industries today will spread to many others tomorrow. As the NICs climb up the industrial ladder, will they not attract more markets away from the developed countries? And if they do, will not the MNEs become increasingly involved? In this respect, the participation of MNEs in audio and video equipment, in synthetic fibres and auto components in some countries in Asia and Latin America is cited as a foretaste of the pattern of the future. But here the experience of Japan is salutary. Japan increased her share of world trade in manufactured goods from 6.9 per cent in 1960 to 16.0 per cent in 1978 with the minimum contribution from foreign MNEs. Yet to achieve this resurgence to industrial strength she imported a very substantial amount of technology, while building up an indigenous strength in the ability to absorb, alter and adapt that technology. For example, between 1950 and 1970 the Japanese government approved 8,324 contracts made by Japanese concerns involving purchases of technology from Western enterprises (Ozawa, 1972).[46]

It is a moot point whether Europe and the USA would have been better off without the Japanese economic miracle; but, the point at issue is that it would have been difficult, if not impossible, for these countries to have used normal commercial channels to have arrested the miracle. At the same time, it is at least arguable that the USA and Europe would have been better off had they been allowed a stake in this miracle. The contrast to Japan is Brazil and Mexico, whose rate of growth of industrial production since the late 1960s has outpaced that of Japan, but in whose prosperity foreign based (particularly US) MNEs have fully participated. The dictum 'if you can't beat them join them' seems very apt in this case.

The World Bank estimates that exports of manufactured goods from developing countries will rise by about 12 per cent per annum between 1975 and 1985 (Keesing, 1978). At the same time exports of manufactured goods, particularly capital goods, from industrialised countries to developing countries are likely to increase almost as quickly. Assuming this prediction to be accurate, the EICs will be affected differently. Low wage cost developed countries might be expected to be penetrated less than high wage countries, for example, the USA and Sweden. On the other hand, low wages are often a symptom of low productivity and lack of industrial competitiveness, in which case the weaker developed countries might suffer more than the stronger. The Foreign and Commonwealth Office study estimates that between 1978 and 1988, the increase of UK imports from the NICs could be of the order of 8 per cent of the present output of manufactured goods. It suggested that the gross labour displacement might be more than this proportion of the manufacturing labour force because the industries likely to be most affected are those of higher than average labour intensity, and that firms react to additional NIC competition by adopting more capital or technology intensive methods of production. To some extent, this labour displacement will be offset by increased employment in the industries serving the NICs, but as the study argues, it is the *gross* labour displacement that is the relevant indication of the adjustment task.

Different industries will be differently affected, but the study asserts that in spite of the inroads into the UK's (revealed) comparative advantage by the changing comparative advantage of the developing countries (Donges and Riedel, 1977) there are many sectors in which the UK's competitive position should (or perhaps one should say could) improve.

VII

It should be clear from the preceding paragraphs that the impact of transfer of technology carried out by MNEs on the economies of the home countries is but a tip of the iceberg of the adjustment problems now facing and likely to face the EICs in the foreseeable future. The fact is that, although MNEs continue to account for the bulk of the commercial R & D carried out in the Western world, only a small amount of this is directly or immediately relevant to the *present* industrialisation programme of the developing countries. Most of the product, process, materials, production, marketing, managerial marketing and organisational know-how currently required for much of this industrialisation is not proprietary to individual firms but is generally available in the market place.

However, in the next decade, the picture may change quite dramatically as the NICs become more sophisticated in their product structure and production techniques. The first question to which EICs have to address themselves − provided they are allowed to − is how far do they wish to be involved in this industrialisation programme? This chapter has no more than hinted that the net social benefits of being involved through technology transfer by their own MNEs may be higher than any alternative action they may pursue.

In response to increasing and more pervasive competition from the NICs there are basically three policies open to governments of EICs. First, they can resort to some kind of protectionism; second, they can enter into agreements with the new industrialised competitors to control their increase in manufacturing exports or to allow them to import from the EICs as much as they export to them (the assurance of fair trading comes into this category); and third, they can seek to identify their future comparative advantage in resource allocation in the future and introduce policies to encourage the necessary adaptation and restructuring. In the long run, assuming the last is judged the first best solution, to be successful it would need more decisive and far-reaching strategies to stimulate productivity, encourage innovation and promote the development of service activities than most OECD countries have introduced up to now.[47] But in the interim, the problem is how to minimise the adjustment costs of market disruptions to maximise the smoothness of the adaptation and restructuring, and, where appropriate, to encourage firms affected by competition from NICs to be more efficient. To solve these problems, which because of of market rigidities may well mean controlling the speed of the restructuring process, some form of import control should not be ruled out.[48]

It is, however, difficult to understand how controlling the activities of manufacturing MNEs in NICs can advance these goals, any more than the controls exerted by the UK on the export of technology in the nineteenth century helped its objective (Rosenberg, 1978).[49] If attention is needed in this direction, it should be towards removing any distorting influences which may encourage MNEs to transfer different amounts or types of technology than they might otherwise have done, or which may interfere with their returning the maximum benefits to the home country. Again, action may involve changes to international patent, monetary or tax systems, etc., some of which at least would operate against the interests of the technology receiving countries.

The area where home governments need to pay most attention, apart from that of defence and national security (Hawkins and Gladwin, 1981) is where their own firms, acting in a mainly consultative capacity, are transferring technology which cannot be obtained from other sources. Here the social opportunity costs of transfer may be considerably greater than the private opportunity costs, and ways may need to be found of redressing this difference.

We have argued that EICs are likely to be differently affected by the industrialisation of the developing world.[50] The role of their own MNEs in this process and the attitudes of their governments (cf. the US and Japanese cases) also differ. We have also asserted that one reason why a particular firm or country may be reluctant to control technology exports is that its competitors may *not* do so. This suggests that the main area of international competition will continue to be *between* countries of the developed world. Only if they adopted a common policy towards the actions of their MNEs would it be possible to control the outflow of technology, which is specific to MNEs, without any EIC feeling it was worse off as a result. While such a policy, at least on economic grounds, seems very unlikely, the efforts of the developing countries, including the NICs, to strengthen their bargaining power *vis-à-vis* MNEs from the developed world may eventually provoke a countervailing reaction on the part of EICs to redress the balance which they believe to be against their own interests (Bergsten, 1974). A less controversial route to follow might be the search for harmonised policies between North and South designed to smooth the adjustment process, which might be of benefit to both older and newer industrialised countries.

One final observation. This chapter began with the expression of concern of developed countries about the possible adverse effects of exporting technology to developing countries through their own MNEs. It ends by asking the question: Can developed countries *not* afford to export technology to developing countries through their own MNEs? For if the activities of MNEs are seen not as a threat to domestic investment, jobs and technological capacity, but as a way of (1) exploiting international markets, (2) ensuring a stake in the prosperity of developing countries, (3) financing technological capacity, and (4) protecting or advancing the *international* competitive position of one EIC relative to another, the question of whether North/South technology transfer is a 'good' or a 'bad' thing takes on a completely new meaning. The case presented is not that this latter proposition is in any way proven, but that it deserves at least as much attention as the alternative thesis which is currently more in vogue and being more vigorously researched.

Notes: Chapter 12

1   For excellent summaries of the main issues involved see Helleiner (1975) and Moxon (1979).
2   Technology is defined as a flow of all kinds of commercial applicable knowledge:

technological capacity is defined as a stock of assets, both physical and human, capable of generating technology flows.

3   For example, in 1975 about 80 per cent of all receipts of royalties and fees by the USA from the sale of technology originated from the foreign affiliates of US MNEs (UN, 1978).

4   We use the nomenclature EICs (existing industrialised countries) to mean the developed industrial countries.

5   These countries' share of world manufacturing exports fell from 36.5 per cent in 1967 to 28.8 per cent in 1977. Of the other industrialised nations, Japan has increased her share from 9.8 per cent to 14.5 per cent while France and Germany have maintained theirs at around 9 per cent and 20 per cent, respectively.

6   Quoted in Meyer (1978). See also National Science Foundation (1974).

7   As has happened in the UK pharmaceutical industry, where the share of output of indigenous firms has risen in the 1970s.

8   That is to say, a firm must expect to earn at least the opportunity cost of the capital invested in technological creating activities.

9   For a discussion of the conditions under which an enterprise may prefer to externalise technology transfers see Telessio (1979) and Robinson (1978).

10 See especially Reddaway *et al.* (1968) and Hufbauer and Adler (1968).

11 A recent study by Kawaguchi (1979) suggests that Japanese joint ventures and subsidiaries in South East Asia buy between 30 per cent and 100 per cent of their inputs (in value terms) from Japan (see especially Table V.3, p. 31).

12 For example, IBM has been one of the main losers of the arrangement made by the US Amdahl Corporation to supply the Japanese computer firm Fujitsu with advanced computer technology; see Baranson (1976).

13 In the macro sense, it is difficult to conceive of unrelated goods as all technology may, indirectly, affect the international competitive position of the recipient country.

14 Such as the French/Mexican nuclear energy project.

15 In 1970, it was estimated that US MNEs accounted for 55 per cent of all the R & D undertaken in US manufacturing industry (US Tariff Commission, 1973).

16 Estimated to have risen to $369 million by the end of 1978.

17 Member countries of the Development Assistance Committee of the OECD.

18 France, West Germany, Italy, Japan, the Netherlands, the UK and the USA.

19 In a symposium organised by *Business International* on the Transfer of Technology, in May 1978, one speaker estimated that as little as 3 per cent of the value of technology transfers took place between the developed and developing countries.

20 In 1976 the outflow of direct investment from the USA was 2½ times greater than in 1967–69; the inflow of direct investment was five times greater. The respective figures for Germany were 4.6 and 2.4, for France 4.3 and 3.0, for the UK 3.3 and 2.2, and for Japan 10.3 and 1.9.

21 In 1972, the USA accounted for 60 per cent of the combined positive balance of technological payments of the OECD countries; by 1976 this proportion had fallen to 45 per cent (OECD, 1977).

22 Some studies (OECD, 1980) also include export of capital goods as a form of technology export. In 1978, such OECD exports to developing countries amounted to $94.6 billion compared with $16.7 billion in 1970.

23 The coverage of NICs varies according to source. The OECD and UNCTAD list Greece, Portugal, Spain, Turkey, Yugoslavia, Hong Kong, Singapore, South Korea, Taiwan, Brazil and Mexico as NICs. However, the UK Foreign and Commonwealth Office, in a recent report (UK, 1979), also includes India, Malaysia, Pakistan, Philippines, Thailand, Argentina, Israel, Malta, Poland, Romania and Hungary. Countries included in the eleven mentioned in the text are Brazil, Mexico, India, Malaysia, Argentina, Singapore, Hong Kong, South Korea and the Philippines.

24 Three-quarters of the inward capital stake of these eleven countries was in manufacturing industry.

25 Since this date the percentage of manufacturing investment directed to Asia has increased significantly.

26 However, as a percentage of GDP some Asian countries, for example, Singapore and Hong Kong, spend more on other forms of technology imports than do Latin American countries (OECD, 1981).

27 In 1972, the ratio between the stock of investment by MNEs in the manufacturing sector and manufacturing exports of Latin American and Caribbean countries was 2.35; the corresponding figure for African developing countries was 2.80 and for Asian and Oceanian developing countries 0.28.

28 See Chapter 4, Table 4.3.

29 Since this date the percentage of manufacturing investment directed to Asia has increased significantly.

30 It is noteworthy that the rate of increase in exports from developing countries has been greatest in sectors where the MNE involvement is small. Had the exports of food, drink and tobacco been included in Group I (Table 12.3) the increase in exports for that group would have fallen from 6.2 to 4.2.

31 Examples include the tropical drugs programme of the WHO, some tyre development (in India and the Philippines), and some product adaptation in toiletries, food products and agricultural and industrial machinery. A recent survey of R & D performed abroad by MNEs showed there were some applied R & D activities in several developing countries including Argentina, Brazil, Mexico, India, Hong Kong and Singapore (Behrman and Fischer, 1980).

32 For example, Keesing (1978) estimated that MNE manufacturing affiliates account for only about 5 per cent of the exports of textiles and clothing from developing countries; and the percentage is even lower for leather goods. Again, the proportions vary between MNEs of different nationalities with the Japanese being the most actively involved in these sectors.

33 Plesch observes that the contribution of MNEs varies considerably between NICs. In Hong Kong foreign investment provided work for 68 per cent of the workforce engaged in electrical engineering in 1972; in Singapore the corresponding figure in 1968 was 67 per cent. In South Korea in the early 1970s foreign firms were supplying 25 per cent of the output and 50 per cent of electronic exports. On the other hand, in Yugoslavia, which is the leading exporter of NICs of domestic electrical appliances and electric power machinery, the role of MNEs is very limited indeed.

34 One estimate of the Netherlands Research Institute (in 1977) is that 70 per cent of all Hong Kong's exports of clothing passes through Western retail traders and import merchants.

35 As defined in the Foreign and Commonwealth Office Study; see UK, 1979, fn. 3, p. 18.

36 This is a lower proportion than in other OECD countries. For example, using the OECD definition of NICs, they accounted for 7.0 per cent of UK manufactured imports, 20 per cent of UK imports, 8.9 per cent of German imports and 8.1 per cent of OECD imports as a whole.

37 i.e. penetration by all MNEs, not just UK MNEs.

38 It is worth observing that an earlier NIC, Japan, is a more important supplier of sophisticated products, for example, cars, motor cycles and consumer electronic goods.

39 Donges and Riedel (1977). Of the thirty-six product groups in which the RCA of developing countries in 1972–73 was greater than 1, in only six was the degree of MNE penetration a high one. Of the fifty-five groups in which the RCA of developing countries was less than 1, the corresponding figure was sixteen.

40 Excepting the technology of marketing or market areas, as made available by MNE buying and sub-contracting groups.
41 See Chapter 11, page 313.
42 Indeed, one of the costs is now being seen in the form of cheap rubber tyre imports from East European economies.
43 For example, it has been estimated that over the period 1962–75 fifty times more jobs were lost through growth of labour productivity as were estimated through growth of imports from developing countries (Keesing, 1978b).
44 The corresponding figure for the USA is 225,000.
45 Of the estimated employment losses in the USA over the period 1964–71, 45 per cent were concentrated in clothing and electrical equipment and supplies. In Germany, between 1970 and 1976, 61.5 per cent were concentrated in the textiles and clothing sector, and 16. 8 per cent in the electrical engineering industry. Across all industries, however, one study (Edwards, 1979) has concluded that only in the case of Canada and the USA have the *net* employment effects of the industrialisation of developing countries been negative; and in some cases, for example, Japan, there has been a sizeable net increase in jobs.
46 For further details of the role of Japan as a technology importer and exporter see Ozawa (1981).
47 For other policy prescriptions see Hogan (1978).
48 Harry Johnson (1975) makes the point that both adjustment assistance and adjustment safeguards should be considered in the *general* context of economic change rather than in the context of change mediated through changes due to international technology transfer.
49 The sluggishness of the UK to adapt to the structural changes required of her industrial economy in the late nineteenth century is an object lesson to EICs faced with the competition from the NICs.
50 See also OECD (1981) and studies quoted therein (e.g. in Chapters 3 and 4).

References

Baranson, J. (1976), 'A new generation of technology exports', *Foreign Policy*, vol. 25 (Winter 1976–77).
Baranson, J. (1979), *Technology Transfer to Developing Countries* (New York: Praeger).
Behrman, J. N., and Fischer, W. A. (1980), *Overseas R and D Activities of Transnational Corporations* (Cambridge, Mass.: Oelgeschlager Gunn and Hain).
Bergsten, C. F. (1974), 'Coming investment wars?', *Foreign Affairs*, vol. 53 (October).
Donges, J. B., and Riedel, J. (1977), 'The expansion of manufactured exports in developing countries: an empirical assessment of supply and demand issues', *Weltwirtschaftliches Archiv*, vol. 113, no. 1.
Donges, J. B., and Muller Ohlsen, L. (1978), *Aubenwirtschafts-strategien und Industrialisierund in Entwicklungsländern* (Foreign Trade Strategies and Industrialisation in LDCs), Kieler Studien No. 157 (Tübingen: Mohr).
Dunning, J. H. (1979), 'Multinational mining companies and governments; a new detente?', *Multinational Business*, no. 1.
Edwards, A. (1979), *The New Industrial Countries and their Impact on Western Manufacturing* (London: Economist Intelligence Unit), Special Report No. 73.

Gilpin, R. (1975), *US Power and the Multinational Corporation* (London: Macmillan).

Graham, E. M. (1978), 'The terms of transfer on technology to the developing nations, a survey of the major issues', unpublished paper prepared for OECD.

Hawkins, R. G., and Gladwin, T. N. (1981), 'Conflicts in the international transfer of technology: a US home-country view', in T. Sagafi-Nejad, R. W. Moxon and H. V. Perlmutter (eds), *Technology Transfer Control Systems: Issues, Perspectives and Implications* (Elmsford, NY: Pergamon Press).

Helleiner, G. K. (1975) 'The role of multinational corporations in the less developed countries' trade in technology', *World Development*, vol. 3, no. 4 (April).

Helleiner, G. K. (1979), *Transnational Corporations and Trade Structure*, mimeo., University of Toronto.

Hill, C. T. (1978), *Technological Innovation, Agent of Growth and Change* (Cambridge, Mass.: MIT Centre for Policy Alternatives).

Hogan, W. G. (1978), *Questions on Structural Adjustment Policies*, Working Papers, Department of Economics, University of Sydney (September).

Horst, T. (1974), *American Exports and Foreign Direct Investment*, Harvard Institute of Economic Research Discussion Paper No. 362 (May).

Hufbauer, G. C., and Adler, M. (1968), *US Manufacturing Investment and the Balance of Payments*, Tax Policy Research Study No. 1 (Washington, DC: US Treasury Department).

Johnson, H. G. (1975), 'Technological change and comparative advantage: an advanced country's viewpoint', *Journal of World Trade Law*, vol. 9 (Jan./Feb.).

Kawaguchi, N. B. (1978), 'The role of Japanese firms in the manufactured exports of developing countries', unpublished manuscript (Washington, DC: World Bank) (November).

Keesing, D. B. (1978), *World Trade and Output of Manufactures: Structural Trends and Developing Countries' Exports* (Washington, DC: World Bank).

Keesing, D. R. (1978b), 'Developing countries' exports of textiles and clothing: perspectives and policy changes', unpublished manuscript (Washington, DC.: World Bank) (May).

Meyer, H. E. (1978), 'Those worrisome technology exports', *Fortune*, May 22.

Moxon, R. W. (1979), 'The costs, conditions and adaptation of MNC technology in developing countries', in R. Hawkins (ed.), *Economic Effects of Multinational Corporations* (Greenwich, Conn.: JA Press).

National Science Foundation (1974), *The Effects of International Technology Transfers on US Economy* (Washington, DC: National Science Foundation).

Nayyar, D. (1978), 'Transnational corporations and manufactured exports from poor countries', *Economic Journal*, vol. 88 (March).

Ozawa, T. (1972), 'Should the United States restrict the technology trade?', *MSU Business Topics*, vol. XX (Autumn).

Ozawa, T. (1981), 'Technology transfer and control systems: the Japanese experience', in T. Sagafi-Nejad, R. W. Moxon and H. V. Perlmutter (eds), *Technology Transfer Control Systems: Issues, Perspectives and Implications* (Elmsford, NY: Pergamon Press).

OECD (1977), *Data Concerning the Balance of Technological Payments in Certain OECD Member Countries: Statistical Data and Methodological Analysis*, unpublished document DSTI/SPR 77.2 (Paris: OECD) (November).

OECD (1981), *North/South Technology Transfer. The Adjustments Ahead* (Paris: OECD).

Plesch, P. A. (1978), 'Developing countries' exports of electronics and electrical engineering products', unpublished manuscript (Washington, DC: World Bank) (February).

Reddaway, W. B., Potter, S. T., and Taylor, C. T. (1968), *The Effects of UK Direct Investment Overseas* (Cambridge: Cambridge University Press).

Robinson, R. D. (1978), *International Business Management* (Hinsdale, Ill.: The Dryden Press).

Root, F. R. (1981), 'The pricing of international technology transfer via non-affiliate licensing arrangements', in T. Sagafi-Nejad, R. W. Moxon and H. W. Perlmutter (eds), *Technology Transfer Control Systems: Issues, Perspectives and Implications* (Elmsford, NY: Pergamon Press).

Rosenberg, N. (1978), 'The international transfer of industrial technology', paper prepared for OECD, Directorate for Science, Technology and Industry, Paris (September).

Sabolo, Y., and Trajtenberg, R. (1976), *The Impact of Transnational Enterprises on Employment in the Developing Countries* (Geneva: International Labour Office) (January).

Teece, D. J. (1977), 'Technology transfer by multinational firms: The resource cost of transferring technological know-how', *Economic Journal*, vol. 87 (June).

Telessio, P. (1979), *Technology Licensing and Multinational Enterprises* (New York: Praeger).

UK Foreign and Commonwealth Office (1979), *The Newly Industrialised Countries and the Adjustment Problem*, Government Economic Service Working Paper No. 18 (January).

UN (1979), *Transnational Corporations and the Long Term Objectives of the Developing Countries* (New York: UN Centre on Transnational Corporations).

UN (1978), *Transnational Corporations in World Development: A Reexamination* (Department of Economic and Social Affairs) E78 II A5 (New York: UN).

UN (1973), *Multinational Corporations in World Development* (Department of Economic and Social Affairs) E73 II A11 (New York: UN).

US Tariff Commission (1973), *Implications of Multinational Firms for World Trade and Investment and for US Trade and Labour* (Washington, DC: US Government Printing Office).

PART THREE

13

Evaluating the Costs and Benefits of Multinational Enterprises to Host Countries: A 'Tool-Kit' Approach

I

Studies undertaken on the consequences and policy implications of the activities of foreign owned MNEs in host countries usually fall into two groups. These are, first, those which attempt, by way of field studies or use of published material, to evaluate the effects of inward direct investment and/or suggest policies which should be pursued in the light of such effects. Known as 'because . . . then' type studies, to be successful they require:

(1) a clearly defined set of criteria by which the contribution of foreign direct investment (fdi) is to be appraised;
(2) precisely identified assumptions about what would have happened to the resources deployed in the absence of fdi;
(3) comprehensive data on the operations of foreign affiliates of MNEs and also those of their parent companies, which might affect the contribution of their affiliates to the local economy.

Studies of the 'because . . . then' kind may be macro- or micro-oriented; they may attempt to examine a broad range of issues or limit themselves to particular effects of fdi, for example, on the transfer of technology, exports, employment, etc. Illustrative of this approach are the writings of Reddaway *et al.* (1968), Steuer *et al.* (1973) and Streeten and Lall (1973).

The second group of studies concerns itself less with appraising the effects of fdi or MNEs as with providing a framework or tool-kit to assist those who may wish to do so. Here attempts are made to theorise about the possible effects of direct investment and other economic variables, and

This chapter is based upon a paper presented at a Conference on the Portuguese Economy held at Lisbon in 1977. The author was asked to write on the effects of foreign direct investment on the Portuguese economy, but because of the paucity of data, he was compelled to write a more conceptual essay.

to suggest possible courses of policy which might be pursued if and when such relationships are established. Such studies are essentially of an 'if . . . then' type; *inter alia* they seek to identify the conditions under which MNEs are most likely to contribute to the goals of host countries. Research by Bos *et al.* (1974) typifies this kind of study, though more often than not, the first group of studies, implicitly or explicitly, assumes some kind of model.

A hybrid of the two approaches begins with second, and then tries to marry up theory with known facts in comparable situations. For example, a study on the impact of fdi on employment in West Germany may be used, within a particular theoretical framework, to suggest the likely effects of fdi on employment in the UK. In our current context, we may hypothesise certain similarities between the structure of the Portuguese and Greek economies, and suggest that some of the known consequences of fdi in Greece may guide Portuguese policy towards foreign affiliates in its economy. Similarly, data on the effects of fdi in the recent past may be used and applied to assist current economic policy. The limitations of this approach are well known and need no elaboration.

Mainly because there are few data on the operations of MNEs in the Portuguese economy, this chapter must be of the second kind. It will summarise, in the following pages, attempts so far made to evaluate the costs and benefits of fdi and formulate a positive policy towards it. In so doing, it will bear in mind two of the questions uppermost in the minds of policy makers, viz.: To what extent and under what circumstances can fdi advance a country's welfare? and How can policy best be framed to accomplish this objective? As far as possible, this analysis will be related to the economic situation in Portugal, particularly in the context of its development planning.

II

In attempting to measure and evaluate the contribution of fdi to host countries, three important points arise which are not always given the attention they warrant. The first is to identify the criteria by which one should assess the contribution of fdi. This may seem obvious, but all too rarely does it appear explicitly in policy statements about fdi. Clearly the criteria, in the sense of what comprises a country's welfare, will vary between countries, in the same country over time, and between different sectors within any country. Without a clear basis for comparison, one can never be sure that when differences arise about the costs and benefits of fdi one is not using different yardsticks to appraise it. Certainly the same effects of foreign owned companies may give rise to different policies in the USA, Taiwan, Mexico and India simply because the criteria by which governments in these countries judge fdi differ. What is good for the UK need not necessarily be good for Portugal; what was good for Portugal in 1950 need not necessarily be good for Portugal in 1976. This would suggest that empirical studies should recognise that host or host/home country-specific factors are as important in evaluating fdi as the characteristics of fdi itself or the behaviour of particular foreign affiliates. Among these one might mention the stage of economic development, cultural values, size, resource and technological capacity, administrative efficiency, political ideology, international involvement (including the extent of fdi), economic expertise, etc. Only now are these factors being explicitly incorporated in models designed to formulate general principles towards fdi. Certainly, the pattern of regulatory action by some developing countries, as set out in Table 13.1, suggests that country-specific variables are as important in determining these as the characteristics of fdi itself.[1]

Attempts to formulate general criteria for gauging the effects of fdi abound in literature. Four groups of host country goals are usually identified: (1) economic (which relates to the type and quantity of products supplied); (2) equity (which concerns the distribution of income and assets); (3) sovereignty (which refers to the right to control one's own destiny); and (4) participation (which suggests the need of people to be involved in the decision taking process). Not always may each of these goals be simultaneously attained, and each must be set within the context of the broadest goal of all, viz. advancing a certain way of life. For example, the volume of certain goods and services might be increased, but only at the cost of more pollution, a change in culture and living habits, and some loss of control over decision taking. On the other hand, economic autarky might rob a country of the main benefits of the international division of labour. It is now being increasingly recognised that the cost/benefit equation of fdi is a very complex thing indeed. But prior to any assessment, a country must try and identify its goals, translate these into operational terms, and decide upon its priorities. Ideally, policies should wait until the trade-offs between the achievement of mutually exclusive goals are known. But if there is one thing which countries, particularly developing countries, have learnt in their experiences with fdi, it is that, in the initial policy forming stage they grossly underestimated the pervading influence of such investment and its wider implications.

While sometimes adding to a country's resource capabilities, it may at the same time lock the country into a pattern of economic interdependence, the costs and benefits of which are only later transparent. Foreign investment transmits a way of life from the investing country to the host country, and strengthens the economic order of which it is part, an order which may not be perceived to be in the best interests of the host country. To argue *ad hominem*, that is, against the conduit of fdi (viz. the MNE), though understandable is not always helpful; the beast is only a creature of its environment. A better appreciation of the goals of host countries

Table 13.1 Patterns of Foreign Direct Investment Regulation in Selected Developing Countries, 1978

Parameter	Pattern I (mostly Asia, excluding India, Africa, CACM)	Pattern II (mostly Middle East. North Africa)	Pattern III (mostly South America)
I Administration	Case-by-case screening largely restricted to award of 'incentives' (non-discriminatory).	Case-by-case screening at establishment (degree of discrimination varies).	Separate administration for foreign investment. Screening at establishment.
II Investment screening criteria	Emphasis on functional contributions of investment. Little indication of extensive cost/benefit analysis. Screening largely for award of incentives.	Emphasis on functional contributions and conditions of investment. Little indication of extensive cost/benefit analysis.	Criteria formulated for cost/benefit analysis, often extensive. Includes social cost criteria in some cases.
III Ownership	Few requirements. Few sectors closed to foreign investment.	Joint ventures prevalent.	Strict regulations on ownership and investment (excl. Brazil). A large number of closed sectors.
IV Finance	Few repatriation limitations.	Few repatriation limitations.	Repatriation ceilings in most areas (excl. Mexico). Screening of foreign loans. Special control of payments to parent company.
V Employment and training	Announced indigenisation policies but little headway in practice.	Local quotas for work force. Few local quotas for management.	Specific across-the-board indigenisation requirements.

VI Technology transfer	No controls.	No controls.	Screening and registration of all technology imported.
VII Investment incentives	Long-term tax incentives for establishment.	Establishment incentives limited to five years – in most cases non-renewable.	Incentives tied to specific contributions, but incentives may be curtailed for foreign-owned firms.
VIII International dispute settlement	Adherence to international dispute regulation. Regional investment regulation: UDEAC, OCAM, EAC, OAMP.	Same as pattern I. Regional investment regulation: Arab Economic Union.	Local adjudication and regional harmonisation of investment regulation: ANCOM, CACM.

and the way in which foreign companies may impinge on these goals, through the technology (including the technology of choice) they transmit and the decisions they take, is badly needed.

The second major methodological issue, which is particularly trouble-some to research workers, and which policy makers are too often apt to ignore, is the problem of evaluating the effects of fdi net of those effects that would have occurred if the resources used by the investing companies had been differently deployed. To illustrate, the effect on UK exports which directly results from the presence of US affiliates in the UK is the actual exports of such affiliates (plus or minus the exports of other companies generated by their activities), minus the exports that would have occurred had not those affiliates been present in the UK. Frequently, it is implicitly assumed that there is no opportunity cost of fdi, that is, in the above case, exports in the absence of US affiliates would have been zero. But rarely is this the actual alternative position; if US firms had not invested in the UK, UK companies may well have invested more, if not in the same sector then in a different one, although admittedly it may have taken a change in government policy to bring this about. And it may make a world of difference which alternative position one chooses. Change the position assumed or the consequences of the same, then, as with changing the criteria by which fdi is appraised, its net contribution to welfare will be different.

It is becoming increasingly recognised that, except for estimating broad macroeconomic effects, the most realistic alternative position will vary between countries, industries and over time. What might happen to the production of computers in the UK in the absence of IBM may be very different to what might happen to the production of petroleum products in the absence of British Petroleum in the USA. The effects of a takeover investment are different from a greenfield investment; those arising from an investment by a well established and integrated MNE are not the same as from a new medium size investor. A sectoral approach is the only way out of this difficulty; alternatively, it may be desirable to classify fdi by origin (is it marketing or cost oriented?) or by the strategies of investing firms. We shall return to this point later.

A final methodological issue concerns policy prescription. Suppose that it has been possible to measure the contribution of MNEs to employment in a particular country (either generally or within a particular sector); and that, in the light of the criteria established, this contribution can be eval-uated. The questions that now arise are: (1) is this the best possible contribution and (2) assuming it is, and it is beneficial, does this mean one should encourage the inflow of direct investment? Whatever the answers, there is a great temptation among policy makers to direct any change perceived necessary as a result of fdi to the foreign investor. If the employment effect of inward investment is negative, how can the foreign firm be made to employ more people? If the balance of payments contribution is negative, how can policy be directed to persuading foreign affiliates to export more or import less, or, failing that, to reduce their capital stake? In some cases, such policies may be the correct ones, particularly where it can be established that the MNE is behaving in a less than optimum fashion (e.g. by not maximising its efficiency). But in others it may not be so, for two reasons. The first is that there may be a trade-off between achieving one national goal and another. Insist that the MNE should employ more labour intensive (but more costly) production methods, and exports may suffer; limit the share of an industry's output an affiliate can supply, and its costs of production may be higher than they might otherwise be; insist on more local research and development and the MNE may be reluctant to relinquish 100 per cent ownership, and so on. This comes back to the first of the methodological problems discussed above. The second reason is that the consequences of fdi reflect the government policies which give rise to it. If these are not what is desired, this may be because the signals given to MNEs are inappropriate. A monopoly rent earned by foreign affiliates may be the direct result of tariff policy which curtails competition from abroad; a capital intensive technology could reflect an unsuitable monetary policy or that labour is overpriced; an ability of companies to juggle transfer prices may be prompted by an overvalued or undervalued exchange rate. Faulty government policies provoke reactions by foreign firms which may themselves generate undesirable effects. In these cases, the remedy may not be to force firms to behave in accordance with the policies but to change the policies themselves.

Moreover, government policies which may have been appropriate in the absence of fdi may require modifications because of it. Just because fdi may cause a balance-of-payments deficit, it does not mean that curbing such investment is the best way to remedy such a deficit. Other options, for example, altering the exchange rate, may be less expensive in terms of the country's primary goals advancing. There is a great temptation to blame or praise MNEs because of the outcome of their operations; but, often, to put right any unwanted results requires macro-policy measures, or measures directed towards other firms which make a lower contribution towards the country's primary goals.

Enough has been written to suggest that the evaluation of the activities of foreign owned firms is a difficult business. Which goals are to be met and in what order of priority and over what time period? In terms of what alternatives are the results of MNEs to be evaluated? Where action by governments is required, to what extent should it be specifically directed to fdi and to what extent to affecting the disposition of resources as a whole?

III

We now turn to the problems of assessing the operational impact of fdi, and will concentrate on the economic consequences. These can be readily identified as they are those by which the contribution of all enterprises may be assessed. They are basically concerned with levels of output, productivity, output stability, long-term growth and structural efficiency. Sometimes more specific goals may be sought, for example, the employment of particular types of labour, a balance-of-payments surplus, or increasing research and development capacity, which may sometimes complement and sometimes compete with general goals.

To measure the contribution of foreign affiliates, information is needed about their activities. Sometimes, this has already been collected from all enterprises independently of their nationality. Examples (in most economies) include data on output employment and wages (suitably classified by skills and industry); exports, imports, R & D expenditures, capital expenditure, sources of finance, profits, advertising, origin of purchases, and so on. The assembling and classification of such basic information by nationality of enterprise is the first priority. In addition, there are data special to foreign affiliates which need collecting. Foremost among these are the transactions of affiliates across national boundaries and between different parts of the same organisation. Statistics on the inflow of capital and technology need to be supplemented by information on profits, royalties and payments for other factor services made to or by parent companies or other parts of the organisation. Separate data on goods and assets traded between the affiliate and other parts of the MNE should be collected to assist the host government in estimating the extent to which transfer pricing manipulations, and the use of leads and lags, etc., are possible and/or likely. Other relevant facts may only be obtained direct from the parent companies of affiliates, for example, the geographical disposition of its capital and R & D disbursements; here the host government is at present reliant on the goodwill of the companies.[2]

In addition to the quantitative data, qualitative information is needed about the relationships between parent and affiliate, for example, with respect to the strategy of the MNE towards product development, marketing, technology transfer, location of R & D, employment of local nationals, and on particular project appraisals. This is especially important in the case of the larger investments and a regular monitoring service may be necessary to alert government to any marked change in strategy. Some kind of permanent liaison with the 100 or so largest investors in a country and/or with those in the most sensitive sectors would help enormously.[3] In some cases, existing machinery might be extended to accommodate these needs, for example, the case of planning agreements in the UK. The important thing is for the host country to be as knowledgeable as possible about everything that goes on in foreign MNEs, which may significantly impinge on the local affiliates' activities.[4]

Given the information what does one then do with it? Here some kind of model of how foreign investment may impinge on domestic economic goals is necessary. Models may vary from the extreme macroeconomic (i.e. national economic) to the microeconomic (i.e. the project) level; they may be general or partial; they may be static or dynamic and of varying degrees of econometric sophistication. Most researchers have contented themselves with measuring the contribution of fdi to fairly specific goals, for example, its effect on employment, balance of payments, output, and so on. Illustrative of the more ambitious macro models is that of Bos and his colleagues (Bos *et al.*, 1974) which both researchers and policy makers are using; somewhat less embracing have been those of Steuer and Streeten and Lall. At a project level, the work of Little and Mirrlees (1974) stands supreme.[5]

Measuring the (gross) economic effects of fdi is essentially an exercise in estimating the local value added and/or employment generated by it, and, in the long run, its contribution to the growth and development of the host economy. Its impact on the balance of payments may affect the extent or speed at which these objectives might be achieved, while the possibility of fdi leading to employment, output or price instability is a risk which must be taken into account. Each of these consequences is measurable, though both the primary and secondary indirect effects of fdi need to be considered. Local value added (lva) equals the gross output of foreign affiliates (= quantity of goods sold multiplied by price) less all imports, less payments made from net output to foreigners (e.g. dividends, royalties, etc.). Lva is thus affected by (1) the technical efficiency of affiliates, and that of indigenous firms from which they purchase, (2) their ability (through market power) to influence price (or inputs and output) and the level of output, and (3) the quantity and price of imported goods and services. The amount of employment necessary to create that lva will be determined by the capital/labour ratio and the efficiency of producing firms. The extent to which the balance of payments (on current account) is affected will be related to the affiliates' export/import ratio, which, in turn, will depend on the investing strategy of the parent company; and also the ability of the affiliate to trade across boundaries at other than arm's length prices. Employment, technology, prices, competitive structure and balance of payments are then the main magnitudes affecting lva; in what way and to what extent, as we have written earlier, will depend on the industrial sector, type of firm investing and government policy.

Expressed in purely economic terms, the (gross) cost of fdi is the loss in value added caused either by the inefficiency of the foreign affiliates and/or the interest, profits, royalties, etc., remitted to the investing company.

Inefficiency might be due to foreign companies investing in the wrong sort of industries, purchasing at less than minimum prices or from the wrong firms, or producing at below technical price or scale efficiency. In turn, such inefficiencies may stem from a protected market structure, entrepreneurial deficiencies, technical or managerial inadequacies, or inappropriate government policies. Usually, since it is the most dynamic and efficient foreign firms which venture abroad, the costs are most likely allied to the domestic or international market conditions which allow foreign affiliates to earn higher than competitive profits, or the strategy of the parent company which requires foreign affiliates to operate in a way that does not optimise their local net output.[6]

It is important to trace through and measure the secondary effects of fdi, for example, their impact on the local value added of suppliers, customers and competitors; and, through the normal course of labour and managerial turnover, information dissemination, etc., their effects on the economy as a whole. In the longer run, their impact on competitive and industrial structure and patterns of development are of key importance. Often the employment impact of fdi may be less in terms of the numbers employed by the foreign affiliate than the additional employment of indigenous firms supplying to it. This is why policy makers try and insist on forward (domestic) linkages in the case of extractive industries and backward (domestic) linkages in the case of final stage manufacturing industries, for example, motor vehicle assembling for foreign investors. Sometimes, as has been suggested, there is a trade-off between (short-run) goals. The most efficient technology may be necessary to penetrate foreign markets; but it may do little to increase employment. A competitive market structure may only be obtained at the price of fragmenting output among firms, such that none is able to produce efficiently. Insisting upon too high a local equity participation may rob indigenous firms of much needed capital.

Throughout the assessment process, a distinction needs to be made between social and private costs and benefits. The problem basically arises because of the different goals of MNEs and the host nations in which they operate and the fact that domestic prices do not always properly reflect the true opportunity cost of the resources involved. While the pursuance of these goals by MNEs may, and often does, advance those of host countries, clashes inevitably occur. These are of three kinds. First, those which are shared by all privately owned firms, independent of their nationality. Since the attainment of private profit and growth do not always advance public welfare, governments must take actions which are not necessarily welcome by such firms; monopoly legislation is the key case in point. Because of their parentage, however, foreign affiliates may create additional problems for governments. Second, the price extracted by the foreign company from the host country in the form of loss of value added may be both destabilising and contain an element of economic rent, part of which may not be easily identifiable. Third, and most difficult both to measure and evaluate, is where an affiliate is locked into a regional or globally oriented production and marketing strategy of the MNE; and decisions are taken, not on the basis of what is best for the affiliate, but on what is the most profitable deployment of resources for the group as a whole.[7] In turn, this strategy may be affected by international market forces or rules and regulations, which, themselves, may not always operate in the interests of individual host countries.

Another problem, explored in depth by Little and Mirrlees (1974) in their work on project appraisal for the OECD, is that the domestic prices which foreign investors face, and sometimes influence, may not accurately reflect the social value of the resources used, either because of market distortions (tariffs, subsidies, inappropriate exchange rates) or because of implicit or explicit price control (e.g. in the labour market, where there is much unemployment, wage rates may exceed the opportunity cost of labour). This means that to properly calculate the costs and benefits of fdi, shadow prices have to be imputed to domestic inputs and outputs which reflect the social cost of resources deployed.

Although the maximisation of local value added per unit of resources used is a convenient yardstick to measure economic welfare, for many purposes it is deficient. Even in purely economic terms it is possible, in any one period of time, to produce more consumption goods but only at the expense of investment goods (including investment in human capital) and, in consequence, future levels of output. If foreign firms diverted resources from investment to consumption activities, lva might be increased in the short run (if productivity were greater in the latter sector) but it would be lower or not rise as fast in the long run. The effect of fdi on the composition of output produced must then also be taken into account.

From a longer-term viewpoint, an economy's development rests on its rate of increase of output per capita. This, in turn, depends on the quality and productivity of its material and human resources and the amount it is prepared to invest to add to these resources, or make them more productive. Productivity increases result essentially from the deployment of more efficient technologies and from improving human skills, assuming other obstacles or disincentives, for example, market distortions, penal tax rates, etc., are removed. Small wonder that most host countries view the main benefit of fdi as increasing their technological and scientific capacities and narrowing any technological or managerial gap which may exist between them and other countries. Small wonder either that the transfer of technology is a crucial issue in the foreign investment debate, particularly as it appertains to the terms of that transfer.

There have been many studies on the technological impact of foreign firms on host countries.[8] The general conclusion is that, while they often introduce technologically advanced products and/or new processes of production (particularly at the raw material extraction or final stages of manufacturing), they rarely find it profitable to transfer technologically advanced or skill intensive manufacturing activities or to establish R & D laboratories. Sometimes this is because of an inadequate technological infrastructure in host economies, although in some countries, at least, this may be remedied over time by appropriate education and training programmes.

In other cases, it may reflect the strategy of the MNE to centralise technology intensive activities in the home or in a few host countries (Behrman and Fischer, 1980).

It may be argued that this, in itself, is not important as long as local firms are encouraged by fdi to increase their own technological capacity. Indeed, this may be preferable as the ownership of the capacity remains domestic. Here, the evidence is mixed. To take one industry – the pharmaceutical industry. In the larger developed countries, foreign companies, particularly the Swiss and American MNEs, have, through competition and example, stimulated local firms in their R & D efforts. Certainly this has been the case in the UK. On the other hand, due to the inability of small countries to finance other than a very limited amount of technological capacity, foreign enterprises in such countries as Sweden, Australia, Canada and Ireland have tended to dominate the supply of local technology and inhibit indigenous R & D effort.[9] Moreover, where foreign affiliates have established R & D facilities, these have usually been either for purely development programmes or as part of integrated R & D strategy of the MNE. Even though this may not necessarily be to the host country's best interest in reducing dependence on foreign technology, it may still be preferable to any feasible alternative.

The question of how far a country should invest in its own technological capacity is rarely decided on economic grounds alone. At the one extreme, it depends on the extent to which it wishes to be involved in international trade and investment, with all its consequential costs and benefits, and on what terms.

Some of the broader costs of fdi are those of other forms of economic interdependence. But since fdi involves domestic resources being directly controlled by non-resident companies – unlike trade, which involves the exchange of goods at arm's length prices between independent domestic and foreign firms – apart from enforcing a change in ownership, there is no way of escaping the fact that *de jure* the locus of decision taking rests outside the country which is most affected by the decisions. And the more global the investing firm is in its activities, outlook and strategy, the more the pattern of output and growth of its affiliates will be determined by forces outside their control. Classically, the fear of many developing countries that they may become permanent satellites to the major investing countries rests on the proposition that the MNEs of these countries find it in their interests to retain their main repositories of knowledge and human capital at home; and that this policy is encouraged by the existing international economic order and the patent system. Be that as it may, in their dealings with foreign investors, host countries are becoming increasingly interested in asking such questions as: What kind of output is to be produced? What is its local content? Who takes the decisions which will determine the affiliate's growth path? What linkages are affiliates likely to have with other economic agents within and outside the host country? Do they aid or inhibit economic or technological independence?

While it is less easy to measure the contribution of fdi to economic growth than to GNP, it is possible to get a fairly good idea of its impact on the capacity for growth, and, given data on its productivity, a reasonable estimate of its contribution to growth itself. It is also possible to assess its effect on economic stability, by examining, for example, trends in output and employment, the export/import ratios of foreign affiliates and their sectoral distribution (are they more or less susceptible to cyclical movements?). The possible destabilising effects of fdi due, for example, to the alleged ability of foreign affiliates to better circumvent national economic controls than domestic firms, and the fact that affiliates are sometimes tied in to a global decision taking system, and their response options are often wider than domestic firms, needs also to be appraised. Such research that has been undertaken suggests that while national economic policies are made more vulnerable by the presence of foreign firms, particularly those which are set up to supply foreign markets, no generalisations are possible on the extent to which fdi makes macroeconomic policy more difficult to implement. While they may sometimes be better equipped than domestic firms to ride over economic difficulties and/or minimise the impact of some government policies, they are often more sensitive to local government needs and subject to government persuasion.[10] Perhaps the best example here is in the field of regional policy.[11]

Moving away from economic to sociological or political questions, it is worth mentioning a number of possible effects of fdi which may or may not concern host countries, according to their goals, ideologies and values. Foremost among these are:

(1) Equity considerations, reflected *inter alia* in the effects of fdi on the distribution of wealth and income, both between capital and labour and between different labour groups. The received literature suggests that inward investment lowers the marginal productivity of capital and raises that of labour, but empirical studies do not generally support this contention. Certainly within the wage sector, it tends to skew the distribution of earnings. And what of its effects on the distribution of economic power? Does it make for a more or less concentrated distribution of output and decision taking?

(2) Cultural considerations, reflected *inter alia* in the type and quality of goods and services produced by foreign affiliates; the way of life reflected in their business practices, dealings with labour, marketing and advertising, respect for the environment; and the value placed upon alternative uses of resources. Does foreign investment erode cultural identity? This is certainly one of the anxieties of countries like Canada, dwarfed by their immediate neighbours, and developing countries in which there is substantial fdi from advanced economies with very different forms of culture.

(3)   Participatory considerations, reflected *inter alia* in the desire of a country's citizens to participate in the making of decisions which affect their own welfare. The cog-in-wheel syndrome is not unique to people working in the branch plants of foreign affiliates. It is as much the fate of the individual worker in any large organisation, publicly as well as privately owned; it is, however, shown in its extreme form in large MNEs, partly because of their intricate organisational hierarchies, partly because they are foreign and partly because of the geographical distance between the decision takers and those affected by the decisions. This anxiety is especially demonstrated at the floor level, and is voice vociferously by organised labour. But it may apply no less at a government level, as portrayed most vividly by the disquiet of the UK government in 1974 and 1975 in being insufficiently consulted by the Ford and Chrysler car companies about their plans for future investment in the UK.

(4)   Political considerations, reflected *inter alia* in any attempt by foreign investors to interfere with the political fabric of host countries – the Chilean case is the most spectacular example; and, at the other extreme, day-to-day attempts by MNEs to influence domestic economic policies to their advantage.

(5)   Ethical considerations, seen *inter alia* by several bribery scandals; the more relaxed policies on the part of some foreign companies to safety standards, for example, in product content and labelling, and in labour practices; in inappropriate advertising and sales techniques, for example, in the case of powdered milk.

(6)   Environmental considerations, seen *inter alia* by the effect of MNEs on pollution. Many of these considerations may be common to all large firms, but MNEs are especially spotlighted when they are seen to export certain practices which are banned in their home countries.

It is some of the above factors which many countries consider especially necessary to control in the pursuit of their development goals, and which, it is believed, are affected in a very specific way by fdi. Sometimes host countries are unaware of these costs (or benefits) prior to fdi; in other cases, fdi brings to the attention of host countries differences in practices and standards between themselves and other countries.

A final effect, which we will do no more than mention, concerns the MNE as an agent or even undertaker of the foreign policy of the home government. The whole question of extraterritoriality is an exceedingly complex one; more significant are the various ways, through both legitimate and other means, that the network of interrelationships between governments and companies of the same nationality may be used, where both are in the interests of the home country but not necessarily in those of the host country. Some of these power relationships have been comprehensively identified in a paper by Vaitsos (1976).

IV

So much for measuring the costs and benefits of fdi. Already the issue is seen to be highly complicated, partly because of the myriad of goals which may be advanced or retarded by fdi, partly because of the difference in objectives between the foreign investor and the host country, and partly because the costs and benefits of fdi are often so intertwined that action taken to reduce one kind of cost may be counterproductive simply because benefits elsewhere are reduced even more. Yet the policy makers must try and identify the key issues and relate the contribution or potential contribution of fdi to these. Where there are clashes in objectives within the host country, these must be accepted as such, and the responsibility for reconciling them placed upon the host government and not on the foreign investor.

The question of evaluating, as opposed to measuring, the costs and benefits of fdi is an even more hazardous task. Basically it comes down to the problem of attribution. It is one thing to associate costs and benefits with fdi. It is another to attribute these costs and benefits to fdi. Put another way, to what extent would the costs and benefits associated with fdi be different if there was no fdi? Questions like this can only be answered by making some assumptions about the alternative position to fdi, that is, what would have happened in its absence? Only by deducting the costs and benefits of the alternative position can one assess the net contribution of fdi to a country's welfare.

Economists have approached this particular problem in a variety of ways. One has been able to identify the unique features of fdi, that is, those that can be attributed to its nationality, and measure the contribution of these compared to that associated with fdi as a whole. For example, in evaluating the export performance of foreign affiliates, their actual exports might be compared with those of domestic firms, and any difference attributed to the nationality of their ownership. Illustrative of this approach is a study by Cohen (1975) of the export performance of foreign affiliates in selected Asian countries, and one by Abdel-Malek (1974) of the export orientation of foreign affiliates and domestic firms in Canada. Though attractive, its usefulness depends heavily on the choice of sample firms. Ideally, everything affecting performance, apart from that which can be attributed to nationality of ownership, should be identical. But this may be asking too much. Even within the same industries, firms have different product or process structures; age and size can rarely be perfectly matched, marketing strategies may reflect the personalities of decision takers, and so on. Moreover, in this kind of exercise one is usually forced to compare the operations of one part of an organisation with that of the whole of another. There is, then, a branch plant effect of fdi, which may no less influence its performance than its nationality. Finally, in some cases, it is the degree of foreignness which may be as important as the foreignness itself. In other words, the costs and benefits of foreign affiliates may as much reflect differences in the multinationality of their parent companies as the fact that they are foreign owned. Research on UK-owned firms in developing countries suggests that differences between the strategies of UK parent companies are as important in explaining the behaviour of their affiliates in host countries as their foreign ownership (Dunning, 1977). Some affiliates were hardly distinguishable from local firms; others were part of a highly integrated network of international activities.

Treated carefully, however, the differential approach can be a useful device for evaluating the contribution of fdi at a micro or sectoral level. More ambitious, though analytically much more difficult, is the alternative situation approach, which is favoured by economists undertaking more macro-oriented assessments of the effects of fdi. The main features of this approach and some of its limitations have already been outlined. Suffice to remind ourselves that the most comprehensive of the macroeconomic models is that prepared by Bos and his colleagues (Bos, 1974), which has been used by Perrakis (1977) to assess the results of fdi on a number of variables in the Greek, Spanish and Turkish economies. Since, in many ways, the Greek economy has a number of structural similarities to that of other parts of Southern Europe, the results of this research are not without interest to the Portuguese authorities.

The other studies have been mainly more specific in objective but they all serve to illustrate the tremendous difference the assumptions make to the outcome of the exercise. Tables 13.2 and 13.3 summarise some results of a selection of studies on the balance-of-payments and employment effects of fdi. They serve to underline the fact that the choice of the most plausible alternative situation, and estimating its costs and benefits, are as relevant as measuring the actual costs and benefits of the operation of foreign affiliates when evaluating the specific contribution of fdi. One difficulty here, to which we shall return in the next section, is to know what are the possible alternative situations that might be pursued. Much depends on government policy, the technology of which is a subject about which little is known. Yet, constraints on the options of governments, through lack of knowledge or understanding, may vitally affect the nature of the alternative situation and hence the answer to the question: Does foreign investment pay?

A third way of approaching the specific contribution of fdi is to try and estimate the costs of obtaining the benefits provided by fdi in other ways. This essentially reduces to unbundling the package of resources supplied *in toto* by fdi and estimating both the costs of obtaining the ingredients separately and of putting them together differently. Instead of

Table 13.2 Best Guess Estimates of Selected Balance-of-Payments Return of UK and US Direct Foreign Investment in Manufacturing Industry

	Reddaway Data (UK 1956/63) % of Net Operating Assets Controlled by UK Firms Abroad		Hufbauer/Adler Data (US 1957/64) % of Total Assets Controlled by US from Abroad	
	Anti-Classical Model	Reverse Classical Model	Anti-Classical Model	Reverse Classical Model
Initial Effect				
1 Capital equipment exports	14	10	27	3
2 Immediate 'multiplier' effect[a]	na	na	2½	3
Specific Recurrent Effect				
1 Exports of parts and components	6	4½	5	1
2 Exports of finished goods (export displacement effect)	−20	−3	−51	2½
3 Trade propensity effect[b]	na	na	6	—
4 Profits and interest	7½	7½	12	12
5 Royalties, fees and services	½	½	1½	1½
6 Imports by investing country from subsidiaries	na	na	−5	−4½
	−6	9½	−31½	12½
Non-specific Recurrent Effect				
1 Sustained multiplier effect[c]	na	na	7	−3
	−6	9½	−24½	9½
Recoupment period (approximate years)	Never	8	Never	8

[a] Attempts to measure the balance-of-payments repercussions (to investing country) of an increase in income in the host country consequent upon the capital transfer (see Hufbauer and Adler, 1968, pp. 52ff).

[b] This effect acknowledges the more general trade effects which accompany any expansion of overseas sales. Under anti-classical assumptions it is simply measured by marginal propensity to import from the USA expressed as a percentage of the capital outflow (see Hufbauer and Adler, 1968, p. 47).

[c] The sustained multiplier effect estimates the multiplier effect of the continuing influence of the various specific balance-of-payments effects on income flows in the host country. For the method of calculation see Hufbauer and Adler (1968, pp. 46ff and Table 4.3).

Source: Reddaway et al. (1968) and Hufbauer and Adler (1968).

Table 13.3 Summary of Studies Relating to Employment Effects of US MNEs

Study	Type of Analysis or Source of Data	Estimate of % of Foreign Production which Could Have Been Retained in USA	Employment Effects				
			US Production Displacement	Export Stimulus	US Parent Employment	Support Firm Employment	Net Employment
Emergency Committee on American Trade	Sample Survey of 74 companies	Not precisely estimated; can be inferred to be low	Not explicitly estimated	+300,000	+250,000	Not considered	Substantially positive
Ruttenberg, AFL-CIO Study	Aggregate Official Data	Not dealt with explicitly; can be inferred to be high	500,000 jobs lost due to adverse trade movements, 1966–69, of which MNEs account for an 'important part'		Not considered	Not considered	Negative by an 'important part' of 500,000
Stobaugh and Associates	Combination of 9 Case Studies of individual investment decisions and aggregate data	Dealt with explicitly in the case studies; was low or zero in the long run in every case	Negligible	+250,000	+250,000	+100,000	+600,000
US Chamber of Commerce	Sample Survey of 158 companies	Not precisely estimated; can be inferred to be low or zero	Not explicitly estimated	+311,245 (based on net trade)	Not considered	Not considered	Positive

Source: Hawkins (1972).

capital, technology, management and entrepreneurship being supplied (and controlled) from a common source, may it not be better for a particular host nation to import capital from (say) the oil states, technology from (say) the Germans, management from (say) the USA, and combine these with indigenous public and private entrepreneurship and control? It is surprising that so little research has been done on the costs and benefits of unbundling and repackaging the package of resources provided by fdi. At one time, it was widely believed that the unique package of fdi produced special benefits over and above those which the ingredients would give if supplied separately. This may still be true in many cases, but it is now also felt that the special costs associated with fdi may exceed those of the ingredients if supplied separately. Yet countries which have expropriated the assets of foreign companies have not always found that they could subsequently import management and technology more cheaply; and that they may have underestimated the advantages of being host to part of a large integrated MNE. It is not too difficult to point to the conditions under which fdi might be an expensive way (relative to other modalities) of importing resources; for example, where high monopoly rents are earned, where there is little attempt at local integration, and where the MNE may be perpetuating a division of labour between home and host country which is not in the latter's long-term interests. But, in other situations, fdi is likely to be the most beneficial way of obtaining capital and know-how; where, for example, the intricate interrelationships between the ingredients of the package of resources confer special benefits, and where there is sufficient competition to prevent the foreign affiliate from making excessive profits. We need much more research about the particular costs and benefits associated with alternative forms of resource transfer. This is especially so as new modalities in the exchange of capital, knowledge and management are opening up.

V

So far in our argument, we have been concerned with measuring the effects of fdi and evaluating it net of what might have happened in its absence. We have considered the alternative situation primarily from an economic viewpoint; but, again, the exercise is no less relevant for appraising cultural, political, etc., impacts. How often is fdi held responsible for something which is not unique to it? Accusations about the export of certain advertising practices or of corruption may apply equally to firms exporting to the country in question or to indigenous firms.

We now come to more normative issues, namely, how best to relate the costs and benefits of fdi to the goals or strategies of host countries. To do this, it is not sufficient to assess whether fdi does promote, or is promoting, national welfare more than some alternative use of resources, though this would, indeed, be a great step forward. It is not sufficient because the actual contribution of fdi may not be the maximum it could make; while the most realistic alternative position may be constrained by lack of local resources or management expertise. To illustrate, a negative contribution by fdi to GNP might suggest that it should be reduced; but it could equally mean that fdi is not efficient, or it is extracting too high a rent from the host country. Increase efficiency and/or reduce economic rent and fdi might become highly desirable. To give another example, the most reasonable alternative situation to fdi in Japan in 1979 is very different from that open to say Peru, Nigeria or Mexico in 1979. Yet a generation ago, Japan had virtually no indigenous industry to compete with the Americans and Europeans. Now, as a result of its development and foreign investment strategy of the 1950s and 1960s, the country is able to profit from importing the ingredients of fdi through non-equity participation quite easily. In other words, a country, by its own policies, can affect its alternative position over time.

The first question prior to the formation of a policy towards (future) fdi is then: Are the benefits of existing fdi being maximised? If not, why not and what can be done about it and at what cost? Policies directed to improving the efficiency of foreign affiliates, their fuller integration with the local economy, adapting product technologies or products to better suit local resource endowments, curbing restrictive practices, for example, on exports and the transfer of technology, eliminating tax evasions by a strong policy towards transfer pricing and payment of royalties and fees, a selective encouragement of local equity participation, or gradual divestment of equity interests, ensuring that the behaviour of foreign affiliates towards employees, consumers and suppliers conforms to local customs (or if preferred, the customs of the investing country) – all these options may be implemented to increase the benefits or reduce the costs of fdi. As has been pointed out, this may be easier said than done, partly because increasing benefits in one direction may increase costs in another, and partly because if the benefits are tilted too far in favour of the host country, there is a danger that future investment might be reduced or cease altogether. The factors which determine the bargaining power of countries and companies is a subject in itself (Streeten, 1974); it is certainly difficult to make any broad generalisations, except that, assuming a range of bargaining points acceptable to both parties, much depends on the options open to the two parties.

The second normative question is the extent to which indigenous resources could be better deployed to do the job at present done by fdi. If they can, these policies should be directed to restructuring local industry, and a conscious and selective industrial development programme and/or technological strategy aimed at strengthening the capacity of indigenous firms. To give just one example, it may be that, in a particular economy, foreign owned motor car companies are more efficient than locally owned motor companies, because the latter are too numerous and far too small to employ the most efficient production techniques. Yet, because they are too small, they may not be able to finance their own rationalisation. Government support may then be needed to promote a viable industry which, ultimately, may yield a higher social benefit than fdi. This belief underlay the UK government's financial involvement in the merger between British Motors and Leyland some years ago. More successful has been the French government's investment in the modernisation of the Renault plants. In the promotion of science and technology, the problem facing economies like Portugal is even greater. Take the pharmaceutical industry again. To what extent should policy be directed to (1) encouraging foreign affiliates to undertake fabricating the processing operations, (2) encouraging them also to produce the chemical ingredients, (3) encouraging them to set up R & D laboratories, or (4) encourage local firms (sometimes under licence to foreign firms) to undertake (1)–(3). Again, the decision may not be as easy as it may seem. Certainly, it should not be taken on only technological grounds. Only by relating a micro-technological decision in the context of macro-industrial strategy and an appreciation of its effects on the total costs and benefits of fdi – with a reasoned assumption about future trends and policy – can a sensible policy be framed.

The third normative question addresses itself to alternative modes of importing resources for development. This was touched upon in the previous section. All that need be added here is that the current stock of knowledge about the options open to host countries in acquiring the resources they need is very inadequate, as, even more so, is that on the costs and benefits of these options. We might suggest similarly that MNEs are not always as aware as they should be of the benefits of forms of foreign involvement other than a 100 per cent equity holding. There is much ignorance and prejudice here, but I believe there is a general tendency for MNEs to over-value the benefits of a 100 per cent or even a controlling equity stake in their affiliates, while governments assign too high a priority to acquiring the ingredients of fdi by contractual routes. Again, a good deal more study is required on this question, even to establish broad principles of the conditions under which, and to whom, which form of international arrangement is likely to be most beneficial.[12]

This section has emphasised that it is not only what is, but also what could be, that ought to be taken into account in evaluating the costs and benefits of fdi. Besides the specific considerations outlined here, there are more general questions relating to the investment climate and government policy of the host country.

VI

We turn finally to policy towards fdi, for at the end of the day, this is what governments are seeking guidance about. The approach in this chapter has been to identify the special ingredients of fdi, pinpoint its main costs and benefits, and then compare these with both the actual and potential benefits of acquiring the same resources, or producing the same or similar output in alternative ways. Policy would then be based upon these findings. It may, however, be argued that, whatever its merits, this procedure would take too much time to give useful results, particularly where there are little or no existing data on the activities of foreign companies. Perhaps a more practical approach would be simply to design policy in such a way as to influence the behaviour of foreign affiliates in the right direction. For example, rather than commission studies to estimate the actual employment effects of fdi, should not policy be directed to ensuring that, as far as possible, fdi does advance manpower goals? Rather than evaluate the extent to which foreign affiliates do earn economic rent, should not steps be taken to minimise the possibility of rent being earned? Rather than set up an inquiry into the extent to which foreign affiliates do engage in adverse transfer pricing manipulation, should not efforts be directed to outlawing this practice? And so on.

This 'if . . . then' approach is likely to be successful when one can reasonably appraise the contribution of fdi to national goals. For example, one may be very clear that one does not wish foreigners to have an equity participation in certain industries, or to allow them to control more than a certain percentage of the output of others. It is also more likely to work where one can draw upon the experience of other countries who have already done some research on the actual costs and benefits of fdi. But it is less satisfactory in helping to formulate long-term strategy towards fdi, or of comparing its contribution to national goals with some alternative uses of resources.

In practice, all countries, explicitly or implicitly, adopt some stance towards fdi; this may range from no policy, or a *laissez-faire* approach to it, to the other extreme of completely outlawing it. Even within a country responses may differ by region (according, for example, to extent of unemployment), institutions (cf. those of trade unions, with those of suppliers to or competitors of foreign affiliates), industrial sector, nationality of investor and extent of foreign participation. It has been suggested that it is possible to identify attitudes of countries towards fdi by such variables as size, stage of development, culture, political ideology. In the past, changes in governments have induced far more dramatic changes in policy towards fdi than any action on the part of MNEs.

It is thus impossible to advise on any definitive policy for all countries to follow at all times towards fdi. Policy needs to be regularly reviewed in the light of changes in a country's goals; its capabilities to meet these goals from indigenous resources; and any changes in the actual or potential costs and benefits of fdi. This suggests the need for a regular monitoring of information about the activities of foreign affiliates, and an acceptance by government that if fdi is to make its best contribution, policies which might have been appropriate in its absence may require modification in its presence. For example, the more a country is internationally involved, the more important it is for its exchange rate and trade policy to be right. If fdi should cause the structure of industry to become more concentrated, the more reason for the government to operate an effective competition policy. The greater the involvement of foreign affiliates in technologically advanced industries, the greater the need for a well-defined source and technology policy. Observe that these are all general policies, that is, not especially directed to foreign affiliates, but which may need modification because of their presence.

When one speaks about policy towards fdi, however, one usually means policies that will specifically affect the behaviour of existing or prospective foreign investors. Yet almost all the surveys done on factors influencing fdi stress the importance of the general economic and political environment of the recipient countries. Tax incentives, tariffs, subsidies, controls on profit remittances, and insistence on local equity participation all matter, but it is the overall environment and market prospects which count in the long run. Most MNEs are risk averse; economic and political instability are risks which such companies are only prepared to undertake (if at all) if the prospective returns are higher (i.e. the benefits accruing to the host country are lower). One way for host countries to increase their share of the benefits of fdi is to create a low risk profile so that foreign firms are content with a lower rate of profit on the capital invested.

A full discussion of the gamut of specific and particular policies towards foreign affiliates which might be pursued by a host country is outside the scope of this paper.[13] But in the context of a cost/benefit exercise, they range from the provision of information to foreign investors about the objectives of host countries (such information may be general or very specific) to outright mandatory control over types of foreign firms admitted, forms of investment, the behaviour of firms once admitted and divestment procedures. In between the 'min–max' extremes are a host of policies open to governments, the appropriateness of which will vary according to circumstances and their likely effect on foreign investors. Guidelines to behaviour are one option which has been endorsed by such bodies as the International Chamber of Commerce, and more recently (with somewhat different intent) by OECD. Several countries and companies have also produced their own guidelines; essentially they are gentlemen's agreements, the success of which depends on the goodwill and co-operation of the parties concerned. One step (but an important step) removed from guidelines are Codes of Conduct, which are more binding on character, and to which sanctions are usually attached. The International Code of Conduct on the Transfer of Technology, promoted by UNCTAD, and the Code of Conduct on TNCs being considered by the Commission on Transnational Corporations (UN, 1976, 1979) are of this kind. From codes, one moves to general economic inducements or constraints, to which foreign investors may or may not respond; and then to very specific rules and regulations which foreign firms must follow, for example, with respect to proportion of equity capital of local enterprises they may own, employment of indigenous labour, import quotas, information and reporting procedures, dividend remissions, and so on. Then, finally, there are more embracing policies directed specifically to foreign companies, for example, those operated by Mexican and Indian governments.

Beyond these unilateral policies are bilateral or multilateral schemes, in which more than one government is involved. These range from a bilateral exchange of information about specific activities of MNEs, or policies adopted towards them, to multilateral treaties on international investment of the GATT variety. Most commentators believe, however, that such generalised agreements, if they ever come about, are a long way in the future. The point of mentioning them here is that multilaterial policies — between home and host or host and host or home and home governments — and the action of such bodies as UNCTAD, OECD, EEC, are likely to become more important in affecting the behaviour of foreign investors. Such a transition from unilateral to multilateral action is not without its costs to individual nation states. Though multilateral policies may increase the benefits of fdi for the participating nations considered, taken as a whole they do not ensure that each and every country will benefit from them. Indeed, in some cases the national sovereignty which countries are seeking to preserve by harmonising their actions may simply be transferred from foreign enterprises to the strongest of the group of countries framing the multilateral action.[14]

Like the fdi they are intended to influence, each of these policy options has its own particular costs and benefits. Once again, what is needed is a model or framework for evaluating such options, and some idea of the conditions under which each of the various options is most likely to be effective.

VII

For reasons stated at the outset, this chapter is not on a subject of the author's choosing. What has been set down is neither directed specifically to the Portuguese situation, nor, except in a very rough and ready sense, does it answer many of the questions which are the concern of all countries. Indeed it poses more questions than it provides answers. In the Portuguese context, when so little is known about fdi, this may not be a bad thing. What is needed by all governments is a kind of tool-kit, from which it would be possible — given the data or a reasonable estimate of same — to build a policy framework.

But the chapter does make a number of quite important general points.

If I had to pick out the most important I would choose five. First, it argues for a sectoral approach to fdi. It really is extraordinarily difficult to generalise about the costs and benefits of fdi. The contribution of foreign affiliates in the extractive industries may be completely different from that in the manufacturing and service industries. Within manufacturing, a distinction needs to be made between import-substituting and export-generating industries, and between the foreign affiliates of MNEs which pursue a global and regional strategy and those which do not. True, if it were found that, *in toto*, fdi had a negative income effect, this might suggest fdi should be restricted; but this policy could be wholly wasteful if, for example, the whole of the negative effect was explained by the behaviour of (say) one large petroleum firm.

Second, arguments have been presented against a series of problem-oriented policy measures towards fdi. The contribution of foreign firms must be looked at as a whole, once one's criteria for evaluating their contribution, with all their implicit trade-offs, have been established. Even if fdi does little to contribute towards a country's technological goals, it does not follow that policies should be implemented to bring this about. For it may be that this can only be accomplished at the expense of the employment and other goals, and, in the end, the country may be worse off than before. There is an interdependence between costs and benefits which requires a macro approach to their evaluation.

Third, it has been stressed that the results of fdi are determined as much by general host government policy and the local economic environment as anything to do with the behaviour of the foreign firms. Once a substantial foreign owned sector exists, governments have a responsibility to reappraise policies implemented in the absence of foreign investment to see whether they are still appropriate. This, of course, governments do not look favourably upon. It is much easier (if not always in the best interests of national welfare) to force the foreign firm to mould itself to existing policies, rather than change the policies so that it can make the best possible contributions. To give an example: if a balance-of-payments deficit appears to be associated with fdi it is tempting to force foreign firms to reduce their investments or to operate in such a way as to eliminate the deficit. But the end result may be a fall in lva. A more sensible reaction might be to try and eliminate the deficit by other means, for example, a change in the exchange rate, or a reduction in the activity of firms which contribute less to lva.

The fourth point is that governments, while evaluating alternative routes of obtaining the benefits of fdi, should not presuppose these routes are necessarily preferable. Many a government has nationalised a foreign investment with the expectancy of getting rid of the control exercised by the foreign investor, only to find that the heart of control was not in the possession of equity capital but of technology, which it had not relinquished. The coming years are likely to witness many new forms of international involvement, and governments seeking to formulate policies should very much be aware of these.

A final point concerns negotiating procedures. There is still a very large gap of understanding between governments and enterprises over the goals each is legitimately seeking to pursue, as there is also over the extent to which fdi can advance these goals. This is especially evident once one moves away from the purely economic consequences (as traditionally conceived) to consider social and cultural effects, where goals and values between investing companies and recipient countries may diverge even more. So often one finds that politicians and businessmen are either not talking about the same thing or disagree with each other because their perceptions are different. Admittedly, some value systems of developing countries have only been consciously identified as a result of fdi, which, if it has done nothing else, has helped them know what they do not want. All too easily, it has been assumed either that fdi has no real impact on the social and cultural habitat of recipient nations or that it is good for them to be inculcated with the economic ethic and aspirations of the home country. But, in many cases, it is clear that fdi has been a conduit of a way of life, which, for perfectly good reasons, recipient countries do not necessarily wish to embrace. No one enterprise is to blame for this, but the fact remains that it might not have occurred, or occurred to the same extent, in the absence of fdi. On the other hand, host countries do not always appreciate the intricacies of the kind of global set-up which may give fdi the very advantages which are sought by it; and to force it to behave like a local firm might rob the MNE of its distinctive contribution. Clearly, the concerns of host countries are not of the same order as those of the MNEs, and there is much to be learned by both parties before full headway can be made on harnessing the benefits of fdi to advance economic and social welfare.

Notes: Chapter 13

1   For further details see UNCTC (1978).
2   It is our belief that this kind of information may be more important for host countries to obtain in the future as the activities of MNEs become increasingly integrated.
3   One suggestion here is for government appointed representatives to be in attendance at the board meetings of affiliates.
4   Other kinds of data include those relating to the activities of MNEs in other countries, including the terms of contracts made.
5   For a discussion of evaluating international projects from a firm's viewpoint see Lessard (1979).
6   Note that even maximising lva does not imply that foreign affiliates should be encouraged to buy from local firms, where it is cheaper to import the inputs and to use the resources saved to produce other goods.
7   Although, in the end, the host country may be better off than if decisions were taken independently in the interests of each affiliate.

8 For a summary of some of the more significant of these, see Moxon (1979).
9 For further details see Dunning, Burstall and Lake (1981).
10 See Chapter 8.
11 See Chapter 9.
12 A subject to which the OECD Development Centre is currently (September 1980) devoting some attention. See Oman (1980).
13 For a description of these, see UN (1978) and Hawkins and Walter (1979).
14 See Chapter 14.

References

Abdel-Malek, T. (1974), 'Foreign ownership and export performance', *Journal of International Business Studies*, vol. V (Fall).

Behrman, J., and Fischer, W. A. (1980), *Overseas R and D Activities of Transnational Corporations* (Cambridge, Mass.: Oelgeschlager, Gunn and Hain).

Bos, H. C., Saunders, M., and Secchi, C. (1974), *Private Foreign Investment in Developing Countries. A Quantitative Study on the Evaluation of Macro-Economic Effects*, International Studies in Economics and Econometrics, Vol. 1 (Boston: Reidil).

Cohen, N. I. (1975), *Multinational Firms and Asian Exports* (New Haven, Conn. and London: Yale University Press).

Dunning, J. H. (1977), *UK Transnational Enterprises in Manufacturing and Resource Based Industries and Trade Flows of Developing Countries*, UNCTAD/ST/MD 18 (Geneva: UNCTAD).

Dunning, J. H., Burstall, M., and Lake, A. (1981), *The impact of MNEs on the Technological and Scientific Capacities of OECD Countries: The Pharmaceutical Industry* (Paris: OECD).

Hawkins, R. (1972), *Job Displacement and the Multinational Firm: A Methodological Review*, Occasional Paper No. 3 (Washington, DC: Centre for Multinational Studies).

Hawkins, R., and Walter, I. (1979), *Multinational Corporations: Current Trends and Future Prospects*, New York University Graduate School of Business Administration, Working Paper No. 79-110 (November).

Hufbauer, G. C., and Adler, F. M. (1968), *US Manufacturing Investment and Balance of Payments*, Tax Policy Research Study No. 1 (Washington, DC: US Treasury Department).

Lessard, D. R. (ed.) (1979), *International Financial Management* (New York: Warren, Gorham and Lamont).

Little, I. M. D., and Mirrlees, J. A. (1974), *Project Appraisal and Planning for Developing Countries* (London: Heinemann).

Moxon, R. W. (1979), 'The costs, conditions and adaptation of MNC technology in developing countries', in R. G. Hawkins (ed.), *The Economic Effects of Multinational Corporations* (Greenwich, Conn.: JAI Press).

Oman, C. (1980), *Changing International Investment Strategies: The 'New Forms' of Investment in Developing Countries*, mimeo (Paris: OECD Development Centre).

Perrakis, C. I. (1977), 'Output, balance of payments and employment effects of private foreign investment in developing countries: an empirical evaluation of the effects of private foreign investment in the manufacturing sector of Southern Europe, Greece, Spain and Turkey', PhD thesis, University of Reading.

Reddaway, W. B., Potter, S. J., and Taylor, C. T. (1968), *Effects of UK Direct Investment Overseas, Interim Report (1967) and Final Report*, Cambridge Department of Applied Economics (Cambridge: Cambridge University Press).

Steuer, M. D., Abell, A., Gennard, J., Perlman, M., Rees, R., Scott, B., and Wallis, K. (1973), *The Impact of Foreign Direct Investment on the United Kingdom*, Department of Trade and Industry (London: HMSO).

Streeten, P. P., and Lall, S. (1973), *Summary of Methods and Findings of a Study of Private Foreign Manufacturing Investment in Six Less-Developed Countries* (in three parts) 1. *Methodology Used in Studies on Private Foreign Investment in Selected Developing Countries*, Document No. TD/B/3 (VI) Misc.6. 2. *Some Reflections on Government Policies Concerning Private Foreign Investment*, Document No. TD/B/C.3(VI)/Misc.7. 3. *Main Findings of a Study of Private Foreign Investment in Selected Developing Countries*, Document No. TD/B/C.3/111 (Geneva: UNCTAD).

Streeten, P. P. (1974), in J. H. Dunning (ed.), *Economic Analysis and the Multinational Enterprise* (London: Allen & Unwin).

UN (1976), *Transnational Corporations: Issues involved in the formulation of a Code of Conduct*, Economic and Social Council E/C 10/17 July (New York: UN).

UN (1978), *National Legislation and Regulations Relating to Transnational Corporations*, Sales No. E 78 II A3 (New York: UN).

UNCTC (1979), 'The code of conduct: latest progress', *CTC Reporter*, vol. 1, no. 6 (April).

Vaitsos, C. V. (1976), 'Power, knowledge and development policy: relations between transnational enterprises and developing countries', in G. K. Helleiner (ed.), *A World Divided* (Cambridge: Cambridge University Press).

14
Alternative Policy Prescriptions and the Multinational Enterprise

I

The dynamism of international economic relations has been vividly evidenced by global events of recent years. The changing roles of the main actors on the world stage has meant that the assumptions underlying their influence and behaviour, as conceived even in the late 1960s, are no longer appropriate for predicting the course of economic events in the 1980s. But, because of time lags, both in perceiving these changes and in adapting policy to them, the actions of politicians and government officials may well have effects very different from those that they had originally intended.

We make this preliminary observation because, although the focus of this chapter is on policies of host countries towards multinational enterprise (MNE), such discussions must be set within a particular frame of reference. The MNE is only one agent (albeit the main one) of international production which, in turn, is only one form of international economic involvement. Until the early 1960s, foreign direct investment, especially in its classical form, was generally welcomed and even encouraged. More important, the global scenario for such investment was one which assumed the virtues of economic interdependence and favoured the relative *status quo* of the main participants (Keohane and Nye, 1974). It was a world of bipolar systems, American hegemony, trade and monetary liberalisation and Keynesian economic dogma. These were features largely accepted by countries outside the Communist bloc, although such compliance on the part of the developing nations was often more by necessity than by choice.

As the international economic order has been increasingly questioned, so too has the MNE — a major product of that order — both as to its impact on international relations and its contribution to the welfare of individual nation states. Moreover, there is a growing appreciation for the need to evaluate the activities of MNEs. For, in the last resort, it is in the area of political perceptions that economic costs and benefits of not only this phenomenon, but of all international economic involvement must be assessed.

This chapter (co-authored by M. Gilman) was first published in G. Curzon (ed.), *The Multinational Enterprise in a Hostile World* (London: Macmillan, 1976).

There can be little doubt of the profound change in the postwar *status quo* that took place in the world economy in the early 1970s. Sparked off by the ending of fixed exchange rates in 1971 and the quadrupling of oil prices in 1973 and 1974, and encouraged by various factions, for example, the environmental lobby, not only is growth of output for its own sake being questioned, particularly in the developed nations, but the international distribution of the output – and the inputs which make it possible – both within countries and between countries, is being seriously challenged. With hindsight, it was unrealistic to have expected the developing nations to remain servile to the economic dominance of the Northern Hemisphere. Most of these nations, politically independent since the Second World War, now have trained, nationally-oriented, and often ambitious elites who have the education and ability to manage their own affairs. After years of interregional rivalries, they have become more united, at least in their dealings with the industrial world. This unity has been fostered, in part, by the increasing need for energy and raw materials found primarily in the developing nations. Rapid improvements in transportation and communications, as well as participation in such organisations as the UN and UNCTAD and OPEC, have helped nations to open new lines of exchange which have promoted a feeling of common cause. This greater dissemination of information, in itself, has helped to improve the self-consciousness and the bargaining power of the developing world.

Differences between the developing nations have increased over time, and they can no longer be classified as a homogeneous group. The oil producers, with their vast and rapidly accumulating wealth, are in a class by themselves. Nations such as Mexico, Brazil and Korea, with their diversified industries and indigenous resources, can hardly be compared economically to the African countries of Chad and Ethiopia, or to the poorer nations of southern Asia. The small island economics like Fiji, the Seychelles and the Dominican Republic whose prosperity is subtantially linked to tourism, and the offshore manufacturing bases like Taiwan, Hong Kong and Singapore, have particularly individual problems of 'dependencia'. Perceptions, the degree of involvement in the world economy, and leverage in international bargaining vary as much within the developing world as between it and the industrial nations. One example of this is the extent to which the origins of international direct investment have diversified in recent years. From being of largely Anglo-American origin, MNEs have now become more broadly based, and we are beginning to see direct investment emerging from the capital-rich but technology-poor oil nations and the more advanced industrialising developing countries. In addition, the socialist nations are participating increasingly in international trade and investment, adding to the diversity and complexity of economic relations. In the 1980s, it is probable that there will be many more state-owned MNEs emerging from both East and West.[1]

A final change of paramount significance has been the changing role of the USA in world economic affairs and the international monetary and commercial order. The fixed exchange rate system no longer exists, and capital flows have been subject to a host of unilateral controls. The non-discriminatory free trade stance espoused by the USA within the GATT has lost support, even within the USA. Although still a powerful influence, the relative weight of the USA in world trade and investment has declined steadily while the economic impact of Japan and the EEC is increasing, even in areas of advanced technology. No less significant is the withdrawal of US moral commitments to maintain institutions which are no longer seen to serve its more narrowly defined national interests (Behrman, 1974a).

The US retrenchment is symptomatic of the generally more inward-looking, nationalistic response on the part of most nations as the ground rules underlying the international economic order have changed. The field has been left open for a redistribution of the means of production and exchange as each nation is consciously striving to protect its own needs and welfare (Bergsten, 1974). This consciousness of limited space and re-sources – most powerfully demonstrated in the context of energy – while long recognised by individual nation states, has never been viewed from a global perspective. Given that the world is a constrained and limited en-vironment, new tactics are evolving as the outer limits in space and re-sources are attained. Foremost among these is the increasing desire of nations for political and cultural identity, which is thought best achieved through economic autarky rather than economic interdependence. Within this context, and specifically with regard to MNEs, countries have become more ethnocentric in their approach, although movements towards regional integration and, on certain specific issues, multilateralism suggest a con-trolled geocentric outlook (Perlmutter, 1972).

This is the scenario of the international environment in which any current analysis of foreign direct investment and the MNE must take place. In this chapter we will examine several possible forms of evolution of the MNE/nation state relationship, and the interaction between the MNEs and the countries in which they invest. Our task will be to analyse the options that host countries have in order to realise maximum benefits from fdi, and the limitations of their options in this respect.

II

Foreign direct investment is hardly a new phenomenon. The classic example of a national company expanding overseas to secure supplies of raw ma-terials, in most cases exported back to the home country, or to develop local markets for home country exports, dates back over two hundred years. The contribution and costs of such investments in terms of employ-ment, capital and trade to the host nations are readily identifiable and can usually be anticipated by the participating parties. Another rather flexible and polycentric agent of direct investment, the international holding company, is also well known but, as the behavioural patterns of such companies in host countries tend to be very similar to those of indigenous firms, their political ramifications are muted (Behrman, 1974b).

International production as an important form of international economic involvement is of fairly recent origin, and that undertaken by enterprises which deliberately coordinate their operations (purchasing, production, finance, R & D, marketing) on a global basis to make the most efficient use of their resources (material, financial, technical and managerial) is still more the exception than the rule. Even on the eve of the Second World War, the value of international production was only one-third that of international trade. In the mid-1950s and 1960s the growth of such production outpaced that of trade, and, in spite of trade liberalisation and rising oil prices, by 1976 it had exceeded that of trade. As the main vehicle of international production, the MNE views (or would prefer to view) the countries in which it operates as one market, ignoring (except where it is forced to do otherwise) the frontiers of nation states. Viewed from this aspect, it performs the same function as international trade, but uses factor flows as well as product flows. However, the economic dimensions of MNEs far outclass those of firms engaged exclusively in trade, and they affect the economic well-being, to some degree, of most states. At the same time, they are largely motivated by private interests, being economic agents in pursuit of profits and growth, even though their effects permeate many other spheres. With the exception of where states are themselves involved in international production, there is no motivation internal to MNEs save goodwill (which should not be underestimated) to have regard to the social implications of their policies.

The real significance of the MNEs involved so intricately in international economic relations derives from the fact that they combine, in a single directing body, an efficient and powerful concentration of financial means, technological know-how and distribution expertise. They have a mobility which is sometimes perceived as an advantage, and sometimes a threat, to the countries in which they operate and to the interests which are at stake. They are the ones who decide, given no outside interference, the manner in which the gains from their activities will be distributed, whether they derive from the exploitation of new technologies or management skills or from the organisation of a worldwide marketing system. This ability to influence the international distribution of resources constitutes a significant modification to the inherited economic power structure and clashes with ideas of national autonomy. Abuses do occur and, when known, have received wide publicity. But it is important to recognise that the problem is an endemic one which would exist with its inevitable tensions and conflicts of interests even if there were no abuses. It is also worth mentioning that similar problems arise from other forms of economic interdependence.

Host country governments generally adopt a schizophrenic attitude towards MNEs (Rubin, 1971). On the one hand, they want to enjoy the benefits of knowledge, capital, entrepreneurship, management skills and economies of scale which can be provided by them (and sometimes only by them); on the other, they do not want to accept the costs involved, particularly those that may erode their political or economic sovereignty. The foreign investment is wanted but not the foreign investor. This clash is most apparent between the developing nations and the MNEs of the developed countries, where the goals of the two participants are most openly in conflict. Yet, ironically, it is the developing countries that most need the resources which are concentrated in the hands of the MNEs.

As the international economic order is being reshaped, we might expect that the role of foreign direct investment and the MNE will change. Before enlarging upon this, however, it may be helpful to take a historical perspective of the world economy, starting at a time when international trade in products was the main form of exchange, free trade was espoused for reasons of efficiency, and the world economy was dominated by a few key countries.

During the retrenchment of the interwar period, suspicion and autarky grew as each country pursued national policies to safeguard domestic priorities. Trade barriers were erected to insulate each nation from the economic perturbations of the rest of the world. Elsewhere a parallel has been drawn between the evolution of trade as a major vehicle of international economic involvement and that of foreign direct investment. As the importance of import controls and other beggar-my-neighbour policies came after a long period of relatively free trade, so the growing suspicion of and occasional hostility to MNEs since the mid-1960s follows an era in which direct investment was largely seen as being a positive benefit with few costs for both home and host countries. Just as the GATT and the IMF were set up in response to the havoc in international commercial and monetary relations during the interwar period, so now a multilateral machinery for direct investment is being talked about for the future.[2]

Given the postwar trends in international production, on the one hand, and the changing attitudes of nation states (and sectors within nation states) to MNEs, on the other, we believe that any analysis of the consequences of direct investment on the welfare of individual countries must proceed along new lines and within a more general framework than has so far been incorporated in most studies on the subject. Nation states are increasingly reluctant to accept the allocation of resources decided upon by the MNE, especially considering the growing preponderance of government and state planning (and trading) even in the Western industrialised nations.

The primary concern of this chapter is to bring a general conceptual treatment to the relationship between the MNEs and their host countries. Heretofore, with a few exceptions, the subject has been treated in a partial or strictly descriptive manner which, given the complexity and integrative features of the subject, has been analytically unwieldy. At the same time, there have been increasing demands from businessmen to establish secure and consistent ground rules for the framework of international production, and from governments for supervision and/or regulation of MNEs.

The scope of the problems and the consequent solutions will, in part, depend upon the unit of analysis that is chosen. The objectives and instruments of the host country will differ from that of a home country or from one that is both; the state of development, the culture and political philosophy of nation states will influence both their goals and the means of achieving them. One can, in turn, analyse the situation from a purely national, regional, global, neoclassical or corporate point of view. Just as the assumptions chosen in an analysis will influence the results, so in this case the perspective assumed will dictate the solutions in terms of the form and degree of regulation of the MNE. Another and perhaps simpler way of looking at this approach is to ask *whose* interests are to be furthered by foreign direct investment.

In many cases, it is unclear whether the perceived conflicts result from the 'multinationality' of these firms or from the fact that they are foreign and, more often than not, big, private, Western, efficient (thus challenging local monopolists) and oligopolistic. Certainly there are ways in which MNEs differ from indigenous firms, such as their ability to realise profits on a global basis even if this procedure results in a loss in any particular market. But many of the perceived differences, such as the exploitation of economies of scale in both human and non-human capital, are more a question of degree than of kind. Nor is it obvious in the literature, much less in the real world, what are the specific attributes of the MNE that are at the root of the concern about them. The problem here seems to be that, just as nation states have different characteristics and methods of attaining national goals, so too MNEs are very heterogeneous. They vary in age, size, reputation, structure, origin, ownership, geographical distribution, management philosophy and type of operation. To lump all these firms into a notional, and possibly erroneous, idea may not advance the analysis unless genuinely common characteristics which apply to the problem at hand can be isolated.

The time framework is no less important. Some of the present tensions between MNEs and nation states are transitory or will fade in importance, while others may prove more intractable; still others may not yet exist. However, since actions taken in the present affect the future, the short-run costs and benefits of certain policies must be weighed against the long-run consequences. There arise the questions of trade-offs and priorities which are too often ignored in policy making by governments and firms. A government's perception of this time continuum will also depend upon its decision-taking horizon and attitudes towards the future scenario of events. For example, is the power of the MNE likely to be an effective challenge to the sovereignty of nation states, dominating production and trade of the free world by 1985, outside the realm of control by governments? Or is it in a state of evolution and adaptation, amenable to both unilateral and multilateral measures which will alter its nature in the coming years? Or are the seeds of its own decline now being sown? These perceptions of the future international order will be crucial when defining the extent and solutions of the problems.

Even if one chooses to regard foreign direct investment from the perspective of the host country, there is the difficulty of establishing a set of goal variables which are applicable to all nation states. Most governments desire to remain in power, but each will choose its own policies towards the attainment of its objectives. Even with no change in government, they may not be consistent in their priorities through time: they may simultaneously seek to achieve possibly conflicting economic, political and social goals with little or no idea of the trade-offs and/or complementarities involved. Perhaps even more important is the need to specify one's assumptions as to the objectives of the home country governments and of the firms themselves. In this framework, other participants in the international economy, such as international organisations and non-government bodies (unions, consumer associations), should also be included.

III

The solutions to the problems posed by MNEs that suggest themselves to the host country are equally diverse. A possible list of solutions might include: do nothing, accepting the resource-allocative pattern decided upon by the MNE; limit the MNE's field of activity or degree or form of its participation; regulate its conditions of operation; nationalise its affiliates; create or strengthen countervailing power to the MNE; enhance national bargaining position *vis-à-vis* the MNE; promote the creation of intergovernmental rules of conduct and multilateral policies; promote the creation or strengthening of machinery to provide technical expertise to host countries in their dealings with the MNE; encourage the incorporation of MNEs under international laws and taxation; reject the MNE altogether. Different countries will respond to the same perceived problems in various ways.

On a small, increasingly interdependent planet, the decisions of any one participant in the world economy will inevitably affect to some degree the economic welfare of the others. The (international) social responsibility that this implies has so far been lacking in an analysis of the problems, although there is a growing body of opinion that co-ordination is necessary. Applied to foreign direct investment, it may be that what is needed is not so much a general code of behaviour or rules (which are difficult to apply) as machinery to bring the participants together to work out common solutions on such specific issues as technology transfer, ownership, taxation, transfer pricing, employment, and so on.

The problem of the MNE and its relations with host countries must be observed, analysed and debated in its totality. A recognition of this need is the first premise on which the future institutional arrangements should be based. But asserting that the problems are complex and should be dealt with in their entirety removes the possibility of positive simple and straightforward solutions. The complicated interrelationships implied by the operations of the MNE will merit an equally complex and thorough response. This means, of course, that quantifying or even estimating orders of magnitude of the costs and benefits of foreign direct investment may not be possible when observed within a general systems framework. At best, the directions of the trade-offs and complementarities may emerge, but we believe this is preferable to more specific, partial and possibly inaccurate decision rules.

Adopting a host country orientation, it has been suggested that there are several strategies which might be adopted for maximising the net benefits of MNEs. We shall now consider three of these: (1) allow the MNEs to decide on the level and pattern of international production; (2) control or influence such decisions by unilateral policies; and (3) control or influence such decisions by supranational solutions.

(a)   *Free international production*

We have seen that attitudes towards trade have evolved through several distinct stages: from free trade to modified free trade with intervention, to autarky, and then to bilateral and multilateral agreements and institutions. The first of these phases was brief, and the honeymoon period of unrestrained international production has been equally so. Even assuming no imperfections, it is questionable if free international production, as with free trade, could ever optimise each country's economic welfare (Kindleberger, 1974). Observe, for example, the likely consequences for the international distribution of income if the location of production were based on decisions taken by MNEs. Global output might be maximised but a country poor in factors and in markets might easily find its real income to be lower. Externalities, such as pollution resulting from production in one country, may adversely affect the welfare of the population in a neighbouring country, yet these would not normally be considered by firms in their allocative decisions.

Both of the above examples can be observed at the regional level within a country but, in this case, the national government can compensate for any adverse effects of national firms by the use of fiscal policies, such as taxing polluters to equalise private and social costs and by the redistribution of income through transfers. There is no such compensatory mechanism available at an international level, nor to our knowledge has any such mechanism been seriously considered, even on a limited scale. Moreover, the distribution of production and trade based on factor endowments is no longer accepted by most countries as they realise that, over time, they can alter their comparative advantage through such vehicles as the MNE. Whereas governments have the necessary instruments to pursue their allocative goals within their borders, there is no such supranational mechanism to effect compensation and redistribution between countries.

In practice, there are many other imperfections which would prevent free international production from optimising economic welfare in each country. Foremost among these are market structures in which MNEs operate. As oligopolists, especially in the resource based and advanced-technology industries, the larger and more integrated MNEs may influence the kind of products produced or processes engaged in in such a way that production and distribution will not be socially optimal. The growth and spread of the MNEs has generally had an integrative effect on the world economy and within regional groupings, but where this has come about through takeovers of indigenous firms and through the exploitation of pseudo-economies of internalisation (Kojima, 1978), the result has sometimes been to restrict rather than advance competition.[3]

At the same time, MNEs themselves operate in an imperfectly structured macro environment which causes their responses to be less than optimal. These distortions arise from national policies designed to achieve goals inconsistent with each other, such as differential tax policies, trade barriers, capital controls and fixed exchange rates. It is important to distinguish between these two types of imperfections. The former are reflections of market failure, well-known in discussions of microeconomic theory, resulting from the fact that knowledge is neither free nor perfect, other resources are neither homogeneous nor perfectly mobile, and the hierarchical decisions of companies do not necessarily promote the best kind of economic interdependence between countries.[4] The latter are geared to meet different national goals and can be altered to adapt to changing circumstances as regards a country's international involvement. Thus, as in the EEC, market imperfections may have been reduced by the opening of national frontiers, but little has been accomplished in terms of policy imperfections as such policies are still oriented towards essentially national goals.

A moment's thought suggests that for free international production to be acceptable (as set out in the Appendix to this chapter) as a means for advancing economic welfare in host countries, it would require wholesale changes in the international economic order. Such changes are neither realistic nor politically feasible. The implications of this solution would involve, among others, a large sacrifice of sovereignty and a much greater mobility of labour and other factors across national boundaries if unemployment or serious distortions in wage structure are to be avoided. What, then, are the alternatives?

One is to accept a second-best solution (or it may be *the* best, practically speaking) by allowing the MNEs free rein in the real world, even with their inherent imperfections. Few, if any, nation states are poised politically to think in these terms. Another possibility is to remove the imperfections surrounding the operations of MNEs so as to create as free a market as is feasible. Again, in practice, this may not be possible; controls would have to be introduced to simulate a free market (monopolies regulation, business practice codes and credit controls). All of these measures are modifications to the basic principle of free international production.

(b)   *Unilateral policies*

The second means of dealing with international production is by unilateral policy. The opposite extreme of free international allocation of resources is national autarky whereby a country would only engage in the minimum amount of international commerce and, where possible, via international trade (in goods and knowledge) rather than by international production. However, in doing so, it will face natural constraints if its economic goals are not compatible with its resources, skills, size, wealth and population. Some countries, such as China, Russia or the USA, may be able to achieve a higher degree of self-sufficiency than others. Europe, *vis-à-vis* the rest of the world, is better placed to achieve self-sufficiency than either the UK or France alone. If each country pursued the goal of maximising its sovereignty through economic isolation, then global economic growth and the efficient use of the world's limited resources would be impossible. National autarky implies no international division of labour and therefore no benefits of specialisation. Each country would rely upon its own factors to produce its requirements, and world gross product would be lower (although some countries might possibly gain at the expense of others). Such autonomy may be worth the economic costs involved where a government values its culture and narrowly defined political aspirations more than growth of output, wealth and a higher material (probably Western) standard of living.

Moving away from complete isolationism, countries must decide how internationally involved they need to be to satisfy their economic goals (implying that there will be a trade-off between economic and non-economic goals). The concern here, however, is not with the classic problem of why countries trade, but to what degree they should accept inward direct investment. A nation may engage in international trade while restricting or excluding international production via direct investment. Japan, until the end of the 1960s, was a classic example. This policy appears to have been successful while Japanese firms were growing rapidly, meeting the buoyant demand of the home market while expanding exports and importing a substantial part of their raw materials. After reaching a certain point of market expansion (and saturation), it became costlier to move goods than factors, so Japanese firms began to expand overseas to profit from lower factor costs and to assure supplies, while foreign investment in Japan could supply cheaper goods than indigenous firms. Countries which pursue this type of restrictionist policy will obviously carefully control inward and outward investment, and also the behaviour of foreign affiliates; they may reject the MNE altogether or impose stringent conditions on its operations. These restrictions are not, however, without their costs as the MNEs react in terms of the amount, direction and quality of their involvement to the measures.

If a nation desires to be less dependent on external forces of decision taking, it must decide upon the degree of international involvement that is acceptable. For it is as much the degree as the form of international involvement that determines the amount of control by foreign affiliates over domestic resources. This will even apply, at least in the short run, to countries which contract out individual components of the MNEs package (such as know-how or patents), especially in highly advanced and rapidly changing technologies. Host countries can take, and have taken, a range of unilateral measures to regulate the affiliates of MNEs in their territory but, as their actions affect only a part of a global system, many of these appear to be inadequate. It should be possible to identify the conditions under which unilateral measures of control are likely to prove successful. Some of these are illustrated in the Appendix.

(c) *Supranational solutions*

A third option open to governments in their treatment of the MNE is the regionalisation or internationalisation of decision taking. From the perspective of the host country, the attractions of this approach stem from the failure of unilateralism to accomplish what is wanted without sacrificing the benefits of international production, whereas the first alternative, that of modified control of the MNE is still too expensive in terms of erosion of sovereignty. The types of MNE/nation state interaction likely to make this type of solution workable are set out in the Appendix.

Clearly, the purpose of supranational action (bilateral and multilateral) can only be achieved by some harmonisation of policies between nation states. This becomes necessary because the repercussions of unilateral policies, both on the MNE and on other nation states, may prompt reactions which can nullify the benefits of such policies. As already observed, an inescapable fact of life on an interdependent planet is that actions taken by any one participant will affect the well-being of the others. Thus there is an effective feedback mechanism which should not be ignored when a host government considers potential policies towards the MNE.

The actors in the international economic setting are often oligopolists (countries controlling vital materials or firms with unique products and skills) or oligopsonists (countries bidding for inward investment or firms dominating a factor market), and MNEs are often more response-elastic than indigenous firms with respect to policies taken to affect their behaviour, if not in the short run then certainly in the long run. This implies that the total response of the MNE must be examined over the appropriate time period. Measures designed to regulate MNEs in one field might serve to accomplish certain objectives but only at the expense of others. For example, a policy designed to prohibit the allocation of export markets might reduce the flow of new technology. Similarly, the reactions of other countries must be considered when policies are introduced which affect dividend repatriation, export controls, investment requirements and the balance of payments, where the goals of home countries are as much affected by host country actions as are those of the MNEs. The treatment of the MNE in its totality requires this incorporation of the goals and behaviour of all the participants in the international economic setting. For, in the end, what we are talking about is the distribution of welfare between people in different countries rather than that between governments or institutions.

The move towards a supranational or multilateral approach to international production stems first from the inadequacy of individual governments, whether they pursue a relatively *laissez-faire* or isolationist policy, to maximise the net benefits flowing from inward direct investment. Second, it stems from the fear that, as with trade in the interwar period, unilateral policies of a beggar-my-neighbour type will, be self-defeating. Under certain conditions, however, host governments can take action to increase their net benefits without inviting an offsetting response. Wherever there is a rent being earned by the MNE (which can take the form of profits above opportunity cost, management slack, inefficiency, and so on) then, by appropriate policies, the host country may gain without affecting the behaviour of the MNE. But the point at which such policies will provoke a response is difficult to discern, as it is possible that the firm is not maximising its profits in the first place. Moreover, it may try to protect existing profits, even if these are above those which it could earn elsewhere, by resorting to other devices such as transfer pricing and the use of leads and lags in intra-group transactions.

IV

In order to evaluate which of these alternative courses of action will best suit the need of particular host countries, it is important to establish the leeway that governments have in policy implementation that affects the behaviour of the MNE or of all firms in its territory. This requires a look at the MNE (or its affiliates), at how it differs from the indigenous firm and its objectives, all within a simple theory of foreign direct investment.

We have seen that the MNE is a means for the international dissemination of factors and output, especially if it is free from outside interference. Normally it will allocate its production and sales so as to maximise its global returns in the long run. We now consider the proposition that the MNE (or its affiliate) is more return- (response-) elastic than its indigenous

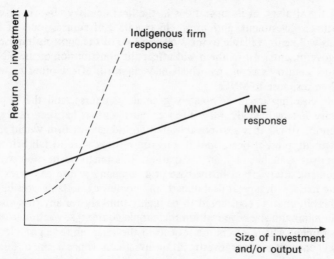

Figure 14.1

competitors. Within a marginal costing framework, any measure taken by the government that alters the relationship between marginal cost and revenue will provoke a compensating response on the part of a profit-maximising firm. Its response or reaction to changes in costs or risk changes, reflected by a change in its return on investment, will be greater in terms of its investment and/or output behaviour than that of an indigenous producer because it deploys more alternatives for investing its resources (managerial, financial and technical), as illustrated in Figure 14.1.

The response—investment (and/or output) curve for the native producer will be fairly inelastic for several reasons. If all of its investment is local, especially in plant and equipment or goodwill, it is a captive firm in that location; viewing its investment as a sunk cost, it will realise whatever profit it can. An MNE, on the other hand, will have its operations spread over several markets and, in consequence, will be less captive in any particular one. Likewise, at little cost, the MNE has more information about the alternatives at its disposal simply because of its international diversification of interests. This same information may be costly for a domestic firm to acquire (if there is a market for such knowledge external to that firm).

Attitudes of managers and owners will also be important. Within the MNE, owners will be less concerned with the source of their income while the managers may be more footloose or indifferent as to their location than in a purely domestic firm. In particular, the MNE is likely to have more behavioural options for reacting to policies which will increase its costs or risks. These include intra-group pricing, dividend remission, external financing, export allocation, source of inputs, the location of new investment, the strategy of its operations in the host country *vis-à-vis* its world operations, divestment, and so on. In practice, of course, some of these options will be unavailable to the MNE because of the controls imposed by host governments. All of them will affect the contribution of the MNE to the host country's economy which may, in turn, affect other countries and their response to MNEs.

This classification is completely general, of course, and the response elasticity between MNEs may differ as much as that between MNEs and indigenous firms. It is also possible that an indigenous firm would rather divest in its present operations if long-run returns were to fall below the alternatives available to it in the market. This might occur even without government intervention in the case of a company whose patent expires, finding itself with a great deal of cash and no new exploitable possibilities; but this situation is considered to be highly unlikely for any firm above a certain minimum size. Even within this simple context, any action taken by a government which lowers the returns in the long run for a given level of risk will encourage lower investment or divestment (once again, in the long run), with MNEs being more responsive than domestic producers.

It should be possible to classify MNEs according to the degree of flexibility of their options, based upon variables such as industry, size, strategy, age and ownership.[5] Certainly a partial takeover by a German steel firm of a French company in order to rationalise operations within the European steel industry is difficult to compare with an IBM or ITT type of investment. Likewise, countries could be categorised by their ability to control the operations of affiliates by unilateral measures.

Using a very simple theory of direct investment, a foreign involvement continuum could be constructed for any particular firm ranging from no foreign involvement (a domestic firm) to integrated international production of the IBM or Philips type, as a function of the returns which might be earned on assets invested, including non-financial assets. Especially in advanced-technology industries there would appear to be a correlation between the returns to the specialised knowledge of the firm and its form and degree of foreign involvement. For example, the greater its stock of knowledge, its degree of market power, and the indivisibilities in the commercialisation of the knowledge, the more likely the firm is to wish to internalise the sale of knowledge downstream within the enterprise. A firm will then produce abroad rather than export because its returns will be higher in the long run. This is illustrated in Figure 14.2.

It can be seen that the curve is not continuous because of the minimum capital requirements (human and non-human) needed to advance from one level of operations to another (although this may not be too significant at earlier stages of the continuum where resource requirements are lowest, which is why most firms keep their form of international involvement modest; in fact, most firms are completely domestic, with no foreign involvement whatsoever). These steps are important in themselves; they

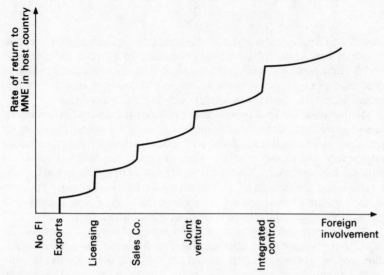

Figure 14.2

indicate the degree of captivity of the firm in that particular country, and thereby the degree to which the host government can raise the cost of doing business within its borders (either of the MNE or of all firms). The government can transfer to itself potential profits of the MNE by raising the costs of its operations to the point where the returns to the firm on the higher step would equal those on the lower step (which involves lower risk and resource requirements). Any further transfer would provoke a major change in its operations and/or investment. Furthermore, this response elasticity need not mean that reactions follow as the government always intends. For example, an increase in selective credit controls might have less effect on investment by affiliates than by indigenous firms because their options to obtain foreign finance are greater.

The length of the steps will be determined by the size of the market in relation to the MNE's global markets, its dependence on factors or raw materials, the size of past investment, certain locational considerations, and the initial profitability of the investment. The higher the step, the more the affiliate of the MNE will act as an indigenous firm, and so the greater the ability of the host government to regulate it by unilateral action without provoking a major offsetting response. In addition, the steps will not be flat because, as noted above, in the short run there are certain options available to the MNE which it can use in response to any changes in policy (transfer pricing, export allocations, and so on). In some cases, where the MNE dominates certain sectors of the host country economy, these options will cause the slope of the steps to be steep; the resulting effect on economic welfare will be correspondingly greater.

V

Now let us apply the analysis to answering the question, How can host countries best treat foreign direct investment to advance their national goals? These goals will usually include more than the neoclassical notion of economic efficiency; most governments, to one degree or another, are concerned with sovereignty, autonomy, equity and cultural values.

At the unilateral level, governments possess an arsenal of policy instruments to regulate affairs autonomously within their borders. These include taxation, tariffs, subsidies, administrative rules, monetary policy, exchange rate policy and capital controls. They can treat the MNE as any other national firm or they can discriminate in favour of or against it. But to properly estimate the domain of unilateral action that a host country has available to it, there needs to be a clear comprehension of how the presence of the MNE affects the effectiveness of national instruments.

As has been said, although countries have a barrage of controls, the MNEs have a barrage of options. These options can be, and often are, modified by government policies but, in the end, the MNE has the ultimate option of not investing. Given the sets of policies and options, it should be possible to specify the circumstances under which bargaining conditions are most likely to favour the MNE and, likewise, when the government's policies will be more or less effective. The more a firm moves away from behaving like an indigenous producer, the less control the government will have by the use of normal unilateral policies. Information as to the alternatives open to the government will be crucial in this area for it will affect the bargaining power between the host country and the MNE. Any help which might be given to a country to make more informed and intelligent decisions is therefore to be welcomed.

Even if the bargaining power of the host country were to be increased, unilateral measures still might not succeed. Some countries are more vulnerable to international involvement than others, such as those with few resources and limited markets, untrained ministry staffs, or those which compete with others for investment of MNEs (Taiwan and South Korea). Moreover, in some cases, all host countries may not benefit as much as they think they should because of the alleged power of MNEs to channel benefits back to their home countries (which assumes that the firms have an overall monopolistic or quasi monopolistic power).

The MNE usually brings a package of capital, services, special skills and technical expertise which may or may not be deployed in a way consistent with national objectives. Thus, within the context of an overall development plan, some nations will search to buy the components of the package separately if this can be done at a lower total cost in political and economic terms. The MNE may affect national goals in the following areas: employment, imports and exports, technological potential, taxation, savings and investment, location of industry, competition, and ownership and control of resources. Unilateral action on the part of the government in pursuit of its objectives is likely to be more successful in some of these areas than others; for example, where the MNE is dependent on the domestic market for its sales and materials, the government can increase taxes, encourage local management, local participation, exports, etc., without an offsetting response on the part of the firm. In small markets, however, or where there is little dependence on resources, the MNE may well see the various countries in the region as equally suitable points for investment. In this case, the steps in Figure 14.2 would be very short and the government would be constrained to take unilateral action. It is only by observing the likely responses of the firms themselves that the limitations of unilateral actions can be properly assessed.

It is just within this area, where the bargaining power of the MNEs is relatively great, that a regional or multilateral solution suggests itself. One obvious point for harmonisation is the domain of fiscal incentives which act as a transfer of income from host countries to the treasuries of the home countries via the MNE. Other types of international action have been urged. Sometimes attention is directed to the international order as such and *inter alia* the reform of the international patent system, the IMF, the international taxation system, etc. Sometimes the emphasis is placed on harmonising standards such as, in the case of industrial relations, pollution, safety, hygiene, consumer protection, and of using the MNEs as a bridgehead of good practice. Home countries, especially, have been urged to unite to solve these problems. Sometimes, as in the Andean Pact countries, there has been an urge to get together to strengthen the bargaining power of the host countries in order to benefit more from the presence of the MNE.

The differences between unilateral and multilateral policies can be conveniently illustrated by reference to Figure 14.3. As in the previous diagram, the vertical axis represents the return on investment for the MNE in the host country while the horizontal axis represents the degree of foreign involvement of the MNE in the host country, that is, the manner in which it chooses to serve the market. The curve will be a function of a particular MNE in a given host country at a specific point in time within a given international setting. Alter any one of these variables and the return–investment (and/or output) curve will suggest a new equilibrium.

For any given rate of return and level of risk attached to its earnings, a firm will choose its degree of foreign involvement as one which enables it to exploit its special knowledge, skills and resources in the most profitable manner. Using Figure 14.3 as an example, for the return R_A a firm will choose to involve itself in this country via direct investment as its most profitable course of action, corresponding to point A in the figure. Unilateral action on the part of the host government will provoke a movement along the curve as it changes the costs and/or risks of the firm's activities. Any measure which increases the costs for a given level of activity will likewise lower the rate of return, effectively transferring the benefits from

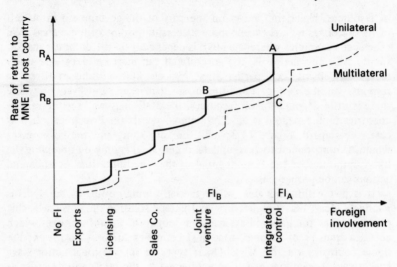

Fig. 14.3

the company to the host country government. As the rate of return on its operations falls relative to what it can earn elsewhere (or by another form of market activity), it will move along the curve to the left, decreasing its foreign involvement (at R_B its most profitable means of serving the market is by FI_B). If the government continues to undertake measures that reduce the return below R_B, then the firm will alter its foreign involvement from a joint venture to licensing.

Examined from the viewpoint of maximising the host country's economic welfare, the lowered returns of the MNE can be seen as the gross benefit to the host country, resembling a tax (area $ABR_B R_A$ is the gain to the host country from its unilateral policies). But there is a cost involved; as the firm decreases its foreign involvement, the host country loses the advantages conferred by the MNE's resources and skills at each step. It is possible that these costs more than offset the potential benefits so that there is no net gain or even a net loss to economic welfare (if $ABFI_B FI_A$ is greater than $ABR_B R_A$ the host country will be a net loser). Thus the more the MNE is like an indigenous firm (where the steps are very high and relatively short), the more likely it is that there will be a net gain for the host country.

It is in the case where the host country becomes a net loser through unilateral policies to control inward direct investment that a multilateral solution suggests itself. So far, it has been assumed that one country acts alone while the others continue their past policies; therefore, if the host country increases the cost of foreign involvement, the other countries become relatively more attractive as investment alternatives. If, however, all the countries of a region coordinate their policies *vis-à-vis* the MNEs then a harmonised change in policy will leave their relative positions the same (or, at least, not consciously altered). Thus instead of a movement along the return–foreign investment curve, there will be a shift in the curve induced by multilateral action. A transfer of benefits to the host country would transpire without an offsetting decrease in the foreign involvement by the MNE. Referring to Figure 14.3, if all nations undertook a multilateral policy (say, special taxes on development) thereby raising the cost of foreign operations, then even though the return would be lower (shifting down to R_B from R_A, for example) the MNE's foreign involvement in the host country would remain at FI_A due to the intersection on the new curve at C. In this case, the net benefit to the host country is the area ACR_BR_A.

Through multilateral co-operation and co-ordination all host countries could benefit. Such actions will affect the amount and distribution of output. Some policies may benefit all, while most will benefit some countries but not others. This is similar to the sharing problem inherent in any national policy, but transposed into an international framework. Just as MNEs differ from indigenous firms in their response, so there are differences between the responses of nations to supranational control of resources and the responses of regions to national policies (for example, Scotland in the UK and the UK within the EEC). There are very considerable differences in goals and aspirations, cultures and states of development, political systems and, perhaps most important, in the mobility of resources, especially labour. Hence, the sharing problem is a crucial one.

Put another way, the problem is similar to that of oligopolists coming together to form a cartel: the total pie may increase but what about the distribution of the larger pie? Will a country that is a weak bargainer *vis-à-vis* the MNE be any stronger when it has to bargain with the rest of the nation states to which it is allied? Ireland may win in the incentive game against Belgium to attract US direct investment. If incentives are harmonised, Ireland plus Belgium may gain relative to the foreign investors, but Ireland's share of the investment may fall to the extent that it is a net loser on the deal. Honduras voiced similar complaints in the now virtually defunct Central American Common Market. Multilateral action may increase the size of the total pie to be shared, but if this is not accompanied by any guarantees as to the size of the share attributable to each, co-operation is unlikely. The achievement of national goals within a multilateral context will only be preferred to unilateral action when the net benefits in terms of output and relative share are clearly foreseen and measurable. The very same kinds of problems have been observed in the negotiations for tariff reductions within the GATT and during the discussions on UK membership in the EEC.

VI

Even in those situations where multilateral policies are suggested, the practical problems of implementation sometimes seem to be overwhelming owing to the difficulty of agreement on *form*, *extent* and *time* dimensions. The *form* dimension is probably the most difficult because there is a large range of conceivable multilateral policies that could be adopted from informal codes of conduct (of the OECD type),[6] to international agreements and form (of the GATT type) (Goldberg and Kindleberger, 1970), to international control and regulation of the MNE through an international body with rule-making and punitive powers. As nation states vary so much in political aspirations, cultural identity and economic development, each one would envisage its own brand of policy to suit its own purposes. Countries that are predominantly recipients of direct investment will differ from those that are capital exporters. From this point of view, the UN has made a pragmatic step by the establishment of a research and information centre to examine the scope of the problems, collect data and promote common terms of reference in such a complex field.

The *extent* dimension poses the same problems for co-operation as the above, mainly stemming from the diverse character of nation states. Some countries will prefer global solutions (especially the smaller and economically weaker ones), whereas others will opt for regional agreements such as the EEC, Andean Pact or ASEAN. Still others will prefer policies formulated by blocs of host or home countries (as paralleled in the oil case).

Finally, there is the difficulty of agreeing on a *time* dimension as the form and extent of the problem of the MNE will alter over time as a consequence of changes in the international economic order and of policies now being contemplated for dealing with the MNE. Therefore, in designing solutions it is necessary either to establish permanent rules and/or institutions whose relevance may quickly fade, or to incorporate the treatment of MNEs within a more general-purpose framework of an existing organisation such as the GATT, OECD, IMF or the UN.

As observed earlier, the purpose of multilateral solutions is to obtain the benefits of foreign direct investment which could not otherwise be recouped by the host countries through the use of unilateral policies. Countries should therefore choose the multilateral policy that maximises the potential difference between benefits thus obtained and those obtained from unilateral policies. To be successful in the achievement of host country objectives, not only must there be agreement and implementation of multilateral policies, but they must be fruitful as well. If pushed too far (if they raise the cost of foreign involvement too much in all countries at the same time), multilateral policies could backfire by changing the nature of foreign investment so that while the costs of the MNE in economic and sovereignty terms are reduced, the potential benefits disappear. If the rate of return is sufficiently reduced with a corresponding transfer to the host countries, then the whole phenomenon to which we are referring may no longer exist.

Will multilateral agreements be more difficult to achieve in the next twenty-five years than in the past quarter-century because of developments in the international order? Not only is the question of the MNE an intractable one for the reasons mentioned earlier, but it will be treated against a whole set of new problems: pollution of the environment, the energy crisis, the depletion of natural resources and the distribution of economic power. At the same time, there are over 140 separate sovereign nation states in the international system, most of which are taking an increasingly active role in the economic, political and cultural lives of their respective countries, as evidenced by the proliferation of ministries, pressure groups and lobbyists. Likewise, there are literally thousands of non-government organisations which influence decision making, officially or unofficially, at the national, regional or international levels. These include labour unions, professional associations, academic institutes, consumer organisations and social welfare groups — and their number is increasing. The existing international organisations will have a role to play in the formulation of an international strategy for the MNE, but there are problems in determining which one is the proper forum.

Thus the administrative and economic limitations of multilateral action are many. Not only is it difficult to get agreement between so many countries (witness the GATT negotiations), but the machinery is usually cumbersome and time-consuming, especially concerning day-to-day questions. Only organisations with some real power of their own (the IMF, the BIS and the EEC, each in its own way) tend to be effective; yet the power conferred on them is in narrowly defined areas and their greatest achievements have been in depoliticised, technical domains.

Just as nation states want to improve their terms of trade, they also want to improve their terms of international production. They will do so through multilateral agreements and organisations when their share of the benefits is clearly delineated. Within this context, however, the focus of our attention must move away from the MNE to the international economic order; in the final analysis, the problem of the MNE is not one of profits versus host country benefits, but one of distribution of costs and benefits between home and host countries.

VII

Unless a nation chooses total autarky, it will always be subject to the vagaries of economic dependence or interdependence. In terms of control of its economic resources, both natural and human, a country can depend on other nations on a bilateral basis to resolve the conflicts between host and home countries concerning the sharing of the benefits and costs of the

MNE, or the country can rely on international agreements and institutions, or it can rely on the MNE itself to allocate global, hence national, resources. Even if they did not question the efficiency of the MNE in terms of production and distribution, there are increasing doubts about the sovereignty, cultural and equity effects of these global firms. Whether the response to this perceived challenge will be unilateral, regional or supranational will depend upon the likely response of each MNE in each country and upon the concrete alternatives made available to the host country through regional or international negotiations.

Appendix 14.1: Alternative Methods of Affecting Behaviour and Impact of MNEs

Unit of analysis: nation state

1 Goals of nation state:
   a economic (GNP, etc.)
   b equity (distribution of GNP)
   c sovereignty (control over decision taking)
   d cultural etc.
2 Alternative means of resource allocation and income distribution to achieve goals:
   a Leave it to the MNE to decide.
      Likely to be most acceptable to nation state where:
         goals are primarily economic;
         its economic structure development is similar to home country;
         MNEs operate in near perfect markets;
         nation state gains net advantages from economic interdependence and operates a free-enterprise economy;
         international economic order and/or multilateral institutions operate efficiently;
         role of MNEs is comparatively insignificant in nation state;
         political ideologies and cultures of home and host countries are similar.
   b Control of investment pattern and extent of MNE's operations behaviour by unilateral measures.
      Likely to prove most successful for nation state where:
         affiliates behave like indigenous enterprises;
         countries do not compete with each other for MNE investment;
         affiliates earn economic rent;
         nation state has good bargaining power *vis-à-vis* MNE and has an efficient economic planning machinery;
         competition exists between MNEs for investment in nation state.
   c Supranational or multilateral measures for controlling MNEs.
      Likely to be encouraged by nation state where:
         above policies (2a and 2b) are ineffective;
         participating countries have broadly similar interests and are at similar stages of economic and cultural development;

individual host countries have good bargaining power in effecting
bilateral regional or international agreements;

MNEs operate an integrated (global) strategy and have a response
elasticity greater than indigenous firms;

there are general advantages of integration and coordinated policies between nation states.

3 Policies consequential upon operations of MNEs:

a Remove all market and policy imperfections (see 3b and 3c).

b (Economic) policies may be directed towards:

affecting behaviour of MNEs to ensure that it is consistent with
national goals and policies (controls over level and pattern of
activity of MNEs' ownership policies, capital inflows and remittances, access to local capital markets, employment of expatri-
ates, location of research and development activities, transfer
of technology, allocation of export markets, transfer pricing,
etc.);

adjusting existing policies (as they affect the behaviour of all
firms) in light of behaviour of MNEs (general demand management policies, exchange rate and balance of payments policy,
monetary policy and interest rates, competition policy, science
and technology policy, etc.).

c Policies may be of three kinds:

adjusting market and institutional mechanisms in which they operate;

harmonising or coordinating policies (general or selective) towards
MNEs (tax incentives, competition and restrictive practices);

direct intra-government negotiations and agreements (concerning
issues of extra-territoriality, or where governments take over
activities of MNEs to protect their own interests).

4 Machinery

This has a form, extent and time dimension:

a form dimension ranges from supply of information to guidelines or
codes of behaviour to binding agreements;

b extent dimension ranges from sectoral (regional or industrial) agreements to global solutions;

c time dimension ranges from what might be accomplished almost immediately to long-term measures.

Notes: Chapter 14

1 For an examination of the international aspects of state owned enterprises see
Vernon (1979).

2 See Chapter 15.

3 See Chapter 8.

4 For a discussion of the similarities and differences between corporate and regional integration see Vaitsos (1979).

5 For a recent discussion of possible MNE reactions to government policy initiat-
ives, see Gladwin and Walter (1980). For a comparative study of some of the
ways MNEs have responded to foreign investment policies and regulations of developing countries see Dymsza (1978).

6   A Code of Conduct for Multinational Companies was adopted by the Council of the OECD on 21 June 1976.

References

Behrman, J. N. (1974a), *Towards a New International Economic Order* (Paris: Altantic Institute).

Behrman, J. N. (1974b), *Decision Criteria for Foreign Direct Investment in Latin America* (New York: Council of the Americas).

Bergsten, C. F. (1974), 'Coming investment wars?', *Foreign Affairs* (October).

Dymsza, W. A. (1978), *Foreign Investment Policies of Developing Countries: Response by Multinational Corporations; Accommodations and Interactions* (mimeo).

Gladwin, T. N., and Walter, I. (1980), *Multinationals under Fire: Lessons in the Management of Conflict* (New York: Wiley).

Goldberg, P. M., and Kindleberger, C. (1970), 'Towards a GATT for investment: a proposal for supervision of the international corporation', *Law and Policy in International Business*, vol. II, no. 2.

Keohane, R. O., and Nye, J. S. (1974), 'World politics and the international economic system', in C. F. Bergsten (ed.), *The Future of the International Economic Order* (Lexington, Mass.: Heath).

Kindleberger, C. K. (1974), 'Size of firm and nation states', in J. H. Dunning (ed.), *Economic Analysis and the Multinational Enterprise* (London: Allen & Unwin). See also Johnson, H. G. (1970), *Guidelines for Relationships between Governments and Multinational Corporations* (London: British-North American Committee).

Kojima, K. (1978), *Direct Foreign Investment* (London: Croom Helm).

Perlmutter, H. W. (1972), 'The multinational firm and the future', *Annals of the American Academy of Political and Social Science*, vol. 403 (September).

Rubin, S. J. (1971), 'Multinational enterprise and national sovereignty: a sceptic's analysis', *Law and Policy in International Business*, vol. III, no. 1.

Vaitsos, C. (1979), *Regional Integration Cum/Versus Corporate Integration* (mimeo.).

Vernon, R. (1979), 'The international aspects of state aimed enterprises', *Journal of International Business Studies*, vol. X, no. 3 (Winter).

15

Multinational Enterprises and the Challenge of the 1980s

I

It was only a decade ago that a distinguished commentator on multinational enterprises predicted that by the mid-1980s the 300 or 400 supergiant companies in the world would account for 60–70 per cent of the world's industrial output (Perlmutter, 1968). Many other analysts, economists, politicians, and even businessmen themselves, believed him. At that time, the MNE seemed to be an increasingly powerful force in the world economy and nothing would stop it in its surge forwards.

Yet in the August 1977 issue of *Fortune* magazine there appeared an article by Sanford Rose, one of the more perceptive writers on MNEs, entitled 'Multinationals in retreat', the main thrust of which was that, faced with a marked slowing down of world economic growth and increasing hostility on the part of both home and host governments to their policies and behaviour, giant companies were cutting back on their international investments and seeking new directions for their future growth.

The events which caused this dramatic turn-about in the prognosis of the future of MNEs are well known. Almost every week, the press reports some incident typifying the confrontation between MNEs and governments, and of new measures introduced to control or regulate their activities. In international fora, particularly at the UN and UNCTAD, demands for stronger multilateral action against the misuse of power by such companies continue to be voiced. In addition to the usually well-publicised cases of expropriation of assets of MNEs, there are many more of voluntary or semi-voluntary divestment, and a refusal on the part of MNEs to accept the demands of host governments — notably in some developing countries: the withdrawal of IBM and Coca Cola from India in 1978 are just two instances. At both a national and international level, attempts to harmonise the activities of MNEs with the goals of the nation states in which they operate continue unabated. While the OECD has contented itself with the

This chapter is based upon two articles by the author, viz. 'The future of the multinational enterprise', first published in *Lloyds Bank Review* (April 1974), and 'Multinational business and the challenge of the 1980s', first published in *Multinational Business*, issue no. 1 (1978).

laying down of guidelines on behaviour to MNEs (at the same time accepting the MNEs should not be discriminated against in relation to
national firms), the UN – notably in the guise of UNCTAD and the Commission on Transnational Corporations – has been pressing for more
formalised codes of conduct. With such attitudes and policies, and within
an uncertain and fragile world economic environment, one might be
forgiven for believing that this particular vehicle of international business
had passed its peak and must give way to other institutional forms more
suited to the needs of the future.

My own reading of the current situation is very different. Just as in
1968 I did not subscribe to the Perlmutter view, so neither do I believe
that MNEs are in retreat today. Rather, it is likely that the peak of the
confrontation between MNEs and governments is now passed and that the
1980s will see a more relaxed and conciliatory relationship emerging,
based on a better perception of the goals and aspirations of each party, a
stronger bargaining capacity of governments, and an acceptance by MNEs
of more involvement by public authorities in the decision-taking process.
In one sense, however, a retreatist view may be correct; that is, that the
traditional role of MNEs (apart from the multinational banks) as providers
of entrepreneurial capital may have reached its zenith. Instead, their future
is likely to rest in the provision of technical, managerial and marketing services bundled together in a variety of ways, the allocation of which will be
increasingly determined by market forces or by government fiat. In the
1970s MNEs, particularly smaller MNEs, have shown themselves adaptable
to new forms of involvement. At the same time, new opportunities, mainly
in the form of joint ventures and technical service agreements, are opening
up in the centrally planned economies. In all these cases, although the
leopard may have changed its spots, it is still very much the same beast.

II

In retrospect, the two decades up to 1975 may be regarded as the matur-
ation of one phase in the evolution of international resource transmission.
This phase began at the turn of the twentieth century, remained inactive in
the interwar years, and blossomed after the Second World War in conditions that were ideally suited to the extension of activities of firms across
national boundaries, through the medium of equity investment. This particular phase followed a much longer era which dated back to the Industrial
Revolution and even before. During this period, capital, labour and technology and entrepreneurship migrated overseas, largely from Europe to the
USA, the Commonwealth and South America. This culminated in the decade before the First World War when Great Britain was investing abroad
three times as much as it was investing at home. International investment
in the nineteenth century had three important characteristics. First, the

resources used were transmitted separately and independently of each other – there was no single organisation packaging them together and arranging for their joint shipment. Second, the resources, or the right to their use, were exchanged between independent parties at arm's length prices. Third, in the main, the exchange was accompanied by a change in the ownership of the *use* of resources, that is, the seller transferred control of the allocation of resources to the buyer.[1]

The *contractual* route of transferring resources remained the dominant mechanism throughout the nineteenth century. It was facilitated by an international economic environment in which there were efficient capital markets and few barriers to the international transfer of resources *between* firms; while there were inadequate mechanisms for transferring resources *within* firms. Only as transport and communications facilities improved did the territorial expansion of business become a practicable proposition. And where it did, it was in areas in which the markets worked the least successfully, for example, in the supply of primary products, where uncertainty over supplies and prices led firms to internalise their activities by operating their own mines and plantations.

Events of the twentieth century changed this situation dramatically. First, the tremendous improvements in transport and communications technology made it as easy for a New York business to operate a branch plant in Frankfurt or Lagos as in Washington or Los Angeles; the jet aircraft and the computer were the culmination of the trend. As a previous chapter has suggested, up to the mid-1960s, at least, technological, economic and political developments increasingly favoured the growth of large-scale business and the penetration of foreign markets. At the same time, the twentieth century markets in capital, technology, information and management failed to provide as adequate a mechanism for the efficient transfer of resources as their nineteenth century equivalents had done.

In the last thirty or so years, policies towards international production have followed a pattern reminiscent of those towards trade in the nineteenth and early twentieth century, which, taken together with changes in the organisational structure of the MNE, have brought this form of international involvement to a point corresponding to the interwar years in the development of trade. At the same time, attitudes to international involvement *per se* are themselves changing.

The period from around the 1950s to the mid-1960s might be described as the honeymoon period of foreign direct investment. The precise timing of this phase differs between countries, but it is identified by the especially favourable environment for international production, and particularly that undertaken by US MNEs. Western Europe, for example, recovering from the Second World War and short of capital, knowledge and human skills had no option but to acquire them from the USA which, in 1950, was, technologically, far and away the most advanced country in the world. American firms were especially welcome for the new resources they provided. In rich developing countries like Canada and Australia the need was no less pressing. It was for money and human capital to develop indigenous national resources and to supply products which could not be economically produced by their own firms. The poorer developing countries, particularly those with unexploited primary products, were just beginning to appreciate their own economic potential but, again, were crucially deficient in the organisational skills and capital by which they could translate this potential into actual wealth. Since the import of goods or technology was not possible because of the shortage of foreign exchange, and as most countries did not have the technological infrastructure or institutional framework (as did Japan) to rely on licensing, foreign direct investment had a flourishing environment in which to operate. These were the years in which the technological and managerial gap between the USA and the rest of the world was at its widest.

Besides these 'pull' factors, there were 'push' factors in the leading capital exporting country — the USA. By the mid-1950s some of the innovatory steam had gone out of the domestic economy. Institutional constraints inhibited domestic expansion by merger. Rates of return on capital and growth prospects seemed more promising in other countries. Scale economies and technological developments were favouring the larger firm. The production of knowledge, often financed by government support, was becoming more enterprise specific and more difficult to assimilate by those who had not produced it. To finance expensive innovatory costs, large markets were necessary, and by the beginning of the 1960s, the dollar was an overvalued currency.

Within this broad economic ambience, international production by US MNEs flourished. Import protection and the need to exploit new markets also encouraged UK foreign direct investment in the same period. Because, too, of the need for the package of resources which the multinational could provide, host countries were willing to offer generous incentives to inward investors. Some attempted to influence the direction of investment and to ensure that it was in conformity with their more pressing national goals, for example, improving the balance of payments, but most imposed few constraints. The cost/benefit ratio was rarely calculated, and the benefits were taken for granted. Little attention was paid to obtaining the resources provided by MNEs in other ways.

For the most part, the strategy of MNEs during this period was simple and straightforward. Outside the primary product sector, most affiliates were set up to supply local or other markets in place of imports. The affiliates operated largely independently of each other and were closely identified with the interests of the local economy. Few firms had yet evolved an integrated or global strategy. Though most decisions, especially those taken by newly established affiliates, were controlled by parent companies, they were usually geared to advance the prosperity and growth of the affiliate. Again, apart from trade in primary products, there was

comparatively little intra-group trading or product or process specialisation within the multinationals. Branch plants were offshoots of parent
companies, and in only a few countries did affiliates do much exporting.

Partly for these reasons, partly because so little was known about the
effects of foreign affiliates, and partly because their involvement in local
economies was generally small, some of the costs of foreign investment
were discounted or not even considered. There was little xenophobia. Free
international production seemed to be the order of the day — the equivalent, for the MNE, of the free trade era.

III

Since the mid-1960s, attention has switched to the costs of, and alternatives to, international production financed by foreign direct investment.
The report of the UN Study Group (UN, 1974) on MNEs identified these
costs. Although it acknowledged the benefits, it recognised that the MNE
was under criticism. The honeymoon period was over. In spite of impressive
research evidence that, on balance, the economic welfare of host countries
had been advanced by foreign direct investment, its net benefits were
being increasingly questioned. Bad news often makes the headlines more
than good news. This certainly has been the case with MNEs, and public
opinion about them has been much coloured by incidents of a disturbing
character, as in Chile, for example.

How has this change in attitude come about in such a remarkably short
period of time? Will it last? What does it foreshadow for the future? How
has it been reflected in government policies towards the MNEs?

On the first question, there are many reasons for the increasing disquiet
about multinationals. Perhaps the most important lies simply in the
growth of their participation both in domestic economies and in the world
economic scene, which previous chapters have described.[2] In almost every
host country, affiliates of foreign firms have increased their share of the
national product; in more than a score, they now account for over one-
third of the output of manufacturing industries.

Second, with this growing international involvement has come a change
in the management style and organisational strategy within MNEs. In the
very industries in which international production has grown the fastest,
product or process specialisation is the most widely practised, intra-group
transactions are the most pronounced and centralised control over resource allocation the most marked. In consequence, in these industries, at
least, foreign affiliates have become less rather than more like their indigenous competitors, for example, in how they behave and react towards
domestic economic policies. The concern lest the international division of
labour, geared to promote the global interests of the MNEs, might operate
against the interests of host countries and make them more rather than less

dependent on industrialised countries, dominated the thinking of developing countries towards MNEs in the 1970s.

Third, the rapid growth of international production has occurred at a time when most governments have become more aware of the need for centralised economic planning. This was already well in evidence in the 1950s and 1960s but it has accelerated and spread in the last decade. Both in developed and developing countries, the State is participating increasingly in economic affairs. Not only has this been undertaken for the usual Keynesian reasons, but on a much broader front, for example, long-term economic planning, urban redevelopment, environmental control, preservation of raw materials, governments now exert much more influence on the way resources are used. It follows, then, that anything which reduces their ability to regulate the behaviour of foreign firms, without having to resort to special measures, is regarded as a challenge to their economic sovereignty.

From the viewpoint of developing countries, the situation has changed even more dramatically. As countries have become politically independent and are searching for their own identity, they have often tended to reject the ties of the past, including direct investment by foreign companies, which they regard as a form of economic imperialism or colonialism. They have also become more aware of the value of the resources they possess, while, at the same time, their knowledge of how to control the use of these resources has increased. Their contacts with the outside world, through education and dealings with international agencies, especially the United Nations, and the technical aid received from such bodies, have made them conscious both of their economic power and of the wider implications of inward investment. They have become better equipped to evaluate the effects of such investment and of the alternatives to it. As they have formulated development plans, their perception of the contribution of MNEs has widened. Not only are they interested in their impact on technology, employment or the balance of payments, but in how they affect consumption patterns, cultural goals and the distribution of income.

In due course, all these misgivings were laid at the door of the *form* of the resource transmission (i.e. the equity investment or non-contractual route) which allowed the transferor of the resources to retain the right to control the use of them. Attention then focused, and continues to be focused, on (1) ensuring either that the centralised control exercised by the MNEs is decentralised or, where this is not possible, that it is used in such a way as is consistent with national goals and policies; and (2) seeking alternative forms of acquiring foreign resources without foreign control over the use of such resources. In the former case, the methods currently used vary from regulating the conditions of inward direct investment, and/ or insisting on certain performance criteria, to laying down a series of guidelines on behaviour to the foreign firms. In the latter, attention has been directed to reducing the equity participation of foreign firms, and to depackaging the resources they provide, with the objective that each resource is bought from a different source on a contractual and arm's length basis.

This process of reorientation in outlook has not always been accompanied by the most sensible policies on the part of host countries. All too frequently the MNE has been made the scapegoat for the failure of host governments to manage their economies properly. Though some developing countries still adopt a liberal approach towards inward investment, most have introduced stringent control procedures on types of investment permitted and conditions of production. In some cases, nationalisation and expropriation have been resorted to; in others, there has been insistence upon local majority ownership and a gradual disinvestment of assets.

Developed countries, too, have attempted to reduce the costs of and increase the benefits from foreign direct investment. In Europe, the fear has been that American direct investment, particularly in research intensive industries, would lead to technological dependence on the USA. The main weapon used to forestall this has been to encourage 'countervailing power', both by the rationalisation of domestic firms and by mergers between European and/or European and US companies. Similarly, there has been disquiet about the effects of foreign investment on the balance-of-payments and competition policy, and the share of the benefits accruing to the local economy.

In part, this reaction against the MNE has nothing to do with its multinationality as such. Nor is it as widespread as may be thought. Those who are most vocal often represent special interests or have particular political axes to grind. There is much less outcry from the man in the street, to whom the benefits of foreign direct investment are more immediately obvious than its costs. Moreover, the MNE is caught up in a general debate about bigness in business, consumer protection and environmental pollution, and, in the developed countries at least, a questioning of economic growth as an end in itself. Greater attention is now being placed on income relativities and on the widening gap between rich and poor countries, the depletion of natural resources, protecting energy supplies, and so on. At every turn, the MNEs seem to be involved and are an easy target for criticism. The recent climate of opinion towards them must be interpreted in this broader context.

How have the MNEs responded to these views and to the efforts made to regulate their activities? On the one hand, they appear to have adapted well to the ownership and control policies of host governments.[3] On the other, because of the widening of investment opportunities, for example, in South East Asia and Eastern Europe, MNEs have not hesitated to divest, or not to increase their investments in uncongenial environments; India is a classic case in point (Dymsza, 1978). More generally, as Chapter 1 has shown, the pace of new MNE activity is slowing down, but it is still impressive, particularly within the developed world. How long this will continue is another matter. In recent years, the macro-political and economic climate facing the world's largest companies has been less favourable to growth. As a result of the realignment of currencies, US companies find foreign investment less attractive than previously. Inflation has produced difficult cash flow situations. Disengagement may be the order of the day, particularly in the uncertain environment of some developing countries. The alternative is for companies to further adapt their involvement to meet the particular needs of host countries, a course especially implemented by some of the smaller multinationals from Japan and developing countries.

IV

It is, at this point, that the Report of the UN Study Group on MNEs is particularly pertinent. It rejects both the view put forward from some quarters that the nation state is dead and that the world is moving towards economic interdependence and unhampered trade and international production, and also the opposite scenario that economic autarky will become the order of the day and international trade and production will be severely constrained.

The group took as its starting point the need to approach the control of international production from a multilateral viewpoint. It observed that, while at present there are organisations such as GATT and the United Nations Conference on Trade and Development (UNCTAD) which help to create orderly conditions for trade and, to a certain extent, influence the terms of trade, there are no such institutions which provide a framework for the flow of international production. In its report, the group proposed that consideration should be given to the conclusion of a General Agreement on Multinational Enterprises (GAME) between governments, which would identify and set out the general conditions for international production. These might include *inter alia* the harmonisation of investment incentives, double taxation agreements, anti-trust legislation, competition policy, controls on capital flows and dividend remissions and questions relating to extraterritoriality. This, I believe, is along the right lines, although, rather than focus attention on particular *institutions*, which possess many characteristics other than that of multinationality, one might consider that any concensus should be 'issue' or 'problem' oriented and that a General Agreement on International Production (GAIP) would be a more appropriate nomenclature.

While acknowledging the benefits of international production, the group's report concentrated on the problems that it may cause, or may seem to cause, countries. It sought to identify these and concluded that some are inherent in the nature of multinationality, while many are due to unsatisfactory terms of international production agreed at the point of entry, resulting from inadequate bargaining power of host countries *vis-à-vis* large international investors. It argued that, for the good of all parties, the terms of entry should be fair and seen to be fair; that companies should know exactly what is expected of them by host countries; that, as far as possible, foreign affiliates should identify themselves with the local economies in which they operate; and that countries should not take discriminatory or retroactive measures against multinationals, which have led to so much bitterness and misunderstanding between companies and governments in the past.

Finally, the group emphasised the need for harmonisation of policies of host countries towards international production. Initially, this might be done by the conclusion of voluntary agreements or codes of conduct, in which respect the multinationals themselves can play an important role,[4] or by bilateral treaties on certain aspects of international production. Eventually, however, a more comprehensive and binding mechanism was needed to avoid distortions and to make possible orderly international production, while allowing flexibility to countries in particular situations.

As an immediate step to this end, the group proposed the establishment of a permanent Commission on Multinational Enterprises responsible to the Economic and Social Council of the UN, to whom it would make an annual report. This commission would have a variety of tasks[5] and would be supported by an information and research centre whose job would be to both collect and analyse data relating to all aspects of international production. The group also felt that the technical advisory services of the United Nations should be strengthened to assist governments, particularly in developing countries, in their dealings with large multinational enterprises. All these functions should be geared to improving the economic environment for direct investment and to acquiring more data about its consequences.

The main recommendations of the Study Group were accepted, and a Commission on Transnational Corporations (the preferred nomenclature of the UN) was set up in 1975 as was a Centre on Transnational Corporations. In the last six years, both the Commission and the Centre have been active both in gathering information and promoting research on MNEs (TNCs) and in preparing a Code of Conduct for TNCs. Another division of the Centre has been concerned with providing technical advisory services, seminars and workshops to assist developing countries in their negotiations with MNEs.[6]

V

In considering the future of MNEs, I believe that a distinction should be drawn between their role in developed and in less developed countries. Concern is greatest where the countries in which foreign production is undertaken are most different — ideologically, politically and economically — from those making the investment. An investment by a powerful industrial nation, with a belief in the free enterprise economy, made in a small centrally-planned developing economy, where there is little indigenous competition and where cultural and other goals are different, may bring far more tensions than where the same investment is made in a similar environment. For these reasons, one foresees that there may be fewer problems connected with transatlantic investment in the next few years than with that made by advanced countries in less advanced countries and that, in the future, the development of foreign investment may take two quite separate courses.

With respect to direct investment within developed countries, I believe that the environment for international production will continue to be generally congenial. Indeed, with the realignment of currencies and the growing technological strength of Europe and Japan there is likely to be a greater symmetry of capital flows between OECD countries, and particularly between Europe and the USA, than there has been in the past. In these countries, the main instruments of policy are likely to be Guidelines on Behaviour (such as those accepted by OECD countries) and regulatory mechanisms of host countries (and of the EEC), for example, with respect to new foreign investment and restrictive practices. In the developed world, the main uncertainty about the future of MNEs surrounds the policies of *home* countries, both towards big business itself — should it be more regulated or broken up? — and to the foreign activities of such companies with respect to their impact on domestic employment, technological capability, and industrial concentration.[7]

A good guide to the approach of the EEC Commission is contained in its document *Multinational Undertakings and Community Regulations*.[8] Basically, the concern of the Commission is to ensure that the monopolistic or oligopolistic power and flexibility of foreign MNEs are not used against the interests of host countries in the Community. There is also some anxiety lest a lack of harmonisation among individual countries on tax, competition and regional incentive policies may induce foreign companies to play one European country off against another. There is, however, less apprehension than there once was that Europe will be economically dominated by US firms, particularly as, in the next decade, European direct investment in the USA is likely to grow faster than US investment in Europe and as the technological and managerial gap may narrow further. Nevertheless, the Commission believes that a united European policy towards foreign investment will strengthen the bargaining positions of individual countries. One is less sanguine about their efforts to promote indigenous competition in some of the high technology industries.

As far as investment between developed and developing countries is concerned, the situation is very different and there are reasons to suppose that the role of the MNE may undergo substantial change. First, the environment which shapes the economic relationships between the developed and less developed world is changing. We can illustrate from recent oil developments, where the developing nations are making concerted efforts to improve their bargaining position and terms of trade *vis-à-vis* consuming countries. This is also happening at a regional level, as seen, for example, by the efforts of the Andean Pact countries. When the supply of basic commodities vital to the prosperity of consuming nations is threatened, governments of these nations inevitably become involved; and this could mean that, in place of market forces, bilateral governmental agreements may determine the conditions and terms of trade. It may well be that international agreements on the supply of a variety of commodities may set the future framework within which multinationals operate. If this is so, the role of multinationals in resource based industries may be much less decisive than in the past.

With respect to specific attitudes by developing countries to foreign direct investment, even when its advantages are undisputed there is a dislike of foreign ownership. This, then, leads countries to consider alternatives to MNEs. In the belief that they can rid themselves of foreign control over their economies, host countries either encourage divestment or, by 'unwrapping the package' of foreign investment, attempt to buy the individual ingredients from separate sources. In some cases, this may not be difficult to do: capital and many kinds of knowledge can be bought on the open market. But such a policy can be successful only if the local economy has the necessary technological expertise to choose exactly what is needed and, once acquired, is able to assimilate the resources and to use them productively. But, as many countries are finding to their cost, the replacement of international production by production undertaken under foreign licence or management contract is not always less expensive; nor does it always lessen economic dependence. Knowledge still has been imported, and, because of imperfections in the diffusion of knowledge and technology, on the one hand, and lack of local capabilities, on the other, the key components of dependence, at least at the firm level, still remain.

Here, it is worth emphasising that the non-contractual (i.e. equity investment) route of transferring resources is very different from the contractual route − or, at least, the contractual route of the nineteenth century. First, the investing firm organises and transmits a package of resources, such that the contributions (or the costs) of the individual ingredients cannot easily be separately identified. Second, the resources are not exchanged on the open market; rather they are channelled within the same firm, that is, they are internal rather than external transmissions. Third, because there is no change in their ownership, a *de jure* control over the allocation of the resources, and local resources used with them, remains with the supplying rather than the receiving firm.

Moreover, although the role of equity capital — certainly the 100 per cent owned affiliate — is likely to become less significant in many developing countries, it will probably not decline as much as was first thought a few years ago. Furthermore, even where it does, this does not necessarily mean that the providers of equity capital will cease to provide the other resources needed for development. The reason for the first statement is that the experience of some developing countries, particularly in Africa, in obtaining technology and management skills through the non-equity investment route have not always been as successful as they had hoped. This is mainly because they *underestimated* the advantages of importing resources as a package or an integrated production and marketing programme, and *overestimated* their own capabilities to organise and complement the separately imported resources. The reason for the second statement is that, in many cases, the MNE remains a unique source of many of the resources and skills, particularly of organisational skills, required by countries. The main difference is that they are no longer unparalleled in their role as capital suppliers and that, apart from joint ventures, the non-contractual route of supplying intangible assets, including knowledge about, and access to, markets, involves the exchange of *services* at arm's length prices. However, it cannot be presumed that these external prices will be lower than the internal prices charged by MNEs; this will depend on the market conditions for the resources in question. Neither can it be assumed that the regulation over decision taking will *de facto* be reduced as a result of a change of the corporate arrangements by which the resources are transmitted.

Indeed, the question: Wherein does control lie? is likely to dominate attitudes of host countries towards the import of resources over the next decade. A lot of preconceptions about control being specific to equity investment have been shattered in recent years. Various studies, *inter alia* by UNCTAD, have suggested that the extent to which the seller is able to direct the use of resources once transferred rests as much on his bargaining power *vis-à-vis* the buyer *at the time the resources are transmitted* as on any continuing relationship between the two parties. Thus, if the licensor of technology is the sole supplier of that technology he may be able to impose conditions over the use of it (or the marketing of the products it produces) by the licencee. Outside manufacturing industry, one classic example of very extensive and detailed supervision over day-to-day resource allocation exercised by a foreign seller of services, without any equity capital being involved, is the international hotel industry. One has only to read the brochures and standard contracts of the Hilton and Intercontinental chains to appreciate this.[9]

The success which host countries *appear* to have had in controlling the activities of MNEs and of finding other sources of resources is essentially a reflection of increased bargaining power *vis-à-vis* the MNEs. This is due, first, to their better appreciation of national goals and policies and of the costs and benefits of foreign direct investment and its alternatives – especially by the larger and more prosperous countries. Second, it reflects the growing competition among MNEs for investment outlets. Particularly significant in this respect has been the growth of 'second league' MNEs and of Japanese MNEs, both of which appear to be more prepared to adapt to the demands of host countries than their predecessors. Third, the alternative sources of capital, technology and management have enormously increased, notably development finance and expert advice from international organisations, technology from the Communist countries, and loan capital from the international banking system.

With political attitudes as they are, with a growing bargaining power of developing countries and with alternatives to such investment becoming available, one might expect the MNE to invest rather less in developing countries in the future. On the other hand, in some kinds of activity involving centralised decision taking they may invest more. The exodus of some firms from high-cost countries to take advantage of lower costs and to concentrate labour intensive parts of their international operations may well continue and intensify. At the same time, there will be pressure from trades unions and others for a gradual upgrading of the type of work delegated to developing countries.

There are other reasons to suppose direct investment might rise in developing countries. As they become wealthier and their markets grow, developing countries become more attractive to foreign companies. Pressures in the oil-producing countries for more petroleum-processing activities may offer great prospects for foreign petrochemical and plant equipment companies. As their governments become more stable and expert at managing their economies, the riskiness of foreign investment declines; firms may then be prepared to accept a lower rate of return. As these countries are seen to accord fair treatment to foreign companies, the incentive to invest will increase.

Host countries have still much to learn about the costs and benefits of direct investment; which is made all the more difficult in developing countries as they struggle to identify their goals of development and the best way to achieve them. In this respect, the advisory services of professional bodies and international agencies can help. So can the multinationals, by a more sensitive understanding of the aspirations of developing countries. The international community can also play its part, by considering whether or not, in the light of international production, existing machinery needs to be modified. Very often, the MNEs have made people in rich countries more aware not only of some of the problems existing between rich and poor countries, but of the inadequacies of existing machineries to deal with them.

VI

What then does this all mean for the future of MNEs and attitudes of host countries towards them? We can draw four principal conclusions.

(1)   Taken separately, the choice to host countries of obtaining resources, once the exclusive province of MNEs and mainly those of US and UK origin, is widening. In consequence, the opportunity to externalise the import of resources is greater than it has ever been and is likely to continue to increase. On the other hand, MNEs still have, and are likely to continue to have, a competitive edge in supplying — as a package or a system — those types of technology, management organisational and marketing skills which are unique to running a large and geographically dispersed operation.

(2)   The terms of the contractual element in any arrangement for the transmission of resources are likely to play a more important role than in the past. This does not only apply to arm's length agreements where there is a trend away from concessions to technical service agreements, but also to the contractual (or quasi-contractual) component of an equity investment. Indeed, I would predict that there will be less concern by host countries about the modality of the transmission of resources and more on the conditions attached to the transmission, particularly as to the use made of resources once transmitted. If it is possible to ensure that these are in the host country's interests and that they can be renegotiated after a period of time long enough to ensure continuity and stability to the company making available the services, then, apart from the purely financial considerations, it may matter little whether the modality takes the form of equity investment or contract. In this respect, codes of conduct and guidelines may be considered as quasi-contracts in as far as they fulfil two main functions. The first is as an informational and a persuasive device, that is, to let MNEs know what is desired of them. The second is to act as a kind of warning signal to potentially offending MNEs. For although, as the situation stands, sanctions may be limited (mainly publicising the 'bad boy' and selective action by individual governments with the backing of others), collective agreement has been reached and a machinery established which may be used to consider further steps which could be much less palatable to MNEs. It is for this reason, together with the fact that governments of very different political persuasions have found it possible to agree on many issues relating to MNEs, that we should not underestimate the significance of this form of international consensus.

(3)   Once the control aspect is settled, the role of MNEs as contractors for governments or consortia of governments opens up tremendously. It is often claimed that MNEs do not meet the basic needs of developing countries. Not only is this a facile statement — MNEs have been directly instrumental in improving agricultural productivity and health, for example, by their production of fertilisers, agricultural

machinery and drugs, as well as providing transportation and communications equipment – but if they do not do so as much as they might, this is as much the fault of governments or international agencies in failing to find the ways and means of harnessing the resources that MNEs do possess to this objective. The exploration of the sea bed, major irrigation schemes, the building of trunk roads, electrification projects, all require the technology and skills which MNEs are particularly well equipped to provide. What is needed is the organisational capacity and entrepreneurial initiative to ensure that the MNEs can play a contractual role in doing just this. Here, the future could be very promising for such companies; they are already playing this role in major constructional petrochemicals and engineering projects in the Middle East, Latin America and South East Asia.

(4)   Both the MNEs and host countries (particularly developing countries) should take note of the Japanese and East European attitudes towards inward direct investment. It is not without relevance that, at the same time as developing countries have been making life more difficult for the MNE, Japan and East European countries have been opening their borders to foreign direct investment. But observe the differences in the two situations. Both Japan and East European countries outlawed foreign investment and strongly regulated the import of resources through the contractual route, until they felt themselves strong enough to absorb the affiliates of MNEs, without being taken over by them. In both cases, with few exceptions, only minority joint ventures were allowed – the few exceptions being where the MNE believes that centralised decision taking is essential for the implementation of its global or regional strategy *and* where the recipient country believes that being part of that strategy will benefit it more than obtaining the resources provided by the MNE through an alternative route, or not importing the resources at all. Observe, too, that in both cases, the technological infrastructure is such that effective use can be made of the resources transferred, that is, there is skilled manpower and supportive technology to know what to do with the resources and maintain them.

The situation in most developing countries is very different, except that a few countries in the Far East, known collectively as the six Japans, are approaching the stage of development of Japan two decades ago. The rest are in a dilemma: on the one hand, if they try and emulate the policies of Japan in the 1960s they may fail because they lack the indigenous technical support capacity to buy the resources for growth by the contractual route; on the other, if they rely on MNEs to provide the package of resources they need, they are in danger of being dominated by and becoming dependent on such companies and tied into their networks. This is precisely the situation from which Brazil and Mexico are trying to extricate themselves at the present time.

The solution is not an easy one, but I believe it lies along the route suggested earlier in this chapter. Developing countries should seek to buy resources from the source, by the modality and in the combination which, taken with their own resources, enable them best to further their longterm objectives. The attainment of control by a country over the direction of resource allocation (as reflected, for example, in its external payments flows or in changes in the nationality of labour inputs) is not inconsistent with its importing resources with the assistance of foreign companies, either through equity investment or through arm's length contracts. The ability to do just this, together with strengthened bargaining power coupled with an efficient administrative machinery, is perhaps one of the most useful ways in which developing countries can help themselves.

The wheel is thus turning full circle regarding the way resources are internationally transmitted. The MNE is not in retreat or, perhaps one should say, need not be in retreat. For every door that closes another opens up. The forms of contractual involvement and the nature of resources provided by MNEs in the last quarter of the twentieth century will be very different from those of the nineteenth century. Resources may be packaged together in various ways, and many different institutions may be involved in particular projects. In particular, one foresees a growing collaboration between state owned enterprises from developing countries and privately owned MNEs from industrialised countries.[10] In addition, although we expect the environment for international investment to improve rather than deteriorate over the next decade or more, the activities of MNEs and other foreign firms are bound to be circumscribed by guidelines, codes, regulations and laws, many of these backed by international consensus. But, hopefully, in exchange for these constraints on behaviour, there will be a greater awareness of governments of their responsibilities to MNEs and a greater perception of their needs, and this may show itself in a more stable environment in which such business may operate. Within these constraints, and if governments take advantage of half the opportunities to make proper use of MNEs, the future for such companies offers both scope and promise.[11]

Notes: Chapter 15

1   Though it has been argued by Houston and Dunning (1976), Wilkins (1977) and Svedberg (1978) that, viewing direct investment in terms of control exercised over the use of assets located abroad, a rather higher proportion of UK foreign investments in the nineteenth century were 'direct' than is commonly supposed.
2   See especially Chapter 1.
3   For an examination of such responses see Gladwin and Walter (1980).
4   In this connection, attention is drawn to the *Guidelines for International Investment* prepared by the International Chamber of Commerce.

5 These include providing a forum for the presentation and exchange of views of governments, inter-governmental and non-governmental organisations about the impact of multinationals on world development; undertaking work leading to the adoption of specific agreements in selected areas relating to the activities of multinationals; conducting inquiries, making studies, preparing reports and organising panels for facilitating a dialogue among the parties concerned; and promoting a programme of technical co-operation, including training and advisory services, aimed, in particular, at strengthening the capacity of developing countries in their relations with MNEs.

6 Perhaps the best description of the ongoing work of the Commission and the Centre on Transnational Corporations is given in the periodic editions of the Centre's 'house' journal – *The CTC Reporter*.

7 For a discussion of these issues in a US context, see Hawkins and Walter (1979).

8 COM 73 1930, Brussels 9 11 73.

9 The early concession agreements concluded by foreign mining companies and host governments are another example of 'control without equity investment'.

10 For an analysis of the comparative advantages of state owned enterprises and MNEs see Vernon (1979).

11 For other views about the future of MNEs, see Malgrem (1978), Franko (1978), Hawkins and Walter (1979) and Keegan (1979).

References

Dymsza, W. A. (1978), *Foreign Investment Policies of Developing Countries: Response by Multinational Corporations; Accommodations and Interactions* (mimeo.).

Franko, L. G. (1978), 'Multinationals: the end of US dominance', *Harvard Business Review* (Nov./Dec.).

Gladwin, T. N., and Walter, I. (1980), *Multinationals under Fire: Lessons in the Management of Conflict* (New York: Wiley).

Hawkins, R. G., and Walter, I. (1979), *Multinational Corporations: Current Trends and Future Prospects*, New York University, Faculty of Business Administration, Working Paper Series (November).

Houston, T., and Dunning, J. H. (1976), *UK Industry Abroad* (London: Financial Times).

Keegan, W. J. (1979), 'The future of the multinational manufacturing corporation. Five scenarios', *Journal of International Business*, vol. 10, no. 1 (Spring/Summer).

Malgrem, H. (1978), 'Multinational business and the decline of overseas investment', *Multinational Business*, no. 1.

Perlmutter, H. V. (1968), 'Super-giant firms in the future', *Wharton Quarterly* (Winter).

Rose, H. (1977), 'Multinationals in retreat', *Fortune* (August).

Svedberg, P. (1978), 'The portfolio-direct composition of private foreign investment in 1914', *Economic Journal*, vol. 88 (December).

UN (1974), *The Impact of Multinational Enterprise on Development and International Relations* (New York: United Nations), Sales No. E.74 II A5.

Vernon, R. (1979), 'International aspects of state owned enterprises', *Journal of International Business*, vol. X, no. 3 (Winter).

Wilkins, M. (1977), 'Modern European history and the multinationals', *Journal of European Economic History*, vol. 6, no. 3.

Index

activities, of firms, government pressure on 229
  of US MNEs in technological industries 73
administrative fiat 96
advantages, natural resource based 100
  see also internalisation
advertising, practices of MNEs 196
  role of 54
affiliate(s), alien status and establishment 267
  behaviour, control of 187, 194–7, 230, 268, 376
  foreign, establishment of 193, 199
  goods produced by, market for 228
  independent and interdependent 186, 187, 193
  and industrial unrest 241
  of MNEs, importance to developing countries 332
  and policy changes 229
  payroll costs per employee 274, 275
  pricing behaviour 208
  and capital subsidies 263
  after-sales service, competitive advantage of 98
agribusiness activities, multinational 4
agricultural investment (UK) 148
allocative efficiency, MNEs and 236
American, enterprise investment 249
  MNE affiliate borrowing 265
  in Europe, investments in assisted areas 253
  see also USA
analysis of variance of wage payments 284, 285
Andean Pact 17, 201, 212, 219, 404
anti-trust legislation of governments 201
Asian countries export performances 371
assets, two kinds 46, 47
Australia, GNP per capita 120
  investment in developing countries 99
average hourly compensation (AHC) 55, 59, 61, 62, 63, 65, 276, 277, 278, 280
  ratio of net income to sales (AVNIS) 58, 60, 61, 62, 64, 65

balance of payments, effect of fdi in 372, 415

returns for UK and US 373
Balance of Payments Yearbook (IMF) 112
bargaining power, affected by capital intensity 289
  of workers 283
bargaining process 15
behaviour, of foreign affiliates 194, 207–8
  alternative methods affecting 406–7
Belgium, fiscal incentives 233
  foreign investment 261
  location of foreign firms 252
Belgium–Luxembourg, industry sales 51
  wage rates 276, 277
BERI Environmental Risk index 127, 128
bilateral or multilateral schemes on policy 202–3, 380
branch plant effect 27, 185, 186
Brazil, industry sales 51
  investment flows 134
break-even subsidy 255–6, 257, 258
British, companies, IRC and 210
  mergers 205, 210
  economy, competition increased by US affiliates 204
  firms redirect to Western Europe 148
  inquiry into location attitude 253
  see also UK
Bureau of Economic Analysis (BEA) 273

Canada, wage rates (1966, 1970) 276, 277
  industry sales 51
capital, controls 90, 159, 393
  flows, impact of MNEs on 224, 242
  formation 221 ff., 227–9, 234, 241
  intensity and wage payments 289
  intensive industries, MNEs and 235, 240
  market imperfections, effect of 98
  movements 236, 237, 238
    theory of 72
  subsidies as incentives 263
  three kinds of 307
capitalisation rates of nationalities 47
cartels, problem of 403
Central Statistical Office data 145–8

classification of manufacturing activity by SIC code 299
codes of conduct 379, 417, 422, 424
for MNEs, demand for 410
Committee of International Investments and Multinational Enterprises 203
communications technology, progress of 411
companies and ownership advantage 119
comparative, advantage 236, 304, 305, 309, 312
growth rates 280
market growth (CMG) of USA 58
trading advantage of exports and imports 145
competition, between developed and developing countries 336–8
new, barriers to 27, 183, 310, 311
competitive, advantage of firms 53
position of firms from mergers 205
strength, factors of 53
computers, innovation of 411
concentration ratios 197, 198, 203
conglomerates, internalising of 28
consumer, electronic industries 344
prices 166–70, 293
contractual resource transfers 110
control of MNEs, problem of 420
see also affiliates, behaviour control
cost-push inflation, impact of MNEs on 240
costs, and benefits, distinction between social and private 366
of MNEs to host countries 357–84
differences, determination of 256
in internalising economic activities 32
country-specific, advantages 13
characteristics 81, 91, 94
determinants of location-specific advantages 91–6
of ownership advantages 86–91
factor in wage payments 284, 286
internalisation advantages 96–8
variables 53
cross-subsidisation 29, 183
crude factor proportions theory 23
cultural considerations affected by fdi 269
cumulated fund flow of US-owned affiliates 222–3

defensive oligopolistic strategy 23
dependencia of small countries 313, 386
dependent variables 52–9
determinants, of export/local production

ratios of US MNEs 65
of participation ratios of US MNEs 60–1
devaluation, effects of 239
developing countries, bargaining powers 421
foreign investment 90
impeded by MNEs 313
industrialisation policies 305
labour-intensive and small-scale technologies 90–1
MNE benefits to 333, 422–3
output potential 305
and resource values 414
trade difficulties, MNEs and 309
use of resources 306
development incentive, effect of 254–5
market economics, stock of direct investment abroad (1967–8) 75
direct international stake position (UK) 146
direct investment 24, 47, 74, 75, 110, 114, 117, 118, 120, 129, 145, 224
in developing countries 421
of MNEs, data on 329
transferred resources 76
discriminant analysis 129, 130
distribution, of income 241–3
of UK direct capital stake 149
distributive trades, investment 151
diversification, by international products 184–5
by an MNE and internalisation gains 111
spatial, of firms 181
domestic, capital formation of MNEs 221–48
economic policies affected by fdi 370
firms and affiliate behaviour 198
markets and investment overseas 92
policy measures for capital spending 231
Dutch MNEs, location 265

earnings base, diversified, advantage to MNEs 36
determinants of average 282
eclectic, model as a general theory 33
theory 133
and economic structure 121
of international economic involvement 24
of international production 33, 48, 50, 72–107, 109, 112, 188

and outward/inward investment changes 136

economic(s), activity of a country and enterprise propensity 112
  agents servicing foreign markets 25
  analysis 8
  development obstacles 306–7
    and output per capita 367
    stages of 117
  of integration 13
  involvement outside boundaries 24, 25
  management difficulties 237
  potential, MNEs help to exploit 236
  power, concentration of 16
    and control 193
    of scale at plant level 259
  structure of countries, differences 120–1
    of home and host countries, MNEs impact on 312–13
    outward direct investment 126, 127
    relationship between investment flows and OLI 130

economists, and behaviour of MNEs 17
  and policy makers, MNEs and 7, 8

efficiency 9, 11–14

electronics, USA export of technology in 323

empirical tests 48–71

employee compensation, dispersion of 278
  differences related to net output 296
  in US multinational and indigenous firms, analysis of 272–303
  problem of comparisons 273–4

employment, in developing areas 257
  effect of fdi on 372
    of US MNEs on 374
  and output, effect of varying exchange rate on 239
  necessary to create lva 365
  patterns and wages 279
  of UK and foreign firms (1963–71) 252

endowments between countries 28, 47, 48

enterprise, and advantages 29
  assets of 46
  characteristics and break-even subsidies 260
  direct investment factors determining 109–10

diversification, effect on market 183
foreign activities of 21
  increase in multinationalities 91
  internalisation of 33, 110, 122–3
    advantage factors affecting 82
  and international production 46
  ownership advantages and 86
    endowments 47
    and profit maximising 50
  size economies 34
  structures and strategies influence of in locational choices 254
  and technology 30
    internalising 30, 31

enterprise-related variables 258, 260–2

enterprise-specific advantages 13, 310
  integration or internalising as 309
  knowledge, obtaining 309

entrepreneur activity 37

environmental considerations affected by fdi 370

equity 9, 14–17, 422
  capital, role of 420
  considerations affected by fdi 369
  to debt ratio in subsidy incentive schemes 262

Eurodollar market and company expansion 235, 238

European countries fiscal incentives for foreign capital 237
  increase in foreign production 99
  and Japan (1950s) import capital 329
  MNE investment 252, 253
  direct investment in USA 418

European Economic Community (EEC) 403, 404, 405
  and allocation of resources 201
  and behaviour of foreign investors 380
  Commission, concern of 418
    and jobs at risk in Europe 345
  economic impact of 387
  policy towards competition and restrictive practices 203
  reduction of market imperfections 393
  specialisation 37, 76

European, firms exploit UK market 162
  savings, outlet for 238
  MNEs, locational patterns 249

exchange of goods and services between countries 21

exchange rate, and dollar rise 98
  policy affected by free capital movements 238

fluctuation 31
realignment, effect of 92
externalising the marketing of raw materials 32
existing industrial countries (EICs) 322, 323, 339, 342, 346
  consultancy contracts 343
  industrial programme 347, 348
  technology exports 344
Expansion Laws, Belgium 252, 253
export(s), ability (UK) 143
  and foreign involvement 110
  incentive 54
  and market structure 182
  of MNEs, intra-group character of 33
  oriented firm and regional development 259
  performance of US affiliates 211
  and production in servicing foreign markets 50
  promotion and growth 306
  ratio 52
  rebates 90
  records on domestic value added basis 26
  revealed comparative advantage 85
  subsidies 268
  underpricing 317
  of US affiliates 207
  of weapons (USA) and technology transfers 323
export/foreign direct investment stake ratio 93
direct investment stock ratio 92
export/import ratio (XMR) 58, 61, 62
export replacing investment 226

factor(s), longer-term for overseas investment 92
price equalisation theorem 22
Finnish companies, foreign direct investment 92
firms, ability and willingness to serve markets 79
  behaviour of influenced by ownership and location 183
  behavioural pattern, changes in 179–80
  in closed economy 180
  diversification and market structure 181, 184
  exploiting advantages over foreign competition 78
  foreign activities, financial aspects 78
  investment behaviour of 225

new, difficulties on entry to market 310
reaction to government policy 179
size of 203–4
  related to markets 86
  and subsidies 265
firm- (ownership) specific factors in wage payments 284, 286
fixed exchange rates 237, 312, 393
flexible exchange rates 14, 237
  undermining fiscal policy 238
Ford Motor Company (UK), horizontal specialisation 76
  wage settlement (1978) 296
foreign affiliates, competitive tactics and devices 195
  entry into a business 198
  evaluating performance of 371, 372
  investing inefficiency 365
  of MNEs, near relations 7–8
  monitoring activities of 378
  ownership, data on 76
  problems for governments 366
  product and process structure 194
  and regional inflation 240
  wages in particular industries 279
foreign based enterprises, locational considerations 249
Foreign and Commonwealth Office study 345, 346
foreign direct investment (fdi) 34, 38, 72, 73, 74, 112, 224, 337, 370, 379, 411
  to acquire foreign technology 118
  costs and benefits, evaluating 371, 387
  costs and economic interdependence 368
  economic effects of 365, 369
  effect concerning host countries 369
  growth and composition 23, 369
  impact on balance of payments 365
  industrial and geographical distribution 48
  operational impact of 364–5
  ownership advantages and 79
  policy towards 376, 377–80
  problem-oriented policy measures towards 38
  research determinants 265, 266
  secondary effect of 366
  and technology, groups of recipients 329, 332
  trade oriented and anti-trade oriented distinction 313

UNCTAD study 315
of US MNEs 189
foreign, divestment of MNEs 74
  firms, effect of influx of 198
    force countries to rent capital 235
    government direct action on in conditions of entry and behaviour 201
    and regional development ideas 267
    in UK, concentration of 171
  investment, adverse affect on UK jobs 172
    by developing countries 90
    outlawed by Japan and Europe 423
    US made to protect oligopolistic position in world market 38
  involvement by enterprises, three main vehicles 110
  markets, process of exploiting 77
  services 28, 50, 78
  participation in selected industries 6
  production dominated by USA (1960s) 72
  sales assets and profits generated by 4
foreign production units, distribution to assisted areas 252
France, average hourly rate 276, 277, 278
  increases in wages and profits 288
  industry sales 51
  investing in Renault by government 377
free, collective bargaining and strict monetary control 297
  international production 392, 413
    changes needed for acceptance 393
  international trade causing adjustment problems 242
  movement of goods and resources 145
freight costs of products in relation to value 259
funds, shifting for high and low tax 235, 239

General Agreement on International Production (GAIP) 416
General Agreement on Multinational Enterprises (GAME) 416
General Agreement on Tariffs and Trade (GATT) 380, 389, 404, 416
  loss of support 387

geographical distribution of outward and inward capital 150
  proximity of home country to main markets and overseas investment 92
Germany, direct investment stock 74
  investment flows 90, 134
  profit and high wages 288
  US foreign investment in 265
government(s), anti-inflationary policies made difficult by affiliates 297
  and benefits of affiliates 202
  and benefits from fdi 387
  control of activities of foreign firms 202
  encourage enterprises to internalise 30, 31
  financing of private research and development 89
  and incomes policy, three main options 298
  influence on labour force 53–4
  intervention in market structure 89, 95, 97, 181
  and level of direction of foreign investment 89
  negotiation procedure with enterprises 382
  persuasive or mandatory policies to foreign firms 201
  policies and MNE options 400
  policy and behaviour of MNEs and affiliates 18, 30, 198, 199, 201–2, 268, 312, 369
    differences across national boundaries 11
    faulty, and reactions of foreign firms 363
    and industrial climate for firms 90
    influencing MNEs 13
    towards fdi 363, 377–80
  protection and assistance for firms gaining commercial knowledge from competitors 201
  pursuing macroeconomic goals, distortion arising 30
  research and development (R&D) programmes 89
  response to mobility of capital by MNEs 239
  skilled labour, type, quality, education and training 89
  three broad aims of 11–18
grant-aided manufacturing plants in Ireland 253

gross, domestic product 25
  inward investment (GII) 115, 119, 130, 132
  national product (GNP) 15, 25, 144, 165
    and NOI per capita variance 129
    per capita variations 120, 122, 123, 124, 128, 133
  outward investment (GOI) 115, 123, 125, 128, 129, 131, 132
    deviation 121, 122
growth in sales per man (GRSPM) 55, 61, 64, 65
guide lines of behaviour (OECD) 418, 422, 424

harmonisation of policies for international production 416, 417
Harvard Multinational Enterprise project data on concentration ratio 73, 192
heteroscedasticity 129
hierarchical, decisions and economic interdependence 393
  diversification 180
  structure of firms related to government policy on mergers 97
high and medium technology industries, importance of foreign affiliates in 332
home country, MNEs, importance of 4
home government policies affecting competition of affiliates 195
Hong Kong textiles and clothing industry 90
horizontal integration, 28
host country(ies), bargaining powers 400
  and direct investment 421
  effect on market structure and performance of firms 185
  and foreign direct investment 400
  policies towards MNEs 385
  solution to problems of MNEs 391
  success in controlling MNEs 420
  transmission of resources 422
host government attitude towards MNEs 389
  unilateral policies 199–200
host/home country-specific factors in evaluating fdi 359
hourly wage packet differences in different firms and industries 275, 282–3
human capital 307

and ownership advantage in knowledge intensive sectors 89

immobility of resources across national boundaries 12
imperfection preventing free international production 393
import(s), competition, effect of 344, 345
  of large and small firms and market structure 182
  over-pricing 317
  replacement of manufactured goods 306
  resources for development, models of 377
import-substituting, manufacturing investment 49, 117, 118, 122, 151, 327, 336
  production 234
incentives, regional, and production costs 252, 253, 255, 263
income, distribution control 16, 241–3, 298
  mobility of capital, main impact of MNEs 238, 239
  multiplier effects in technology transfer 328
incomes policy, rigid, penalising workers in efficient firms 297
independent variables 53–9
indigenous, endowments 26
  knowledge and human skills, MNE demand for 235
  resources, deployment to do job for fdi 376
industrial, enterprises, foreign content ratio 5
  moves in UK 1945–65, regional distribution 251
  organisation theory 77, 79, 185
  policies, direction of 201
  structure of investments and overseas investments 92
  unrest (UK) affecting US investments 165
Industrial Reorganisation Corporation (IRC) 205, 210
  and mergers across national boundaries 209
  and role of MNE 209
industrialised developing countries and investments 99
industries, patterns of involvement 55, 310

industry controlled by integrated company seeking outlets (UK) 308
industry-specific, advantage 13
    factors in wage payments 284, 286
inflation 239–41, 293
    and cash flow situation 416
    checking of, causing unemployment 297
    role played by MNEs 293
information markets, analysis of 78
innovation response 35, 53
innovative activities, distribution of 38
    effect of 196
innovative, capacity and foreign direct investment 78
    centres of enterprise 260
inputs, and outputs, buying and selling 78
    in trade theory 14
    transforming into valuable outputs 22, 47
intangible assets, production and marketing 27, 32
inter-country interest rate differentials influencing investment flows 91
interest-mobile capital 239
interest rates, response to 231
internal organisation of MNEs based on multinational enterprise advantages 264
internal transactions across national boundaries 238–9
internalisation, advantages of 29, 32, 34, 49, 97, 124
    characteristics of OLI 113
    country-specific 96
    of enterprises 110
    incentive advantages 34, 80, 81
    indices of 55–7
    a motive for takeovers and mergers 28, 29
internalising, economic activities, costs 32, 50
    devices and capital formation 233
international, action to control MNEs 401
    allocation of resources 21
    capital flows and inflation 239
        movements, effects of 22, 237, 238
        theory and international production 76
    competitiveness of a country's product 28, 29
    direct investment, diversified 386

direct specialisation 118
diversification of markets and behaviour of firms 183
a division of labour and resource allocation, MNEs and 195, 342
economic involvement 25, 26–7, 50
    order 385
hotel industry and resource allocation 314, 420
integration 111
investment in research intensive industries 310
    and structure of resource allocation 171
    and trade 310
organisation of the enterprise 260–1
patent system, reform of 401
portfolio capital flows 224
production, advantages of internalisation 36, 40
    control 416
    in countries with affiliates 186
    eclectic theory of 80
    financed by fdi 72, 413
    as an international economic involvement 388
    by MNEs 412
    as part of oligopolistic behaviour 36
    policies towards 411
    theories 77, 110
    three strands of economic theory 79
    types of, some determining factors 49
social responsibility applied to fdi 391
spatial diversification 183
technology, diffusion of new, MNEs and 208, 348
    transfer of by MNEs 321–52
transmission of inflation, MNEs and 296
International Monetary Fund, reason for 389, 404, 405
International Chamber of Commerce and behaviour of foreign affiliates 379
International Code of Conduct on the Transfer of Technology 379
International Harvester, horizontal specialisation 70
internationalisation of firms, technology and 30
interrelationship between government and companies 370–1

intra-firm, pricing, arm's length pricing in 317
trade of MNEs 316, 317
intra-group, pricing 18
transactions, effect of 237
investment, allocation in dynamic situations 201
behaviour, variations in 225
difference between portfolio and direct 76
distribution of MNEs 226
to exploit national resources 117
flows for selected countries 134–5
by foreign firms in UK 142
function of firms, domestic and foreign 225
location decisions of MNEs 249
for the local market 340
motivation of 261
outlets, US and UK 34
political risk 267
taking advantage of semi-skilled labour 336
trade generating and trade-destroying 38
United Kingdom 145 ff.
see also inward and outward investment
investment-development cycle of countries 120, 123, 133
inward direct investment benefits and problems 134–5, 311, 312
inward and outward direct investment 119, 133, 142, 423
Ireland, fiscal incentive to attract new foreign capital 231, 233
industrial closures (1960–73) 254
locational pattern of foreign and indigenous plants (1960–73) 53
Irish Republic, behaviour of foreign affiliations 233

Jamaica, GNP per capita 120
Japan/Japanese, affiliates in Western Europe, language and cultural barriers affecting establishment 94
buying resources 39
divestment MNEs 74
economic, impact of 163, 387
miracle, Europe and US and 345–6, 394
increase in foreign production 99
investment 74, 83, 84, 89, 90, 93, 94, 134–5, 423

motor vehicle industry 94
MNEs, growth of 76, 89, 421
protection of domestic iron and steel industry, effect on MNEs 188
purchase of technology for Western enterprise 345
jet aircraft advantages 44
jobs, geographical pattern of redistribution 250
joint ventures 97

knowledge, acquiring 308
capital 235
of a particular market, advantages 100
and resource intensive industries 99
theories of direct investment 32
transmission of productive, costs of 236
which cannot be patented 30
Kozima, Professor on foreign direct investment distinctions 313, 339, 340

labour, and capital, immobility of 12, 22
cost subsidies, MNEs and 264
displacement by transfer of technology 326
force, cost of, in displacement area 255
difference in characteristics 292
government influence on 53–4
intensive industries, effect of technology on exporting of 323
market characteristics of US manufacturing and MNEs 272 ff.
unions, multinational in scope and organisation 297
(UK), unco-operativeness of 142
unskilled, affecting subsidy 263
Labour Government 205
impact on foreign affiliates 209
Latin American Free Trade Union (LAFTA) allocation of resources problem 201
and policy towards competition and restrictive practices 203
less technology intensive (LTI) industries 153, 156, 157, 158, 160
licence to exploit a patent, conditions for 324
Lima Declaration of UNIDO (1975) 322
lines of exchange between countries 386
linkage(s), creation, main determinants 314
domestic, forward and backward 366

liquid assets of MNEs 239
loan raising and size of firm 262
loanable funds, ability to acquire 227, 228, 230
local management and locational decisions 268
local value added (lva) of foreign affiliates 365
location, advantages 49, 53, 57, 99, 113, 143, 229, 340
    attraction of UK as a production base, changes in 142
    in development areas, preference for 250
    differences 13
    endowments advantages 25, 26, 48
    and mode of foreign involvement 111
    of new US affiliates, inducements for 231
    and production impact of MNE on 36
    theory 12, 35, 54, 77, 81, 229
    variables 35, 55−8
locational attraction improvement for UK and foreign producers 172
    choices, multinationality 266
    efficiency of MNEs 267
    mobility 265
    patterns on European MNEs 249
    strategies and regional development 249−71
location-specific, advantages 35, 52, 81, 122, 143
    endowments, 27, 32, 35, 47
    factor and country-specific characteristics, links between 95
    resources 32
    variables 58

Malaysia investment flows 134
management decentralisation, MNEs and 264
    organisational change in MNEs 413
manufacturing, exports and imports (UK) 162
    investment 151, 153, 156
mark, upward revaluation, effects of 92
market, boundaries and international spatial diversification 183
    failure, causing internalisation 96
        theory and foreign direct investment 78, 96, 97
    forces, influence on wages 296
    growth in host countries 58, 64
    imperfections or failures 14, 29, 32,
35, 78, 97, 228, 309−10
    mechanisation replaced by administrative fiat, reasons for 96
    and production units, spatial deployment of 179
    structure 181, 182, 188, 199, 203−6
        affected by competitive tactics 195−6
        of affiliates of MNEs in host countries 188
        and behaviour, policies affecting 200−1
        of particular industries 201
        in wage payments 291
mergers involving US firms 204, 205
    and takeovers, US and UK firms 205, 208−9
methodology in empirical texts, note on 66
Mexico industry sales 51
microeconomic effectiveness of regional subsidies 255, 256
mining industry, skill and proprietary assets 88
    investments in (UK) 148
    and technology transfer 343
monetary integration 238
Monopolies Commission 204, 205, 208, 209
    and behaviour of affiliates 206, 207, 210, 211
monopolistic, behaviour and trade barriers 305
    competition theories of trade 24, 26, 32
monopoly, legislation 366
    power of MNEs 27, 37, 235
more technology intensive (MTI) industry 289
    sector 153, 156, 157, 158, 163, 166
motor vehicle industry concentration ratios 203
multicollinearity, problems of 58, 316
multidivisional structure and organisation advantage 264
multilateral, bodies affecting behaviour of foreign investors 380
    policies, problem of implementation 403, 404
multilocation domestic enterprise (MLDE) 7, 12, 255, 258
    and labour subsidies 264
    shifting tax burden 267
    transfer policy 267
multinational, behaviour influencing

government policy 14
companies, bargaining position 14, 16, 17
enterprise(s) (MNE) affiliates, competitive position in UK 231
    percentage of industries 4
    and standardised commodities 264
avoiding taxation 201
bargaining power 16, 401
and barriers facing developing countries 309
capital deployment consistent with national objectives 400
competition for investment outlets 421
competitive practices 195–6, 422
conditions of sale of resources, determination of 185
as contractors or consortia of governments 422, 423
demands for supervision and regulation of 390
and developing countries 422
differences from indigenous firms 390
direct investment 329, 386
distinctive behaviour 7
a distorting force in resource allocation 21, 37, 39
and distribution of income 17
and domestic capital formation 221–48
effect of industrial concentration 192
as foreign policy agent 370
and foreign production 26
and government policies 14, 200, 234, 397
growth of explained 99, 143, 413
in host countries 28, 385
hostility to 389
impact on, income distribution 297
    industrial structure within particular industries 189
    regional disequilibria 254
    takeovers 189–99, 192
    world output 11
incentive to manipulate transfer prices 97
and industrial structure and policy 174–220
and inflation 240, 293, 296
influence in free international

production 393
    market structure 185, 188
influencing domestic economic policies 370
    resource allocation and economic policy 10
an integrating force in world economy 37
internalising imperfect markets 36
in international economic relations 388
location strategies of 249ff., 265–6
market control and exploitation 309, 311
and nation states, tension between 390
operations in labour market and inflation 272
ownership advantage 341
payroll costs 274
post-tax profit maximising 226
reasons for intermediary operations 31
reducing tax burden 31
regional office functions 228
resources provided by 424
'second league' 421
and specialisation 37
state-owned, future of 386
strategy (1960) 412
a target for criticism 415–16
traditional role of 410
transfer of income across national boundaries 31
transferring technology 324, 327, 328–32
transmission of resources 321
as wage leaders 275, 296, 297, 298
multinational investments 16
institutions, liquid assets 3
Multinational Undertakings and Community Relations (EEC) 418
multinationality of a company, advantages for 27
of firms and wage payments 283
and ownership advantages 82
multi-plant and multi-product firms 181–2
    response to regional development incentives 254–5
multiregional national enterprise operation compared with MNE 312

multi-sourcing and economics of location 264

nation states, changing attitudes to MNEs 389
national, economic management 237–9
    government controls, MNEs and 237
    policies causing distortions 393
nations, different groups and classes 386
natural resources, possession of and ownership advantages 88
neofactor, trade theories of 23, 26, 52
neotechnology theories of trade 26, 32, 52, 82
net outward investment, flow (NOI) 116–36 *passim*
    and indicators of OLI-specific advantages 126, 127
New International Economic Order 322
newly industrialised countries (NICs) 322, 333, 338, 342, 347
    pattern in technology transfer 332
New Zealand GNP (1971) per capita 120
Northern Ireland, foreign firms in 252
North Sea oil, and balance of payments 142
    capital flow 152

oil, industry and vertical integration 31
    investment data 148
    prices increases and world economy 386
oil-producing countries demand for petroleum processing activities 421
oligopolists in international economics 395
    internalisation and 28
openness of an economy 182–5, 237, 241
operating costs assisted by non-assisted location 256
Organisation for Economic Co-operation and Development (OECD) 112, 404
    and behaviour of foreign investors 203, 379, 380
    Commodity Trade Statistics 55
    countries and technology exports 329
    guideline to MNE behaviour 409–10
    and regionally differentiated depreciation allowance 262, 263
organisations influencing decision making 405

Organisation of Petroleum Exporting Countries (OPEC) 17, 212, 329
outward and inward investment 82, 83, 149, 151, 152, 153, 154–5, 165, 170, 171, 326
overseas, controlled manufacturing employment shift in geographical distribution 250
    investment, evaluation of spatial 255
    ratio of UK investment in manufacturing industry 160–1
ownership 12, 113
    advantages 23, 26, 27, 33, 49, 56, 82, 111, 143, 340
    country-specific, determinants of 86–91
    of enterprises 79, 90, 91
    of firms 32
    of foreign investment 78
    possession of and exploitation of foreign markets 48
    possession of natural resources 88
    systemic theory of 33
    and tangible assets 79
    transference of 97
    variables affecting 35
        characteristics of OLI 113
        effect 185, 186
        endowments 25, 26, 35
        and internalising advantages, distinction between 111
        structure of international production 76
ownership-location-internalisation (OLI) 110
    advantage 113, 123, 124, 125–30, 133
ownership-specific, advantage 27, 46, 52, 80, 81, 82, 88–9, 109–10, 119, 143
    assets 47
    endowments 48
    variables 55–8

participation, rates of MNE affiliates in manufacturing sectors 27, 330–1
    ratios, determination of 60–1, 63, 227
patent and trademark legislation 89, 98, 401
patterns of foreign direct investment regulations 360–1
payroll costs of foreign affiliates 274, 275
petrochemical, know-how, transfer of 343

and plant equipment companies prospects 421

petroleum and non-fuel sector participants 4

pharmaceutical industry, study of 24, 377

Philips, horizontal specialisation 76
major restructuring of worldwide operations 344

physical and psychic barrier affecting overseas investment 94

plant and equipment expenditures by US foreign affiliates 221, 225

political, aspirations and economic sovereignty 17–18
considerations affected by fdi 370
and cultural identity, increasing desire of nations for 387

policy(ies), inducing reaction from firms 200
makers, three objectives of 8–9
prescription of MNE 385–408
towards affiliates 208–11

pollution from product affecting neighbouring country 392

population size influencing inward investment 128

portfolio, capital 224, 234
theory 78

Portuguese economy similarity to Greek economy 358, 380

post-tax profit, maximising 226

predatory pricing 183, 195

price, behaviour of MNEs 295
control, implicit and explicit 367
determination of 8, 10
rise through wage movement 240

Price Commission and behaviour of affiliates 206, 208, 210–11

Prices and Incomes Board 208, 211

private enterprise, commodities and services as public goods 30

product, cycle theory 47, 77, 94, 305
differentiation 23, 78, 192, 193, 205–6
diversification or integration 29
particular, servicing market for 12
and process structure 192
rationalisation following takeover 192
specialisation 76

production, costs 55, 95, 225
extension outside boundaries 304
financed by foreign direct investment 21

for home market servicing 25
and marketing, government and 30
of US affiliates in UK manufacturing industry 190–1
units, UK set-up in European markets 162
operation of 180

product-related variables and subsidies 258–60

productive knowledge as capital 307–8

profit variable 226

profitability, of foreign investment in UK 168–9
UK domestic firms 168–9
of UK and foreign firms in UK manufacturing industry 167
of UK overseas direct investment 168–9

promotional and marketing expenditure and policies 205–6

property rights and vertical integration theory 79

protectionism and control 347

public intervention in allocation of resources 29

purchasing and market policies of MNEs affecting trade flows 313–14

quality control as competitive advantage 98

regional policy incentives 250, 252, 255, 256, 263

regions, development production costs 255

regulatory mechanisms of host countries (EEC) 418

regression, analysis results 59, 60–1
methodology 129, 131

relative, export shares (RES) 58, 60, 62
market size (RMS) 58, 60, 61, 62
wages (RW) 58, 60, 62, 64, 65

research and development 325, 340
activities 35, 37–8, 207, 208, 325
cost recoup 323
facilities 325, 368

resource, allocation 29, 30, 37, 235, 306, 311, 318, 424
based industries 31, 49
based investment 88, 341
capability and usage 27
endowment 25, 88, 89, 123
imports by host countries 422
international distribution of 36
transmission 321, 414, 422

restrictive trade practices of unions 165
revealed comparative advantage (RCA)
    indices 82–98 *passim*, 339
Ricardian type assets 47
risk diversification and factor 92, 95

sales per man (SPM) 63, 64
sanctions on MNEs, limitation of 422
Scotland, foreign firms in 252
self-sufficiency, achieving 394
servicing markets, alternative routes 111
Singapore, investment flows 134
    market advantages 100
single product, single plant firms 180–1
size of the firm influencing subsidies 27,
    261
skilled and/or capital intensity 256–9
skilled employment ratio (SER) 55
skills and technology of MNEs 423
South East Asia investment in 76
South Korea construction industry 90
    investment flows 134
specialisation 37, 38, 76, 316, 341
specialists, technology supply 324
state participation in economic affairs
    414
state-owned MNEs, role of 89
structural imperfections 29
subsidies, as incentives 255–6
    and size of firm 262
supranational solutions to treatment of
    MNEs 395
Sweden, investment 83, 84, 90, 93
Switzerland 45, 265
systemic theory of ownership advantage
    33, 35

takeovers 12, 189, 193 *see also* mergers
tariffs 58, 236
taxation, avoidance 201, 236, 393
    variables 125
tax, burden, shifting 31, 267
    changes, response of MNEs to 231
    on foreign profit 90
    rates affecting conduct of MNEs 312
technology 23, 24, 25, 30, 34, 78, 323,
    324, 343, 355, 367, 368, 415,
    420
    advantage of sales of 324
    export of 322, 329, 344, 348
    industry, high wages in 289
    production and marketing 31
    transfer 39, 321–52
textile and clothing industry compe-
    tition, effect of 344

trade, across boundaries 21
    advantages 27
    barriers 54, 307, 308, 393
    basis between countries 81, 82
    distribution of international pro-
        duction 49
    flow theories and technology 304,
        305
    location of economic activity 21–45
    and production theories 12, 13, 22,
        23, 24, 54
trade unions 142, 239
    and employee compensation 272
    membership in capital intensive in-
        dustries 289
    and wage negotiations 240, 283,
        291–2
trade-oriented and anti-trade oriented
    activities of MNEs 38
trading pattern of US MNEs 39
transfer, price manipulation 31, 98, 195,
    208, 211, 231, 267
    of production, effects of 8, 242
Transnational Corporations (TNCs) 325,
    332, 337, 338, 343
    Commission 379, 410, 417
transport costs 94
types of foreign investment and tech-
    nology transfer 332–6

unemployment, causes of 142, 297
unilateral policies 394
United Kingdom (UK), acquire US firms
    98
    companies, failure to invest 344, 345
        profit from foreign operators 148
    exploitation of European market 162
    exports 85, 163
    in EEC, economic implications 24
    firms, competitiveness 151, 159, 163,
        171, 203 ff., 346
    and foreign MNE export restrictions
        207
    imports origination from NICs 338
    increase in foreign production 99
    industry sales 51
    investments 73, 83, 84, 90, 93, 97–
        8, 142–75, 377
    locational strategy 165, 250, 252,
        253
    as a production base 165
    production penetration by foreign
        affiliates 144
    retailing business reaction to MNEs
        198

technology transfer, income from 328
unemployment problem 142
unions, unco-operative policies 142
wages 276, 277, 278, 283
United Nations Centre on Transnational
Corporations 76, 112, 314, 332
United Nations Conference on Trade and
Development (UNCTAD) 380,
410, 416, 420
United Nations Study Group on MNEs
416
United States of America (USA) 51,
73–4, 203, 204, 207–8, 278–80
as capital exporter 329
company, transfer of production 242
wages 281–2, 283
domination of foreign production 72,
73
exports 51, 85, 93, 226–7
firms, main advantages 54, 59
investment 72, 73, 76, 77, 83, 84,
90, 99, 163, 165, 204, 263, 411,
412
and the motor industry 91
MNEs exploit ownership advantages
89
Related-Party Imports 335
research and development in UK 207
specialisation 37
technological capacity and lead in
industry 35, 73
wages 278, 281

United States Tariff Commission report
55, 73, 227, 229, 253, 273, 274,
299

variables 10, 17, 35, 55–8, 226
vertical, direct investment 54
expansion forwards 88
integration 28, 31, 78, 261, 265
specialising of US firms 226–7

wages, attracting labour 240
and conditions of work parity 272
costs 64
determinants 272, 274, 275, 283,
346
policies 272, 274, 275, 298
rates, collective bargaining and trade
union practices 240, 255, 283,
284
by US MNEs and affiliates 275, 287–
9, 290–2
West Germany 51
exports 85
investment 83, 84, 93
Western Europe, firms exploit UK market 160–1, 171
recovery from war, USA and 411
World Bank 343, 346
world economy, factors changing 386
MNEs an integrating force 37

yen, upward revaluation, effect of 92

By the same author

American Investment in British Manufacturing Industry
(Allen & Unwin, 1958; reprinted by Arno Press, 1976)
(with C. J. Thomas) *British Industry* (Hutchinson, 1961, 1963, 1966)
Economic Planning and Town Expansion: A Case Study of Basingstoke
(Workers Educational Association, 1963)
Studies in International Investment (Allen & Unwin, 1970)
(ed.) *The Multinational Enterprise* (Allen & Unwin, 1971)
(with E. V. Morgan) *An Economic Study of the City of London*
(Allen & Unwin, 1971)
(ed.) *International Investment* (Penguin, 1972)
(ed.) *Economic Analysis and the Multinational Enterprise*
(Allen & Unwin, 1974)
United States Industry in Britain (Wilton House Publications, 1976)
(with T. Houston) *UK Industry Abroad* (Financial Times, 1976)
*United Kingdom Transnational Enterprises in Manufacturing and
Resource Based Industries and Trade Flows of Developing Countries*
(United Nations, 1977)
(with G. Norman) *Factors Influencing the Location of Offices of
Multinational Enterprises* (Location of Offices Bureau, 1979)
(with J. Stopford and K. Haverich) *The World Directory of Multinational
Enterprises* (Macmillan Reference Books, 1980)
(with R. D. Pearce) *The World's Largest Industrial Enterprises 1962–1978*
(Gower Press, 1981)
(with M. Burstall and A. Lake) *Multinational Enterprises, Governments
and Technology: the Pharmaceutical Industry* (O.E.C.D., 1981)

Have you enjoyed this book?
If so, why not write a review on your favourite website?

If you're interested in finding out more about our
books, find us on Facebook at **Summersdale Publishers**
and follow us on Twitter at **@Summersdale**.

Thanks very much for buying this Summersdale book.

www.summersdale.com